Lecture Notes in Computer Science 8853

Commenced Publication in 1973
Founding and Former Series Editors:
Gerhard Goos, Juris Hartmanis, and Jan van Leeuwen

More information about this series at http://www.springer.com/series/7412

- real-time capturing, compression, and rendering
- real-time gesture reconstruction
- body and facial animation
- behavioral simulation
- game design and development
- immersive gaming
- serious games
- VR/AR in minimally invasive surgery
- medical imaging processing, analysis, and visualization
- VR in preoperative surgical planning
- VR in surgical training
- VR in rehabilitation
- virtual patient
- VR/AR in education
- VR/AR in cultural heritage
- virtual museums and exhibitions
- VR in military simulation
- VR in spatial simulation
- VR in industrial simulation

We received 76 submissions from 15 countries. Each was been evaluated by at least two members of the Program Committee and external reviewers. Based on these reviews, 28 papers were selected for long oral presentations and 9 for poster talks. In addition to the contributed papers, 2 tutorials and 3 keynote speaker presentations were included in the conference program.

The geographical spread of the different institutions presenting their research was: Belgium, Brasil, Canada, Estonia, Italy, Kazakhstan, Latvia, Lithuania, Mexico, Pakistan, Poland, Sweden, Taiwan, UK and USA.

We are very grateful to Program Committee members for volunteering their time to review and discuss the submitted papers and doing so in a timely and professional manner. We extend our thanks to University of Salento and other sponsors for providing support in the organization of the event. Last but not least, we would like to thank all authors for presenting their work at the conference and we hope that all participants enjoyed the stimulating discussion as well as the opportunity to establish fruitful interactions.

September 2014

Lucio Tommaso De Paolis
Antonio Mongelli

Lucio Tommaso De Paolis · Antonio Mongelli (Eds.)

Augmented and Virtual Reality

First International Conference, AVR 2014
Lecce, Italy, September 17–20, 2014
Revised Selected Papers

 Springer

Editors
Lucio Tommaso De Paolis
University of Salento
Lecce
Italy

Antonio Mongelli
University of Salento
Lecce
Italy

ISSN 0302-9743
Lecture Notes in Computer Science
ISBN 978-3-319-13968-5
DOI 10.1007/978-3-319-13969-2

ISSN 1611-3349   (electronic)

ISBN 978-3-319-13969-2   (eBook)

Library of Congress Control Number: 2014957958

LNCS Sublibrary: SL6 – Image Processing, Computer Vision, Pattern Recognition, and Graphics

Springer Cham Heidelberg New York Dordrecht London
© Springer International Publishing Switzerland 2014

Printed on acid-free paper

Springer International Publishing AG Switzerland is part of Springer Science+Business Media
(www.springer.com)

Preface

This book contains the written contributions to the First International Conference on Augmented and Virtual Reality (SALENTO AVR 2014) that has held in Lecce (Italy), during September 17–20, 2014.

The aim of the SALENTO AVR 2014 has been to bring a community of researchers from academia and industry, computer scientists, engineers, physicians together in order to share points of views, knowledge, experiences and scientific and technical results, related to state-of-the-art solutions and technologies on virtual and augmented reality applications for medicine, cultural heritage, education, industrial sectors, as well as the demonstration of advanced products and technologies.

The papers spans topics from virtual/augmented/mixed reality (VR/AR/MR) to 3D user interfaces and the technology needed to enable these environments to a wide range of applications (medical, entertainment, military, design, manufacture, maintenance, arts, and cultural heritage).

The topics of the SALENTO AVR 2014 Conference were:

- input devices for VR/AR/MR
- 3D interaction for VR/AR/MR
- computer graphics techniques for VR/AR/MR
- advanced display technology
- haptic interfaces
- audio and other nonvisual interfaces
- tracking and sensing
- distributed VR/AR/MR
- VR toolkits
- modelling and simulation
- physical modelling
- perception and presence in virtual environment
- human-computer interface
- human-computer Interaction
- teleoperation and telepresence
- intuitive interactions and interfaces
- artificial life art
- interactive art
- navigation
- natural user interface
- gestural-based interaction
- interaction techniques for AR/MR
- collaborative learning environment
- augmented and mixed reality
- augmented visualization on mobile
- real-time 3D body reconstruction

Organization

Scientific Committee

Conference Chair

Lucio Tommaso De Paolis   University of Salento, Italy

Conference Co-chair

Patrick Bourdot   CNRS/LIMSI, University of Paris-Sud, France

Honorary Chair

Giovanni Aloisio   University of Salento, Italy

Scientific Program Committee

Andrea Abate	University of Salerno, Italy
Angelos Amditis	Institute of Communication and Computer Systems (ICCS), Greece
Bruno Arnaldi	IRISA, France
Selim Balcisoy	Sabancı University, Turkey
Roland Blach	Fraunhofer IAO, Germany
Davide Borra	NoReal.it, Italy
Pierre Boulanger	University of Alberta, Canada
Massimo Cafaro	University of Salento, Italy
Sergio Casciaro	IFC-CNR, Italy
Bruno Carpentieri	University of Salerno, Italy
Marcello Carrozzino	Scuola Superiore Sant' Anna, Italy
Mario Ciampi	ICAR/CNR, Italy
Pietro Cipresso	IRCCS Istituto Auxologico Italiano, Italy
Fernando Arambula Cosio	Universidad Nacional Autónoma de México (UNAM), Mexico
Mirabelle D'Cruz	University of Nottingham, UK
Yuri Dekhtyar	Riga Technical University, Latvia
Alessandro De Mauro	Vicomtech-IK4, Spain
Giorgio De Nunzio	University of Salento, Italy
Alessandro Distante	ISBEM, Italy
Aldo Franco Dragoni	Università Politecnica delle Marche, Italy

Themis Exarchos	University of Ioannina, Greece
Dimitrios Fotiadis	University of Ioannina, Greece
Francesco Gabellone	IBAM ITLab, CNR, Italy
Jaume Segura Garcia	Universitat de València, Spain
Osvaldo Gervasi	University of Perugia, Italy
Luigi Gallo	ICAR/CNR, Italy
Viktors Gopejenko	Information Systems Management Institute (ISMA), Latvia
Alexander Glaz	Riga Technical University, Latvia
Mirko Grimaldi	CRIL, University of Salento, Italy
Tomas Krilavičius	Vytautas Magnus University, Lithuania
Torsten Kuhlen	RWTH Aachen University, Germany
Salvatore Livatino	University of Hertfordshire, UK
Luca Mainetti	University of Salento, Italy
Arianna Menciassi	Scuola Superiore Sant' Anna, Italy
Daniel R. Mestre	Aix-Marseille University/CNRS, France
Roberto Paiano	University of Salento, Italy
Giorgos Papadourakis	Technological Educational Institute of Crete, Greece
Sofia Pescarin	CNR ITABC, Italy
Paolo Proietti	MIMOS, Italy
James Ritchie	Heriot-Watt University, UK
Oliver Staadt	University of Rostock, Germany
Robert Stone	University of Birmingham, UK
Doru Talaba	Transilvania University of Brasov, Romania
Franco Tecchia	Scuola Superiore Sant' Anna, Italy
Carlos M. Travieso–González	Universidad de Las Palmas de Gran Canaria, Spain
Manolis Tsiknaki	Technological Educational Institute of Crete, Greece
Virginia Valzano	CEIT, Italy
Krzysztof Walczak	Poznań University of Economics, Poland
Charles Woodward	VTT Technical Research Centre, Finland
Domenico Zungri	Future Labs, Italy

Local Organizing Committee

Antonio Mongelli	University of Salento, Italy

Tutorials

Virtual Reality and Augmented Visualization in Medicine and Surgery

Lucio Tommaso De Paolis

AVR Lab, University of Salento, Lecce, Italy

In medicine and surgery the Virtual Reality technology has made available new tools for diagnosis and therapy definition by translating the information contained in the medical images of the patients into 3D virtual models who are realistic replicas of real patients with their actual pathologies. This has allowed the development of a new form of medical education and training and the use of patient-specific surgical simulators has permitted to practice and rehearse the surgical procedures on digital clones of the real patients. New applications of Augmented Reality technology, by means of the overlapping of virtual information on the real patient, provide systems that help surgeons in the intra-operative phase and permit to perform their tasks in ways that are both faster and safer. The use of the augmented visualization in surgery has the potential to bring the advantages of the open-surgery visualization also in the minimally invasive surgery.

Lucio Tommaso De Paolis is an Assistant Professor of Information Processing Systems and the scientific responsible of the Augmented and Virtual Reality Laboratory (AVR Lab) at the Department of Engineering for Innovation of the University of Salento, Italy; he is also the responsible of the "Advanced Techniques of Virtual Reality for Medicine" research group of the DReAM (Laboratory of Interdisciplinary Research Applied to Medicine) located at the Hospital of Lecce, Italy.

He received the Master Degree in Electronic Engineering from the University of Pisa (Italy) in 1994 and after, first at the Scuola Superiore S.Anna of Pisa and then at the University of Salento, his research interest concerns the study of realistic simulators for surgical training and the development of applications of Virtual and Augmented Reality in medicine and surgery.

De Paolis has been in 2014 visiting professor at the Tallinn Technical University of Tallinn (Estonia), in 2012 visiting professor at the Vytautas Magnus University of Kaunas (Lithuania), in 2011 visiting professor at the University of Tallinn (Estonia), in 2007 and 2010 visiting researcher at the Centro de Ciencias Aplicadas y Desarrollo Tecnológico (CCADET) – Universidad Nacional Autónoma de México (UNAM) – Mexico City (Messico), and in 2007 and 2009 visiting researcher at Computer Graphics Laboratory, Sabanci University of Istanbul (Turkey).

Development of Immersive VR Applications Using XVR

Marcello Carrozzino

PERCRO Lab, Scuola Superiore S. Anna, Pisa, Italy

The tutorial will explain the basics on how to program a in immersive VR application using the XVR technology, tackling general VR framework considerations and focusing on the most recent development in the field of managing immersive devices such as CAVEs and HMDs. Live examples of CAVE and Oculus Rift-based XVR applications will be provided, together with interesting insights on the uses of such technologies for mixed reality applications.

Marcello Carrozzino is an Assistant Professor of Computer Graphics and Virtual Reality. His activities deal with the integration of Virtual Reality systems and Cultural Heritage applications. Since 2005 he has been teaching the course of Virtual Environments held at the Computer Science Department of the University of Pisa. In 2006 he attained a Ph.D. at Scuola Superiore S. Anna in Pisa with a thesis on Efficient Management of Complex Virtual Environments. From 2006 to 2009 he has been Assistant Professor at IMT Lucca in the area of Technology and Management of Cultural Heritage. He is a founder of VRMedia s.r.l, a spin-off company of Scuola Superiore S. Anna in Pisa. Since 2000 he has been collaborating with Scuola Superiore S. Anna, where he is currently heading the Art, Cultural and Education Group of PERCRO Lab. He is a founder of the Mnemosyne Digital Culture association and has participated to several EU research projects, leaded regional projects, and authored or co-authored more than sixty publications in journals, conference proceedings and book chapters.

Keynote Speakers

Fully Immersive Modification of Native CAD Data During Project Reviews: Recent Results and Remaining Issues

Patrick Bourdot

CNRS/LIMSI, University Paris-Sud, France

This talk focuses on recent results on VR and CAD integration to make possible direct and interactive modifications of CAD objects in immersive Virtual Environments (VE). Using CAD software requires some skills (experience and knowledge), on its function-alities and representations, as well as on objects (principally on their design history). On the other hand, VR brings new interactive paradigms of 3D interaction, and one needs intelligent middleware to manage CAD objects in immersive VE

After an overview of the main approaches in the VR-CAD integration field, we focus on an extension of one of our previous work which proposed a mechanism al-lowing implicit edition of the Construction History Graphs (CHG) of CAD objects via a direct manipulation of their 3D visual representations. Based on labelling technique of the Boundary Representations (B-Rep) elements, and coupled with an inference en-gine, this mechanism is providing a backward chaining of B-Rep elements towards the operators of the CHG. However, we had demonstrated that this approach up today only on a dedicated CHG and specific persistent naming developed in the OpenCASCADE framework. Recent results on the generalization of our approach makes possible to ap-ply it to marketed CAD systems, software generally chose by industrials for a number of years.

Firstly, this generalization aims to propose an architecture based on a VR-CAD data model to apply our backward chaining mechanism to any CAD system based on B-Rep and CHG models. Several encapsulations structures are proposed, to manage CHG op-erators and their parameters, as well as the B-Rep components. Secondly, the B-Rep labelling, now attached to these structures, has been extended to enable multiple back-ward chaining, as some B-Rep elements may be the result of several CHG operators, so that alternate decisions may be inferred from their manipulation. These improvements make it possible to access direct and interactive modifications of existing CAD objects by parsing their CHG to fill our structures with useful data. Moreover the multiple backward-chaining mechanism grants the manipulation of CAD objects to non-experts through the inference engine. As a proof of concept of our VR-CAD model, we detail the application of our approach on CATIA, then we conclude on the remaining issues and future works.

Patrick Bourdot is Research Director at CNRS and head of VENISE team (http://www.limsi.fr/venise/), the Virtual & Augmented Reality (V&AR) research group he has created in 2001 at CNRS/LIMSI lab. Architect graduated in 1986, he received his PhD in Computer Sciences at the University of Aix-Marseille in 1992, joined the CNRS/LIMSI lab in 1993. His main research focuses are multi-sensorimotor, multi-modal and collaborative V&AR interactions, and the related issues for users' perception and cognition. He coordinated the scientific partnership of his Lab or led a number of research projects that have been or are currently funded by French government (RNTL, ANR), or by national or regional research institutes (CNRS, DIGITEO). He has been the founding secretary of AFRV, the French association of V&AR, and co-chaired its 5th conference (http://afrv2010.limsi.fr/). At the international level, one of his actions has been to manage the CNRS Labs involved in INTUITION, the NoE of the 6th IST framework focused on V&AR, where he was member of the Core Group. He is founding member of EuroVR (www.eurovr-association.org), and has been re-elected last year to its Executive Board. He organised the first Special Interest Groups meeting of EuroVR (http://eurovr-eve-2010.limsi.fr/), during the inauguration of the EVE system, an innovative CAVE-like setup, whose he defined the specification and implemented with the VENISE team. He is presently organizing JVRC 2013, the 5th Joint Virtual Reality Conference of EGVE and EuroVR (http://jvrc2013.sciencesconf.org/), which will take this December in Paris area. Patrick Bourdot has a large number of international publications in most important V&AR conferences such as IEEE VR, ACM VRST, IEEE 3DUI or EGVE, and many others international or national papers in the fields of 3D modelling, 3D reconstruction, and HCI. He has been or is reviewer or expert for several national and international journals, conferences or research agencies.

Simplifying Creation of VR/AR Applications for Domain Experts

Krzysztof Walczak

Department of Information Technology
Poznan University of Economics, Poland

One of the main obstacles, which currently limits wider use of virtual and augmented reality applications on everyday basis is the difficulty associated with the creation of useful 3D content. Non-trivial, interactive 3D multimedia content is inherently difficult to create. Not only geometry and appearance of particular elements must be properly represented, but also temporal, structural, logical and behavioural aspects must be taken into account. Moreover, creation of useful content requires participation of domain experts in this process. For example, a virtual museum exhibition should be set up by a museum curator, while an augmented reality lesson should be designed by an experienced teacher.

In this presentation, a range of methods aiming at simplification of the creation of interactive 3D content by domain experts are discussed. These methods include:

- content componentisation – which enables the content to be configured from pre-designed – possibly parameterised – blocks (geometrical, logical or behavioural);
- narrowing the application domain – which enables to increase the quality of the created content, but at the same time limits the generality of the solution;
- narrowing content variability – which enables creating more complex content at the cost of limited possibilities of content customisation.

Content can be also created collaboratively by groups of authors resulting in smaller and more manageable tasks assigned to particular designers. Moreover, the whole content creation process can be divided into distinct phases, which can be performed by designers with different responsibilities, skills and tools.

A promising research direction aiming at simplification of 3D content creation is semantic content modelling. Semantic modelling enables creation of 3D content using domain-specific ontologies, which domain experts are familiar with. Creation of an interactive 3D scene consists then in building a semantic knowledge base using known domain-specific concepts. Such a knowledge base may be created using a variety of tools – from text-based semantic editors to semantically-enabled graphical 3D authoring packages.

Krzysztof Walczak received the M.Sc. degree in Electronics and Telecommunications in 1992 and in Computer Science in 1994, both from the Technical University of Poznan. He received the Ph.D. degree in Computer Science in 2001 from the Technical University of Gdansk. From 1992 to 1996 he was with the Franco-Polish School of New Information and Communication Technologies in Poznan. He spent over one year as an invited researcher at the Syracuse University, NY, USA. In 1996 he joined the Department of Information Technology at the Poznan University of Economics, where currently he is an associate professor. His current research interests include virtual reality systems, multimedia systems, distance learning and semantic web. He was acting as a technical coordinator in numerous research and industrial projects in these domains.He is a member of Executive Committee of EuroVR Association, ACM (Association for Computing Machinery), Web3D Consortium and Board of Directors of VSMM (International Society on Virtual Systems and Multimedia).

Virtual Worlds: A Perfect Convergence Between Real and Virtual Life

Davide Borra

NoReal.it, Italy

In a future work, daily life, health, and social relationships will be mediated by our virtual alter-ego. Is the "metaverse" or "virtual world", a sintetic on-line environment, when our avatar can explore and build our space, van exchange, buy and sell our creations and abilities, when my expressions will be replicate in real-time on my avatar's face. It is virtual, aumented or mixed reality? What is difference from what we already know about the cybernetic suites, the oculus visors, the immersive caves used in the differents manifacture fields?

Second Life, Active Worlds and the others on-line platforms are always operatives?

I think we are in front to a singularity point of the digital humanism: we can be immersed in a metaverse in a real-scale, with a series of good wearable devices, in a very confortable psycological status, with a realistic multisensorial feedbacks.

The technology is quite ready to offer a domestic environment and we are ready to offer to our avatar, a series of personal "messages" that it (or he/she?) can use in a social relationships to be more natural the communication.

Real-scale, device usability, humanization of communication. Three impact factors to make the perfect convergence between real and virtual worlds.

Davide Borra is an architect with PHD in Environment and Territory (Politecnico di Torino) and has about twenty years of experience in designing and creating of multi-platform 3D contents in the area of cultural heritage, architecture and communications company.

The 3D model genesi and the importance of the user in the information cycle based on virtuality, are the main topics of his research in both academic and vocational education, which resulted in applications for museums and exhibit and in a number of scientific articles published.

The last experiments concern the latest Mobile 3D, 3D Metaverses on-line and the Augmented Reality.

For a decade, he taught 3D in the Faculty of Architecture of the Politecnico di Torino and Milan.

In 1999 he founded NoReal [www.noreal.it], a company specialized in Virtual Cultural Heritage, which currently manages.

Since 2008 he is the President of MIMOS (Italian Movement of Modelling and Simulation) [www.mimos.it].

Actually he is one of the international experts invited to discuss about the principles of the Virtual Cultural Heritage around the London Charter and the Sevilla Principles.

Contents

Cultural Heritage

Visualization and 3D Modelling

Posters

Education

A MAR Game Design via a Remote Control Module

Chi-Fu Lin[1(✉)], Pai-Shan Pa[2], and Chiou-Shann Fuh[1]

[1] Department of Computer Science and Information Engineering,
National Taiwan University, Taipei, Taiwan
daky1983@gmail.com, fuh@csie.ntu.edu.tw
[2] Graduate School of Toy and Game Design,
National Taipei University of Education, Taipei, Taiwan
myhow@seed.net.tw

Abstract. This paper intends to propose an interactive system that allows users to remotely control device and combine augmented reality content with the application. It is possible to generate games or education applications. Using augmented Reality and remote-control module as starting point, we design a MAR (Mobile Augmented Reality) game that contains shooting game, roadblock hindrance, and traffic signal game. Then use the mobile remote-control module to control the device. Finally, use augmented reality technology to allow real objects to interact directly with the virtual objects. As a platform to integrate mobile phone, we complete the development of augmented reality remote-control module application. The difference from the general AR applications is that our proposed method combines the remote-control objects to interact with virtual objects.

Keywords: MAR · Game design · Remote control

1 Introduction

1.1 Background and Motivation

With the development of mobile Augmented Reality (AR) enabling technology, there have been many mobile AR applications, services, and contents. Due to the demand for software resources in recent years, more and more large, relatively rising smartphone hardware, augmented reality technology in the past can only be used on the computer, because the pixels of the camera to enhance graphics processing progress, can now also be applied in the mobile phone software. Because the phone is easy to carry, augmented reality is able to generate more interactive applications, such as interactive advertising, navigation, books, and games.

Nowadays augmented reality still needs to use the mark to reach a recognition target. Mark setup as well as mark portability still has much room for improvement. Thus many studies aim to improve recognition technology. For example, use the mark to replace a specific image augmented reality, or to replace the electronic information other than the image tag identification, such as geographic information to achieve the effect of augmented reality and Global Positioning System (GPS).

Lack of dynamic expansions of the new features or styles is disadvantage of physic toys. If we want to add new features or a new style must be additional to buy, but it

© Springer International Publishing Switzerland 2014
L.T. De Paolis and A. Mongelli (Eds.): AVR 2014, LNCS 8853, pp. 3–18, 2014.
DOI: 10.1007/978-3-319-13969-2_1

will waste space and increase costs. Thus, the concept is to make augmented reality mobile platform. Use digital content within the practical function of the mobile device to match hardware and software to achieve the effect of human-computer interaction.

This paper consists of five sections. In Section 2, we will summarize related works. The system overview is in Section 3. Then, we describe implementation of the system in Section 4. Finally, we will conclude in Section 5.

2   Related Work

2.1   Development and Application of Augmented Reality

Definition of the Augmented Reality
Augmented reality is a form of virtual reality. Virtual reality allows users to fully integrate into the computer-generated virtual environment. We cannot see the reality of its surrounding environment. Augmented Reality allows the user to see the reality of the environment, as well as the synthesis of virtual objects in the real environment superimposed or contrasted with virtual reality. Therefore, Augmented Reality augments real environment rather than completely replaces real environment. Augmented reality has the following three characteristics: combination of real and virtual, real-time interactivity, and three-dimensions [1].

Principle of the Augmented Reality
Real and virtual images are combined and displayed to the user on the small screen inside the helmet [1, 2]. The equipment and technology, coupled with immaturity, high cost, inconvenience to carry, cannot be accepted for general users. But the popularity of PC and network cameras makes a new way to achieve augmented reality. Use a webcam to identify the real environment. The video is output to PC monitors. Hardware price in this mode of operation is quite cheap. Therefore the popularity of augmented reality increases [3]. Another paper describes an RF-based approach to mobile augmented reality [4].

Because of the rapid development of mobile devices, augmented reality has extended from personal computers to mobile devices. The highly interactive nature of augmented reality with its user has given rise to various augmented reality applications for mobile devices [5]. AR can be used in handheld games, it has more novel play experience for people [6]. After integrating the virtual and real world, it can improve the convenience for people. AR can be used in classroom as teaching tool. A study analysis by the use of the AR book in classroom indicates that the interaction can strengthen the study result for all ages [7]. The authors research how augmented reality can increase the selective and sustained attention of children with autism during object discrimination therapies and elicit more positive emotions [8].

There are several SDKs and platforms to realize augmented reality. Qualcomm Vuforia [9] is a software platform for Android, iOS, and package for Unity3d [23] that enables app to recognize mark from a Vuforia target database or in the Vuforia Cloud Recognition Service. It allows users to track objects such as two-dimensional planar mark, three-dimensional cube, and cylinder-shape object. It also supports real-time text recognition. ARtag and ARtoolkit are C/C++ open source platforms which support tracking 2D mark and displaying openGL [10]. BazAR is a computer vision library based on matching and feature point detection. In particular, it is able to quickly detect and register known planar objects in images [11].

2.2   Analyses and Discussions

The human-computer interaction toys can be classified into two types. The first type is mobile device combined with Augmented Reality. Another one is physical toy communication with mobile device. We discuss and analyze two types below.

Interactive Mobile Device and Augmented Reality
Use the camera on mobile device to recognize target and generate 3D models on the screen. Augmented reality has for years been one of the focuses in mobile phone application development, ranging from mere interaction to marketing, games, navigation, and so on. The highly interactive nature of augmented reality with its user has given rise to various augmented reality applications for mobile phones.

With Hoops AR [12], user simply views the ticket using a mobile device, and then the basketball ticket turns into an interactive basketball game. By using user's finger to shoot the basketball to control the speed of the shot. An iPad app, Barbie Digital Mirror [13] uses augmented reality to let kids try on makeup. When user looks in the interactive mirror, user dips a make-up tool into pretend makeup, and it appears on her face. The iButterfly [14] app generates a butterfly on the screen combining AR with Global Positioning System (GPS) information, and then user can catch butterfly which becomes a coupon. Popar [15] Toys uses Augmented Reality technology to create an immersive reading experience. It is designed to change the way users interact and experience stories, adventures, and learning. Table 1 shows a comparisons of various AR software.

Interactive Toys and Mobile Device
It generates different experiences by interactive toys and mobile device using sensor on mobile device connected to toys and interacting with each other.

The first type is mobile device connected with toy via Bluetooth, Infrared Module, Wireless, and so on by using mobile device for remote control. User can control toys through mobile device remotely when the connection is successful. Helicopter and remote-control car use this type. Table 2 shows comparisons of various toys combined with mobile software.

The second type uses toys to control game. Apptivity [16] action games include toys and an iPad app. The iPad recognizes the toy thanks to Mattel's patented "Active Touch" technology when kids use the physical toys to play the app game. The Apptivity action games will include several popular themes such as Fruit Ninja, Angry Birds, and Batman: The Dark Knight Rises. Adding different shapes of touch points to toy's bottom to achieve recognition. It recognizes shapes and triggers the corresponding event by touching the toy on iPad.

Augmented reality interactions have been classified into three categories. The first category uses computer and webcam to identify the specified tag. The disadvantage is lack of mobility in this method. The second category is a popular method in recent years. This method uses mobile device and camera to identify the specified tag, then generates 3D models on the screen. A user clicks on the touch screen to interact with digital content on the mobile device. The advantage is more mobility in this method. However the real interaction experiences are not enough. The third category is similar to the second category, but it provides more realistic experiences. Through augmented reality detection effect, user directly uses fingers to interact with digital content in a real environment. Table 3 shows a comparison of augmented reality interactions.

Table 1. Comparisons of Various AR Software

	Advantage	Disadvantage
AR Drone [17]	The effect of the AR and play against other players.	Need to buy expensive AR Drone aircraft.
Word Lens [18]	Simple and practical translation software can be used without Internet.	Four translation languages (English, Italian, French, and Spanish) are too few.
iButterfly [14]	Butterfly shape combined with advertising, marketing effect by capturing various butterflies.	Single marketing function, low user viscosity.
Hoops AR [12]	A basketball court for the mark, to enhance game play.	Need to prepare a mark for the game.
Layar [19]	Intuitive navigation screen.	Need to turn on the camera and Internet connection to use navigation, consume much electricity.

Table 2. Comparisons of Various Devices Combined with Mobile Software

	Mobile Device	Devices
AR Drone [17]	Bluetooth: Mobile device connects with toy via Bluetooth.	Bluetooth: Receive mobile device's signal to control toy.
RoboMe [20]	Microphone: voice command recognition, and remote video control. Camera: Face detection and tracking	User will be able to change the face that appears on the screen and the voice to different accents.
Apptivity [16]	The iPad recognizes the toy thanks to Mattel's patented "Active Touch" technology.	Touch point with different shapes at toy bottom.

Table 2. (*Continued*)

Silverlit R/C Car [21]	Bluetooth: Mobile device connects with toy via Bluetooth.	Bluetooth: Receive mobile device's signal to control toy.
Silverlit helicopter [21]		

Table 3. Comparison of Augmented Reality Interactions

	Illustration pictures	Description
Virtual button of AR [9]		Through setting the virtual buttons on the marker, when virtual button occlusion is detected, our system triggers corresponding event.
Popular augmented reality on the mobile device.		A user clicks on the touch screen to interact with digital content on the mobile device.
Augmented reality on an early computer		Webcam identification of the main tag. Users also need to use other specified tag to interact with digital content.

3   System Overview

Our proposed system enables the user to remotely control device by mobile device and let physical remote control device or toy to interact with virtual object. We analyze operational processes summarized into two modes in Figures 1 and 2. There are five major roles in the system consisting of user, mobile device, remote-control device, tag, and virtual object. In Mode 1, user can use mobile device to remotely control device. Use the mobile device's camera to recognize the predefined tag and render virtual object. The remote-control device via virtual button interacts with virtual object.

The difference between Modes 2 and 1 is that Mode 2 adds a tag in the remote-control device. When mobile device identifies the tag, it will produce a corresponding virtual object, allowing original device to have more diversification. The concept is somewhat similar to the movie "Transformers [22]" and each device can be transformed into any types. Mode 2 allows more interesting interaction.

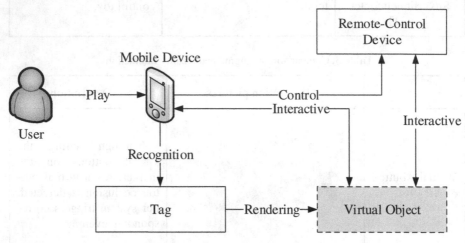

Fig. 1. System process diagram - Mode 1

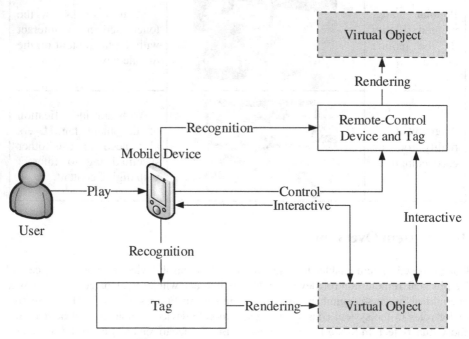

Fig. 2. System process diagram - Mode 2

4 Results and Discussions

4.1 Structure and Process

In this study, we use augmented reality features and interactive games to construct a remote-control module. We choose a remote-control car in our design MAR game. Traffic signal theme features the design of the interactivity of the users and remote car. The system's hardware and software architecture is shown in Fig. 3. The mobile application can be divided into two platforms generally, Apple's iOS and Google's Android. We use Unity 3D [23] to develop a mobile AR game.

4.2 Development Tools

The design tools of the game are categorized into the following four items:

1. 3D computer graphics software: Autodesk Maya
2. Augmented Reality: Unity 3D, Augmented Reality (Vuforia™)
3. Arduino software: Arduino 1.0.5
4. Eclipse: Eclipse 3.6.2 with Android Development Tools (ADT)

Table 4 shows a classification of the various augmented reality game design tools.

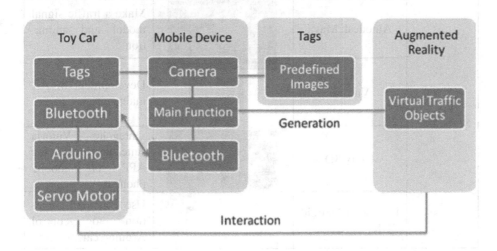

Fig. 3. Hardware and software architecture

Table 4. Analysis of Hardware and Software

	Name	Diagram	Description
Hardware	Arduino Uno		Arduino is an open-source electronics prototyping platform based on flexible, easy-to-use hardware and software.
	Arduino Shield		Shields are boards that can be plugged on top of the Arduino PCB extending its capabilities.
	Car		It consists of two servomotors and a power device.
	Bluetooth module		Receiving and transmitting signals via Bluetooth.
Software	Autodesk Maya		Make a traffic signal model and animation.
	Vuforia		Development of AR main suite.
	Unity 3D		Integrate Vuforia suite, and output the APP on mobile phone.
	Eclipse (Android SDK)		Use Bluetooth function to control Arduino car.

4.3   The Development Flow

Remote-Control Car Assembled

Remote-control car companies in the market do not release any Software Development Kit (SDK). The toy company only releases a control app to allow user to use. In order to have much flexibility and programmability, we choose Arduino finally.

Arduino is a single-board microcontroller designed to make the process of using electronics in multidisciplinary projects more accessible. User can connect the board with many different devices, such as Light-Emitting Diode (LED), temperature sensor, speaker, servo motor, infrared sensor, Bluetooth chip, Ethernet, XBee, Radio Frequency Identification (RFID), Global Positioning System (GPS), and so on. Arduino is great development tool intended for everybody who wants to easily and quickly create his own application. For example it could be a blinking LED or a system to control home appliances via Wireless network.

The following are brief assembly steps:

1. Assemble Arduino Uno board and Arduino Shield board.
2. The servomotors connect with corresponding pins on Arduino Shield board.
3. Assemble car and Arduino boards.
4. Add battery power supply.
5. Connect Bluetooth module with corresponding pins on Arduino Shield board.

After assembling the car, then write an Arduino blink program. We write a control servo code in setup function and loop function. After finishing remote-control car assembly in Fig. 4, we start to implement connection function in mobile device and remote-control car. After remote-control car modification in Fig. 5, the "Cars" outfit is virtual.

Fig. 4. Remote-control car

Fig. 5. After remote-control car modification

Mobile Device and Remote-Control Car
There are many different ways to implement connection function, such as Bluetooth, Wi-Fi, infrared, RFID, and so on. Because the Bluetooth has been widely utilized in mobile device, we choose it as our connection module.

Bluetooth connections comprise mobile device and Arduino car.

Implement connection function in mobile device.
1. Mobile device scans the Bluetooth device and connects with it.
2. Send control signals to Arduino car.

Implement connection function in Arduino car.
1. Add a function control to the Arduino car consisting of forward, backward, left turn, right turn, and stop.
2. Receive signals from mobile device and trigger the corresponding event.

Augmented Reality Interaction Design
Use Unity 3D and Qualcomm Vuforia SDK to develop the application. The game aims to construct traffic signals for education. We design some tags to be recognized.

With Image Recognition AR, user holds camera over tags, and event happens in a virtual environment. The following are brief development steps:

1. Launch the Unity and load Vuforia kit.
2. Use the material dragged into the Unity project library.
3. Identify tag loading Unity.
4. Set up a virtual button on the scene.
5. Combine the connection function in Unity.

The Car Tracked via a Marker
After remote-control car modification in Fig. 5, we use the car's pattern as marker by Vuforia kit. When mobile device's camera recognizes target, we can get the car's position. Via a car's position, we can calculate distance between a car in real world and the object in virtual world or collision detection.

Game Mechanism and Interface
The game mechanism created from Augmented Reality integrates real and virtual features. There are three scenarios in our game mechanism that contains shooting game, roadblock hindrance, and traffic signal game.

Shooting game
Shooting game scenario uses a tag on remote-control car and sets a corresponding 3D model. This scenario's system process diagram uses Mode 2 in Fig. 2. When mobile device's camera recognizes target, the weapon will appear at the top of the car in Fig. 6. It is similar to the movie "Transformers" that cars can transform into the other type. We design some virtual enemies in the game and player can control the car and shoot to be a winner.

Roadblock hindrance
This scenario's system process diagram uses Mode 1 in Fig. 1. The game scenario to identify tags is roadblock hindrance in Fig. 7. When a user drives and crashes into roadblocks, a car will stop forward in Fig. 8. In this scenario, we realize the virtual objects to interact with physical objects.

Traffic signal game
This scenario's system process diagram uses Mode 1 in Fig. 1. The screen of game playing is shown in Fig. 9. There are five buttons consisting of "forward", "left", "right", "back", and "stop" on the screen. User can control car via those buttons and the virtual objects shown on the screen. The use of a set of virtual buttons in the program allows the game to generate feedback on the car's behavior. We design a game situation when the user drives through a green light then the pass has been shown on the screen in Fig. 10. On the other hand, when the user drives through a red light, then the warning has been shown on the screen in Fig. 11. By this way, user will learn the traffic rules.

Fig. 6. The weapon will appear at the top of the car

Fig. 7. A roadblock hindrance on the screen

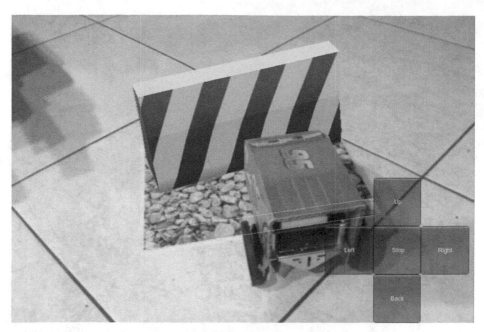

Fig. 8. Drive and crash into roadblocks

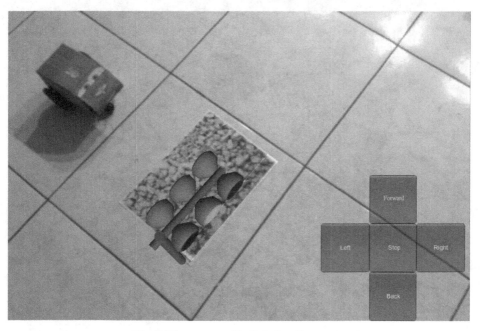

Fig. 9. The green traffic light is safe to pass

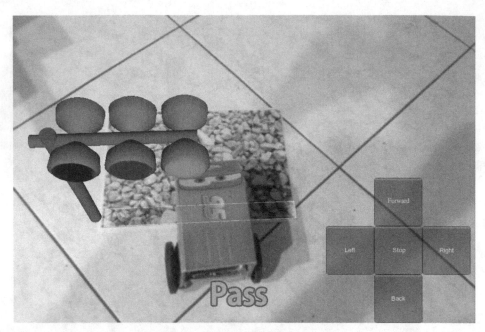

Fig. 10. The green traffic light is safe to pass

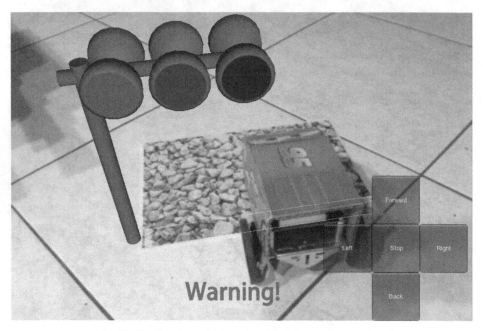

Fig. 11. Passing through the red traffic light causes warning

5   Conclusions

We construct virtual object settings and create the appearance by traffic signal as well as various animation of virtual traffic light, for the reality and remote toys as starting point. We uses the mobile device to control the car. Finally, it allows the car to interact directly with the virtual traffic light, using augmented reality technology. We complete the development of augmented reality car application with a platform to integrate mobile phone. It combines the real toys with virtual objects.

Our proposed remote-control module can be a car, robot, boat, helicopters, and so on. AR interaction with different devices produces more interesting applications. In this paper, we propose two system process modes and design three play scenarios. Combining AR and remote-control car gets more different experience and pleasure. Future studies should further investigate user friendliness and usability with respect to remote-control toys and AR system. The development of additional interaction technology to create Augmented Reality content allows users to understand and use easily.

Acknowledgment. This research was supported by the National Science Council of Taiwan, R.O.C., under Grants NSC 98-2221-E-002 -150 -MY3 and NSC 101-2221-E-002 -194, by Winstar Technology, Test Research, and Lite-on.

References

1. Azuma, R.: A Survey of Augmented Reality. Presence: Teleoperators and Virtual Environments **6**(4), 355–385 (1997)
2. Milgram, P., Kishino, F.: A Taxonomy of Mixed Reality Visual Displays. IEICE Transactions on Information System **77**, 1321–1329 (1994)
3. Roland, J.P., Holloway, R.L., Fuchs, H.: A Comparison of Optical and Video See-through Head-Mounted Displays. Proceedings of Society of Photographic Instrumentation Engineers: Telemanipulator and Telepresence Technologies **2351**, 293–307 (1994)
4. Regen, H.T., Specht, R.: A Mobile Passive Augmented Reality Device-mPARD. In: Proceedings of International Symposium on Augmented Reality, pp. 81-84. Munich (2000)
5. Wagner, D., Schmalstieg, D.: First Steps towards Handheld Augmented Reality. In: Proceedings of IEEE International Symposium on Wearable Computers, White Plains, NY, pp. 127–135 (2003)
6. Chang, Y.N., Koh, R.K.C., Duh, H.B.L.: Handheld AR Games—a Triarchic Conceptual Design Framework. In: Proceedings of ISMAR, Basel, Switzerland, pp. 29–36 (2011)
7. Billinghurst, M., Duenser, A.: Augmented Reality in the Classroom. Computer **45**(7), 56–63 (2012)
8. Escobedo, L., Tentori, M., Quintana, E., Favela, J., Garcia-Rosas, D.: Using augmented reality to help children with autism stay focused. In: Proceedings of Pervasive Computing, Budapest, Hungary, vol. 13, pp. 38–46 (2014)
9. Qualcomm: Vuforia (2014). http://www.vuforia.com
10. Abawi, D.F., Bienwald, J., Dorner, R.: Accuracy in Optical Tracking with Fiducial Markers: An Accuracy Function for ARToolKit. In: Proceedings of the IEEE/ACM International Symposium on Mixed and Augmented Reality, Washington DC, pp. 260-261 (2004)
11. EPFL, Bazar (2014). http://cvlab.epfl.ch/software/bazar/

12. Bigplayar, Hoops AR (2014). http://www.bigplayar.com/hoopsar.html
13. Mattel, Barbie® Digital Makeover (2014).
    https://itunes.apple.com/us/app/barbie-digital-makeover/id549872444?mt=8
14. Dentsu, iButterfly (2014). http://ibutterfly.hk/chi/
15. Digital Tech Frontier, Popar Toys (2014). https://popartoys.com/
16. Mattel, Inc. Apptivity (2014). http://www.mattelapptivity.com/
17. Parrot SA, AR Drone (2014). http://cdn.ardrone2.parrot.com/
18. Quest Visual, Word Lens (2014).
    http://itunes.apple.com/tw/app/word-lens/id383463868?mt=8
19. Layar, Layar (2014). https://www.layar.com/
20. WowWee, Robome (2014). http://www.wowwee.com/robome/
21. Silverlit, Interactive Bluetooth R/C (2014).
    http://silverlit.com/brand/interactive-bluetooth-rc
22. IMBD, Transformers (2014). http://www.imdb.com/title/tt0418279/
23. Unity, Unity3D (2014). http://unity3d.com/

Investigation on Player and Virtual Environment Interaction

Aušra Vidugirienė[1]([✉]), Aistė Pranckevičienė[2], Egidijus Vaškevičius[1],
and Minija Tamošiūnaitė[1]

[1] Faculty of Informatics, Vytautas Magnus University, Kaunas, Lithuania
{a.vidugiriene,e.vaskevicius,m.tamosiunaite}@if.vdu.lt
[2] Faculty of Social Sciences, Vytautas Magnus University, Kaunas, Lithuania
a.pranckeviciene@smf.vdu.lt

Abstract. The paper introduces an investigation on player and virtual environment interaction. A computer game (spaceship navigation through randomly flying asteroids) with different levels of difficulty was created in order to elicit and test human emotions when playing. Emotional responses (excitement, frustration, and engagement/boredom) to the computer game were recorded using Emotiv Epoc device. Spaceship manoeuvring speed and acceleration were included in the investigation as well. Significant relationships between some of the personality traits, emotional reactions and manoeuvring characteristics were found. Emotional responses were significantly increasing when the density of asteroids was increasing. Excitement and frustration signals showed correlations when gaming. Significant increase in manoeuvring speed and acceleration were observed after spaceship and asteroid collision. Positive correlations were found between extraversion and excitement during experiment. The gaming experience and manoeuvring acceleration was strongly negatively related when the difficulty of the game was lower and strongly positively related when it was higher.

Keywords: Virtual environment · Computer game · Emotions · Personality · Player's affective state

1 Introduction

Computer games became a common form of entertainment, so they are expected to generate emotional involvement, excitement and motor or cognitive challenges. Game developers spend a great deal of effort trying to create technology that would be able to create this rich experience. However this task is harder than it sounds, because a player is not just a blank table that mechanically responds to provided stimulations. Decision to play or not to play, preference for certain game genre, response to game appearance, visual and auditory stimulations, persistence of play, reactions to challenges and fails depend on many individual factors like previous game and life experience or personality traits. Research findings support an idea that we play the way we are. For example, study of Wohn and Wash [1] show that observer could identify personality traits of the player by simply looking at a screenshot of created virtual

© Springer International Publishing Switzerland 2014
L.T. De Paolis and A. Mongelli (Eds.): AVR 2014, LNCS 8853, pp. 19–34, 2014.
DOI: 10.1007/978-3-319-13969-2_2

environment. In another study, persistence during game play predicted person's persistence in other life tasks, such as learning [2].

On the other hand computer games are also not passive. They create new reality and offer opportunities for players to meet their needs [3]. The more game corresponds with the needs of the player, the more motivated he or she is to play. Findings of Tone et al. [4] show that certain characteristics of games may even cause player to become addicted.

Thus, as Khong and Thwaits [5] state, video games constitute a genre of software that involves interface and user experiences, it makes sense that it should be studied from the perspective of Human-Computer Interaction (HCI). Looking from the perspective of game developers, knowledge about HCI might help to develop responsive technologies that will be able to adapt to player needs. From the psychological perspective a comprehensive knowledge about interaction between player characteristics and game features is needed for a better understanding of the process of game play and its impacts on users [6].

There are quite a lot of different studies done in the field of computer games and affective states of a player using various means to evaluate them. Shaker et al. [7] investigate self-reflected player experiences (engagement, challenge and frustration) and player movements when playing Super Mario Bros computer game, but the affective states of the players are not measured from bio-signals in real time. Holmgard et al. [8] describe a study where a computer game is dedicated to help people with post traumatic stress disorder. A player is given different stressful situations (usually caused by previous experiences in a war) and his skin conductance is measured to objectively evaluate his stress level during a game in real time. Gutica and Conati [9] present a research where students were playing educational mathematical game and their emotions were observed and evaluated by judges. The improved mathematical skills correlated to the observed emotional states as engaged concentration. Chanel et al. [10] describe a Tetris game study when player's affective state is evaluated according to physiological signals as electro-dermal activity, blood volume pulse, skin temperature, and chest cavity expansion. The purpose is to keep a player engaged and regulate the level of game complexity according to the changes of the player's affective state – to decrease difficulty if a player becomes anxious and to increase it if a player is bored. Some studies propose affective models or game engines [12,13] for collaborative virtual environment games. Pröll [13] examines Emotiv Epoc device for various gaming purposes.

This research is dedicated to investigate the relationship between player personality traits, emotional (EEG-based) response to a computer game when playing, and user manoeuvring characteristics (speed and acceleration) during a game. A computer game was created for this purpose and Emotiv Epoc device was used to measure emotional reactions (excitement, frustration and engagement/boredom).

2   Virtual Environment – "Spaceship" Computer Game

A virtual environment (computer game) with different levels of intensity was created to investigate its influence on player's emotions and behaviour, and game play experience relations with personality traits.

A player controls a spaceship using keyboard buttons (left, right, up, and down) and tries not to collide with asteroids that are flying to the spaceship. The principle of a game is shown in Fig. 1.

Fig. 1. Randomly generated asteroids flying to the spaceship

The generator of the asteroids is programmed so that the asteroids are randomly generated in a limited rectangle area (Fig. 1, back rectangle) and can appear in any point of the rectangle with the same probability. In this way a dispersion of the asteroids on the screen is created and they are spread in the whole space area. The generated asteroids are of different sizes within the predefined size limits. The asteroids fly in the same velocity but their number differs in different phases of a game. When the asteroids reach the front (monitor) plane, they are invisibly destroyed to avoid "wondering" asteroids and accidental collisions. If an asteroid is not destroyed, it can begin flying back after reaching the front plane.

The distance between the plane where asteroids are generated and the front plane, where they are invisibly destroyed is more than ten seconds long if evaluating it by the speed of an asteroid. The generated asteroid becomes visible to a player 4-5 s later after the generation. After it becomes visible it reaches the possible collision (with a spaceship) plane in 6-7 s and a few more seconds are needed to reach the front plane where they are invisibly destroyed. The spaceship is not situated on the front plane; it is placed on a potential collision plane and is all visible to the player. It is important to note that if an approaching asteroid is in the centre and the spaceship is in the centre at that moment, it is not possible to avoid a collision two seconds before the potential collision. In order to elicit stronger emotional reaction to a collision of a spaceship and an asteroid visual (fire) and audible (strong crash sound) effects are produced.

Fig. 2 and Fig. 3 demonstrate two scenes and situations of a game.

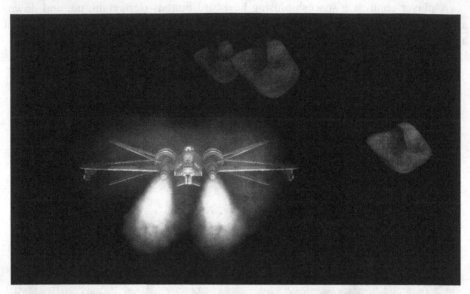

Fig. 2. Asteroids flying to the spaceship without a collision

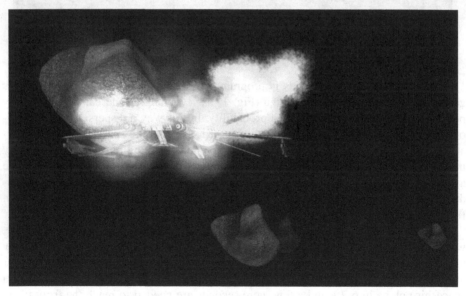

Fig. 3. A collision of a spaceship and an asteroid (with visual fire effect)

Fig. 2 illustrates asteroids flying to the spaceship without a collision (the spaceship leaves a smoke band behind it) and Fig. 3 shows a collision of a spaceship and an asteroid when a fire visual effect is present together with a collision sound. However the spaceship is not visually affected after a collision and the game is continued.

Game simulator was created using Unity 3D engine and C# programming language. A PC with i7 processor 8 GB RAM and Nvidia GeForce 8600 GT video card was used. The computer game was played using full HD 65" diameter monitor (screen resolution 1920x1080), and surround 5.1 sound system.

3   Experiment and Data

3.1   Sample

15 university students (nine (60.0%) males, six (40.0%) females, age M=22.9 (1.3), range 21-26) participated in the study. Ten (66.7%) participants reported that they play computer games regularly, every day. Other participants reported playing computer games from several times a week to several times a year. There were no participants who had no gaming experience. Average hours per week spent gaming was 12.5 (11.8) and ranged from 0 to 35. All the participants preferred using their personal computer for gaming (19 (100%)), one (6.7%) participant also used mobile phone as gaming platform in his daily life. Participants mention playing almost all game genres: strategy – 9 (60.0%), RPG – 8 (53.3%), MMO – 7 (46.7%), simulations – 3 (20.0%), action – 2 (13.3%), other – 3 (20.0%).

3.2   Psychological Tests and Data Collection

Several aspects of personality, sensation seeking and Big Five personality traits, were measured in this study.

Sensation seeking was evaluated using Sensation Seeking Scale – form V (SSS-V, [14], Lithuanian translation by Pranckevičienė, Ružas, 2012). Reliability of the SSS-V was acceptable for the data analysis (Cronbach α = .77). The SSS-V score addresses extent to which participants are drawn towards feelings and experiences that are novel, varied, thrilling, possibly risky and intense. Trait of sensation seeking is related to low tolerance of routine and boredom. Previous research shows that sensation seeking might be related to players emotional response and playing behaviour. In Fang and Zhao [6] study sensation seeking had significant positive effect on enjoyment of computer game play. Sensation seeking is found to be a good predictor of high or even pathological involvement in online games [15].

Big Five personality traits were evaluated using The Big Five Inventory (BFI; [16,17,18], Lithuanian translation by Vytautas Magnus university, Psychology Department, 2009). Reliability of all BFI scales was acceptable for the data analysis (Cronbach α ranged from .65 to .88). BFI measures five core personality dimensions: extraversion vs. introversion, agreeableness vs. antagonism, conscientiousness vs. lack of direction, neuroticism vs. emotional stability, openness vs. closeness to experience. Big Five personality traits are often analyzed in relationship with gaming behaviour [19,20].

Participants were also asked about frequency of computer game play, hours per week spent playing, types of the games played and game platforms used.

After the experiment participants were asked to subjectively evaluate their general emotional state, satisfaction with their performance during the game play and to express their opinion about game characteristics.

3.3   Stages of the Experiment

At first the whole procedure of the experiment was explained in details to the volunteer and if he or she did not want to participate in the experiment, it was possible not to take part in it. Before the beginning of the experiment, a volunteer signed an agreement to participate in the experiment and to let using his or her data in the study.

The experiment started with psychological tests that were described in 3.2. A volunteer was given as much time as he or she needed to fill the tests. He or she was also asked to choose a nickname and to use it in the tests instead of his or her real name to assure confidentiality of the data. The same nicknames were used later during a game play to strengthen the impression of a usual computer game.

After the tests were completed the Emotiv Epoc device that records EEG inputs from 14 channels (according to international 10-20 locations: AF3, F7, F3, FC5, T7, P7, O1, O2, P8, T8, FC6, F4, F8, AF4) [21] was put on the head of the volunteer, making sure that all the contacts are in the right places and properly attached to the skin. The computer game was started when the bio-signals were steady.

The environment of the experiment aimed to create a cosy home type atmosphere. A volunteer was sitting on a sofa-bed and the play was performed on a large screen monitor in the special laboratory for virtual reality experiments. The game was controlled by a wireless keyboard. At the same time only a volunteer and a person responsible for the experiment was in the room. The lights were off to minimise any possible visual distraction.

The computer game had several intensity stages. At first one minute was given for getting used to the game environment. Only one asteroid in ten seconds was generated. The second phase was more intense and one asteroid in two seconds was generated in the next four minutes. The third stage was the most intense and aimed to cause stressful situations for the volunteer. Two asteroids in one second were generated for five minutes. The last phase that lasted one and a half minute was aimed for relaxing and again only one asteroid in ten seconds was generated.

After the computer game, the volunteers were asked to reflect their emotional state after the game play and to report their impressions of various game characteristics as quality, ease of game control, as well as frustration level induced by background, sound, speed, density of asteroids, smoke, explosions, and video discrepancies.

3.4   Emotional and Game-play Data Processing

During the experiment three pre-processed emotional signals – excitement, frustration and engagement/boredom – were recorded using Emotiv Epoc device. Values of the three signals varied from zero to one. If excitement, frustration and engagement were low, the value was close to zero and if they were high, the values of parameters were close to one. The signals were recorded with the sampling period of $T_0=0.5$ s.

The coordinates of a spaceship two times per second and the exact time of the collision were recorded as well. Two derivative parameters were calculated and added after the experiment. Using the coordinates of the spaceship, manoeuvring speed and acceleration of a spaceship were calculated and later used in the statistical analysis.

SPSS 13.0 software was used for statistical analysis. Nonparametric correlations and criteria for two related samples comparison were used because of the small sample size. Matlab software was used for processing the required data for later statistical analysis.

Relations between personality traits, gaming experience, emotional signals and spaceship manoeuvring speed as well as acceleration were calculated using the data from the second (two asteroids per second were generated) and the third (ten asteroids per second were generated) stage of the game.

There was more specific analysis performed, using excitement, frustration, and spaceship manoeuvring speed and acceleration signal intervals of 14.5 s around the collision action (seven seconds before the collision and seven seconds after the collision). Interval of seven seconds before the collision was chosen as an asteroid becomes visible on the monitor screen six-seven seconds before the possible collision. The same length interval was taken after the collision as the reaction time to visual and audible stimuli for every person is different.

These intervals were selected from each volunteer data, but the statistical analysis was performed for the whole group at once. Only single collisions in the selected intervals were analysed. There were lots of cases where several collisions were present in the 14.5 s length interval, but they were not taken into the analysis as there is a need of larger amounts of data for more complex analysis.

Fig. 4 shows all the single intervals of frustration signal around the collision for one of the volunteers in the experiment Stage II. Vertical dotted lines denote the collision moment and the time is set to zero at this point. Fig. 5 shows all the single intervals of frustration signal around the collision for the same volunteer in the experiment Stage III. It can be seen from the figures that the signals behave differently. To analyse the data in detail the intervals of 14.5 s around the collision were divided into three smaller intervals. The first sub-interval included signal values from -7 to -2.5 s before the collision; the second sub-interval included the values from -2 s to 1.5 s – the close collision environment and the third included values from 2 s to 7 s after a collision. Such sub-intervals were selected based on the fact that the collision starts to become unavoidable 2 s before a collision and taking into account that it takes some time for the sound and visual collision effects to disappear. Maximal values from each sub-interval were calculated for excitement, frustration, manoeuvring speed, and acceleration signals to analyse the changes in the sub-intervals that is to investigate if there are significant changes in the signals before the collision, during it and after it. Engagement/boredom signals were not analysed this way as they did not vary in the vicinity of the collisions.

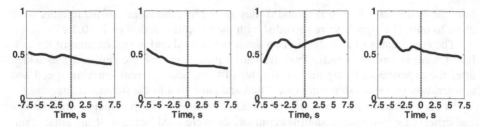

Fig. 4. Samples of frustration signal around the collision in the experiment stage 2. Vertical dotted lines denote the collision moment.

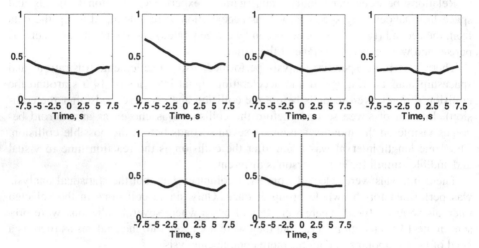

Fig. 5. Samples of frustration signal around the collision in the experiment stage 3. Vertical dotted lines denote the collision moment.

4   Results

4.1   Impact of Computer Game on Player

Emotional signals of the players during different computer game stages (with different asteroid generation frequency) were compared. Sub-intervals of spaceship-asteroid collisions environment were investigated when emotional signals as well as spaceship manoeuvring speed and acceleration were taken into account.

Significant changes in frustration and engagement were registered between Stage II and Stage III of the computer game (Table 1). At Stage II frustration increased while boredom decreased. A statistical tendency observed that excitement also increased ant Stage III. At Stage III manoeuvring speed was faster, but no significant changes in manoeuvring acceleration were observed.

Table 1. Changes in excitement, frustration, engagement, manoeuvring speed and acceleration during the experiment. Wilcoxon Signed Ranks Test.

Stage of the experiment (III-II)		N	Mean rank	Z	p
excitement III - excitement II	Negative Ranks	4	7.50	-1.70	0.09
	Positive Ranks	11	8.18		
frustration III - frustrationII	Negative Ranks	3	7.00	-2.22	0.03
	Positive Ranks	12	8.25		
engagement III - engagement II	Negative Ranks	13	8.38	-2.78	0.01
	Positive Ranks	2	5.50		
speed III – speed II	Negative Ranks	5	6.20	-1.65	0.10
	Positive Ranks	10	8.90		
acceleration III - acceleration II	Negative Ranks	7	7.86	-0.28	0.78
	Positive Ranks	8	8.13		

The test for the sub-intervals of collision interval in excitement signal showed that there are significant change between sub-interval 1 and sub-interval 3 (Table 2). Excitement signal is increasing more often than decreasing after spaceship collision with an asteroid (comparing pre-collision and post-collision sub-intervals).

Table 2. Changes in excitement in collision interval when evaluating their sub-intervals. Wilcoxon Signed Ranks Test.

Excitement		N	Mean rank	Z	p
	Negative Ranks	39	49.77		<0.000
sub-interval 3 – sub-interval 1	Positive Ranks	73	60.10	-3.551	
	Ties	3	-		
	Negative Ranks	65	56.30		
sub-interval 2 – sub-interval 1	Positive Ranks	48	57.95	-1.258	0.209
	Ties	2	-		

The test for the sub-intervals of collision interval in frustration signal showed that there are significant change between sub-interval 1 and sub-interval 2 (Table 3). Frustration signal is decreasing more often than increasing if comparing the pre-collision and collision sub-intervals.

Table 3. Changes in frustration in collision interval when evaluating their subintervals. Wilcoxon Signed Ranks Test.

Frustration		N	Mean rank	Z	p
	Negative Ranks	60	54.43		
sub-interval 3 – sub-interval 1	Positive Ranks	54	60.92	-0.03	0.97
	Ties	1	-		
	Negative Ranks	77	60.48		
sub-interval 2 – sub-interval 1	Positive Ranks	35	47.74	-4.33	<0.00
	Ties	3	-		

Table 4. Changes in manoeuvring speed in collision intervals when evaluating their sub-intervals. Wilcoxon Signed Ranks Test.

Speed		N	Mean rank	Z	p
	Negative Ranks	48	61.99		
sub-interval 2 – sub-interval 1	Positive Ranks	65	53.32	-0.702	0.483
	Ties	2	-		
	Negative Ranks	39	59.74		
sub-interval 3 – sub-interval 1	Positive Ranks	71	53.17	-2.155	0.031
	Ties	5			

Analysis of speed and acceleration changes in subintervals before and after collision revealed, that significant increase in speed is observed after collision (sub-interval 3) comparing with speed before collision (sub-interval 1) (Table 4)

Changes in acceleration in three collision sub-intervals more frequently resembled U-shape form: acceleration decreased in sub-interval 2 comparing with sub-interval 1, and increased again in sub-interval 3 comparing with sub-interval 1 (Table 5).

Table 5. Changes in acceleration in collision intervals when evaluating their subintervals. Wilcoxon Signed Ranks Test.

Acceleration		N	Mean rank	Z	p
sub-interval 3 – sub-interval 1	Negative Ranks	68	62.76	-2.604	0.009
	Positive Ranks	47	51.11		
sub-interval 2 – sub-interval 1	Negative Ranks	43	61.53	-1.923	0.055
	Positive Ranks	72	55.89		

The comparison of excitement, speed and acceleration sub-intervals showed negative correlations between some sub-intervals of the signals (Table 6). Post-collision sub-intervals of excitement signal correlate with all three speed sub-intervals.

Table 6. Relationship between excitement and speed and acceleration. Spearman rho.

Excitement	Speed			Acceleration		
	Sub-interval 1	Sub-interval 2	Sub-interval 3	Sub-interval 1	Sub-interval 2	Sub-interval 3
Sub-interval 1	-0,010	-0,091	-0,123	-0,105	0,111	0,075
Sub-interval 2	-0,045	-0,123	-0,121	-0,143	0,138	0,096
Sub-interval 3	-0,217**	-0,246***	-0,205**	-0,066	0,158	0,053

**Correlation is significant at $p<0.05$, (2-tailed)
***Correlation is significant at $p<0.01$, (2-tailed)

The comparison of frustration, manoeuvring speed and acceleration sub-intervals showed positive correlations between pre-collision and collision sub-intervals of frustration and collision sub-interval of speed as well as pre-collision sub-intervals of acceleration signals (Table 7).

Table 7. Relationship between frustration and manoeuvring speed and acceleration. Spearman rho.

| | Speed | | | Acceleration | | |
Frustration	Sub-interval 1	Sub-interval 2	Sub-interval 3	Sub-interval 1	Sub-interval 2	Sub-interval 3
Sub-interval 1	0,127	0,194**	0,151	0,243***	0,169	0,025
Sub-interval 2	0,118	0,196**	0,167	0,213**	0,166	0,094
Sub-interval 3	0,009	0,111	0,034	0,141	0,162	0,023

**Correlation is significant at $p<0.05$, (2-tailed)
***Correlation is significant at $p<0.01$, (2-tailed)

4.2   Player's Contribution to Gaming Experience

Relationships between personality traits and gaming experience as well as emotional signals and game properties (manoeuvring speed and acceleration) in different stages of the game were investigated.

Statistical analysis revealed that personality traits were not significantly related to frequency of computer game play, but correlated with hours per week spent gaming (Table 8). More expressed trait of neuroticism correlated with more gaming hours per week, while negative relationship was observed between more expressed sensation seeking, extraversions, agreeableness and conscientiousness.

Table 8. Relationship between personality traits and involvement in computer gaming. Spearman rho.

| | Involvement in computer games | |
Personality traits	Frequency	Hours per week
Sensation seeking	-0.08	-0.52**
Extraversion	-0.21	-0.47*
Agreeableness	-0.12	-0.54**
Conscientiousness	-0.22	-0.51**
Neuroticism	-0.04	0.55**
Openness	-0.37	-0.24

*Correlation is significant at $p<0.1$, (2-tailed)
** Correlation is significant at $p<0.05$, (2-tailed)

As can be seen in Table 9 extraversion positively correlated with excitement during all stages of experiment. Observed correlations were relatively strong taking into account small sample size.

Data analysis revealed unexpected results. Openness to new experiences was related to higher levels of frustration during experiment. Contrary to expectations, negative correlation was found between frustration and trait of neuroticism.

No statistically significant relationships were observed between personality traits and Emotic Epoc measures of engagement (Table 10), although some tendencies that are in line with previous research were found: sensation seeking and openness to new experiences correlated positively with higher engagement, while neuroticism showed tendency to be negatively related to engagement.

Table 9. Relationships between personality traits and excitement and frustration. Spearman rho.

Personality traits	Excitement			Frustration		
	Stage I	Stage II	Average	Stage I	Stage II	Average
Sensation seeking	0.07	0.28	0.23	0.35	0.31	0.34
Extraversion	0.68***	0.43	0.50*	0.09	-0.09	-0.06
Agreeableness	-0.03	-0.15	-0.11	0.27	0.35	0.37
Conscientiousness	0.36	0.30	0.33	0.03	0.08	0.06
Neuroticism	0.13	0.11	0.10	-0.37	-0.41	-0.43
Openness	-0.13	-0.19	-0.23	0.49*	0.56**	0.53**

*Correlation is significant at $p<0.1$, (2-tailed)
**Correlation is significant at $p<0.05$, (2-tailed)
***Correlation is significant at $p<0.01$, (2-tailed)

Table 10. Relationship between personality traits and engagement. Spearman rho.

Personality traits	Engagement		
	Stage I	Stage II	Average
Sensation seeking	0.26	0.01	0.35
Extraversion	0.30	-0.22	-0.03
Agreeableness	-0.16	0.08	0.02
Conscientiousness	0.00	0.02	0.10
Neuroticism	0.08	-0.11	-0.25
Openness	0.26	0.08	0.28

Table 11. Relationship between personality and speed during experiment. Spearman rho.

Personality traits	Speed			Acceleration		
	Stage I	Stage II	Average	Stage I	Stage II	Average
Sensation seeking	-0.15	-0.19	-0.12	-0.22	-0.15	-0.22
Extraversion	0.23	0.22	0.17	0.24	0.19	0.59**
Agreeableness	0.00	0.25	0.13	0.01	-0.06	0.08
Conscientiousness	-0.05	0.18	0.03	0.29	0.04	0.51**
Neuroticism	0.23	0.17	0.17	0.31	-0.16	0.08
Openness	0.20	0.03	0.12	0.29	0.46*	-0.04

*Correlation is significant at $p<0.1$, (2-tailed)
**Correlation is significant at $p<0.05$, (2-tailed)

No statistically significant correlations were observed between spaceship manoeuvring speed and personality traits (Table 11). However positive correlations between extraversion, conscientiousness and acceleration were found.

Hours per week spent gaming were negatively correlated with excitement during the experiment (Table 12), indicating that more experienced players are less likely to feel satisfaction during computer game, especially when the game is not very challenging. Frequency of computer gaming and hours spent gaming correlated negatively with frustration. These results might indicate that more experienced players feel more comfortable and relaxed even facing new game and user interface and might be used to such forms of stimulation. No relationship was found between computer game experience and engagement during the experiment.

Table 12. Relationship between gaming frequency and excitement. Spearman rho.

Involvement in computer games	Excitement			Frustration		
	Stage I	Stage II	Average	Stage I	Stage II	Average
Frequency	-0.22	0.15	0.00	-0.62**	-0.49*	-0.52**
Hours per week	-0.37	-0.18	-0.28	-0.47*	-0.33	-0.37

*Correlation is significant at p<0.1, (2-tailed)
**Correlation is significant at p<0.05, (2-tailed)

Frequency of computer gaming did not correlate with manoeuvring speed during experiment (Table 13). The more experienced a player was, the less he or she accelerated during non intensive phase of experiment, and were more prone to acceleration during more challenging phase of the game.

Table 13. Relationship between gaming frequency and manoeuvring speed and acceleration. Spearman rho.

Involvement in computer games	Speed			Acceleration		
	Stage I	Stage II	Average	Stage I	Stage II	Average
Frequency	-0.12	0.07	0.01	0.52**	0.63***	0.07
Hours per week	0.18	0.15	0.19	-0.32	0.15	-0.31

**Correlation is significant at p<0.05, (2-tailed)
***Correlation is significant at p<0.01, (2-tailed)

5   Conclusions and Discussion

Emotional responses are changing between the stages of the game when the density of asteroids is increasing. More challenging tasks evoke higher levels of frustration but at the same time generate higher engagement and excitement. Frustration and engagement/boredom signals are changing in larger extent than excitement and spaceship manoeuvring speed signals.

Analysis of changes in emotional responses in sub-intervals before, around, and after collisions with the asteroid supported the idea that collision experience has significant impact of player's emotional response. Although collision might be considered as negative and unpleasant event, data of this study show increase of excitement after collision. The highest level of frustration was before a collision and it shows tendency to decrease just after a collision. This data supports the idea that excitement and frustration during the game play are correlated phenomena and some level of frustration is needed for game to evoke excitement. Trajectories of changes in frustration an excitement let us speculate, that high frustration before collision is replaced by decrease of the tension just after collision, when player understands that he or she could not change this situation and followed by increased excitement and motivation to play.

Changes in spaceship manoeuvring speed and acceleration in sub-intervals before, around and after collision with the asteroid reflect expected players behaviour – significant increase in speed and acceleration were observed after the collision because they where decreased by the collision incident. However speed and acceleration of the spaceship were related to player's emotional responds as well. Analyzing the pre-collision, collision and post-collision sub-intervals, weak inverse correlations were found between all three subintervals of speed and post-collision subinterval of excitement. Weak direct correlations were found between pre-collision and collision sub-intervals of frustration and collision sub-interval of speed as well as pre-collision subintervals of acceleration. These results indicate that players who experience higher levels of frustration might be linked to higher manoeuvring speed and acceleration during computer game; however this does not directly convert to higher level of excitement. Although small sample size and very simple statistical procedures do not let us draw very strong concussions, these results are in line with Yerkes–Dodson law of optimal emotional arousal [22] indicating that optimal balance between challenge of the task and level of frustration must be found for player to feel excited. This is the place where HCI might make impact. Personality traits were not strongly related with emotional responses to a computer game. The strongest relationship was found between extraversion and excitement. Extraversion was positively related to excitement during experiment. These results are in line with psychological theories because it is known that extraverts are in general more prone to experience positive emotions. Extraversion is found to be related to more frequent technology use [20]. However not all studies find relationship between extraversion and gaming behaviour [23].The study showed that higher neuroticism is related to a lower frustration what contradicts with usual psychological rules, but this result could be explained by a sample of the experiment as the most experienced players had the highest neuroticism scores while the gaming experience had inverse correlation to frustration signals. Positive correlation between neuroticism and hours spent gaming are in line with studies that report positive relationship between expressed neuroticism and game addiction [24]. There were no correlations found between personal characteristics and manoeuvring speed, manoeuvring acceleration was related to consciousness as well as to extraversion.

Although sensation seeking is found to be related to gaming behaviour in other studies [6], [15], this study failed to replicate these results. Contrary to expectations, sensation seeking was negatively related to hours spent gaming and did not correlate with excitement during experiment.

The gaming experience was not statistically significantly related to excitement signal, but there is a tendency that more experienced players experience less excitement and less frustration especially in the second stage of the game (2 asteroids/s are generated). There was no correlation between gaming experience and engagement found. These results support our speculations about importance of frustration-excitement relationship for enjoyment of a computer game. Although more experienced players showed less frustration during the game, their excitement was lower.

The gaming experience and acceleration was strongly negatively related in the second stage of a game and strongly positively related in the third stage of a game. That means that more experienced players accelerated less where the density of asteroids was smaller (two asteroids per second were generated) and accelerated more where the density of the asteroids was larger (ten asteroids per second were generated). These results indicate that more experienced game players get used to certain levels of stimulation and it becomes harder to achieve higher levels of excitement. Small sample size does not let us to perform more precise analysis where various personality traits and level of game experience were controlled. However our data supports the idea that the player contributes to the game experience and personal factors may impact excitement and frustration levels during the game.

Game properties' relations with user's personality traits and physiological signals lead to the development of emotion-oriented adaptive computer games. Objective information about the preferences and reactions of the payers would allow constructing game scenarios of continuous engagement without using excessive elements.

Acknowledgements. Postdoctoral fellowship of Aušra Vidugiriene is funded by European Union Structural Funds project "Postdoctoral Fellowship Implementation in Lithuania" within the framework of the Measure for Enhancing Mobility of Scholars and Other Researchers and the Promotion of Student Research (VP1-3.1-ŠMM-01) of the Program of Human Resources Development Action Plan.

References

1. Wohn, D.Y., Wash, R.: A virtual Room with a cue: Detecting personality through spatial customization in a city simulation game. Computers in Human Behavior **29**, 155–159 (2013)
2. Ventura, M., Shute, V.: The validity of a game-based assessment of persistence. Computers in Human Behavior **29**, 2568–2572 (2013)
3. Homer, B.D., Hayward, E.O., Frye, J., Plass, J.L.: Gender and player characteristics in video game play of preadolescents. Computers in Human Behavior **28**, 1782–1789 (2012)
4. Tone, H.-J., Zhao, H.-R., Yan, W.-S.: The attraction of online games: An important factor for Internet Addiction. Computers in Human Behavior **30**, 321–327 (2014)
5. Khong, C.W., Ng, Y.Y., Thwaites, H.: A Review of Affective Design towards Video Games. Procedia – Social and Behavioral Sciences **51**, 687–691 (2012)
6. Fang, X., Zhao, F.: Personality and enjoyment of computer game play. Computers in Industry **61**, 342–349 (2010)
7. Shaker, N., Asteriadis, S., Yannakakis, G.N., Karpouzis, K.: A Game-Based Corpus for Analysing the Interplay between Game Context and Player Experience. In: D'Mello, S., Graesser, A., Schuller, B., Martin, J.-C. (eds.) ACII 2011, Part II. LNCS, vol. 6975, pp. 547–556. Springer, Heidelberg (2011)
8. Holmgard, C., Yannakakis, G.N., Karstoft, K.-I., Andersen , H.S.: Stress Detection for PTSD via the StartleMart Game. In: Proc. of the 5th Bianual Humaine Association Conference on Affective Computing and Intelligent Interaction, pp. 523–528 (2013)
9. Gutica, M., Conati, C.: Student Emotions with an Edu-Game: A Detailed Analysis. In: Proc. of the 5th bianual Humaine Association Conference on Affective Computing and Intelligent Interaction, pp. 534–539 (2013)
10. Chanel, G., Kalogianni, K., Pun, T.: GamEMO: How Physiological Signals Show your Emotions and Enhance your Game Experience. In: Proc. of the 14th ACM international conference on Multimodal interaction, pp. 297–298 (2012)

11. Manninen, T.: Rich interaction model for game and virtual environment design, academic dissertation (2004)
12. Popescu, A., Broekens, J., van Someren, M.: GAMYGDALA: an Emotion Engine for Games. IEEE Transactions on Affective Computing **5**(1), 32–44
13. Pröll, M.: Using a low-cost gyro and eeg-based input device in interactive game design, Master's Thesis, Graz University of Technology (2012)
14. Zuckerman, M.: Sensation Seeking: Beyond the Optimal Level of Arousal. Lawrence Erlbaum Associates, Hillsdale, N.J. (1979)
15. Barrault, S., Varescon, I.: Impulsive sensation seeking and gambling practice among a sample of online poker players: Comparison between non pathological, problem and pathological gamblers. Personality and Individual Differences **55**, 502–507 (2013)
16. John, O.P., Naumann, L.P., Soto, C.J.: Paradigm Shift to the Integrative Big-Five Trait Taxonomy: History, Measurement, and Conceptual Issues. In: John, O.P., Robins, R.W., Pervin, L.A. (eds.) Handbook of personality: Theory and research, pp. 114–158. Guilford Press, New York (2008)
17. John, O.P., Donahue, E.M., Kentle, R.L.: The Big Five Inventory-Versions 4a and 54. University of California, Berkeley, Institute of Personality and Social Research, Berkeley (1991)
18. Benet-Martinez, V., John, O.P.: Los Cinco Grandes across cultures and ethnic groups: Multitrait multimethod analyses of the Big Five in Spanish and English. Journal of Personality and Social Psychology **75**, 729–750 (1998)
19. Collins, E., Freeman, J., Chamarro-Premuzic, T.: Personality traits associated with problematic and non-problematic massively multiplayer online role playing game use. Personality and Individual Differences **52**, 133–138 (2012)
20. Witt, E.A., Massman, A.J., Jackson, L.A.: Trends in youth's videogame playing, overall computer use, and communication technology use: The impact of self-esteem and the Big Five personality factors. Computers in Human Behavior **27**, 763–769 (2011)
21. Emotiv Epoc specifications. Brain-computer interface technology. http://www.emotiv.com/upload/manual/sdk/EPOCSpecifications.pdf
22. Yerkes, R.M., Dodson, J.D.: The relation of strength of stimulus to rapidity of habit-formation. Journal of Comparative Neurology and Psychology **18**, 459–482 (1908). doi:10.1002/cne.920180503
23. Collins, E., Freeman, J.: Do problematic and non-problematic video game players differ in extraversion, trait empathy, social capital and prosocial tendencies? Computers in Human Behavior **29**, 1933–1940 (2013)
24. Huh, S., Bowman, N.D.: Perception of and addiction to online games as a function of personality traits. Journal of Media Psychology **13**, 1–31 (2008)

Real-Time Single Camera Hand Gesture Recognition System for Remote Deaf-Blind Communication

Giuseppe Airò Farulla[1]([✉]), Ludovico Orlando Russo[1], Chiara Pintor[1],
Daniele Pianu[2], Giorgio Micotti[3], Alice Rita Salgarella[4], Domenico Camboni[4],
Marco Controzzi[4], Christian Cipriani[4], Calogero Maria Oddo[4], Stefano Rosa[1],
and Marco Indaco[1]

[1] Politecnico di Torino, Turin, Italy
{giuseppe.airofarulla,ludovico.russo,stefano.rosa,
marco.indaco}@polito.it,chiara.pintor@studenti.polito.it
[2] Institute of Electronics, Computer and Telecommunication Engineering,
National Research Council of Italy, Padova, Italy
daniele.pianu@ieiit.cnr.it
[3] Politecnico di Milano, Milano, Italy
giorgio.micotti@mail.polimi.it
[4] The BioRobotics Institute, Scuola Superiore Sant'Anna, Pisa, Italy
{a.salgarella,d.camboni,m.controzzi,ch.cipriani,oddoc}@sssup.it

Abstract. This paper presents a fast approach for marker-less Full-DOF hand tracking, leveraging only depth information from a single depth camera. This system can be useful in many applications, ranging from tele-presence to remote control of robotic actuators or interaction with 3D virtual environment. We applied the proposed technology to enable remote transmission of signs from Tactile Sing Languages (i.e., Sign Languages with Tactile feedbacks), allowing non-invasive remote communication not only among deaf-blind users, but also with deaf, blind and hearing with proficiency in Sign Languages. We show that our approach paves the way to a fluid and natural remote communication for deaf-blind people, up to now impossible. This system is a first prototype for the PARLOMA project, which aims at designing a remote communication system for deaf-blind people.

Keywords: Real-time Markerless Hand Tracking · Hand Gesture Recognition · Tactile Sign-Language Communication · Haptic Interface

1 Introduction

The problem of tracking human hands joints, recognizing a wide set of signs, from single marker-less visual observations is of both theoretical interest and practical importance. In the last years promising results in terms of performances and robustness have been achieved due also to rapid advances in modern sensing technologies.

© Springer International Publishing Switzerland 2014
L.T. De Paolis and A. Mongelli (Eds.): AVR 2014, LNCS 8853, pp. 35–52, 2014.
DOI: 10.1007/978-3-319-13969-2_3

Many approaches have been presented in the hand gesture recognition area [16,20,27]; they differ in the used algorithm, in the type of camera, in the theoretical justifications, etc. Due to recent lowering in prices, new data sources have become available for mass consumers, such as time-of-flight [7] and structured light cameras [5], which ease the task of hand gesture recognition. Indeed, a robust solution has yet to be found, as existing approaches very often require an intensive tuning phase, the usage of coloured or sensitized gloves, or a working framework which embed more than one imaging sensor. Currently, traditional vision-based hand gesture recognition methods do not achieve satisfactory performances for real-life applications [15]. On the other hand, the development of RGB-D cameras, able to generate depth images with few noise also in very low illumination conditions, has recently accelerated the process of investigating for innovative solutions. In addition, the advent of modern programming frameworks for GPUs enable real-time processing even for complex approaches (i.e., that do not rely on too simplistic assumptions), that otherwise would be much slower if executed in CPUs.

Hand gestures are a natural part of human interaction, both with machines and other humans. As they represent a simple and intuitive way of conveying information and commands (e.g., zoom in or out, drag...), hand gesture recognition is of great importance for Human Machine Interaction (HMI) as well. Human interaction is widely based on hand gestures, above all when subjects with severe disabilities are involved and speech is absent, as in Sign Language (SL) based interaction. In both these fields (HMI and SL based interaction) it is necessary to provide support for real-time unaided gestures recognition, as markers or gloves are cumbersome and represent a hindrance to natural interaction. It is preferable to develop a system which relies on a single camera and does not require any calibration or tuning phase. Extensive initialization would represent a barrier for users which are not comfortable with technology, in particular when severe disabilities such as deaf-blindness are targeted.

Indeed, deaf-blind people can use neither vocal mean nor standard SLs, in the latter case because they are not able to perceive the meaning expressed by the signer. For this reason their communication is based on a different mechanism: the receiver's hands are placed on the ones of the signer in order to follow the signs made. Since the communication is still based on SL, but with tactile feedback, this variant is called tactile SL (tSL). Therefore, while it is possible for two normal speakers or two deaf signers to communicate in presence or remotely (either through phone calls or video-calling systems), as of now, there is no way for two deaf-blind persons to communicate with each other if they are not in the same place, given the basic need to touch each other's hands. Moreover, one-to-many communication is not possible, and the same signs must be repeated in front of each *listener* if the same message should reach many different persons [19].

In this context, the PARLOMA project[1] aims at designing a system able to capture messages produced in SL and reproduce them remotely in tSL, in order

---

[1] http://www.parloma.com

to overcome the spatial limitation posed by tSL communication. Indeed, the project poses the bases for the experimentation of a "telephone for deaf-blind people".

In this paper, we present a sophisticated approach to make the remote communication between deaf-blind people feasible. The proposed solution is based on a reliable marker-less hand gestures recognition method, which is targeted to recognize static signs from Italian SL (LIS) and is able to work up to 30 fps, that is the maximum operating frequency of the Kinect sensor[2].

To show its effectiveness, in addition to a quantitative and qualitative analysis, we also present an experimental apparatus in which signs from a subset of LIS hand spelling alphabet are recognized and sent remotely over the Internet, so that a compatible robotic actuator can reproduce them and any *listener* with proficiency in LIS can understand the meaning of what is signed. This work is a first step toward complete remote deaf-blind communication, in which more complex and also dynamic signs will be recognized.

This paper is organized as follows: Section 2 lists already existing related works, Section 3 discusses theoretical background and practical implementation of our solution, Section 4 presents results from our experiments and summarizes the pipeline of the remote communication system we developed and finally Section 5 presents some conclusion.

2   Related Works

This paper relies on hand tracking, anthropomorphic robots and data transmission over the web. In this Section, state-of-the-art approaches on these topics are briefly discussed.

2.1   Hand Tracking

Object tracking techniques can be divided into two main classes: *invasive* approaches, based on tools physically linked to the object (e.g., sensitized gloves [18] or markers [28]), and *non-invasive* approaches. The former are usually fast and computationally light, but also very expensive and cumbersome. The latter require more computational resources, but are based on low-cost technologies and do not require a physical link to the object to be tracked.

Non-invasive approaches proposed in literature (as in [22]) can be classified according to the kind of information in input they need (2D or 3D) and output they provide. Obviously, as real world life is embedded in a 3D universe, best performances are obtained when 3D features characterization is performed. Moreover, relying on 3D input information makes a visual system more robust and accurate [13].

Thanks to technology evolution though, it is nowadays possible to obtain reliable features extraction from confused backgrounds by trying to isolate and

---

[2] http://msdn.microsoft.com/en-us/library/jj131033.aspx

segment the object to be recognized (e.g., a human hand). In fact, 3D information may be obtained by depth maps that are automatically calculated by acquisition system using cheap RGB-D cameras.

Non-invasive approaches are classified into *partial tracking* and *full tracking*: tracking is defined as partial when it requires only information on a subset of input DoF [22] (e.g., only thumb and index in case of partial hand tracking), while it is said to be full when all the DoF are taken into account for computation. Of course, full tracking approaches are the best in terms of accuracy and robustness, but they also require a lot of computational resources [10]. Full tracking solutions can be divided into *model-based* and *appearance-based* approaches.

Model-based approaches [12] are based on a 3D model representing the object to be tracked. These approaches seek for the 3D model parameters that minimize the discrepancy between the appearance and 3D structure of hypothesized instances of the model and actual observations. The problem is usually solved using probabilistic optimization approaches [25] or evolutionary algorithms [20], leading to accurate results, but requiring a lot of computational resources.

Appearance-based techniques are based on special points (features) extracted from input data. An algorithm tries to directly map the extracted features to the hand configuration (i.e., the pose). Appearance-based algorithms are often implemented using machine learning [24] or database-retrieval [4] techniques. Learning how to map features and model configurations is the most computational intensive phase. Since this task is performed off-line, appearance-based techniques easily achieve real-time performances. The accuracy of these algorithms is strongly related to the quality of the training set or database, particularly to its variety and capacity to cover the set of poses.

2.2 Anthropomorphic Haptic Interfaces

Haptic devices elicit human perception through the sense of touch. Haptics therefore extends the communication channels for human-machine interaction, in addition to the typical senses, such as vision and hearing. Haptics includes wearable devices, such as gloves, and robotic devices, such as arms and hands. With respect to robotic hands, despite the significant progress in the last decades in electronic integrated circuits and in applied computer science, current systems still lack in dexterity, robustness and efficiency, as well as in matching cost constraints [9]. Examples of dexterous robotic hand for humanoid robotics are the Awiwi Hand [14] and the Shadow hand [26].

In prosthetics, electro-actuated hands have been commercially available since the early 70s: the major manufacturer is Ottobock (Austria), followed by other few companies. Recently two commercial prosthetic hands with greater Degree of Freedom (DoF) have been introduced to the market: the i-limb (developed by Touch Bionics in 2007) and BeBionic (developed by RSL Steeper in 2010) prostheses. Both hands are capable of different grasping patterns thanks to five individually-powered digits, but their functionality is limited by the passive movement of the thumb abduction/adduction joint. Most of current commercial prosthetic hands are very simple grippers with few active DoF and poor cosmetic appearance, however major research progresses are being achieved [21].

2.3   Transmission

Remote control of robotic actuators is nowadays a well studied task, investigated above all in surgery [3]. For what concerns the transmission of human movements to the robotic hand in this project, we evaluated different scenarios trying to maintain the infrastructure as simple as possible, as this will naturally lead to a simple, fast to develop and robust pattern of communication.

3   The Developed Solution

The proposed system is designed in order to accomplish to three different tasks: (1) sign acquisition and recognition (front-end), (2) sign conversion and transmission, (3) sign synthesis (back-end); that are performed by three different sub-blocks, i.e., the *input module*, the *transmission module* and the *robotic hand module*.

The input module is connected to a depth camera (the acquisition device) and is able to identify signs made by the human hand in front of the device. The transmission module is in charge of encoding the information generated by this first block, sending them through the web, and decoding them in a way that is suitable for the last block. Finally, the robotic hand module is composed by the robotic haptic interface and by a controller that uses the information from the first module to control robotic hand in a proper way.

3.1   The Input Module

The proposed implementation of the input module follows the work proposed in [16], where authors propose a full-DoF appearance-based hand tracking approach that uses a random forest (RF) classifier [23]. RF is a classification and regression technique that has become popular recently due to its efficiency and simplicity [16].

In the proposed system, a low-cost depth-camera (see Fig. 1), is used as only input to the hand segmentation phase, that is the task of isolating hand from the background (RGB information is discarded). Once foreground pixels have been recognized and separated from background, the hand pose can be reconstructed, resorting to two main blocks, that are the *hand labelling block* and the *joints position estimating block*. Hand labelling is an appearance-based method that aims at recognizing single sub-parts of the hand in order to isolate the joints, while the joints positions estimation block aims at approximating the joints 3D position starting from the noisy labelling and depth measurements. As done in [23], in our approach the RF classifier is employed to label pixels of the depth-image according to the region of the hand they should belong to, and than clusters each region in order to find the position of the centre of that

Fig. 1. The hand tracking input system

region. Regions are chosen in order to be centred over the joints of the hand, so that, at the end of the clustering process, the algorithm outputs the 3D position of each joint of the hand.

The developed code can recognize 22 different sub-parts of the hand, which are palm, wrist and 4 joints for each of the fingers. Each part is centred around a specific joint. Parts are tagged with different encoding and the tags are visually represented by different colours.

The hand is first segmented by thresholding depth values. The segmented hand is isolated from the background and tracked resorting to OpenNi tracker [1]. Finally, a point cloud for further processing is obtained, taking into considerations all the points within the sphere centred in the centre of the tracking and with a conservative radius τ.

To label the hand, an approach based on machine learning algorithms has been developed. Basically, at the very beginning, a RF classifier [6] is trained on thousands of different hands performing different signs, also turned or oriented differently. The classifier reads and examines such signs, and calculates the same feature for all of them; then, it keeps the more discriminative features. Such features can be later used to distinguish, with a certain confidence, the different hand sub-parts, and especially pixels that belong to different labels. Finally, the joints position is approximated applying the mean shift clustering [8] algorithm on the hand sub-parts. This approach provides promising results: first experiments with real-world depth map image show that it can properly label most parts of the hand in real time without requiring excessive computational resources.

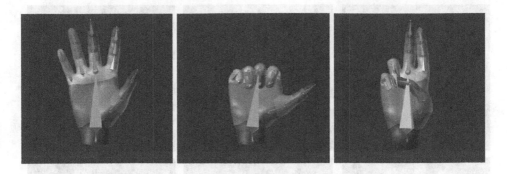

Fig. 2. 3D model in different poses used to generate the synthetic training set

In our approach we perform a per-pixel classification, where each pixel $\mathbf{x}$ of the hand is described using the following feature

$$\mathcal{F}(\mathbf{x}) = \left\{ F_{\mathbf{u},\mathbf{v}}(I,\mathbf{x}) = \sum_{\mathbf{j}\in(\mathbf{u},\mathbf{v})} I\left(\mathbf{x} + \frac{\mathbf{j}}{I(\mathbf{x})}\right), ||\mathbf{u}|| < R, ||\mathbf{v}|| < R \right\}, \quad (1)$$

where I is the depth-image so that $I(\cdot)$ represent the depth value of the image at a given point, while $\mathbf{u}, \mathbf{v}$ are two offset limited to a finite R length.

We use this feature because, in combination with RF, it has proved to very quickly succeed in discriminating hand parts, as shown in [16]. Hand poses can be estimated by labelled segmented hands resorting on mean shift [8]. Also, we resort on the mean shift local mode finding algorithm (as in [24]) to reduce the risk of outliers, that might have a large effect on the computation of the centroids for the pixel locations belonging to a hand part. In such a way, we obtain a more reliable and coherent estimation of the joints set $\mathcal{S}$.

Note that (1) is not invariant to rotations, while in the other hand it is invariant to distance and 3D translations (thanks to the normalization factor $I(\mathbf{x})$). So, it is necessary to build a wide training set composed of the same sign framed from different point of view; for this reason, we have also investigated ways to effectively and automatically build comprehensive large train sets.

To train the algorithm, a training set with labelled samples is necessary. Since manually building a dataset is a tedious, time-consuming and error-prone process, a system able to create a synthetic training set was developed. Such system is based on the 3D model of a human hand shown in Fig. 2. Some examples of the outcomes of the synthetic training tool are shown in Fig. 3.

Main parameters describing the RF we trained were chosen as the ones providing best results after several tests and are summarized in Table 1. Each tree we use is trained with 2'000 random pixels from each training image. Offset vectors u and v from (1) are sampled uniformly between -30 and 30 pixels.

Finally, using a look-up table, the module converts the recognized hand pose in a list of 19 joints positions, that represents the angular positions that each

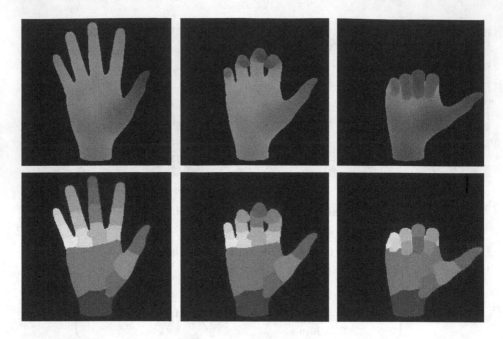

Fig. 3. Outcomes from the synthetic training tool: depth images and related labeling in 3 different poses

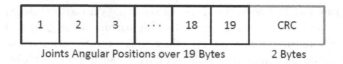

Fig. 4. Structure of the packet with the joints positions

joint of the hand have to reach in order to perform the sign. Global hand rotation (3 DOF) is at the moment discarded as the robotic hand used cannot rotate over the palm base.

3.2 The Transmission Module

Remote communication is implemented using a client - server socket architecture. The client is in charge of coding the sign coming from the input module, creating a proper packet for remotely sending needed data; this packet is also encrypted for secure communication. On the other side, the server is in charge of receiving and decrypting packets, and to decode commands in a suitable way for the hand control module.

The client gets the 19 joints positions, coming from the input module (as shown in Section 3.1). Each position ranges from 0 to 180 degrees, so it is encoded

Table 1. Optimal values we propose to train the RF classifier

Parameter	Value
U,V Offsets	30 pixel
Features extracted per image	2'000
Threshold	10
Sample pixels per image	2'000
Tree depth	18
Number of trees	3

with an unsigned Byte, where the value "180 degrees" is mapped with the maximum number representable (255) and linear scaling is used. Then a 16-bit CRC check is applied to detect potential errors in the transmitted packet. The generated CRC signature is joined to the packet (as in Fig. 4), and then encrypted using a robust cipher algorithm, AES [11]. The output of the cypher operation is an unintelligible string over 108 Bytes.

A TCP socket is opened to build a communication bridge between the client itself and the server, to send the encrypted list of positions.

The server is in charge of receiving and decrypting packets in order to retrieve the position of each of the robotic fingers. Finally, the received information are shared with the hand controller. Then, the robotic hand module is triggered when new data are available.

Failures in the network, such as unilateral unattended errors or crashes within the communication, are well managed by the code, in which ad-hoc exceptions handlers are implemented.

3.3 The Robotic Hand Module

Particular attention must be paid on what concerns the robotic hand, as this is one of the most important points in the solution communicative chain. The hand must be solid, very precise and user-friendly, combining well packaged mechanical components with a cosmetic glove able to mimic as much as possible the characteristics of human skin.

To develop a first prototype of the solution, a programmable anthropomorphic human-sized hand, EH1 Milano series, has been used. This is a versatile device for multiple research scenarios, produced by Prensilia s.r.l..

Such hand comes with 6 DoF, and the five compliant fingers are independently driven by electrical motors, by means of tendon transmission. The thumb abduction/adduction actuator is placed within the palm, whereas the fingers bending/extension motors are hosted into what could be thought as the forearm, a mechanical platform that represents a support for the hand itself and contains all the electronics needed to control the six motors and to communicate with a PC [2].

Communication with the hand is performed using the serial standard; in order to connect the hand to a standard laptop, an USB to serial converter has been used. The serial commands that have to be sent to the hand-side serial port, in order to make the hand move and reproduce signs, have been encoded in a demo program by means of a vocabulary that associates the list of six motor positions with the sign to be reproduced.

Each time the controller is triggered by the transmission module, it synthesizes the joints position in the commands needed by the actuators of the robotic device. Finally, it sends the commands to the robotic hand.

3.4 Implementation of the System

For the tests that are described in the next Section, a Raspberry Pi acts as server and hand controller, while a Laptop PC is used as client-side to compute sign acquisition.

Raspberry Pi[3] is a credit card size computer with low-cost hardware running Linux. The choice is motivated by the fact that, operations such as package decrypting and hand controlling do not require a powerful device.

A Notebook PC equipped with Intel Core i5-2450M @2.50GHz and 8 GB of RAM, running Ubuntu 13.10 OS is used to run all the algorithms regarding the input module, since image processing (coming from a PrimeSense[4] depth camera) requires much more computational power. On this machine, the whole acquisition system processes 30fps, thus achieving real-time performances. All the code is written in C/C++ and Python 2.7, using Open Source Software.

A video showing the proposed solution can be seen at the PARLOMA YouTube channel page[5].

4 Experimental Results

This Section summarizes results of some of the experiments we have performed to test the effectiveness of the proposed approach. These experiments aimed at: (1) evaluating the ability in recognizing signs in LIS (input module); (2) tuning the remote control of the robotic hand (robotic hand module); (3) assessing the effectiveness in transmitting the information over the whole pipeline; (4) getting feedbacks in order to fix potential errors and problems. In particular, the input module has been more intensively tested, as the ability of recognizing reliably and quickly SL signs is of crucial relevance for the whole system.

4.1 Input Module Validation

For what concerns the classification, we report both the average per-class accuracy and the hand gesture recognition accuracy. The first metric highlights how many times each pixel is labelled correctly by the classification layer. Results,

---

[3] http://www.raspberrypi.org
[4] http://www.primesense.com
[5] http://www.youtube.com/watch?v=6MGJb_GqauU

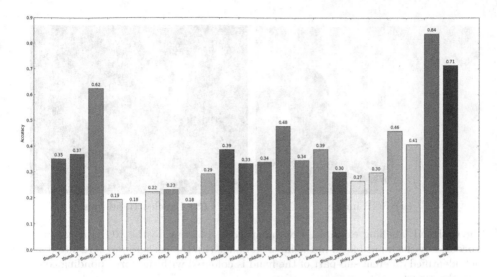

Fig. 5. Average per-pixel classification accuracy for each hand part. In the x axis, for each finger, palm subscripts identify the metacarpophalangeal joints (MCP), while indexes 1, 2 and 3 identify respectively proximal interphalangeal joints (PIP), distal interphalangeal joints (DIP) and fingertips. The y axis represent, in percentage, how many time the hand part is correctly labelled.

presented in Fig. 5, show that our system is usually able to discriminate among fingers and reach peaks of accuracy in discriminating palm and wrist. Little fingers, as ring and pinky, are obviously more difficult to track, especially for the self-occlusions that are experimented in many poses, and so the accuracy in their labelling is lower. Data presented in Fig. 5 represent the average accuracy of our system with respect to a ground truth set composed by 42 depthmaps, manually labelled. Hand labelling example is given in Fig. 6.

Average accuracy obtained by of our system in per-pixel classification is slightly worse than the one achieved in [16], but this is just due to the fact that we used a much smaller training set, composed of less than 15'000 images, while in [16] 200'000 images are used (and authors could not use more for memory constraints).

However, the experiments confirm that the average accuracy reached by our approach is sufficient to effectively track the hand and discriminate among hand gestures, even if similar. To this extent, Fig. 7 shows a graph summarizing the hand gesture recognition accuracy. Such data are computed using one against everything else cross-correlation validation, a process in which data from one subject is used for testing and all the others are used for training. This is the same metric used in [17] and allowed us a comparison between our approach and the results obtained by Kuznetsova et al. on real data. Error rate that authors report for multi-layered RF relying on decision trees with depth fixed to 20 do

(a) RGB image   (b) Labeled Hand image

Fig. 6. Hand labelling example. Depthmap corresponding to the RGB image (a) is processed by the input block: in the labelled image (b), the background is removed and each identified different sub-part of the hand is coloured with the corresponding colour from the model.

not go below 49%. Such results are outperformed by our approach, since we achieve an average error rate of 46% in the same operating conditions.

As shown in Fig. 7, our approach is able to accurately recognize a sign most of the times. Even if accuracy is practically never over 90% in our experiment, we notice that a precision of nearly 35% is always guaranteed and it is sufficient to accurately recognize signs. For instance, Fig. 8 shows two example of a hand labelled by our approach. As it is shown in Fig. 8d, the T letter is easily discriminated even if average classification accuracy is slightly more than 40%.

4.2   Experimental Method

To test the whole pipeline of the system, comprehensive experiments were performed. In these experiments, subjects, not expert in TSL (blindfolded and with ears covered with headphones), are required to recognize the signs performed by the robotic hand, while a proficient in SL performs the signs in front of the input device in another room of the same building.

Each test subject is visually trained for five minutes on the subset of chosen signs with the proficient in LIS (the robotic hand is not used in this phase). After this first phase, the subject is blindfolded and his/her ears are covered; then, the subject is introduced in the room where there is the robotic hand. Note that the subject does not see the robot hand when training.

The message is sent to the robotic hand through a net (local network in the experiments). The results collected so far show that most of the times signs are correctly sent over the network and successively recognized in few seconds touching the robotic hand, even by non expert people.

In these experiments, we use only a subset of the LIS alphabet, consisting of characters S, U, V, W, F, because these are the signs recognized with more

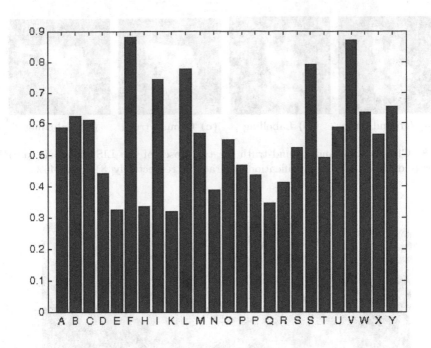

Fig. 7. Average percentage classification accuracy for different hand gestures, the sign is on the x-axes; please note that signs P and S are repeated two times because LIS admits two ways of performing those signs

accuracy and are also reproducible by the robotic hand, which is a first prototype with 6 DoF and cannot reproduce the whole possible static signs from LIS.

In particular, the experiments show that the system is able to work without errors for hours, and pose the basis for a more intensive session with deaf-blind subjects.

A test application collects data about the experiments. An example of recorded data is provided in Table 2. The test application randomly produce a List of 40 Signs (LoS) and the signer is asked to perform these signs, one by one, in front of the acquisition device. Moreover, it records the list of Signs Recognized by the Input module (SRI).

Recognized signs are transmitted to the controller of the hand by the transmission module. The robotic hand performs the sign and holds it for 5 seconds, and then it comes back to a rest position (open hand) and waits for the next sign. The subject has to recognize the sign by touching the robotic hand (using one or both hands), and then pronouncing the sign he/she understands. An experimenter records the Signs Performed by the Hand (SPH) and the relative Signs Recognized by the Subject (SRS). Each experiment lasts about 20 minutes

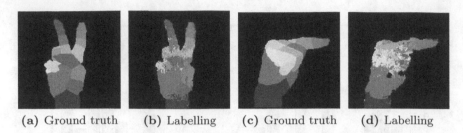

| (a) Ground truth | (b) Labelling | (c) Ground truth | (d) Labelling |

Fig. 8. Classification and ground-truth for two poses of the LIS alphabet. (a,b) V letter; (c,d) T letter. The classification accuracy is, respectively, 81% and 46%.

Fig. 9. Subject (blindfolded and with headphones) interacting with the robotic hand during the test session (V letter is performed in the picture)

per subject. Fig. 9 shows a subject during a test, while Fig. 10 illustrates the pipeline of the described experimental apparatus.

The experiments consist in repeating the procedure previously described for 10 subjects, for total amount of 400 signs produced. At the end of the experiments, four list of signs (LoS, SRI, SPH and SRS) are available. Hence, the recorded lists have been compared among each other and the results summarized in Table 3.

LoS VS SRI refers to the percentage of signs correctly recognized by the input module. This comparison to evaluate the effectiveness of recognition module. Here errors are due to finger occlusions, that sometimes deceive the recognition algorithm, but mainly to mistakes of signer. An example of erratic recognition is shown in column 3 of Table 2.

SRI VS SPH refers to the percentage of signs correctly sent to the hand. This comparison to evaluate the effectiveness of transmission module and the robotic hand module. No errors happened in this stage during the experiments.

Table 2. Example of recorded data during real experiments. Here are reported the List of Sign (LoS) to be produced, the list of Signs Recognized by the Input module (SRI), the list of Signs Performed by the Hand (SPH) and the list of Signs Recognized by the Subject (SRS).

#	1	2	3	4	5	6	7	8	9	10	...
LoS	F	W	V	S	V	F	S	S	V	S	...
SRI	F	W	W	S	V	F	S	S	V	S	...
SPH	F	W	W	S	V	F	S	S	V	S	...
SRS	W	W	W	S	V	F	S	S	V	S	...

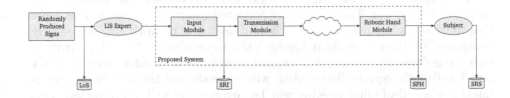

Fig. 10. Pipeline of the experimental apparatus

SPH VS SRS refers to the percentage of signs correctly recognized by the subjects. More of the errors in this phase can be ascribed to the subjects' lack of experience in Tactile LIS. In particular, the sign W is often confused with the sign F, since in both cases three fingers are opened.

Finally, LoS VS SRS measures the efficiency of the whole experimental apparatus. Here the percentage of success synthesizes the other percentages.

As shown in Table 3, overall success rate is 91%. Such result proves the general robustness of our system. In addition, we are confident that success rate will be higher in communication with real deaf-blind persons, that would surely make less mistakes in both performing and recognizing signs and letters from their SL alphabet.

Table 3. Reliability performances of the proposed system

LoS VS SRI	95%
SRI VS SPH	100%
SPH VS SRS	96%
LoS VS SRS	91%

5 Conclusions

This paper presents a system to allow non-invasive remote control of a robotic hand by using low-cost acquisition devices. The system is able to recognize human hand poses and can send them over the Internet, in order to control a robotic hand, that is able to reproduce poses in real time. This system does not require any tuning phase. Despite further optimizations which are still required, our approach shows great accuracy in discriminating even similar poses and achieves real-time performances.

Such system can be useful in many different fields, as for example human-machine interaction, and may easily and intuitively allows interaction with 3D virtual environments.

The paper presents also an early set of experiments demonstrating the efficiency of the system. The preliminary collected results demonstrate that more than 90% of times signs are correctly sent over the network and successively recognized by the test subjects touching the robotic hand. Note that errors in sign recognition by the subjects are not a validation penalty, since they are not Tactile LIS experts. The system will be evaluated through future experiments, when deaf-blind persons will be involved as well. Nevertheless, performed experiments were very useful to preliminarily assess the feeling of the subjects in touching the haptic interface while performing the sign recognition task.

References

1. Openni. http://www.openni.org/
2. Prensilia s.r.l., datasheet eh1 milano series (2010). http://www.prensilia.com/index.php?q=en/node/41
3. Abbou, C.C., Hoznek, A., Salomon, L., Olsson, L.E., Lobontiu, A., Saint, F., Cicco, A., Antiphon, P., Chopin, D.: Laparoscopic radical prostatectomy with a remote controlled robot. The Journal of Urology 165(6), 1964–1966 (2001)
4. Athitsos, V., Sclaroff, S.: Estimating 3d hand pose from a cluttered image. In: Proceedings of 2003 IEEE Computer Society Conference on Computer Vision and Pattern Recognition, vol. 2, p. II-432. IEEE (2003)
5. Bray, M., Koller-Meier, E., Van Gool, L.: Smart particle filtering for 3d hand tracking. In: Proceedings of Sixth IEEE International Conference on Automatic Face and Gesture Recognition, pp. 675–680. IEEE (2004)
6. Breiman, L.: Random forests. Machine Learning 45(1), 5–32 (2001)
7. Breuer, P., Eckes, C., Müller, S.: Hand gesture recognition with a novel ir time-of-flight range camera–a pilot study. In: Gagalowicz, A., Philips, W. (eds.) MIRAGE 2007. LNCS, vol. 4418, pp. 247–260. Springer, Heidelberg (2007)
8. Comaniciu, D., Meer, P.: Mean shift: A robust approach toward feature space analysis. IEEE Transactions on Pattern Analysis and Machine Intelligence 24(5), 603–619 (2002)

9. Controzzi, M., Cipriani, C., Carrozza, M.C.: Design of artificial hands: A review. The Human Hand as an Inspiration for Robot Hand Development. STAR, vol. 95, pp. 219–246. Springer, Heidelberg (2014)
10. Erol, A., Bebis, G., Nicolescu, M., Boyle, R.D., Twombly, X.: Vision-based hand pose estimation: A review. Computer Vision and Image Understanding 108(1), 52–73 (2007)
11. Frankel, S., Glenn, R., Kelly, S.: The aes-cbc cipher algorithm and its use with ipsec. RFC3602 (2003)
12. Gavrila, D.M., Davis, L.S.: 3-d model-based tracking of humans in action: A multi-view approach. In: Proceedings of the IEEE Computer Society Conference on Computer Vision and Pattern Recognition, CVPR 1996, pp. 73–80. IEEE (1996)
13. Goncalves, L., Di Bernardo, E., Ursella, E., Perona, P.: Monocular tracking of the human arm in 3d. In: Proceedings of Fifth International Conference on Computer Vision, pp. 764–770. IEEE (1995)
14. Grebenstein, M.: The awiwi hand: An artificial hand for the DLR hand arm system. In: Grebenstein, M. (ed.) Approaching Human Performance. STAR, vol. 98, pp. 67–136. Springer, Heidelberg (2014)
15. Han, J., Shao, L., Xu, D., Shotton, J.: Enhanced computer vision with microsoft kinect sensor: A review (2013)
16. Keskin, C., Kıraç, F., Kara, Y.E., Akarun, L.: Real time hand pose estimation using depth sensors. In: Consumer Depth Cameras for Computer Vision, pp. 119–137. Springer (2013)
17. Kuznetsova, A., Leal-Taixe, L., Rosenhahn, B.: Real-time sign language recognition using a consumer depth camera. In: Proceedings of the IEEE International Conference on Computer Vision Workshops, pp. 83–90 (2013)
18. Lorussi, F., Scilingo, E.P., Tesconi, M., Tognetti, A., De Rossi, D.: Strain sensing fabric for hand posture and gesture monitoring. IEEE Transactions on Information Technology in Biomedicine 9(3), 372–381 (2005)
19. Mesch, J.: Signed conversations of deafblind people
20. Oikonomidis, I., Kyriazis, N., Argyros, A.A.: Efficient model-based 3d tracking of hand articulations using kinect. In: BMVC, pp. 1–11 (2011)
21. Raspopovic, S., Capogrosso, M., Petrini, F.M., Bonizzato, M., Rigosa, J., Di Pino, G., Carpaneto, J., Controzzi, M., Boretius, T., Fernandez, E., Granata, G., Oddo, C.M., Citi, L., Ciancio, A.L., Cipriani, C., Carrozza, M.C., Jensen, W., Guglielmelli, E., Stieglitz, T., Rossini, P.M., Micera, S.: Restoring natural sensory feedback in real-time bidirectional hand prostheses. Science Translational Medicine 6(222), 222ra19 (2014)
22. Rehg, J.M., Kanade, T.: Digiteyes: Vision-based hand tracking for human-computer interaction. In: Proceedings of the 1994 IEEE Workshop on Motion of Non-Rigid and Articulated Objects, pp. 16–22. IEEE (1994)
23. Rodriguez-Galiano, V., Ghimire, B., Rogan, J., Chica-Olmo, M., Rigol-Sanchez, J.: An assessment of the effectiveness of a random forest classifier for land-cover classification. ISPRS Journal of Photogrammetry and Remote Sensing 67, 93–104 (2012)
24. Shotton, J., Sharp, T., Kipman, A., Fitzgibbon, A., Finocchio, M., Blake, A., Cook, M., Moore, R.: Real-time human pose recognition in parts from single depth images. Communications of the ACM 56(1), 116–124 (2013)

25. Stenger, B., Thayananthan, A., Torr, P.H., Cipolla, R.: Model-based hand tracking using a hierarchical bayesian filter. IEEE Transactions on Pattern Analysis and Machine Intelligence **28**(9), 1372–1384 (2006)
26. Walkler, R.: Developments in dextrous hands for advanced robotic applications. In: Proc. the Sixth Biannual World Automation Congress, Seville, Spain. pp. 123–128 (2004)
27. Wang, R., Paris, S., Popović, J.: 6d hands: markerless hand-tracking for computer aided design. In: Proceedings of the 24th Annual ACM Symposium on User Interface Software and Technology, pp. 549–558. ACM (2011)
28. Wang, R.Y., Popović, J.: Real-time hand-tracking with a color glove. ACM Transactions on Graphics (TOG) **28**, 63 (2009)

Measuring the Student's Success Rate Using a Constraint Based Multi-modal Virtual Assembly Environment

Inam Ur Rehman$^{(\boxtimes)}$, Sehat Ullah, and Ihsan Rabbi

Department of Computer Science and IT, University of Malakand,
Chakdara, Pakistan
inam.btk@gmail.com, {sehatullah,ihsanrabbi}@uom.edu.pk

Abstract. Personnel Training is considered as the most important pre-requisite in the assembly operations of any kind of equipment/apparatus ranging from simple nut-bolt assembly to complex equipment (e.g., aircraft engine) assembly. This paper presents a novel Virtual Reality Training System (VRTS) for the constraint based assembly of a 3phase step down transformer. The ARToolKit [1] markers are used for interaction with the VRTS. The system improves the technical skills of students in the real assembly environment. The analysis shows that the average success rate of untrained students is 35.7% while that of trained students increased to 81.5%.

Keyword: Virtual assembly environment

1 Introduction

Virtual Reality (VR) technology appears to be the most dominant learning tool due to its distinctive scientific nature which can be used to model real or non-real situations by using artificial, extremely interactive 3 dimensional (3D) worlds [2]. Virtual reality learning environment are more useful than traditional black-board teaching methodology where knowledge acquisition takes place due to the exchange of technical interactions with other people or systems. The use of VR in education is a great branch in teaching techniques with different forms such as virtual teaching and training, virtual labs, and virtual schools after multimedia, computer, and cyberspace [3]. One of the most critical cause of the limited use of VR in school education is the unaffordable cost [4] [5]. The cost of availability, establishment, and maintenance of highly immersive systems and related devices prevent the large scale use of this technology [6]. Low level instruction design of virtual teaching environments is another concern [5] [7] [8].

In developing countries engineering universities and polytechnic institutes are following traditional teaching methodology. In traditional techniques, teachers follow textbooks, chalk and board, and 2D drawings for teaching. These techniques fail to represent the real world phenomena's and facts. Furthermore there is a lack of student's interest in these teaching techniques.

© Springer International Publishing Switzerland 2014
L.T. De Paolis and A. Mongelli (Eds.): AVR 2014, LNCS 8853, pp. 53–64, 2014.
DOI: 10.1007/978-3-319-13969-2_4

This paper addresses the development of a desktop based 3D Virtual Reality Training System (VRTS) for students of polytechnic institutes/colleges. This system guides students in the assembly of a 3Phase step-down power transformer. VRTS is a multi-modal user friendly 3D virtual environment that allows users to improve their learning process in an interactive manner with reasonably low cost. The interaction includes free navigation, object selection and manipulation in the virtual environment. This interaction is achieved through ARToolKit markers based on its visibility and movement. During interaction with the system the user is given multi-modal (Audio-Textual) information about a particular object such as its name, properties and functions. The objectives of the development of VRTS are the following:

- To study the effect of VRTS on students' learning of the theoretical aspects of technical education.
- The effect of VRTS in technical skills acquisition.
- The applicability of skills acquired through VRTS in real situation.

The rest of the paper is organized as: section 2 describes related work, section 3 presents VRTS, section 4 presents experiments and evaluation and section 5 describes result analysis. Finally in section 6 conclusion and future work is described.

2   Related Work

Immersive virtual reality technology is widely in use since 1960. "Sinsorama" was the first single user console system used in entertainment to capture spectators' attention. It also had the ability to use different human senses to provide the illusion of reality [9]. The use of VR in teaching and training began in 1980 [10]. In 1990's the scope of VR extended to educational projects such as Science Space, Safety World, Global Change, Virtual Gorilla Exhibit, Atom World, and Cell Biology [11]. Currently the use of VR in education is an active research area.

Ng et al. [12] have developed a virtual environment which helps users in cable routing and designing in electro-mechanical products. Head Mounted Display (HMD) was used for display and 3D mouse for interaction. The system is immersive in nature, but the high cost of HMD and 3D mouse limits its applicability in education. Angelov et al. [13] have presented a computer generated 3D virtual training system. The system was used for training and learning about power system operation to its workers. A 2D Mouse is used for interaction with no 3D navigation in the environment.

Wang et al. [14] have made a math learning virtual environment system which helps students to understand mathematical concepts. Menus and 2D buttons are used for interaction with environment. Here 2D mouse and keyboard are used for interaction. Pasqualotti et al. [15] developed mathematical representations for modeling buildings and virtual city. The system uses 2D mouse for interaction and there is a lack of free navigation in the environment.

Real Time Relativity (RTR) presented by Savage et al. [16] is a 3D simulation software for physics that provides interactive game-based experience. There is no direct interaction with objects. Kaufmann et al. [17] designed the PhysicsPlayground, an Augmented Reality application. It was a real time 3D virtual environment for physics experiments in the area of mechanics. The system used costly HMD for display, a wireless pen and a Personal Interaction Panel (PIP) for interaction. Dede et al. [18] have developed an immersive 3D virtual environment for physics education. The environment contains virtual objects and students can perform experiments on these objects. This system used (HMD) for display, 3Ball or stylus for interaction which makes the environment highly expensive. Loftin et al. [19] developed a physics based virtual laboratory where students could observe the virtual environment as well as the virtual object's properties. The system also used a head mounted color stereoscopic Silicon Graphics 4DD20VGX display, a 3D auditory system, a hand gestures obtaining system (hand glove) and a Polhemus (magnetic position and orientation system) for observing user eye's direction, head and hand position. The use of specialized devices makes the system complex, costly and unaffordable in real situations.

Virtual Radioactivity Laboratory (VRT) developed by Crosier et al. [20] for teaching the radioactivity in secondary school level. A comparison is also made between VR with traditional teaching methodology. The system used 2D mouse to perform different tasks. Zhang et al. [21] designed a multisensory feedback Virtual Assembly Environment (VAE), in order to assess the user efficiency, satisfaction and consistency. The system used Trimension's V-Desk 6, highly immersive L-shaped workbench, shutter glasses and infrared emitter, and Wand for interaction. The system can't be adopted in education due its high cost and complex nature. Yao et al. [22] presented an immersive virtual assembly planning and training system (I-VAPTS) in order to train and guide workers in a pump assembly process. Data glove and 3D mouse were used for interaction and HMD for display. The system cost was very high. According to Bryson [23], the complications associated with glove devices are imprecise measurements and need of standard gestural lexis.

Dunne et al. [24] presented the Pulse!! The Virtual Clinical Learning Lab for teaching and training in medical education. Using mouse and keyboard user could navigate in the environment. The environment was 3D but used 2D mouse and keyboard for interaction. The system could provide only textual information about the patient. Virtual Body Structures-Auxiliary Teaching System (VBS-ATS) designed by Huang et al. [25] is an interactive Web-based 3D system for teaching human physiology in medical. It provides two versions i.e. desktop for single user and projection-based VR for multiple users. User could navigate in the environment, rotate, and zoom in and out the objects. A 3D ear model of the central and inside of the ear is presented by Nicholson et al. [26]. The model is 3D in nature but interaction with it is carried out using the 2D mouse. There is no interaction with the individual parts of the ear. The system gives only the textual information to the user.

Mikropoulos et al. [27] presented the creation and assessment of 3D biological virtual learning environment. Here traditional 2D Mouse is used for interaction.

In Shima et al. [28] 3D Webmaster software (3DWS) is used for the development of Virtual Reality Biology Simulations (VRBS) program. The system is used to educate middle school students. The VRBS studies the structure and working of eye. Here keyboard is the only way of interaction. Bakas et al. [29] created a learning environment to educate the students about the universe and planets. This system doesn't support 3D interaction with objects, all is made through mouse and menus.

The devices used for interaction with these systems have many problems such as cost, availability, weight and size, need of electric charge, cabling and space constraints. Also most of the existing systems are not the virtual worlds but the simulation software. This paper presents a realistic 3D virtual environment called VRTS that uses ARToolKit marker for interaction. The ARToolKit markers are printed patterns (see Fig. 1) that can work as low cost, flexible and real-time positional and orientation input device.

Fig. 1. ARToolKit markers' patterns

Marker has many advantages, such as tracking in 3D space, fast detection, wireless nature, can be used anywhere and need not be built into objects, wide range of movements and styles of interactions, no hardware cost, easy calibration, and supported by specific software [30].

3 Virtual Reality Training System

We have developed a 3D Virtual Reality Training System (VRTS). It is a desktop based virtual environment that is used to train students in assembly of 3phase step-down transformer. The VRTS is a room like structure and contains all 3D components of the transformer as shown in Fig. 2. These component are designed in 3d studio max and loaded and placed in the virtual environment. The high quality of these models increases the realism of the environment. Just like a real environment the user can navigate, select and manipulate the objects. Whenever a user selects an object he/she is provided various audio/visual information about that object i.e. name, properties and function of the object. Interaction with VRTS is made via the ARToolKit [9] markers which are printed patterns. These markers provide 6 degree of freedom.

3.1 Software Architecture of VRTS

The complete model of the system is shown in Fig. 3. This model represents the working mechanism of VRTS, and consists of the following principle modules.

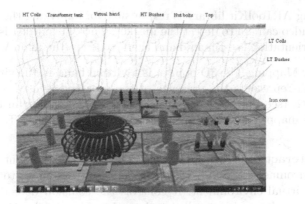

Fig. 2. Overview of the VRTS environment

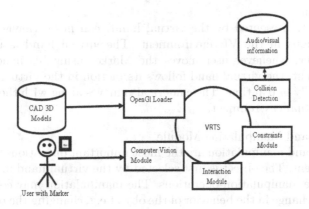

Fig. 3. Software architecture of VRTS

CAD 3D MODELS. The whole environment and all the parts of 3 phase step down transformer were first designed in 3D Studio Max 2009 package. These high quality objects were then translated to .obj file format along with color, material and texture information. The .obj file is then exported to OpenGl Loader software.

OpenGl Loader. This module is used to translate the .obj file into the VR environment. It places all the objects at specific positions in the VR environment.

Computer Vision Module (CVM). In order to make the VRTS system simple, realistic, and reduce its cost and complexity so that it can easily be adopted and used in many organization, we use computer vision based interaction system. This system has three main components: (i) ARToolKit markers (ii) ARToolKit library and (iii) a video camera. ARToolKit markers are special black and white markers printed on a paper that can be detected by a normal camera. The algorithm developed using ARToolKit library is responsible for analyzing the input stream taken by the video camera to detect the marker. Once the marker is detected, its position and orientation is estimated and then passed to the main VRTS module.

– 3D Pointer Mapping The 3D pointer is a virtual hand in the virtual environment which represents the presence of the user and is used for interaction with the VE (see Fig. 2). The physical pose of the marker in the real environment is mapped into the pose of the 3D pointer in the VE.

The User Interaction Module (UIM). UIM controls different operations in the virtual environment. It allows the 3D pointer (virtual hand) to navigate and interact with virtual environment. It controls the collision detection of virtual hand with objects, inter-object collision detection, object selection, and manipulation in the virtual environment.

– Navigation
The user (represented by the virtual hand) can move (navigate) freely in all directions in the VR environment. The virtual hand is mapped with the marker, whenever user moves the Marker using his hand in the real environment, the virtual hand follows its motion in the virtual environment dynamically in real time. The camera also moves along with the virtual hand in the virtual environment.

– Selection and Manipulation Module
Selection and manipulation are the most important operations in any virtual environment. The object is first selected by the virtual hand in order to perform some manipulation operations. The manipulation may consist of making some change in the behavior of the object e.g. changing the position of the object. ARToolKit marker is used for navigation, identification and selection of objects in the virtual environment. The virtual hand follows the movement of the real world marker. A single marker is simply used for the free navigation and identification of objects in the virtual environment(Fig. 4 (a)). If an object collides/intersects with the virtual hand while the user has a single visible marker, the audio/visual information related to that object are provided. If the second maker is also made visible to the camera and the virtual hand collides/intersects with an object, then the virtual hand picks/grabs that object (see Fig. 4 (b)). So in this way user can select, move, and rotate the object dynamically. To release the object, simply make the second marker invisible to camera. The Fig. 5 shows the algorithm for interaction using the markers.

Collision Detection. Collision detection is the most important issue in complex virtual assembly environments. Different types of techniques are used for collision detection. VRTS measures collision by calculating the distance between the centers of objects. The system performs different actions when the collision occurs in the virtual environment. If the virtual hand collides with an object, the audio/visual information related to the object is provided by the system or

(a)   (b)

Fig. 4. Interaction via ARToolKit markers (a) Single marker (b) Two markers both visible

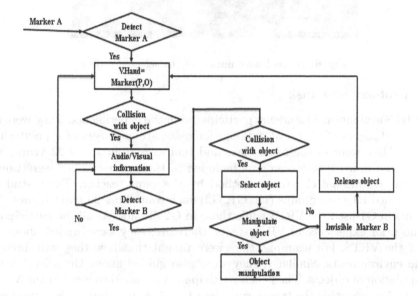

Fig. 5. Flow diagram for object selection and manipulation using markers

the object is selected. If a selected object collides with any other object in the environment, the object blocks moving further.

Audio and Visual Information. The system provides audio/visual information as cognitive aids to the user. The objective of using audio/visual information is to enhance the user learning about the system and the objects. When the virtual hand touches an object in the virtual environment, the object related information both in audio/textual forms are provided to the user (see Fig. 6). These information are stored in audio/textual databases.

4 Experiments and Evaluation

In order to investigate the effects of using VRTS on students learning, we performed subjective evaluation.

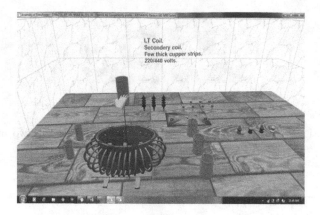

Fig. 6. Textual information of the selected object

4.1 Protocol and Task

For VRTS evaluation 40 students participated in the experiments. They were the 3rd year students of electrical diploma for associate engineers of a polytechnic college. They were in the same class and had ages from 19 to 22 years. The 3phase step down transformer was included in their course. They were taught using the traditional classroom method by the same teacher. These students were divided into two groups (i.e. G1, G2) each containing 20 participants. The students in G1 used the VRTS while those in G2 did not. As all the participants had no prior experience of VR systems, therefore, they were briefed about the use of the VRTS. For example, they were taught that how they will navigate in the environments. Similarly, they were also guided about the selection and manipulation of objects. Then each participant was asked to work in the VRTS. They had to assemble the transformer (see Fig. 7. a user during the experiment using VRTS). Each participant filled a questionnaire after getting experience in VRTS. Then both G1 and G2 were taken to a workshop where they had to perform the assembly of the 3phase transformer. Here the data of the students performance were collected again through a questionnaire.

5 Result Analysis

In this section we present the analysis of the questionnaire filled by students in G1 (group 1). There were four questions in this questionnaire. The objective of these questions was to evaluate the following aspects of VRTS:

- The role of VRTS in technical skills learning.
- Realism of the system.
- Ease of interaction.
- Its role in students confidence building in real situations.

The students had to answer these questions on a scale of 1 to 5. Where 1= low and 5 = very high level. The analysis of these responses is given below.

Fig. 7. A user during the experiment using VRTS

The first questions was related to realism for which 85% students selected the highest level (see Fig. 8).The next question which was related to the easiness of interaction in VRTS which got the 60% vote for the highest option (see Fig. 9). Similarly, 80% students selected the highest level for confidence (they got using VRTS) of VRTS, in technical education (see Fig. 10). The second part of the questionnaire was filled by both the groups (G1 and G2) during their session in the workshop (real situation). The data recorded in the second section were consist of their ability to perform the assembly task in the real environment. Comparing the VRTS trained group (G1) with untrained group (G2) we observed a great difference in their success rate graph (see Fig. 11). Here the mean learning score of G1 is 81.5% while that of G2 is only 35.75%.

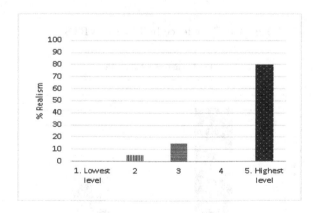

Fig. 8. Realism in VRTS

The result shows that the VRTS system is more helpful in students learning, confidence building, and improving their practical skills if it is employed in technical colleges as a supplement with the traditional teaching methodology.

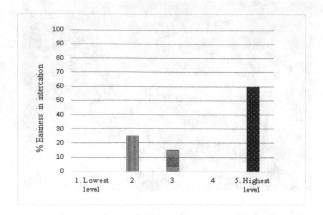

Fig. 9. Easiness in interaction

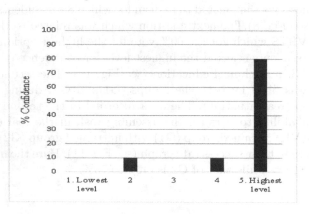

Fig. 10. Confidence building in VRTS

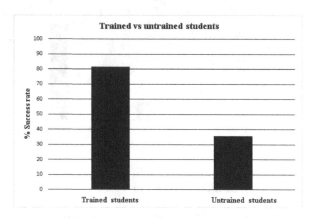

Fig. 11. Comparison of trained vs. untrained students

6   Conclusion and Future Work

In this paper we presented a novel learning system called Virtual Reality Training System (VRTS) for polytechnic colleges students in assembling a 3 phase transformer. VRTS is a Virtual Reality environment where we visualized the 3 phase transformer parts through 3D objects. The user could easily interact with VRTS through fiducial markers. The audio visual information about each object/part of transformer were given to its users. The system improved the practical skills of students in technical education. The analysis showed that the average success rate of untrained users is 35.75% while that of trained (using VRTS) students is 81.5%.

References

1. Kato, H.: How does ARToolKit work?, ARToolKit Documentation (2/4/14). http://www.hitl.washington.edu/artoolkit/documentation/userarwork.htm
2. Mikropoulos, T.A., Natsis, A.: Educational virtual environments: A ten-year review of empirical research (1999–2009). Computers & Education **56**, 769–780 (2011)
3. Jou, M., Wang, J.: Investigation of effects of virtual reality environments on learning performance of technical skills. Comput. Hum. Behav. **29**, 433–438 (2013)
4. Mantovani, F., Castelnuovo, G., Gaggioli, A., Riva, G.: Virtual reality training for health-care professionals. CyberPsychology & Behavior **6**, 389–395 (2003)
5. Riva, G.: Applications of virtual environments in medicine. Methods of Information in Medicine **42**, 524–534 (2003)
6. Merchant, Z., Goetz, E.T., Cifuentes, L., Keeney-Kennicutt, W., Davis, T.J.: Effectiveness of virtual reality-based instruction on students' learning outcomes in K-12 and higher education: A meta-analysis. Computers & Education **70**, 29–40 (2014)
7. Chen, C.J., Toh, S.C., Ismail, W.M.F.W.: Are learning styles relevant to virtual reality? Journal of Research on Technology in Education **38**, 123–141 (2005)
8. Wong, B., Ng, B., Clark, S.: Assessing the effectiveness of animation and virtual reality in teaching operative dentistry. Journal of Dentistry 1 (2000)
9. Heilig, M.: Sensorama simulator. united state patent office (3,050,870) (Patented August 28, 1962)
10. Hawkins, D.G.: Virtual reality and passive simulators: the future of fun. L. Erlbaum Associates Inc., Hillsdale (1995)
11. Youngblut, C.: Educational uses of virtual reality technology. IDA Document D-2128, i.o. d. analysis, ed., Alexandria (1998)
12. Ng, F.M., Ritchie, J.M., Simmons, J.E.L., Dewar, R.G.: Designing cable harness assemblies in virtual environments. Journal of Materials Processing Technology **107**, 37–43 (2000)
13. Angelov, A.N., Styczynski, Z.A.: Computer-aided 3D Virtual Training in Power System Education. In: Power Engineering Society General Meeting, pp. 1–4. IEEE (2007)
14. Wang, Y., Cui, S., Yang, Y., Lian, J.-a.: Virtual Reality Mathematic Learning Module for Engineering Students. Technology Interface Journal **10** (Fall 2009)
15. Pasqualotti, A., Freitas, C.M.S.: MAT3D: A Virtual Reality Modeling Language Environment for the Teaching and Learning of Mathematics. CyberPsychology & Behavior **5**, 409–422 (2002)

16. Savage, C., McGrath, D., McIntyre, T., Wegener, M., Williamson, M.: Teaching Physics Using Virtual Reality. In: American Institute of Physics Conference Series, pp. 126–129 (2010)
17. Kaufmann, H., Meyer, B.: Simulating educational physical experiments in augmented reality. In: SIGGRAPH Asia 2008 ACM SIGGRAPH ASIA 2008 Educators Programme. ACM (2008)
18. Dede, C., Salzman, M.C., Loftin, R.B., Sprague, D.: Multisensory Immersion as a Modeling Environment for Learning Complex Scientific Concepts. In: Feurzeig, W., Roberts, N., (eds.) Modeling and Simulation in Science and Mathematics Education Modeling Dynamic Systems, pp. 282–319. Springer, New York (1999)
19. Loftin, R., Bowen, M.E., Benedetti, R.: Applying virtual reality in education: A prototypical virtual physics laboratory. In: Proceedings of the IEEE 1993 Symposium on Research Frontiers in Virtual Reality, pp. 67–74. IEEE Computer Society Press (1993)
20. Crosier, J.K., Cobb, S.V.G., Wilson, J.R.: Experimental comparison of virtual reality with traditional teaching methods for teaching radioactivity. Education and Information Technologies 5, 329–343 (2000)
21. Zhang, Y., Travis, A.R.L., Collings, N.: Evaluation of Multi-sensory Feedback on the Usability of a Virtual Assembly Environment. Journal of Multimedia 2 (February 2007)
22. Yao, Y.X., Xia, P.J., Liu, J.S., Li, J.G.: A pragmatic system to support interactive assembly planning and training in an immersive virtual environment (I-VAPTS). Int J Adv Manuf Technol 30, 959–967 (2006)
23. Bryson, S.: Virtual Reality in Scientific Visualization. Communications of the ACM 39(5) (1996)
24. Dunne, C.J.R., McDonald, C.L.: Pulse!!: A Model for Research and Development of Virtual-Reality Learning in Military Medical Education and Training MILITARY MEDICINE 175 (July Supplement 2010)
25. Huang, H.-M., Liaw, S.-S., Lai, C.-M.: Exploring learner acceptance of the use of virtual reality in medical education: a case study of desktop and projection-based display systems, Interactive Learning Environments. Interactive Learning Environments (2013)
26. Nicholson, D.T., Chalk, C., Funnell, W.R.J., Daniel, S.J.: Can virtual reality improve anatomy education? A randomised controlled study of a computer-generated three-dimensional anatomical ear model. US National Library of Medicine National Institutes of Health 40, 1081–1087 (2006)
27. Mikropoulos, T.A., Katsikis, A., Nikolou, E., Tsakalis, P.: Virtual environments in biology teaching. Journal of Biological Education 37, 176–181 (2003)
28. Shima, Kew-Cheol: J.-S.P., Hyun-Sup Kima, Jae-Hyun Kima, Young-Chul Parka, Hai-Il Ryua Application of virtual reality technology in biology education. Journal of Biological Education 37, 71–74 (2003)
29. Bakasa, C., Mikropoulos, T.: Design of virtual environments for the comprehension of planetary phenomena based on students ideas. International Journal of Science Education 25, 949–967 (2003)
30. Hornecker, E., Psik, T.: Using ARToolKit Markers to Build Tangible Prototypes and Simulate Other Technologies. In: Costabile, M.F., Paternó, F. (eds.) INTERACT 2005. LNCS, vol. 3585, pp. 30–42. Springer, Heidelberg (2005)

The Effect of Multimodal Virtual Chemistry Laboratory on Students' Learning Improvement

Numan Ali$^{(\boxtimes)}$, Sehat Ullah, Ihsan Rabbi, and Aftab Alam

Department of Computer Science and IT, University of Malakand,
Chakdara, Pakistan
{numan,sehatullah,ihsanrabbi,alam}@uom.edu.pk

Abstract. This paper presents a novel Multimodal Virtual laboratory (MMVL) for the learning of chemistry experiments. MMVL is a Virtual Reality environment where the user can perform chemistry experiments like a real world chemistry lab. The user can easily interact with MMVL through 3D interaction interface. The audio and visual information about each chemical objects are provided to its users. The system improves the learning capabilities of students in chemistry education. The analysis shows that the average learning of untrained student is 32.7% while that of trained students increased to 83.5%. Experiments reveal that confidence level in practical field of students who got training in MMVL is much better than those who did not use it.

Keywords: Virtual reality environment · 3D virtual chemistry laboratory · Multimodal

1 Introduction

Guided methods of learning process have given little opportunities for students to motivate them. The intelligence, individual abilities and innovative thinking of the students can be obtained by doing something practical by them. In this framework laboratory applications perform an important role for students motivation. In the field of science education (chemistry, physics, biology and engineering) a lot of researchers admitted that laboratory activities increase the students capabilities and interest [1,2]. Especially in chemistry education, the role of laboratory is clearly understandable [3]. Students take more interest in learning by performing and observing the experiments in the chemistry laboratory [4]. Laboratory activities enhance and stabilize students learning capabilities [7]. However due to financial problems and other several hurdle most of the institutions cannot establish and utilize chemistry laboratories, particularly in developing countries. These include the followings

☐ To arrange all equipments and chemicals for experiments in the laboratory are more costly for institutions.

☐ For a student it is difficult to perform the experiments individually.

© Springer International Publishing Switzerland 2014
L.T. De Paolis and A. Mongelli (Eds.): AVR 2014, LNCS 8853, pp. 65–76, 2014.
DOI: 10.1007/978-3-319-13969-2_5

☐ It is also difficult for teacher to check the performance and learning process of every student if the number of students is high in a class.

☐ Repetition of an experiment will require more time and resources.

☐ Consumption of chemicals and breaking of glass ware is also an issue.

☐ A little mistake in real laboratory environment may hurt the student or may cause damage to the laboratory.

The solution of these challenges is the use of Virtual Reality (VR) technologies in education and laboratory activities [5]. Virtual environments allow users to have real time interactions with computer generated objects and perform the desired task while getting the illusion of reality. It fulfills the deficiency of chemical items and other equipment which appear in the real chemistry laboratories. There are many benefits of virtual laboratories especially in distance learning education, because it can be accessed anywhere and anytime for experiments without any cost [6]. Virtual laboratories provide safe environment for students to simulate their experiments [9]. There is a need to design fully equipped virtual chemistry laboratory for students to easily simulate their chemistry experiments virtually. This paper examines the development of MMVL where the students can simulate their chemistry experiments like they perform a real world chemistry experiment. The paper is organized as follows: Next section will present previous studies. Section 3 presents the development of MMVL. Section 4 is about the experiment and evaluation of the MMVL. Section 5 presents the whole work. Final section 6 presents the conclusion.

2   Literature Review

This section presents the literature review which is related to the development of virtual chemistry laboratories.

The Virtual Reality Undergraduate Projects Laboratory (VRUPL) is a 3D virtual chemistry environment developed for the training purposes of undergraduate students. VRUPL enables students to learn that what apparatuses will be used and what will be their proper assembly in a particular experiment. In addition students are guided about how to take various safety measures while working in real chemistry labs both in industrial and educational settings. Although the environment is helpful for learning safety principles but not suitable for traditional teaching where it is important to learn that how a particular experiment is done in actual [8].

Similarly VRAL (Virtual Reality Accidents Laboratory) is another 3D web-based virtual chemistry lab developed for the training of undergraduate chemical engineering students to learn how to safeguard themselves from accidents in chemical laboratories setups [9].

At Charles Sturt University a virtual chemistry laboratory has been developed. The main objective of this environment is to make the students familiar with real laboratory environment. It allows a student to know about the procedure of an experiment and assembling of various apparatus. The main limitation of this environment is its inability to simulate any chemical reaction [10].

Virtual ChemLab is a part of Y science laboratories developed by the Brigham Young University. ChemLab allows a student to select a chemical product and see its various properties like molecule structure, color etc. In addition, movie metaphor is used to simulate a chemical reaction. Evaluation of the ChemLab showed that the environment was helpful for students to improve their exams scores and the capability of problem solving [11].

An online virtual chemistry laboratory system is developed by Oxford University England for harmonizing their first year undergraduate teaching. This system contains a number of chemical reactions experiments in the form of video clips. The user can view the video clips by selecting two reactants. In this system the user can repeat the reaction many times. The system was also suitable for users to learn about the safety rules during the experiments in the real laboratory. The system was suitable for undergraduate students and was very less interactive environment due to video clips [12].

The iVirtualWorld is a web-based environment where various 3D objects required for an experiment are selected from 2D menus using traditional mouse based interaction. Similarly different properties of the selected object are also set using 2D graphical user interface (GUI), which makes the environment less realistic and hence it becomes difficult to achieve more immersion of the user [2].

The above related works stated that the previous virtual chemistry laboratories were developed in a way that user can identify and select the chemicals but there were no multimodality (textual and audio information) system to know about the physical and chemical properties of chemicals and apparatuses. Besides this interaction with previous laboratories was possible only through keyboard and mouse and resultantly they were less realistic and immersive.

3   Multimodal Virtual Laboratory (MMVL)

The objective of this research work is to study the effect of simulating chemistry experiments in a computer generated world on the learning of students. Our 3D virtual chemistry laboratory provides some advantages over previous virtual chemistry laboratories:

☐ It is a multimodal (visual and audio) system which provides the detail information about the physical and chemical properties of chemical objects. Through multimodality users will improve their learning capabilities about the theory of chemistry.

☐ Both the visual and audio information are combined in MMVL which guides users to increase their learning which is very useful for their exam score improvement.

MMVL is a 3D virtual environment like a real chemistry room/lab as shown in figure 1. All the chemical items are placed in the cupboards where user can easily identify them. The environment contains all the apparatuses, chemical and glassware that are required for the high school and college level experiments. The environment has a table in the center where experiments are performed as like the real chemistry lab. Some apparatuses like burette, spirit lamp, digital balanceetcare permanently laying on the table. Similarly the chemicals and other glassware have been placed in their respective shelves as shown in figure 1(a). In order to perform an experiment, a student can select and bring a chemical/glassware to the table. The environment also contains a virtual board on which the equation of the chemical reaction is shown. For example when the user selects the experiment of standardization of sodium hydroxide by oxalic acid the following equation is displayed as shown in figure 1(b).

$$
\begin{array}{c}
COOH \\
| \\
COOH
\end{array}
\; 2H_2O + 2NaOH \; \rightarrow \;
\begin{array}{c}
COONa \\
| \\
COONa
\end{array}
\; + 4H_2O
$$

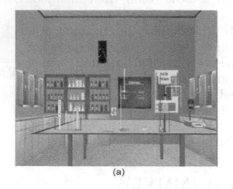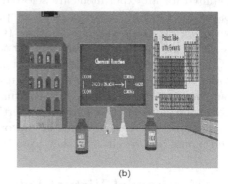

(a)   (b)

Fig. 1. The inside scenario of MMVL

The user can navigate in the environment either to know about the properties of various chemical and glassware or to select an item (chemical or apparatus) to perform an experiment using the simple virtual hand (SVH) technique. He/she can identify the required chemical items and other instruments according to the experiment. In addition, the user can pick up and place the selected item on the table as shown in figure 2.

For one-column wide figures use

By selecting any item in the MMVL, the student gets multimodal (textual and audio) information about the selected chemical items as shown in figure 3. This information is very useful for student learning enhancement where he/she comes to know about the properties of chemical items.

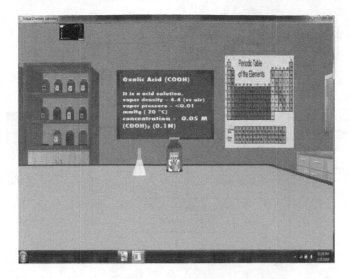

Fig. 2. Simulating virtual experiment

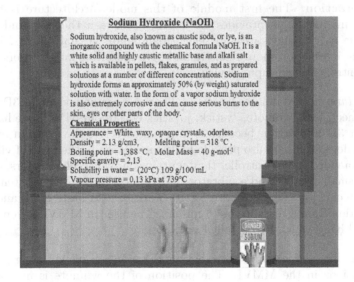

Fig. 3. Visual/audio information

3.1   Software Architecture

In this section we are going to discuss the principle components of the software architecture as shown in figure 4, on which the MMVL is based. For one-column wide figures use

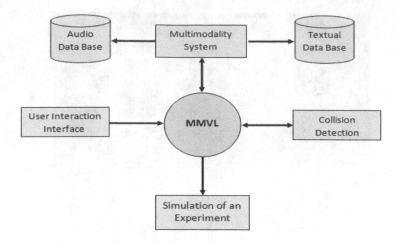

Fig. 4. Software Architecture of MMVL

User Interaction. The first module of this model/architecture is the user interaction module. This provides an interface between the user and MMVL enabling the user to navigate and select/manipulate virtual objects. In order to make the interaction more realistic and give more freedom to users, we use wiimote controller as an input device.

Wiimote's Interface. Wiimotes Interface. There are many devices for 3D interaction like kinect, leap, wiimote, ?ystick, joystick etc. In our MMVL we have used wiimote for 3D interaction because it is a cost e?ective device than other 3D interaction devices, it can also provide haptic sensation in the form of vibration. Wiimote is a video game controller that contains on two accelerometers, multiple buttons, a small speaker and a vibrator. For connection with the system it uses Bluetooth technology (see in figure 5). Its workspace is quite large and allows the interaction from a distance of 18 meters. The user in MMVL is represented by a virtual hand which is controlled via wiimote.

Navigation. The virtual hand representing the user can move (navigate) freely in all directions in the MMVL. The position of the wiimote is mapped onto the virtual hand and whenever the user moves the wiimote in the real world environment, the virtual hand follows its motion in the MMVL. The navigation of virtual hand along X-axis is achieved through the rotation of wiimote along its Y-axis as shown in figure 6(c). Similarly the movement of virtual hand along Y-axis is controlled through the rotation of wiimote along its X-axis as shown in figure 6(a). The Z-axis movement of virtual hand is controlled through the up and down buttons of wiimote. Figure 6 shows the 3D coordinates of MMVL.

Selection & manipulation. Selection and manipulation are the important activities in any virtual environment. For the manipulation of an object it needs to

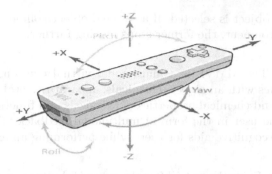

Fig. 5. Wiimote Motion Sensing [13]

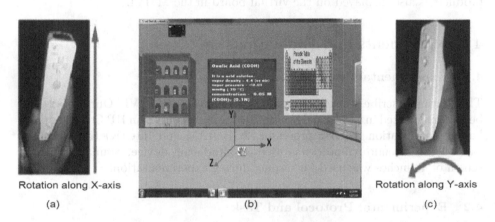

Rotation along X-axis

(a)

(b)

Rotation along Y-axis

(c)

Fig. 6. 3D Coordinates of MMVL

be selected first. In MMVL an object becomes selectable when the virtual hand collides with it. After collision if the user presses the button "A" of the wiimote, the object is selected. After selection the user is able to manipulate it i.e. to change its position or orientation and other attributes. For example he/she can bring the selected chemical or glassware to the table and can place it anywhere by just pressing the wiimote "A" button again.

Collision Detection. It is a natural matter that one solid object cannot inhabit the space of another solid object. In a simulated virtual environment an object needs realistic responding collision with other objects to show solidity [14]. In MMVL the collision detection module is responsible to check the collision of the virtual hand with all other objects such as chemical and apparatuses. The system performs different actions when the collision occurs. If the virtual hand collides with an object, the audio/visual information related to the object is provided by the system or the object is selected. If a selected object collides with any other object in the environment, the former stops moving further.

Multimodality. The MMVL is a multimodal virtual environment when the virtual hand collides with an object (chemicals, apparatuses etc) its information (such as physical and chemical properties of chemicals and function of glassware etc) is given to the user in the form of multimodal feedback. The multimodal feedback works as cognitive aids for users while performing an experiment.

Simulation of an Experiment. After the successful performance of an experiment the user obtains the simulated reaction and the equation of the resultant products is also displayed on the virtual board in the MMVL.

4   Experiments and Evaluations

4.1   Experimental Setup

This section describes the experiment and evaluation of MMVL. Our MMVL has been implemented in MS Visual Studio 2010 using OpenGL on HP Corei3 Laptop having specification 2.4GHz processor, 2GB RAM and Intel(R) HD Graphics card. The Nintendo wiimote was used as interfacing device. Similarly, a LED screen of 40 inches was used for display during experimentation.

4.2   Experimental Protocol and Task

In order to evaluate the MMVL, fourteen students participated in the experiments. They were the 10th class students of government high school. They were in the same class and had ages from 16 to 18 years. We selected one of their course experiments The Standardization of Sodium Hydroxide. They were taught using the traditional classroom method by the same teacher. These students were divided into two groups (i.e. G1, G2) each containing seven participants. The students in G1 used the MMVL while those in G2 did not. As all the participants had no prior experience of VR systems, therefore, they were briefed with the help of 20 minutes demonstration about the use of the MMVL. For example, they were taught that how they will navigate in the environments. Similarly, they were also guided about the selection and manipulation of chemicals and apparatuses. Then each participant was asked to work in the MMVL. One of a participant performs the virtual experiment as shown in figure 7. Each participant filled a questionnaire after getting experience in MMVL. Then both G1 and G2 were taken to a chemistry laboratory where they had to perform the simulation of experiment. Here the data of the students performance were collected again through a questionnaire.

Fig. 7. Simulation of an experiment by one of the participants in MMVL

4.3 Analysis

This section describes the data analysis accumulated from the evaluation. The analysis of the questionnaire filled by students in G1 (group 1). There were seven questions in this questionnaire. The objective of these questions was to evaluate the following aspects of MMVL:

☐ The effect of MMVL on students learning in chemistry education.

☐ Realism of the system.

☐ Ease of interaction in MMVL.

The students had to answer these questions on a scale of 1 to 5. Where 1= low and 5 = very high level. The analysis of these responses is given below.

Statistical and Subjective Assessment. This subsection presents the statistical results of the MMVL which we obtained from participants. By using MMVL all of the participants completed their virtual experiments in an average time of 12 minutes.

The first question which are related to learning for which 75% students selected the highest level as shown in figure 8(a).

For question 2 which are related to realism of MMVL, 68% students selected for the very highly real option as shown in figure 8(b).

The next question which was related to the easiness of interaction in MMVL got the vote 67% students for the highest option as shown in Figure 9.

Similarly 75% students selected the highest level for usefulness and 67% students selected the highest level of confidence they feel after performing the experiment in MMVL as shown in figure 10(a) and 10(b) respectively.

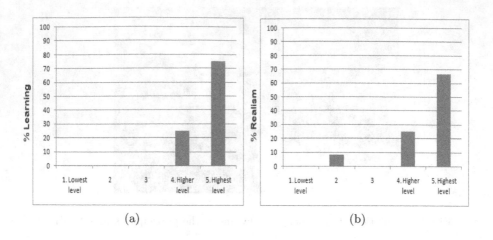

Fig. 8. Learning and realism in MMVL

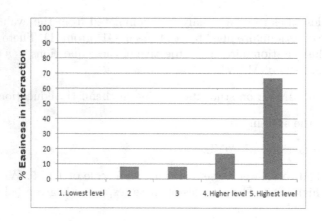

Fig. 9. Easiness of interaction in MMVL

The second part of the questionnaire was filled by both the groups (G1 and G2) during their session in the laboratory (real situation). The data recorded in the second section were consisting of their ability to identify various chemicals, apparatuses and their function and to perform the experimentin the real environment in the correct manner. Comparing the MMVL trained group (G1) with untrained group (G2) we observed a great difference in their success rate (see Fig.11). Here the mean success rate of G1 is 83.5% while that of G2 is only 32.7%.

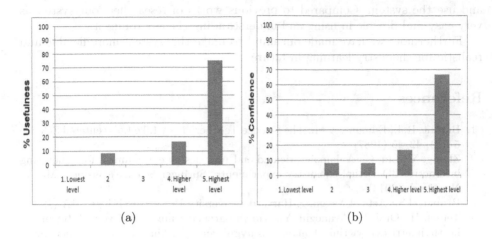

(a)   (b)

Fig. 10. Usefulness and confidence of MMVL

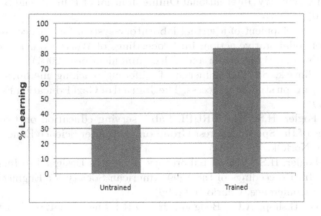

Fig. 11. Comparison of trained vs. untrained students

5   Conclusion

In this paper we presented Multimodal Virtual Laboratory which we have developed for high schools. In most of the education institutions there are not so much laboratory facilities due to financial problems. Our developed MMVL is very helpful for educational institutions where students can simulate their chemistry experiments like the real chemistry laboratory and to improve their learning which is very useful for exam score improvement. We evaluated the MMVL through students to find the usefulness and efficiency of the MMVL. Overall evaluations prove that the MMVL is very useful and efficient for chemistry practical learning and for students learning improvement. The user can easily understand

and use the system. Compared to previous works of researchers our system is very easy and flexible in using and understanding the environment.

Furthermore we have made our mind to make this system more flexible and realistic for chemistry learning in future.

References

1. Bryant, R.J., Edmunt, A.M.: The Science Teacher. They Like Lab-centered Science **54**(8), 42–45 (1987)
2. Zhong, Y., Liu, C.: A domain-oriented end-user design environment for generating interactive 3D virtual chemistry experiments. Springer Science+Business Media, New York (2013)
3. Bruner, J.S.: Acts of Meaning. Harvard University Press, Cambridge, MA (1990)
4. Temel, H., Oral, B., Avanoglu, Y.: Kimya ogrencilerinin deneye yonelik tutumlari ile titrimetri deneylerini planlama ve uygulamaya iliskin bilgi ve becerileri arasndaki liskinin degerlendirilmesi. Journal of Contemprory Education **264**, 32–38 (2000)
5. Cengiz, T.: The Effect of the Virtual Laboratory on Students Achievement and Attitude in Chemistry. International Online Journal of Educational Sciences **2**(1), 37–53 (2010)
6. Jensen, N.: Development of a virtual laboratory system for science education and the study of collaborative action. In: Proceedings of World Conference on Educational Multimedia, Hypermedia and Telecommunications (2004)
7. Bagci, N., Simsek, S.: The influence of different teaching methods in teaching physics subjects on student's success. The Journal of Gazi Education Faculty **19**(3), 79–80 (1999)
8. Bell, J.T., Fogler, H.S.: The VRUPL Lab - serving education on two fronts., In: Proceedings of the Special Interest Group on Computer Science Education Annual Conference, Norfolk, VA (2004)
9. Bell, J.T., Fogler, H.S.: Virtual Laboratory Accidents Designed to Increase Safety Awareness. In: Proceedings of the 1999 American Society for Engineering Education Annual Conference, Charlotte (1999)
10. Dalgarno, B., Bishop, A.G., Bedgood Jr., D.R.: The potential of virtual laboratories for distance education science teaching: reflections from the development and evaluation of a virtual chemistry laboratory. In: UniServe Science Conference Proceedings (2003)
11. Woodfield, B.F.: The virtual ChemLab project: a realistic and sophisticated simulation of organic synthesis and organic qualitative analysis. Journal of Chemical Education **82**, 1728–1735 (2005)
12. Oxford University Virtual Chemistry Lab. http://www.chem.ox.ac.uk/vrchemistry (accessed on February 05, 2014)
13. http://embeddedcode.wordpress.com/2010/12/07/wiimote-and-glovepie/ (accessed on March 02, 2014)
14. Olwal, A., Feiner, S.: The Flexible Pointer: An Interaction Technique for Selection in Augmented and Virtual Reality. In: Conference Supplement of UIST 03 (ACM Symposium on User Interface Software and Technology), Vancouver, BC, pp. 81–82 (November 2003)

Medicine

Virtual Reality Surgical Navigation System for Holmium Laser Enucleation of the Prostate

Giuseppe Lo Presti[1,2(✉)], Cinzia Freschi[1], Sara Sinceri[1], Girolamo Morelli[3],
Mauro Ferrari[1], and Vincenzo Ferrari[1]

[1] EndoCAS Center, Department of Translational Research on New Technologies
in Medicine and Surgery, University of Pisa, Pisa, Italy
giuseppe.lopresti@endocas.org
[2] Scuola Superiore di Studi Universitari e Perfezionamento S'Anna, Pisa, Italy
[3] Urology Department, Cisanello Hospital, Pisa, Italy

Abstract. Holmium Laser Enucleation of the Prostate (HoLEP) is an endoscopic transurethral surgical technique for Benign Prostatic Hyperplasia (BPH) treatment that carries significant benefits compared with the traditional Trans-Urethral Resection of the Prostate (TURP). In HoLEP procedure the portion of the prostate with hyperplasia (adenoma) is cut under endoscopic view. Only a few experts in the world perform HoLEP, since the adenoma borders are not clearly visible in the 2D endoscopic images and consequently the clinicians have difficulties to orientate the laser.

Virtual reality navigators demonstrated their potentialities in many fields of surgery to show hidden structures to direct vision and to restore surgeon's orientation.

3D trans-rectal ultrasound (US) probe allows acquiring volumetric information containing prostate and adenoma borders, which can be segmented and represented in a virtual environment. To coherently and real-time render the surgical instrument in respect to the patient anatomy, we can employ a tracking system. A crucial aspect of each navigation system regards the virtual scene ergonomics.

We designed and implemented a pilot surgical navigation system to support the surgeons to accomplish the HoLEP, showing them the cutting plane and the outlines of adenoma and the prostatic capsule in respect of the surgical tool.

Under supervision of an expert urologist we studied and tested the optimal way to realize an anthropomorphous US phantom. Furthermore our virtual reality surgical navigator provides various visualization modalities studied on the basis of clinical requirements.

On the basis of our results it will be possible to perform in-vitro trails to evaluate the usability of our solution to precisely enucleate the adenoma along its borders.

Keywords: HoLEP · Virtual Reality · Navigation system · Benign Prostatic Hyperplasia

© Springer International Publishing Switzerland 2014
L.T. De Paolis and A. Mongelli (Eds.): AVR 2014, LNCS 8853, pp. 79–89, 2014.
DOI: 10.1007/978-3-319-13969-2_6

1   Introduction

Trans-Urethral Resection of the Prostate (TURP) is considered the first choice for the removal of obstructing Benign Prostatic Hyperplasia (BPH). Although TURP has been the gold standard for almost fifty years [1] until now the morbidity is still about 15% [2-3]. Even though TURP procedure evolved in order to reduce its morbidity [4], a solution to decrease patient dissatisfaction and collateral damages is missing [5]. Ideally, to reduce patient's morbidity, an adenoma complete and one shot enucleation is better than the traditional slice-by-slice TURP resection. To perform this kind of intervention the Holmium Laser Enucleation of the Prostate (HoLEP) procedure was developed. The holmium laser is a pulsed solid-state laser, with a wavelength of 2140 nm strongly absorbed by water, making it ideal for safe use in aqueous environment. An end-firing bare laser fiber is inserted through the urethral channel. It delivers the laser energy to the prostatic tissue. The laser simultaneously cuts and coagulates blood vessels and its effect is circumscribed with a penetration of approximately 0.2 mm and very little thermal spread [6-7].

Although HoLEP potential benefits, this procedure is performed only by a few experts in the world, since the adenoma borders are not clearly visible in the 2D endoscopic images and consequently the clinicians have difficulties to orientate the laser. These difficulties determine the risk to partially remove the adenoma and consequently the need of reintervention. The best performed HoLEP procedure is to cut as big as possible the adenoma without injuring the patient's prostate healthy tissue.

Virtual reality navigators demonstrated their potentialities in many fields of surgery to identify hidden structures to direct vision and to restore surgeon's orientation.

In this paper we propose a navigation system that shows three dimensional (3D) models of prostate, adenoma, urethral channel and medical instruments in a virtual reality scene.

2   Materials and Methods

We designed and implemented a surgical navigator based on virtual reality. Our navigator provides the clinician a software application with a 3D virtual scene. In this scene the surgical instrument is coherently visualized in respect to a 3D representation of the 3D model of the anatomy. To know the right position of the rendered object, we used an electromagnetic localizer. Furthermore we studied and developed the optimal way to obtain a phantom for in-vitro system testing.

2.1   Prototypal System Architecture

The prototypal system architecture was realized with: a Philips iU22 ultrasound system, an electromagnetic localizer (Aurora®, Northern Digital Inc., Canada), a sensorized surgical instrument and a laptop running a home-developed software application. Figure 1 shows the prototypal architecture.

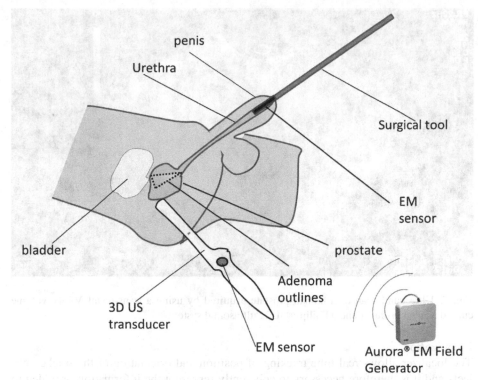

Fig. 1. General description of the architecture: an EM sensor is embedded in the surgical tool; an EM sensor is fixed to the US transducer

Several basic problems have been addressed to design and implement the US navigation system: the virtual information representation, instruments tracking and calibration, design and implementation of the Graphical User Interface (GUI).

Virtual Information Representation

To obtain the 3D model of the anatomy it is necessary an imaging source: we chose to use an intraoperative imaging to avoid the critical registration problem. We chose 3D Ultrasound (US) because presents some advantages with respect to other imaging modalities: it is portable, less expensive, non-invasive, it does not require a dedicate room.

To acquire the ultrasound (US) volumetric dataset we used the trans-vaginal V9-4v volume curved array transducer connected to Philips® iU22 ultrasound system. The transducer has an operating frequency range between 9 to 4 MHz, 150 degrees field of view and 2D, 3D, 4D imaging including Doppler, STIC, PW Doppler, M-mode and CPA. We verified that the transducer was right for our purpose, acquiring four volumetric dataset of the prostate during four male patients US examinations (through anus). The patients suffered from benign prostatic hyperplasia (BPH). First of all we converted the US voxel size to obtain cuboid voxels with constant size. Figure 2 shows the prostate of a patient. Furthermore, we elaborated the volumes in order to build up a virtual 3D model of the prostate, and the adenoma. The patient specific 3D models were used to build up a phantom, required to validate the navigation system.

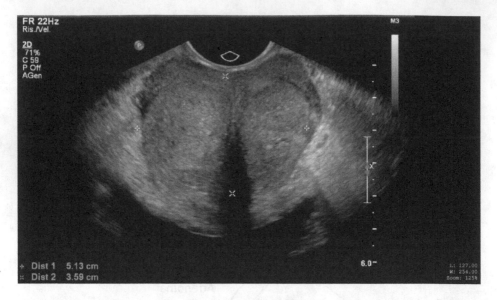

Fig. 2. Ultrasound scan of a human prostate acquired by using a trans-rectal V9-4v volume curved array transducer and a Philips® iU22 ultrasound system

Localization

The localizer allows real-time tracking of position and orientation of the tracked objects and it is therefore necessary to coherently represent the information provided to the user in the virtual reality scene.

We chose EM tracking due to the poor visibility and limited space of the surgical environment that does not allow direct line of sight, required by more precise optical technologies.

We fixed a six-degree of freedom (DOF) electromagnetic sensor to the V9-4v volume curved array transducer. In the prototypal system we used a cylindrical shape instrument simulating the surgical cutting device. We embedded an Aurora® 5 DOF electromagnetic sensor (0.5 mm diameter) in the instrument to track its position and orientation.

Calibration

Reading the position and the orientation of the sensors fixed on the objects, the localizer permits to refer all the sensors in the same reference frame (fixed on the localizer itself). It is necessary to determine the relationship between each sensor and the object on which this sensor is mounted. In particular, in our case, a calibration procedure was necessary to know the position and orientation of the US scan volume starting from the 3D position and orientation of the sensor attached to the US probe. To this aim, we implemented a software routine and we realized a calibration phantom. The phantom was a simple three points' phantom. It was placed in an aqueous environment and we acquired the US volumetric dataset and simultaneously electromagnetic (EM) measures with acquisition rate of 1 second. We acquired the data in ten different positions. We adopted a closed form to solve the problem (Figure 3). The problem is conducible to solve an equation of the type: AX=XB, well known in robotics. The A matrices are determined by localizer measurements, the B matrix by means of a point based rigid registration routine applied to the points' coordinates in the US volume reference frame system in two poses. A detailed description of these routines can be found in our previous works [8-9]. Using a cylindrical shape instrument its calibration has been performed easily since the embedded sensor was aligned with the object main axis.

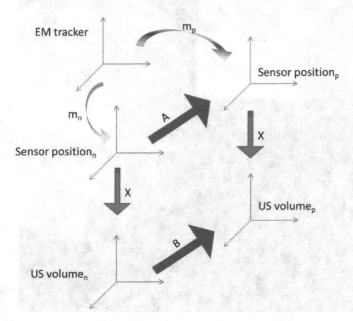

Fig. 3. Schematics of the calibration procedure to solve the position and orientation of the US scan volume starting from the 3D position and orientation of the sensor attached to the US probe. The variables n and p varied from 1 to 10 with the condition $n \neq p$.

Graphical User Interface (GUI)
Our navigator provides two kinds of visualization: a classical 3D virtual scene where the clinician can change the point of view, and one where the camera and the light of the scene are fixed on the tip of the instrument realizing an endoscopic view. Figure 4 shows the GUI of the navigation system.

2.2   Phantoms (Feasibility Study)

We studied and tested two types of phantom.

Agar Based Phantom
We arranged a prostate phantom composed of a prostate capsule, a prostatic hyperplasia, and surrounding tissue combining agar, distilled water, Psyllium and chlorhexindine

0.2%. The chemical composition of sections differed on the percentages of the cited ingredients. Table 1 shows the optimal compositions obtained after experimental trials under US examination.

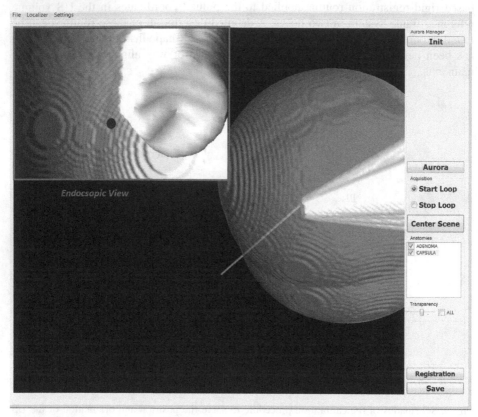

Fig. 4. Screenshot of the navigation system visualizations: at the top left corner the endoscopic visualization; at the bottom the lateral 3D view of the prostate and the surgical tool

Table 1. Composition of agar-based phantom

Phantom	Agar (g)	Psyllium (g)	Distilled water (g)	Chlorhexidine (g)
Prostate	0.6	2.6	95.6	0.2
Adenoma	1.5	0.7	97.6	0.2
Surrounding tissue	15	7	976	2

To prepare the prostatic capsule we added 0.6 g of agar and 2.6 g of Phylum to 95.6 g of distilled water and then we stirred until the ingredients were completely dissolved. We boiled the mixture. After two minutes cooking we added 0.2 of chlorhexidine, we poured it in a realistic mold and we refrigerated it for 30 minutes [10-11].

We prepared the adenoma and the surrounding tissue using the same concentration. We combined 15 g of agar, 7 g of psyllium and 976 g of distilled water. We added 488 ml of cold water to the agar and we stirred to dissolve the agar. We stirred 7 g of psyllium with 488 ml of cold water. After boiling the agar solution for two minutes we mixed it with psyllium solution adding 2 g of chlorhexidine and stirring the mixture to make it homogeneous. Figure 5 shows the phantom acquired by an US linear transducer: the boundaries are evident and it is possible to distinguish the prostate, the urethra and the adenoma that occluded the urethral channel. The materials chosen had same acoustic impedance in respect of human soft tissue. On the other hand the stiffness of adenoma and prostate were too different oversimplifying the enucleating performance.

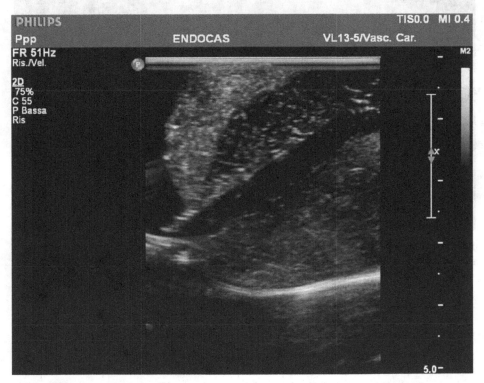

Fig. 5. Ultrasound scan of the phantom in aqueous environment: the prostate capsule, the adenoma and urethral channel are well distinguished from the surrounding environment

Wilkin and Hamm like Phantom

We investigated the optimal way to preserve the acoustic impedance of the phantom and to employ materials that simulate the density and the stiffness ratio of the real structures. We exploited the method described by Wilkin and Hamm to develop a cheap prostate phantom making use of cornstarch, beets, corned beef and gelatin [12]. Figure 6 shows the phantom acquired by using the trans-vaginal V9-4v volume curved array transducer. The inner adenoma appeared high-echogenic: in real patients the inner gland usually results hypo-echoic compared to the peripheral zone of the prostate and the central zone is often discernible. Despite the different US features, our phantom allowed to well distinguish the zones and thanks to its comparable densities it simulated the operative conditions to enucleate the prostate.

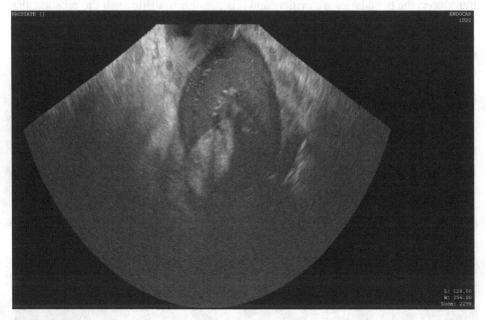

Fig. 6. Ultrasound scan of phantom obtained by using Wilkin and Hamm recipe: the conic shape adenoma is clearly visible in respect of the surrounding prostate

3   Results

We designed and implemented a pilot surgical navigation system to support the surgeons to perform the HoLEP. Our system required a-priori trans-rectal US acquisition and a subsequent realization of the patient specific 3D model of the prostate (capsule and adenoma). Our system provides a view showing a 3D rendering scene in which the instruments and the prostate with the planned cutting surface are visualized. Figure 7 shows the 3D prostate model obtained by segmenting US trans-rectal images and the outlines of the adenoma and the external prostate capsule. Our system is able to support different types of visualization.

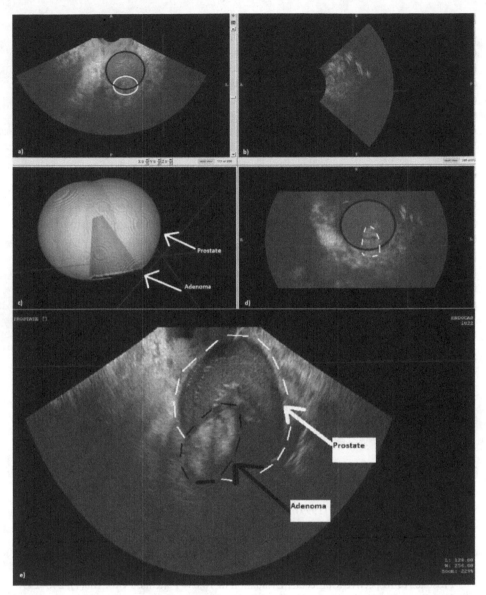

Fig. 7. Ultrasound scan of the prostate phantom and 3D model; a), b), d) show the prostate in the three anatomical planes; c) shows the 3D model built up and e) is a zoom of prostate capsule and adenoma from axial view in respect of the transducer

We conducted a feasibility study by using a prostate phantom containing a benign hyperplasia. Firstly we investigated the mechanical features and the acoustic impedance of a massive number of materials. Our studied led us to the agar/psyllium solution. The US investigation was acceptable but the densities between central and peripheral zones were too different. Consequently the surgical simulation performed to the phantom resulted not comparable with real cases. Then we availed ourselves of one urologist expert advices in order to find the materials and the right composition of those to obtain a plausible prostate phantom. We focused our attention to duplicate the stiffness that surgeons contend with. We found an optimal solution: it exploits cornstarch, corned beef and beets: the cited work is cheap and permits the recognition of the anatomical structures. Although the echogenicity achieved by this latter solution was not exactly the one of the real diagnostic scenario, the phantom simulated well the prostate and the adenoma in terms of density and stiffness.

4   Conclusions

We implemented a virtual reality navigation system for HoLEP. Surgeons currently use only endoscopic images to advance with medical instrumentation during HoLEP. Our solution is a preliminary surgical navigator that helps surgeons to orientate the laser fiber used during the intervention and to follow the hyperplasia borders. Our navigation system provides surgeons a virtual scene showing in real time the relationship between the anatomy and the instrument tip. Different types of visualization are provided. We are designing a validation study to evaluate also the best visualization.

To validate the navigation system we studied different ways to build up a plausible US prostate phantom, taking into account the acoustic impedance, the mechanical features and the stiffness ratio between the adenoma and the external prostatic capsule. Future works are required to validate the proposed solution by urologists.

Acknowledgment. This work has been supported by Regione Toscana within the Scientific Project "MILoRDS" (PAR FAS 2007-2013 Azione 1.1 P.I.R. 1.1.B).

References

1. Medersbacher and Marberger: Is transurethral resection of the prostate still justified? BJU International **83**, 227–237 (1999)
2. Leyh and Necknig: Transurethral prostatectomy: management of complications. Urologe A. **53**(5), 699–705 (2014). doi:10.1007/s00120-014-3483-7
3. Reich, O., Gratzke, C., Bachmann, A., Seitz, M., Schlenker, B., Hermanek, P., Lack, N., Stief, C.G.: Morbidity, Mortality and Early Outcome of Transurethral Resection of the Prostate:A Prospective Multicenter Evaluation of 10,654 Patients. J Urol 180(1), 246–249
4. Horninger, W., Unterlechner, H., Strasser, H., Bartsch, G.: Transurethral prostatectomy: mortality and morbidity. Prostate **28**, 195–200 (1996)
5. Gilling, P.J., Cass, C.B., Cresswell, M.D., Fraundorfer, M.R.: Holmium laser resection of the prostate: preliminary results of a new method for the treatment of benign prostatic hyperplasia. Urology **47**(1), 48–51 (1996a)
6. Cynk, M.: Holmium laser enucleation of the prostate: a review of the clinical trial evidence. Ther Adv Urol. **6**(2), 62–73 (2014). doi:10.1177/1756287213511509
7. Gilling, P.J., Cass, C.B., Cresswell, M.D., Malcolm, A.R., Fraundorfer, M.R.: The use of the holmium laser in the treatment of benign prostatic hyperplasia. J Endourol. **10**(5), 459–461 (1996b)

8. Megali, G., Ferrari, V., et al.: EndoCAS navigator platform: a common platform for computer and robotic assistance in minimally invasive surgery. Int J Med Robot Comp **4**(3), 242–251 (2008)
9. Freschi, C., Troia, E., et al.: Ultrasound Guided Robotic Biopsy Using Augmented Reality and Human-Robot Cooperative Control. Conf Proc IEEE Eng Med Biol Soc **2009**, 5110–5113 (2009)
10. Zell, K., Sperl, J.I., Vogel, M.W., Niessner, R., Haisch, C.: Acoustical properties of selected tissue phantom materials for ultrasound imaging. Physics in medicine and biology **52**, N475–N484 (2007)
11. Ahmadi, R., Kalbasi-Ashtari, A., Oromiehie, A., Yarmand, M.S., Jahandideh, F.: Development and characterization of a novel biodegradable edible film obtained from psyllium seed (Plantago ovata Forsk). J Food Eng **109**, 745–751 (2012)
12. Wilkin, R., Hamm, R.: How to make a cheap and simple prostate phantom. J Ultrasound Med **29**, 1151–1152 (2010)

Development of a Serious Game for Laparoscopic Suture Training

Lucio Tommaso De Paolis[1(✉)], Francesco Ricciardi[1,2], and Francesco Giuliani[2]

[1] AVR Lab, Department of Engineering for Innovation,
University of Salento, Lecce, Italy
{lucio.depaolis,francesco.ricciardi}@unisalento.it
[2] Unit of Information Systems, Innovation and Research,
Casa Sollievo della Sofferenza Hospital,
San Giovanni Rotondo, FG, Italy
f.giuliani@operapadrepio.it

Abstract. Surgeon training in laparoscopic suturing is very important because this task generally requires an high level of experience from the surgeon. Serious gaming refers to a computer games technology where the primary goal is to train the player. In this kind of training the education goal is achieved also ensuring the entertainment and the engagement factors typical of a traditional game. This paper presents the development of a serious game for training on suturing in laparoscopic surgery that is focused on the physical modeling of the virtual environment and on the definition of a set of parameters used to assess the level of skills developed by the trainees.

Keywords: Serious game · Simulation · Surgical training · Laparoscopic suturing.

1 Introduction

The spreading of Minimally Invasive Surgery (MIS) reduced the trauma and surgical cut on patients. The use of this type of surgical technique has led to an increasing demand of education and training of surgeons. Furthermore traditional approach to learning and teaching based on the use of animals, cadavers or dummies appears obsolete.

As compared to traditional surgical techniques (i.e. open surgery), in MIS surgeons operate in a very small workspace, without having a direct view of the organs that are visualized by means of a camera. For this reason, in this context, some skills such as eye-hand coordination are fundamental for the success of the surgical operation. Surgeons need to have an accurate training with this type of technique.

The introduction of the simulation based on the Virtual Reality (VR) technology has completely changed the education and training tools and, since 1998, the virtual simulators are officially accepted as training tools for surgeons. Several studies have demonstrated how the virtual reality-based simulators, compared to training based on traditional methods, can significantly reduce the intra-operative errors [1].

© Springer International Publishing Switzerland 2014
L.T. De Paolis and A. Mongelli (Eds.): AVR 2014, LNCS 8853, pp. 90–102, 2014.
DOI: 10.1007/978-3-319-13969-2_7

The VR-based simulators allow reproducing different surgical scenarios without risks for the patient. They have also the advantage of the repeatability of the training sessions in order to evaluate and study the mistakes. In addition, these simulators provide an objective measurement of the developed skills. It is also possible to reuse many times the simulator because the virtual environment does not undergo the degradation of the traditional toolbox used for training.

Nowadays VR-based laparoscopic simulators have achieved a high level of accuracy. The use of haptic devices able to provide a force feedback to the user has contributed to the spread of the virtual simulators developed for surgery training.

Laparoscopic suture is one of the most frequently performed task in minimally invasive surgery. It is used to close the incisions made during the surgical procedure. This task need an high level of surgeon experience in order to be carried out correctly reducing unwanted side effects. It needs much training.

A new trend in the development of virtual surgical simulators is represented by "serious games". A serious game is a computer game whose primary purpose is not entertainment, but teaching and learning. Although virtual simulators and serious games are conceptually similar and the same technology (hardware and software) can be used, the serious game approach introduce an entertainment factor and include some of the highlights typical of a videogame: challenge, risk, reward and defeat.

Serious gaming in healthcare and surgery has the goal to educate and train people about treatments, medical and surgical procedures, involving them with an entertainment factor typical of a videogame.

In this paper we present a serious game for training surgeons on suturing in laparoscopic surgery. In particular, our system is focused on an accurate physical modeling of the virtual environment and on the definition of a set of parameters used to assess the level of skills developed by the trainees. A pair of haptic devices has been utilized in order to simulate the manipulation of the surgical instruments. NVIDIA PhysX physics engine is used to simulate the physics of the simulated environment and Ogre3D is used for graphical rendering.

2   Surgical Training

Medical professionals for centuries have used a training model based on apprenticeship. With this training approach the trainee observes a procedure made by an expert physician and then practices it under the teacher or an expert supervision.

With this traditional approach, many different tools and techniques have been deployed to provide added value to the training process, such as using animals or cadavers or by practicing on mannequins. However, the interactions that occur in an animal's or cadaver's tissues differ from those of living humans due to varying anatomy or absence of physiological behaviour. This type of training can also raise some ethical issues. Mannequins that simulate part or all of a patient anatomy provide a limited range of anatomical variability and also a different response from the living human tissue.

An alternative approach that is becoming more and more accepted by the medical community consists in the use of a virtual reality simulators that can train practitioners on a virtual patient and permit to have a live feedback on the performed procedure. This feedback can then be used to refine the required skills until the operator reaches a target level of proficiency before doing the required procedure on the real patient. In addition, virtual simulations can provide the user the possibility to practice the surgical procedure on rare or difficult medical cases or on virtual models of patients with unconventional anatomy.

3D virtual models offer also the opportunity to be customized. In fact they can be derived from patient medical data in order to replicate the patient's real anatomy and produce a realistic simulation environment.

Laparoscopy is a minimally invasive surgical procedure performed on the patient body through small incisions on the patient skin using long thin tools. The surgeon's view is provided by means of a camera inserted into the patient body. With this kind of "indirect" view and with the manipulation of long surgical instruments, the distance between surgical tool and the organ is difficult to be estimated. For this reason in this surgery field training with virtual simulator is very important [2]. Practitioner needs a long training period using commercial simulators before performing the operation on the real patient.

3   Virtual Surgical Simulators

In the field of surgical simulation, Wang et al. [5] present a physics-based thread simulator that enables realistic knot tying at haptic rendering rate. The virtual thread follows Newton's law and considers main mechanical properties of the real thread such as stretching, compressing, bending and twisting, as well as contact forces due to self-collision and interaction with the environment, and the effect of gravity.

Webster et al. [6] describe a new haptic simulation designed to teach basic suturing for simple wound closure. Needle holders are attached to the haptic device and the simulator incorporates several interesting components such as real-time modeling of deformable skin, tissue and suture material and real-time recording of state of activity during the task.

Le Duc et al. [7] present a suturing simulation using the mass-spring models. Various models for simulating a suture were studied, and a simple linear mass-spring model was determined to give good performance.

Choi et al. [8] explore the feasibility of using commodity physics engine to develop a suturing simulator prototype for manual skills training in the fields of nursing and medicine. Spring-connected boxes of finite dimension are used to simulate soft tissues, whereas needle and thread are modeled with chained segments. The needle insertion and thread advancement through the tissue is simulated and two haptic devices are used in order to provide a force feedback to the user.

Lenoir et al. [9] propose a surgical thread model for surgeons to practice a suturing task. They first model the thread as a spline animated by continuous mechanics. Moreover, to enhance realism, an adapted model of friction is proposed, which allows the thread to remain fixed at the piercing point or slides through it.

Shi et al. [10] present a physics-based haptic simulation designed to teach basic suturing techniques for simple skin or soft tissue wound closure. The objects are modeled using a modified mass-spring method.

LapSim [24] is a commercial surgical simulator that offers a complete portfolio of laparoscopic procedure exercises. It has a modular structure and comprises also a module for laparoscopic suture training.

4   Serious Games

Serious games usually refer to games developed for user training and education. In 2005 Stokes [3] defined serious games as: "games that are designed to entertain players as they educate, train, or change behaviour". They are designed to run on personal computers or videogame consoles. Today they can be played also on smartphones.

Serious games provide an high fidelity simulation of particular environments and situations that focus on high level skills that are required in the real world. They present situations in a complex interactive context coupled with interactive elements that are designed to engage the trainees.

Strengths and weaknesses of videogames are also transferred to serious games. Further benefits of serious games include improved self-monitoring, problem recognition and solving, improved short-and long-term memory, increased social skills and increased self-efficacy [4].

In contrast to traditional teaching environments whereby the teacher controls the learning (teacher centered), the serious games present a learner centered approach to education in which the trainee controls the learning through interactivity.

Serious game engagement may allow the trainee-player to learn via an active, critical learning approach. Game-based learning provides a methodology to integrate game design concepts with instructional design techniques with the aim to enhance the educational experience.

Virtual environments and videogames offer students the opportunity to practice their skills and abilities within a safe learning environment, leading to a higher level of self-efficacy when faced with real life situations where such skills and knowledge are required.

Serious games should provide a balanced combination between challenge and learning. Playing the game must excite the user, while ensuring that the primary goal (acquiring knowledge or skills) is reached seemingly effortlessly, thus creating a 'stealth mode' of learning. Players are challenged to keep on playing to reach the game's objective.

Although game-based learning is becoming a new form of healthcare education, scientific research in this field is limited.

Dental Implant Training Simulation [11], developed for the Medical College of Georgia and funded through a grant by Nobel Biocare, is a groundbreaking project created to better teach and train dental school students and dental professionals on patient assessment and diagnosis protocol and to practice dental implant procedures in a realistic, 3D virtual environment. The game-based simulation has the aim to improve dental student learning outcomes in the area of diagnostics, decision-making and treatment protocols for enhanced patient therapy outcomes and risk management.

Total knee arthroplasty [12] is a commonly performed surgical procedure whereby knee joint surfaces are replaced with metal and polyethylene components that serve to function in the way that bone and cartilage previously had. The serious game has been designed to train orthopedic surgical residents on surgical procedures, and to gauge whether learning in an online serious gaming environment will enhance complex surgical skill acquisition.

Qin et al. [13] realized a serious game to train blood management in orthopaedic surgery context to orthopaedic surgeons. The serious game uses two haptic interface for the user interaction and comprises two practice games where the player develop the required hand-eye coordination using the haptic interface. In the third game the user play as a surgeon and three modality were provided: training mode, time-attack mode and collaborative mode. The game uses a Mass-Spring model for tissue deformation modeling and a blood flow distribution model based on human physiology.

Cowan et al. developed a serious game for off-pump coronary artery bypass grafting cardiac surgical procedure (OPCAB) training [14]. In the game the player is placed in the operating room with the role of cardiac surgeon and must execute surgical procedure.

Qin et al. presented another serious game [15] to train radiologist in the ultrasound-guided needle placement procedure. They used a block based construction scheme in order to generate game scenarios and a novel texture-based image synthesis technique in order to simulate corresponding ultrasound images. The game was evaluated over a group of 21 participants and this study shows that the serious game approach is useful for surgical skills teaching to surgical novices.

Serious gaming can be used to enhance surgical skills. Ideally, these training instruments are used to measure certain parameters and to assess the trainees' performance. In these games, strict requirements should be met and the interpretation of the game metrics must be reliable and valid. Games used to train medical professionals need to be validated before they are integrated into teaching methods and applied to surgical training curricula [17].

5   Technological Platform

The serious game for laparoscopic suturing training was developed using OGRE 3D graphics engine [16], NVIDIA PhysX for physical modeling of the objects and HAPI library for haptic interactions and force feedback rendering.

PhysX [17] is a real-time physics simulation framework developed from NVIDIA. A major advantage of this physics engine is the support of hardware acceleration when a compatible Graphics Processing Unit is installed. Developers can instruct the engine to utilize the processing power of the GPU in order to perform physics computation and to relieve the CPU for other tasks.

PhysX uses a position-based approach for the body dynamics management in order to reduce the instability problems that could make unnatural the results of simulation and so the resulting environment [18].

The PhysX engine supports the simulation of both rigid bodies and soft objects, including cloth and fluids. It employs a scene graph to manage the objects in a virtual environment.

In order to provide a force feedback to the user, an haptic interface is used in our simulation. In our developed solution it is possible to use two SensAble Phantom Omni or two Novint Falcon haptic devices.

The choice of the preferred haptic devices is possible through the use of the multi-device HAPI library. This library has the advantage to be open-source and cross-platform. It supports many commercial haptic interface and the user can extend this compatibility writing its own library extension. In order to improve simulation results it is better to use two Phantom Omni devices that have a larger workspace and are provided of 6 DOFs [19].

6   Simulation Models

One of the most important thing in surgical simulation is the real-world reproduction fidelity. The reproduction fidelity is measured not only in terms of graphical rendering fidelity but also in terms of physical behaviours simulation. Objects and materials should react to forces and solicitation like in the real world.

To achieve this goal it is necessary to use a physically-based simulation. This approach considers the physical properties of the object materials as well as its geometrical shape in a mathematical model that tries to reproduce the real world. Generally more are real world reproduction fidelity constraints more computational resources are needed in order to obtain an accurate simulation. These constraints are generally in contrast with the requirement to have a "real-time" interactive simulation which can responds to the user interaction.

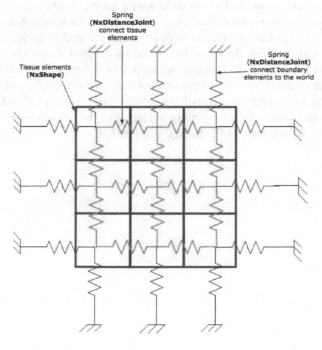

Fig. 1. Tissue modeling using the mass-spring method

Tissue Modelling

In the simulation, virtual tissues has been modeled using the mass-spring method [20]. Other models were also developed for this purpose but this one was chosen for its computational complexity. The tissue is represented as a three-dimensional net of point masses connected each other with springs.

Tissue deformation is based on the dynamics of the masses, and on the elasticity and damping factor of the springs that connect these masses. The law that describes the dynamic of each single point of mass (node) is the Newton law:

$$m_i \frac{d^2 x_i}{dt^2} + c_i \frac{dx_i}{dt} + F_i^{int} = F_i^{ext} \qquad i = 1, \dots, m$$

with

$$F_i^{int} = \sum_{j \in N_s} \frac{k_{ij}(|d_{ij}| - l_{ij})}{|d_{ij}|} d_{ij}$$

In these equations x_i represents the displacement of i-th node with respect its position in quiet state, m_i is the mass of the point, c_i is the damping factor of the i-th node, d_{ij} is the distance vector between i-th and j-th points, k_{ij} and l_{ij} are respectively the stiffness and length of the spring in the quiet state between i-th and j-th nodes and F_i^{ext} is the sum of the external forces that acts on the i-th node. N_s is the set of the nodes directly connected to i-th node with a spring. These equations are discretized and solved iteratively on the computer with a 4th order Range-Kutta method.

Additional springs have been used in order to fix the grid of springs in the virtual space. These springs allow the tissue to resume its original shape when the effect of deformation is removed. Fig. 1 shows the model of the tissue with the mass-spring method. In the intersection point of the springs there are the ideal point masses. Usually, in this kind of modeling masses have infinitesimal size, but PhysX engine does not allow the definition of dimensionless objects. For this reason a box of finite size has been used for the creation of a single tissue element.

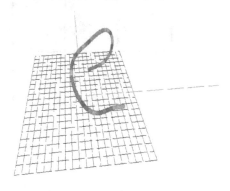

Fig. 2. Thread model

Another advantage that comes with the use of a mass-spring model is that a topological modification of the net produce a simple modification of the model equations. For example, the cut of the tissue surface produces a modification of the equations of the only nodes directly connected to those involved in the cut. Anyway this produces also a disadvantage because global modifications are hard to propagate because they require many simulation iterations.

Tissue rendering is obtained using Ogre3D [21]. Ogre3D is a scene oriented, open source 3d graphics engine. It supports only graphical rendering process and is compatible with many library for haptic, sound, etc. rendering and also physics computation. Ogre3D is a cross-platform library and can be used with Windows, Mac OS X and Linux platforms.

In Fig. 2 is shown the model of the thread.

Thread Modelling

The main technique used to model the dynamics of the surgical thread in virtual simulations is known in literature as "follow-the-leader" [22]. With this technique the thread is modeled by means of a chain of cylinders connected by joints that allow to simulate the bending of the thread.

At each step of simulation, when an external force is applied to a cylinder, the new position of this cylinder is calculated, and, using the follow-the-leader approach, the new positions of all cylinders are computed. In addition also the collisions between elements of the thread are detected and the new configuration of the entire thread is displayed.

As for the tissue, also for the thread the PhysX features are exploited in order to manage the dynamics of the thread (calculation of position and collision detection).

To simulate the flexibility of the thread, two adjacent cylinders are connected through a spherical joint, which allows the rotation of the elements relative to each other. A spherical joint, as shown in Fig. 3, is a constrains where two points located on two different rigid bodies must coincide in one point in space; a spherical joint has 3 free DOFs and 3 blocked DOFs. The visual model of the suturing thread is achieved through the rendering of all elements of the chain.

The use of spherical joints could led to strong oscillations when the thread is subjected to strong stretching forces. This is because spherical joints are temporarily disconnected when subjected to strong forces. To reduce this problem we modified the inertial tensor of thread elements to increment the inertia of each element.

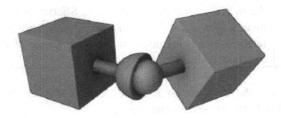

Fig. 3. The spherical joint used in order to simulate the flexibility of the thread

7   Serious Game for Laparoscopic Suturing Training

The aim of the developed serious game is to teach to surgeons the laparoscopic suture technique in minimally invasive surgery. An assessment module in the game were also provided to evaluate surgeon performance during the training phase.

To execute the surgical procedure two clamps are provided in the virtual environment. They are controlled by two haptic interfaces and should be used in order to pick the needle and execute the suture like in the real world.

After playing the serious game simulation the user should:

- acquire a good eye-hand coordination, that is very important in laparoscopic surgery;
- improve the ability to manipulate the surgical instruments;
- learn the techniques for performing the suture node.

Table 1. Parameters used to assess the player's performance

Parameter	Description
Duration time	It is the time elapsed between the first contact of the needle with the tissue and the completion of the node. Less time the surgeon spends to complete the procedure and greater is the evaluated skill.
Accuracy error	This parameter describes the maximum distance between the ideal point (indicated by a marker) and the real point of entry of the needle into the tissue. Smaller is the error and higher is the quality of the node.
Force peak	This number is the value of the maximum force used during the simulation in order to pierce the tissue by means of the needle.
Tissue damage	This value represents the sum of the forces applied to the tissue over the threshold of breakage of the tissue.
Angle of entry	This parameter is the difference between the normal to the surface and the tangent at the point of the needle entry.
Overall score	This parameter is determined by the average of all previous specified parameters.
Needle total distance	This value represents the total distance traveled from the needle in order to complete the task. Shorter is this distance and greater is evaluated the skill of the surgeon. Anyway this parameter is not included in the calculation of the quality assessment of the suture task.

Before developing the serious game some requirements were defined. These guided the entire development process and are:

- Simulation: the system should simulate as much as possible the real appearance and behavior of a real human tissue and suture thread;

- Configuration: the size of the tissue, the number of elements of the thread, the number and position of the fiducial points on the tissue and the time duration of the simulation must be specified before starting the simulation. These parameters are all stored in an XML configuration file;
- Haptic device - surgical forceps interaction: the user must to be able to move the virtual surgical forceps by means of the haptic device;
- Skill evaluation: the game must implement algorithms for measuring the skill of the user during the execution of the surgical procedure.

In the assessment of a suturing procedure it is necessary to consider some parameters that should be evaluated. These parameters are not extracted from the medical literature, which does not specify any quantitative metrics for evaluating the performance of this task, but were expressly defined for this serious game.

Some numerical indicators can be achieved by the physically-based virtual simulation. The Table 1 summarize the parameters used to assess the player's performance.

The software architecture of the serious game has been developed using the architectural pattern Model-View-Controller (MVC), whose use is not limited to the development of web applications, but also to virtual simulators [23].

The model manages the behavior and objects of the virtual environment, responds to requests for information about its state and responds to instructions to change state (Fig.4).

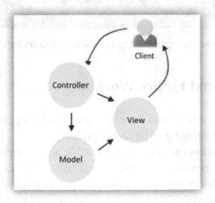

Fig. 4. Model-View-Controller pattern representation

The view renders the model into a form suitable for interaction and is managed by OGRE 3D graphical engine.

The controller accepts input from the user and instructs the model to perform actions based on that input. There are two subcontrollers:

- The controller of the physical simulation that applies the laws of the physics to the elements of the model (by changing the position, velocity and acceleration of the objects) and handles the collision detection between objects in the scene. This controller is implemented by the PhysX library.

- The controller of the haptic simulation that allows the communication between the model and the haptic device. This controller returns the forces, but is not responsible for the calculation of these that are computed by the controller of the physical simulation.

In Fig. 5 is shown the monitor of a pc with the serious game interface loaded and the two Novint Falcon haptic devices.

Fig. 5. The serious game using two Novint Falcon haptic devices

8   Conclusions and Future Work

This work describes the design and development of a first prototype of serious game for training surgeons on suturing in laparoscopic surgery.

We focused our attention on as more as possible accurate physical modeling of the objects involved in the serious game (the virtual tissue, the suture thread and needle). Then we defined a methodology to evaluate and measure the skills of the trainee. The surgical instruments manipulated by the surgeon are replaced in the serious game by two haptic interfaces. These interfaces control the movements of the virtual tweezer that are used in order to manipulate suture thread and needle.

We cannot compare our surgical simulator with complete and complex commercial products like the LapSim. The first reason is that we focused our attention on a particular step of the laparoscopic procedure (suturing) and ignored all the other steps of laparoscopic surgery that require however an accurate training. This choice and the use of commercial haptic interfaces permitted to mantain very low the cost of the simulator. The second reason is that we've structured our simulator as a serious game to engage and motivate the players to improve their performance. We made this choice because we want to evaluate in a successive study the usefulness of a serious game training approach in laparoscopic suture training.

In the future the system can be improved with a more accurate modeling of the interaction between the tissue and suture thread. Algorithms for skills evaluation can also be improved with a software module that stores the results of users training sessions in order to evaluate the progress of performance in the execution of suturing task. We also plan to substitute the current haptic interfaces with more expensive ones to ensure a bigger dimension of the player's workspace. These interfaces can be then modified to include real surgical instruments in the handle in order to obtain a more realistic simulation. Last we want try to evaluate the game training usefulness with medical students and expert surgeons to understand if this can represent a valid training approach.

References

1. Seymour, N.E., Gallagher, A.G., Roman, S.A., O'Brien, M.K., Bansal, V.K., Andersen, D.K., Satava, R.M.: Virtual reality training improves operating room performance: Results of a randomized, double-blinded study. Annals of Surgery **236**(4), 458–464 (2002)
2. Liu, A., Tendick, F., Cleary, K., Kaufmann, C.: A Survey of Surgical Simulation: Applications, Technology, and Education. Presence: Teleoperators and Virtual Environments **12**(6), 599–614 (2003)
3. Stokes, B.: Video games have changed: time to consider "serious games". The Development Education Journal **11**(108) (2005)
4. Susi, T., Johannesson, M., Backlund, P.: Serious Games – An Overview. Technical Report HS- IKI -TR-07-001, School of Humanities and Informatics, University of Skövde, Sweden
5. Wang, F., Burdet, E., Vuillemin, R., Bleuler, H.: Knot-tying with Visual and Force Feedback for VR Laparoscopic Training. In: Proc. of 27th Annual International Conference of the IEEE Engineering in Medicine and Biology Society (IEEE-EMBS), China (2005)
6. Webster, R.W., Zimmerman, D.I., Mohler, B.J., Melkonian, M.G., Haluck, R.S.: A Prototype Haptic Suturing Simulator. In: Westwood, J.D. et al. (eds.) Medicine Meets Virtual Reality 2001. IOS Press (2001)
7. LeDuc, M., Payandeh, S., Dill, J.: Toward Modeling of a Suturing Task. In: Graphics Interface, pp. 273–279 (2003)
8. Choi, K.-S., Chan, S.-H., Pang, W.-M.: Virtual Suturing Simulation Based on Commodity Physics Engine for Medical Learning. Journal of Medical Systems, 1–13 (2010)
9. Lenoir, J., Meseure, P., Grisoni, L., Chaillou, C.: A Suture Model for Surgical Simulation. In: Cotin, S., Metaxas, D. (eds.) ISMS 2004. LNCS, vol. 3078, pp. 105–113. Springer, Heidelberg (2004)
10. Shi, H.F., Payandeh, S.: Suturing Simulation in Surgical Training Environment. In: The 2009 IEEE/RSJ International Conference on Intelligent Robots and Systems, St. Louis, USA, October 11-15 (2009)
11. Dental Implant Training Simulation. http://www.breakawaygames.com
12. Sabri, H., Cowan, B., Kapralos, B., Porte, M., Backstein, D., Dubrowskie, A.: Serious games for knee replacement surgery procedure education and training. Procedia - Social and Behavioral Sciences **2**(2), 3483–3488 (2010)
13. Qin, J., Chui, Y.-P., Pang, W.-M., Choi, K.-S., Heng, P.-A.: Learning blood management in orthopedic surgery through gameplay. IEEE Computer Graphics and Applications **30**(2), 45–57 (2010)

14. Sabri, H., Cowan, B., Kapralos, B., Moussa, F., Cristanchoi, S., Dubrowski, A.: Off-pump coronary artery bypass surgery procedure training meets serious games. In: 2010 IEEE International Symposium on Haptic Audio-Visual Environments and Games (HAVE), pp. 1–5 (2010)
15. Chan, W.-Y., Qin, J., Chui, Y.-P., Heng, P.-A.: A serious game for learning ultrasound-guided needle placement skills. IEEE Transactions on Information Technology in Biomedicine **16**(6), 1032–1042 (2012)
16. OGRE 3d. http://www.ogre3d.org
17. NVIDIA Corporation, PhysX SDK 2.8 Reference (2008)
18. Müller, M., Heidelberger, B., Hennix, M., Ratcliff, J.: Position based dynamics. J. Vis. Comun. Image Represent **18**, 109–118 (2007)
19. Chan, L.S.-H., Choi, K.-S.: Integrating Physx and Openhaptics: Efficient Force Feedback Generation Using Physics Engine and Haptic Devices. In: Joint Conferences on Pervasive Computing (JCPC), Tamsui, Taipei, pp. 853–858, December 3-5 (2009)
20. Cotin, S., Delingette, H., Ayache, N.: Real-time elastic deformations of soft tissues for surgery simulation. IEEE TVCG **5**(1) (1999)
21. Junker, G.: Pro OGRE 3D Programming. Apress (2006)
22. Brown, J., Latombe, J.-C., Montgomery, K.: Real-time knot tying simulation. The Visual Computer **20**(2-3), 165–179
23. Maciel, A., Sankaranarayanan, G., Halic, T., Arikatla, V.S., Lu, Z., De, S.: Surgical model-view-controller simulation software framework for local and collaborative applications. International Journal of Computer Assisted Radiology and Surgery, 5 (2010)
24. http://www.surgical-science.com/lapsim-the-proven-training-system/

A Method of Three-Dimensional Visualization of Molecular Processes of Apoptosis

Ravil I. Muhamedyev[1], Vlad Gladkikh[1], Viktors I. Gopejenko[2],
Yevgenia A. Daineko[1(✉)], Alma T. Mansharipova[3],
Elena L. Muhamedyeva[4], and Aleksejs V. Gopejenko[5]

[1] CSSE and T Department, International IT University, Almaty 050040, Kazakhstan
{ravil.muhamedyev,yevgeniya2001}@gmail.com
[2] Information System Management Institute, Riga LV-1019, Latvia
viktors.gopejenko@isma.lv
[3] Kazakh-Russian Medical University, Almaty 050004, Kazakhstan
[4.] Riga Technical University, Riga, Latvia
[5] Institute of Solid State Physics, University of Latvia,
Kengaraga str. 8, Riga LV-1063, Latvia

Abstract. Apoptosis or programmed cell death plays an important role in many physiological states and diseases. Detection of apoptotic cells, tracing the development of apoptosis, drug development and regulation of apoptosis are an important parts of basic research in medicine. A large number of models have been developed that are based on the differential equations of the chemical kinetics, and can be expressed in a uniform notation using some XML-based languages, such as SBML and CellML. We describe the CellML and the simulation environment OpenCell herein. These tools can display models schematically and output results in the form of graphs showing time dependencies of component concentrations. However, at the present time we do not have a software that could represent the results of the modelling in a form of animations as well as in the form of 3-D models. Using descriptive as well as quantitative models we discuss approaches to visualize the biological processes described by the apoptosis models. The quantitative method was implemented using a 3-D visualization of the molecular biological processes modelled by chemical kinetic equations. The quantitative parameters in our visualization scheme are determined based on the kinetic equations governing the participating components, so our visualization is not only qualitative but also quantitative. To implement this visualization, the C# software and a database of 3-D forms that model molecular complexes are developed. We present 3-D visualization of the molecular processes described in the mathematical model for the mitochondria-dependent apoptosis proposed by Bagci et al. [22] as a case study.

Keywords: Apoptosis · Visualization · Chemical kinetics · Molecular biology

© Springer International Publishing Switzerland 2014
L.T. De Paolis and A. Mongelli (Eds.): AVR 2014, LNCS 8853, pp. 103–112, 2014.
DOI: 10.1007/978-3-319-13969-2_8

1   Introduction

Visualization of biomolecular processes is essential for understanding of the biological mechanisms' interaction principles. Chemical composition is not the only factor that determines the interactions between proteins, organelles and other biological molecular complexes. Their shape, i.e. the spatial configuration of the chemical components included in the composition of the macromolecules has significant role. Computer visualization of such interactions will have an important role in understanding the processes and will help to solve the problem of the chemicals' synthesis in order to control the biological processes in the cells; this might lead to the creation of the new medical products. E.g, the diphtheria toxin produced by the Corynebacterium diphtheriae bacteria that is diphtheria pathogenic agent may create pH-dependent pores or channels in the cell membranes. However, the mechanism of the diphtheria toxin permeation through the membrane is currently unknown. In order to answer this question, the understanding of the spatial forms that can be shaped by diphtheria toxin during the interaction with the membrane is required. It is a very difficult to determine experimentally and no one was able to do this yet. This is the reason why the computer modeling and the visualization of the given interaction may cast the light on this problem. The understanding of the mechanisms of the diphtheria toxin penetration through the cellular membrane may lead to the development of the medical products to cure the diphtheria. The study of the diphtheria toxin is also important because this molecule has the same spatial configuration as the Bcl-xL proteing, which has an important role in the process of apoptosis of the mammals' cells including humans [1].

Apoptosis is the process of programmed cell death (PCD) that may occur in multicellular organisms [2]. In contrast to necrosis, which is a form of traumatic cell death that results from acute cellular injury, in general apoptosis confers advantages during an organism's lifecycle.

Despite the chemical composition of the Bcl-xL protein is significantly different from that of the diphtheria toxin the spatial forms of these complexes are very similar and their main functions come to the light during their interactions with the lipid membranes. Besides Bcl-xL the mammal cells' apoptosis is controlled by some other proteins of the Bcl-2 super-family [3-6]. The question of their interaction with mitochondria membranes is opened for all of them for over 20 years as it is very difficult to determine experimentally. Several different hypothesis were proposed [7-9] but it is unknown which one is correct. Computer modelling and visualization may have an important role in the verification of the existing hypothesis as well as in the creation of the new ones and they may lead to the new ideas in conducting the experiments.

The detailed study of the apoptosis process is important as the dysfunction of the apoptosis dynamics leads to the oncological diseases as well as to the neural and endocreanal system diseases. The studies in this field already lead to the creation of the new medical products [10].

In spite of the existing progress, the problem of visualizing biochemical processes and models of apoptosis is not resolved completely. Therefore we propose both qualitative and also quantitative approaches to visualization of apoptosis models in [11].

In the work mentioned above, the languages and tools of computational biology that are used for modeling of apoptosis are considered. Then we described and discussed three possible ways to visualization biological processes and had proposed system for visualization of biomolecular models based on CellML modeling language.

This work contains explanation of the system named as parser-visualizator in details.

2   Basic Features of CellML and OpenCell

There are several popular languages to describe the biological processes: SBML, CellML, FieldML.

One of the popular languages is CellML. It is a compact format to describe the computational models and has a modular structure that facilitates the description of the complex interconnected cell models. Basic features of CellML were described in [12]. The model of the biological processes described by CellML has unique identifier, which can be used to refer to the model. A CellML document can include the elements of one of the following types: units; components; connections; groups; import; or metadata.

- Units are used to measure the quantities. Conversion of one unit to another would be done by CellML framework software.
- Components are the parts of CellML model that are related to one another. Component frequently includes units definitions, variable declarations, equations. Mathematic equations are written using MathML specification.
- Connection establishes mapping between two components, which means that the variables declared in one component might be accessed from another one.
- Groups provide mechanisms to organize components into hierarchies that support geometric containment and logical encapsulation.
- Metadata or data about data can be embedded in the CellML document by using the Resource Description Framework. This type of the information is intended for later usage, for example to search models and components.

A variety of tools exists for the CellML model creation and modification (editors) as well as for their debugging and verification (validators). One of the most famous tools is the OpenCell (Physiome). OpenCell is a framework for working with CellMLmodels (Fig. 1).

It is a uniform way of working with CellML documents including all basic steps of simulation from the creation of new models, editing of existing models and running [13]. OpenCell's main features are:

- Integration of CellML models that includes ordinary differential equations.
- Ability to work in a variety of operating systems, Linux, Windows and Mac OS.
- Ability to build and edit graphics.
- Support of metadata modeling and graphics draft specifications.
- Support of principles of Open Source.

- Based on this possibilities of framework we can create the models in a form of a set of differential equations and obtain results as a list or diagram of proteins concentration that are dependent on the time. By using repository of CellML models users can download and insert some of them into the OpenCell and obtain results from existing ones.

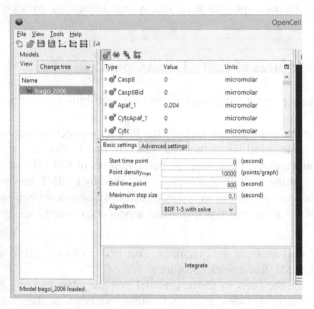

Fig. 1. The screenshot of OpenCell framework

3   Apoptosis Models Based on CellML

There are about 27 papers describing apoptosis in the form of mathematical models constructed on the basis of CellML on the portal http://models.cellml.org/cellml. This repository shows the possibilities of the language to represent wide categories of molecular biological models. The models are devoted to the analysis of the impact of various factors on the process of apoptosis. For example, the mathematical model which includes TNF-initiated survival and apoptotic cascades is presented in the article [14]. The model is capable of predicting the vitality of the cells in condition of DNA damage within the duration of the stimulus TNF-a.

The mathematical model to simulate the effects of nitric oxide (NO) on apoptosis is proposed in [15]. Biochemical apoptosis in combination with NO-related reactions is described with ordinary differential equations using the mass action kinetics. In the absence of NO, the model predicts either cell survival or apoptosis (bistable behavior) with changes in the early apoptotic response times depending on the strength of the extracellular stimuli.

The case study of our discussion is the model described in [16]. Authors of this model considered the role of Bax and Bcl-2 synthesis and degradation rates as well as the number of mitochondrial permeability transition pore (MPTP) in the cell response to apoptotic stimuli. They simulate so-called mitochondria-dependent apoptosis as a bistability process.

The models described in [16] consist of a set of ordinary differential equations (ODEs) and parameters adopted in the model. Part of them are shown below as illustrations.

ODEs:

$d[Apaf\text{-}1] / dt = -J1 + JApaf\text{-}1$

$d[cyt\ c * Apaf\text{-}1] / dt = J1 - 7J1b$

$d[apop] / dt = J1b - J2 + J4b$

$d[apop * pro9] / dt = J2 - J3$

$d[apop * (pro9)2] / dt = J3 - J3f$

$d[apop * (casp9)2] / dt = J3f - J4 - J5c - J6b + J6bf$

$d[apop * casp9] / dt = J4 + J4b - J5b$

$d[casp9] / dt = J4 - J4b - J5 - J6 + J6f + Jcasp9$

$d[pro9] / dt = -J2 - J3 + Jpro9$

$d[IAP] / dt = -J5 - J5b - J5c - J7 + JIAP$

$d[casp9 * IAP] / dt = J5$

$d[apop * casp9 * IAP] / dt = J5b$

...

Reaction rates (or fluxes):

$J_0' = k_0^+ [casp8][Bid] - k_0^- [casp8 * Bid]$

$J_0^f = k_0^f [casp8 * Bid]$

$J_1 = k_1^+ [cyt\ c][Apaf\text{-}1] - k_1^- [cyt\ c * Apaf\text{-}1]$

$J_{1b} = k_{1b}^+ [cyt\ c * Apaf\text{-}1]^P - k_{1b}^- [apop]$

$J_2 = k_2^+ [apop][pro9] - k_2^- [apop * pro9]$

$J_3 = k_3^+ [apop * pro9][pro9] - k_3 [apop * (pro9)_2]$

$J_3^f = k_3^f [apop * (pro9)_2]$

$J_4 = k_4^+ [apop * (casp9)_2] - k_4^- [apop * casp9][casp9]$

$J_{4b} = k_{4b}^+ [apop * casp9] - k_{4b}^- [apop][casp9]$

$J_5 = k_5^+ [casp9][IAP] - k_5^- [casp9 * IAP]$

$J_{5b} = k_{5b}^+ [apop * casp9][IAP] - k_{5b}^- [apop * casp9 * IAP]$

$J_{5c} = k_{5c}^+ [apop * (casp9)_2][IAP] - k_{5c}^- [apop * (casp9)_2 * IAP]$

...

Production-degradation rates:

$J_{Apaf\text{-}1} = \Omega_{Apaf\text{-}1} - \mu[Apaf\text{-}1]$

$J_{IAP} = \Omega_{IAP} - \mu[IAP]$

$J_{pro3} = \Omega_{pro3} - \mu[pro3]$

$J_{pro9} = \Omega_{pro9} - \mu[pro9]$

$J_{Bid} = \Omega_{Bid} - \mu[Bid]$

...

All equations shown above were proposed in [16]. The models were described by CellML (Fig. 2).

```
<?xml version="1.0"?>
<!--
This CellML file was generated on 21/08/2009 at 9:19:39 at a.m. using:

COR (0.9.31.1309)
Copyright 2002-2009 Dr Alan Garny
http://cor.physiol.ox.ac.uk/ - cor@physiol.ox.ac.uk

CellML 1.0 was used to generate this model
http://www.cellml.org/
    --><model xmlns="http://www.cellml.org/cellml/1.0#" xmlns:cmeta="http://www.cellml.org/metadata/1.0#" cmet
    <documentation xmlns="http://cellml.org/tmp-documentation">
    <article>
    <section id="sec_status">
    <title>Model Status</title>
    <para>This CellML model is able to run in PCEnv and COR to reproduce published results in the original pap
    </section>
    <sect1 id="sec_structure">
    <title>Model Structure</title>
    <para>ABSTRACT: We propose a mathematical model for mitochondria-dependent apoptosis, in which kinetic coo
    </para>
    <para>The original paper is cited below:</para>
    <para>
    Bistability in Apoptosis: Roles of Bax, Bcl-2 and Mitochondrial Permeability Transition Pores. E.Z. Bagci,
    <ulink url="http://www.ncbi.nlm.nih.gov/entrez/query.fcgi?db=pubmed&amp;cmd=Retrieve&amp;dopt=AbstractPlus
    </para>
    <informalfigure float="0" id="fig reaction diagram">
```

Fig. 2. The part of .cellml file that describes model from the [16]

The results (Fig.3) were obtained using OpenCell the .csv (comma separated value) file. The file shows the change of the protein concentrations.

```
time(second),Casp8/Casp8(micromolar),Casp8/Casp8Bid(micromolar),Bid/Bid(micromolar),Apaf_1/Apaf_1(micromolar
0,0.004,0.004,0.004,0.004,0.004,0.004,0.004,0.004,0.004,0.004,0.004,0.004,0.004,0.004,0.004,0.00
0.00219920946112976,0.004004865752954688,0.003995081401813386,0.004008092582346884,0.004004858312971695,0.00
1.0095460286195062,0.0055759788083823494,0.0023944224301139807,0.00653232627294662,0.010284202591929916,0.01
2.009546028619507,0.0062959363102923823,0.0016385690141474416,0.0075312454400186202,0.01836111525735253258,0.018
3.009546028619508,0.0066184153907890189,0.00127721694992635,0.00784525430407250,0.025305910379076733,0.0184
4.009546028619509,0.0067575863179828718,0.0010978581726486468,0.0078675284638080659,0.030808102973462904,0.018
5.069100745746848,0.006814523765704431,0.0009977474635505866,0.007763277333233398453,0.0351238456261861259,0.01
6.109546028619501,0.0068294519385610719,0.00094021828207803561889,0.0076126929994040367,0.0381039928303153,0.01884
7.1691007457468405,0.006825753256298184,0.0009005049273084257,0.0074434044829029215,0.040174839401373376,0.0
8.209546028619494,0.006813417364251582509,0.0008702653730612177,0.007274133660493076,0.0415362543412729609,0.018
9.269100745746833,0.0067965232284806079,0.0008438964626758578,0.0071036219195535350,0.0424561543233124,0.018
10.309546028619486,0.00677769490123329709,0.000820354250547011409,0.0069398151584302129,0.043054038104634210,0.018
11.369100745746826,0.006757199474404312,0.00079786263981334589,0.006777327400615075509,0.0434591996879994709,0.01
12.409546028619479,0.006736220369608169,0.0007766878480142678109,0.006622181719872480,0.0437269156868664920,0.01895
13.469100745746818,0.0067142100063415375,0.00075594313452601830,0.0064686690528666259,0.04391399196685466,0.01
14.509546028619472,0.0066920740115155089,0.0007362333641828027,0.0063222527787224809,0.0440434269352985640,0.018
15.569100745746681,0.0066690623780455690,0.00071677419343663590,0.0061774551508290920,0.0441396303718363309,0.01895
16.56910074574681 6,0.006649694508323345509,0.0006989432786780145,0.006004686052586662509,0.043913991966585466,0.01
17.56910074574683,0.006624463629298691,0.0006816103291893394,0.005915598938918643,0.04426463587204934609,0.018
18.56910074574684 4,0.0066016359807763279,0.0006647595098086729,0.005790100262832143509,0.044311165782883945,0.01
19.569100745746806,0.006578477608513845,0.0006483773795628461,0.0056680979199313039,0.044351551662968349,0.01896
20.569100745746873,0.006555002661717236259,0.000632451730606993709,0.0055494980090931333035,0.0443877543046597859,0.0
21.569100745746887,0.006531224550591064509,0.0006169710118389723,0.00543421225658546209,0.0442106501527101,0.01
22.56910074574 69,0.0065071562311945099,0.0006019240469685663,0.005322150976542997,0.0444523377494616509,0.01896
23.569100745746915,0.006482810341739164,0.0005872999010349179,0.005213226801756471,0.0444821404686537509,0.0189
24.569100745746 93,0.006458199263008047,0.00057308782141249409,0.005107354065524492,0.0445108538101146940,0.0189
25.569100745746944,0.0064333354201007109,0.00055927721567263929,0.00500444888825556349,0.0445387354276102109,0.018
```

Fig. 3. The .csv file of results

All of these models are illustrated by the schemas and diagrams that show the details of the simulations.

4   3D Visualization of the CellML Models of Apoptosis

The changes of the modeling parameters are converted by the system into the changes of the visual objects. Due to the lack of the comprehensive mathematical model of the apoptosis and due to the complexity of the system this approach is the most difficult one, however it seems to be the most promising approach on the other hand. Currently the model can be displayed schematically using the modeling environment [17].

The "game" showing the processes at the molecular level is the first step towards the 3-D visualization. The processes described within the models can also be represented as the results of the simulation. 3-D visualization of the molecular biological processes modeled by chemical kinetic equations is created by this method. Kinetic equations governing the participating components determine the quantitative parameters. This approach is illustrated in Fig. 4.

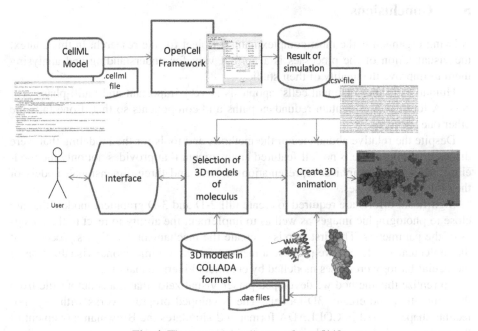

Fig. 4. The parser-visualizator scheme [11]

.cellml file contains the description of the model, which can be opened by the OpenCell Framework. Simulation results are saved in the .csv file that can be obtained along as with the required information from this file by the parser. The user using a simple interfacing form can chooses the necessary molecule. Selected molecules are shown in the graphical window if they are graphically represented in the COLLADA format. The Brownian movement of the molecules can be observed in the window. The number of molecules corresponds to the concentration of proteins during the modeling.

The advantage of these approaches is the possibility to create visualization that corresponds to the modeling parameters.

Of course, there are some hardships in the simulation. For example, in the case of the model taken from [16] the .csv the file contains the concentrations of 31 molecules. It will be difficult to analyze the visualization because of the number of different molecules. Secondly, graphics card requirements will be very high due to the very large number of molecules. Therefore, user must select several molecules to visualize and the number of the selected molecules is limited to 7. Also, user can specify the characteristics of the molecules, if they are known.

Another problem is that the concentrations of the different molecules vary in 1000 and even more times. The solution is to provide logarithmic visualization. Therefore user must specify the type of visualization before it starts.

The third problem is the necessity to use a huge amount of 3D-models of proteins. Therefore the special mechanism is required to access the protein data bank [18].

5   Conclusions

A living organism is the most complex natural object for the research. In this context the visualization of the processes is a normal way for understanding and analysing them to improve the quality of their studies.

Human and other mammal cells' apoptosis is very important and multi-phase process. A lot of phases contain redundant paths and components so that if one fails the other one succeeds.

Despite the relative abundance of the methods and tools for the modeling that were discussed earlier there is no full-featured environment that provides not only the modeling but also the graphical representation of two- and three-dimensional models of the biological processes.

Significant efforts are required to create full 2-D and 3-D graphical models that are close to photographic images as well as to implement the ability to react to the changes of the parameters. The first step is to create the mechanism that shows processes at the molecular levels. So, we propose a method for three-dimensional visualization of molecular biology processes modelled by chemical kinetic equations.

To realize this method we developed parser-visualizator that reads output file from the simulation and creates 3D-models. The developed program works with any molecular shapes stored in COLLADA format and simulates the Brownian movement of the proteins and changes of their concentration.

Note that cell apoptosis in simpler organisms is more simple with a smaller number of redundant paths. However, it is possible to make homologies between the corresponding phases of the apoptosis in all multicellular organisms from the simplest ones to the most complex ones. This is the reason why the study of the apoptosis features in the simpler organisms if important in order to study their correspondence with the more complex ones.

One of the simplest multicellular organisms that has many of its biological processes well studied is Caenorhabditis elegans or C. elegans free-living nematode (roundworm), which is about 1 mm long [19-21].

It has 959 cells and has the simplest neural system, which consists of 302 neurons only and of about 5000 connections between them [22]. During the process of the C. elegan evolution, 131 cell dies exposed to apoptosis. Currently C. elegan is chosen as the first multicellular organism that will be fully modeled using the computers. This is the international project called OpenWorm (http://www.openworm.org/). The participants of the project have already finished the modelling of the neural system of the grown-up C. elegan and the new project Devoworn (http://syntheticdaisies.blogspot.com/2014/06/now-announcing-devoworm-project.html) that is devoted to the C. Elegan evolution and to the process of its cells division from embryo to grown-up organism was started in June 2014. 131 cell are exposed to apoptosis exactly during this process. Computer modelling and the visualization of the apoptosis in C. elegan are planned in the framework of the further studies. In order to perform not only qualitative modelling but quantitative as well the model that describes the dynamics of the components engaged in the process is required, e.g. if this process is described but the system of the equations of the chemical kinetics. Such system of the equation was developed for the apoptosis process in mammals but this was not performed for C. elegans. The development, the quantitative solution and further computer modelling and visualization of the corresponding mathematical model are planned. Despite the fact that C. elegan organism is well studied there still are unsolved problems including the process of its cells apoptosis [23]. E.g., it is unknown whether cytochrome participates in this process as it happens with mammals. We hope that computer modelling and visualization of these processes will help in the studies of this and other similar problems.

Acknowledgements. The work is funded by grant № 1758 GF-OT13 for basic research in the natural sciences of the MES RK Science Committee.

References

1. Muchmore, S.W., Sattler, M., Liang, H., Meadows, R.P., Harlan, J.E., Yoon, H.S., Nettesheim, D., Chang, B.S., Thompson, C.B., Wong, S.-L., Ng, S.-C., Fesik, S.W.: X-ray and NMR structure of human Bcl-xL, an inhibitor of programmedиcell death. Nature **381**(6580), 335–341 (1996)
2. Green, D.R.: Means to an End: Apoptosis and other Cell Death Mechanisms, p. 250. Cold Spring Harbour Laboratory Press, NY (2010)
3. Antonsson, B., Conti, F., Ciavatta, A.M., Montessuit, S., Lewis, S., Martinou, I., Bernasconi, L., Bernard, A., Mermod, J.-J., Mazzei, G., Maundrell, K., Gambale, F., Sadoul, R., Martinou, J.-C.: Inhibition of Bax channel-forming activity by Bcl-2. Science **277**(5324), 370–372 (1997)
4. Minn, A.J., Vélez, P., Schendel, S.L., Liang, H., Muchmore, S.W., Fesik, S.W., Fill, M., Thompson, C.B.: Bcl-x(L) forms an ion channel in synthetic lipid membranes. Nature **385**(6614), 353–357 (1997)
5. Schendel, S.L., Xie, Z., Montal, M.O., Matsuyama, S., Montal, M., Reed, J.C.: Channel formation by antiapoptotic protein Bcl-2. Proc. Natl. Acad. Sci. U.S.A **94**(10), 5113–5118 (1997)

6. Schlesinger, P.H., Gross, A., Yin, X.-M., Yamamoto, K., Saito, M., Waksman, G., Korsmeyer, S.J.: Comparison of the ion channel characteristics of proapoptotic BAX and antiapoptotic BCL-2. Proc. Natl. Acad. Sci. U.S.A. **94**(21), 11357–11362 (1997)
7. Peixoto, P.M., Ryu, S.-Y., Bombrun, A., Antonsson, B., Kinnally, K.W.: MAC inhibitors suppress mitochondrial apoptosis. Biochem. J. **423**(3), 381–387 (2009)
8. Czabotar, P.E., Westphal, D., Dewson, G., Ma, S., Hockings, C., Fairlie, W.D., Lee, E.F., Yao, S., Robin, A.Y., Smith, B.J., Huang, David C.S., Kluck, R.M., Adams, J.M., Colman, P.M.: Bax crystal structures reveal how BH3 domains activate Bax and nucleate its oligomerization to induce apoptosis. Cell **152**(3), 519–531 (2013)
9. Kushnareva, Y., Andreyev, A.Y., Kuwana, T., Newmeyer, D.D.: Bax activation initiates the assembly of a multimeric catalyst that facilitates Bax pore formation in mitochondrial outer membranes. PLoS Biol. **10**(9), e1001394 (2012)
10. Souers, A.J., Leverson, J.D., Boghaert, E.R., Ackler, S.L., Catron, N.D., Chen, J., Dayton, B.D., Ding, H., Enschede, S.H., Fairbrother, W.J., Huang, D.C.S., Hymowitz, S.G., Jin, S., Khaw, S.L., Kovar, P.J., Lam, L.T., Lee, J., Maecker, H.L., Marsh, K.C., Mason, K.D., Mitten, M.J., Nimmer, P.M., Oleksijew, A., Park, C.H., Park, C.-M., Phillips, D.C., Roberts, A.W., Sampath, D., Seymour, J.F., Smith, M.L., Sullivan, G.M., Tahir, S.K., Tse, C., Wendt, M.D., Xiao, Yu., Xue, J.C., Zhang, H., Humerickhouse, R.A., Rosenberg, S.H., Elmore, S.W.: ABT-199, a potent and selective BCL-2 inhibitor, achieves antitumor activity while sparing platelets. Nat. Med. **19**(2), 202–208 (2013)
11. Muhamedyev, R., Mansharipova, A., Muhamedyeva, E.: Visualization of Biological Processes Described by Models of Apoptosis. Life Science Journal **11**(10), 320–327 (2014). ISSN:1097-8135
12. Garny, A., Nickerson, D.P., Cooper, J., dos Santos, R.W., Miller, A.K., McKeever, S., Nielsen, P.M., Hunter, P.J.: CellML and associated tools and techniques. Phil. Trans. R. Soc. A **2008**, 366 (2008). doi:10.1098/rsta.2008.0094. Published 13 September
13. OpenCell (May 20, 2014). http://www.cellml.org/tools/opencell/
14. Rangamani, P., Sirovich, L.: Survival and apoptotic pathways initiated by TNF-alpha: modeling and predictions. Biotechnology and Bioengineering **97**(5), 1216–1229 (2007)
15. Bagci, E.Z., Vodovotz, Y., Billiar, T.R., Ermentrout, B., Bahar, I.: Computational insights on the competing effects of nitric oxide in regulating apoptosis (2009) (May 20, 2014). http://www.ncbi.nlm.nih.gov/pmc/articles/PMC2386238/
16. Bagci, E.Z., Vodovotz, Y., Billiar, T.R., et al.: Bistability in Apoptosis: Roles of Bax, Bcl-2 and Mitochondrial Permeability Transition Pores. Biophysical Journal **90**, 1546–1559 (2006). PubMed ID: 16339882
17. Wimalaratne, S.M., Halstead, M.D.B., Lloyd, C.M., Cooling, M.T., Crampin, E.J., Nielsen, P.F.: A method for visualizing CellML models. Bioinformatics **25**(22), 3012–3019 (2009). doi:10.1093/bioinformatics/btp495
18. Protein Data Bank (2014). http://www.rcsb.org/pdb/home/home.do
19. Brenner, S.: The genetics of Caenorhabditis elegans. Genetics **77**(1), 71–94 (1974)
20. Sulston, J.E., Horvitz, H.R.: Post-embryonic cell lineages of the nematode. Caenorhabditis elegans. Dev. Biol. **56**(1), 110–156 (1977)
21. Sulston, J.E., Schierenberg, E., White, J.G., Thomson, J.N.: The embryonic cell lineage of the nematode Caenorhabditis elegans. Dev. Biol. **100**(1), 64–119 (1983)
22. White, J.G., Southgate, E., Thomson, J.N., Brenner, S.: The structure of the nervous system of the nematode Caenorhabditis elegans. Phil. Trans. R. Soc. Lond. B, Biol. Scien. **314**(1165), 1–340 (1986)
23. Wang, X., Yang, C., Chai, J., Shi, Y., Xue, D.: Mechanisms of AIF-mediated apoptotic DNA degradation in Caenorhabditis elegans. Science **298**(5598), 1587–1892 (2002)

AGITO: Virtual Reality Environment for Power Systems Substations Operators Training

Tiago Ramos Ribeiro[1]([✉]), Paulo Roberto Jansen dos Reis[1],
Geraldo Braz Júnior[1], Anselmo Cardoso de Paiva[1], Aristófanes Corrêa Silva[1],
Ivana Marcia Oliveira Maia[2], and Antônio Sérgio Araújo[3]

[1] Applied Computing Group (NCA), Federal University of Maranhão (UFMA),
Av. dos Portugueses, SN, Campus do Bacanga, São Luís, MA, Brazil
{tiagoribeiro,jansen,geraldo,anselmo.paiva,ari}@nca.ufma.br
[2] Design Department, Federal Institute of Maranhão - IFMA,
Av. Marechal Castelo Branco, 789 - São Francisco, São Luís, MA, Brazil
ivana@nca.ufma.br
[3] São Francisco Hydroelectric Company - CHESF,
Rua Delmiro Gouveia, 333 - San Martin, Recife, Pernambuco, Brazil
asergio@chesf.gov.br

Abstract. This paper presents the architecture and development of a virtual reality environment for powers systems substations operators training. The proposal intents to reduce the training time for new operators and increase the effectiveness of the continuous training of operators. Using the simulation, the operator can interact with a virtual reality interface (immersive or non immersive) viewing the state of the power system captured through the supervisory system and acting through the virtual environment operating the substation, without exposing the system to dangerous situations, avoiding the occurrence of injuries of any kind. Also, the training sessions can be analyzed offline by an instructor.

Keywords: Virtual Reality Systems · Power Systems Training

1 Introduction

Power systems have a complex operation, needing qualified professional that are able to take complex decisions in order to maintain the compromise between safety and economy.

These systems must be working continuously. The monitoring and correct actions are fundamental for keeping it working. The capacity of identify the correct electric power system state depends on several factors, such as emergency and restoration procedures and continuous training.

Beyond power system complexity there are the inherent risks associated with the operation of power transmission and distribution systems. This training becomes a priority for a growing number of electricity companies. This continuous training is needed to keep the operator updated with the maneuvers,

© Springer International Publishing Switzerland 2014
L.T. De Paolis and A. Mongelli (Eds.): AVR 2014, LNCS 8853, pp. 113–123, 2014.
DOI: 10.1007/978-3-319-13969-2_9

procedures and norms. This is fundamental to ensure the efficiency when performing procedures and also to maintain the operation process continuously.

Simulation-based training is an interesting option as they are safe for both personnel and equipment. Also, it offers to the trainee the opportunity to be exposed to several scenarios and critical conditions, even if them occur rarely or are hazardous to reproduce. The graphical environment may contribute considerably as they offer a better visualization of the electrical system state and guarantees a more effective training process.

Virtual Reality are one of the disruptive technologies. It may be seen as an interaction way between users and computers, where to the users is allowed to navigate and interact with a world represented graphically in 3D using multisensory devices [4].

Initially used for entertainment, this technology is largely perceived as an important tool in the process that involves content and procedures learning. This way, this technology emerges as a possibility for the construction of training environments in several areas, favoring the assimilation and experience of virtual situations comparable to real ones.

The application of virtual reality systems in training process has become an important application of this technology in industrial environment ([10], [14] and [6]).

Thus, we may verify that there is a need for simulation systems dedicated to the training of operators of power systems that are based on 3D graphical visualization and integrated to an electrical system simulation tool. The main goal is to allow training sessions creating mental images of the electrical system state and the spatial configuration of the electrical facilities.

This work aims to present the architecture and development of an virtual reality system that uses interactive 3D enviroments and gamification to provide a rich and objective interface for power systems operators training. It is done throught the integration to the Open System Supervision and Control (SAGE) [8] and simulated by a reference training implementation of EPRI/OTS, called SIMULOP [13] implemented in the context of the São Francisco Hydroelectric Company (CHESF) [2].

The remainder of this paper is organized in three sections. The Background section presents aspects of the SAGE system and its training using EPRI/OTS simulator. Then the system architecture AGITO presented as well as its main features. Lastly, held a discussion about the results previously found and on the following work that will be undertaken to improve the system.

2   Related Works

Several works have been proposed using virtual reality and simulation systems for the training of technical personnel in electrical systems companies.

The ESOPE-VR is a virtual reality environment representing an electrical substation with a two level interface representing the electrical panels (control room) and supervisory software [3]. It has an architecture based on the Expert

System Operations Planning Environment - ESOPE where the operators may interact with a line diagram representation of the substation system.

In [9] is presented a system for the training of operators focused on the simulation of faults to train the operators in diverse types of occurrences. The system is integrated with SAGE (Open System For Supervision and Control) and is composed of three modules to: edit scenarios, simulate the operation and analyze the performance. It does not offer a virtual environment.

A simulator developed for training electric systems operators is presented in [1]. The simulator allows training on the operation of substation panels as well as on supervisory systems. It presents the representation of a supervisory system and a tutor module that allows planning, implementing and evaluating of training programs. The simulator underwent a functional evaluation, with the participation of users, representing both the tutor and the operator under training.

In [15] is presented an application designed to train electrical sub-station operators using virtual reality. The application offer functionalities for visualization of the substation and navigation in the virtual environment interacting with the elements, with the complete functionality of the sub-station.

In [13] is presented the architecture and development experience of a training system, named SIMULOP, used in electrical companies in Brazil. The system consists of an integration of an Energy Management System named SAGE with Operator Training Simulator (OTS). The integration was done based on the Common Information Model (CIM) [5], and developed a training infrastructure. Also, the paper presents general aspects about the experience of implantation of this training system and its use for operators training.

Thus we may see that several research groups are looking for the proposal of virtual reality systems for electrical operators training, integrated to the companies architecture of supervisory and control system.

3 Background

This section presents the basic concepts that are involved in the description and comprehension of the proposed system. This consists of the supervisory system description and of its integrated training system, respectively SAGE and SIMULOP.

3.1 Open Supervisory and Control System (SAGE)

SAGE is an open system, in the sense of its architecture that is portable, expandable, modular and interconnected [8]. It implements the functionalities of energy management in control centers. Also, these functionalities may be configured for diverse applications from the automation of local facilities as substations or plants, till the application in complex operational centers based on heterogeneous network. Thus, SAGE system is presented as a unified solution for all supervision levels, reducing implantation costs.

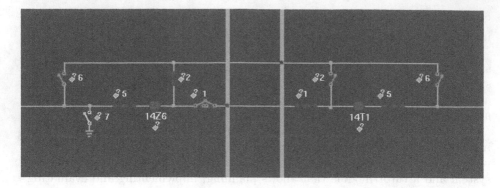

Fig. 1. Basic SLD diagram presented by SAGE interfaces

The substations could be operated by interfaces that represent the information in Single-line diagrams (SLD's) as exemplified in Figure 1. This kind of interface requires high level of application domain knowledge. That's one of the reasons why exhaustive training are conducted by the companies to enhance the operating capacity of correct acting when it is necessary.

3.2 Simulop

Simulop was developed to allow the use of the SAGE system for operators training [13]. It is a training simulator that allow the inclusion of scenarios in the context of CHESF, implemented as an integration of SAGE and EPRI-OTS (Operator Training Simulator) [11].

Simulop main objectives are: primary training of operators; adaptation to control room environment; complementary training, confronting the operator with extraordinary situations; qualification for operator upgrading and for procedures and network changes; and finally increasing the knowledge about the system.

The integration of SAGE and OTS was achieved through the use of a database compatible with the Common Information Model specification [5]. Simulop has been used successfully for operator training and certification in CHESF. But, it presents some limitations as the absence of trainee automatic evaluation, reinforcement learning and real contextualization of the scenario situations. These limitations may be overcome by using virtual reality techniques and information analysis, as a way to broaden the effectiveness of SAGE training scenarios.

4   Proposed System

As already stated, the main objective of the system proposed in this paper is the contribution to the enlargement of the effectiveness of a simulation based operators training system, through the use of virtual reality environments. This must be achieved, through the increment of the trainees capacity of synthesize and knowledge assimilation, elaborating associations between the real world and the simulated situations.

The system architecture was designed based on the following principles:

- Use of data collectors to acquire information from external systems, based on push events. This will allow that electrical system state modifications may be seen in the virtual reality interface, minimizing the communication overload of multiples clients to the central server, making the architecture scalable;
- Temporal labeling of all information collected, enabling its presentation in correct time;
- Development based on three layers - server, client and legacy systems, introducing facade elements for inter layers communication. This allows flexibility in the development making easier the change of layers and the reorganization or redefinition of roles in the system;
- Use of a 3D game engine to ease the activities of virtual world construction and interaction with its components;
- Extension by the use of plug-ins of the game engine to support the implementation of new functionalities.

Based on these requirements, we present in Figure 2 the architecture of the proposed system. The Figure 2 presents the role division as server modules that are in charge of the interoperability between the client modules (editor, viewer and supervisor) and the external systems SAGE/OTS.

The architecture is organized in three layers: SAGE/OTS, Interoperation and Client. SAGE/OTS layer represents the API and legacy systems that are integrated to the AGITO system. The Interoperation layer implements the middleware AgitoServer for the communication between SAGE/OTS and Client layer. Finally, the client layer has the software artifacts responsible for interaction through the AgitoViewer and AgitoSupervisor.

Layers Interoperation and Client are better described in the following sections

4.1 AgitoServer - Interoperation Layer

AgitoServer component is responsible for the communication to the SAGE/OTS offering a unique communication interface that enables an easy integration of services. The communication with the interface is done through a facade interface implemented on socket commands. To simplify, we grouped the information capture commands in four functionalities:

1. Equipment operation state, including measures and alarms
2. Record of equipment state change based on user actions
3. Notifications of equipment state change based on events triggered from the real time database. The viewer record these state changes, and stay in a loop. The feedback is done at every second, if any change is perceived. This is done to avoid an overhead of state requests by the viewer
4. OTS simulation scenario load and execution.

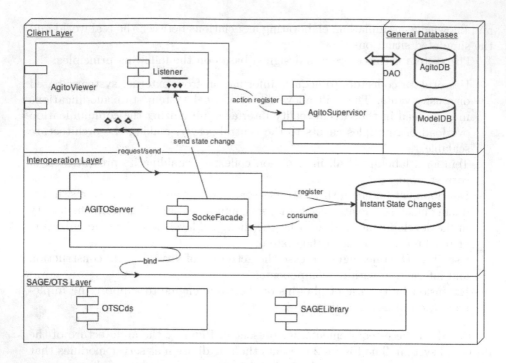

Fig. 2. Components view of Agito architecture

The communication is formatted through JSON to make easier the integration with other components of Agito: AgitoViewer and AgitoSupervisor.

4.2   AgitoViewer - Client Layer

It is implement using Unity game engine [16], being in charge of the visualization and interaction with electrical substations and all of their components. Figure 3 presents AgitoViewer initial interface when an specific substation is selected. The interface is organized in 6 functional regions, identified in Figure 3 by the letters A to F.

The region A represents the area where the equipment state is shown (Equipment State Control Panel). The equipment may be viewed individually in the pre-visualization panel (region B) where the selected one is shown. In C area is presented the minimap of the virtual world and the layers selection area (at the right). The layers are associated with predefined visualizations options, such as alarm or cables visualization. There is also a panel for equipment selection where is possible do change some settings of the equipment. In Figure 3, there are in this panel a voltage converter, with the option do adjust the TAP value. Also, there are two navigation control panels (regions E and F). One of them (region E) allow the control of zoom, pan and camera change. The channel of region F, permits the navigation through the power systems, changing the current substation to be visualized.

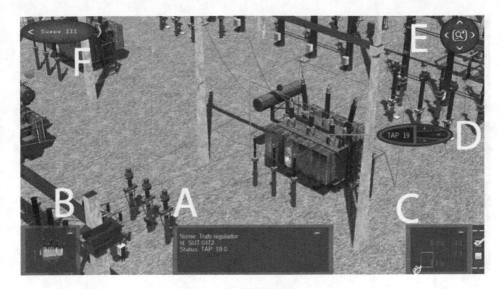

Fig. 3. AgitoViewer initial interface

All interface panels may be minimized to maximize the screen view area. Also, it is possible to visualize the scene in an immersive screen with passive stereo vision, as shown in Figure 4.

The viewer must be connected to the AgitoServer. This is necessary to acquire the equipment status and data making possible the visualization of them in the interface. Thus, there are in AgitoViewer, a listener module that is a multithreading system for information collection from AgitoServer. As new information is collected they are sent to the actually rendered scene.

To improve the responsive capacity of the system and to provide more interactivity, we implemented in separate threads the commands for equipment state change information acquisition, data request and users events collection.

Thus, we may see that AgitoViewer present as main functionalities a realistic visualization of an electrical substation (Figure 5a), with navigation through the virtual world (Figure 5b) and interaction possibilities. The user may set to maneuver equipments, visualizing the signalization of correct and wrong operations. Also it is possible to interact with simulation scenarios. During a trainning session the trainee actions are recorded and can be analyzed posteriorly by AgitoSupervisor. The alarm notifications are presented, with the representation of its location context and its cause (Figure 5c-d).

4.3 AgitoSupervisor

A simulation scenario, already defined in OTS, is a simulation of a real situation that is planned and defined by the supervisor, to create situations that can teach the trainees in the process of decision making. A scenario is compound by a sequence of actions that generates, in general, abnormal situations in the

Fig. 4. View of a user visualizing the substation in a immersive room

system. Thus there is an expected response by the system operator to react to these situations.

As each situation can generate different operator response, and actions sequences, it was developed a module to enable the achievement of a qualitative evaluation of the trainee performance. This was done in the supervisor and evaluation module, named AgitoSupervisor.

This module aims the evaluation of user actions during a training scenario, assigning a score to him accordingly with his performance. Also, this module aims the support to the supervisor to perform a qualitative evaluation of the operator training session in a clear and short manner.

The implementation of AgitoSupervisor is based on gamification approach [12]. Each user action is recorded by the AgitoViewer module and is analyzed to see if it is appropriated for the situation. Depending on training configuration the system may give an immediate feedback indicating the wrong decision. Otherwise, the system can reward the user with score points that make possible a rank.

The simulation scenario previously created by the training supervisor could be started at any time in AgitoViewer and assisted by the automatic Supervisor at any time, making possible an offline training with automatic feedback. The proposal is that the training could be repeatedly perform for better understanding of simulated scenarios based on reinforcement learning [7].

Also the training supervisor could use more precise tools to analyze the learning and better optimize the scenarios directing efforts to situations that proven to wanting during the training.

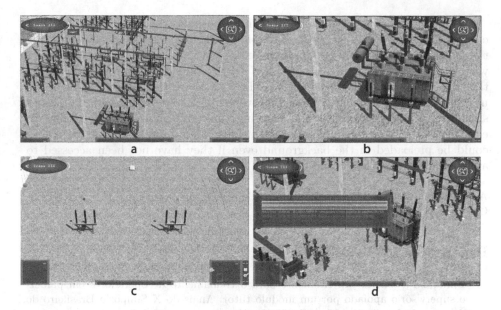

Fig. 5. Examples of AgitoViewer functionalities. (a) Initial screen with all panels minimized (b) Illumination and texture mapping aspects that improve the scene realism. (c) Visualization of alarms layers over the scene (d) Alarm menu with the alarm recognition option.

5   Discussion and Future Works

The use of interfaces with low usability and based on schematic diagrams such as SAGE, cause an cognition overhead in the learning stage. It is known that it is necessary rapid responses to a large number of situations. The process of reinforcement learning is applied to many companies as a way to turn simple those responses based on simulated experience.

The possibility of a virtual environment as a second view of the real world makes possible interactions with the environment, greater contact and visual appeal. Also we believe that the use of an environment similar to a game makes the training activity more pleasant. The AGITO work as second view, which does not replace the SAGE to operate the system during training sessions but increases the assimilation through visual representations of the real world.

Another improvement achieved by AGITO is the capacity of make a simulated scenario at any time. So, the operator could repeat any times he want the simulation and with this enhance his capacity of better handle real-time events when needed. The strategy of include the idea of games concepts also creates a healthy environment of competition to overcome the challenges that are characterized by the simulation scenarios. The expectation is that when implanted is to make training more efficient by conducting a more enjoyable activity.

As future work we intend to implement the visualization of internal electrical components allowing directly operating, simulating manual changes and allowing the inclusion of information to operator field. Another task is integrate the viewer with the rules of procedures adopted by CHESF to include a tutor mode during the execution of scenarios where the AGITO notice restlessness or doubt of the user by analyzing feelings. Some improvements in the runtime of the scenes should be added to decrease the charging time and allow more flexibility in exchange for substations and other operations. The proposal is that the scenes could be preloaded in the background even if they have not been accessed to allow quick access when requested.

Acknowledgments. Our research group acknowledge financial support from CAPES, CNPQ, FAPEMA and CHESF.

References

1. Filho, T.F., Vieira, M.: Ambiente para o treinamento de operadores em painéis e supervisório apoiado por um módulo tutor. Anais do X Simpósio Brasileiro de Automação Inteligente **10**, 857–862 (2011)
2. Companhia Hidro Elétrica do São Francisco (CHESF) site. http://www.chesf.gov.br/ (last access 2014)
3. Okapuu-von Veh, A., Marceau, R.J., Malowany, A., Desbiens, P., Daigle, A., Garant, E., Gauthier, R., Shaikh, A., Rizzi, J.C.: Design and operation of a virtual reality operator-training system. IEEE Transactions on Power Systems **11**(3), 1585–1591 (1996)
4. Ryan, M.-L.: Narrative as virtual reality: Immersion and interactivity in literature and electronic media. Johns Hopkins University Press (2001)
5. Lima, L., Oliveira, A., Pereira, L, Azevedo, G., Ghelman, C.A., Azevedo, P.: Information Sharing in Power System Control Centers. In: First EPRI Latin American Conference and Exhibition, November 28–30, Rio de Janeiro, Brazil (2001)
6. Sousa, M.P.A., Nunes, M.V.A., da Costa Lopes, A.: Maintenance and operation of a hydroelectric unit of energy in a power system using virtual reality. International Journal of Electrical Power and Energy Systems **32**, 599–606 (2010)
7. Barto, A.G.: Reinforcement learning: An introduction. MIT press (1998)
8. Pereira, L.A.C., Lima, L.C., Silva, A.J.R.S., Machado, P.A., Amorim, M.F.P., Filho, L.O.A., Azevedo, G.P., Lambert, N., Zarur, P.D., Tavares, V.V.: SAGE-Um Sistema Aberto para a Evolução
9. Silva, V.N.A.D., Linden, R., Ribeiro, G.F., Pereira, M.D.F.L., Lannes, R.S., Standke, C.R.: Simuladores para treinamento de operadores de sistema e de instalações do setor elétrico. In: XII ERIAC Encontro Regional Iberoamericano de Cigré, Puerto Iguazú, Argentina
10. Arroyo, E., Arcos, J.L.L.: SRV: a virtual reality application to electrical substations operation training. In: International Conference on Multimedia Computing and Systems, vol. 1, pp. 835–839. IEEE (1999)
11. Lee, S.T.: The EPRI common information model for operation and planning. In: Power Engineering Society Summer Meeting, vol. 2, pp. 866–871. IEEE (1999)
12. Kapp, K.M.: The gamification of learning and instruction: game-based methods and strategies for training and education. John Wiley and Sons (2012)

13. Oliveira, J.J.R., Lima, L.C., Pereira, L.A.C., Sollero, R.B., Leite, C.R.R., Muniz, R.B., Costa, C.A.B., Cavalcante, M.S., Carmo, U.A., Araújo, A.S.: Treinamento e certificação de operadores no sistema SAGE empregando o simulador EPRI/OTS. In: Grupo de Estudos de Operação de Sistemas Elétricos, XVIII SNPTEE, Curitiba-Paraná (2005)
14. Yao, F., Luo, D.-S., Zhao, J., Wang, H.-C., Kuang, S.-L.: Virtual Interactive Training System for Power Safety Regulation Based on Torque Engine. In: Proceedings of the Chinese Society of Universities for Electric Power System and Its Automation, vol. 4, pp. 15 (2012)
15. Romero, G., Maroto, J., Félez, J., Cabanellas, J.M., Martínez, M.L., Carretero, A.: Virtual reality applied to a full simulator of electrical sub-stations. Electric Power Systems Research 78(3), 409–417 (2008)
16. Unity: Unity Game Engine-Official Site. http://unity3d.com (last access 2014)

Lossless Compression of Multidimensional Medical Images for Augmented Reality Applications

Bruno Carpentieri[✉] and Raffaele Pizzolante

Dipartimento di Informatica, Università degli Studi di Salerno,
84084 Fisciano, SA, Italy.
bc@dia.unisa.it, rpizzolante@unisa.it

Abstract. Medical digital imaging technologies produce daily a huge amount of data (data obtained by magnetic resonance, computed tomography and ultrasound examinations, functional resonance magnetic acquisitions, etc.), which is generally stored in ad-hoc repositories or it is transmitted to other entities, such as research centers, hospital structures, etc.. These data need efficient compression, in order to optimize memory space and transmission costs. In this work, we introduce an efficient lossless algorithm that can be used for the compression of volumetric multidimensional medical image sequences. This approach can be also used, in conjunction with Augmented Reality techniques, to save in a database or to transmit on a communication line the outcomes of surgical decisions or medical applications. We experimentally test our approach on a test set of 3-D computed tomography (CT), 3-D magnetic resonance (MR) images, and of 5-D functional Magnetic Resonance Images (fMRI). The achieved results outperform the other state-of-the-art approaches.

Keywords: Multidimensional medical images compression · Multidimensional medical images coding · Multidimensional data compression

1 Introduction

Digital medical images are widely used in a large range of medical applications, research tasks, medical related studies, etc.. The acquisition technologies are continuously evolving and are becoming always more sophisticated. On the other hand, the amount of memory space required for the storing and the time needed for the transmission is growing proportionally to the size of the images. The new expectations in medicine that are arising from the application of augmented reality techniques (see [6], [7]) will increase the need for memory space or the transmission time for medical data.

It is evident that data compression is essential, in order to minimize the implicit transmission costs involved. Since the compression layer is generally transparent or semi-transparent to the end-users, it is important to adopt models that can have high-level profiles (as for instance an *higher compression at lower speed* profile, or a *lower compression at higher speed* profile, etc.) or that are related to the hardware on which the compression process will be performed (as for instance *use resources as parsimoniously as possible*, etc.).

© Springer International Publishing Switzerland 2014
L.T. De Paolis and A. Mongelli (Eds.): AVR 2014, LNCS 8853, pp. 124–136, 2014.
DOI: 10.1007/978-3-319-13969-2_10

The design decisions related to the compression techniques need to consider which strategy (lossy or lossless) could be used in the delicate medical contexts. Today, lossy compression strategies are in a few case used, but lossless compression techniques are generally preferred, since they guarantee that the coded data, once decoded, are identical to the original data and this cheers and satisfies doctors.

In this paper, we consider lossless techniques that are based on the predictive model, described in [18]. We focus on multidimensional medical image sequences (such as 3-D computed tomography images, functional resonance magnetic images, etc.), which have considerable space memory requirements (many hundreds of megabytes/gigabytes per acquisition). These techniques can be also used coupled with Augmented Reality applications in medicine and tele-medicine.

State-of-the-art predictive-based schemes can be subdivided into two distinct and independent steps: modeling and coding [4]. The digital file is observed in a predefined order and modeling is aimed at gathering information in the form of a probabilistic model that is then used for coding. The modeling step can be carried out via a predictive structure, in which a value x^{t+1} is guessed for the next sample to be coded: x^{t+1}, based on a finite subset of the available past data. The prediction residual (or prediction error) can then be encoded conditionally on the context of x^{t+1}. The usual interpretation of prediction, which is the most important step of this scheme, is that it de-correlates the data samples, thus allowing the use of simple models (i.e. entropy coders) for the coding of prediction errors.

The purpose of this paper is to introduce a novel multidimensional, configurable, predictive structure that can be used for the compression of multidimensional medical images. The predictor we propose is scalable, adjustable, and adaptive. We present experimental evidences of its performance on multidimensional medical images: 3-D Computed Tomography (CT) images, 3-D Magnetic Resonance (MR) images and 5-D functional Magnetic Resonance Images (fMRI).

This paper is organized as follows: Section 2 focuses on the description of the proposed N–D predictive structure. In Section 3, we report the experimental results achieved on the different typologies of N–D data. Finally, we highlight our conclusions and outline future research directions (Section 4).

2   A Predictive Structure for Multidimensional Data

Formally, we can define a multidimensional (N-D) dataset as a collection of bi-dimensional components (such as images, data matrices, etc.) [11]. The dimensions of an N-D dataset ($N \geq 3$) can be described as $<M_1, M_2, ..., M_{N-2}, X, Y>$, where X and Y are respectively the width and the height of the bi-dimensional components and M_f is the size of the f-th dimension ($1 \leq f \leq N - 2$). A specific bi-dimensional component can be univocally identified through a vector of N–2 elements: $[p_1, p_2, ..., p_{N-2}]$, where $p_i \in \{1,2,...,M_i\}$ [11].

By considering the formal definition of an N-D dataset, we can describe the dimensions of a three-dimensional (3-D) dataset as $<Z, X, Y>$. This means that the dataset is composed of Z components (among the third dimension), where each component has respectively width X and height Y.

According to the above definitions of N-D data, let's suppose that the current sample has coordinates $(m_1, m_2, ..., m_{N-2}, x, y)$ (where $1 \le x \le X$, $1 \le y \le Y$ and $1 \le m_i \le M_i$, $\forall i \in \{1,2,..., N-2\}$). Consequently, the vector $[m_1, m_2, ..., m_{N-2}]$ identifies the current component.

For each of the $N-2$ dimension, we define a *references set*, denoted as $R_i = \{r_1^i, r_2^i, ..., r_{t_i}^i\}$ (for the i-th dimension, with $1 \le i \le N-2$), where $r_j^i \in \{1,2,...,M_i\} \cup \{-1,-2,...,-M_i\}$, $t_i = |R_i|$, $1 \le j \le t_i$, and $\left| \bigcup_{i=1}^{N-2} R_i \right| > 0$.

Such references sets are univocally set up at the beginning of the algorithm and they are used in the prediction step.

In detail, a generic element $r_j^i \in R_i$ (where $1 \le i \le N-2$) will be used to denote a specific bi-dimensional component. In particular, we will use the following notation: if $r_j^i > 0$, then the denoted component is the one identified through the vector $[m_1, m_2, ..., m_{i-1}, r_j^i, m_{i+1}, ..., m_{N-2}]$, or, if $r_j^i < 0$, then the denoted component is the one identified through the vector $[m_1, m_2, ..., m_{i-1}, m_i - |r_j^i|, m_{i+1}, ..., m_{N-2}]$.

The proposed predictive model is based on the least squares optimization technique. In particular, the prediction is formed by using the current component and all the (valid) components of the *references sets*.

If we consider $N = 3$ and suppose that we have a 3-D medical image with dimensions: $M_1 = 48$ (Z dimension), $X = 256$ and $Y = 256$ (formally denoted as <48, 256, 256>). For example, we can set up the references set for the M_1 dimension (Z dimension) as $R_1 = \{-1, -2\}$ and we suppose that the current sample has (23, 45, 67) as coordinates ($m_1 = 23$, $x = 45$ and $y = 67$). Therefore, in this example, the prediction is formed by using the neighboring samples of the current sample in the current component, identified by the vector *[23]*, and in the components identified by the vectors *[22]* (*[23 − |−1|]*) and *[21]* (*[23 − |−2|]*). In detail, these latter vectors, *[22]* and *[21]*, are obtained by considering respectively the element −1 and the element −2 of R_1.

Let E denotes a 2-D enumeration, which has as objective the relative indexing of the samples in a bi-dimensional context, with respect to a specific reference sample. The fundamental requisites that the enumeration E needs to satisfy are that the specified reference sample has 0 as index and that any two samples (with different coordinates) do not have the same index.

Let $x_j^{(e)}(r_s^j)$ (where $r_s^j \in R_j$) denotes the e-th sample in the bi-dimensional context according to the enumeration E, with respect to the sample with coordinates $(m_1, m_2, ..., m_{j-1}, r_s^j, m_{j+1}, ..., m_{N-2}, x, y)$ when $r_s^j > 0$, or $(m_1, m_2, ..., m_{j-1}, m_j - |r_s^j|, m_{j+1}, ..., m_{N-2}, x, y)$ when $r_s^j < 0$.

3	2	$x_1^{(3)}(-2)$	$x_1^{(2)}(-2)$	$x_1^{(3)}(-1)$	$x_1^{(2)}(-1)$	$x^{(3)}$	$x^{(2)}$
1	0	$x_1^{(1)}(-2)$	$x_1^{(0)}(-2)$	$x_1^{(1)}(-1)$	$x_1^{(0)}(-1)$	$x^{(1)}$	$x^{(0)}$
(a)		(b) 21-th slice		(c) 22-th slice		(d) 23-th slice	

Fig. 1. (a) An example of an enumeration; Examples of the bi-dimensional prediction contexts for: (b) the 21-th, (c) the 22-th and (d) the 23-th slice

Finally, let $x^{(e)}$ denotes the e-th sample in the current component, according to the enumeration E, with respect to the current sample. Notice that $x^{(0)}$ denotes precisely the current sample.

By taking into consideration the previous example, we consider, for instance, the enumeration E graphically defined in Figure 1(a). Figures 1(b), 1(c) and 1(d) show the bi-dimensional prediction contexts, obtained by using the enumeration of Figure 1(a), respectively for the 21-th, 22-th and 23-th slices (formally identified respectively through the vectors [21], [22] and [23]) and highlight how the samples are addressed according to our notations.

The T-order prediction (where $T = \sum_{i=1}^{N-2} t_i = \sum_{i=1}^{N-2} |R_i|$) of the current sample $x^{(0)}$ is obtained through the equation (1).

$$\hat{x}^{(0)} = \sum_{i=1}^{N-2} \sum_{j=1}^{t_i} \alpha_i^j \cdot x_i^{(0)}(r_j^i). \qquad (1)$$

The coefficients $\alpha_0 = [\alpha_1^1,...,\alpha_1^{t_1},...,\alpha_i^1,...,\alpha_i^{t_i},...,\alpha_{N-2}^1,...,\alpha_{N-2}^{t_{N-2}}]^t$ are chosen to minimize the energy of the prediction error:

$$P = \sum_{i=1}^{H} \left(x^{(i)} - \hat{x}^{(i)} \right)^2. \qquad (2)$$

In detail, H indicates the number of samples used, for the current and for each one of the components specified in the references sets. Thus, $H \cdot (T + 1) + T$ samples are used for the prediction.

The coefficients α_0 are obtained by using the optimal linear prediction method, as in [17]. In detail, we can rewrite the equation (2) in the form $P = (C\alpha - X)^t \cdot (C\alpha - X)$, by using matrix notation, where:

$C =$
$$\begin{bmatrix} x_1^{(1)}(r_1^1) & \cdots & x_1^{(1)}(r_{t_1}^1) & \cdots & x_i^{(1)}(r_{t_i}^i) & \cdots & x_i^{(1)}(r_{t_i}^i) & \cdots & x_{N-2}^{(1)}(r_1^{N-2}) & \cdots & x_{N-2}^{(1)}(r_{t_{N-2}}^{N-2}) \\ \vdots & \ddots & \vdots & & \vdots & \ddots & \vdots & & \vdots & \ddots & \vdots \\ x_1^{(H)}(r_1^1) & \cdots & x_1^{(H)}(r_{t_1}^1) & \cdots & x_i^{(H)}(r_{t_i}^i) & \cdots & x_i^{(H)}(r_{t_i}^i) & \cdots & x_{N-2}^{(H)}(r_1^{N-2}) & \cdots & x_{N-2}^{(H)}(r_{t_{N-2}}^{N-2}) \end{bmatrix}$$

and $X = [x^{(1)} \cdots x^{(H)}]^t$.

The linear system of the equation (3) is obtained, as in [17], by taking the derivate of the equation (2), in matrix notation, with respect to α, and by setting it to zero.

$$(C^t C)\ \alpha_0 = (C^t X).\tag{3}$$

Thus, by computing the coefficients α_0, which solve the linear system (3), it is possible to determinate the prediction of the current sample, $\hat{x}^{(0)}$, by using the equation (1).

In particular, the prediction error is computed by means of the equation (4). This latter can then be sent to an entropy encoder.

$$e = \left\lfloor x^{(0)} - \hat{x}^{(0)} \right\rfloor.\tag{4}$$

The proposed predictive model is easily scalable through an adequate configuration of the references sets. By selecting the wideness of the multidimensional prediction context, which depends on H, it is possible to configure the predictive model in order to prefer the parsimonious use of the computational resources, so to make the model suitable for low-complexity applications, or it is possible to reward the accurateness of the prediction. It is important to note, that if we use only past information there is no need to send any side information to the decompression algorithm during the prediction step.

If the linear system of the equation (3) has no solutions or if it has infinitely, many solutions [9], our approach cannot perform the prediction. We called these scenarios *exceptions* and the exceptions can be managed through another predictive model (for example DPCM, Median Predictor, etc.).

3   Experimental Results

We have tested our predictive model by implementing a predictive-based compression scheme, and then we have experimented this algorithm on different types of N-D data: 3-D computed tomography and 3-D magnetic resonance images (Sec. 3.1), and 5-D fMRI medical images (Sec. 3.2).

The algorithm takes as input the N-D images and predicts the current sample, by using the previously coded samples. In this way, it is possible to have a consistent prediction for both compression and decompression algorithm.

After the prediction step, the prediction error is obtained as the difference between the current sample and its prediction. Finally, the prediction error can be encoded by using an entropy or a statistical coder.

In our experiments, we have used as error encoder the PAQ8 algorithm, which is a state-of-the-art lossless compression algorithm [10]. In particular, the PAQ8 method belongs to the PAQ family, which is an Open Source compression family. As discussed in [10], such family of encoders is strictly related to the well-established *Prediction by Partial Matching* scheme (PPM), which is described in [18].

		32	26	24	27			
	29	20	16	14	17	21	30	
31	19	11	8	6	9	12	22	
25	15	7	3	2	4	10	18	28
23	13	5	1	(0)				

Fig. 2. Example of the resulting enumeration E of the first 32 samples, based on the function defined in (5)

From the design point of view, some architectural aspects could vary depending on the particular version of PAQ8. In detail, we used the *paq8l* version (released by Matt Mahoney) that uses 552 predictive structures. Such predictive structures are modeled in a single prediction through a *Model Mixer*. Once the prediction is computed, the result of such step is passed to an *Adaptive Probability Map* (APM). After this, the obtained prediction error is used by the arithmetic encoder scheme [18]. The main objective of an APM is to reduce the prediction error of 1% [10]. Furthermore, in order to improve the accuracy, the values composing an APM are adjusted according to the prediction error, after the encoding of each bit of the input data [10]. Generally, all the versions of the PAQ8 algorithm achieve a high degree of compression performances. On the other hand, the complexity is over the average of other lossless approaches.

In detail, the implementation of the proposed method uses the 2-D Linearized Median Predictor (2D-LMP) [15], for all the components which have no component references (for instance, the first slice of a 3-D medical image), and our N-D predictive structure, for all the other components.

As enumeration E, similarly to [17], we have used the one that is based on the distance function d, defined as:

$$d((m_1,...,m_{N-2},u,v),(m_1,...,m_{N-2},w,z)) = \sqrt{(u-w)^2 + (v-z)^2} \; .$$

Figure 2 shows an example of the resulting enumeration E for the first 32 samples, by using as reference sample the sample that has 0 as index (highlighted in parenthesis in Fig. 2).

In order to improve the readability, we use the mnemonic name of the dimension instead of its index for the references sets. For example, R_Z indicates the reference set for the Z dimension.

3.1   3-D Medical Images

We have performed experiments on the test set described in Table 1, which is composed by four 3-D CT images and four 3-D MR images. It is important to outline that each slice has 256 columns, 256 lines and each sample is stored by using 8 bits.

Table 1. Description of the used test set

3-D Computed Tomography Images		
Description – Age – Gender	**Image Name**	**Number of slices**
Tripod fracture – 16 – M	CT_skull	192
Healing scaphoid dissection – 20 – M	CT_wrist	176
Internal carotid dissection – 41 – F	CT_carotid	64
Apert's syndrome – 2 – M	CT_Aperts	96
3-D Magnetic Resonance Images		
Description – Age – Gender	**Image Name**	**Number of slices**
Normal – 38 – F	MR_liver_t1	48
Normal – 38 – F	MR_liver_t2e1	48
Left exophthalmos – 42 – M	MR_sag_head	48
Congenital heart disease – 1 – M	MR_ped_chest	64

In the next two sub-sections, we report the experimental results achieved respectively for the 3-D CT and 3-D MR images.

In both cases, as in [12], we have mapped the prediction error before coding through the PAQ8 scheme. Furthermore, we have managed the exceptions with the 3-D Differences-based Linearized Median Predictor (3D-DLMP) [15].

3-D Computed Tomography Images. Computed Tomography (also known as TC, CT, TAC and CAT) uses X-rays to obtain many radiological images. During this process is used a computer, in order to produce different cross-sectional views. It is also possible to obtain three-dimensional views of internal organs of the body.

One of the most common medical application is generally related to identify normal or abnormal structures of the human body. Generally, an X-ray scanner generates many different X-ray images at various angles around the body. All of these images are processed through the dedicated computer, which outputs cross-sectional images, generally referred as slices.

Thus, each slice is a graphical representation of a cross-section of the part of the human body that is undergoing analysis.

We have experimented our approach on the four 3-D CT images of the test set. In particular, in Table 2 we report the experimental results we have achieved, in terms of *bits-per-sample* (BPS), and we compare our results with other state-of-the-art techniques (first column), and we do this for each one of the four 3-D CT images (from the second to the fifth columns). Finally, the sixth column reports the average results for each method. It is important to remark that we have tested our approach by using different configurations for the H parameter and the references sets.

Figure 3 summarizes the results of Table 2. On the Y-axis we have the average bits-per-sample obtained on the 3-D CT images and on the X-axis we have the methods we are comparing. The configuration shown for our approach is: $H=8$, $R_Z=\{-1, -2\}$.

As it is clear in Figure 3, our approach outperforms, all the other state-of-the-art techniques.

Table 2. Comparison of different compression methods on the CT data set. The results are reported in *bits-per-sample* (BPS).

Methods / Images	CT_skull	CT_wrist	CT_carotid	CT_Aperts	*Average*
Proposed $H=32, R_Z=\{-1, -2, -3\}$	1.4836	0.8979	1.2783	0.7283	*1.0970*
$H=16, R_Z=\{-1, -2, -3\}$	1.5309	0.9290	1.2976	0.7350	*1.1231*
$H=8, R_Z=\{-1, -2, -3\}$	1.6258	1.0042	1.3421	0.7587	*1.1827*
$H=32, R_Z=\{-1, -2\}$	1.5393	0.9527	1.3363	0.7265	*1.1387*
$H=16, R_Z=\{-1, -2\}$	1.5688	0.9737	1.3448	0.7271	*1.1536*
$H=8, R_Z=\{-1, -2\}$	1.6196	1.0110	1.3496	0.7349	*1.1788*
3D-ESCOT [19]	1.8350	1.0570	1.3470	0.8580	*1.2743*
MILC [15]	2.0306	1.0666	1.3584	0.8190	*1.3187*
AT-SPIHT [5]	1.9180	1.1150	1.4790	0.9090	*1.3553*
3D-CB-EZW [3]	2.0095	1.1393	1.3930	0.8923	*1.3585*
DPCM+PPMd [1]	2.1190	1.0290	1.4710	0.8670	*1.3715*
3D-SPIHT [19]	1.9750	1.1720	1.4340	0.9980	*1.3948*
3D-EZW [3]	2.2251	1.2828	1.5069	1.0024	*1.5043*
JPEG-LS [4]	2.8460	1.6531	1.7388	1.0637	*1.8254*

In details, only for "*CT_carotid*", by using $H=8$ and $R_Z=\{-1, -2\}$, our approach achieves a slightly worse results with respect to 3-D ESCOT, which is he most performing competitor.

3-D Magnetic Resonance Images. Magnetic Resonance Imaging (MRI) techniques are widely used for the investigation of the anatomy and the function of the body. In particular, the MRI scanners are able to produce three-dimensional images of the body, by using magnetic fields.

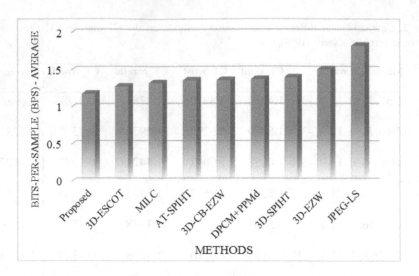

Fig. 3. Graphical comparison of different compression methods on the CT data

Table 3. Comparison of different compression methods on the MR data set. The results are reported in *bits-per-sample* (BPS).

	Methods / Images	MR_liver_t1	MR_liver_t2e1	MR_sag_head	MR_ped_chest	*Average*
Proposed	H=32, R_Z={-1, -2, -3}	1.8511	1.2539	1.4890	1.2920	*1.4715*
	H=16, R_Z={-1, -2, -3}	1.8850	1.2783	1.5311	1.3498	*1.5111*
	H=8, R_Z={-1, -2, -3}	1.9894	1.3360	1.6020	1.4669	*1.5986*
	H=32, R_Z={-1, -2}	1.8996	1.3101	1.5477	1.3740	*1.5329*
	H=16, R_Z={-1, -2}	1.9089	1.3232	1.5737	1.4053	*1.5528*
	H=8, R_Z={-1, -2}	1.9471	1.3482	1.6094	1.4694	*1.5935*
	3D-ESCOT	2.0760	1.5100	1.9370	1.6180	*1.7853*
	MILC	2.1968	1.7590	2.0975	1.6556	*1.9272*
	3D-SPIHT	2.2480	1.6700	2.0710	1.7420	*1.9328*
	3D-CB-EZW	2.2076	1.6591	2.2846	1.8705	*2.0055*
	DPCM+PPMd	2.3900	2.0250	2.1270	1.6890	*2.0578*
	3D-EZW	2.3743	1.8085	2.3883	2.0499	*2.1553*
	JPEG-LS	3.1582	2.3692	2.5567	2.9282	*2.7531*

There are many medical and medical-related fields, in which MRI techniques are involved. In particular, their most common use is related to medical diagnosis and treatments.

Table 3 reports the experimental results, in terms of *bits-per-sample* (BPS), achieved by our approach on the four 3-D MR images of our test set, by using different configurations for both the *H* parameter and the references set. We compared these results with the other state-of-the-art techniques.

Figure 4 summarizes the results of Table 3 and demonstrates that our approach outperforms all the other state-of the-art methods.

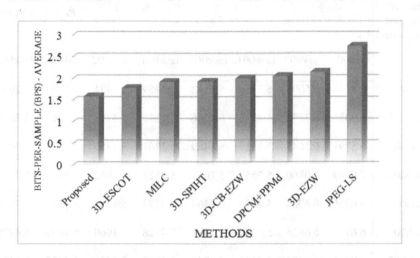

Fig. 4. Graphical comparison of different compression methods on the MR data

3.2   5-D Functional Magnetic Resonance Images

Functional Magnetic Resonance Imaging (functional-MRI or fMRI) is a technology used in different medical and research fields. fMRI permits, for example, the measurement of the brain activity through the measure of the changes of the cerebral blood flow [8], which is strongly coupled with the neuronal activation. An fMRI dataset consists in a collection of 3-D data volumes (*T* dimension). Each of them can be viewed as a collection (on the *Z* dimension) of bi-dimensional images (*X* and *Y* dimensions). Analyzing these data it is possible to determinate the regions of the brain that are activated by a particular task. Generally, multiple trials of experiments are performed (*R* dimension) to improve the accuracy of the examination. Therefore, these are 5-D data.

We have tested our approach on a test set, named *"Stop-signal task with unconditional and conditional stopping"* [2], that is currently available from the OpenfMRI project site [14]. The test set is composed of thirty 5-D fMRI images and has the following organization: there are two 5-D fMRI images (*task001* and *task002*) for each one of the fifteen studied subjects. *task001* and *task002* have respectively the following dimensions $R=3$, $T=182$, $Z=30$, $X=64$, and $Y=64$ and $R=3$, $T=176$, $Z=30$, $X=64$ and

Y=64; except for few exceptions where R can be different (*i.e.* R=1 or R=2). Each sample is stored by using 16 bits. Table 4 reports the experimental results we have achieved in terms of *bits-per-sample* (BPS). We have tested our approach with different parameters for the references sets. H is equal to 32. The exceptions are managed by DPCM [1] on the Z dimension.

Table 4. The 5-D fMRI data test set results are reported in *bits-per-sample* (BPS)

Dataset/ Proposed (Parameters)	3-D (Z) $R_Z=\{-1\}$		3-D (T) $R_T=\{-1\}$		4-D $R_Z=\{-1\}$ $R_T=\{-1\}$		5-D $R_R=\{-1\}R_T=\{-1\}$, $R_Z=\{-1\}$	
	task001	task002	task001	task002	task001	task002	task001	task002
sub001	6.5155	6.5095	5.3550	5.3513	5.3459	5.3421	5.3104	5.2983
sub002	6.8036	6.7873	5.4296	5.4266	5.4277	5.4238	5.3687	5.3844
sub003	6.5791	6.5641	5.3857	5.3469	5.3761	5.3385	5.3338	5.3032
sub004	7.0789	7.0860	5.7552	5.7686	5.7523	5.7662	5.7064	5.7046
sub005	6.6956	6.6908	5.4645	5.4463	5.4574	5.4395	5.4384	5.3989
sub006	6.6714	6.6638	5.5046	5.5081	5.4928	5.4960	5.4601	5.4779
sub007	6.9816	6.9473	5.4636	5.4745	5.4642	5.4761	5.4315	5.4434
sub008	6.6152	6.6119	5.3296	5.3266	5.3239	5.3211	5.3239	5.2853
sub009	6.8820	*N.P.*[1]	5.4410	*N.P.*[1]	5.4437	*N.P.*[1]	5.4265	*N.P.*[1]
sub010	6.7509	6.7450	5.4445	5.4342	5.4385	5.4281	5.4171	5.4176
sub011	6.6081	6.5977	5.3399	5.3252	5.3312	5.3162	5.3158	5.3184
sub012	6.8235	6.8583	5.4756	5.5145	5.4763	5.5150	5.4440	5.4990
sub013	6.6585	6.6492	5.4835	5.4825	5.4722	5.4705	5.4303	5.4403
sub014	6.7979	6.8154	5.5139	5.5319	5.5070	5.5259	5.4711	5.5150
sub015	6.6019	6.5900	5.4626	5.4543	5.4505	5.4426	5.4234	5.4248

[1]*N.P.*: Such data is not present into the test set.

The experimental results show that our approach achieves better results when our predictive model uses all the five dimensions: X, Y, Z, T and R (fifth column). When the predictive model uses X, Y, Z and T (fourth column), the results are generally slightly better with respect to the results achieved by using X, Y, T (third column) and they are significantly better with respect to when we have used X, Y, Z (second column). For such test set, to the best of our knowledge, there are no published results for other compression methods.

4   Conclusions and Future Work

In this paper, we have proposed an N-D predictive model that can be used for efficient lossless compression of multidimensional medical image. We have experimentally tested our method on 3-D computed tomography images, 3-D magnetic resonance images and 5-D functional Magnetic Resonance Imaging (fMRI) data.

Future work will include further testing of our approach, both for lossy and lossless compression, on other multidimensional data (eg. 4-D medical ultrasound images, etc.). We will also focus on the execution performances. In particular, we will outline a parallel implementation of our proposed approach, that can be executed on heterogeneous devices, such as Graphics Processing Units (GPUs), Central Processing Units (CPUs), Field Programmable Gate Arrays (FPGAs), etc.. We will finally design a multidimensional component or volume reordering algorithm, that will improve the compression performances [13, 16] without altering the complexity of the decoder.

References

1. Ait-Aoudia, S., Benhamida, F., Yousfi, M.: Lossless Compression of Volumetric Medical Data. In: Levi, A., Savaş, E., Yenigün, H., Balcısoy, S., Saygın, Y. (eds.) ISCIS 2006. LNCS, vol. 4263, pp. 563–571. Springer, Heidelberg (2006)
2. Aron, A.R., Behrens, T.E., Smith, S., Frank, M.J., Poldrack, R.A.: Triangulating a Cognitive Control Network Using Diffusion-Weighted Magnetic Resonance Imaging (MRI) and Functional MRI. The Journal of Neuroscience 27(14), 3743–3752 (2007)
3. Bilgin, A., Zweig, G., Marcellin, M.W.: Three-Dimensional Image Compression with Integer Wavelet. Applied Optics 39(11), 1799–1814 (2000)
4. Carpentieri, B., Weinberger, M., Seroussi, G.: Lossless Compression of Continuous Tone Images. Proceeding of IEEE 88(11), 1797–1809 (2000)
5. Cho, S., Kim, D., Pearlman, W.A.: Lossless Compression of Volumetric Medical Images with Improved Three-Dimensional SPIHT Algorithm. Journal of Digital Imaging 17(1), 57–63 (2004)
6. De Paolis, L.T., Pulimeno, M., Aloisio, G.: Advanced Visualization and Interaction Systems for Surgical Pre-operative Planning. CIT 18(4) (2010)
7. De Paolis, L.T., Ricciardi, F., Dragoni, A.F., Aloisio, G.: An Augmented Reality Application for the Radio Frequency Ablation of the Liver Tumors. In: Murgante, B., Gervasi, O., Iglesias, A., Taniar, D., Apduhan, B.O. (eds.) ICCSA 2011, Part IV. LNCS, vol. 6785, pp. 572–581. Springer, Heidelberg (2011)
8. fMRI Wikipedia English Page. http://en.wikipedia.org/wiki/Fmri (accessed on July 2014)

9. Golub, G.H., Van Loan, C.F.: Matrix Computations, 3rd ed. Baltimore. MD: The Johns Hopkins Univ. Press (1996)
10. Knoll, B., De Freitas, N.: A Machine Learning Perspective on Predictive Coding with PAQ8. Data Compression Conference (DCC) 24(8), 377–386 (2012)
11. Lalgudi, H.G., Bilgin, A., Marcellin, M.W., Nadar, M.S.: Compression of Multidimensional Images Using JPEG2000. IEEE Signal Processing Letters 15, 393–396 (2008)
12. Motta, G., Storer, J.A., Carpentieri, B.: Lossless Image Coding via Adaptive Linear Prediction and Classification. Proceedings of the IEEE 88(11), 1790–1796 (2000)
13. Motta, G., Rizzo, F., Storer, J.A.: Hyperspectral Data Compression. Springer Science, Berlin (2006)
14. OpenfMRI Site. https://openfmri.org (accessed on July 2014)
15. Pizzolante, R., Carpentieri, B.: Lossless, low-complexity, compression of three-dimensional volumetric medical images via linear prediction. Digital Signal Processing (DSP), 1–6 (July 1-3, 2013)
16. Pizzolante, R., Carpentieri, B.: Visualization, Band Ordering and Compression of Hyperspectral Images. Algorithms 5, 76–97 (2012)
17. Rizzo, F., Carpentieri, B., Motta, G., Storer, J.A.: Low-complexity lossless compression of hyperspectral imagery via linear prediction. IEEE Signal Processing Letters 12(2), 138–141 (2005)
18. Salomon, D., Motta, G.: Handbook of Data Compression, 5 edn. Springer (2010) ISBN: 978-1-84882-902-2
19. Xiong, Z., Wu, X., Cheng, S., Jianping, H.: Lossy-to-lossless compression of medical volumetric data using three-dimensional integer wavelet transforms. IEEE Trans. on Medical Imaging 22(3), 459–470 (2003)

Low-Cost Motion-Tracking for Computational Psychometrics Based on Virtual Reality

Pietro Cipresso[1(✉)], Silvia Serino[1], Irene Alice Chicchi Giglioli[1], Igor Giuliano[2], Davide Borra[3], Andrea Farina[4], and Giuseppe Riva[1,5]

[1]Applied Technology for Neuro-Psychology Lab, IRCCS Istituto Auxologico Italiano, Via L. Ariosto 13, 20145 Milano, MI, Italy
p.cipresso@auxologico.it
[2]Regola, Corso Turati 15/H, 10128 Torino, TO, Italy
[3]NoReal.it, Via Ugo Foscolo 4, 10126 Torino, TO, Italy
[4]Partner and Partners, Corso Brescia 9, 10152 Torino, TO, Italy
[5]Department of Psychology, Università Cattolica del Sacro Cuore, L.go Gemelli 1, Milano, MI, Italy

Abstract. Virtual Reality (VR) is a computer-based simulation designed to expose users to environments in order to replicate real world objects and events. In this framework, video games are one of the most popular forms of VR media all over the worlds. Their popularity has been fuelled by advancements in gaming technology and interactive devices at a low cost in home gaming market but also in clinical and research settings. In clinical and research virtual rehabilitation, the user should be able to interact (directly or indirectly) with the environment via a wide array of input technologies. These include activation of computer keyboard keys, a mouse or a joypad (indirect) and even by using special sensors or visual tracking (direct). For example, Microsoft Kinect provides low-cost motion tracking sensors, allowing to clinicians to interact with rehabilitation applications in the most natural and flexible way. This flexibility can be employed to tailor the user interaction to the specific rehabilitation user aims. According to this perspective, the paper aims to present a potential new platform, NeuroVirtual3D, which intends to develop a software interface for supporting assessment and rehabilitation of cognition function through several input/output devices, such as data gloves, joypad and Microsoft Kinect.

Keywords: Psychometrics · Virtual Reality · Biosensors · Psychophysiology

1 Introduction

Virtual Reality (VR) usually concerns the application of interactive simulations produced by computer hardware and software for engaging users in environments that are similar to the events and objects of the real world. [1]. Users interplay with virtual images and objects being able to perform several actions (such as handle and shift the objects) in a virtual environment, which elicits a sense of immersion and *presence*. In general terms, a first group of researchers defined presence as "Media Presence", by

© Springer International Publishing Switzerland 2014
L.T. De Paolis and A. Mongelli (Eds.): AVR 2014, LNCS 8853, pp. 137–148, 2014.
DOI: 10.1007/978-3-319-13969-2_11

focusing on the disappearance of the medium from the conscious attention of the individual during the human-computer interaction [1-7]. According to a second group of researcher, an individual is present in a space – real or virtual – when he/she can successfully acts in and performs his/her intentions. According to this perspective, presence can be envisaged as "Inner Presence", defined as the sensation to be in a sense external world around the self: it is a broad psychological phenomenon, not necessarily linked to the experience of a technology [8-10].

Advanced simulations are used to trigger broad empowerment processes induced by a strong sense of presence, leading to greater agency and control over one's actions and environment. In rehabilitation, advanced simulations can reveal in the user/patient what is defined as "transformation" of flow, which affects a person's ability to exploit the best (flow) experience for recognizing and utilizing new and unforeseen psychological abilities as source of engagement. [11]. A powerful sense of presence can be generate by the user through the interaction with virtual objects and events being, thus, able to perform several actions (such as handle and shift the objects) in the virtual environment. Virtual environment are typically experienced with special hardware and software for input (move information from the user to the system) and output (move information from the system to the user). The choice of appropriate hardware is essential since its characteristics may enormously condition the way users respond to a virtual environment [12].

Recent advances in video game technology have made available a large number of low-cost devices that can track the movement of the user, such as Nintendo Wiimote (TM), the Playstation Move (TM) and Microsoft Kinect (TM).

On these premises, the NeuroVirtual 3D platform aims at exploiting these potentiality by designing, developing and testing a low-cost integrated virtual reality solution for applications in clinical psychology and neuropsychological rehabilitation [13]. The platform has been developed expanding the features of the software NeuroVr 2.0 (http://www.neurovr.org/neurovr2/) [14] thanks to the development of a software plug-in allowing the interaction with external devices Microsoft Kinect (TM).

2   A New Platform for Assessment and Neurorehabilitation: NeuroVirtual 3D

Video games are one of the most popular forms of media all over the worlds. Their popularity has been fuelled by advancements in gaming technology, a persisting trend that is producing advanced gaming consoles such as such as Nintendo Wiimote (TM), the Playstation Move (TM) and Microsoft Kinect (TM). Thanks to this incredible spread on home gaming market, in the last years there are a wide series of interactive devices at a low cost also in clinical and research settings [15-18]. A key feature of these consoles is multimodal interaction, achieved through specialized low-cost hardware. In particular, Xbox One includes an advanced version of the motion sensing Kinect camera, updated with the ability to read biometric data and see using infrared. A PC version of the same camera is also available – Kinect for Windows sensor and the Kinect for Windows software development kit (SDK). This offers new opportunities for virtual neuropsychological assessment and rehabilitation. Sophisticated VR systems employ more than specialized visual displays. Engaging the user in the virtual environment may be enhanced via audio display, either ambient or directed to specific stimuli [19]. VR hardware that facilitates the input and output of information, in combination with programmed virtual environments provide the tools for designing tasks that enable users to perform in ways that help them achieve established assessment and rehabilitation goals. When creating a specific virtual rehabilitation tool the clinician and technical team face the challenge of choosing and integrating the software and hardware, and the input and the output methods. Likewise, in a virtual environment, for reaching an experience similar to the real one, is essential for the user be able to navigate and handle objects within it. Thus the user must be able to interact (directly or indirectly) with the environment via a wide array of input technologies. A first class consists of indirect ways for users to manipulate and navigate within a virtual environment, such as the start up of computer keyboard keys, a mouse or a joypad or even virtual buttons being present in the environment. [12]. A second class of input technologies may be considered as direct methods since users behave in a natural way, and the system tracks their actions and responds accordingly. Generally, this is achieved by using special sensors or by visual tracking. With the sensor approach, such as used by Intersense's (www.isense.com) InterTrax2, a three degree of freedom, inertial orientation tracker used to track pitch, roll and yaw movements, the user wears a tracking device that transmits position and orientation data to the VR system. With the visual tracking approach, such as used by VividGroup's video-capture VR system, the user's motion is recorded by video cameras, where special software processes the video image, extracts the user's figure from the background in real-time, and identifies any motion of the body. On this basis, the NeuroVirtual 3D platform is a low-cost integrated virtual reality solution for creating virtual environments useful for neuropsychological assessment and neurorehabilitation by interacting with real-like artifacts (Fig. 1). Actually, NeuroVirtual 3D platform includes two virtual environments: a VR-home for neuropsychological assessment and a VR-city for rehabilitation. VR-home is a two-story home with garden including a living room and kitchen on the ground floor and a bedroom, a bathroom and a studio on the first floor. Instead, VR-city is a small town made-up by 3x3 streets including a square, shops, and buildings. In this two virtual environments patients can carry out several ecological tasks: for example, in the VR-home participants can distribute playing cards, serve tea, or look for clothes in the wardrobe; in the VR-city, participant can look for stores, trash bin or people in the square. The main aim of NeuroVirtual 3D platform is to offer a wide range of interactive contents and rehabilitative exercises. Moreover, the platform now has a specific interface for interaction with external devices like Microsoft Kinect (TM), allowing users to interact in the most flexible with virtual environments. In the following paragraph, the technical features of Kinect-NeuroVirtual 3D interaction interface will be detailed.

Fig. 1. Through NeuroVirtual 3D, users are able to interact with real-like artifact. In this figure it is possible to see a kitchen containing many objects users can move and re-organize by the means of a Microsoft Kinect. Also further interaction and manipulation are developable.

2.1   Microsoft Kinect-NeuroVirtual 3D Interaction Interface: Technical Features

The interaction of the patient with the scene is detected analyzing movements and poses, which are defined relating to each peripheral to be interfaced to. These actions are processed and normalized before creating a new instance of the controller object, which is interpreted by the NeuroVR platform.

Acting on the configuration parameters is possible to perform an accurate tuning of the Microsoft Kinect detections with respect to user's biometric measures in the scene. Considering the data acquired from the Microsoft Kinect is possible to modify configuration parameters to proportionally bias the reactivity and the precision of movement, reported in the scene by the Avatar.

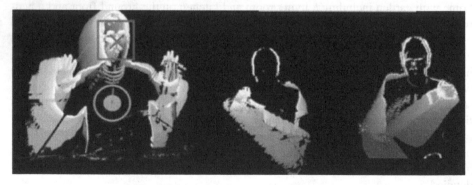

Fig. 2. Video signal processing from kinect

The Avatar's interaction in the virtual scene can be summed up through the following concepts:

Table 1. Avatar's interaction in the virtual scene

Translation	It defines the Avatar's spatial movement in the scene and it is featured by the following actions: go Ahead, go Back, go Right, and go Left.
Rotation	It defines the Avatar's point of view movement and it is featured by the following actions: Tilt Up, Tilt Down, Pan Left and Pan Right.
Command	It defines the recognition of the "poses" the Avatar takes, which are used for recognition of coded actions. e.g.: Left Click, Center Click, Right Click. This element is necessary to implement the Avatar's interaction with items in the scene, e.g.: take the pot, put down the pot.

It can be considered that the intensity of the movements performable in the scene can range from a minimum to a maximum (parametric) and that the movement speed be linearly proportional to the straight line (Fig.3), which links these two values. The Dead Zone (red), defined by the perception thresholds, is identified through the values (N_0, P_0) defined in the configuration. Values related to the upper (or lower) movement threshold are identified by N_0 e N_1 and are specularly acquired by Kinect in rest state. For movements performed within the Dead Zone no movement is notified, outside of it, the maximum value or a fraction of it.

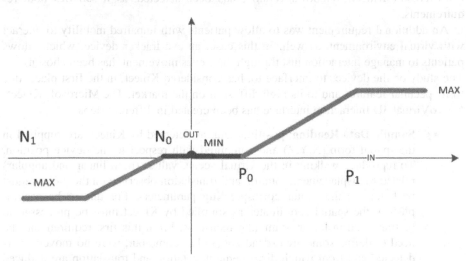

Fig. 3. The behaviour of the transfer function between the data acquired by Microsoft Kinect and the ones supplied to the platform can be made dependent from used parameters. When needed, it is possible to obtain a non-specular behavior with respect to the rest state.

Configuration parameters allow to fine tune the measurements acquired by Microsoft Kinect, when necessary, hence they have to be modified upon reading some biometric measurements of the patient in the studio. Microsoft Kinect reads these data on the user in rest state, and, in case of commands, in poses which the patient would consider natural and spontaneous. Acquired data constitute the threshold values beyond which the movements and the commands for that specific patient are taken into account. For each controllable axis some parameters have been defined, named in the form with the label Axis_ParameterName, with the following meaning for parameters:

- P0: positive value of lower threshold for the movement detection
- P1: positive value of upper threshold for the movement detection
- N0: negative value of lower threshold for the movement detection
- N1: negative value of upper threshold for the movement detection
- OutPut: maximum output value
- Bias: input correcting factor
- Gain: input multiplication factor

Furthermore, two different requirements have been considered to choose the suitable peripherals to be used in the project:

- Low cost and consequent widespread diffusion on the market

- Precise acquisition of patient's movements in the scene to reproduce them in the virtual scene

Microsoft Kinect, Windows version, has been selected, as it satisfies both requirements.

An additional requirement was to allow patients with impaired mobility to interact with virtual environment, as well. In this case, an eye tracker device, which allows patients to manage interaction just through their eyes movement, has been chosen.
The study on the devices to interface to, has considered Kinect, in the first place, due to its peculiar features and to its high diffusion on the market. The Microsoft Kinect-NeuroVirtual 3D Interaction interface has been created in different steps.

- **Sample Data Reading**: position data, as detected by Kinect, are supplied in the spatial form (X,Y,Z) and computed with respect to the device position. To reproduce walking in the virtual scene, values (both linear and angular) related to displacement, rotation and translation observed on the patient must be bound to the avatar corresponding parameters. For this to be accomplished, the spatial coordinates as supplied by Kinect must be processed to be translated in linear or angular measures. From this first requirement, the need to define some area (dead zones) has come out, were no movement is detected and from which displacement, rotation and translation are deduced by difference when going out of the zone itself.

  In the first place, dead zones with a fixed amplitude have been defined, but the use experience has pointed out that is not possible to reposition them when the patient stops moving, producing some "drift" effects, hence errors, in the patient position measurements, or that even distinguish between immobility and movement could be impossible. For such a reason, position and movement have to be determined in a relative fashion, correlating some patient's skeleton elements rather than setting fixed measure points in the deambulation environment (e.g.: marks on floor). The processing algorithm that has come out, allows recognizing the patient's moving will with respect to relative immobility positions.

- **Acquired Data Normalization**: as human body is always moving, even in an apparent rest position (for example the erect one), and since Kinect can detect even the smallest movement of the patient's skeleton, the need to "filter" acquired data has come out, so that the virtual scene representation would be as realistic as possible and not affected by the amplification of such oscillations. To accomplish this, the movement has to be analyzed to determine, for each sample to be acquired, some threshold values, above which the real movement could be detected.

- **Movement Analysis**: to detect the movements performed by the patient, the position she/he takes with respect to the device, and the quality of the process performed analyzing her/his posture, are taken into account. Some movement (particularly the patient's back movements) can be better detected by an accurate selection of the points marked on the patient's skeleton on which the elaboration is performed. To this end, by analyzing experimentally the movement, couples of measurement points that could lead to more accurate patient's position and movement measures, have been identified.

A further constraint, resulting from the movement thresholds setting, has come out, by evaluating the interaction of patients with different build. In these cases, the definition of preset thresholds causes a movement detection that could differ from reality, producing unwanted amplification or attenuation effects. At this end, and to limit these consequences, parametric thresholds, which are bound to patient's biometric features, have been introduced. In this way, a double result is obtained: first, reproducing the movement in the most accurate way, and second, exploiting these chances to introduce voluntarily some amplifications or attenuations on the detected movements (useful, for example, in case of reduced mobility patients).

In the movement analysis context, some studies have been conducted aimed to the actions sequence, or "gestures" recognition. These studies have pointed out big difficulties in this recognition, and, above all, in the univocal identification of gestures, since in a movements sequence many factors can affect negatively the recognition, although not visible at a first sight. Examples are:

- Gesture execution speed

- Gesture execution amplitude

- Subject performing the gesture (child, elderly, adult, …)

In this regard, it seems more useful to concentrate on the recognition of "Poses", which are static movements, that is, not affected by the above-mentioned issues. Even in the Poses recognition, a thorough study on the patient position, so that all the defined ones do not introduce any ambiguity in the recognition, is necessary.

- **Transfer Functions**: at the conclusion of the studies and of the experimentations performed, through the definition of recognition thresholds, acquired data normalization and information filtering, real Transfer Functions have been defined, which are applied to the data coming from Kinect, when it detects the patient posture. The features of such functions will be discussed hereinafter.

To allow some abstraction on the used peripheral, an interface component (between the NeuroVR and the physical device) has been implemented, by which a generic object, on which the interaction is mapped and managed, has been defined. The communication between systems has been managed using the VRPN framework, by means of which, a device-independent architecture to interconnect peripherals in Virtual Reality applications, has been defined.

The two main devices selected for NeuroVirtual 3D are:

- **Kinect**: to be used in context where body movements can be used to interact with the NeuroVR platform.

- **Eyetracker**: to be used in context where body movements are not possible, due to patient impairments. In this case the interaction with the NeuroVR platform is carried out just moving eyes.

The implemented abstraction has defined a set of actions allowed in the scene, which are mapped on the VRPN object (controller) needed to perform the communication.

The use of the selected devices is always mutually exclusive and does not contemplate a concurrent use of both devices.

3   The Potentiality of NeuroVirtual 3D for Psychology

Sophisticated VR systems employ more than specialized visual displays. Engaging the user in the virtual environment may be enhanced via audio display, either ambient or directed to specific stimuli [19]. VR hardware that facilitates the input and output of information, in combination with programmed virtual environments provide the tools for designing tasks that enable users to perform in ways that help them achieve established assessment and rehabilitation goals. When creating a specific virtual rehabilitation tool the clinician and technical team face the challenge of choosing and integrating the software and hardware, and the input and the output methods. Likewise, in a virtual environment, for reaching an experience similar to the real one, is essential for the user be able to navigate and handle objects within it. Thus the user must be able to interact (directly or indirectly) with the environment via a wide array of input technologies. A first class consists of indirect ways for users to manipulate and navigate within a virtual environment, such as the start up of computer keyboard keys, a mouse or a joypad or even virtual buttons being present in the environment. [12]. A second class of input technologies may be considered as direct methods since users behave in a natural way, and the system tracks their actions and responds accordingly. Generally, this is achieved by using special sensors or by visual tracking. With the sensor approach, such as used by Intersense's (www.isense.com) InterTrax2, a three degree of freedom, inertial orientation tracker used to track pitch, roll and yaw movements, the user wears a tracking device that transmits position and orientation data to the VR system. With the visual tracking approach, such as used by VividGroup's video-capture VR system, the user's motion is recorded by video cameras, where special software processes the video image, extracts the user's figure from the background in real-time, and identifies any motion of the body.

Fig. 4. A virtual room designed for the object interactions with a Kinect

Fig. 5. A room, and in particular a wardrobe with the task of intercting with the virtual dresses using a Kinect

NeuroVirtual3D intends to develop a software interface for supporting assessment and rehabilitation of cognition function through several input/output devices, such as data gloves, joypad and Microsoft Kinect. Traditionally, the assessment and rehabilitation of impairments of cognitive functions (language, spatial perception, attention, and memory) have been carried out with pen-and-paper methods. Psychology has worked to develop several measures to effectively evaluate several cognitive abilities. On one side, traditional measures are generally reliable and have adequate validity. On the other side, however, a critical challenge for psychology has been to find new way to better evaluate and predict everyday abilities. In addition to a precise evaluation, indeed, there is a need for cognitive assessments that reflect real-world situations, in order to better assess functional impairment. Recently, the need for a more ecological and functional evaluation has been the focus of considerable research interest. In this perspective, NeuroVirtual 3D may be used in psychology to allow user to interact with immersed in a computer-generated environment in a naturalistic fashion. Furthermore, the full-body tracking allows selecting among various combination of gestures and limbs without wear any markers, carry any additional device or using specific limbs to interact with the system in an ecological environments. For example, Microsoft Kinets provides low-cost motion tracking sensors, allowing to clinicians to interact with rehabilitation applications in the most natural and flexible way. This flexibility can be employed to tailor the user interaction to the specific rehabilitation user aims [20].

Fig. 6. Using low-cost motion tracking sensors, like Kinect, it also possible to navigate in Virtual environment using body gesture (e.g., a foot ahed), making also this task the most natural and flexible possible

To sum, the future development of application of NeuroVirtual 3D-based therapy to rehabilitation could be very effective in many realms of medicine and psychology. Furthermore, NeuroVirtual 3D could be extremely effective to supply different modality of feedback in sensory deficits such as motion and tactile signals for patients with severe deficits through interactive virtual environments. In conclusion, the cost of tools is dropping, the software is more accessible than before and by now it is much easier to adopt this new technology. As mentioned above, VR systems are becoming very important in the assessment and intervention for cognitive-motor rehabilitation thanks to their specific and unique characteristics.

These characteristics make it highly suitable for the achievement of many rehabilitation aims including the encouragement of experiential, active learning, the provision of challenging but safe and ecologically valid environments, the flexibility of individualized and graded treatment protocols, the power to motivate patients to perform to their utmost capability and the capacity to record objective measures of performance.

Acknowledgements. This study was supported by the research project "NeuroVirtual 3D," funded by Regione Piemonte (Grant No. FA 211-432C- 2012).

References

1. Sheridan, T.B.: Musings on telepresence and virtual presence. Presence-Teleop Virt. **1**, 120–126 (1992)
2. Schloerb, D.: A quantative Measure of Telepresence. Presence-Teleop Virt. **4**(1), 64–80 (1995)
3. Sadowski, W.J., Stanney, K.M.: Measuring and Managing Presence in Virtual Environments. In: Stanney, K.M. (ed.) Handbook of Virtual Environments Technology, pp. 791–806. Lawrence Erlbaum Associates, Mahwah, NJ (2002)
4. Ijsselsteijn, W., de Ridden, H., Freeman, J., Avons, S.E.: Presence: Concept Determinants and Measurement. In: P SOC PHOTO-OPT INS, San Jose, CA (2000)
5. Lombard, M., Ditton, T.: At the Heart of It All: The Concept of Presence. J. Comput-Mediat Comm. **3**(2) (1997)
6. Sheridan, T.B.: Further Musing on the Psychophysics of Presence. Presence-Teleop Virt. **5**, 241–246 (1996)
7. Marsh, T., Wright, P., Smith, S.: Evaluation for the Design of Experience in Virtual Environments: Modeling Breakdown of Interaction and Illusion. Cyberpsychol. Behav. **4**(2), 225–238 (2001)
8. Riva, G., Davide, F., IJsselsteijn, W.: A Being There: Concepts, Effects and Measurements of User Presence in Synthetic Environments. In: Riva, G., Davide, F. (eds.) Emerging Communication: Studies on New Technologies and Practices in Communication. Ios Press, Amsterdam (2003)
9. Riva, G., Waterworth, J.A., Waterworth, E.L., Mantovani, F.: From Intention to Action: The Role of Presence. New Ideas Psychol. **29**(1), 24–37 (2011)
10. Waterworth, J.A., Waterworth, E.L., Mantovani, F., Riva, G.: On Feeling (the) Present: An Evolutionary Account of the Sense of Presence in Physical and Electronically-Mediated Environments. J. Consciousness Stud. **17**(1–2), 167–178 (2010)
11. Riva, G., Castelnuovo, G., Mantovani, F.: Transformation of flow in rehabilitation: the role of advanced communication technologies. Behav. Res. Methods **38**(2), 237–244 (2006)
12. Rand, D., Kizony, R., Feintuch, N., Katz, N., Josman, N., Rizzo, A.A., Weiss, P.L.: Comparison of two VR platforms for rehabilitation: video capture versus HMD. Presence-Teleop Virt. **14** (2005)

13. Cipresso, P., Serino, S., Pallavicini, F., Gaggioli, A., Riva, G.: NeuroVirtual 3D: A Multi-platform 3D Simulation System for Application in Psychology and Neurorehabilitation. In: Ma, M. (ed.) Virtual, Augmented Reality and Serious Games for Healthcare 1, pp. 275–286. Springer (2014)

14. Riva, G., Gaggioli, A., Grassi, A., Raspelli, S., Cipresso, P., Pallavicini, F., Vigna, C., Gagliati, A., Gasco, S., Donvito, G.: NeuroVR 2-a free virtual reality platform for the assessment and treatment in behavioral health care. Stud. Health. Technol. Inform. **163**, 493–495 (2011)

15. Giakoumis, D., Drosou, A., Cipresso, P., Tzovaras, D., Hassapis, G., Gaggioli, A., Riva, G.: Using activity-related behavioural features towards more effective automatic stress detection. PloS One **7**(9) (2012b)

16. Giakoumis, D., Drosou, A., Cipresso, P., Tzovaras, D., Hassapis, G., Gaggioli, A., Riva, G.: Real-time monitoring of behavioural parameters releted to psychological stress. St Heal T. **181**, 287–291 (2012)

17. Lee, J., Chao, C., Thomaz, A.L., Bobick, A.F.: Adaptive Integration of Multiple Cues for Contingency Detection. In: Salah, A.A., Lepri, B. (eds.) HBU 2011. LNCS, vol. 7065, pp. 62–71. Springer, Heidelberg (2011)

18. Rigas, G., Tazallas, A.T., Tsalikakis, D.G., Konitsiotis, S., Fotiadis, D.I.: Real-time quantification of resting tremor in the Parkinson's disease. In: Conf. Proc. IEEE Eng. Med. Biol. Soc., pp. 1306–1309 (2009)

19. Vastfjall, D.: The subjective sense of presence, emotion recognition, and experienced emotions in auditory virtual environments. Cyberpsychol. Behav. **6**(2), 181–188 (2003)

20. Lange, B., Chang, C.Y., Suma, E., Newman, B., Rizzo, A.A., Bolas, M.: Development and evaluation of low cost game-based balance rehabilitation tool using the Microsoft Kinect sensor. In: Proc. IEEE Int. Conf. Eng. Med. Biol. Soc. (2011)

Augmented and Mixed Reality

A Design and Evaluation Framework
for a Tele-Immersive Mixed Reality Platform

Simon Crowle[1(✉)], Michael Boniface[1], Benjamin Poussard[2],
and Stylianos Asteriadis[3]

[1] IT Innovation Centre, University of Southampton, SO16 7NS, Southampton, UK
sgc@it-innovation.soton.ac.uk
[2] ARTS Presence and Innovation Team, Ingénierium - 4, Rue de l'Ermitage,
53000, Laval, France
benjamin.poussard@ensam.eu
[3] Centre for Research and Technology Hellas,
Information Technologies Institute, Paiania, Greece
stiast@iti.gr

Abstract. Tele-immersive, mixed reality interactive systems bring remote users
together to share a common experience in an environment that synthesizes aspects of the real and virtual worlds. The 3D-LIVE platform is an example of
one such system that synthesizes 3D models, audio, motion capture and activity
recognition from a number of geographically separated sources into a single
gaming environment to support a variety of sports based activities. The design
and evaluation of such systems is challenging since factors relating to the technical quality of service (QoS) and quality of experience (QoE) are difficult to
identify and measure. In this paper we present a novel QoS/QoE model and
evaluation methodology that is being used in the development and testing of the
3D-LIVE mixed reality platform. Our initial results provide some insights into
the quality of user experience (UX) we observed from users interacting with
3D-LIVE and are evaluated in the light of QoS data captured. We conclude by
discussing the impact of these findings on future platform developments.

Keywords: Teleimmersion · Mixed reality · Quality of experience · Quality of
service · Co-creation

1   Introduction

Contemporary consumers' computing technologies found at home or in mobile devices are typically capable of providing rich user interfaces that offer virtual or augmented reality presentations. In the computer games market, these experiences are
enriched through shared collaborative or competitive game play with friends connected via the Internet. A range of interactive modalities including virtual reality (VR);
augmented reality (AR); voice based group communication; and body motion tracking are now integrated in popular, modern computer game design. The 3D-LIVE
project [1] is developing a platform for real-time, interactive teleimmersion that

© Springer International Publishing Switzerland 2014
L.T. De Paolis and A. Mongelli (Eds.): AVR 2014, LNCS 8853, pp. 151–158, 2014.
DOI: 10.1007/978-3-319-13969-2_12

connects augmented, interactive experiences situated in real-world activities with corresponding, simulated activities realised in virtual environments elsewhere. Our goal is to generate a shared sense of presence, co-location and engagement between all users taking part in mixed reality sporting activities and to gain insight into what design and technical considerations must be taken into account to realise this UX. In the following sections we present a high level overview of the UX driven design process and model based approach that is being used to progressively refine, improve and evaluate the 3D-LIVE system. Following this, we present results from our preliminary evaluation work and discuss how the early findings have helped direct prototype developments for enhanced UX.

2   Background

Mixed reality teleimmersion is a progression of conventional 3D virtual environments through interaction with the inclusion of full body motion capture and augmented reality presentation technology. Unlike more conventional systems, mixed reality platforms necessarily include real world contexts that introduce inherently more complex and distributed interactions that are challenging both technically and also in terms of understanding their impact on UX [2][6]. Technology used in an attempt to increase the user's perception of full tele-immersion includes the use of CAVE based environments [3], full body motion capture and reconstruction [4] [17] and mobile, augmented reality applications [5]. Variations of traditional sporting activities have been explored using mixed reality technologies. Sports games have either been replicated in a virtualised form [7] [8] or redesigned for remote interaction and training [9] [10].

In 3D-LIVE, we extend this work by exploring the realisation of three sports related scenarios (golfing, jogging, skiing) that engage users situated both outdoors and indoors. In the real world, outdoor users interact via augmented reality presentations on a mobile device and wearable sensors. Two deployments exist for indoor users using virtual reality, in order to assess the impact of different configurations on UX: a 'high end' configuration which includes a CAVE environment, wearable motion sensors, dedicated simulators and rendering of full-body reconstruction of remote users [17]. The consumer level or 'low end' configuration displays the virtual environment on a large, conventional display and integrates Nintendo's Wii for simulation, while simple avatars represent the remote users. In both cases, Microsoft's Kinect depth sensors are used to capture motion, 3D information of user silhouette and evaluate activity using fuzzy engines [20]. A typical test case for a 3D-LIVE scenario is to include one outdoor user with two indoor (but geographically separate) users. An outdoor user is connected to indoor users using a mobile application that operates as a sensor gateway and voice communication channel. Outdoor human activity is acquired by a combination of inbuilt mobile device sensors (e.g. GPS position, direction) and wearable inertia-based wearable sensors (e.g. motion analysis). Local environment data is acquired by a combination of wearable environment sensors that is aggregated with in-situ weather sensors and wide area weather services. All data is captured and communicated in real time to a 3D virtual environment for rendering to the indoor users. Each indoor sees himself as a 3D avatar in the virtual environment along with the other players; his direction of travel is captured using a combination of motion capture sensors and activity recognition algorithms. Each scenario is based on an interaction design that aims to enhance UX associated with distant collaboration within the context of shared sporting activities.

- Golf (Laval, France): Players collaborate in a 'scramble play' variation of the golfing game in which indoor and outdoor players take shots towards the hole and then select the ball judged to be in the most favorable position for the next stroke.
- Jogging (Oulu, Finland): The outdoor jogger initially leads a short jogging route around streets in Oulu whilst the indoor users follow. The aim is for all runners to keep together as a group and achieve the best possible time for the route.
- Skiing (Schladming, Austria): Players race down a slalom course led by the outdoor skier. The slalom course is positioned on the real and virtual slopes. The outdoor skier leads the group down the slope whilst the indoor users attempt to keep up by following their path.

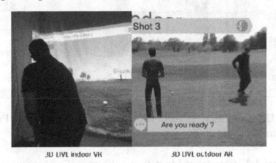

Fig. 1. Golfing scenario indoor golf simulator (VR) and outdoor view (AR)

3   3D-LIVE Design Process and Evaluation Model

3D-Live uses an iterative process of user-driven design and prototype based evaluation to develop an understanding of the necessary interaction design and technical characteristics that combine to deliver a compelling UX. Engagement of users throughout the development life-cycle using scenario based approaches is a well-established design practice for VR design [15][14]. Specialisations of these approaches that introduce a formal model to represent system behaviour and UX have been created to evaluate usability experimentally [16]. We build on this work by instantiating an 'experiential model' that includes concepts that are used formatively in the design process as a structure for engaging user groups in 'co-creation activities' associated with the real-world contexts of scenarios. The outcomes allowed us to update the experiential model based on users' views experiential priorities and to direct ongoing design and implementation of the system itself.

From co-creation activities and research work about UX, we built the 3D-LIVE Immersive User eXperience (IUX) model. IUX can be described by two engines: The

Rational Engine, and the Experiential engine (see Fig. 2). The Rational engine mainly reuses the DIME (Distributed Interactive Multimedia Environment) indicators of UX [16]. It includes the three following elements: Psychological Flow, Telepresence and Technology Acceptance. The Experiential engine is based on emotion and intuition as described in the CEST (Cognitive Experiential Self Theory) [18], and includes the following constructs: Social Presence, Social Emotion, and Emotional Response. The QoS constructs cover the technological aspects of the platform and are derived from DIME's QoS model. Among those constructs are Interactivity (Speed, Range), Vividness (Breadth, Depth) and Consistency (Temporal, Spatial). A model of QoS and QoE that is aligned with the IUX constructs are required to evaluate UX.

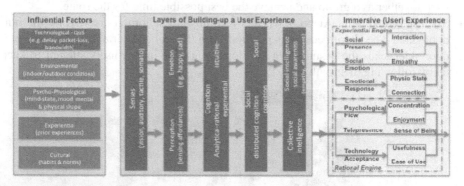

Fig. 2. Immersive UX Constructs aligned with Influential Factors and Process Layers (UX Model extended from Wu et al., 2009)

Applying this model starts from identifying the specific metric set representative of the UX to be assessed. Users have been involved in the iterative design process for the three scenarios (Golfing, Jogging, and Skiing). User needs and requirements have been gathered to define the set of metrics related to the constructs of the QoE/QoS table, as shown by two example metrics on the Table 1, to assess the experience they do expect, and what is really important for them.

Table 1. Example sets of metrics for corresponding 3D-LIVE QoE/QoS constructs

Dimensions	Criteria	Constructs	Metrics	Nature
QoS	Consistency	Spatial	Path Accuracy of the outdoor avatar (m)	Log: GPS positions compared to avatar position
QoE	Performance Gains	Hedonic	Pleasure	Semantic differential scale

4   Observational Methodology

3D Live has developed an observational method for carrying out evaluation trials in real-time tele-immersive environments. Tele-immersive systems pose challenges due to the need to coordinate and collect data from geographically distributed system components and users. A coordinated approach to these trials requires unified control over an experimental workflow to orchestrate participants and the ability to monitor and aggregate synchronized metric data from multiple sources. A central human co-ordinator provides executive control over the experimental process to support work-flow execution and data gathering. Communication between the coordinator and local support teams was achieved using a shared, on-line workflow defining the process model and the ability to collect fine-grained notes on the status the game as it pro-gressed. The process model contained all steps needed to consistently set-up, execute and tear-down the system under test including distributed interactions with remote users in a repeatable way.

In addition to the workflow management described above, a systematic approach to metric data collection was provided using an experiment data management system called the EXPERIMonitor (EM) developed as part of the EXPERIMEDIA project [19]. The EM is a web service and data visualisation tool that offers support for real-time automatic metric based data acquisition and aggregation from remotely connected sources. Selected technical components within the 3D-LIVE system were instrumented using the EM API to provide specific sets of QoS data during each game, live at run-time. The coordinator used the EM to step through an experiment based process where connected components (or 'EM clients') are managed through specific phases that perform coordinated set-up, live data collection and tear-down related activities. Orthogonal to the quantitative observations, qualitative data was gathered in the form of video recordings of participating users, and post-game user interviews. Video data and interview based feedback provided us with early, rapid insights into the overall QoE and their perceptions of system performance.

5   Preliminary Results

Initial trials of all three scenarios have been carried out, each of which involving a series of repeated evaluation runs (between 15 and 20 games were typical). The pur-pose of these trials was two-fold; first to act as verification of system behaviour when deployed in the real-world and the second to gather a preliminary data-set of QoS measures and actual UX from which a 'baseline' of system behaviour and accompa-nying UX could be defined. Our QoS data set covered a range of measurements mapped to interactivity, including graphics rendering; human motion capture and reconstruction; voice communications and environment reconstruction data. Inspec-tion of some of the principal QoS criteria defined for 3D-LIVE has revealed useful insights. Spatial-temporal consistency is one such criterion in our UX model: it pro-vides an indication of closeness of mapping between indoor and outdoor interactions.

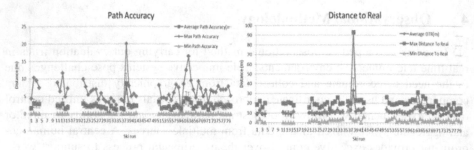

Fig. 3. Average distance of real-world skier to virtual avatar

An example of spatial-temporal QoS data, from the skiing scenario, can be seen in Fig. 3. We show two sets of measures that relate the actual position of real-world skier and that of his avatar rendered to indoor users on the virtual slope. The path taken by the avatar representing the outdoor user is estimated using remote GPS data combined with a skiing motion simulation within the 3D-LIVE system. In the 'pathaccuracy' series we see the average deviation of the avatar's path from the actual position of the outdoor for each run. This data indicates that the path of is replicated virtually on average is 2.5m. We visualize the spatial consistency using a path repre-

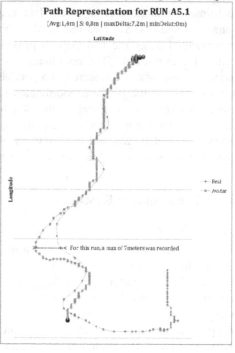

sentation shown below. A temporal analysis of the path data, shown in the 'distance to real' (DTR) series shows the distance between the outdoor ski-er's last known position on the real-world slope and the estimated position of his avatar. Here a wider discrepancy is evident (10m) suggesting that update latency is impacting spatial accuracy over time; an average calculation of skiing speed at 10m/s suggests a delay of around one second.

In addition to collecting metrics reflecting technical performance, quali-tative feedback was gathered from participants during trials. Here users were quick to identify issues that af-fected their overall UX; these included inaccuracies in movement reconstruc-tion and update latencies (i.e. delays in voice communication). Interestingly, in both the skiing and jogging scenarios, the mapping between the physical movement of indoor users and their perceptions of their corresponding avatar behaviour was considered as unsatisfactory. In technically replicating the physical behaviour of users, a 1-to-1 mapping is applied as closely as possible in the virtual world - these avatar motions are displayed in the third person.

However, in some cases the apparent changes to avatar motion (viewed at a third person distance) did not result in the 'expected' progress through the game (avatars were considered to be moving too slowly). This was mainly observed in the ski scenario, where the users were looking for a stronger link between their body pose on the simulator or the Wii balance board and the speed of their avatars. Overall the evaluations of the prototypes were enthusiastically received by users both formatively during co-creation and during summative trials. Early evaluation of the use of the technology was productive in that it revealed real-world performance and technical issues to be addressed as well as new ideas for future interaction design.

6   Conclusion

Our approach to design and evaluate complex tele-immersive systems combines user-centric co-creation and a distributed observation methodology. Using constructs from the IUX model, qualitative user input can be captured and used to drive design and implementation allowing for refinement of understanding of technical requirements and how UX can be enhanced. Qualitative and quantitative observations captured during trials have served to identify the aspects of actual UX that were considered important and a means by which system performance (QoS) can be understood and improved. Lessons learnt include an updated experiential model; changes and improvements to the 3D-LIVE interaction design; and better QoS and QoE metrics including a structured QoE questionnaire to provide formal validation of the experiential model. The lessons will be factored into our second phase of experimentation.

Acknowledgements. The authors would like to thank the staff of Schladming 2030 GmbH (Austria) and Laval Golf, La Mayenne (France) for supporting our experimental work.

References

1. 3D Live Project. http://3dliveproject.eu/wp/
2. Yang, Z., Wu, W., Nahrstedt, K., Kurillo, G., Bajcsy, R.: Enabling multiparty 3D tele-immersive environments with ViewCast. ACM Transactions on Multimedia Computing, Communications, and Applications 6(4), article 29 (2010)
3. Nakevska, M., Vos, C., Juarez, A., Hu, J., Langereis, G., Rauterberg, M.: Using Game Engines in Mixed Reality Installations. In: Anacleto, J.C., Fels, S., Graham, N., Kapralos, B., Saif El-Nasr, M., Stanley, K. (eds.) ICEC 2011. LNCS, vol. 6972, pp. 456–459. Springer, Heidelberg (2011)
4. Normand, J.M., Spanlang, B., Tecchia, F., Carrozzino, M., Swapp, D., Slater, M.: Full body acting rehearsal in a networked virtual environment - a case study. Presence: Teleoper. Virtual Environ **21**(2), 229–243 (2012)
5. Gervautz, M., Schmalstieg, D.: Anywhere Interfaces Using Handheld Augmented Reality. Computer **45**(7), 26–31 (2012)

6. Dickey, C.G.: Blending games, multimedia and reality. In: Proceedings of the First Annual ACM SIGMM Conference on Multimedia Systems (MMSys 2010), pp. 209–214. ACM, New York (2010). doi:10.1145/1730836.1730862, http://doi.acm.org/10.1145/1730836. 1730862

7. Oshima, T., Sato, K., Yamamoto, H., Tamura, H.: AR2 Hockey: A case study of Collaborative Augmented Reality. In: Proceedings of the Virtual Reality Annual International Symposium. IEEE (1998)

8. Vaïkkynen, P., et al.: Using exercise cycle as a haptic input device in a virtual environment. In: EGVE 2001 Proceedings of the 7th Eurographics Conference on Virtual Environments & 5th Immersive Projection Technology, pp. 229–235 (2001)

9. Mueller, F.F., Agamanolis, S.: Sports over a distance. Computers in Entertainment 3(3), 4 (2005)

10. Göbel, S., Geiger, C., Heinze, C., Marinos, D.: Creating a virtual archery experience. In: Proc. of The International Conference on Advanced Visual Interfaces (AVI 2010), Rome, Italy (2010)

11. Pallot, M., Eynard, R., Poussard, B., Christmann, O., Richir, S.: Augmented sport: exploring collective user experience. In: Proceedings of the Virtual Reality International Conference: Laval Virtual (VRIC 2013), Article 4, 8p. ACM, New York, (2013). doi:10.1145/2466816.2466821 http://doi.acm.org/10.1145/2466816.2466821

12. Pallot, M., Trousse, B., Senach, B., Scapin, D.: Living Lab Research Landscape: From User Centred Design and User Experience towards User Cocreation. In: Proceedings of the Living Lab Summer School, Paris, Cité des Sciences (August 2010)

13. Kim, S.J.J.: A User Study Trends in Augmented Reality and Virtual Reality Research: A Qualitative Study with the Past Three Years of the ISMAR and IEEE VR Conference Papers. In: 2012 International Symposium on Ubiquitous Virtual Reality (ISUVR), pp. 1–5 (2012)

14. Gabbard, J.L., Swan, E.: Usability Engineering for Augmented Reality: Employing User-Based Studies to Inform Design. IEEE Transactions on Visualization and Computer Graphics 14(3) (May/June 2008)

15. Rosson, M.B., Carroll, J.M.: Scenario-based design. In: Jacko, J.A., Sears, A. (eds.) The human-computer interaction handbook, pp. 1032–1050. L. Erlbaum Associates Inc., Hillsdale (2002)

16. Wu, W., Arefin, A., Rivas, R., Nahrstedt, K., Sheppard, R., Yang, Z.: Quality of experience in distributed interactive multimedia environments: toward a theoretical framework. In: Proceedings of the 17th ACM International Conference on Multimedia (MM 2009), pp. 481–490. ACM, New York (2009) doi:10.1145/1631272.1631338 http://doi.acm.org/10. 1145/1631272.1631338

17. Doumanoglou, A., Alexiadis, D., Zarpalas, D., Daras, P.: CERTH/ITI Towards Real-Time and Efficient Compression of Human Time-Varying-Meshes. IEEE Transactions on Circuits and Systems for Video Technology and 105th MPEG meeting,Vienna (July-August 2013)

18. Epstein, S.: Cognitive-Experiential Self-Theory of Personality. In: Millon, T., Lerner, M.J. (eds.), Comprehensive Handbook of Psychology, Personality and Social Psychology 5, pp. 159–184. Wiley & Sons, Hoboken

19. Boniface, M., Osborne, D.S., Voulodimos, T., Murg, S.: Technology Enablers for a Future Media Internet Testing Facility, NEM Summit (2013)

20. Poussard, B., Richir, S., Vatjus-Anttila, J., Asteriadis, S., Zarpalas, D., Daras, P.: 3DLIVE: A Multi-Modal Sensing Platform Allowing Tele-Immersive Sports Applications. In: 22nd European Signal Processing Conference (EUSIPCO 2014), pp. 2–5. Lisbon, Portugal (September 2014)

Hand Orientation Regression Using Random Forest for Augmented Reality

Muhammad Asad$^{(\boxtimes)}$ and Greg Slabaugh

City University London, London EC1V 0HB, UK
{Muhammad.Asad.2,Gregory.Slabaugh.1}@city.ac.u

Abstract. We present a regression method for the estimation of hand orientation using an uncalibrated camera. For training the system, we use a depth camera to capture a large dataset of hand color images and orientation angles. Each color image is segmented producing a silhouette image from which contour distance features are extracted. The orientation angles are captured by robustly fitting a plane to the depth image of the hand, providing a surface normal encoding the hand orientation in 3D space. We then train multiple Random Forest regressors to learn the non-linear mapping from the space of silhouette images to orientation angles. For online testing of the system, we only require a standard 2D image to infer the 3D hand orientation. Experimental results show the approach is computationally efficient, does not require any camera calibration, and is robust to inter-person shape variation.

Keywords: Orientation estimation · Random forest regression · Silhouette image · Hand

1 Introduction

Technological advancements over the recent years have made computing devices powerful, portable and inexpensive. This has given the possibility to rethink how devices are designed to work with us. One of the major hurdles faced by existing technology is the requirement for humans to adapt and learn to use it. This is particularly true for the existing tangible human-computer interaction interfaces, such as keyboard and mouse, which have not seen significant change since their first introduction. Researchers and manufacturers are trying to think of ways technology can adapt to our lifestyle so it does not get in the way but works with us [1].

Recent years have seen increased interest in wearable devices that utilize an egocentric approach for acquiring interaction input from multi-modal sensors and performing everyday computing tasks. These include devices like augmented reality glasses, where a combination of an augmented display and a number of tangible and voice activated interfaces are used for interaction [2]. Such devices lack a novel interaction method which is both computationally efficient and robust. There is a need for an interaction method which can intuitively utilize the egocentric perspective to realize a natural interaction experience.

© Springer International Publishing Switzerland 2014
L.T. De Paolis and A. Mongelli (Eds.): AVR 2014, LNCS 8853, pp. 159–174, 2014.
DOI: 10.1007/978-3-319-13969-2_13

The human hand is already an effective interaction tool, as a number of hand gestures and postures are used for both communication and manipulation tasks [3]. Most of the previous research on hand-based interaction focussed on recognition of hand gestures and 3D hand pose [3] [4] [5] [6]. Some methods extract the orientation of hand for augmented reality [7] [8] [9] [10]. Our work is closely related to [7], which uses a calibrated camera and recovers a single person's hand geometry in addition to the camera pose. However our approach differs in that it does not require camera calibration, rendering it suitable for a much wider array of applications. In addition, by training the system on data from multiple people, it naturally handles person-to-person hand variations. Our method does not recover the camera pose, instead we focus on acquiring the orientation of the hand itself, which can be used to render an augmented object.

Our method utilizes silhouette images to extract relevant features for regression. Silhouette images have been previously used to extract features for regressing 3D human pose [11] [12]. Multi-view silhouette images have also been used for 3D modelling [13]. Albert *et al.* [14] used multi-view silhouette images to estimate hand pose. Our approach differs from these methods as in our case, we only regress the 3D orientation using hand silhouette images.

We propose a method to regress hand orientation from a dataset of hand images. This method first extracts contour distance features from the hand silhouette images and then uses these features along with the ground truth (GT) orientation angles to train a set of Random Forest regressors. The hand orientation dataset is captured using a commodity depth sensor, where for each hand orientation we have a pair of color image and GT orientation angles. These angles are generated by fitting a plane on the depth image. The dimensionality of contour distance features is then reduced using Principal Component Analysis (PCA). Offline training of a set of Random Forest regressors is performed using the dimensionally reduced features and GT orientation angles. Online testing involves using only dimensionally reduced contour distance features from silhouette images (as shown in Fig. 1) to predict orientation angles. The proposed method is evaluated using single fold and leave-one-out cross-validation.

The rest of the paper is organised in subsequent sections. Section 2 provides the details of the proposed method, while section 3 details the experimental evaluation. Discussion of the evaluation results is presented in section 4. An augmented reality based application of the proposed method is illustrated in section 5. The paper concludes with section 6.

1.1   Our Contribution

A considerable amount of existing research has focused on gesture and pose estimation of human body and hand [3]. However there has been significantly less work done to extract the 3D orientation of a hand from a 2D image [7]. To the best of our knowledge our proposed method is the first to recover hand orientation using silhouette images only. Moreover our proposed method does not require camera calibration and is capable of generalizing variations in hand shape, size and orientation.

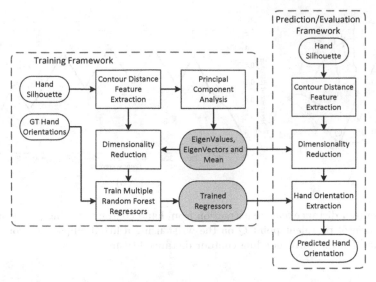

Fig. 1. Flowchart for training and evaluation of the proposed hand orientation method

We also contribute a method for extracting GT hand orientation angles from a depth image. We note this GT orientation is only used for training of the regression model.

2   Method

Given a set of color images and GT orientation angles of hands, we are interested in finding the mapping between segmented silhouette images and the corresponding orientation angles. The framework is designed to work with uncalibrated cameras and across a range of different shapes, size and style variations of hand.

The flowchart in Fig. 1 presents the different steps in our proposed method. The framework consists of two stages, namely, training and prediction stage. Training is done offline while prediction is done online. Both training and predication require contour distance features to be extracted from hand silhouettes. For the training stage, Principal Component Analysis (PCA) of the training dataset is computed and the corresponding mean, eigenvalues and eigenvectors are used to reduce the dimensionality of the contour distance features in both training and prediction stages. Next, a set of Random Forest regressors are trained using the dimensionally reduced features and GT orientation angles [15]. For the prediction stage these regressors are used to infer the orientation using silhouette images only. The proposed approach is presented in further detail in the subsequent sections below.

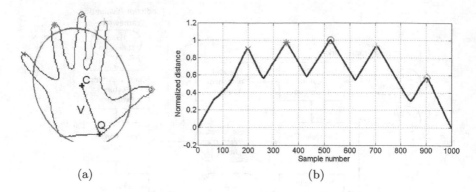

(a)   (b)

Fig. 2. Contour distance feature extraction from hand contour showing (a) the method for extraction of prevalent point Q on the wrist using a fitted ellipse, centroid C and a ray V and (b) the corresponding contour distance features

2.1   Feature Extraction

Our method utilizes the contour distance features which are extracted from hand silhouette images. Contour distance features have been previously used for hand shape based gesture recognition [16]. While the main aim of our proposed method is not gesture recognition, contour distance features provide sufficient hand shape variations that can directly correspond to changes in orientation of the hand. Additionally we also employ a method for aligning and normalizing these features. Details on these feature extraction techniques are depicted in the following subsections.

Contour Distance Features. Let $\mathbf{S}_n = \{S_k\}_{k=1}^{K}$ be a set of hand silhouette images for the nth person. We propose a method to compute a corresponding distance feature set $\mathbf{D}_n = \{\bar{D}_k\}_{k=1}^{K}$.

The contour extracted from each silhouette image consists of points $P_k = \{P_{ki}\}_{i=1}^{I}$. The Euclidean distance of each of these contour points $P_{ki} = \{P_{ki}^x, P_{ki}^y\}$ to a prevalent point on the wrist $Q = \{Q^x, Q^y\}$ is determined as:

$$D_{ki} = \sqrt{(Q^x - P_{ki}^x)^2 + (Q^y - P_{ki}^y)^2},\qquad(1)$$

where $D_k = \{D_{ki}\}_{i=1}^{I}$ is the contour distance feature vector for a set of contour points P_i. This method is illustrated in Fig. 2. The extracted features have different number of samples and magnitude depending on the scale changes and inter-person hand shape variations. To deal with this we normalize a given feature vector as:

$$\bar{D}_k = \frac{D_k}{\sum_{i=1}^{I} D_{ki}}.\qquad(2)$$

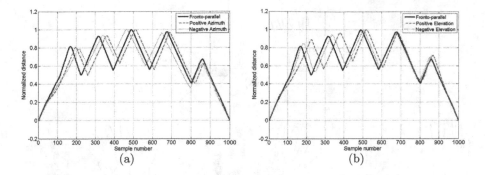

Fig. 3. Variation in the contour distance features with varying orientation in (a) Azimuth (ϕ) axis and (b) Elevation (ψ) axis only

All extracted feature vectors are resampled to a specified number of samples ρ, in order to use PCA and train Random Forest regressors. For our experimental evaluation we empirically choose $\rho = 1000$.

Extraction of a Prevalent Point on the Wrist. To align the values in the distance feature vectors, we propose a method to extract a prevalent point on the wrist. Given an orientation θ between x-axis and the major axis of an ellipse that fits the hand contour and centroid C, an equation of a ray emanating from C can be defined by:

$$V = \xi\lambda\hat{v} + C, \tag{3}$$

where $\hat{v}$ is the unit vector encoding the direction,

$$\hat{v} = \frac{\begin{bmatrix} 1 \\ \tan\theta \end{bmatrix}}{\sqrt{1^2 + \tan^2\theta}}, \tag{4}$$

ξ is a scalar for correcting the direction of $\hat{v}$,

$$\xi = \begin{cases} +1 & \text{if } \theta < 90° \\ -1 & \text{if } \theta \geq 90°, \end{cases} \tag{5}$$

and λ is a parameter that changes the length of the ray. The direction scalar ξ is calculated using Eq. 5 based on the assumption that the in-plane orientation θ of hand will always be within a predefined range of an upright hand pose with $\theta = 90°$. We define this range to be $0° < \theta < 180°$. This corrects the direction of the ray V so that it is always propagating towards the wrist.

The proposed method increases λ until the ray intersects with the contour at a point $Q \in P_{ki}$ on the wrist. This point is then used as a starting point for distance feature calculation. θ represents the in-plane rotation of the hand, and is used along with the other predicted angles to define a complete hand orientation.

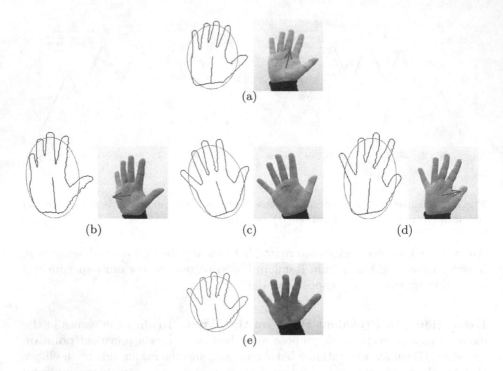

Fig. 4. Variation in the contour corresponding to contour distance features in Fig. 3 along with the normal vector encoding the GT Azimuth (ϕ_g) and Elevation (ψ_g) orientation angles. From Fig. 3 each plot corresponds to the contours in the following manner: (a) Negative Elevation: $\phi_g = +12.60°$ and $\psi_g = -38.96°$, (b) Negative Azimuth: $\phi_g = -36.67°$ and $\psi_g = +8.59°$, (c) Fronto-parallel: $\phi_g = +2.29°$ and $\psi_g = -0.57°$, (d) Positive Azimuth: $\phi_g = +47.56°$ and $\psi_g = +2.29°$ and (e) Positive Elevation: $\phi_g = +10.31°$ and $\psi_g = +41.83°$.

We note that changes in the hand orientation can directly induce variation in the contour distance feature. Fig. 3 shows these variations in contour distance feature corresponding to different orientations of hand. To visualize these variations effectively, we only show the contour distance feature for orientations near the ends of our defined orientation space. These orientations are called positive elevation, negative elevation, positive azimuth and negative azimuth. The corresponding hand contour and images, depicting the direct hand shape changes for each angle combination are shown in Fig. 4.

2.2   Dimensionality Reduction

The contour distance features extracted from the hand silhouettes have a large number of dimensions. To extract the prominent variations in the dataset, we use PCA for projecting the feature vectors onto a reduced feature space.

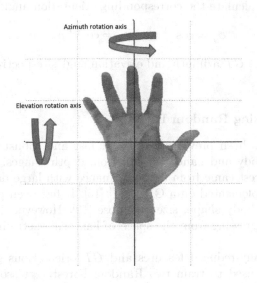

Fig. 5. Rotations axis about which Azimuth (ϕ) and Elevation (ψ) angles vary in the dataset. Image rendered using libhand [18].

We first extract the eigenvectors and eigenvalues of the corresponding feature vectors in the training data. The dimensions of these feature vectors are then reduced by selecting a set of eigenvectors E, that result in 90% energy for corresponding eigenvalues, and projecting the feature vectors onto a reduced space defined by:

$$\check{\mathbf{D}}_n = E^T \left(\mathbf{D}_n - \mu \right), \tag{6}$$

where μ is the mean of all the samples and $\check{\mathbf{D}}_n$ is a set of dimensionally reduced feature vectors [17].

2.3   Ground Truth (GT) Data Generation Using Depth Maps

The dataset contains color images and GT orientation angles. These GT orientation angles are only used during training phase and are extracted from aligned depth images by fitting an equation of a plane. For our dataset collection we use an outstretched hand pose which is roughly planar.

We use RANSAC to fit an equation of a plane defined by:

$$n_0 = x n_x + y n_y + z n_z, \tag{7}$$

where the individual coefficients form a normal vector N such that:

$$N = [n_x, n_y, n_z]^T . \tag{8}$$

This N is used to calculate the corresponding orientation angles:

$$\phi_g = \cos^{-1} n_x, \quad \psi_g = \cos^{-1} n_y, \tag{9}$$

where ϕ_g and ψ_g are GT azimuth and elevation angles respectively, as shown in Fig. 4 and Fig. 5.

2.4   Training Using Random Forest

Random Forest has been previously used for fast and robust pose estimation for both the full-body and hand [19] [20] from depth images. The motivation to use Random Forest came from its performance with large datasets and that it can be easily implemented on a GPU [21] [15]. It has been proven to handle large variations in body shape, size and pose [19]. However, in this paper we are interested in regressing from the space of hand silhouette images to that of orientation angles.

The dimensionally-reduced features and GT orientations extracted in the previous steps are used to train two Random Forest regressors, one for each orientation angle. In our experimental evaluation we use Random Forest with 1000 trees and 2 features are sampled for splitting at each node.

We generate a dataset which contains 1624 color images and GT orientation from a total of 13 participants. The choice of hand orientation variations used to record the dataset holds significance in depicting the contribution of the proposed method. To generate this dataset we asked our participants to use an outstretched open hand pose throughout the data capture process. They were asked to rotate the hand back and forth, first along the azimuthal axis and then along the elevational axis only (as shown in Fig. 5). Color images and GT hand orientations were recorded while the participants performed these manipulations. As a result of different participants, the dataset contains significant variations in hand size, shape and style of rotations. This current dataset only contains data from participants' right hand, however taking the advantage of mirror symmetry the same dataset can be reflected to generate images for left hand.

The GT orientation angles are only used for the training step and are not part of the final prediction method, where only hand silhouettes from color images are used. In the dataset both ϕ_g and ψ_g are limited from $-45°$ to $+45°$.

3   Experimental Evaluation

Evaluation of the proposed approach is done using two different methods. A single fold evaluation is done using 70% of the data for training while holding out 30% data for independent testing. Next, we perform a leave-one-out cross-validation, where in each trial we left one participant's data out for training the system, and tested the resulting system on the left out participant. This latter technique demonstrates how the system performs on unseen individuals. For comparison all experiments are also repeated using Neural Network regressor

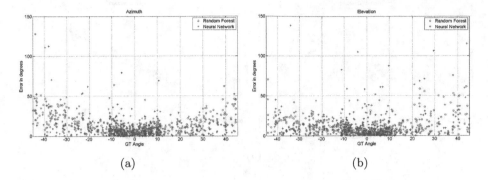

Fig. 6. Absolute prediction error (in degrees) illustrating error (a) ϕ_e and (b) ψ_e in single fold validation using Random Forest and Neural Network regression techniques

Table 1. Average error in degrees for experimental evaluation in section 3

Evaluation method	Regressor Used	Azimuth (ϕ_a)	Elevation (ψ_a)
Single Fold	Random Forest	11.44°	9.57°
	Neural Network	15.31°	14.19°
Leave-one-out	Random Forest	12.93°	12.61°
	Neural Network	20.14°	18.85°

with 1 hidden state containing 1000 neurons. In our experiments, we varied the number of trees in Random Forest and neurons in Neural Network regressors. However changing these parameters did not significantly affect the output of our method. Therefore we empirically fixed the number of trees and neurons to be 1000 for all the experiments. The results are presented below which are then compared and discussed in Section 4.

3.1 Single Fold Validation

To evaluate the overall performance of the proposed method, we randomly divide the dataset into training and testing sets. The system is then trained and evaluated using the corresponding sets of data.

The absolute predicted errors for this validation are presented against GT orientation angles in Fig. 6. We also present plots of GT orientation angles against corresponding predicted angles in Fig. 7. For comparison, both these figures include results from Random Forest and Neural Network. Average error for orientation angles ϕ_a and ψ_a are presented in Table 1.

3.2 Leave-One-Out Cross-Validation

We further evaluate our method against a scenario where in each trial, we leave one participant's data out from the training dataset. This left out data is then

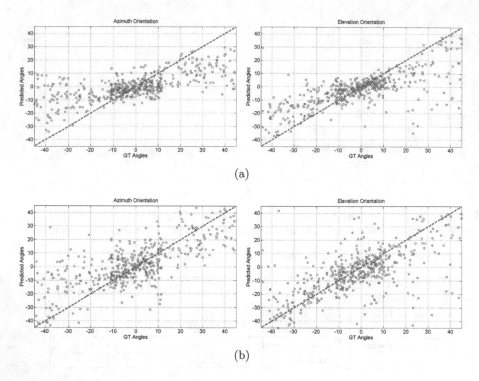

(a)

(b)

Fig. 7. *GT* vs Predicted Angle plots showing the accuracy of different regressors for predicted angles ϕ_p and ψ_p in single fold validation. The predicted angles are illustrated using (a) Random Forest regressors with number of trees = 1000 and (b) Neural Network regressor with 1 hidden state containing 1000 neurons.

used for testing. This is a scenario where an unseen hand is used with our method. It is also able to evaluate the ability of the method to handle variations in hand shape, size and orientation without the need for an additional calibration step. The average prediction error for each participant using Random Forest and Neural Network are presented in Fig. 8 (a) and (b) respectively, while Table 1 shows the results for average prediction error for all participants' cross-validation.

4   Discussion

Experimental results show that the proposed method is able to learn the mapping of 2D silhouettes to orientation angles. The method performs well when using Random Forest in both single fold and leave-one-out cross-validation. The average prediction error for single fold evaluation using Random Forest is close to 10° for both ϕ and ψ angles (as shown in Table 1). The average execution time of the proposed method for the given set of input silhouette images is found to be 16.93 ms per frame in Matlab implementation on 3.2 GHz Core-i5 CPU.

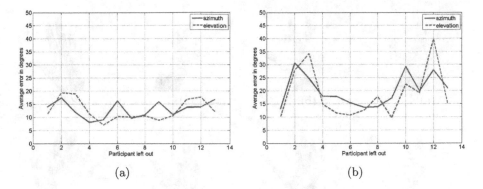

(a)   (b)

Fig. 8. Absolute prediction error in degrees for leave-one-out cross-validation of each participants' data using (a) Random Forest and (b) Neural Network regression techniques

Fig. 6 shows the absolute prediction errors against GT orientation angles for both Random Forest and Neural Network regressors. It can be seen from this figure that Random Forest is able to model the underlying data well, with significantly less number of outliers as compared to Neural Network. Looking at the range $-10°$ to $+10°$ Random Forest is able to predict with exceptional accuracy, while Neural Network regressor has significant number of outliers falling within the same range.

In Fig. 7 we establish the relationship between GT and predicted orientation angles to illustrate the performance of different regressors in single fold validation. The diagonal line represents the region with optimum results, where we have correct predictions. The closer the predicted data is packed around this diagonal, the better the performance of the regressor is. It can be seen from this figure that for both ϕ and ψ, Random Forest is able to perform better with fewer outliers.

Leave-one-out cross-validation results show that the method is able to produce compelling results for the prediction of orientation for unseen hands. This evaluation method illustrates how well the system can perform with a training data containing different variations in hand shape, size and style. Comparing the average prediction errors for leave-one-out cross-validation with single fold validation in Table 1, there is a significant decrease in the performance of the Neural Network regressors. This highlights the inability of the Neural Network to model the variations in the dataset. Fig. 8 further validates these cross-validation results for each individual participant. In this validation Random Forest produces relatively lesser errors, which indicates its ability to generalize the inter-person variations.

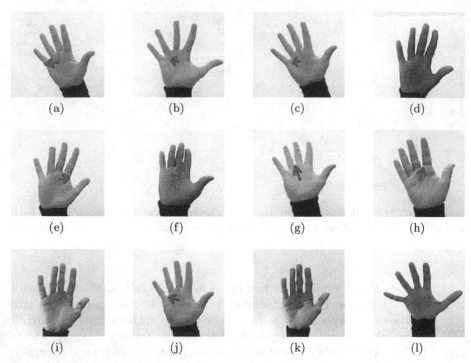

Fig. 9. Success cases for our proposed method. The GT normal vectors are superimposed on each image to depict the orientation. Error for each case is presented separately in Table 2

Table 2. Absolute prediction error in degrees for success cases shown in Fig. 9

Fig. 9	Abolute Error ϕ_e	Abolute Error ψ_e	Fig. 9	Abolute Error ϕ_e	Abolute Error ψ_e
(a)	0.89°	3.61°	(g)	5.17°	1.35°
(b)	4.33°	0.39°	(h)	9.08°	0.04°
(c)	1.18°	0.52°	(i)	7.83°	1.31°
(d)	0.81°	8.69°	(j)	7.12°	0.20°
(e)	1.17°	0.34°	(k)	1.07°	0.86°
(f)	3.18°	0.88°	(l)	7.18°	1.22°

As shown above our method performs well to recover 3D hand orientation despite of a number of underlying variations in hand shape, size and style. In Fig. 9 we present different success cases using Random Forest in single fold validation. Table 2 shows the absolute error for each of these success cases. The variations in the dataset and the capability of our method is clear from these results.

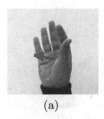 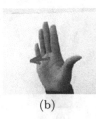 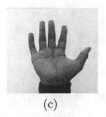 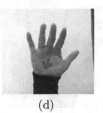

(a)   (b)   (c)   (d)

Fig. 10. Failure cases for our proposed method. The GT normal vectors are super-imposed on each image to depict the orientation. Error for each case is presented separately in Table 3.

Table 3. Absolute prediction error in degrees for failure cases shown in Fig. 10

Fig. 10	Predicted		Ground Truth		Abolute Error	
	ϕ_p	ψ_p	ϕ_g	ψ_g	ϕ_e	ψ_e
(a)	2.96°	−7.90°	−43.46°	−7.26°	46.42°	0.64°
(b)	−0.54°	2.29°	−43.29°	5.85°	42.75°	3.56°
(c)	−3.86°	−11.16°	−1.15°	−41.17°	2.71°	30.01°
(d)	−4.88°	−17.85°	−7.00°	20.97°	2.12°	38.82°

While our method works well for most of the cases, it does produce errors. Fig. 10 shows some of the cases where our method fails, while Table 3 presents the corresponding error. These failure cases can easily be identified as outliers in the dataset as they do not have outstretched hand pose. In Fig. 10 (a), (c) and (d) the hand does not follow the planar surface assumption which directly affects the calculation of GT orientation angles, whereas in Fig. 10 (b) the fingers are placed too close together making it impossible to extract a contour distance feature that corresponds to the ones in the training dataset. Furthermore by analysing the absolute prediction errors for each failure case in Table 3 it can be seen that our method only fails for the orientation where these assumptions fail. Since our method is regressing both orientation angles independently therefore, even in these failure cases, the unaffected angle is predicted with good accuracy.

5   Application to Augmented Reality

The proposed method can be applied to a number of different application scenarios. In our work, we present an augmented reality based application for visual inspection of virtual objects (shown in Fig. 11). In this application the digital content is overlaid on an augmented layer. Orientation changes from the hand movements are captured using our method and the corresponding orientation transformations are applied to the augmented object.

This kind of visual inspection of virtual objects is useful in scenarios where user does not have access to the actual object, however they want to view it from different perspectives. When applied to an online shopping scenario, a person can effectively view the object they are going to buy. Using this application they will

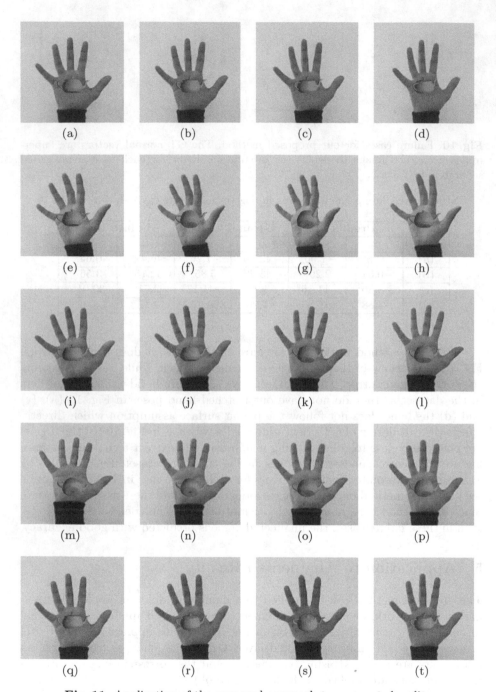

Fig. 11. Application of the proposed approach to augmented reality

be able to inspect it from different angles in 3D, so as to get the real impression of how the object looks like.

6 Conclusion

A hand orientation regression approach was proposed. This method used a dataset of hand silhouettes only to predict the orientation of the hand in azimuthal and elevational axes. Contour distance features were extracted from hand silhouettes and used along with the GT orientation from depth images to train two Random Forest regressors, one for each angle. The online testing of the system required only a standard 2D image to infer the 3D hand orientation. Comparison of Random Forest with Neural Network based regression shows that the Random Forest is better suited for generalizing the variations in the dataset The system performs well with an average error of 10° with single fold evaluation and 12° for leave-one-out cross-validation. The proposed method has an average execution time of 16.93 ms per frame in a matlab implementation.

Our future aim is to extend this approach with hand in a number of different poses across different orientations. While contour distance features are able to encode variation related to orientation changes, we endeavour to explore other features as well which might further improve the overall performance of the proposed method. A major challenge for this will be to extract GT orientation. Our existing GT orientation data generation approach can be extended for such scenarios by introducing a palm extraction method. This way, assuming that the palm is rigid, we can again extract the GT orientation of hand. We also envision to use temporal correlation methods such as Kalman filtering to further increase the performance of the proposed method.

References

1. Allison, S.: Wearable tech - the future, or just a fad? (February 2014) (Online; posted February 13, 2014)
2. Olsson, M.I., Martin, M.W., Hebenstreit, J.J., Cazalet, P.M.: Wearable device with input and output structures. US Patent App. 14/037, 788 (2013)
3. Erol, A., Bebis, G., Nicolescu, M., Boyle, R.D., Twombly, X.: Vision-based hand pose estimation: A review. Computer Vision and Image Understanding 108(1), 52–73 (2007)
4. Wu, Y., Huang, T.S.: Capturing articulated human hand motion: A divide-and-conquer approach. In: The Proceedings of the Seventh IEEE International Conference on Computer Vision (ICCV), vol. 1, pp. 606–611. IEEE (1999)
5. Rosales, R., Athitsos, V., Sigal, L., Sclaroff, S.: 3d hand pose reconstruction using specialized mappings. In: Proceedings of Eighth IEEE International Conference on Computer Vision (ICCV), vol. 1, pp. 378–385. IEEE (2001)
6. de La Gorce, M., Fleet, D.J., Paragios, N.: Model-based 3d hand pose estimation from monocular video. IEEE Transactions on Pattern Analysis and Machine Intelligence 33(9), 1793–1805 (2011)

7. Lee, T., Hollerer, T.: Handy ar: Markerless inspection of augmented reality objects using fingertip tracking. In: 11th IEEE International Symposium on Wearable Computers, pp. 83–90. IEEE (2007)
8. Lee, T., Hollerer, T.: Hybrid feature tracking and user interaction for markerless augmented reality. In: IEEE Virtual Reality Conference (VR 2008), pp. 145–152. IEEE (2008)
9. Lee, T., Hollerer, T.: Multithreaded hybrid feature tracking for markerless augmented reality. IEEE Transactions on Visualization and Computer Graphics 15(3), 355–368 (2009)
10. Kato, H., Kato, T.: A marker-less augmented reality based on fast fingertip detection for smart phones. In: IEEE International Conference on Consumer Electronics (ICCE), pp. 127–128. IEEE (2011)
11. Agarwal, A., Triggs, B.: Recovering 3d human pose from monocular images. IEEE Transactions on Pattern Analysis and Machine Intelligence 28(1), 44–58 (2006)
12. Elgammal, A., Lee, C.-S.: Inferring 3d body pose from silhouettes using activity manifold learning. In: Proceedings of the 2004 IEEE Computer Society Conference on Computer Vision and Pattern Recognition (CVPR), vol. 2, pp. II-681. IEEE (2004)
13. Franco, J.-S., Boyer, E.: Fusion of multiview silhouette cues using a space occupancy grid. In: Tenth IEEE International Conference on Computer Vision (ICCV), vol. 2, pp. 1747–1753. IEEE (2005)
14. Causo, A., Ueda, E., Kurita, Y., Matsumoto, Y., Ogasawara, T.: Model-based hand pose estimation using multiple viewpoint silhouette images and unscented kalman filter. In: The 17th IEEE International Symposium on Robot and Human Interactive Communication, RO-MAN, pp. 291–296. IEEE (2008)
15. Breiman, L.: Random forests. Machine Learning 45(1), 5–32 (2001)
16. Yoruk, E., Konukoglu, E., Sankur, B., Darbon, J.: Shape-based hand recognition. IEEE Transactions on Image Processing 15(7), 1803–1815 (2006)
17. Leventon, M.E., Grimson, W.E.L., Faugeras, O.: Statistical shape influence in geodesic active contours. In: Proceedings of IEEE Conference on Computer Vision and Pattern Recognition (CVPR), vol. 1, pp. 316–323. IEEE (2000)
18. Šarić, M.: Libhand: A library for hand articulation, Version 0.9 (2011)
19. Shotton, J., Girshick, R., Fitzgibbon, A., Sharp, T., Cook, M., Finocchio, M., Moore, R., Kohli, P., Criminisi, A., Kipman, A., et al.: Efficient human pose estimation from single depth images. IEEE Transactions on Pattern Analysis and Machine Intelligence 35(12), 2821–2840 (2013)
20. Keskin, C., Kıraç, F., Kara, Y.E., Akarun, L.: Real time hand pose estimation using depth sensors. In: Consumer Depth Cameras for Computer Vision, pp. 119–137. Springer (2013)
21. Sharp, T.: Implementing decision trees and forests on a gpu. In: Forsyth, D., Torr, P., Zisserman, A. (eds.) ECCV 2008, Part IV. LNCS, vol. 5305, pp. 595–608. Springer, Heidelberg (2008)

Visualization of Power Systems Based on Panoramic Augmented Environments

Paulo Roberto Jansen dos Reis[1]([✉]), Daniel Lima Gomes Junior[1],
Antônio Sérgio de Araújo[2], Geraldo Braz Júnior[1], Aristófanes Correa Silva[1],
and Anselmo Cardoso de Paiva[1]

[1] Applied Computing Group (NCA), Federal University of Maranhão (UFMA),
Av. dos Portugueses, SN – Campus do Bacanga, São Luís, MA, Brazil
{jansen,daniellima,geraldo,ari,anselmo.paiva}@nca.ufma.br
http://nca.ufma.br
[2] São Francisco's Hydroelectric Company (CHESF), Rua Delmiro Gouveia,
333 – San Martin, Recife, PE, Brazil
asergio@chesf.gov.br
http://www.chesf.gov.br

Abstract. Interactive and contextualized applications have been aimed to support professionals in the field of engineering in order to deal with the difficult of understanding technical diagrams related to power systems when there is a vast amount of information represented on them. Augmented Reality (AR) and Static Panoramic Augmented Environments have been considered promising approaches to build solutions in this field. This paper presents an application that uses Panoramic Augmented Environments to extends the way information is shown to power systems operators supporting data interpretation, monitoring and manipulation. This application is connected with a real power system database and uses images from substations of CHESF, a Brazilian power systems company.

Keywords: Panoramic Augmented Environment · Power Systems · Augmented Reality

1 Introduction

In power systems management, substation operators are required to monitor a vast amount of information and to respond fast to system changes. An effective visualization of these data are very important to help them to get an overall perspective of the system state without bloating the interface [18].

Single-line diagrams (SLD's) are widely used to represent the electrical scheme, because they can provide a holistic view of the system. These diagrams consist of a 2D drawing that shows equipments and it's connections using a variety of symbols. SLD's by themselves, cannot provide to professionals real world context and as the complexity of the system increase, the quantity of information rises up, overwhelming operators and becoming more complex to analyze and interact to solve problems [8].

© Springer International Publishing Switzerland 2014
L.T. De Paolis and A. Mongelli (Eds.): AVR 2014, LNCS 8853, pp. 175–184, 2014.
DOI: 10.1007/978-3-319-13969-2_14

Augmented Reality (AR) is a technology that consists in adding virtual elements to the real world, overlapping objects in real time and enriching perception and interaction with the real world [9]. In industrial fields, this technique can help in operators training besides maintenance and repair of equipments [1][12].

Applications using Augmented Reality to support data visualization in Architecture, Engineering and Construction (AEC) fields are on the rise [16]. One of the reasons for this is that AR annotations are one of the most efficient and intuitive ways to provide information contextualized with the real world environment, considering that the data contained in these annotations appears on the same place of the object related to it [17]. However applications used in engineering areas require high precision and real time processing, and these features are arduous to achieve using AR due to the complexity of detection and tracking of equipments [3].

One of the ways to avoid detection and tracking of these elements is to insert artificial markers on them, which are polygon images usually detected using corner detection algorithms and that are substantially easier to detect [10]. Although, in some fields of power systems, such as a substation, the use of these markers are not viable, because most of these equipments cannot be turned off and is not safe to be next of them during their operation. As a result, applications in this area need to use only natural markers. In other words, they should process the image to detect the equipment itself using only the image features [7].

Another factor that makes AR hard to apply in a context of power systems is that since professionals cannot be in the area of equipments in use, the only way to visualize then in real time is to install cameras in a environment that should be augmented. This approach can be very expensive in consequence of a large area of these installations.

Static Panoramic Augmented Environments are environments where images are used as a background to virtual elements. In this approach images can be processed offline, allowing the use of more accurate methods of pattern recognition than those used in real time. Therefore, the results tends to be more reliable and with less or no jitter. On the other hand, the main disadvantages of this approach are that the images become out of date from the moment they are captured and that they cannot incorporate dynamic events [4].

In [3] is reported an experience of building a system with an offline panoramic video augmentation due to the difficulties of an efficient augmented reality in real time and in [4] is described an approach able to perform real time augmentation using a 360° camera to capture the images and a 3D model of the place to augment the panorama.

The main disadvantage of the abovementioned works, is that the 3D models used to augment the panoramas should be accurate and detailed to achieve better results. However, this is not an easy feature to accomplish, due to changes in the environment and the time required to create these models.

As shown in [14], GPS sensors and compasses have limited accuracy and cannot provide precise pose information. This fact is another motivation to encourage the use of panoramic images. The possibility of using the internet to provide a robust application is a similar feature to the application presented in this work.

Finally, in [6] is presented an application that uses spherical panoramic technology on power system equipment visualization, which is also the objective of this work.

As stated in the literature, the application of AR technology for visualization of industrial systems are largely investigated. Also, for the conditions of use in an electrical facility, the use of static images are very adequate, as the layout and conditions of the equipments are changed with low frequencies. Thus the use of static panoramas for the visualization of these industrial systems is an open question for research.

This work proposes an application that aims to extends the visualization of power systems diagrams by supporting interpretation and monitoring of data, and an alternative way to manipulate equipments through a flexible environment that uses static augmented panoramas to support real world context.

The remainder of this paper is organized in two sections. Section 2 shows details about the implementation of the application and Section 3 concludes the paper and discusses about some future works to be done.

2   Power System - Panoramic Augmented Environment (PS-PAE)

This paper proposes an application to visualize a panoramic augmented environment to improve the way power systems informations are shown to professionals, given a real context of the equipments to them. This application is called Power System - Panoramic Augmented Environment (PS-PAE).

PS-PAE is described in two parts. The first one explains the architecture developed to access the power system database and the second presents the viewer of the panoramic environment and informations.

2.1   Power System Data Acquisition

To provide the visualization of the updated status of equipments is essential to integrate this application with the legacy systems used to access the Real Time Database (RTDB) of a power system. In this work, is used the database of the São Francisco's Hydroelectric Company (CHESF) controlled by the legacy systems: Open System Power Management (SAGE) and Operator Training Simulator (OTS).

SAGE is used by several companies in Brazil and can be used to control substations and power plants supporting various hardwares from different manufacturers [13]. OTS is a software used to simulate all power systems sensors and networking measurements providing an environment to train operators without a connection with real equipments [11].

The architecture to retrieve data from the power system database is implemented to communicate with the main legacy systems of CHESF. This architecture is shown in Fig. 1.

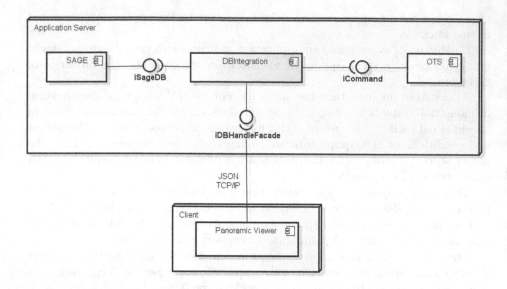

Fig. 1. Component Diagram of PS-PAE, showing the architecture of power system data acquisition

The viewer is represented as a component called *Panoramic Viewer* on the client side. On the *Application Server*, the object *DBIntegration* provides a facade to handle the database, allowing the client to receive the current status of equipments and to manipulate them. This data exchange is made using JSON format via TCP/IP protocol.

DBIntegration is a socket server implemented in Java and running on the same machine of SAGE and OTS. This object implements access to read and write in the SAGE database, which is the database used for real applications, and it also provides, access to read and write in the simulation database of the OTS.

The architecture proposed has allowed the application to monitor and manipulate equipments of all substations contained in CHESF power system database. In addition, there are two different types of actions that the system can perform, the first is to open/close switches and circuit breakers. The second is to change numerical values, such as the value of a TAP in a transformer. The flexibility to use both, SAGE and OTS, gave us an advantage to use this application in a real scenario or in a simulation. This application was tested using a simulation database, which is a clone of the power system database used in a real scenario.

2.2 Panoramic Viewer

The Panoramic Viewer is the component of PS-PAE that implements visualization, navigation and interaction with the panoramic elements. This component is implemented in C# using the Unity 3D engine, that provides portability to multiple platforms [15].

The main features proposed to the viewer are:

- Flexibility in the use of panoramas: The panoramas can be captured from a variety of cameras with different aspect ratios, and the application can work with different types of panoramas;
- Real time information: The application can contain points of information with unique identifiers that corresponds to the ones in the power system database. these points are represented by icons of information and show the current status of the equipment. To increase context, they should be located in the image at the same place that the information is referring to;
- Interaction with equipments: The user can use buttons that appear inside the equipment panel information to interact with equipments;
- Links between panoramas: A panorama can contain arrows that load another specified panorama setting.

There are several types of panoramas that can be adjusted to be used in this application. In the scope of this work, only Planar, Cylindrical and Spherical Panoramas are focused, by the reason that Planar and Cylindrical Panoramas are relatively easy to create using basically a camera and a simple tripod, and the Spherical Panorama is the most immersive type of panorama that enables a 360° field of view and can be created using a variety of techniques [5][2][4].

The Fig. 2 shows the different types of panoramas focused in this approach. The method to view these panoramas consists in add images as textures of the objects. A plane is used to visualize Planar Panorama (Fig. 2.a), this plane should be scaled to match with the aspect ratio of the image. The Cylindrical Panoramas 360° and 180° (Fig. 2.b and Fig. 2.c) are visualized using a cylinder and a half cylinder, respectively, and also scaling this object to be at the same proportion of the image. Spherical Panoramas (Fig. 2.d) uses a sphere as a model to be textured.

AR can be achieved by the same methodology, but using a live video as a texture rather than static images.

In order to enhance the reuse of elements used in this application, prefabs of the main elements was created. Prefabs are objects that reuse components and properties and acts like templates from which it is possible to create new object instances using the previous configuration [15].

The creation of new panoramas is simple since the prefabs of the models to be textured are ready with their camera and scripts to handle it. In this case, is only necessary to choose the type of panorama and set the image as a texture, after that it is possible to use the prefabs to create links between panoramas and points of information. The communication with the server is made through a script that implements a socket client and it is also a prefab that can be configured to work in another IP or port and with a different delay to update the data.

The navigation through panoramas is made by manipulating the camera. In the Planar Panoramas the camera is located in front of the plane and translated

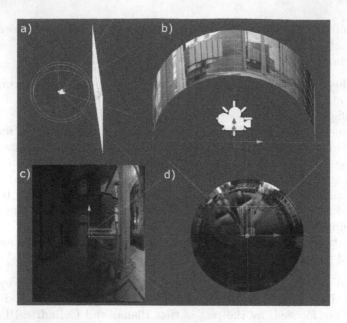

Fig. 2. Types of panoramas implemented in PS-PAE. a) Planar Panorama; b) Cylindrical Panorama 180°; c) Cylindrical Panorama; d) Spherical Panorama.

through one axis and limited by the end of the object. In Cylindrical and Spherical Panoramas the camera is placed in the center of the object and it is rotated to navigate through the panorama.

The methodology to create a new augmented environment is illustrated in Fig. 3. This process starts with the images acquisition and after that these images should be applied as textures in the objects corresponding to the panorama type. Next the elements are added manually in their contextualized place, if the elements are links between panoramas, the information of what panorama this link opens should be given, and if the elements are points of information, the identifier of the equipment is required. Finally, the basic configuration to access the database should be provided and after that the build of the application can be made and the executable to visualize the augmented environment is generated.

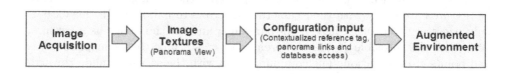

Fig. 3. Creation methodology of augmented environments using PS-PAE

The panoramic images used in this application was captured in five substations of CHESF using a tripod and two distinct cameras with their own embedded software to create 180° Cylindrical Panoramas. If any change occurs in the environment, a new set of images should be acquired to avoid inconsistency between the images and the data exhibited on screen.

The visualization process occurs as shown in Fig. 4. The camera can be rotated to visualize the panoramic image and the data augmented on it.

Fig. 4. Panoramic visualization in the development environment

In Fig. 5 is demonstrated the application running with a link to load other panorama represented by an arrow, points of information with a button to open/close equipments and data retrieved from the power system database. The diagram below is the SLD of SAGE that contains the data of a transformer shown in the panorama.

Fig. 5. Panorama of a substation visualized in PS-PAE showing real time information
retrieved from SAGE

3   Conclusion and Future Works

The work presents a solution to visualize power systems equipments measurements and manipulating them using panoramic images. This solution supports
professionals in this area, by giving real context of the installation and extending
the traditional view of SLD's without aiming to substitute them, because these
diagrams can visualize a system in a holistic view that cannot be viewed in a
single panorama.

This type of application has the advantage of reduced cost and shorter development time compared to systems using virtual reality, as a consequence of a
variety of equipments that demands more time to create the 3D models than the
time to acquire images and insert points of information.

The disadvantage of approaches that use static images are that they prevents the display of dynamic events, such as opening and closing of switches, circuit breakers or other possible events to be monitored as fire, lightning occurrence, wrong operations, disruption of cables, among others. Though this situation can be overcame with the use of video textures to create Augmented Reality applications.

Future works will be focused on augment a live video instead of static images, implement an authoring tool for creating applications to use panoramic images applied in other domains and conduct usability tests with operators of the power system to improve the application.

Acknowledgments. Our research group acknowledge financial support from CAPES, CNPQ, FAPEMA and CHESF.

References

1. Azuma, R.T.: A Survey of Augmented Reality. Presence **6**(4), 355–385 (1997)
2. Cogal, O., Popovic, V., Leblebici, Y.: Spherical Panorama Construction Using Multi Sensor Registration Priors and Its Real-Time Hardware. In: 2013 IEEE International Symposium on Multimedia (ISM), pp. 171–178. IEEE (2013)
3. Côté, S., Barnard, J., Snyder, R., Gervais, R.: Offline Spatial Panoramic Video Augmentation for Visual Communication in the AEC Industry. In: Proceedings of the 13th International Conference on Construction Applications of Virtual Reality, London (2013)
4. Côté, S., Trudel, P., Desbiens, M., Giguère, M., Snyder, R.: Live Mobile Panoramic High Accuracy Augmented Reality for Engineering and Construction. In: Proceedings of the Construction Applications of Virtual Reality (CONVR), London, England (2013)
5. De Carufel, J., Laganiere, R.: Matching Cylindrical Panorama Sequences Using Planar Reprojections. In: 2011 IEEE International Conference on Computer Vision Workshops (ICCV Workshops), pp. 320–327 (2011)
6. Gao, S., Chen, Z., Fan, H., Pan, J., Liu, W., Geng, J.: Research and Application of 3D Panoramic Technology on Equipment Visualization. In: 2012 International Conference on Computer Science and Electronics Engineering (ICCSEE), vol. 1, pp. 562–565. IEEE (2012)
7. Kim, J., Jun, H.: Implementation of Image Processing and Augmented Reality Programs for Smart Mobile Device. In: 2011 6th International Forum on Strategic Technology (IFOST), vol. 2, pp. 1070–1073. IEEE (2011)
8. Klump, R., Schooley, D., Overbye, T.: An Advanced Visualization Platform for Real-time Power System Operations. In: Proc. of the 14th Power Systems Computation Conference, vol. 2 (2002)
9. Maidi, M., Preda, M.: Markerless Tracking for Mobile Augmented Reality. In: 2011 IEEE International Conference on Signal and Image Processing Applications (ICSIPA), pp. 301–306 (2011)
10. Meng-meng, C., Xiao-wu, C., Yi-li, L.: Integration of 3D Registration Methods Based on Multiple Natural Features. In: 2010 International Conference on Audio Language and Image Processing (ICALIP), pp. 1279–1283. IEEE (2010)
11. Operator Training Simulator - OTS. http://www.simulationrsi.com/process-simulation-expertise-1/ots-operator-training-simulator.html

12. Schönfelder, R., Schmalstieg, D.: Augmented Reality for Industrial Building Acceptance. In: Virtual Reality Conference, VR 2008, pp. 83–90. IEEE (2008)
13. Sistema Aberto de Gerenciamento de Energia - SAGE. http://sage.cepel.br
14. Spohrer, J.: Online Creation of Panoramic Augmented-reality Annotations on Mobile Phones (2012)
15. Unity3D Documentation. http://docs.unity3d.com
16. Wang, X., Kim, M.J., Love, P.E., Kang, S.C.: Augmented Reality in Built Environment: Classification and Implications for Future Research. Automation in Construction **32**, 1–13 (2013)
17. Wither, J., DiVerdi, S., Höllerer, T.: Annotation in Outdoor Augmented Reality. Computers & Graphics **33**(6), 679–689 (2009)
18. Yan, Z., Liu, X., Sun, P., Zhu, G., Zhang, H., Zhang, Y.: Practical Research of Visualization in Power System. In: 2013 7th Asia Modelling Symposium (AMS), pp. 247–251. IEEE (2013)

A Workflow Analysis for Implementing AR-Based Maintenance Procedures

Federico Manuri[1]([✉]), Andrea Sanna[1], Fabrizio Lamberti[1],
Gianluca Paravati[1], and Pietro Pezzolla[2]

[1] Dipartimento di Automatica e Informatica, Politecnico di Torino,
C.so Duca degli Abruzzi 24, 10129 Turin, Italy
{federico.manuri,andrea.sanna,fabrizio.lamberti,
gianluca.paravati}@polito.it
[2] Fidia S.p.A., C.so Lombardia 11, 10099 San Mauro Torinese, Turin, Italy
p.pezzolla@fidia.it

Abstract. The widespread adoption of mobile devices is giving everyone access to augmented reality systems, possibly involving a huge number of people in AR-based apps, with a pervasive social impact that cannot be neglected. AR systems are becoming affordable to everyone and especially useful in the maintenance field. This report aims to describe in a clear and accessible way the workflow to design and develop an augmented reality (AR) application for supporting maintenance procedures. The main focus of this paper is the evaluation of markerless tracking systems, as they could provide environment-independent solutions. The tests performed on a real use case outline the robustness of 3D CAD tracking with respect to other solutions.

Keywords: Augmented Reality · Maintenance · Tracking Systems · Robustness

1 Introduction

The main purpose of an AR-based system is to allow users to "experience" the real world enriched by a set of overlapping computer-generated contents and eventually other sensory inputs, such as audio augmentation through earplugs or speakers [1]. The augmentation generated by the computer is strictly related to the user context, both in terms of view and location: the virtual objects are aligned to the real ones in a meaningful way to provide the user a better understanding of the surroundings. As augmented reality is something strictly related to the experience of the real world, an AR system should collect a wide range of information from different sensors (e.g. camera, GPS, and so on). Another peculiarity of AR systems is to be real time, so a device should provide enough computing power to interactively run an AR application.

Until some years ago, the lack of cost-efficient devices was the main barrier to a wider adoption of AR applications. Nowadays, the widespread adoption of

© Springer International Publishing Switzerland 2014
L.T. De Paolis and A. Mongelli (Eds.): AVR 2014, LNCS 8853, pp. 185–200, 2014.
DOI: 10.1007/978-3-319-13969-2_15

mobile devices has removed this limitation, as smartphones and tablets feature all the sensors and processing units needed to develop and deploy AR applications. Moreover, the technology innovations that affect mobile devices can produce new challenging products, commonly referred to as 'wearables', and industries are making steady progress in developing new categories of AR devices, such as the Google Glass project [2] and contact lenses from Innovega [3]. The global market for augmented reality is growing fast and the pervasive adoption of AR technologies implies an undeniable impact on today's society. Industrial applications for maintenance, repair and manufacturing have always been an interesting domain for AR and the benefits that these solutions could offer are investigated into details in [4] and [5]. In addition, current AR applications could effectively replace the traditional maintenance solutions such as paper manuals and handbook instructions.

This manuscript aims to present a workflow for implementing markerless AR maintenance procedures, evaluating challenges, opportunities and limitations of the latest AR technologies. The main focus of this research is evaluating the robustness of different tracking systems, thus assessing the applicability of AR-based maintenance procedures with respect to variable environmental conditions.

The paper is organized as follows: Section 2 briefly outlines the state of the art of AR applications, with a focus on the maintenance procedures area. Section 3 presents a workflow diagram for implementing an AR application for maintenance, whereas evaluation of experimental data is provided in Section 4. Finally, open problems and future works are discussed in Section 5.

2   Background

Over the years, developers and researchers investigated many different domains that could profit from AR systems. Industrial, military and medical applications were the first area of research, followed soon after by commercial and entertainment apps.

In recent years AR technologies were used in many different domains, such as tourism, shopping, social networks and advertisement. SnapShop Showroom [6] allows users to capture an image of the room they wish to furnish, quickly browse through a vast catalogue of furniture from big retailers like IKEA [7] and position items in the virtual environment to see how the room may look like. Google's Ingress [8] is a MMO strategy game where players, grouped in two factions, fight for the control of virtual territories simply walking around and looking for points of interest in the real world, such as sculptures, libraries, post offices, memorials and so on. Wikitude World Browser [9] is an AR browser that offers geographically-relevant information of the surroundings that could be valuable for the user, detailing restaurants, ATM location and many other information.

One important domain for AR is the development of applications for maintenance procedures. The use of AR systems to provide instructions to maintainers and technicians was first investigated in the early 1990s [10][11]. Since then several experiments led to prototypes and evolutions in this field using head-mounted displays to perform maintenance procedures [12]. The usefulness of

AR-based systems for training and maintenance applications was investigated in several studies, with the development of prototypes to maintain PCs [13] and other industrial contexts such as plant maintenance [14] or facility management [15]. The latest works further investigate AR-based solutions for car maintenance and suggest the use of AR applications to replace instruction manuals or handbooks.

This paper focuses on conceiving and designing a workflow for developing AR applications that could be applied to various domains, including maintenance procedures. While other researches usually point out the AR solutions that best fit with their domain or peculiar requirements, this research aims to provide a methodology to adopt when planning the development of an AR application, independently of the specific domain.

Nowadays, the market offers a wide range of AR frameworks, which differ for license (commercial, free, open source), tracking systems (marker, markerless) and target devices (computer, mobile devices) [16]. A framework based on Metaio SDK [17] is presented in this paper; Metaio offers the wider set of tracking systems among its competitors (such as Vuforia [18], Layar [19] and many others) and it provides a free SDK and well documented APIs. Nonetheless the workflow proposed in this manuscript aims to be unbounded from the AR platform of choice and easily adaptable to any AR framework. The AR market is drastically increasing and the spreading of AR applications and the pervasive adoption of AR technologies provide significant areas of research for AR developers [20]: this paper aims at filling the gap between users and AR technology, focusing on the application development and providing a clear and accessible workflow to create AR applications, and particularly maintenance apps.

3   The Workflow

Several issues and problems have to be considered when developing an AR application for maintenance, repair and assembly. First of all, an efficient tracking system has to be identified. The tracking system can be based on the object (or objects) to be tracked or it can be based on artificial features (e.g., markers), which can be added to the object itself. Moreover, the focus can be either on just one tracking system or on a hybrid approach, depending on the steps of the procedures to be performed. For example, it can be necessary to recognize an object with a complex geometry (by using 3D CAD or 3D Map tracking) and then a flat surface with several textures (by using 2D image tracking). Depending on the tracking system, a set of configuration files needs to be created. These files can consist of several 2D images, such as photos or computer-generated renderings, or 3D models of parts of the object to be tracked.

The next step involves the description of the procedure to be used for supporting the end-user during the maintenance/assembly task. Computer-generated (sometimes called virtual) hints can be: text labels, images, 3D static models, 2D and/or 3D animations, videos, audio messages.

During the last step, all the code to perform the above mentioned contents (and possibly extra features depending on the user requirements) has to be implemented for the chosen AR technology. Figure 1 provides a high-level visualization of the workflow for developing an AR application.

3.1 Tracking Process

The tracking process is the core feature of every AR application. Among the different tracking solutions available, markerless systems do not require to add any artificial feature to the scenario and they depend only on the object to be tracked. These characteristics are fundamental when developing an application that should be reliable independently of the environment and other context conditions, such as illumination.

2D Image Tracking. This tracking system is based on providing an image to match with the current scene framed from the camera. The image could either be a photo of the object or a rendering of a 3D model of the object itself. Depending on the provided image, the environment would be part of the recognition process, but it could be excluded for better re-usability of the application. The 2D Tracking System recognizes the object when the camera frame "matches" the provided image; of course, the point of view of the camera has to be as similar as possible to the one used to gather the reference image. The recognition will go on till the tracked object is inside the area of the camera, even stretching the camera view (to some extent).

3D Map Tracking. 3D maps markerless tracking allows users to use any object as a tracking reference. This technique is based on creating a map of points by the Toolbox app. This map will be used in the developed application to match with the current viewed frame for positive recognition. The first step is to use the Toolbox app provided by Metaio to create a 3D map of the desired object or environment. The output of this process is a *.3dmap file, which is intended to be used with the Creator or the SDK.

The points created by the mapping are based on geometry and texture and they could come from both the object and the environment. All visible features in the proximity of the object are detected from the smartphone camera during the 3D map creation task. For this reason, it is better to manage the entire operation on a neutral background, avoiding any undesired interference with the surrounding environment. The map could be edited to improve its robustness, thus removing useless points and trying to focus on the object itself. As the texture information is used for the tracking, light condition and texture of the objects should be considered and could limit the object tracking.

3D CAD Tracking. 3D Markerless Tracking based on CAD data allows a precise pose localization based on a given 3D model of an object or a part of the environment; for example, a small object that should be tracked or a building that the tracking system should recognize when the camera frame "matches" the

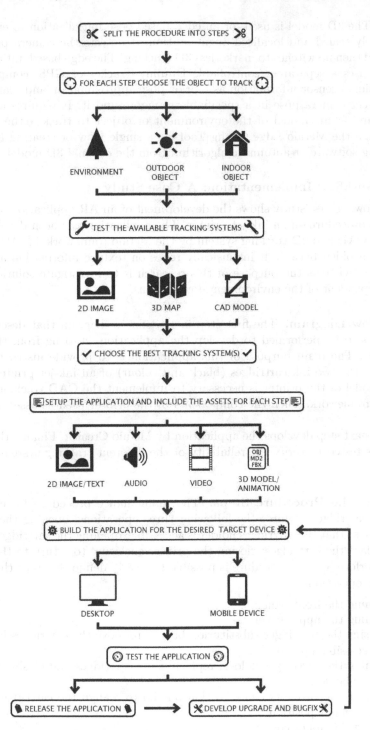

Fig. 1. The Workflow Diagram

model. The 3D model is used for an edge based pose initialization to enable an accurately scaled and localized augmentation. It detects the camera pose only once and then it switches to markerless 3D tracking. The edge based initialization process uses a separately controllable Dummy Tracker or GPS, compass and gravitational sensor information as a prior pose approximation and searches for the correct camera pose in a specifiable range around it. It requires a surface model and a line model of the environment or object to track, either getting it through the Metaio Edge Config Tool for a single view or creating it with a modeling software or automatic algorithm from the original 3D model.

3.2   Workflow Implementation: A Case Study

The following case study shows the development of an AR application for maintenance procedure on an ink-jet printer. The application has been developed to test the CAD and 2D tracking system by the Metaio framework. 3D Map tracking was avoided because it intrinsically relies on texture information and light condition, whereas the purpose of this research is to investigate solutions that are independent of the environmental conditions.

Workflow Diagram. The first step is to define a diagram that describes all the steps to be performed to develop the application, starting from the specifications. The main purpose of this application is to provide instructions for changing the two ink cartridges (black and colour) of an ink-jet printer. A 3D CAD model of the printer is necessary to implement the CAD tracking by the Metaio framework. Then the components of the printer used as assets are animated.

The next step develops the application by Metaio Creator. Finally, the application is tested to verify the reliability of the different tracking systems implemented.

Defining the Procedure Steps. The maintenance procedure for changing the ink cartridges requires the following three operations: opening the printer enclosure so that the cartridges holder is accessible; opening the cartridges holder and replace the cartridges; closing the printer enclosure to return to the initial state. Performing the procedure is possible to clearly define the steps that make up these operations:

1. opening the front panel;
2. opening the upper cover;
3. pressing the cartridges substitution button to move the cartridges holder to an accessible position;
4. opening the cartridges holder, replacing the cartridges and closing the cartridges holder;
5. pressing the cartridges substitution button to realign the cartridges holder to its default position;
6. closing the upper cover;
7. closing the front panel.

Choosing the Object to Track. The next step is to define what will be tracked to identify the different steps of the procedure. Since the printer is normally used indoor, environment and outdoor objects can be excluded as tracking. Moreover, performing the procedure pointed out that the printer configuration could be uniquely defined by the printer chassis in steps 1, 2, 3, 5, 6 and 7. Steps 4 is defined by the cartridge holder configuration and its position related to the printer chassis. For these reasons the printer chassis will be the tracking object for steps 1, 2, 3, 5, 6 and 7, while the printer chassis and the cartridge holder will define the tracking object for step 4.

Testing the Tracking Systems. At this point it is necessary to choose the most suitable tracking system. Among the three available tracking systems, the 3D map system has been avoided for the given case as it is the one that most relies on the light condition and texture of the objects. As the printer presents no texture of any kind and the light conditions could vary depending on the environment, the 3D map system could limit the object tracking and will be poorly effective. 2D Image and CAD model could equally fit for the given case study and the preliminary tests did not point out clearly which system would fit better. A procedure would usually require a lot of effort for producing the tracking object configuration for each available tracking systems and for each step of the procedure itself, so it is recommended to test only some of the most significant steps with different tracking systems at this phase of the workflow. The simpleness and shortness of the given case study allowed to develop the entire procedure with both 2D Image and CAD model tracking systems: this is the reason why all the testing results are evaluated later in the tests section. For the 2D Image tracking system, photos of the printer were taken for each steps of the procedure, while for CAD model tracking system the CAD of the printer was created, as detailed in the next section.

Modeling the Object. A 3D mesh of the printer is modeled, by using Blender [21], as similar as possible to the real printer. The model is used for: real-time tracking recognition with the 3D CAD tracking system; rendering some poses of the model to test the reliability of the 2D tracking system; creating animations that will be used as assets in the AR application.

In order to provide a better visualization of the assets in the final application, the texture "baking procedure" is used (Fig. 2). This procedure allows to: define a texture for the model, setup a lighting/shading system in Blender and perform a UV mapping of the texture that includes light parameters. This feature is not used by the 3D CAD tracking system, because it relies only on a wireframe representation (also called line object model) of the model.

When the model is ready, it is then necessary to setup poses identifying the steps of the procedure. In this example, four different poses of the printer define the procedure (Fig. 3), as steps 5, 6 and 7 are the mirror of steps 1, 2 and 3. Each pose is then exported as an .obj file, the format required by Metaio Creator. The four poses are also rendered to be used in the 2D Image tracking system.

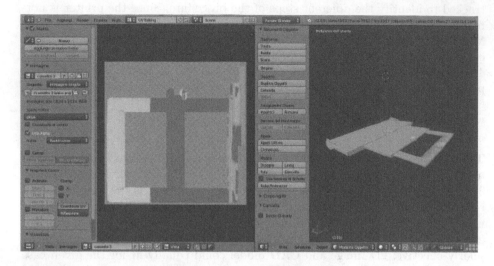

Fig. 2. The texture baking procedure: a texture is mapped by the UV mapping system to add texture, lightning and shading to the 3D model

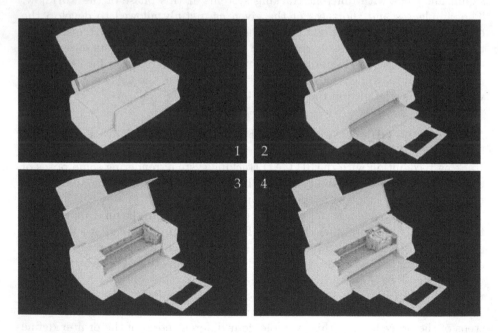

Fig. 3. The four poses defining the four different steps of the maintenance procedure

Creating the Assets. The last step to obtain all the resources for developing the application is to create the assets, a set of computer-generated hints that describe the procedure and support the end-user during the maintenance/assembly task. The Metaio SDK offers content creation guidelines in three major areas: images, movies and 3D animations. At first only a set of animations has been produced as assets for the procedure to speed up the developing process. After the first set of tests, text, audio and video instructions have been prepared as part of the "develop upgrade and bugfix" step to offer a wider set of assets for future usability tests. Each animation represents one of the task that the final user should perform for the specific maintenance procedure. The following animations are implemented in Blender: top panel opening/closing; front panel opening/closing (Fig. 4); toner case left/right translation; toner case opening/closing; toner extraction; toner insertion. When all the animations are ready, it is necessary to convert the resulting FBX files by the FBX Mesh Converter tool provided by Metaio. The output will be an MFBX package compatible with Metaio Creator.

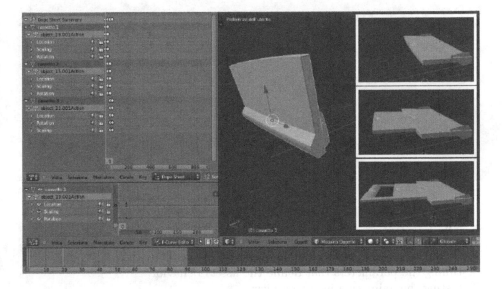

Fig. 4. The front panel animation implemented in Blender

Creating the Application with Metaio Creator. For each pose defined for the procedure, the following steps have to be performed:

1. creating a new scene;
2. importing and positioning the .obj file that represents the pose to be tracked in the scene (see Fig. 5);
3. creating a line object model through the edge tool utility (see Fig. 6);
4. tuning the parameters that define the tracking system;

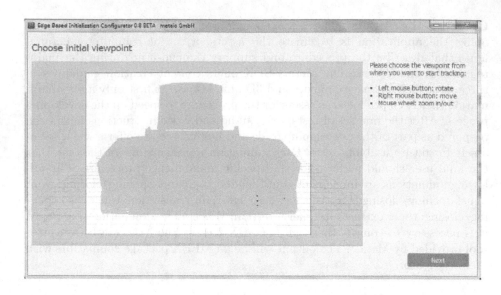

Fig. 5. An example of tracking object model

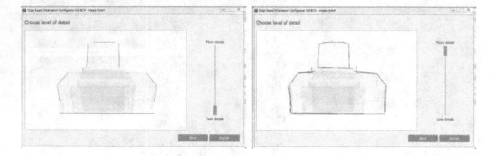

Fig. 6. An example of line model object (wireframe) representation

5. importing the assets and aligning them to the real object;
6. tuning the parameters that define the assets behavior;
7. testing the animation in the preview.

When all the scenes are ready, it is possible to export the project as an application available for the main platforms (Windows, iOS, Android). In the context of this work, the application has been tested on an Android device. To develop another version of the application that relies on the 2D Image tracking system, the previous steps are performed with the following differences: in step 2 renderings are imported as .jpeg files, instead of the .obj model, whereas step 3 is not performed as it is specific for the 3D CAD tracking system.

4 Tests

The developed application has been tested by using the real object in order to assess the efficiency of the proposed tracking systems. Tests on the real object have been repeated using 3D CAD tracking and 2D tracking. The second solution has been tested with both renderings and photos of the real object. As one of the main focus of the research is that the procedure should be repeatable independently of the environmental conditions, the photos were taken through the tracking camera and edited to remove all environmental information. As detailed before, since the last three steps of the procedure (5,6 and 7) are specular to the first three ones, only steps 1-4 were taken into account for these tests.

Four parameters have been considered in each test, in order to evaluate the performance of the two solutions: tracking object quality, recognition threshold, luminosity, alignment precision. The tracking object quality defines the quality of the image or CAD model for the tracking algorithm. Both systems have their own rules to finely craft the tracking object. Metaio Creator rates with a three star system how much the chosen tracking object is suitable. The better the rating, the easier for the system to recognize the object and avoid false positive, providing a robust solution. Recognition threshold evaluates the similarity parameter used to calibrate the matching between the tracking virtual object and the real one ranging from 0.00 to 1.00. Metaio suggests the range 0.30 - 0.70 for better results, as values below 0.30 will lead to a too inaccurate recognition and values over 0.7 could make it difficult to recognize the object. A low value means that the system is less robust: false positives or alignment errors of the assets might occur in this case. Luminosity has been evaluated to test the robustness of the systems in different situations. The tests have been performed with low light (30 lux), medium light (160 lux) and high light (300 lux), where low light represents a nearly dark room and high light represents a well illuminated office desk. The luminosity value is approximated and it is evaluated through the luminosity sensor of a Nexus 10" Tablet. 3D CAD recognition should always work, as it does not rely on the color information, such as texture or grayscale, but only on the object geometry: while the first parameter could change with different luminosity, the second should be independent of it. Alignment precision defines how precisely the system overlaps the assets when it correctly tracks the object. This parameter could only be estimated by the final user on a range of 0.00 - 1.00, where 0.00 means the object is not recognized and 1.00 means that all the assets are always perfectly aligned to the real object.

The tests were performed with the applications deployed through Metaio Creator (v.3.2.2) and a Logitech HD Webcam C310 to track the printer. Table 1 shows the results of the tests performed for the four steps of the printer maintenance procedure.

The first evaluation is that the 2D image tracking based on the renders of the model does not work properly for the proposed real object. The tests were performed changing the recognition threshold from 0.70 to 0.30, to check if a feeble value could provide some significant results for the alignment quality parameter. The main issue could be that the 3D model of the printer does not

Table 1. Results of the tests performed on the printer maintenance procedure, with different luminosity conditions and tracking configurations, for the four steps of the procedure. Legend: TOQ = Tracking Object Quality, RT = Recognition Threshold, AQ = Augmentation Quality.

STEP 1									
	LUX 40			LUX 160			LUX 300		
Tracking Configuration	TOQ	RT	AQ	TOQ	RT	AQ	TOQ	RT	AQ
3D CAD	3	0.70	0.80	3	0.70	0.80	3	0.70	0.80
2D Image with Render	2*	0.30	0.00	2*	0.30	0.00	2*	0.30	0.00
2D Image with Photos	2*	0.30	0.00	2*	0.50	0.40	2*	0.35	0.20
STEP 2									
	LUX 40			LUX 160			LUX 300		
Tracking Configuration	TOQ	RT	AQ	TOQ	RT	AQ	TOQ	RT	AQ
3D CAD	3	0.70	0.90	3	0.70	0.90	3	0.70	0.90
2D Image with Render	2*	0.30	0.00	2*	0.30	0.00	2*	0.30	0.00
2D Image with Photos	2*	0.30	0.00	2*	0.45	0.35	2*	0.30	0.00
STEP 3									
	LUX 40			LUX 160			LUX 300		
Tracking Configuration	TOQ	RT	AQ	TOQ	RT	AQ	TOQ	RT	AQ
3D CAD	3	0.70	0.90	3	0.70	0.90	3	0.70	0.90
2D Image with Render	2*	0.30	0.00	2*	0.30	0.00	2*	0.30	0.00
2D Image with Photos	2*	0.60	0.65	2*	0.85	0.90	2*	0.75	0.80
STEP 4									
	LUX 40			LUX 160			LUX 300		
Tracking Configuration	TOQ	RT	AQ	TOQ	RT	AQ	TOQ	RT	AQ
3D CAD	3	0.70	0.90	3	0.70	0.90	3	0.70	0.90
2D Image with Render	2*	0.30	0.00	2*	0.30	0.00	2*	0.30	0.00
2D Image with Photos	2*	0.60	0.65	2*	0.85	0.90	2*	0.75	0.80

*since the 2D image contains transparency, Metaio could not provide an exact evaluation of the Tracking Object Quality.

provide enough texture or visual references for the tracking algorithm to match the real object.

The 2D image tracking based on the photos provides better results but it is not robust enough. First of all, if the photo does not provide rich texture data (step 1 and 2), the recognition threshold drops significantly. As a consequence, also the alignment quality drops: alignment errors may occur in terms of deviation between the real object and the expected virtual asset position.

Moreover, the alignment might change when moving the camera from the tracking view. This problem worsen when the luminosity is changed: in step 2 the recognition fails for darker or lighter environment conditions; in step 1 it is necessary to reduce the recognition threshold significantly to obtain a minimum alignment in the lighter environment. In step 3 and 4, the printer provides better photos in terms of recognition algorithm and the alignment is possible even when the luminosity parameter changes. Finally, this solution is still feeble if the object does not provide enough texture data and it would need an algorithm to dynamically change the recognition threshold on luminosity variation. On the other hand, this solution provides the simpler and faster way to create the tracking object, as taking the photos and doing some image editing are the only requirements. Moreover, it does not require modeling skills to produce a model of the real object, which takes more time and could be onerous.

The 3D CAD tracking is the most robust solution. Changing the luminosity of the environment does not affect the alignment quality, without the need to loosen the recognition threshold. Moreover, this system provides the best alignment quality results in each step of the procedure and it is the more suitable for the maintenance domain. On the other hand, the 3D CAD-based tracking is the most onerous system because it needs a model of the real object to properly work. If the manufacturer could not provide a 3D model of the object, it is necessary to create it with a 3D modeling software: this could be difficult depending on the complexity of the object and the skills of the user. Furthermore, 3D modeling could not be possible for a variety of reasons: the original model could not be available, the object could be too tiny or simple to provide suitable recognition features and the tracking object could be too complex to provide a 3D model similar enough to the real one.

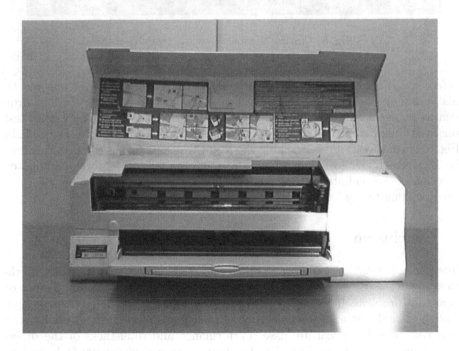

Fig. 7. Lightening the real object with a torch

To further evaluate the robustness of these solutions, other tests were performed for the three proposed luminosity conditions: the first test consisted of casting shadows over the real object in order to change the luminosity of the

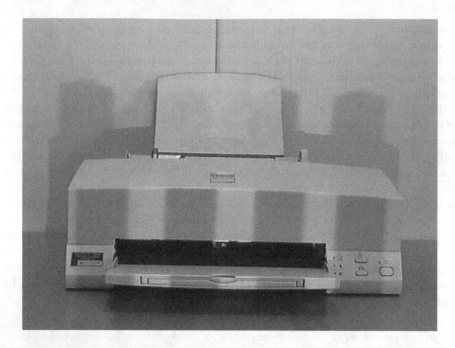

Fig. 8. Casting shadows over the real object

surface not linearly (Fig. 7). While the 3D CAD tracking was not affected by this variation, with the 2D image tracking the alignment quality would drop even more, eventually leading to not recognize the real object. The second test consisted of lightening the real object with a torch, a Maglite 3CELL D flashlight (Fig. 8): with the 2D image tracking the result was the same as the previous test; the 3D CAD tracking was sometimes affected, especially if the torch highlighted a section of the real object that defined the geometry (such as an edge section corresponding to the line object).

5   Conclusions

This paper presents a workflow to efficiently develop augmented reality markerless applications, with a special focus on the maintenance domain. The most important problems have been evaluated, investigating all the steps to design, implement and test an AR application. Finally, two markerless solutions have been compared by a real use case. Performance and robustness of the different systems have been evaluated to identify the best environment-independent tracking solution.

The problems found with the 2D image tracking based on render could originate from either the quality of the 3D model or the lack of tracking features by the real object or both of them. Moreover, image tracking based on render should be further investigated as the advantage of using renders relies on the possibility to simulate different texture conditions, such as shadows, dirt, brightness, dust and so on.

Future works could include further research on the 3D CAD tracking system when future releases of the Metaio SDK occur, since this tracking solution is now provided in a not stable version. Moreover, 2D tracking could be improved with a system to better evaluate the quality of the images used as trackables and an algorithm could be developed to dynamically change the recognition threshold on luminosity variation.

Acknowledgments. This work is founded by the EASE-R[3] project [22]: Integrated framework for a cost-effective and ease of Repair, Renovation and Re-use of machine tools within modern factory, FP7, FoF.NMP.2013-8, Grant agreement no: 608771.

References

1. Van Krevelen, D.W.F., Poelman, R.: A Survey of Augmented Reality Technologies, Applications and Limitations. The International Journal of Virtual Reality **9**, 1–20 (2010)
2. The Google Glass project web site. http://www.google.com/glass/start/
3. The Innovega web site. http://innovega-inc.com/
4. Henderson, S.J., Feiner, S.: Exploring the Benefits of Augmented Reality Documentation for Maintenance and Repair. IEEE Trans. on Visualization and Computer Graphics **17**, 1355–1368 (2011)
5. Terenzi, G., Basile, G.: Smart Maintenance: An Augmented Reality Platform for Training and Fields Operations in the Manufacturing Industry. ARMEDIA Augmented Reality Blog (2014). http://arblog.inglobetechnologies.com/?p=1370
6. The SnapShop web site. http://www.snapshopinc.com/
7. The Ikea web site. http://www.ikea.com/
8. The Ingress web site. https://www.ingress.com/
9. The Wikitude Web Browser site. http://www.wikitude.com/app/
10. Ong, S.K., Yuan, M.L., Nee, A.Y.C.: Augmented Reality Applications in Manufacturing: A Survey. Intl. J. Production Research **46**, 2707–2742 (2008)
11. Neea, A.Y.C., Onga, S.K., Chryssolourisb, G., Mourtzisb, D.: Augmented reality applications in design and manufacturing. CIRP Annals - Manufacturing Technology **61**, 657–679 (2012)
12. Feiner, S., Blair, M., Dorée, S.: Knowledge-based Augmented Reality. Communications of the ACM **36**, 52–62 (1993)
13. Ke, C., Kang, B., Chen, D., Li, X.: An Augmented Reality-based application for equipment maintenance. In: Tao, J., Tan, T., Picard, R.W. (eds.) ACII 2005. LNCS, vol. 3784, pp. 836–841. Springer, Heidelberg (2005)
14. Savioja, P., Järvinen, P., Karhela, T., Siltanen, P., Woodward, C.: Developing a Mobile, Service-Based Augmented Reality Tool for Modern Maintenance Work. In: Shumaker, R. (ed.) HCII 2007 and ICVR 2007. LNCS, vol. 4563, pp. 554–563. Springer, Heidelberg (2007)
15. Kahn, S., Olbrich, M., Engelke, T., Keil, J., Riess, P., Webel, S., Graf, H., Bockholt, U., Picinbono, G.: Beyond 3D "As-Built" Information Using Mobile AR Enhancing the Building Lifecycle Management. In: 12th International Conference on Cyberworlds, pp. 29-36. IEEE Press (2012)

16. Augmented Reality SDK Comparison. http://socialcompare.com/en/comparison/augmented-reality-sdks
17. The Metaio web site. http://www.metaio.com/
18. The Augmented Reality Trends web site. http://www.augmentedrealitytrends.com/
19. The Vuforia web site. https://www.vuforia.com/
20. The Layar web site. https://www.layar.com/
21. The Blender web site. http://www.blender.org/
22. The EASE-R3 project web site. http://www.easer3.eu/

Augmented Reality at the Industrial Shop-Floor

Anna Syberfeldt$^{(\boxtimes)}$, Oscar Danielsson, Magnus Holm,
and Tom Ekblom

Virtual System Research Centre, University of Skövde, Skövde, Sweden
anna.syberfeldt@his.se

Abstract. This paper describes a study of the potential of using augmented reality at the industrial shop-floor with the aim of improving the capability of the shop-floor operators. In the study, a prototype system for augmented reality is developed based on the Oculus Rift platform. The system is evaluated through an experiment in which a physical three-dimensional puzzle is to be assembled.

Keywords: Augmented reality · Industrial shop-floor · Assembling · Oculus rift

1   Introduction

Manufacturing companies of today face a global and rapidly changing market. To stay competitive, it is of critical importance for companies to continuously improve their shop-floors. A powerful, yet extensively overlooked, mean to improve shop-floor performance is to enhance the capability of its operators. In their daily work, shop-floor operators constantly face complex and uncertain situations due to unpredictable events and uncontrollable variations (such as machine breakdowns, fluctuating product demand, re-prioritizations, etc.). There is a need of finding new methods and tools that increase productivity and quality by supporting the operators in making the right decisions and optimally operating the shop-floor.

This paper describes a study of improving the capability of shop-floor operators by using augmented reality. With augmented reality, artificial information about the environment and its objects can be overlaid on the real world in order to enhance the operator's perception of reality. Augmented reality is today mainly used in application areas such as gaming, sports and tourism. The topic has also recently begun to be discussed within the context of industrial shop-floors, but so far mainly as a concept and there exist few practical demonstrators. This study aims to advance the research on augmented reality within the manufacturing domain by developing a prototype system. The study is part of the research project "Young Operator 2020" at the University of Skövde in Sweden. The aim of this project is to technically improve the industrial shop-floor and provide industrial operators with better tools in order to support the operators in making the right decisions and work optimally. The authors are certain that augmented reality is a key to fulfill this aim, and also that the technique will be part of all modern, high-tech shop floors of the future. This idea is also supported by previous studies of using augmented reality within industry, see for example Henderson and Feiner (2009) and Henderson and Feiner (2011).

© Springer International Publishing Switzerland 2014
L.T. De Paolis and A. Mongelli (Eds.): AVR 2014, LNCS 8853, pp. 201–209, 2014.
DOI: 10.1007/978-3-319-13969-2_16

The next section continues by describing the approach used in the study for implementing augmented reality. In Section 3, the equipment developed in the study is presented, followed by a description of the experiment performed in Section 4. In Section 5, results from the experiment are discussed. Section 6, finally, outlines conclusions from the study and possible future work.

2   Approach for Implementing Augmented Reality

There exist a number of methods to implement augmented reality. Krevelen and Poelman (2010) divides the various implementations into three general categories: a) hand-held, b) head-worn, and c) spatial. Head-worn implementations are in turn divided into retina projection, optical, video and projective. Spatial implementations are also divided into sub-categories: video, optical and projective. In this study, a head-worn implementation is selected. This is since such implementation frees the user's hands, which is seen as a necessary feature when considering shop-floors. It could be noted that a spatial implementation also frees the user's hands, but as this implementation requires fixed equipment in the working environment (Krevelen and Poelman, 2010) it is considered as too inflexible.

For realizing the head-worn implementation in the study, the choice stood between a video-based solution and an optical solution (retina projection and projective solutions were not considered for practical reasons). Rolland and Fuchs (2000) describe the trade-off between optical and video-based solutions in the following manner:

"Optical see-through HMDs take what might be called a "minimally obtrusive" approach; that is, they leave the view of the real world nearly intact and attempt to augment it by merging a reflected image of the computer-generated scene into the view of the real world. Video see-through HMDs are typically more obtrusive in the sense that they block out the real-world view in exchange for the ability to merge the two views more convincingly." (Rolland and Fuchs, 2000, page 293)

Both solutions clearly have advantages, and in selecting between them the decisive factor was set to image updating performance at head moves. This is considered important as an industrial operator will move frequently and not seldom rapidly. Jeon and Kim (2008) have performed studies on head movements and they found that the slowest head moves correspond to an angular velocity of 8 degrees per second, while the fastest were up to 80 degrees per second. Jeon and Kim (2008) also found that in approximately 95% of the cases the users rotated their heads with a speed of approximately 40 degrees per second. In a similar study, Azuma (1997) found that the average speed of moving the head was 50 degrees per second. With a latency of 100 milliseconds in a system, Azuma (1997) state that the dynamic error is about 5 degrees. At a distance of 68 centimeters this accumulates to an error of 60 millimeters. Considering these findings, it is obvious   an optical solution where the virtual information is projected directly on the real world objects, even normal head moves will require an extremely fast and frequent image updating in order to avoid visual lag.

Visual lag is caused by, for example, communication or rendering delays and means that the virtual objects do not stay in the correct real-world position when the user moves. To avoid the problem of lag, a video-based solution is chosen in the study. With this solution, the real world and the virtual world are merged into the same view, and the user's view is completely digital. In this way, the real world and the virtual world can be easily synchronized. A video-based solution is, however, far from perfect as there will always be a mismatch between what the user sees and what is happening in the real-world. This is since the process of capturing the video stream, convert it into digital format and rendering it on a screen impossibly can be made at the speed of light. This means that there is always a delay of the user's sight which might cause body coordination problems.

In the next section, the equipment used to implement the video-based solution is described.

3   Equipment

The hardware platform used in the study is the first version of Oculus Rift (http://www.oculusvr.com/), see Figure 1. The Oculus Rift is selected since it is easy to work with, comes with a low price and is available on the public market.

Fig. 1. Oculus Rift

Since Oculus Rift is developed for virtual reality where the real-world is totally blocked-out, modifications are needed for using it for augmented reality. Such modifications have previously been made by Steptoe (2013). Steptoe mounted two web cameras in front of the Oculus Rift and showed their video streams on the Oculus's screens. With such solution, one achieve video-based, digital view of the real world on which it is possible to place virtual objects. The same solution as proposed by Steptoe is used also in this study.

The modified Oculus Rift used in the study is shown in Figure 2. As can be seen in the picture, there are two sets of a bowed aluminum plates that can be slipped on from the side. These make it possible to adjust the cameras laterally which is important in order to compensate for different users having different distances between their eyes. Each aluminum plate has three holes in it and each hole has a nut screw. The screws are used to hold a plastic disc on which the cameras are glued. The plastic discs can be adjusted laterally by tightening or loosening the screws. For each screw hole in the plastic disc, there is a 25 mm slits that allows adjusting the cameras in height. adjusting the cameras in height as this has been considered as important in previous studies by Park et. al. (2008). Park et al. studied the effect of eye-hand coordination with different camera positions. They tested a number of different positions and found that a height displacement of 35 mm above or below the eyes gave a better user experience compared to when the cameras were placed at eye level.

Fig. 2. Cameras mounted on Oculus Rift

The next section describes how the modified Oculus Rift has been used to in an experiment meant to imitate an industrial assembling process.

4   Experiment

As the study aims to investigate the use of augmented reality for aiding industrial shop-floor operators, a scenario imitating an industrial assembling process is set up. In this scenario, the task of the user consists of assembling a three-dimensional puzzle with nine pieces (see Figure 3). The pieces are to be placed in a certain order and at specific positions, just like in industrial assembling. Similar assembling tasks for studying augmented reality have previously been used by Sääski et al. (2008) and Woodward et al. (2012).

When undertaking the assembling of the puzzle, the user wears the modified Oculus Rift. The user then sees the real world digitally and virtual information is added on physical objects, creating an augmented reality effect. For handling the virtual information a library called Metaio is used (www.metaio.com).

Fig. 3. Three-dimensional puzzle used in the experiment

At the Oculus's screens, the piece to select next is highlighted in green and the place to put it is marked with the same shape and color. Figure 4 presents a screenshot illustrating the effect. In the screenshot, the user holds piece number one, which is overlaid with green color and pointed on with a virtual arrow. The piece is to be placed at the position marked with the same shape, color and number as the piece itself. As a the reference for determining positions of objects a reference image is used. In this case, the reference image is a photo of a team of budo girls as can be seen in the screenshot. A full demonstration of the augmented reality function and a complete assembling of the puzzle can be found at http://youtu.be/tuP28sZ6EZM.

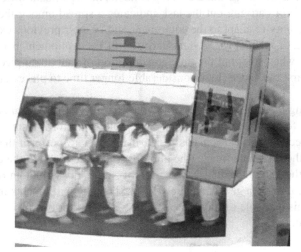

Fig. 4. Screenshot from Oculus's screen

In the study, six persons were participating in the experiment and given the task of assembling the puzzle wearing the modified Oculus Rift. The participants were given a short introduction to the task before starting, but did not receive any information about the equipment. During the assembling, there was no guidance given except in the case that a participant asked for it (which happened twice). After the assembling was completed, the participant was asked to fill in a questionnaire in order to assess their experience. The questionnaire was developed based on the questionnaire used in Looser et. al (2007) and consists of the following seven questions, each to be graded on a Likert scale from 1 to 7 (1 = totally disagree, 7 = totally agree):

Question 1: I found the system easy to understand.

Question 2: I found it easy to place a piece of the puzzle.

Question 3: I felt like I performed efficient with this system.

Question 4: If I had to use equipment like this on a regular basis, I would appreciate having access to.

Question 5: I found the system physically exhausting.

Question 6: I found the system mentally exhausting.

Question 7: I found the system frustrating.

In the next section, results from the experiment are presented in the next section.

5   Results

All six participants succeeded in assembling the puzzle, but needed different amounts of time for carrying out the task. The fastest assembling was performed within 3 minutes and 37 seconds, while the slowest assembling took about three times as long - it was completed within 10 minutes 30 seconds. The significant difference in amount of time needed for carrying out the task indicates a spread among the participants regarding their ability to adapt to the equipment and/or their previous experience in handling this type of technology. A familiarity with the equipment being advantageous becomes clear when studying the time consumption of individual pieces. As shown in Figure 5, the first two pieces took considerable longer time to place correctly compared to the rest.

After placing the first two pieces of the puzzle, the test participants had learned the basics of how to use the equipment and were able to perform faster. The single most important aspect for the participants to learn in order to perform the task efficiently was to retain the reference image (the photo of the budo girls) in the camera's field of view. When the reference image gets out of sight, no virtual information can be shown and the user then gets completely lost. All of the participants in the experiment experienced this a couple of times, especially with the first two pieces before learning how to avoid it.

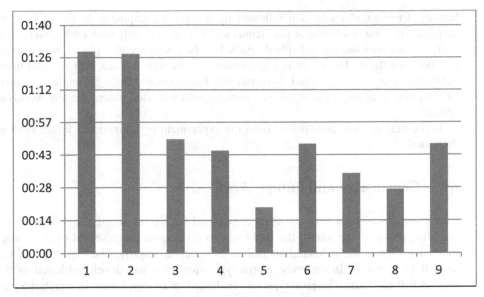

Fig. 5. Time consumption of each of the nine pieces of the puzzle (average values)

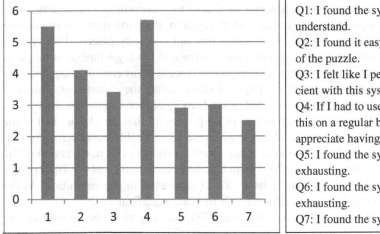

Q1: I found the system easy to understand.
Q2: I found it easy to place a piece of the puzzle.
Q3: I felt like I performed efficient with this system.
Q4: If I had to use equipment like this on a regular basis, I would appreciate having access to.
Q5: I found the system physically exhausting.
Q6: I found the system mentally exhausting.
Q7: I found the system frustrating.

Fig. 6. Questions and average results (1 = totally disagree, 7 = totally agree)

Although there was a learning curve for the participants, all of them considered the system easy to understand as shown in Figure 6 were average results from the questionnaire are presented. Furthermore, the participants thought that they would appreciate having access to system like this it if faced with a work task that needed it. However, as also can be seen in the figure, the participants experienced that the system was both physically and mentally stressful, and also that it made them frustrated to some extent. The main cause mentioned for the negative experience was the heavily deteriorated vision that followed by using the equipment. In fact, this is no surprise since the resolution of the Oculus Rift's screens is only 640 x 800 pixels. The user cannot only see the individual pixels, but the pixels are also placed with a small gap between them. The result is a quite blurry sight with a black grid net laid upon everything the user sees, which is disturbing. Furthermore, the sight angle is significantly reduced as the angle of the web camera (which is used record the real-world) is limited.

In the next section, conclusions from the experiment is outlined and future work is discussed.

6   Conclusions and Future Work

This paper described a study of using augmented reality for aiding the user in an assembling process. The aim of the study was to investigate the potential of using augmented reality at the industrial shop-floor in order to improve the capability of the shop-floor operators. In the study, a prototype equipment was developed based on the Oculus Rift platform. The prototype was evaluated in an experiment in which the participants were presented with the task of assembling a physical three-dimensional puzzle.

Results from the experiment showed that the participants were guided by visual information in the assembling process and were able to successfully assemble the puzzle. An important point to raise is that with the system, the participants were not able to move on with the puzzle in case a piece was not correctly placed. This type of built-in control helps to protect against human error and is very valuable in industry. In general, the participants believed that augmented reality was easy to grasp, but they experienced considerable mental and physical stress during the experiment. This negative experiences were mainly connected to the heavily reduced sight that comes with the Oculus Rift. However, it is important to keep in mind that the Oculus Rift at the moment is at a very early stage and that it will have considerable better screen resolution and refresh rate when released as a commercial product. The next version of the Oculus Rift is coming already in 2014 with a screen resolution of 960 x 1080 pixels, and the commercial version coming later on will have even higher resolution. As the technology advances, the user experience will increase significantly.

However, in an industrial setting the Oculus Rift, or any video-based solution for augmented reality, will most probably not be useful. This is since the industrial shop-floor is generally a high-risk environment with automated machines, robots, trucks, chemicals, etc. With a video-based solution the operator's sight is completely digitized and technology-dependent, which is too risky in case of, for example, a power failure in the equipment. However, while waiting for the head-worn solutions for augmented reality to become further developed and available at the market (for example, Google glasses), the video-based approach is perfectly fine to use for experimenting in safe environments.

In the near future, the authors intend to assess the actual improvements gained by using augmented reality in comparison with not doing so. This can, for example, be done by using the same task of assembling the three-dimensional puzzle but only letting the participants use paper instructions for how to place the pieces. For comparative results, differences in time consumption and error rates should be measured. Extensions of the study could also preferably involve a larger number of participants and several other assembling tasks with higher complexity. If possible, it would be advantageous to study ergonomic aspects as part of such extended study, for example related to head and hand movements. Body coordination with and without equipment would also be interesting to investigate.

References

Azuma, R.: A Survey of Augmented Reality. Hughes Research Laboratories, Malibu (1997)

Henderson, S., Feiner, S.: Evaluating the Benefits of Augmented Reality for Task Localization in Maintenance of an Armored Personnel Carrier Turret. In: Proceedings of IEEE International Symposium on Mixed and Augmented Reality (ISMAR 2009), pp. 135–144 (October 2009)

Henderson, S., Feiner, S.: Exploring the Benefits of Augmented Reality Documentation for Maintenance and Repair. IEEE Transactions on Visualization and Computer Graphics (TVCG) 17(10), 1355–1368 (2011)

Jeon, S., Kim, G.J.: Providing a Wide Field of View for Effective Interaction in Desktop Tangible Augmented Reality. VR 2008, pp. 3–10 (2008)

Looser, J., Billinghurst, M., Cockburn, A., Grasset, R.: An Evaluation of Virtual Lenses for Object Selection in Augmented Reality. In: Proceedings of the 5th International Conference on Computer Graphics and Interactive Techniques in Australia and Southeast Asia, New York, pp. 203–210. ACM (2007)

Rolland, J., Fuchs, H.: Optical Versus Video See-Through Head-Mounted Displays in Medical Visualization. Presence: Teleoperators and Virtual Environments 9(3), 287–309 (2000)

Steptoe, W: AR-Rift: Stereo camera for the Rift & immersive AR showcase. Oculus Developer Forums. Available on Internet: https://developer.oculusvr.com/forums/viewtopic.php?f=28&t=5215 (retrieved June 15, 2014) (2013)

Sääski, J., Salonen, T., Hakkarainen, M., Siltanen, S., Woodward, C., Lempiäinen, J.: Integration of design and assembly using augmented reality. Micro Assembly Technologies and Applications 260, 395–404 (2008)

Woodward, C., Hakkarainen, M., Billinghurst, M.: A client/server architecture for augmented reality on mobile phones. Handbook of research on Mobile Software Engineering - Design, Impementation and Emergent Applications, volume I. In: Alencar, P., Cowan, D. (eds.) Engineering Science Reference, pp. 1–16 (2012)

Robust Global Tracking Using a Seamless Structured Pattern of Dots

Lode Jorissen[✉], Steven Maesen, Ashish Doshi, and Philippe Bekaert

Expertise Centre for Digital Media, Hasselt University - tUL - iMinds,
Wetenschapspark 2, 3590 Diepenbeek, Belgium
{lode.jorissen,steven.maesen,ashish.doshi,philippe.bekaert}@uhasselt.be

Abstract. In this paper, we present a novel optical tracking approach to accurately estimate the pose of a camera in large scene augmented reality (AR). Traditionally, larger scenes are provided with multiple markers with their own identifier and coordinate system. However, when any part of a single marker is occluded, the marker cannot be identified. Our system uses a seamless structure of dots where the world position of each dot is represented by its spatial relation to neighboring dots. By using only the dots as features, our marker can be robustly identified. We use projective invariants to estimate the global position of the features and exploit temporal coherence using optical flow. With this design, our system is more robust against occlusions. It can also give the user more freedom of movement allowing them to explore objects up close and from a distance.

Keywords: Optical tracking · Structured pattern · Projective invariant · Augmented reality

1 Introduction

Estimating the pose of a camera accurately and robustly is essential to achieve a stable augmented image. It is the basis of any Augmented Reality application, ranging from entertainment to medical visualization. In many cases, the image to be augmented is also the basis for the tracking system. These optical trackers provide an inexpensive solution to the pose estimation problem.

The majority of camera based tracking systems use markers placed in the environment. These markers need to be completely visible to the camera to identify and calculate the transformation of the camera. Most systems fail when even a tiny portion is occluded. To compensate for this, they use multiple markers to have redundant information. This poses a trade-off between the number of markers and the minimum size for the information to be read out which translates into robustness versus accuracy.

We propose to use a seamless pattern of spatial coded dots. Individual dots are identified by the spatial relation between them using projective invariant properties. As long as a minimum set of identifiable dots is visible anywhere in the image, a global pose (the absolute pose in a predefined coordinate system,

© Springer International Publishing Switzerland 2014
L.T. De Paolis and A. Mongelli (Eds.): AVR 2014, LNCS 8853, pp. 210–231, 2014.
DOI: 10.1007/978-3-319-13969-2_17

e.g. defined by the marker) can be estimated. This makes our system more robust against occlusions than other marker based systems while maintaining an accurate pose estimate. Using a virtual and real test setup, we show that our tracking system reports a camera pose with an accuracy up to 1 mm and 0.06°, even with large occlusions. This results in a stable augmented image.

2   Related Work

There are different kinds of trackers, such as acoustic and mechanical trackers, that are able to estimate an object's pose. These trackers, however, are often too expensive or difficult to setup correctly. Optical trackers, on the other hand, can be made cheaply and the required cameras can be found in a wide range of devices these days.

Optical trackers can be classified into categories using different conditions. First, one can classify optical trackers as 'outside-looking-in' and 'inside-looking-out' trackers [27]. Outside-looking-in trackers use multiple calibrated cameras to determine the pose of one or more objects that move through the environment, while inside-looking-out trackers use one camera to determine its own pose with the help of the environment. Since inside-looking-out trackers are more suitable for applications such as augmented reality and virtual reality, and are more readily available than outside-looking in trackers (only one camera is needed), we will focus on this kind of optical trackers.

A second categorization is whether the tracker uses markers or natural features. Trackers can use natural features, such as corners and edges, as reference points. These trackers can be subdivided into different categories. PTAM[14], PTAMM [5] and vSLAM[12] for example build a feature map, used for tracking, at runtime. Visual Odometry[22] on the other hand only uses the information from the last few frames to determine the movement of the camera. Natural feature based trackers make it possible to determine the pose of the camera without adding markers in the environment, which means that they can work in unknown environments. These trackers, however, usually have several disadvantages. Most natural feature trackers only return a pose relative to the starting position instead of an absolute pose. This can make it difficult to align augmented reality objects with the real world. A solution to this problem could be to create a feature map first and reuse this map in subsequent executions in the same environment or to add a fiducial marker to the environment for initialization. Another disadvantage of natural feature trackers is that they often need to determine the positions of the features at run-time using only new features relative to existing features. This leads to an accumulation of errors and thus a decreased accuracy over time resulting in the estimated camera pose drifting away from the true pose. Again, this can be countered by providing a feature map of the environment, but creating an accurate map is often a time consuming and difficult task not suitable for most people. Natural feature trackers also need to detect a good amount of unique features, otherwise they will fail to determine the pose of the camera. Some control over the scene, for example adding more

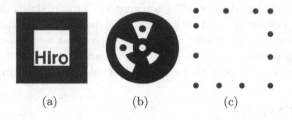

(a)   (b)   (c)

Fig. 1. A few different markers: (a) ARToolKit. (b) InterSense's marker. (c) PiTag (from [13], [19] and [2]).

textured objects, can resolve this problem, but this is contrary to the purpose of natural feature tracking.

Marker-based trackers are trackers that use artificial features that are placed in the environment. These features, called markers, often contain an identification pattern, or some other method to identify them, they can serve as reference points that are used to estimate the camera's extrinsic parameters. These extrinsic parameters relate world space coordinates to camera space coordinates, and thus describe the position and rotation of the camera. The markers deliver reference points or 2D-3D correspondences between the image plane and the real world that can be used to estimate the pose. Since the world position of these points is already known, the pose can often be estimated more accurate than with natural feature trackers. Markers can have different shapes, as can be seen in Figure 1, and those shapes have different advantages. Square markers, such as ARToolKit markers [13] and ARTag markers [9], usually have a thick black border, which is used to detect the marker while the inner part of the marker contains an identification tag. This tag often is an image or a binary code. Since the world-space position of the marker's four corners can easily be determined, they can be used to estimate the extrinsics of the camera. Circular markers such as TRIP [15] and InterSense's markers[19] also contain an identification tag, but the pose must be estimated using the shape of the projected circle, or with the help of multiple markers. According to Rice et al. [20] square markers can contain more data, but the pose can be calculated more accurately with the help of circular markers. Another more recent form of fiducial markers are marker fields [23]. Marker fields can be described as a grid of mutually overlapping partial markers, which allows the fiducial marker to be partially occluded.

Another possibility is to only use dots as markers and store the identification in the relation of the positions of the dots. This is the case for marker systems such as Pi-Tag [2] and Random Dot Marker [25], which both use a projective invariant, i.e. a property that does not change under a projective transformation, to identify the points. Another example is RUNE-tag, which can be seen as a hybrid between dot based markers and circular markers [1]. These dot-based trackers have the advantage that the markers take up a relatively small area in comparison to the square and circular markers. The biggest part of the area that these dot-based markers span is empty, which means that those areas often can be occluded without too much negative effects for the pose estimation algorithm. Square and circular markers on the other hand fill the area which means that even a small occluding object can already result in a failed detection or identification.

The previously mentioned trackers have a limited tracking span. Maesen et al. [17] proposed a system that uses dots, but does not store any identification information in these features. This results in a system that can be easily extended to larger areas, but as a trade-off only returns a pose relative to the starting position and not to a fixed predefined coordinate system. Maesen et al. [18] recently proposed a new system that encodes the position of the dots using De Bruijn codes and decodes the positions with the help of cross-ratios. This allows the tracker, contrary to their earlier system, to estimate the pose in relation to a predefined coordinate system. While they can support a very large tracking area accurately, their system has little redundant information to handle large occlusions. Saito et al.[21] created a system that encodes the position in the rotation and relative position of images that are placed on a plane. The result is a system that feels less artificial than other marker-based systems but is also less accurate.

Another way of increasing the tracking space is to place multiple markers in the environment, such that at least one marker is viewable from the camera. The main disadvantage of this method is that the position of each marker needs to be determined after placing it. One could also place the markers in a grid, but still needs to find a good balance between tracking distance and robustness against occlusions. Decreasing the size of the markers also decreases the tracking distance but allows more markers to be visible. Increasing the size, decreases the chance that a complete marker is visible in the frame and therefore reduces robustness against occlusions. Libraries such as ARToolKitPlus [26] and ARUco [10] allow this kind of setup. Chen et al. [6] proposed a system where they use a map of random dot markers to track the camera over a larger area. While their system is able to handle occlusions very well, it also inherits a drawback of random dot markers. Because of the exponential increase of invariant relations that the tracker can find between detected points, the computation time can increase dramatically in cases where the detector finds a lot of points.

Our proposed system of a seamless spatial encoded pattern is designed so that any part of the pattern can be used for tracking. In contrast to the state of the art approaches, our system does not require a whole marker to be visible but only multiple distributed parts. This makes it more robust for large occlusions than most other marker designs. The design is partly based on the grid of dots that Maesen et al. [17] proposed, but introduce a robust spatial coding scheme for global pose estimation. We encode the position of each line in the grid with a unique relative placement of the dots on the lines. Thanks to the cross-ratio projective invariant [7], we are able to reconstruct this placement which allows the identification of the lines. This in turn allows us to identify the position of each visible dot, which is used to give an accurate estimate of the pose of the camera. Our system is especially designed to be robust against large occlusions as can be seen in the next sections.

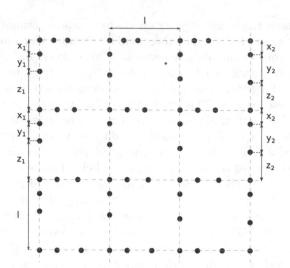

Fig. 2. The structure of our marker. Only a small part of a possible setup is shown here. Each line has a different set of distances between the points. The set (x_1, y_1, z_1) for example is not equal to the set (x_2, y_2, z_2) since both y_1 and z_1 are not equal to y_2 and z_2 respectively.

3   Structured Dot Marker

Our tracking pattern consists of a spatially encoded set of dots. Compared to conventional marker systems, the dots themselves do not contain any identification information. This makes them very small, easily detectable and harder to occlude than large markers. The identification of a single dot requires the spatial relationship between its neighbors. The dots are placed on a grid structure consisting of two sets of parallel lines and are uniquely spaced to create a coded pattern. Figure 2 shows part of the structure of our marker. The dots on each line are repeatedly spaced according to three distances x, y and z. Each line has a unique set of distances and the sum of those distances is always equal to the line distance l, which is the distance between two subsequent parallel lines. This means that for two different lines l_1 and l_2 the corresponding sets of distances (x_1, y_1, z_1) and (x_2, y_2, z_2) are never equal to each other. Each intersection of two perpendicular lines also corresponds with a dot. By utilizing these properties it is possible to determine the world-space position of each dot, which allows us to accurately estimate the camera's true pose.

4   Tracking

As can be seen in Figure 3, the algorithm consists of four important steps: image capture, detection, identification, and pose estimation. The image capture step acquires an image from the input system. The captured image is passed on to the

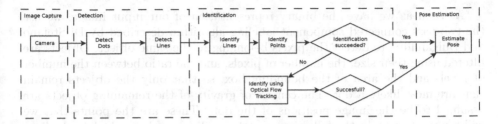

Fig. 3. Overview of our tracking algorithm. Our system consists of 4 steps, more specifically image capture, detection, identification, and pose estimation.

detection step, which consists of a dot detection step and the detection of (virtual) lines passing through the detected points. This information is then passed down to the identification step, which identifies the lines and the points lying on those lines. Using the identified points we can estimate the extrinsic parameters of the camera. In some cases where it is not possible to identify enough points, we switch to an optical flow tracking algorithm which uses information from earlier frames to track previously identified dots. The following sections describe each step in more details.

4.1 Image Capture

The first step in the algorithm acquires an image from the input device. Input can be taken from a camera, a video or a virtual scene. Because we assume that we are working with a standard pinhole camera model, we need to undo the lens distortion on the image. It is more efficient to only undistort the positions of the detected points right after the dot detection step. The first option will take more computing time than the latter, but it can be more suitable for certain applications such as augmented reality, where one needs to display the input image in the background.

Both lens distortion and intrinsic camera parameters (focal length, principal point, etc.) can be calculated in a preprocessing step as they do not change when using a fixed focus camera. We do this by using a checkerboard pattern provided by the OpenCV framework [4].

4.2 Dot Detection

After acquiring the image we need to detect the dots that are visible in the image. This step consists of a thresholding algorithm which creates a binary representation of the image, and a connected component labeling algorithm which groups the pixels belonging to the same object together. We used the adaptive thresholding algorithm described by Bradley and Roth[3] to create a detection algorithm that can handle to varying lighting conditions. This makes it possible to detect dots that are hulled in shadows, or to use the tracker in most environments without the need to manually change the thresholding parameters.

As soon as we have the binary representation of our input image, we use the two-pass connected component labeling algorithm described by Di Stefano and Bulgarelli[8] to detect the pixels belonging to the same object. Objects are filtered using their size, the number of pixels, and the ratio between the number of pixels and the area of the bounding box, so that only the objects remain that are most likely a dot. The centers of gravity of the remaining objects are assumed to be the image positions of the dots. These are the points that we will try to identify. In the following step they will be used to calculate the lines passing through the points.

4.3   Line Detection

In this step, we determine the lines passing through the points. This is done by iterating over each point that is not yet part of a line, and selecting its two nearest neighbors. We then generate the two lines that pass through the selected point and each of its neighbors. For each line we determine the detected points that lie on it: the distance from the point to the line should be smaller than a certain threshold. We update the parameters of the line for each point that lies on it to make sure that we find most of the points on the line. A line will only be passed to the line identification step when there are enough points associated with it. The line identification step will filter out falsely detected lines.

4.4   Line Identification

After detecting the lines we must identify them. We use the projective invariant cross-ratio, which, combined with the fact that the distances between the points on the same line are repeated, allows us to identify the lines.

Cross-Ratio. The cross-ratio of four collinear points can be calculated as follows[7]:

$$\tau(A,B,C,D) = \frac{d(A,C)}{d(B,C)} \Big/ \frac{d(A,D)}{d(B,D)} = \frac{d(A,C)}{d(B,C)} \cdot \frac{d(B,D)}{d(A,D)} \tag{1}$$

where $d(A,B)$ is the signed distance from A to B such that $d(A,B) = -d(B,A)$. The cross-ratio is projective invariant, i.e. if we look at the projection of four collinear points on the image plane, the cross-ratio of those projections is always the same and thus it is independent of the camera's pose. This means that in Figure 4, $\tau(A,B,C,D) = \tau(A',B',C',D') = \tau(A'',B'',C'',D'')$. Calculating the cross-ratio using a different order for the points can result in a different value. In fact there are six different cross-ratio values for each set of four collinear points, but these values are all dependent on each other. If we use the same order of points or if we reverse the order, the resulting value will always be the same.

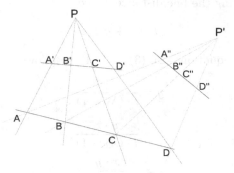

Fig. 4. Illustration of the projective invariance of the cross-ratio τ. In this example, according to the property of the cross-ratio, $\tau(A, B, C, D) = \tau(A', B', C', D') = \tau(A'', B'', C'', D'')$.

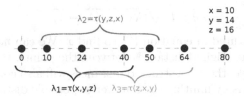

Fig. 5. For six subsequent points there are three independent cross-ratios ($\lambda_1, \lambda_2, \lambda_3$) as shown in this example

Identification. It would be easy to identify the lines if we knew the true distance between the points, but it is well known that under a projective transformation the distance between two points is not preserved. Since the cross-ratio of four collinear points is dependent on three variables, namely the three distances between the points, one needs to have three cross-ratios that are dependent on these distances to reconstruct the original distances. For the repeated dot pattern on a line one can find three cross-ratios for six subsequent points, as can be seen in Figure 5. These cross-ratios can be written as:

$$\lambda_1 = \tau(x, y, z) = \frac{(x+y)}{y} \Big/ \frac{x+y+z}{y+z} = \frac{(x+y) \cdot (y+z)}{y \cdot (x+y+z)} \tag{2}$$

$$\lambda_2 = \tau(y, z, x) = \frac{(y+z)}{z} \Big/ \frac{x+y+z}{z+x} = \frac{(y+z) \cdot (z+x)}{z \cdot (x+y+z)} \tag{3}$$

$$\lambda_3 = \tau(z, x, y) = \frac{(z+x)}{x} \Big/ \frac{x+y+z}{x+y} = \frac{(z+x) \cdot (x+y)}{x \cdot (x+y+z)} \tag{4}$$

Since scaling the distances with a constant gives the same cross-ratio (thus $\tau(x, y, z) = \tau(kx, ky, kz)$), we need to make sure that we find the correct solution.

This can be done using the line distance, since

$$l = x + y + z \tag{5}$$

We can now rewrite equations (2), (3) and (4) as follows:

$$y = \frac{x \cdot z}{l \cdot (\lambda_1 - 1)} \tag{6}$$

$$x = \frac{y \cdot z}{l \cdot (\lambda_3 - 1)} \tag{7}$$

$$z = \frac{x \cdot y}{l \cdot (\lambda_2 - 1)} \tag{8}$$

If we replace y in (7) by (6) and z by (8) we respectively find:

$$z = l \cdot \sqrt{(\lambda_1 - 1)(\lambda_3 - 1)} \tag{9}$$

$$y = l \cdot \sqrt{(\lambda_2 - 1)(\lambda_3 - 1)} \tag{10}$$

which can be substituted in equation (7) to find x. We can now use these equations to calculate the original distances between the points. Because of measurement errors and noise, the reconstructed distances will also contain noise. We are able to cope with this by limiting the number of possible distances, i.e. rounding the calculated distances (x, y, z) towards the nearest available correct distance values $(\tilde{x}, \tilde{y}, \tilde{z})$.

It is a good idea to limit the number of positions on which a point can be placed by dividing the length l in intervals, and placing the dots only at those intervals. Assuming that the line distance l is set at 80mm, and every point is placed at one of the 80 different intervals: the maximum allowed error for the calculated distances is 0.5 mm. If we would only allow 40 intervals of 2 mm, the maximum allowed error would be 1 mm. This means that we can increase the robustness against noise by decreasing the number of positions on which a point can be placed at the cost of a smaller set of lines that can be used by the marker. We can achieve this by replacing l by the number of intervals between two subsequent lines and setting the distances x, y and z equal to the number of intervals between the points.

The calculated distances are used to construct a unique hash-value to identify the lines:

$$h = d_1 + d_2 \cdot l + d_3 \cdot l^2 \tag{11}$$

where d_1, d_2 and d_3 are the corresponding distances $\tilde{x}$, $\tilde{y}$ and $\tilde{z}$ sorted in ascending order:

$$(d_1, d_2, d_3) = \text{sorted}(\tilde{x}, \tilde{y}, \tilde{z}) \tag{12}$$

The resulting value can be used to lookup information about the line, like whether the line is a horizontal or a vertical line and the position of the line along the axis. This hash-value also adds the constraint during the generation of the setup that the sum of the distances has to be unique for each line. One should always check that the sum of the distances is equal to l before checking the hash as this will filter out most outliers.

The set of distances where $d_3 - d_1 \leq 1$ should be avoided to encode a line in the setup. The reason for this is that these distances result in cross-ratios that are almost equal to those of lines with evenly spaced dots, which turns out to be very common in our setup (for example diagonal lines passing through the intersection of perpendicular lines).

Each group of six subsequent points that is identified is stored for that line, and will be reused in the point identification stage. We ignore a line if there are conflicting identifications for it.

It might be possible that, at the end of this step, there still are some incorrectly identified lines. This is something that we have to take into consideration in the point identification step.

4.5   Point Identification

It is possible to identify the points if we have at least three correctly identified lines, where one line is perpendicular to the other two. We are able to determine at least one coordinate of the points on these lines since we know the horizontal or vertical location of the lines. This means that we only have to find the position of the point along the line.

We used a RANSAC approach to determine the positions of the detected points. First, we randomly select three identified lines, where two (E_1 and E_2) of them are parallel to each other and the other one L is perpendicular to them. This means there are two intersection points, whose positions, on the marker plane and on the image plane, we know: the intersections of E_1 and E_2 with L. We call these points the anchor points, as they help us determine the absolute world positions of the detected points. Using this information it is possible to determine the directions of the axes of the coordinate system. For example, if we know the position of E_1 along the x-axis is smaller than the position of E_2, then we know that x-axis of the coordinate system is parallel to L and that it increments in the direction of E_1 to E_2. Because of this we also know the direction of the y-axis. After determining the directions, the points on the lines are ordered in ascending order.

For each line L, E_1 and E_2 we can now determine the positions of the points by looking at each group $\{G\}$ of six subsequent points. Each group $\{G\}$ was found during the line identification step. An example of this calculation is given in Figure 6:

1. Determine the relative positions of the points in $\{G\}$ such that one point, which lies on the intersection of two lines (not necessarily the anchor points), is placed at the origin of this relative system (its position along the line is zero).
2. Use these relative world positions of the points in $\{G\}$ and their positions along the projected line to determine the homographic transformation H which maps points on the projected line to the original line. We describe a method to determine H later on.

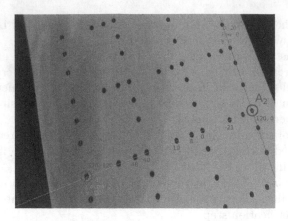

Fig. 6. The world positions of the two intersection points are determined using the lines' information. Note that this position is not yet coupled to the underlying dot. The relative positions of the points in a group is determined, and this information is used to determine the offset. Considering anchor-point A_1 the displacement equals $120 - 80 = 40$ where 120 is the true position along the line and 80 is the relative position determined using $\boldsymbol{H}$.

3. Map the image position p of one of the anchor points to this relative world space using $\boldsymbol{H}$. Call this position p'.
4. The displacement from the relative positions to the true positions is given by $a - p'$ where a is the true position of the anchor point.
5. The true displacement δ can be found by rounding of the calculated displacement to the nearest multiple of l.
6. Add δ to the relative positions of the points in $\{\boldsymbol{G}\}$ to find the true world position.

We need to do these steps for each $\{\boldsymbol{G}\}$ because $\boldsymbol{H}$ is too inaccurate to determine the location of the points on the lines outside of group $\{\boldsymbol{G}\}$. This is also the reason why we place the relative coordinate system at an intersection: since the distance between this intersection and the selected anchor point always is a multiple of l it is possible to remove the error in the displacement $a - p'$ by rounding it to the nearest multiple of l.

The transformation $\boldsymbol{H}$ can be calculated in a similar way as the Direct Linear Transformation (DLT) for obtaining the 2D homography[11]. The matrix $\boldsymbol{H}$ is given as:

$$\boldsymbol{H} = \begin{bmatrix} h_{11} & h_{12} \\ h_{21} & h_{22} \end{bmatrix}$$

The linear system to be solved is:

$$\boldsymbol{A}h = 0$$

with

$$A = \begin{bmatrix} -e_1' & -1 & e_1' \cdot e_1 & e_1 \\ \vdots & \vdots & \vdots & \vdots \\ -e_n' & -1 & e_n' \cdot e_n & e_n \end{bmatrix}$$

where e_i are the signed distances to a reference point along the projected line, e_i' are the signed distances to this reference point along the line in world space and

$$h = \begin{bmatrix} h_{11} & h_{12} & h_{21} & h_{22} \end{bmatrix}^\mathsf{T}$$

This equation can be solved using the Singular Value Decomposition (SVD). A position on the projected line can be mapped to the world line as follows:

$$\lambda \begin{bmatrix} e' \\ 1 \end{bmatrix} = H \begin{bmatrix} e \\ 1 \end{bmatrix}$$

After calculating the positions of the points on the three selected lines we can calculate the positions of the other points in the image by using a 2D homography that maps the points in the image to the marker plane. If an unprojected point is close enough to another point on the plane the unprojected point is assumed to be that point and the image point is assigned that position.

Because of the fact that some lines may be falsely identified it is necessary to select multiple sets of three lines and only keep the results of the best set. We can use these image-space and world-space correspondences to determine the pose of the camera as in section 4.7.

4.6   Optical Flow Tracking

Even if not enough points are detected to establish full identification, we still want to identify those points. This situation happens for example when the camera moves too close to the marker plane, in which case we are unable to find enough points to detect and identify lines. Another situation where this can happen is when the camera view is occluded, leaving only very few markers visible. By exploiting the temporal coherence between frames, we can still identify these detected dots using optical flow tracking. By keeping track of the pose of the camera in the last few frames, it is possible to estimate the new image-space position for the current frame using extrapolation. This new pose can be used to estimate the new position of the points that we identified in the previous frame. Next, we map the points detected in the new frame to the estimated locations which gives us new 2D-3D correspondences, which are used to estimate the real pose. The mapping is done by finding the nearest detected point in the new frame for each estimated position. It is possible that during the mapping step some point are falsely identified. These outliers can be detected by reprojecting the position of the dots on the image. Assuming that we have more inliers than outliers, the outliers will have a larger reprojection error than the inliers. The inliers can then be used to determine a homography between the image plane and the marker plane, so that the newly detected points can be identified.

4.7 Pose Estimation

Given the 2D-3D correspondences, we minimize the reprojection error with the help of the projection equation that projects a given 3D point (X, Y, Z) on the image plane using the estimated extrinsic parameters $\boldsymbol{R}$ and $\boldsymbol{t}$. The reprojection error can be calculated using the sum of squared differences (SSD):

$$e = \sum_{i=1}^{N} \left((x_i - x_i')^2 + (y_i - y_i')^2 \right) \tag{13}$$

where N is the number of points, (x_i, y_i) is the true projection of the ith point and (x_i', y_i') is the projection of the point which is calculated from the projection equation and the estimated extrinsics:

$$\lambda \begin{bmatrix} x' \\ y' \\ 1 \end{bmatrix} = \boldsymbol{K}[\boldsymbol{R}|\boldsymbol{t}] \begin{bmatrix} X \\ Y \\ Z \\ 1 \end{bmatrix} \tag{14}$$

where (X, Y, Z) is the 3D world point, $\boldsymbol{K}$ are the intrinsic and $\boldsymbol{R}$ and $\boldsymbol{t}$ are the extrinsic parameters of the camera. These extrinsic parameters relate world coordinates to a camera coordinate system where the camera is placed at the origin.

To solve this problem, we first estimate the homography between the image plane and the marker plane [11]. This method gives us a good initial estimate for the camera's pose. We can use this to initialize the Levenbergh-Marquardt algorithm which refines the pose iteratively by minimizing Equation (13).

5   Results

Our tracking system is implemented using the OpenCV framework [4]. We used the Levenbergh-Marquardt implementation of Lourakis[16] the estimate the pose. Both a virtual and real world setup are constructed to test the accuracy of the algorithm as well as the influence of the different parameters of the setup on the accuracy. We also looked at the processing time and the robustness of the tracker.

5.1   Virtual Setup

The virtual setup consisted of an OpenGL scene that contained our marker. This allowed us to compare the calculated position and orientation against the ground truth. We used a reference setup to compare the influence of the different parameters. This reference setup had a line distance of 45 mm, and the dots had a radius of 2 mm. The setup consisted of 10 horizontal and 10 vertical lines. The segments between two adjacent lines were split up into 40 intervals. Dots were

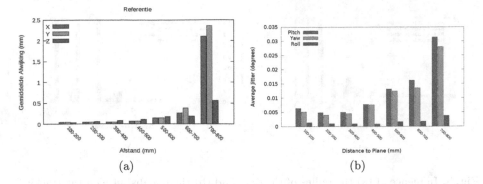

Fig. 7. Both the accuracy of the position (a) and the rotation (b) decrease if the distance to the marker increases

placed on the lines with a minimum distance of 8 intervals between each other to prevent overlapping dots. The camera had a resolution of 640×480 pixels and a horizontal field of view of $75°$.

We first tested the accuracy of our tracker in the given setup. As we can see in Figures 7(a) and 7(b), the accuracy decreases if the distance to the plane increases. The maximum distance to the marker was approximately 70cm. Beyond 70cm, failure rate increases due to the inability to detect the dots. During the tests with this setup the average deviation was about 0.1 mm for the position and $0.01°$ for the rotation.

5.2   Real World Setup

We also tested the tracker in real world conditions. We used a low-cost camera with a resolution of 640×480 pixels and a horizontal field of view of $53°$. The camera was placed on a tripod to determine the jitter. We used different poses for the camera and did this calculation for different setups. From this information we found that increasing the dot radius decreases the jitter for poses closer to the marker plane, but increases the jitter for poses further away from the plane. This can be explained by the fact that each dot now fills a larger area on the image plane, which reduces the influence of the noise in the image, and thus result in a more stable pose when the camera is closer to the marker. This also means that the distance between two points becomes smaller, which will lead to points blurring into each other when the camera is situated at a greater distance to the plane, which results in an increased jitter. Increasing the number of intervals or decreasing the line distance also increased the jitter since the maximum allowed deviation for the calculated distances in the line identification step decreased. The average jitter for a typical desktop setup was about 1 mm for the position, and $0.06°$ for the rotation. From these results we can conclude that both noise and blur effects influence the accuracy of the tracker.

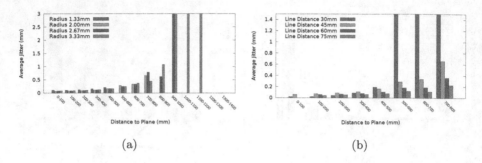

Fig. 8. Influence of (a) the radius of the dots and (b) the line distance on the tracking distance and the accuracy

5.3   Increasing Tracking Distance

It turns out that there are two main possibilities to increase the tracking distance: increase both the line distance and the radius of the dots simultaneously, or increase the camera resolution. As we can see in Figure 8(a), simply increasing the radius already increases the tracking distance, but the accuracy decrements dramatically at a certain point. Increasing only the line distance doesn't increase the tracking distance, but it does increase the accuracy as one can see in Figure 8(b). This can be explained by the fact that, at a certain distance, the distance between the projected points becomes too small to give an accurate result. Increasing both the line distance and the radius of the dots will thus increase the tracking distance while maintaining a decent accuracy, as can be seen in Figure 9(a). Increasing the camera resolution results in a similar behavior as can be seen in Figure 9(b). Another method to increase the tracking distance is to decrease the field of view, but this might be impractical in the real world.

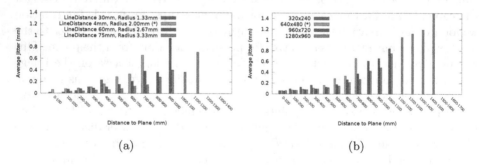

Fig. 9. (a) Influence of both the line distance and the radius on the tracking distance and the accuracy. (b) Increasing the camera resolution increases both the accuracy and the tracking distance.

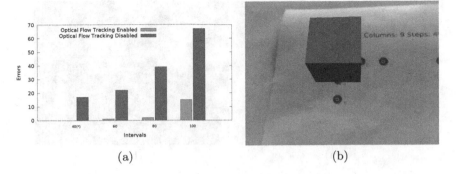

(a)   (b)

Fig. 10. (a) Optical flow tracking can help to determine the pose for an image when insufficient dots are visible for full identification. This histogram shows the number of frames where the pose could not be detected in function of the number of intervals, while the camera was moving away from the marker. The path consisted of 661 frames. (b)

5.4   Robustness

Next, we examined the influence of the optical flow tracking algorithm on the number of frames for which a pose could be determined. On a prerecorded path existing of 1758 frames the number of failed identifications dropped from 81 frames to six frames when we enabled the optical flow tracking algorithm. Figure 10(a) visualizes the decrease of failures when optical flow tracking is enabled. Similar results were obtained for other paths, which clearly shows that the optical flow tracking algorithm increases the robustness of the tracker.

Using optical flow tracking, it is possible to estimate the pose with at least four non-collinear points, which makes it possible to track the pose in more unusual cases. This allows us, for example, to move the camera close to the marker plane, as can be seen in Figure 10(b).

The small area of the points compared to the area of the plane on which they are placed and the redundancy of the encoded positions already allows us to estimate the pose in cases where big parts of the setup are occluded. It can happen that the occluding object makes it impossible to identify at least three lines, in which case the tracker can again rely on the optical flow tracking step. This means that both marker design and the optical flow tracking algorithm helped to create a tracking system that is more robust against occlusions than most other marker based trackers. Examples of this are given in Figure 11.

Since we use an adaptive thresholding algorithm to create the binary image in the dot detection step, the tracker is able to detect dots under varying lighting conditions. This allows the usage of the tracker in an environment where the lighting is not controlled.

(a)   (b)

Fig. 11. Even when big parts of the marker are occluded, it is still possible to determine the camera's pose

5.5 Number of Lines

One of the factors that determines the area that can be tracked is the number of available lines, since they define the height and the width of the marker's plane. The number of lines is dependent on the number of intervals we divide the line distance l in, and the minimum number of intervals between two adjacent points. Table 1 gives the number of available lines for a given number of intervals and a minimum distance. One should be careful when choosing these values, since an increase in the number of intervals may lead to a decreased number of successful identifications as can be seen in Figure 10(a). These failures can be limited with the help of optical flow tracking. A decrease of the minimum distance between the points may result in overlapping points or may increase the negative influence that motion blur has on the detection step: if the distance is too small two nearby dots may blur into each other, and may thus be detected as just one point. This can of course be mitigated by decreasing the radius of the dots, but this will also lead to a decreased tracking distance.

Table 1. The number of available lines is dependent on the number of intervals in which the line distance is split and the minimum offset between the points

Intervals	Offset (intervals)	Number of Lines
20	1	31
20	4	8
40	1	132
40	4	79
40	8	29
60	8	126
60	12	60
80	1	531
80	8	288
80	16	100

5.6   Processing Time

On our test system[1] the processing time for each frame, with a resolution of 640x480 pixels, was on average 13ms or 77 frames per second. When a very large part of the pattern becomes visible, the processing time could go up to 24ms. In our current implementation the dot detection step was approximately 6 ms, while the line detection and the line identification step was 0.3 ms and 0.6 ms respectively. Identifying the individual dots took on average 6 ms, including the optical flow algorithm when not enough lines are identified. The processing time of the dot detection is highly dependent on the resolution of the images, which means that it will increase if the resolution increases. The dot identification step on the other hand seems to be dependent on the number of selected groups of three lines.

5.7   Comparative Analysis

In this section, performance comparisons were made between Structured Dot Markers (SDM) and two well known trackers. The first tracker was ARToolkit [13] with its default multimarker setup and 65mm wide markers. The other tested tracker was ARUco [10]. Its setup was a 6 × 8 marker grid and 35mm wide markers. The SDM grid setup consisted of 9 rows and 6 columns, with a line spacing of 45mm. Each dot had a radius of 2mm.

The first experiment relates to performance analysis without occlusions. For each tracker, 1000 frames were captured whilst the camera was moved along a set path. The experimental results are presented (red columns) in Figure 12. The green columns relate to the second experiment of performance analysis with occlusions.

Both ARToolKit and ARUco had reasonable success rates of 78.4% and 96.9% respectively, for the first experiment and lowered successes for the second experiment, with ARToolKit only recording a 34.3% success rate. In comparison, SDM had a 100% success rate for marker identification without occlusion and a

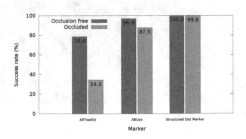

Fig. 12. A comparison of the success rate of marker identification and tracking with and without occlusions

---

[1] Desktop workstation with 2.80GHz Intel Core i7 CPU.

fairly high success rate of 99% with occlusion. Though the performance results were surprising, it was not entirely unexpected that SDM would outperform ARToolKit and ARUco. As outlined earlier, this is because our marker design is organized in a structured grid, with easily recognized features (dots) and the ability to identify individual lines. However, our tracking system is susceptible to abrupt movements that cause the optical flow algorithm to fail, thereby needing to reinitialize or when the camera is hovering too close over the marker. It is also susceptible to large motion blurs, as with any other tracker in the field.

6   Applications

We implemented both an augmented reality and a virtual reality application to show how well it can perform in a real world situation. For example, in Figure 11(a) we can see that our tracking solution can still produce a stable augmented image, even with most of the dots occluded by the hand of the user. When the camera moves closer to the pattern, the optical flow algorithm makes sure that tracking can still be continued, as shown in Figure 10(b). Our system can also cope with objects being placed on top of our pattern. Figure 11(b) shows that it has little effect on the tracking stability and accuracy. We would like to refer to our accompanying video for more results demonstrating the use of AR with our tracking system.

We added the ability to start a Virtual-Reality Peripheral Network (VRPN) server [24] to our system. This allows (already existing) virtual reality applications that implement the VRPN protocol to connect to our tracker. This means that the tracker can easily be integrated into other applications. An example of this is shown in Figure 13.

The supplementary video[2] shows these applications in action.

(a)   (b)

Fig. 13. (a) The image taken by the camera. (b) A screenshot of a VRPN client using the calculated pose.

---

[2] http://research.edm.uhasselt.be/%7Esmaesen/pubs/AVR14/StructuredDotMarker. mp4

7 Conclusion

We proposed a novel tracking approach using a seamless structured pattern of dots that can estimate the global position and orientation of a camera accurately and robustly. The tracker works over relatively large areas without relying on individual identifiable markers as used in related systems. Instead our dots are encoded using the spatial relationship with its neighbors which can be identified using projective invariants. We can also exploit the temporal coherence between frames to establish a robust tracking result in cases where other systems fail. We have shown that our system is able to handle large occlusions, either by objects placed on top or by dynamic occlusions of users. This makes it very useful in Mixed or Augmented Reality applications where occlusions are frequent.

We have conducted extensive tests in a virtual scene to identify the major parameters that contribute to the accuracy of our system. Using the ground truth of the tracking data in a virtual scene, we established that we could achieve a global accuracy of 0.1 mm and 0.01°. In our real world setup, we used a standard low-cost camera with a resolution of 640x480 to test the accuracy in a typical desktop AR scene. These cameras suffer from measurement noise, motion blur and lens distortion. Under these conditions, the average jitter of our system was measured to be 1 mm for the position and 0.06° for the rotation of the estimated camera pose. This gives a stable augmented image, even under large occlusions, as shown in our results. Compared with other marker based tracking systems, we showed that our system outperformed ARToolkit and ARUco at handling occlusions. Our tracking system can process camera images at a rate of 77 frames per second (average of 13 ms per frame).

Further work is planned to include hierarchical based structured dots, optimization for mobile devices and expanding our system for more diverse applications.

References

1. Bergamasco, F., Albarelli, A., Rodola, E., Torsello, A.: Rune-tag: A high accuracy fiducial marker with strong occlusion resilience. In: 2011 IEEE Conference on Computer Vision and Pattern Recognition (CVPR), pp. 113–120 (June 2011)
2. Bergamasco, F., Albarelli, A., Torsello, A.: Pi-Tag: A fast image-space marker design based on projective invariants. Machine Vision and Applications 24(6), 1295–1310 (2013)
3. Bradley, D., Roth, G.: Adaptive Thresholding using the Integral Image. Journal of Graphics, GPU, and Game Tools 12(2), 13–21 (2007)
4. Bradski, G.: Dobb's Journal of Software Tools (2000)
5. Castle, R.O., Klein, G., Murray, D.W.: Video-rate Localization in Multiple Maps for Wearable Augmented Reality. In: Proc. 12th IEEE Int. Symp. on Wearable Computers, Pittsburgh PA, September 28-October 1, pp. 15–22 (2008)
6. Chen, L., Fu, H., Ho, W., Li, A., Ian Tai, C.: Scalable Maps of Random Dots for Middle-scale Locative Mobile Games (2013)

7. Courant, R., Robbins, H.: What is Mathematics? Oxford University Press (1996)
8. Di Stefano, L., Bulgarelli, A.: A simple and efficient connected components labeling algorithm. In: Proceedings of the International Conference on Image Analysis and Processing, pp. 322–327 (1999)
9. Fiala, M.: ARTag revision 1, a fiducial marker system using digital techniques. Technical Report NRC 47419/ERB-1117 (November 2004)
10. Garrido-Jurado, S., Muoz-Salinas, R., Madrid-Cuevas, F., Marn-Jimnez, M.: Automatic generation and detection of highly reliable fiducial markers under occlusion. Pattern Recognition **47**(6), 2280–2292 (2014)
11. Hartley, R., Zisserman, A.: Multiple View Geometry in Computer Vision. Cambridge University Press (2004)
12. Karlsson, N., Di Bernardo, E., Ostrowski, J., Goncalves, L., Pirjanian, P., Munich, M.: The vSLAM Algorithm for Robust Localization and Mapping. In: Proceedings of the 2005 IEEE International Conference on Robotics and Automation (ICRA 2005), pp. 24–29 (2005)
13. Kato, D.H.: ARToolKit (1999). http://www.hitl.washington.edu/artoolkit/
14. Klein, G., Murray, D.: Parallel tracking and mapping for small AR workspaces. In: Proc. Sixth IEEE and ACM International Symposium on Mixed and Augmented Reality (ISMAR 2007), Nara, Japan (November 2007)
15. López de Ipiña, D., Mendonça, P.R.S., Hopper, A.: TRIP: A Low-Cost Vision-Based Location System for Ubiquitous Computing. Personal Ubiquitous Comput. **6**(3), 206–219 (2002)
16. Lourakis, M.: levmar: Levenberg-Marquardt nonlinear least squares algorithms in C/C++ (July 2004). http://www.ics.forth.gr/lourakis/levmar/ (accessed on January 31, 2005)
17. Maesen, S., Bekaert, P.: Low-Cost, Wide-Area Tracking for Virtual Environments. In: IEEE VR 2007 Workshop Trends and Issues in Tracking for Virtual Environments, pp. 16-21, Charlotte, NC, USA. IEEE, Shaker Verlag (2007)
18. Maesen, S., Goorts, P., Bekaert, P: Scalable optical tracking for navigating large virtual environments using spatially encoded markers. In: Proceedings of the 19th ACM Symposium on Virtual Reality Software and Technology, VRST 2013, pp. 101–110. ACM, New York (2013)
19. Naimark, L., Foxlin, E.: Circular data matrix fiducial system and robust image processing for a wearable vision-inertial self-tracker. In: Proceedings of the 1st International Symposium on Mixed and Augmented Reality, ISMAR 2002, p. 27. IEEE Computer Society, Washington, DC (2002)
20. Rice, A.C., Harle, R.K., Beresford, A.R.: Analysing fundamental properties of marker-based vision system designs (2006)
21. Saito, S., Hiyama, A., Tanikawa, T., Hirose, M.: Indoor Marker-based Localization Using Coded Seamless Pattern for Interior Decoration. In: IEEE Virtual Reality Conference, VR 2007, pp. 67–74 (2007)
22. Scaramuzza, D., Fraundorfer, F.: Visual odometry [tutorial]. IEEE Robotics Automation Magazine **18**(4), 80–92 (2011)
23. Szentandrási, I., Zachariáš, M., Havel, J., Herout, A., Dubská, M., Kajan, R.: Uniform Marker Fields: Camera localization by orientable De Bruijn tori. In: Proceedings of ISMAR (2012)

24. Taylor, II, R.M., Hudson, T.C., Seeger, A., Weber, H., Juliano, J., Helser, A.T.: VRPN: A device-independent, network-transparent VR peripheral system. In: Proceedings of the ACM Symposium on Virtual Reality Software and Technology, VRST 2001, pp. 55–61. ACM, New York (2001)
25. Uchiyama, H., Saito, H.: Random dot markers. In: Proceedings of the 2011 IEEE Virtual Reality Conference, VR 2011, pp. 271–272. IEEE Computer Society, Washington, DC (2011)
26. Wagner, D., Schmalstieg, D.: ARToolKitPlus for Pose Tracking on Mobile Devices (2007)
27. Welch, G., Bishop, G., Vicci, L., Vicci, R., Brumback, S., Keller, K., Place, M.: High-Performance Wide-Area Optical Tracking: The HiBall Tracking System, pp. 1–21. MIT Press (2001)

Lightweight Augmented Reality Tools for Lean Procedures in Future Factories

Francesco Capozzi, Valerio Lorizzo$^{(\boxtimes)}$, Gianfranco Modoni, and Marco Sacco

Institute of Industrial Technology and Automation,
National Research Council, Milan, Italy
{francesco.capozzi,valerio.lorizzo,gianfranco.modoni,
marco.sacco}@itia.cnr.it

Abstract. The aim of this paper is to introduce the main outcomes of the application of Augmented Reality (AR) features to manufacturing and industrial scenarios under a new perspective. While the request of industrial mixed reality technologies is continuously growing, the research community is still facing the crucial challenge to give a convenient answer to such needs. The problem of the development of adaptable and inexpensive AR solutions is herein addressed by proposing a new approach for the application of AR technology to lean-based visual communication transfer and exchange. This work starts from the concept of virtual factory, a place where the real production of future factories becomes fully merged with virtual reality features and utilities. AR applications may then be reinterpreted as lightweight tools that continuously interact with the virtual factory to support manufacturing and management tasks, providing just-in-time and adaptive augmented information to users. As a case study, several AR tools designed following these principles to support a real production process are presented.

Keywords: Augmented reality · Interoperability · Human-machine interface · Lean manufacturing

1 Introduction

Augmented reality (AR) is a form of mixed reality technology where physical and virtual objects coexist and interact in the real time with the aim of enriching the informative content a user perceives from the real scene. This represents an undeniable advantage in certain scenarios, such as manufacturing, where operators may need to handle large amounts of technical and safety information while guaranteeing high production performance.

As matter of fact, manufacturing is a globalized market where the ever growing competition, especially from emerging markets, forces to adopt the leading principle of "continuous improvement" in order to enhance production performance and quality and to reduce risks, costs and delivery time. Therefore, speeding up the rate of industrial transformation to high added-value products, processes and services is a fundamental milestone for the entire academic and industrial research community in this area.

© Springer International Publishing Switzerland 2014
L.T. De Paolis and A. Mongelli (Eds.): AVR 2014, LNCS 8853, pp. 232–246, 2014.
DOI: 10.1007/978-3-319-13969-2_18

For this reason, technological solutions based on AR and Virtual Reality (VR) are being deeply investigated and explored as a key driver for a performance boost in several spheres of production and management processes. Under this perspective, future factories are widely foreseen as places where virtual world is fully integrated within real production, letting operators and managers overview the production, take actions and control over the machines and operate constant and intuitive real-time monitoring [15]. The concept of Virtual Factory (VF) is widely discussed in literature [10] as a new model for factories of the future, where real factory is merged with virtual tools, in order to operate advanced planning, simulation, decision support and validation capability, and to facilitate the sharing of resources, manufacturing information and knowledge. The VF paradigm, moreover, can assist to answer the needs for innovation in industrial context by addressing several key factors such as (i) the reduction of production time and material waste, thanks to the analysis of virtual mockups of new products, (ii) the enhancement of interoperability capabilities of factory digital tools, (iii) the improvement of workers efficiency and safety through training and learning on virtual production systems and, (iv) the creation of a collaboration network among people concurrently working on the same project in different places.

Within this definition, AR represents a fundamental tool for integrating real-time adaptive visual controls to the factory environment, being adopted to merge visual-based procedures with the factory information and communication technologies (ICT). As already covered in [5], only a small percentage of AR applications developed so far was successfully deployed in practical scenarios and actually used within industrial contexts. Despite the enormous amount of demonstrators and working solutions, in fact, most of them result noncompliant with some simple requisites, such as the practical ability to be applied in real contexts and their actual cost benefits [6]. A functioning AR application for manufacturing should be first of all interoperable with existing applications and easily portable in several contexts [3], in order to cover development and deployment costs. Moreover, its design should be carefully addressed, as users must find it safe and easy to set up, learn, use, and customize in order to avoid misuses and aversion toward the new technologies.

Therefore, the aim of this paper is to propose the experimentation of AR into real industrial contexts under a new perspective, where AR applications are not anymore seen as decoupled tools for assisting specific manufacturing tasks, but rather as totally integrated within future factory workplaces. This approach has been used to design a series of low costs AR tools that can easily been integrated in several production and managements processes of a real factory, spanning from assisting workers under various circumstances, to deploying lightweight and low impact production progress control tools and to enable easy and automatic integration for supply control management. As it will be further detailed in next sections, the coordination role carried out by the Virtual Factory Framework (VFF) is of fundamental importance [12][2]; thanks to a semantic technology based architecture [13], in fact, it enables full interoperability and interaction among AR tools, that can then be relieved from all duties regarding the business logic management and can simply act as lightweight client interfaces.

The rest of the paper is organized as follow: next section briefly overviews the fundamental aspects of AR technology. In section 3, the new approach of augmented factory as an innovative visual workplace is presented along with a system architecture proposal. Section 4 covers the design and development of some AR applications based on such paradigm and deployed on the field. Section 5 draws the conclusion and presents the future works.

2 Augmented Reality: Technology Overview

AR is a variation of reality where something virtual is added to the human natural perception of the real world. The most common form involves the eyesight: In this case, virtual objects are overlaid on the real scene viewed by a user.

Azuma defined in 1997 [4] AR as system that (i) combines real and virtual environments, (ii) interacts in real time and (iii) is registered in 3D. AR requires a certain degree of interaction with the system (for instance, changing its properties depending on camera position) and their geometric coherence to the viewer position and movements, besides the mere introduction of virtual objects within the real view. In particular, an AR system must be aware of the environment it has to augment, in order to match virtual and real world. This is usually done tracking down objects movements in both worlds.

The difference between AR and VR becomes here more evident: while in VR everything is artificially created and objects positions are clearly defined, in AR the system has to follow changes in real-world and properly adapt virtual objects to match those changes.

AR has been applied, in some cases with success, to many fields, from marketing to architecture, from industrial to military applications. The common concept to aforementioned areas is that AR is used to increase the amount of information contained in the real world scene, for instance by adding objects, colors or text.

Research community has soon started to show AR potentialities in production processes and manufacturing, where it can be used to enhance all levels of control in both tangible and intangible functions of production, including assembling, maintenance, cost deployment, process planning, scheduling, quality control, and management information system [10]. As an example, AR providing additional instructions to the human operator, thus reducing both the assembling time and the error probability, can aid assembly tasks. In the same way, typical warehouse picking operations usually performed by operators with common "shopping lists" can be supported with the use of HMDs that highlight the correct items on the shelves.

3 AR for Visual Factories

This paper deals with the concept of visual factory, which is a workplace where communication is strongly based on visual approach that guides and helps the operators to carry out their own tasks.

Visual approach is commonly used for information transfer in productive environments where many management and production operations are guided/ helped/ facilitated by visual information. This approach is immediate and, when properly designed, it stimulates the right parts of the human brain without the need of further elaborations. It strongly differs from simple text messages whose comprehension requires an elaboration time, depending on many factors such as the culture, the known languages and the responsiveness of the reader [9][8][16]. In industrial environments, visual approach is widely used to provide just-in-time information delivering, following the principle of transferring the right information at the right person at the right time.

In authors' opinion, AR is naturally applicable to merge visual-based lean procedures with ICT, leading to the concept of augmented factory, that is a factory where visual controls are displayed through AR technologies, meaning that every visual content can be updated in real-time and can be customized depending on the viewer himself. This approach would guarantee personalized and updated solutions for the operators, with the final result to keep production running smoothly and safely. Moreover, the integration of virtual objects within real scenes can be also fruitfully operated in lean manufacturing and strictly productive scenarios, allowing a human operator to keep under control a series of information depending on the specific task he is carrying out.

In next sections it will be shown how augmented content can support specific tasks by providing the right timing of several operation such as assembling components and moving materials; it can visually advise where and how to store specific items, with the advantage that such visual information would be non-invasive towards other worker that probably will need a different set of information.

In [5] authors already overviewed the issues connected to the development of a system architecture capable of enabling such augmented workplace. The basic idea is that shared information related to the factory processes should be stored in a semantic data repository located on a remote server and then accessed on a real-time basis in order to provide the right visual information to the requiring user. In Fig. 1 it is proposed a general scheme of such architecture, that merges together AR enabling technologies, an information retrieval system, an information harvesting system (IHS) and a data input interface. From an high level perspective, the IHS stores all relevant information concerning production, quality and safety, and the AR Engine retrieves a subset of such information depending on position and duties of every user.

Because of the widespread incompatibility of different hardware and operating systems and the enormous amount of heterogeneous data handled by involved software applications, it is quite hard to develop universal AR applications running on different devices. Therefore, this work has focused on integrating AR tools in a multi-platform and multi-channel environment, that share the same working flow regardless the specific technology, thus allowing easy creation of practical AR systems on a broad range of end devices, spanning from mobile devices (such smartphones and tablets) to more sophisticated instruments such as Head Mounted Displays (HMD) and laser projectors.

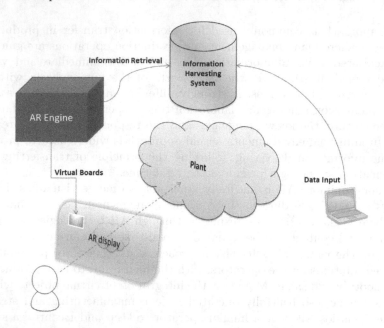

Fig. 1. General architecture for augmented factory framework

4   AR Tools on the Field

In this section a series of case study applications are presented. The work is being carried out within the iSofas project [1], funded by the Italian Ministry of Economic Development with the aim of improving several aspects of the production process of "made in Italy" brands.

In particular, presented works have been conducted in cooperation with Natuzzi S.p.A., worldwide leader in sofas and leather upholstery production and marketing. This specific environment represents a very interesting case study, as from one side there still is large space for improvements thanks to the application of innovative technologies, on the other side the specific context of a home fashion brand, that makes of hand-made production the most important value proposition to customers, significantly reduces the freedom of action in terms of processes automation and innovation deployment. This means that most of the process innovation needs to be addressed towards the direct support of human operators activities rather than towards sophisticated machinery. Under this perspective, visual approach and AR are the most suitable intervention that can be applied in different areas of interest with the aim of:

- reducing non-value adding activities;
- reducing mistakes from employees and suppliers;
- reducing time for employee orientation and training;
- reducing search time in navigating the facility and locating tools, parts and supplies;

- reducing unnecessary human motion and transportation of goods;
- improving floor space utilization and employee safety.

The work has been mainly focused on the production process of the wooden part of Natuzzi sofas, including activities of wood saw, packaging and delivering of wooden components, warehouse management and final assembling. All these activities are performed by (or require strong involvement of) human operators, and all of them are characterized by several problems due to the necessity to work with very high numbers of wooden pieces that are often quite similar among them.

This scenario seems to perfectly fit with the potentiality of augmented reality, which can be used as a Human-Machine Interface (HMI) with the scope of helping and facilitating the user in performing his tasks. On the other hand, releasing several different AR applications becomes an expensive tasks with nowadays methodologies, since they would require specific settings and development approaches depending on the information set they deal with and the required displaying technologies.

As already mentioned, this represents the typical problem of the development of AR application since it strongly limit deployment scalability in terms of both numbers and scenarios. The proposed approach, instead, is based on the framework illustrated in Fig. 1 where all factory and production knowledge is stored in the IHS and the AR tools work as lightweight HMI modules capable of support the operator with the aim of reducing all possible waste in terms of flow time and information delivery and exchange.

In the rest of the section, the system architecture of the virtual factory that enables data centralization and interoperability will be detailed and an overview on the developed AR tools will be provided.

It is important to note how all developed tools have been designed with the specific aim of having an high added value while being low cost, highly scalable and easy to integrate in the system. The value proposition of this tools has been thought to be something more than simple advantage in terms of support to the operators; in authors opinion, in fact, AR-based tools should be rather seen as an enablers of more efficient work flows and organizational approaches.

4.1 The System Architecture

The concept of digitally storing, collecting, organizing and elaborating a huge multitude of factory-related information is a hot topic for the research community involved in finding ICT solutions capable of boosting manufacturing and industrial performance. Bringing these solutions to reality and designing proper user interactions and interfaces leads to the idea of virtual factory, that is a place where production and management, at several levels, take advantage of a strong interaction with digital and virtual tools.

This paradigm is exploited by the Virtual Factory Framework [12], developed within the VFF project [2], that is a new modular, open source, extensible architecture to support interoperability and factory data exchange.

The architecture of VFF makes use of semantic web technologies in order to store an integrated representation of the factory objects and knowledge domain through a set of coherent, standard and extensible set of ontologies (VF Data Model) [14][7]. All the data and knowledge related to the factory are stored in repositories and governed by the Semantic Virtual Factory Manager (VFM), that represents the data access tier and provides the functionalities of access control, data versioning and selective data query [11]. Such data can be accessed and modified by several decoupled software tools, called VF modules, in order to support specific activities in the product/process/factory life-cycles by interacting with the VFM.

Therefore, VFF provides the central governance and data management system that let both software applications and people to insert and retrieve useful data. While all VF modules connected to the virtual factory share the VF Data Model and the VF Manager, each module will present custom implementations of the presentation and business tier.

The augmented factory can fruitfully exploit the performance and the structure of VFF. Under this perspective, the AR engine would work as a VF module capable of selectively retrieve desired data (business tier) and visualize useful information on virtual boards in the real factory (presentation tier).

The abstraction of the AR part of the system has been chosen on purpose, as the excess of customization represents the main limit to scalable frameworks. In this case, instead, once every single component of the information system is available and the communication interface among them is implemented, every AR application would be reduced to a sort of plug-in of the AR Engine.

Such a multi-tier architecture makes the development of tools based on different platforms simple and inexpensive, concentrating the shared business logic on common tiers (and therefore reusable by all tools) thus enabling easy customization only on the specific layers . This approach is proposed to reach the important goal to develop industrial AR solutions that are reproducible and scalable, in terms of capability to deploy the same core application to a wide variety of scenarios and fields of application [5].

4.2   Augmented Reality Tools for Sofas Production Support

The internal structure of each sofa is given by a combination of several wooden components that differ in terms of geometry and type of wood.

In the phase of wood saw, most of the attention of this work has been given to the pantograph, that is an automatic machine with 2D cutting capability responsible to cut a wide panel in several components. The output of a pantograph cutting cycle is represented by a certain number of components that an operator should properly group to aliment the following step of the production flow. Several issues arise from this operation of unloading the pantograph. In particular: (i) components on the machine can belong to different models of sofa, (ii) components on the machine can have different destinations (local production, further processing steps, outbound shipping) and (iii) pantograph cutting cycles

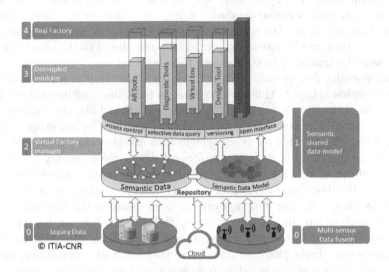

Fig. 2. Conceptual scheme of the Virtual Factory Framework

always differ from each other, meaning that the task of the operator can become quite difficult due to the absence of common patterns of pieces recognition.

This operation is commonly performed only with support of papers reporting the current composition, with the consequences that the job is time expensive and significantly error-prone, especially when it comes to sort the pieces depending on their final destination. In terms of performance, the cost of this inefficiency is very high and it is clearly demonstrated by the fact that the pantograph is the only machine working on a 24h basis and represents the bottleneck of the entire production cycle.

This situation can then be overtaken in terms of efficiency by providing an AR tool capable of displaying (either on a computer screen or with a tablet) all necessary information to unload the pantograph directly on every single component, by augmenting the real scene. Following this approach, it is possible to meet the main requirement of a lean procedure, that is the minimization of time waste connected to every single procedure, as the operator has no more need to move around the working table to check his papers and to signal potential problems to his supervisors.

It is important to note that this application can be implemented considering that all unloading logic and data are already available in digital format (and modeled within the VF Data Model) as they represent the same input given to the pantograph to perform the cutting cycle. Therefore, the basic idea is that the AR application will only work as a client HMI, since the VF Manager will provide all the data and the business logic in real time.

Figure 3 and 4 represent some moments of the AR-supported unloading activity by an operator. The application was implemented as a desktop software running on a common personal computer using free software libraries. Information provided on screen are the same information commonly printed on supporting papers, but they can be much easily read and associated to the exact component that has to be unloaded in the current time interval.

The working flow is quite simple. The very first step is represented by the AR application setup. In this singular case, in fact, the tracking system does not need to be continuously working due to the fact that both the camera and the table are fixed. The geometry setup is only done once by selecting a reference origin of the 2D cartesian reference system that matches the pantograph working table. Once the setup is correctly performed, the same geometry references can be used whatever the size and the configuration of wooden panels are.

During the daily production process, once the 2D nesting has been completed, data regarding a specific cutting cycle are sent both to the pantograph and to the AR application. In this phase, then, the AR application has the duty to guide the operator in the unloading process, supporting him step by step and signaling every single piece to unload together with all information needed to detect the position of the wooden component and its next destination.

Moreover, thanks to the introduction of ICT tools on the field, it is possible to integrate many other applications with the same final aim of reducing time waste and error probabilities. As already shown in the pictures, in fact, also a lightweight messaging system was introduced within the AR application to send alert messages to work supervisors. This functionality is quite useful when dealing with cutting errors or any other problem occurring in the unloading phase, since the operator can just signal the problem to the proper colleague without leaving his workplace and keeping working on following items.

4.3   AR Assisted Picking Procedure

As already pointed out, AR tools should be seen as enabler of more efficient working flows and organizational approach. In fact, thanks to the useful on-the-job support that AR application can give to operators, it is possible to re-design both workplace and materials handling in a more efficient way.

Following the same approach, it was possible to develop an application for supporting the user in the operation of selective picking into the warehouse. This kind of picking is performed as the first step of the production of a single sofa. The operator, in fact, has to collect on a cart all the wooden components needed to assemble the sofa. As described before, also this action is currently performed with the exclusive help of paper sheets reporting the list of components to collect, causing high flow time and high error probability.

It is important to note that picking operations in the described scenario are quite hard to perform, due to the high variety of very similar wooden pieces on these shelves and the difficulty to distinguish the right item to pick among components of the same material (see Fig. 5). The consequence of such situation

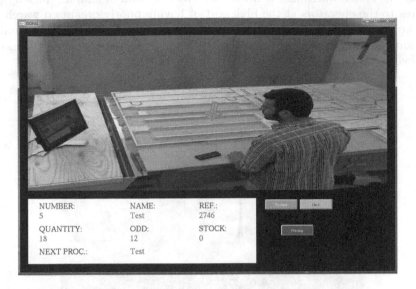

Fig. 3. Example of the application state during unloading phase

Fig. 4. View of the pantograph workstation after AR application deployment

is that the entire warehouse is filled with the only aim of simplify picking procedures to the operators at the high cost of having poorly organized warehouse with no space optimization and where each component is not located in a unique position but rather positioned in several different areas depending on the models of sofas to produce.

Fig. 5. View of a shelf in the production warehouse

This scenario is quite explicative of how augmented reality can be used to both support users to perform certain tasks and, at the same time, enable a new and optimized organizational approach that would have been impossibile to achieve otherwise.

Within the works carried out for iSofas project, in fact, it was possible to re-think the warehouse organization thanks to the combination of the VFF approach and the AR tools deployment. This objective can be accomplished by properly associating an AR marker to each wooden component version, and storing this information in the central repository, offering the possibility to locate every item in a specific location with the unique aim to optimize the warehouse spaces at no risk for picking performance. Starting from this point, in fact, it is easy to design an AR tool able to signal to the user which component (and how many of it) he needs to pick to complete the assembling kit for the current sofa version without knowing in advance any item location. This means that even if items location varies in time depending on the expected production and other parameters, this will not affect in any way picking operation efficiency.

The application, tested on a virtual warehouse environment and whose performance results are included in projects deliverables [1] (see a screenshot in Fig. 6), was developed for common low-cost tablets, and represents again an example of the proposed approach. The work flow is the typical one of a common marker-based AR application, but its functionalities are extended thanks

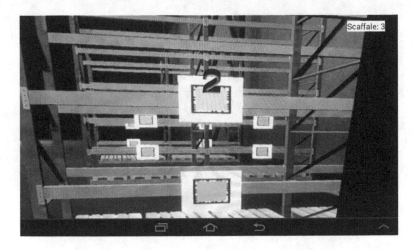

Fig. 6. Example of AR supported picking

to the strong difference that both markers to track and 3D object to display are time variant and dependent on the particular input condition.

The idea, in this case, is that all information connected to tracking and 3D visualization should be part of the factory knowledge and accessible through the VFM. The central plant repository, in fact, holds the information about the sofa that should be produced in a particular moment and communicates to the AR application the list of items to pick and all related information. The AR tool, then, would only work as an interface signaling picking information to the user depending on the sofa model to produce, guaranteeing high scalability properties. Fig. 7, represents the high level architecture of this application and clearly shows how the AR tool only acts as a HMI since all data regarding tracking information and models to be displayed are retrieved from the central repository.

4.4   Augmented Reality Tools for Production Progress Control

AR tracking technologies can also be fruitfully used for implementing light production progress control. A typical image recognition system, for instance, can help in keeping trace of the progress status of a specific activity. Within the present work, these kind of technologies were adopted to implement low cost tools useful to support several phases of the production cycle.

On the assembling phase in the sofa production flow, simple marker-based tracking systems have been applied for the implementation of a virtual interface totally immersed in the working environment where users can interact and control virtual buttons with light and simple movement of their hands. The assembling procedure, in particular, is mainly characterized by a series of operations such as laths gluing and stuff handling. Nevertheless, workers often need to check out the instruction sheets due to the strong difference among assembling sequences of different sofa models, and the time spent by workers in consulting

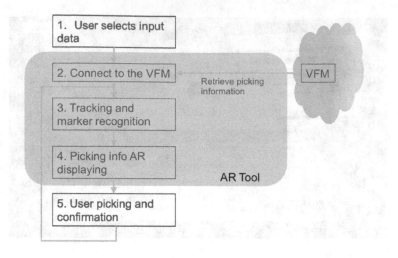

Fig. 7. Conceptual working flow of the AR tool for picking support

such manuals can significantly grow depending on their experience and on the frequency of production of different models, leading to large waste of time for non-added value operations.

An AR tool has therefore been developed to address aforementioned issues with the objective of reducing the waste of resources and facilitating the interaction of the user with his instruments. This was accomplished by equipping the workspace with a screen to display assembly instructions and a virtual keyboard to easily browse the guide. The virtual keyboard, in particular, is a controller tool where virtual buttons can be activated without the need of physical pression but rather with simple hands movement. Typical implementations of a virtual button consists in deploying tracking technologies that look for markers occlusions. This application can be implemented in a total general way, meaning that each marker occlusion can launch a generic procedure, and the association between marker and procedure can be loaded on-line depending on the current needs. The connection of this tool to Natuzzi Product Data Management (PDM) via the VFM, in fact, made possible both the real-time on-the-job instruction sheets retrieval, as well as the implementation of specific procedure such as internal messaging and alert delivery.

Based on same working principles, image tracking technologies have been applied to production flow control and to improve the interaction with suppliers. In this case, such technologies were used to keep trace of the state of processing of every single step of production on the moving line. Furthermore, by allowing the supplier to access to a subset of the factory information stored through the VFM, the supplier itself can interact seamlessly with the semantic data storage with the objective to signal the state of production of supplies.

The possibility to share a subset of the overall information managed by the VFM, in fact, providing cross-platform services that can be accessed by remote applications, gives a series of opportunities of cooperation and enables interoperability among modules installed by different companies belonging to the same supply chain.

5 Conclusions and Future Works

This work focused on illustrating a new methodology for applying augmented reality technology to industrial and manufacturing scenarios, based on the use of a central framework where a shared semantic data model facilitates the interoperability among different AR tools. The main objective of this approach is to make AR applications scalable and easy to port in different scenarios, thus lowering the cost of development and of technology acquisition.

AR perfectly fits in the concept of visual factory, that is a workplace where visual controls and information exchange enable a series of lean-based procedure with the aim of reducing the production flow time. Furthermore, AR can be used as a lean HMI capable of both providing just-in-time information to users and keeping trace and reporting the state of production.

An overall system architecture, based on the Virtual Factory Framework, as well as the design of some applications of such paradigm to the production of sofas are also provided, in order to demonstrate how this methodology can guarantee high scalability and reduced costs of developed AR tools.

Implemented application were successfully tested on the field in real production scenarios and showed the potential that AR tools can have in improving performance of procedures that require strong involvement of human operators.

Future works will focus on expand this approach to the supply chain control and to the development of a feedback systems capable of reporting production information acquired on the field through the AR tools back to the factory management.

Acknowledgments. This work has been carried out within "iSofas", a project funded by Italian Ministry of Economic Development within the program "Industria 2015".

References

1. iSofas Project. http://isofas.eng.it
2. VFF Project. http://www.vff-project.eu/
3. IEEE Standard Computer Dictionary: A Compilation of IEEE Standard Computer Glossaries. IEEE Std **610**, 1–217 (January 1991)
4. Azuma, R.: A Survey of Augmented Reality. Teleoperators and Virtual Environments **6**(4), 355–385 (1997)
5. Capozzi, F., Sacco, M.: Exploiting Augmented Reality in Lean Manufacturing: Opportunities and Challenges. In: Advances in Sustainable and Competitive Manufacturing Systems - Proc. FAIM 2013, p. 1361 (2013)
6. Fite-Georgel, P.: Is there a reality in Industrial Augmented Reality? In: 2011 10th IEEE International Symposium on Mixed and Augmented Reality (ISMAR), pp. 201–210 (2011)

7. Ghielmini, G.: Virtual Factory Manager of Semantic Data. In: Proc. of 7th International Conference on Digital Enterprise Technology, Athens, pp. 268–277 (2011)
8. Hirano, H.: 5 Pillars of the Visual Workplace, p. 365. Productivity Press (1995)
9. Inc., B.: Visual Workplace Handbook. Brady, p. 21 (2012)
10. Khan, W.A.: Virtual Manufacturing. Springer Series in Advanced Manufacturing (2011)
11. Modoni, G., Sacco, M., Terkay, W.: A survey of RDF store solutions. In: 20th International Conference on Engineering, Technology and Innovation (2014)
12. Pedrazzoli, P., Sacco, M., Jönsson, A., Boër, C.: Virtual Factory Framework: key enabler for future manufacturing. In: 3rd International CIRP Sponsored Conference on Digital Enterprise Technology, pp. 83–90 (2006)
13. Shadbolt, N., Berners-Lee, T., Hall, W.: The semantic web revisited. IEEE Intelligent Systems 21(3), 96–101 (2006). http://eprints.soton.ac.uk/262614/
14. Terkay, W., Pedrielli, G., Sacco, M.: Virtual Factory Data Model (VFF Ontology). In: 2nd International Workshop on Ontology and Semantic Web for Manufacturing, OSEMA 2012 (2012)
15. Viganò, G., Greci, L., Mottura, S., Sacco, M.: GIOVE Virtual Factory: A New Viewer for a More Immersive Role of the User During Factory Design. Springer, London (2011)
16. Wang, Y., Qi, E.: Enterprise planning of Total Life cycle Lean Thinking. In: IEEE International Conference on Service Operations and Logistics, and Informatics, IEEE/SOLI 2008, vol. 2, pp. 1712–1717 (October 2008)

Interactive Augmented Omnidirectional Video with Realistic Lighting

Nick Michiels$^{(\boxtimes)}$, Lode Jorissen, Jeroen Put, and Philippe Bekaert

Expertise Centre for Digital Media, Hasselt University - tUL - iMinds,
Wetenschapspark 2, 3590 Diepenbeek, Belgium
{nick.michiels,lode.jorissen,jeroen.put,
philippe.bekaert}@uhasselt.be

Abstract. This paper presents the augmentation of immersive omni-directional video with realistically lit objects. Recent years have known a proliferation of real-time capturing and rendering methods of omni-directional video. Together with these technologies, rendering devices such as Oculus Rift have increased the immersive experience of users. We demonstrate the use of structure from motion on omnidirectional video to reconstruct the trajectory of the camera. The position of the car is then linked to an appropriate 360° environment map. State-of-the-art augmented reality applications have often lacked realistic appearance and lighting. Our system is capable of evaluating the rendering equation in real-time, by using the captured omnidirectional video as a lighting environment. We demonstrate an application in which a computer generated vehicle can be controlled through an urban environment.

Keywords: Omnidirectional video · Realistic lighting · Product integral rendering · Structure from motion

1 Introduction

Omnidirectional video is an emerging medium that gives viewers a 360° panoramic experience. Previous work focused on the real-time capturing and rendering of omnidirectional video on a 360° projection screen [5,24], in a head-mounted display like Oculus Rift [29] or other applications like Illumniroom [14]. We demonstrate the use of structure from motion on omnidirectional video to reconstruct the trajectory of the camera. The structure is used to accurately track the camera poses in a large environment. Extending this omnidirectional content with camera position tracking creates a global coordinate system in which virtual objects can be augmented. This makes it possible to bridge the gap between video and computer graphics. Possible applications are interactive worlds, architectural modelling and marketing.

Up until now, most augmented reality applications have often lacked realistic lighting [13]. This paper shows how to leverage tracking information and use that to feed the correct environment frame to a realistic renderer. The existing environment lighting from the captured 360° video can be used to augment

© Springer International Publishing Switzerland 2014
L.T. De Paolis and A. Mongelli (Eds.): AVR 2014, LNCS 8853, pp. 247–263, 2014.
DOI: 10.1007/978-3-319-13969-2_19

realistic objects in the scene in real-time. For this, the augmented virtual objects need to be synchronized with the lighting information of its position. Our goal is to render virtual objects with lighting that is consistent with the captured video, so that the objects are seamlessly integrated into the environment. An example of a technique is to find the main light source of the scene using the shadows in the original image [2]. This way, realistic shadowing can be achieved, but all high frequency lighting information is lost. Since we are working with an omnidirectional camera, we have lighting information from all directions for all camera poses. This paper explores how that lighting information can be used to feed to the rendering. As explained before, tho achieve this, a proper renderer that is able to render distant view-dependent high frequency lighting and detailed spatial and angular reflection is required. Our proposed system is capable of evaluating the rendering equation for distant light in real-time, based on precomputed radiance transfer using spherical radial basis functions. Our system is demonstrated with an application in which an augmented vehicle can be controlled through an urban environment (Figure 1).

Fig. 1. Illustration of real-time augmented rendering of virtual objects in an omnidirectional environment. The 360° video is used as environment map for realistic lighting.

The paper is organized as follows. The first section describes the related work. Then, we present the three steps necessary to achieve our goal of a real-time augmented renderer. Section 3.1 explains how to capture, process and render the omnidirectional data with a custom camera. Section 3.2 describes how to extract the camera poses of the omnidirectional camera using structure from motion. Section 3.3 gives a solution for a real-time renderer that uses the tracked frames to realistically render lighting and reflectance effects. The results of this work and an application are shown in Section 4. Finally, in Section 5, we conclude and discuss the future work of this paper.

2   Previous Work

Debevec [4] was one of the first to propose image-based lighting (IBL), where the capturing of real-world lighting is used to render virtual objects. The environment lighting is described as a single light probe image. A nice overview of photorealistic and non-photorealistic augmented reality applications is made by Haller et al. [13]. They compare both approaches using ARToolKit markers to track the camera its pose. In the photorealistic approach, they show how to use shadow volumes and bump mapping.

Agusanto et al. [1] show an application where image-based rendering techniques are used to incorporate virtual objects in augmented reality content using environment illumination maps. They do not capture any environment map, but use existing single shot light probes. The disadvantage is that they are not able to render with interactive and dynamic lighting.

Other techniques [2,16] focus on shadow effects in augmented reality applications. They identify the most important light sources in the light probe and use them to cast shadows of the augmented objects so that they are consistent with the real world. In terms of other lighting and reflectance effects, they lack visual realism.

Grosch et al. [11] showed how to make the light of a room consistent with the rendered virtual objects by reconstructing the geometry of a single light probe. The reconstruction makes it possible to add new lights sources to the light probe as well as place new objects in the room and project the light probe for different positions in the room. They mainly focus on consistency of the light conditions in a room, but not on how to realistically render objects with these new light conditions. Additionally they only use one light probe for the entire scene, which makes their algorithm not applicable to larger scenes. Later, Grosch et al. [12] studied how to use irradiance volumes to place virtual objects in a real-life Cornell Box. The external illumination is captured with a HDR camera and a fisheye lens. Direct and indirect lighting effects are simulated for the virtual objects. The rendering is done at interactive frame rates, but the geometry of the objects cannot change easily which makes the rendering of dynamic scenes not possible.

Papagiannakis et al. [23] and Gierlinger et al. [9] have integrated the full precomputed radiance transfer (PRT) [21,22,27] in a mixed reality application using HDR input images. They use spherical harmonics to precompute the three factors of the radiance transfer. They are able to render high quality and realistic lighting in real-time but require a great amount of precomputation. Since precomputation of visibility is necessary, the results are limited to static scenes. Additionally, the use of spherical harmonics are suboptimal for high frequency lighting conditions.

This paper will also use precomputed radiance transfer to render the scene with accurate environment lighting. To make sure that the high frequency light conditions are preserved, the three factors of the radiance transfer are represented with spherical radial basis functions (SRBFs) instead of spherical harmonics [30]. Furthermore, using this spherical radial basis representation, the amount of precomputation will decrease drastically: the bidirectional reflectance distribution function (BRDF) is approximated with few SRBFs; the visibility can be traced using cone tracing where the cones are approximated with SRBFs; and the environment frame can be efficiently transformed into a SRBF representation using an hierarchical approximation algorithm. Since almost no precomputation is required, the three factors can change at any time making the rendering system very flexible and interactive. This is particularly important since our application of driving a virtual vehicle in an urban environment requires a frequent change in all three factors.

3   Our Approach

The goal of this paper is to augment omnidirectonal video (ODV) with new virtual objects that are realistically lit by their environment. The user must be able to interact with the video by moving around the virtual object, while at the same time the lighting and reflectance conditions stay consistent with the captured environment. This requires a system with the following three stages:

1. Stitching and rendering of ODV
2. Offline reconstruction the camera trajectory of ODV using structure from motion
3. Real-time realistic rendering of virtual objects using the ODV for lighting

These three stages will now be explained in more detail.

3.1   ODV Capturing and Rendering

Capturing is performed with a custom designed camera, built with six cameras at 60° intervals with approximately 50% coverage between adjacent cameras. The omnidirectional camera is depicted in Figure 2(a). Each camera has a resolution of 1600×1200. All six cameras are synchronized and capture at 25 frames per second. Next, we mounted the camera on top of a vehicle and drove through a local city, which is demonstrated in Figure 2(b). The stitching and rendering of the different camera frames are performed in real-time on the graphics card. Figure 2(c) depicts an example of such stitched frame in an equirectangular representation. The rendering of such frames requires the warping of the equirectangular stitched frame onto a sphere where the virtual camera is positioned within the sphere. This way, the camera can be rotated in any direction, so that the user can freely experience a 360° walkthrough in the video environment, as illustrated in Figure 3. This step is performed in real-time, but for this application it is not required.

3.2   Camera Tracking Using Structure From Motion

The ability of adding new virtual objects in the captured video of the previous section requires the pose estimation of the omnidirectional camera throughout the sequence. This step is of significant importance and aims to determine the alignment between synthetic objects and the real world in order to render them at the correct position. Once the alignment is complete, an appropriate omnidirectional video frame can be identified for each virtual object which will serve as environment lighting so that realistic lighting can be achieved. This section

(a)   (b)

(c)

Fig. 2. Capturing of omnidirectional video. (a) Our custom designed omnidirectional camera consists of 6 cameras, all capturing at 25 fps with a resolution of 1600×1200. (b) The omnidirectional camera mounted on a vehicle to capture the streets of an urban environment. (c) The full panoramic stitched frame of all six cameras, which can be done in real-time.

will explain how to adapt a structure from motion algorithm to make it work with omnidirectional content. The result is accurate tracking information of the omnidirectional camera for a large environment.

The first step of a structure from motion algorithm is feature tracking. Since the stitched omnidirectional video frames have still some ghosting artifacts which will possibly degrade the tracking accuracy, feature tracking was done on the individual camera images (the frames from the cameras that make up the omnidirectional camera). Since the poses of the individual cameras relative to the center of the ODV camera are already known (this information is extracted during ODV camera calibration), we do not need to estimate the pose of each individual camera for each frame. Instead, the pose of the complete ODV camera

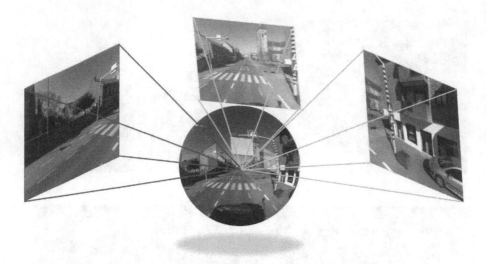

Fig. 3. Rendering of omnidirectional content. A virtual camera (red, yellow or green) can be placed in the spherical warped ODV frames. This gives the viewer a full 360° interactive experience, since one can freely look around with the camera.

is estimated using only the image information of the individual cameras, resulting in a more accurate pose estimation.

As explained earlier the algorithm works on the individual cameras of the ODV camera. The first step in this process is to remove the distortion from the images. In our current implementation we apply a Shi-Tomasi corner detector on the undistorted input images [26]. Only features of good quality are stored. The features are then tracked to the next frame of the corresponding camera using Lucas-Kanade optical flow tracking [20]. We chose the Lucas-Kanade tracker instead of a descriptor based matching method because we want the number of frames in which a feature is tracked to be as high as possible. Longer feature tracks result in more shared information between the poses of the ODV camera and thus result in a more stable pose estimation. In case of short feature tracks there is less shared information and the estimated poses often show more jitter when rendering synthetic objects. The optical flow algorithm can however result in erroneous matches. Therefore, we use the trifocal tensor constraint to filter out incorrect matches. The trifocal tensor is calculated for three adjacent ODV frames with a RANSAC approach [7]. The input of the RANSAC step consists of the features that are visible in all three frames. A subset of these features is used to determine a trifocal tensor, and the trifocal tensor is used to check whether a feature is an inlier or not (the position in the third frame needs to be close to the estimated position).

For each feature a SIFT descriptor [19] is extracted, necessary to match the features between the cameras. Feature matching between the cameras allows us to connect shorter feature tracks into longer tracks. This is especially useful when a feature leaves one camera and shows up in another one. A cross-check is applied to make sure that the features match in both directions. The remaining features are checked against the epipolar constraint.

Estimating the trifocal tensor for outlier removal also has the advantage that one can extract the fundamental matrices (from camera 1 to 2 and from camera 1 to 3). These encode the relative position and orientation of the cameras and thus can be used to determine an estimate of the poses of the ODV camera. This process is similar to visual odometry (VO) [8,25] and, as is to be expected with VO, the resulting positions are far from optimal since the pose of the camera is only estimated in relation to the previous pose. The initial estimation of poses is shown in Figure 4. A better option is to globally estimate the pose using the information gathered in all ODV frames. This is done by applying bundle adjustment.

Fig. 4. Initial reconstruction of the camera poses using visual odometry without sparse bundle adjustment. The accuracy of the poses is very poor.

Bundle adjustment simultaneously updates the poses of the cameras and the 3D world positions to minimize the mean error between the reprojected world points and their corresponding features. The error metric is defined as a function of the distance between the position of the feature and the reprojection. The sparse bundle adjustment implementation of Lourakis and Argyros [18] is used. As input, the algorithm requires initial estimates of the poses and the world positions of the features. These initial world positions are obtained by doing a SVD based triangulation, followed by an optimization step that also reduces the reprojection error

The results of bundle adjustment are refined ODV camera poses and a sparse 3D structure that aligns to objects in the world. Figure 5 shows the poses and the structure of the track after bundle adjustment as well as examples of the structure rendered on top of the omnidirectional video using an estimated pose. One can clearly see that the 3D points are aligned with their corresponding features in the video and that the estimated positions of the camera better

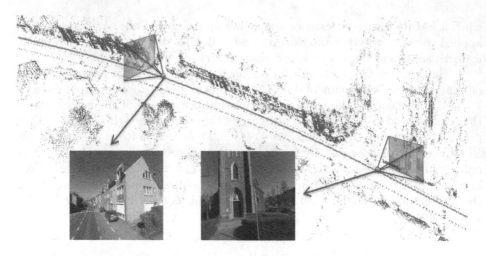

Fig. 5. Structure from motion is used to reconstruct the trajectory of the road (depicted in orange). The trajectory is used to align the rendered objects with the real-world scene.

represent the true positions of the camera compared to the initial poses of visual odometry in Figure 4.

3.3   Real-Time Augmented Rendering

High quality and realistic rendering of objects will drastically increase the immersive experience of augmented reality applications. To achieve this, the rendering requires detailed natural lighting and realistic reflectance of materials. View-dependent effects like a change in eye direction across surfaces will improve visual realism. This dynamically varying viewpoint will require a reflectance representation defined in 6D (light direction, view direction and surface position). Since detailed variations in reflectance will visually impact the end result, the 6D functions needs to be evaluated densely. Naive sampling of the rendering equation [15] at every point in the scene will result in a correct calculation of the radiance reaching the observer, but will also be very intractable. Solutions using precomputed radiance transfer (PRT) [21,22,27] are able to render efficiently under the above mentioned conditions. Here the light transport is precalculated in a factored form. The rendering equation is then evaluated at each point x, with view direction ω_0 by calculating the triple product integral over the hemisphere of the factored representation:

$$B(x, \omega_o) = \sum_i \sum_j \sum_k V_i \; \rho_j(\omega_o) \; L_k \int_\Omega \Psi_i(\omega) \; \Psi_j(\omega) \; \Psi_k(\omega) d\omega \qquad (1)$$

with visibility V, reflectance ρ, environment lighting L.

Previous methods used Haar wavelets as a representation for the three factors of the triple product rendering equation [22]. An important disadvantage of wavelet-based methods is the absence of an efficient rotation operator in the wavelet domain, which is required to rotate the environment in the local frame for each vertex. Additionally, a per-vertex 2D slice of the bidirectional reflectance distribution function (BRDF) needs to be sampled at execution time. We use spherical radial basis functions (SRBF) to represent each element of the rendering equation [30]. A SRBF is a rotation-invariant function depending on the parameter v describing a direction on the sphere S^2:

$$G(v; p, \lambda, \mu) = \mu e^{-\lambda} e^{\lambda(v \cdot p)} \qquad (2)$$

where $P \in S^2$ is the center of the SRBF, $\lambda \in (0, +\infty)$ is the lobe sharpness and $\mu \in \mathbb{R}$ is the lobe amplitude. This spherical radial basis function can now be used to approximate any spherical function to an arbitrary degree of accuracy by mixing various SRBFs with different lobe sizes and positions:

$$F(v) = \sum_{l-1}^{n} G(v; p, \lambda_l, \mu_l) \qquad (3)$$

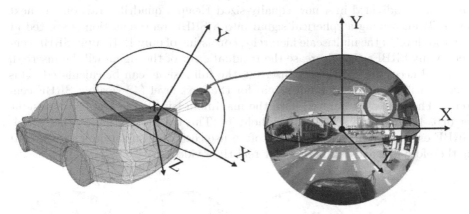

Fig. 6. Rotation of a SRBF of an environment map defined in the global frame (right) to a SRBF of an environment map defined in the local frame of a vertex is done by simply rotating its center

Unlike Haar wavelets, spherical functions represented with SRBFs can easily be rotated on the sphere by simply rotating its SRBF lobe centers (depicted in Figure 6). Furthermore, as shown by Tsai et al. [28], the product and convolution of Gaussians can be evaluated analytically. By using these characteristics, the convolution of three Gaussians results in a scalar, making the triple product integral calculations of the rendering equation straightforward:

$$\int_{S^2} G_1(v; p_1, \lambda_1, \mu_1) G_2(v; p_2, \lambda_2, \mu_2) G_3(v; p_3, \lambda_3, \mu_3) dv$$
$$= \frac{4\pi\mu_1\mu_2}{e^{\lambda_1 + \lambda_2 + \lambda_3}} \frac{\sinh(\|r\|)}{\|r\|} \qquad (4)$$

where $r = \|\lambda_1 p_1 + \lambda_2 p_2 + \lambda_3 p_3\|$. Once all three factors of the rendering equation are represented in the SRBF basis as described above, efficient rendering of a realistically lit virtual object is possible and the object can be integrated in the omnidirectional scene in real-time. The next sections show how to obtain the basis transformations for lighting, reflectance and visibility.

Environment Map. Using the tracking information of Section 3.2, we can map the reconstructed 3D positions to an appropriate omnidirectional video frame. These omnidirectional video frames can then be used as environment lighting for virtual objects for that specific position. The environment map frames are approximated with a multi-level hierarchical SRBF model. The domain of the spherical function is subdivided in different hierarchical layers of SRBFs with increasing density and decreasing lobe size. The SRBF centers of a specific level are uniformly distributed over the spherical surface. This paper uses the Healpix [10,17] distribution on the sphere. Healpix is optimal for distributing the spherical surface in equal area parts (see Figure 7). Moreover, it is suitable for hierarchical algorithms, since one Healpix quadrilateral on a specific level can be easily subdivided in 4 new equally-sized Healpix quadrilaterals on the next level. Transforming a spherical signal into a SRBF representation is started at the root level of the multiscale hierarchy, consisting of only 12 Healpix SRBF centers. Only SRBFs that decrease the residual error of the signal will be inserted. Once all necessary SRBFs are inserted, the full residue can be calculated. This residue will serve as the input signal for the next level (48 Healpix SRBF centers). The process is iterated until the maximum level is reached or the residue error is lower than a specified threshold [6]. This transformation process avoids SRBF estimation procedures which often use costly optimization algorithms. It is therefore fast and can happen for real-time video.

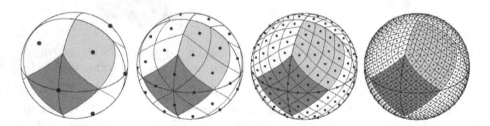

Fig. 7. Healpix distribution scheme subdivides the sphere in equal area parts. The Healpix quadrilaterals of a specific level can be subdivided in 4 new equally-sized Healpix quadrilaterals on the next level [10].

BRDF. Instead of sampling the 2D slices of the BRDFs in the pixel domain, these can now be directly approximated with few SRBFs. The BRDF models used in this paper all are based on microfacet theory, meaning that the specular lobe ρ_s can be described in terms of a normal distribution function (NDF) $D(h)$, with h the halfway vector and a remaining factor $M_o(i)$:

$$\rho_s(o, i) = M_o(i)D(h) \quad h = \frac{o + i}{\|o + i\|} \tag{5}$$

BRDFs that are expressed in terms of the normal distribution (NDF) can be approximated with spherical Gaussians. $D(h)$ can be approximated using a single spherical Gaussian for isotropic models or multiple spherical Gaussians for anisotropic models. $M_o(i)$ is very smooth and can be approximated by a constant. We implemented multiple BRDF models. For example, fitting the Blinn-Phong model with a Gaussian lobe is done as follows:

$$M_o(i) = \frac{n + 2}{2\pi}$$
$$D(h) = (h \cdot n)^\lambda \approx G(n; h, \lambda, 1) \tag{6}$$

To obtain the 2D BRDF slice $\rho_s(o, i)$ for a specific view direction o, we first need to warp the lobe described in terms of the halfway vector into the lobe defined in terms of the view direction. The warp for every lobe is specified as:

$$p_i^W = 2(o \cdot h)h - o$$
$$\lambda_i^W = \frac{\lambda_i^D}{\tau(p_i^D)} \tag{7}$$
$$\mu_i^W = \mu_i^D$$

where the differential area of the warp $\tau(h) = 4\|h \cdot o\|$ is defined as the determinant of the Jacobian of the warp function. The details of fitting different BRDF models and warping them on the sphere are described in detail by Wang et al [30].

Visibility. The visibility can be traced in real-time using voxel cone tracing [3]. Voxel cone tracing requires virtual objects to be rasterized using a real-time voxelization algorithm. This is done by rasterizing the geometry along the three main axes of the scene. The viewport resolution defines the resolution of the 3D voxel volume. We have observed that a 256^3 voxel volume yields plausible visibility. The voxel volumes are stored in OpenGL 3D textures in contrast with the sparse octree representation of Crassin et al. [3]. The main advantage of using 3D textures is that they require no octree traversal, making them ideal for parallelism on GPU. In the future, sparse 3D textures will become available, allowing the algorithm to work with bigger objects. A next step is to generate MIP-maps for the 3D texture. These MIP-mapped versions of the volume will be extensively used in the cone tracing for LOD, since the footprint of cones will increase with the distance to the center, allowing lower resolution MIP-maps to be used. We use importance sampling in order to know where to trace cones for visibility. For every product of a lighting SRBF and reflectance SRBF, the support can be determined and used to sample the directions for cone tracing. The cone can then be seen as a SRBF on its own, and can be applied in the triple product integral.

4   Results

Our real-time augmented renderer is implemented on a system with an Intel Xeon^{TM} dual six core processor and a nVidia GeForce GTX 780 graphics card. The stitching and rendering of the omnidirectional video is performed on the GPU in GLSL shaders. We created a viewer where the user can walk through the video and can manipulate the viewing direction of the camera. This viewer can be outputted to a normal screen or to more immersive hardware like Oculus Rift or a omnidirectional cave.

Structure from motion is done offline as a preprocessing step. The focus of this step lies on quality and accuracy and not so much on time performance since the application requires only the reconstructed trajectory of a video that is not captured at runtime.

The transformation of the omnidirectional video frames to spherical radial basis functions is done on the CPU and later passed to the GPU. In GLSL shaders, the different models of the BRDF and the spherical warp are implemented and together with the SRBFs of the environment lighting and possibly the visibility, they are used to evaluate the triple product integral of Section 3.3. At this time, we have not integrated the visibility factor into the renderer. Our cone tracing is not optimized to work in real-time yet, but, as explained in Section 3.3, once the cone tracing is fully operational, the integration is straightforward. For basic ambient occlusion, the cone tracing is working, since only few cones are traced over the hemisphere. An example of ambient occlusion of a car using cone tracing is depicted in Figure 11(a). When we render the same car with our real-time renderer and scale with this ambient occlusion factor we get Figure 11(b). In the future, more detailed geometry of the SfM from Section 3.2 can be used to integrate occlusions from the environment.

A main advantage of using SRBFs as a representation is that BRDFs can easily be approximated with few SRBFs which can be reconstructed at real-time using only the parameters of the BRDF model. For each point in the virtual object, the system only needs to know its BRDF parameters and then an appropriate BRDF radial basis function can be assigned. We have support for the Lambertian, Phong, Blinn-Phong, Ward and Cook-Torrance BRDF models. In Figure 8, we show a sphere model inside our captured environment, all rendered with different material parameters. The top row of the Figure shows the Phong BRDF with a exponent parameter ranging from 10 to 10000. The bottom row shows the mixing of a specular Phong BRDF with a Lambertian BRDF. Now the percentage of mixing the diffuse Lambertian is ranging from 0.25 to 1.00. Figure 10 depicts the results of a more realistic model, i.e. a vehicle. A model of a Mercedes with texture mapping is inserted into the scene. Furthermore, we assigned a realistic material with a mixture of BRDFs to the model. The figure clearly shows accurate view depended lighting and detailed spatial and angular reflections when the car is moved in the environment. We provide a video of our

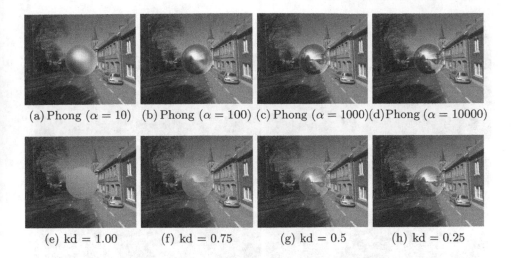

(a) Phong ($\alpha = 10$)   (b) Phong ($\alpha = 100$)   (c) Phong ($\alpha = 1000$)(d)Phong ($\alpha = 10000$)

(e) kd = 1.00   (f) kd = 0.75   (g) kd = 0.5   (h) kd = 0.25

Fig. 8. Rendering with different material properties. Top row: Phong BRDF whith an exponent α ranging from 10 to 10000. Bottom row: mixing of materials with a kd percentage of a Lambertian BRDF added to a $(1 - kd)$ percentage of a Phong ($\alpha = 10000$) BRDF.

Fig. 9. Rendering of a sphere. Different positions of the sphere will result in different lighting conditions.

application[1]. In Figure 9 we show the same sphere and assigned a high specular material to make sure all lighting effects of the environment onto the sphere can be seen. We chose a Phong BRDF with a big exponent factor ($N = 10000$). It is now possible to perceive a change in reflection when the sphere is moved around in the urban environment.

---

[1] http://www.youtube.com/watch?v=gwftfqfY9WM

Fig. 10. Rendering of a user-controlled vehicle in an urban environment. Row 1 shows the change in reflection when the user is horizontally moving the vehicle. Row 2 and 3 depict the change in reflection when driving the car forward. Row 4 and 5 show the car from different angles.

(a)   (b)

Fig. 11. Rendering of (a) ambient occlusion using cone tracing and (b) environment map, BRDF and ambient occlusion

5   Conclusion

This paper presented an approach for augmenting omnidirectional video with interactive virtual objects rendered with realistic lighting and reflectance properties. The method used offline feature tracking to align positions of virtual objects with positions of the real-world. We proposed to use the omnidirectional video frames as environment lighting for the virtual objects and showed how to use the tracking information to synchronize the correct environment map with the virtual objects. Furthermore we explained how to transform the environment lighting, BRDF properties and possibly the visibility to spherical radial basis functions in order to render the virtual objects in real-time and with realistic reflectance and lighting integrated over the hemisphere. Currently, visibility is not entirely integrated in the rendering, but we showed how to use cone tracing to solve this issue. Future work is to integrate our cone trace approach in the renderer. Further development of the structure from motion step can result in more dense geometry. This geometry can be used to cast shadows onto the objects as well as correct occlusions. For now, the renderer is limited to distant light. But near-field lighting can be sampled, similar to the cone tracing algorithm of the visibility factor.

Acknowledgments. This work has been made possible with the help of a PhD specialization bursary from the IWT and FWO. The authors acknowledge financial support from the European Commission (FP7 IP SCENE).

References

1. Agusanto, K., Li, L., Chuangui, Z., Sing, N.W.: Photorealistic rendering for augmented reality using environment illumination. In: Proceedings of the Second IEEE and ACM International Symposium on Mixed and Augmented Reality, pp. 208–216 (October 2003)
2. Arief, I., McCallum, S., Hardeberg, J.Y.: Realtime estimation of illumination direction for augmented reality on mobile devices. In: Color and Imaging Conference, pp. 111–116. IS&T and SID, Los Angeles, CA, USA (November 2012)

3. Crassin, C., Neyret, F., Sainz, M., Green, S., Eisemann, E.: Interactive indirect illumination using voxel-based cone tracing: An insight. In: ACM SIGGRAPH 2011 Talks, SIGGRAPH 2011, pp. 20:1–20:1. ACM, New York (2011). http://doi.acm.org/10.1145/2037826.2037853

4. Debevec, P.: Rendering synthetic objects into real scenes: Bridging traditional and image-based graphics with global illumination and high dynamic range photography. In: Proceedings of the 25th Annual Conference on Computer Graphics and Interactive Techniques, SIGGRAPH 1998, pp. 189–198. ACM, New York (1998)

5. Dumont, M., Rogmans, S., Maesen, S., Frederix, K., Taelman, J., Bekaert, P.: A spatial immersive office environment for computer-supported collaborative work - moving towards the office of the future. In: Proceedings of the 25th Annual Conference on Computer Graphics and Interactive Techniques, SIGMAP 2011, pp. 212–216 (2011)

6. Ferrari, S., Maggioni, M., Borghese, N.: Multiscale approximation with hierarchical radial basis functions networks. IEEE Transactions on Neural Networks 15(1), 178–188 (2004)

7. Fischler, M.A., Bolles, R.C.: Random sample consensus: A paradigm for model fitting with applications to image analysis and automated cartography. Communications of the ACM 24(6), 381–395 (1981)

8. Fraundorfer, F., Scaramuzza, D.: Visual odometry : Part ii: Matching, robustness, optimization, and applications. IEEE Robotics Automation Magazine 19(2), 78–90 (2012)

9. Gierlinger, T., Danch, D., Stork, A.: Rendering techniques for mixed reality. Journal of Real-Time Image Processing 5(2), 109–120 (2010)

10. Gorski, K., Hivon, E., Banday, A., Wandelt, B., Hansen, F., et al.: HEALPix - A Framework for high resolution discretization, and fast analysis of data distributed on the sphere. Astrophys. J. 622, 759–771 (2005)

11. Grosch, T.: PanoAR: Interactive augmentation of omni-directional images with consistent lighting. In: Mirage 2005, Computer Vision / Computer Graphics Collaboration Techniques and Applications, pp. 25–34 (2005)

12. Grosch, T., Eble, T., Mueller, S.: Consistent interactive augmentation of live camera images with correct near-field illumination. In: Proceedings of the 2007 ACM Symposium on Virtual Reality Software and Technology, VRST 2007, pp. 125–132. ACM, New York (2007)

13. Haller, M.: Photorealism or/and non-photorealism in augmented reality. In: Proceedings of the 2004 ACM SIGGRAPH International Conference on Virtual Reality Continuum and Its Applications in Industry, VRCAI 2004, pp. 189–196. ACM, New York (2004). http://doi.acm.org/10.1145/1044588.1044627

14. Jones, B.R., Benko, H., Ofek, E., Wilson, A.D.: Illumiroom: Peripheral projected illusions for interactive experiences. In: Proceedings of the SIGCHI Conference on Human Factors in Computing Systems, CHI 2013, pp. 869–878. ACM, New York (2013). http://doi.acm.org/10.1145/2470654.2466112

15. Kajiya, J.T.: The rendering equation. In: Proceedings of the 13th Annual Conference on Computer Graphics and Interactive Techniques, SIGGRAPH 1986, pp. 143–150. ACM, New York (1986)

16. Kanbara, M., Yokoya, N.: Real-time estimation of light source environment for photorealistic augmented reality. In: Proceedings of the 17th International Conference on Pattern Recognition, ICPR 2004, vol. 2, pp. 911–914 (August 2004)

17. Lam, P.M., Ho, T.Y., Leung, C.S., Wong, T.T.: All-frequency lighting with multiscale spherical radial basis functions. IEEE Trans. Vis. Comput. Graph. 16(1), 43–56 (2010). http://dblp.uni-trier.de/db/journals/tvcg/tvcg16.html

18. Lourakis, M.I.A., Argyros, A.A.: Sba: A software package for generic sparse bundle adjustment. ACM Trans. Math. Softw. 36(1), 2:1–2:30 (2009). http://doi.acm.org/10.1145/1486525.1486527
19. Lowe, D.G.: Object recognition from local scale-invariant features. In: Proceedings of the International Conference on Computer Vision, ICCV 1999, vol. 2, p. 1150. IEEE Computer Society, Washington, DC (1999). http://dl.acm.org/citation.cfm?id=850924.851523
20. Lucas, B.D., Kanade, T.: An iterative image registration technique with an application to stereo vision. In: Proceedings of the 7th International Joint Conference on Artificial Intelligence, IJCAI 1981, vol. 2, pp. 674–679. Morgan Kaufmann Publishers Inc., San Francisco (1981). http://dl.acm.org/citation.cfm?id=1623264.1623280
21. Ng, R., Ramamoorthi, R., Hanrahan, P.: All-frequency shadows using non-linear wavelet lighting approximation. ACM Trans. Graph. **22**(3), 376–381 (2003)
22. Ng, R., Ramamoorthi, R., Hanrahan, P.: Triple product wavelet integrals for all-frequency relighting. In: ACM SIGGRAPH 2004 Papers, SIGGRAPH 2004, pp. 477–487. ACM, New York (2004)
23. Papagiannakis, G., Foni, A., Magnenat-Thalmann, N.: Practical precomputed radiance transfer for mixed reality. In: Proceedings of Virtual Systems and Multimedia 2005, pp. 189–199. VSMM Society (2005)
24. Raskar, R., Welch, G., Cutts, M., Lake, A., Stesin, L., Fuchs, H.: The office of the future: A unified approach to image-based modeling and spatially immersive displays. In: Proceedings of the 25th Annual Conference on Computer Graphics and Interactive Techniques, SIGGRAPH 1998, pp. 179–188. ACM, New York (1998). http://doi.acm.org/10.1145/280814.280861
25. Scaramuzza, D., Fraundorfer, F.: Visual odometry : Part i - the first 30 years and fundamentals. IEEE Robotics Automation Magazine 18(4) (2011)
26. Shi, J., Tomasi, C.: Good features to track. In: 1994 Proceedings of the IEEE Computer Society Conference on Computer Vision and Pattern Recognition, CVPR 1994, pp. 593–600 (June 1994)
27. Sloan, P.P., Kautz, J., Snyder, J.: Precomputed radiance transfer for real-time rendering in dynamic, low-frequency lighting environments. In: Proceedings of the 29th Annual Conference on Computer Graphics and Interactive Techniques, SIGGRAPH 2002, pp. 527–536. ACM, New York (2002)
28. Tsai, Y.T., Shih, Z.C.: All-frequency precomputed radiance transfer using spherical radial basis functions and clustered tensor approximation. In: ACM SIGGRAPH 2006 Papers, SIGGRAPH 2006, pp. 967–976. ACM, New York (2006). http://doi.acm.org/10.1145/1179352.1141981
29. Vr, O.: Oculus rift - virtual reality headset for 3d gaming (2012). http://www.oculusvr.com/ (accessed May 7, 2014)
30. Wang, J., Ren, P., Gong, M., Snyder, J., Guo, B.: All-frequency rendering of dynamic, spatially-varying reflectance. In: ACM SIGGRAPH Asia 2009 Papers, SIGGRAPH Asia 2009, pp. 133:1–133:10. ACM, New York (2009). http://doi.acm.org/10.1145/1661412.1618479

Cultural Heritage

Natural Interaction and Wearable Augmented Reality for the Enjoyment of the Cultural Heritage in Outdoor Conditions

Giuseppe Caggianese$^{(\boxtimes)}$, Pietro Neroni, and Luigi Gallo

Institute for High Performance Computing and Networking,
National Research Council of Italy (ICAR-CNR), Naples, Italy
{giuseppe.caggianese,pietro.neroni,luigi.gallo}@na.icar.cnr.it

Abstract. In this paper, a first prototype of a wearable, interactive augmented reality (AR) system for the enjoyment of the cultural heritage in outdoor environments, is presented. By using a binocular see-through display and a time-of-flight (ToF) depth sensor, the system provides the users with a visual augmentation of their surroundings and with touchless interaction techniques to interact with synthetic elements overlapping with the real world. The papers describes the hardware and software system components, and details the interface specifically designed for a socially acceptable cultural heritage exploration. Furthermore, the paper discusses the lesson learned from the first public presentation of the prototype we have carried out in Naples, Italy.

1 Introduction

In recent years, Augmented Reality (AR) has developed into a cutting edge technology. It allows researchers and visual artists to investigate a variety of application possibilities in domains not commonly associated with computer technologies, such as the cultural heritage and tourism. One of the reasons that has made AR an ideal approach for so many different types of applications is the possibility of introducing computer-generated information into the real world without occluding it. This aspect has the potential to reduce the gap between intention and action [26]: the user who needs information does not have to execute a search on her/his smartphone, because the information is automatically proposed to her/him organized in a computer-generated world overlapping with the real one.

These aspects have attracted the attention of researchers who have started to apply this technology to enhance the enjoyment of the cultural heritage. Another reason for this increased attention has also been the widespread adoption of smartphones and *mobile-AR* which have dominated the scene making AR one of the top 10 emerging technologies [25]. In fact, smartphones provide all the required hardware to develop a video-based AR application. However, they also present some important limitations, such as the need to frame the real world with the camera of the phone and watch the augmented information merged with the

L.T. De Paolis and A. Mongelli (Eds.): AVR 2014, LNCS 8853, pp. 267–282, 2014.
DOI: 10.1007/978-3-319-13969-2_20

real world through its display. This last aspect negatively affects enjoyment and forces the user to have at all times at least one hand occupied.

Nowadays, the release of new wearable hardware has increased the potential of AR in the cultural domain providing new possibilities to explore. New devices such as wearable see-through displays, increasingly similar to common sun glasses, have led to the redesigning of AR applications to exploit the opportunity to project digital imagery directly into the field of view (FOV) of the user. Particularly in the cultural heritage domain, this provides a means to develop applications in which ultimately technology becomes an on-demand service for the citizen/tourist, who can fully enjoy the cultural heritage without being distracted by the technology itself.

AR, when combined with wearable devices, becomes *mobile-wearable-AR*, a new platform that allows the development of applications characterized by full mobility, invisible technology, and hands-free interaction. A tourist can wear the AR device at the start of the tour without having to remove it to see the real world. In addition, the device will be completely invisible to the user, who will not need to use any type of controller to interact with it.

The possibility of placing information in the field of view of the user actually joining real and synthetic information, combined with the absence of a physical controller or touch displays, has immediately connected this platform with the the natural interaction domain, extending exponentially the design opportunities. The main challenge with this kind of touchless interface for AR environments is that the interface itself has to disappear, so as to allow the user to focus only on the cultural heritage and architecture of the city. Moreover, the time-consuming training required to learn how to use the interface has also to be considered as a priority for the specific domain of the cultural heritage. In fact, in this domain users can be extremely differentiated including many with no experience about natural user interfaces; this means that the interface has to be easy to use, taking advantage of interaction metaphors that require almost no learning curve. Accordingly, gestural interfaces, namely interfaces that recognize the gestures made by the user, seem to be suitable for this type of application.

However, the design of such a kind of interface for outdoor environments presents at least two main difficulties due to the actual hardware inefficiency: the brightness of current see-through displays, which is still too low in conditions of direct sunlight; and the inadequacy of current tracking technologies, since the cameras used to track the hands are still too big to be integrated into a pair of glasses and inertial sensors are still affected by many interference problems that make them inaccurate for registering synthetic and real worlds.

In this paper, we describe a complete AR system for a fully-featured, interactive exploration of the cultural heritage, thanks to a custom-made wearable AR device and a gestural interface based on the use of an inexpensive depth camera and inertial sensors. We detail the design of the interface, discuss open problems and report the lessons learned from the first public presentation we have carried out in Naples, Italy.

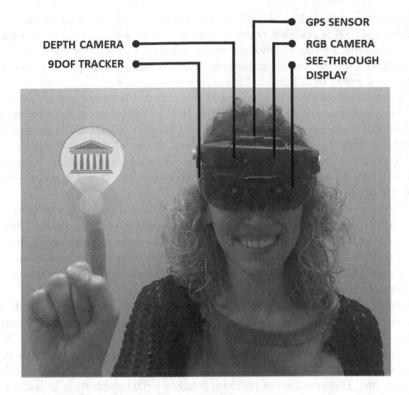

GPS SENSOR

DEPTH CAMERA

RGB CAMERA

9DOF TRACKER

SEE-THROUGH
DISPLAY

Fig. 1. The wearable AR system

The rest of the paper is structured as follows. In Section 2, we give an overview on related work and summarize the advantages and challenges of using wearable devices in AR applications. In Sections 3 and 4, we introduce the AR system and explain the main components of the user interface, respectively. After that, in Section 5, a detailed description of the implementation is presented, while Section 6 focuses on users' feedback. Finally, in Section 7 we present our conclusions.

2   Related Work

In recent years, many research activities have been carried out with the goal of designing a fully-featured, interactive augmented reality both minimally intrusive and suitable for use in indoor and outdoor environments. The first generation of outdoor user interfaces for mobile augmented reality systems was based on a combination of a head-tracked, see-through, head-worn display used in conjunction with a hand-held computer.

In [14], a prototype that assists users who are interested in a university campus was presented. The system overlays information about items of interest in the user's vicinity. As the user moves about, she/he is tracked through a combination of GPS position tracking and magnetometer orientation tracking. Another example of this technology was presented by Hollerer et al. [17]. The system allows users to access and manage information that is spatially registered with the real world by a hand-held pen-based computer.

Concerning application in the field of the cultural heritage and tourism, one of the first systems was Archeoguide [27]. It is an AR system for tourism and education built around the historical site of Olympia, which offers personalized augmented reality tours of archaeological sites, using HMD connected to a laptop, pen-tablet or palmtop. However, recent advantages in mobile computing, computer graphics and wireless and sensor technologies allow for a new generation of AR application mobile devices.

AR frameworks such as Wikitude [7], Layar [3] and Junaio [2], can be used to design mobile applications in which digital representations of points of interest (POI) are superimposed over the real world. In this case, the computer-generated content is shown over the smartphone's live video view of the real world, and the integrated GPS and compass sensors are used to locate the smartphone and the object of the user's interest [9].

Tuscany+ [6], is a mobile AR application that operates like a digital tourist guide, developed specifically for the Tuscany region by Fondazione Sistema Toscana. Taking information from Internet sources, such as Google Places, Wikipedia, and the region's official portal, Tuscany+ provides tourists with information in Italian and English regarding accommodation, restaurants and the city's nightlife. The application provides tourists with information in Italian and English regarding accommodation, restaurants and the city's nightlife taking information from Internet sources, such as Google Places, Wikipedia, and the region's official portal. In the same direction, within the project Augmented Reality for Basel [1] a mobile AR application has been developed that allows users to retrieve valuable information about the city of Basel and the surrounding area, and more specifically regarding its sites, museums, restaurants and hotels, with information for events and shopping centres also being available. It is built on top of Layar.

A similar AR application is Streetmuseum [5], developed by The Museum of London in 2012. It is a mobile AR application that allows users to view archival images exactly in the locations where they were taken. Using the application in Victoria Street, for example, users can view the images captured at the time a building was collapsing during a bombing raid in 1941. In [19], a wearable AR system that uses a monocular see-through HMD and a smartphone for hand gesture input is presented.

Using a smartphone to visualize an augmented world attracts the user's focus to the device rather than to the cultural heritage. On the contrary, smart AR glasses keep the user focused on the work of art, and with her/his hands free. However, while the touch interaction paradigm of smartphones is now well-assessed, wearable AR systems require a completely different approach to let the user interact with synthetic data. Accordingly, in recent years many researchers have been working on the design of a natural interface for wearable AR applications.

In [21], an AR interface that combines free-hand gesture and speech input using a multimodal fusion architecture, was presented. The interface is used in an AR application to select 3D synthetic objects and change their shape and colour. In [12], a free-hand gestural interface for crime scene investigator application using AR was described. Shumaker et al. [23] proposed a method for tracking a hand with a near-range depth camera attached to a video see-through head-mounted display (HMD) for digital object manipulation in an AR environment. An interface that combines natural 3D free-hand gestures with touch input on wearable computers has recently been introduced in [8]. Nonetheless, the use of gestural interaction in a wearable AR interaction context has not been investigated in detail.

3   System Description

3.1   Goals and Motivation

In this paper, we describe a wearable augmented reality system for a fully-featured, highly interactive enjoyment of the cultural heritage in outdoor environments. Most wearable AR applications have been designed and tested in indoor environments. On the contrary, the proposed system has been designed to be used outdoors, without limiting the user's position. The objective is to allow users to navigate within the tangible cultural heritage, such as buildings and monuments and at the same time to visualize and manipulate with hand gestures additional information about them. The realization of a system of this type has become possible thanks to the recent availability of a new generation of wearable AR displays which can be coupled with low consumption inertial sensors and RGB-D cameras (see figure 1) [24].

In more detail, the proposed application allows a citizen/tourist to:

- visualize georegistered points of interest (POI) overlaid on the real world view;
- filter the POI visualizations by POI type and distance from the user;
- visualize additional information about each POI;
- visualize navigation aids to reach a POI; and
- interact with the computer generated information by means of head movements and hand gestures.

In particular, the POIs are created and georegistered in real time using web services and the user's position and direction of sight.

The custom-made wearable device has been realized by integrating a binocular see-through display, a depth sensor and low-cost inertial sensors. Before detailing the interface, in the following sections we will describe the hardware components used.

See-through display   9DOF tracker   RGB-D camera   GPS sensor   Mini PC

Fig. 2. The components of the wearable AR system

3.2   Visual Augmentation

To augment the user's field of view with computer generated content, we have used the Vuzix STAR 1200XLD, a see-through augmented reality display system (see figure 2). This device uses a quantum optic see-through display technology so that the user can see the real world directly through its transparent wide screen video displays while the computer content is overlaid in full colour. The computer images are visualized on two high-resolution WVGA (852 x 480) LCD displays with 24-bit true colour and 35°of diagonal field of view, able to display 2D and stereoscopic 3D content.

The maximum resolution supported by the device is 1280×720, reproduced on a synthetic display of 75 inches as seen from about 3 meters. Included in the glasses are a removable head-tracker with a compass, audio support with a pair of headphones, an HDMI computer interface and a rechargeable battery powered interface for composite and component audio/video devices.

3.3   Depth Sensing

Since the interaction area is limited by the user's arm length, and the sensor is mounted on the user's head, we have used a short range depth sensor to track user hand movements. In the system, we have used the Softkinetic DepthSense 325 camera (see figure 2), since it is one of the smallest off-the-shelf sensors. With a dimension equal to $10.5cm \times 3cm \times 2.3cm$ it represents an optimal solution for the purpose of the project where the camera has to be worn by the user. It provides a horizontal field of view of 74°, a 58°vertical field of view, an operating distance range between 0.15 m and 1.0 m, and a resolution of 320×240 (QVGA).

Basically, the depth sensor measures the time it takes for infrared light emitted from the camera to return and transform the ToF positional data into real-time depth map images. The sensor also allows you to capture RGB images using a standard, low cost and low power consumption CMOS sensor. The RGB sensor specifications are a horizontal field of view of 63.2°, a 49.3° vertical field of view and a HD resolution at 720p. In the following, we will call the plane on which the depth sensor resides XY, and the axis orthogonal to this plane directed towards the user Z.

3.4   Tracking

To track the head movement of the user, we have used an accelerometer, a magnetometer, a gyroscope and a GPS sensor (see figure 2). These sensors allow you to keep track of the movement of the user's head and so build a synthetic world superimposed on the real one.

4   User Interface Description

In the system's interface all the interaction commands are mapped to head movements or hand gestures, which can be executed without having to touch any device. To let the user directly point at a synthetic object, she/he has to introduce her/his physical hand in the line of her/his point of view. So the interaction area has been formalized as the reachable workspace of the hand, defined as the volume within which all points can be reached by a chosen reference point on the wrist [20], posed on the look direction of the user. The user's hand movements executed in the physical space in front of her/his involve a corresponding movement of a cursor in the augmented space.

During the execution the system can be put in different states which are described below together with the conditions to execute transitions between them.

Idle. In this state the system is completely switched off, with the glasses and the depth camera used for the tracking being in fact disabled. This state allows you to save energy and extend the battery life of the device because the power consumption of the device is almost zero. The only exception is for the head tracker component, which remains active all the time to allow the user to turn on the system.

To activate the system the user should tilt (incline) back her/his head by a few degrees. The system detects the motion through the tracker attached to the glasses and automatically turns on the two see through displays of the glasses and the depth sensor. At this moment the system also performs a check of all the devices and, in the case of any malfunction or of any not detected devices, the system sends an error message to the user. At any time the user can put the system in the Idle state by tilting back her/his head using the same movement performed to turn it on.

Active. In this state the system tracks the position of the user through the GPS sensor to visualize all the surrounding POIs. The system arranges the POIs in the augmented space according to their relative position with respect to the user. From the user's point of view, the real world becomes augmented by a bunch of computer-generated information represented as POIs; when, for instance, the user looks at a monument or a building, she/he will be able to visualize a POI placed on it (see figure 3.a).

In the active state, the user can only visualize the POIs georeferenced in the real world view. To start the interaction with the synthetic content, the user has to move a hand (left or right as she/he prefers) inside the interaction area. In fact, in this state the depth sensor delivers all the captured depth images to the system, which analyzes these images to detect the user's hand. If the user's hand is detected, the system enters the pointing state.

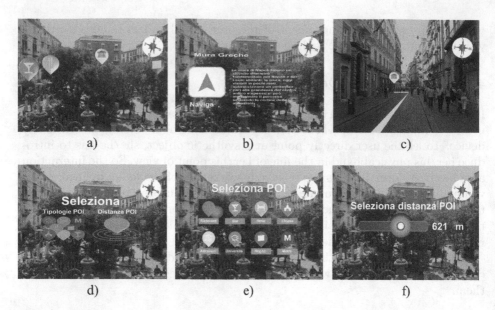

Fig. 3. Overview of the system's features: a) POIs overlapped to the real world view; b) POI information sheet; c) navigation path toward a POI; d) first level of the system menu; e) selection of the POI categories; f) selection of the POI coverage area

Pointing. In this state, the user can interact with the synthetic elements of the augmented environment. Choosing the appropriate interaction metaphors is a key activity in the design of a gestural interface, since you have to keep in consideration both the hardware characteristics of the input device and the applicative domain in which the interaction tasks take place, as well as human factors such as user fatigue and the social acceptance of the required hand and arm movements.

We have chosen the metaphorical gesture of pointing at an object; this gesture turns out to be familiar to users because it is usually used in classic desktop oriented applications. While the user executes the pointing gesture (hand posed with all the fingers closed, except for the index finger) the system maps to the point of the finger position a spherical computer-generated object that will work as a pointer. To use the pointing metaphor in a synthetic space which is bigger than the working space of the user, defined as the area reachable with the maximum extension of arm and hand, we have used the *ray casting* technique [22]. In the ray casting approach the pointer controlled by the user is connected to a computer-generated ray that works like a picking ray, since each time it intersects a digital object this object is returned to the system as the selected one.

Finally to improve the user's experience, the selection task is associated with a visual feedback which consists in a graphical highlight of the POI; in this way the user receives an immediate feedback about the object currently intersected by the ray. Each time the user moves her/his index fingertip to point at an object in the scene and the picking ray sends back a new synthetic element, the state of the system switches to a selection state to manage the associated trigger action.

Selection. The system continuously switches between the pointing and selection states each time the user points at a different object. The selection is in charge of managing the trigger action associated with the selection. We have chosen to implement the selection task by following the *wait to click* paradigm. To select an object, the user's index finger should remain still on the desired object for 2.5 seconds. A visual feedback of the elapsing time necessary to trigger the selection is the colour of the pointer, which changes from green to red.

When the user selects a POI the information encoded in it is visualized to the user in the form of a 2D digital paper posed on the look direction of the user (see figure 3.b), whereas when the user selects a button the system executes the associated action. For instance an user after reading the information of a POI can decide to reach the monument, so she/he can select the navigation button, visualized on the side of POI information, whose action will draw a route path overlapped on real streets (see figure 3.c).

System Control. The system control state is activated by using a single movement of the head that is different from the one used to activate the system. When the user tilts forwards her/his head, a system control menu is visualized on the whole FOV of the user (see figure 3.d). The system control state allows the user to modify certain system parameters such as the type of POI visualized and the surrounding area, centred in the user position, to be considered during the creation of the POIs (see figure 3.e and 3.f).

To exit from this state, the user should perform again the same movement of her/his head as that used in the activation, and the system will switch back to the active state.

5   Design and Implementation Details

In this section we introduce how the technology works, the problems encountered during the development and the proposed solutions to solve them.

A principal issue for any AR application is how be certain that the proposed information is embedded in the user's real world, how the system renders an icon in the synthetic environment that sticks exactly on the corresponding object in the real world. That is one of the fundamental challenges addressed in the development of the proposed system. To better lead the user into a merged computer-generated world accurately overlaid with the real one we have used georegistered information and the orientation tracking system. This provides the facility of knowing where the user is located and where she/he is looking when she/he is outdoors, so the system can upload only the relevant information. To put this information on top of the real world in correspondence with the

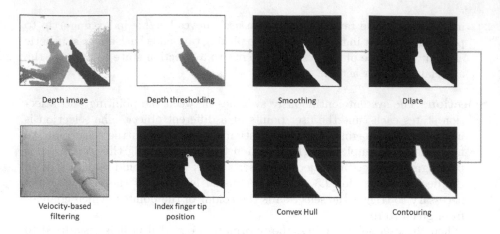

Depth image   Depth thresholding   Smoothing   Dilate

Velocity-based filtering   Index finger tip position   Convex Hull   Contouring

Fig. 4. The index fingertip detection and tracking pipeline

physical element, the system exploits the georeferentiation of the POIs obtained from OpenStreetMap [4]. Basically, the system receives latitude, longitude, and elevation, three pieces of information, for both the user's position and the POIs georeferenced in the same area; this information combined with the information about the look direction allows the building of the synthetic environment registered on the real one.

However, exploiting only the georeferenced information of the POIs to arrange them in the synthetic environments does not produce, in itself, a satisfactory result. In fact, in situations where a dense population of POIs is present, the augmentation is not clear and the interaction becomes unmanageable. In these cases, the user cannot distinguish the POIs since many of them are occluded by the others. Our proposed solution is to use not the elevation information of the georeferenced POIs, but an ad-hoc function that computes the elevation of the POIs based on their distance from the user. The closest POIs will be rendered at the same height as the user's position while those further away will be rendered with a height value that grows exponentially for the first 100 meters and linearly for more distant POIs.

The proposed system provides users with a natural interaction interface based on the tracking of the user's index fingertip. In the system, the hand tracking is executed using the depth map combined with computer vision algorithms realized to improve the performances of the recognition algorithms in outdoor conditions. Using a depth camera strongly facilitates the segmentation of hands, also in gloves, and cluttered backgrounds. However, when in outdoor conditions, the depth sensor shows an excessive level of noise due to the presence of direct sunlight, which makes it difficult to accurately detect and track the hand.

The index fingertip detection and tracking pipeline we have implemented is depicted in figure 4. At the first step of the pipeline there is a threshold procedure carefully calibrated to subtract unnecessary information due to cluttered backgrounds. For the threshold procedure our idea comes from the fact that anything more distant than the maximum extension of the user's arm in the same direction as that in which the user is looking can be cut off without any loss of information. Our experiments show up that the best results are achieved using a threshold posed to 80 cm from the sensor. So the area between 15 cm and 80 cm corresponds to a comfortable interaction area that does not require the user to completely stretch her/his arm. This prevents any feeling of fatigue and/or discomfort to the arm after a period of prolonged use, an aspect also known as the *Gorilla arm* effect [10].

The second step is the smoothing procedure to remove the excessive noise captured in the open space [13]. For the smoothing we have achieved our best performance, finely tuned between the computational time and the quality of the result, using the Gaussian filter with a kernel size of 15 × 15 and a standard deviation in the X and Y direction equal to 6.0.

Since the system really tracks only the index finger to manipulate a synthetic cursor, in the proposed algorithm we have improved the stability of the tracking by applying a morphological operator after the smoothing operator. We have used the dilate operator, which improves the depth image in which, due to the noise introduced by the sunlight, the fingers are difficult to detect. After the dilation of the image, we track the contours of the hand shape and also its convex hull.

Finally, the point on the contour boundary with the highest Y value is considered as the finger position and filtered before being rendered. To smooth the cursor movement and filter out any hand tremors, we used the *Smoothed Pointing* filter [15,16], which adopts a user's hand velocity-based control-to-display ratio adaptation. It uses two speed thresholds to filter the index fingertip motion: a minimum speed (v_{min}) below which any motion is considered a tracking error; and a maximum speed (v_{max}) above which the fingertip speed remains constant. This filter allows you to mitigate the movement of the cursor when the velocity is between v_{min} and v_{max}, and to remove the flickering due to rapid movements of the fingertip, enabling you to achieve more fluid, gradual and precise movements.

In order to facilitate the interaction of the user with the interface, the proposed system does not consider any hand movements of the user in the Z axis. This aspect improves the user's comfort, since she/he is free to choose the most comfortable extension of the arm to point at POIs and buttons.

The interaction approach applied to deal with the selection problem, as introduced in the previous section, is the pointing metaphor that exploits the ray casting technique to reach all the elements in the computer-generated scene. The ray used is an outgoing ray that moves from the cursor connected to the hand inside the scene like a picking ray that returns to the user any element it intersects. This metaphor has been chosen because it is a simple and computationally convenient approach that works well also in the performance of precise selections, but presents some issues with dense scenarios. In fact, as previously mentioned, it may happen that two or more POIs result grouped together. This happens because these POIs are more or less at the same distance from the user's position and, from this particular point of view, are very close to each other.

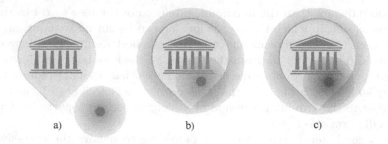

Fig. 5. The selection procedure: a) pointer approaching a POI; b) graphical highlight of the POI when the pointer is on it; c) the pointer becomes red when the selection has been confirmed

In these situations the ray cast metaphor needs to be associated with a disambiguation approach. At the moment, the system exploits a heuristic method to choose a single element from a group of objects in the scene. The selected object is the one whose central position is closest to the ray. Since all the elements in the scene have the same shape and size this approach works very well, allowing the user to easily select even a partially occluded object; in fact, it is sufficient, after the initial positioning, to slightly move the hand and so the cursor until the desired POI is highlighted.

In addition to the selection, it is also necessary to adopt an approach to confirm the selection. For this task, we have chosen the *wait to click* paradigm, which allows you to confirm a selection by keeping your hand still for a defined time. This technique is not affected by the *Heisenberg* effect [11], because the user does not need to execute any movement of the hand to confirm the selection. However, this selection technique is affected by the *Midas Touch* effect [18], since the confirm selection task can result in an unwanted selection. To deal with this problem we propose a double strategy; first of all, we take advantage of visual feedback to better inform the user about the POI currently selected (see figure 5); and secondly, we use a smoothing filter, which stabilizes the cursor position, to simplify the task of keeping the cursor still.

The choice of the time required to trigger the confirmation of the selection becomes an important issue because with an excessively short time window the user does not have enough time to realize her/his selection and, on the contrary, an excessively long time window results in more fatigue. We have chosen a time equal to 2.5 seconds, which has proved to be an adequate trade-off.

A common issue in applications for see-through displays is the lag introduced by the software that displays the synthetic content on top of the user's real-world vision. Latency is something that cannot be eliminated because the ground truth, the reality, is always behind the glass and it is instantaneous. The problem arises from the fact that the system needs time to transfer measurements from the sensor acquisition, process them, and finally render them. In the proposed application, the only component that is affected by a perceptible lag (higher than $33ms$) is the movement of the cursor attached to the user's real hand. In this case, the time needed to take the depth image, to apply the computer vision algorithms to detect and track the hand and finally to render the cursor, turns out to be around 100 ms. However, since the smoothing filter is based on hand velocity, it partially hides the lag, especially during fast movements.

The entire system has been developed by using Unity, which is a cross-platform render engine equipped with a built-in IDE. This development environment supports different scripted languages to develop the necessary behaviours that will be mapped to the synthetic elements in the scene. The interface has been written entirely in C# language, also exploiting open source and cross-platform libraries like OpenCV, which have been combined and extended to support the use of a ToF camera to track the user's hands. To use the OpenCV library with the C# language and to integrate the code in the Unity render engine, we have taken advantage of opencvsharp, a cross-platform wrapper of OpenCV for .NET Framework written in C#.

6 Lessons Learned

The AR system was presented at the public event "OR.C.HE.S.T.R.A. Napoli Smart City Day 2014"; where was possible to collect feedback from subject which tried our application. In this section we briefly summarize the lessons learned by following a talk aloud protocol.

We received negative feedback about the continuous tilting backwards and forwards of the head to enable and disable the interface and the menu. In particular, the users judged it to be uncomfortable when having to change the POI category or distance. In fact, they had to tilt their head backwards and forwards, perform the operation, and then again tilt head backwards and forwards to confirm it. Therefore, new interaction techniques for enabling/disabling the menu will be investigated.

Moreover, users complained of a poor brightness of the smart-glasses display in bright sunlight. We partially solved this problem by superimposing a polarized lens onto the glasses lens to improve sunlight absorption. In this way, however, although the use of these lenses improved the visibility of the synthetic content,it worsened the visibility of the real world.

Finally, when the smart glasses were worn by people who wear ferromagnetic-rimmed glasses, the POIs were placed in the wrong positions. This was because the magnetometer sensor is affected by noise every time a magnetic source is close to it, which throws the user's azimuth estimate off slightly with a substantial affect on the POIs positions. To better assess the azimuth, we will investigate algorithms that combine the magnetometer information with other sources, such as the RGB image.

7 Conclusions and Future Work

Wearable AR technology is now rapidly evolving. This is probably due to the release of Google Glass [26]. Although they are not exactly an augmented reality solution, they have opened up the market. Now many other vendors are going to release low-cost, wearable technologies that will have the potential to enter into everyday life.

In this paper, we have described a first prototype of a wearable, interactive AR system for the outdoor enjoyment of cultural heritage. The system comprises a home-assembled pair of glasses and a touchless interface. It operates as a digital tourist guide, by providing users with tourist and cultural information in the form of POIs with which the user can interact by using touchless interaction techniques. To the best of our knowledge, this is one of the first wearable AR systems oriented to outdoor environments.

Our future work will focus on the enhancing of the accuracy of the user's azimuth estimation, by designing algorithms that use the RGB camera to improve magnetometer and GPS data. For example, georeferenced pictures relating to physical elements of the real world can be used as landmarks. This approach to the estimation of the user's gaze direction would also be useful when the user wears a pair of glasses with a ferromagnetic spectacle frame. However, these approaches require computationally expensive algorithms, so can only be used on devices that have an adequate computing power and battery.

Furthermore we will also focus on encouraging a more active participation of users in the production of information; for instance, an user will be able to advertise an exhibition by sharing this information with her/his friends. However this opens up new issues such as the generation, the sharing control and especially the validation of this information.

Finally, in order to better detect and track the user's hand when exposed to direct sunlight, we will integrate depth data with other sources (RGB and/or thermal). We will also improve the user's experience by making the interaction as natural as possible, and minimizing her/his using fatigue; for this purpose we will investigate different interaction metaphors in an empirical study.

Acknowledgments. The proposed system has been developed within the project OR.C.HE.S.T.R.A. - ORganization of Cultural HEritage for Smart Tourism and Real-time Accessibility, funded by the European Community, Regione Campania, the Ministry of Education Universities and Research (MIUR), and the Ministry of Economic Development, under the Call for Smart Cities and Communities and Social Innovation.

References

1. Augmented Reality for Basel. http://www.perey.com/AugmentedRealityForBasel/
2. Junaio. http://www.junaio.org/
3. Layar. http://www.layar.com/
4. Openstreetmap. http://www.openstreetmap.org/
5. Streetmuseum. http://www.museumoflondon.org.uk/
6. Tuscany+. http://www.turismo.intoscana.it/allthingstuscany/aroundtuscany/
7. Wikitude. http://www.wikitude.org/
8. Bai, H., Lee, G., Billinghurst, M.: Using 3d hand gestures and touch input for wearable ar interaction. In: CHI 2014 Extended Abstracts on Human Factors in Computing Systems, CHI EA 2014, pp. 1321–1326. ACM, New York (2014)

9. Billinghurst, M.: Augmented reality interfaces in human computation systems. In: Michelucci, P. (ed.) Handbook of Human Computation, pp. 317–331. Springer, New York (2013)
10. Boring, S., Jurmu, M., Butz, A.: Scroll, tilt or move it: Using mobile phones to continuously control pointers on large public displays. In: Proceedings of the 21st Annual Conference of the Australian Computer-Human Interaction Special Interest Group: Design: Open 24/7, OZCHI 2009, pp. 161–168. ACM, New York (2009)
11. Bowman, D.A., Wingrave, C.A., Campbell, J.M., Ly, V.Q., Rhoton, C.J.: Novel uses of pinch gloves for virtual environment interaction techniques. Virtual Reality 6(3), 122–129 (2002)
12. Datcu, D., Lukosch, S.: Free-hands interaction in augmented reality. In: Proceedings of the 1st Symposium on Spatial User Interaction, SUI 2013, pp. 33–40. ACM, New York (2013)
13. Essmaeel, K., Gallo, L., Damiani, E., De Pietro, G., Dipanda, A.: Temporal denoising of kinect depth data. In: 2012 Eighth International Conference on Signal Image Technology and Internet Based Systems (SITIS), pp. 47–52. IEEE (2012)
14. Feiner, S., MacIntyre, B., Hollerer, T., Webster, A.: A touring machine: Prototyping 3d mobile augmented reality systems for exploring the urban environment. In: Proceedings of the 1st IEEE International Symposium on Wearable Computers, ISWC 1997, p. 74. IEEE Computer Society, Washington, DC (1997)
15. Gallo, L., Minutolo, A.: Design and comparative evaluation of smoothed pointing: A velocity-oriented remote pointing enhancement technique. International Journal of Human-Computer Studies 70(4), 287–300 (2012)
16. Gallo, L., Ciampi, M., Minutolo, A.: Smoothed pointing: a user-friendly technique for precision enhanced remote pointing. In: 2010 International Conference on Complex, Intelligent and Software Intensive Systems (CISIS), pp. 712–717. IEEE (2010)
17. Hollerer, T., Feiner, S., Terauchi, T., Rashid, G., Hallaway, D.: Exploring mars: Developing indoor and outdoor user interfaces to a mobile augmented reality system. Computers and Graphics 23, 779–785 (1999)
18. Jacob, R.J.K., Leggett, J.J., Myers, B.A., Pausch, R.: An agenda for human-computer interaction research: Interaction styles and input/output devices (1993)
19. Kerr, S.J., Rice, M.D., Teo, Y., Wan, M., Cheong, Y.L., Ng, J., Ng-Thamrin, L., Thura-Myo, T., Wren, D.: Wearable mobile augmented reality: Evaluating outdoor user experience. In: Proceedings of the 10th International Conference on Virtual Reality Continuum and Its Applications in Industry, VRCAI 2011, pp. 209–216. ACM, New York (2011)
20. Kumar, A., Waldron, K.J.: The workspaces of a mechanical manipulator. Journal of Mechanical Design 103(3) (1980)
21. Lee, M., Billinghurst, M., Baek, W., Green, R., Woo, W.: A usability study of multimodal input in an augmented reality environment. Virtual Reality 17(4), 293–305 (2013)
22. Mine, M.R.: Virtual environment interaction techniques. University of North Carolina at Chapel Hill, Chapel Hill, NC, USA, Tech. rep. (1995)

23. Park, G., Ha, T., Woo, W.: Hand Tracking with a Near-Range Depth Camera for Virtual Object Manipulation in an Wearable Augmented Reality. In: Shumaker, R., Lackey, S. (eds.) VAMR 2014, Part I. LNCS, vol. 8525, pp. 396–405. Springer, Heidelberg (2014)
24. Placitelli, A.P., Gallo, L.: Low-cost augmented reality systems via 3d point cloud sensors. In: 2011 Seventh International Conference on Signal-Image Technology and Internet-Based Systems (SITIS), pp. 188–192. IEEE (2011)
25. Pulli, K., Chen, W.C., Gelfand, N., Grzeszczuk, R., Tico, M., Vedantham, R., Wang, X., Xiong, Y.: Mobile visual computing. In: International Symposium on Ubiquitous Virtual Reality, ISUVR 2009, pp. 3–6 (July 2009)
26. Starner, T.: Project glass: An extension of the self. IEEE Pervasive Computing **12**(2), 14–16 (2013)
27. Vlahakis, V., Karigiannis, J., Tsotros, M., Gounaris, M., Almeida, L., Stricker, D., Gleue, T., Christou, I.T., Carlucci, R., Ioannidis, N.: Archeoguide: First results of an augmented reality, mobile computing system in cultural heritage sites. In: Proceedings of the 2001 Conference on Virtual Reality, Archeology, and Cultural Heritage, VAST 2001, pp. 131–140. ACM, New York (2001)

Virtual Reality Visualization for Photogrammetric 3D Reconstructions of Cultural Heritage

Heiko Herrmann$^{(\boxtimes)}$ and Emiliano Pastorelli

Institute of Cybernetics at Tallinn University of Technology, Tallinn, Estonia
{hh,pastorelli}@cens.ioc.ee
http://www.ioc.ee

Abstract. In this paper the authors review the design of a self-build general-purpose Virtual Reality environment, which presents all relevant features of a full-size CAVE-like system, yet at a fraction of the financial and space requirements. Further, the application of this system to the development of a virtual museum is presented. The objects in the museum are models, reconstructed via photogrammetry from a set of pictures. For this process cost-free software is used. The presentation of the 3D models in the Virtual Environment is done using BlenderCAVE, a multi-screen extension of the Blender game engine. The main contributions of this paper are the discussion of the design choices for a small and low-budget but feature-rich virtual reality environment and the application of the system for cultural heritage. In this area tools for creation of 3D models and their presentation in a VR environment are presented.

Keywords: Virtual Reality · CAVE-like system · Cultural Heritage

1 Introduction

In the last year, affordable personal Virtual Reality devices like the Oculus Rift or Google Glasses pushed Virtual Reality, almost unexpectedly, in the public eye, suddenly reviving a trend that seemed to be ready to blossom already twenty years ago but that never did, giving the delusion that the topic was dead.

The truth is, that Virtual Reality never ceased to slowly move on with the development in research, far from the spotlights, patiently waiting for hardware to improve in power and decrease in price to support its features.

In 1993, with the Cruz-Neira CAVE [7], research institutes and private engineering companies slowly started building their own Virtual Environments, with a pace dictated mainly by the still high budget requirements those systems implied. Nowadays, a semi-immersive CAVE-like system price ranges from several hundred-thousand Euro up to several million Euro. The resolution, user interaction and quality of all their characteristics obviously improved enormously compared to their first ancestors from the 90s, but the price is still far from being an easily accessible one. Several research institution that could make use of the

© Springer International Publishing Switzerland 2014
L.T. De Paolis and A. Mongelli (Eds.): AVR 2014, LNCS 8853, pp. 283–295, 2014.
DOI: 10.1007/978-3-319-13969-2_21

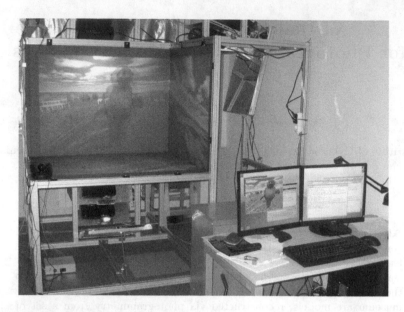

Fig. 1. The "Kyb3" Virtual Reality Environment, showing a 3D model in Blender-CAVE

potentialities of employing VR-oriented visualization systems, wouldn't still be able to afford a full CAVE system.

At the same time, the limitations of lower cost personal VR devices like Head Mounted Displays (HMD) are still hindering their use in environments meant for cooperative research involving multiple users.

From all this premises come the reasons that persuaded us to build our own customized VR system at the Institute of Cybernetics of Tallinn University of Technology in 2012, the Kyb3 [11], Fig. 1. The system has been designed to be a space and budget contained virtual environment with the flexibility of being both a tool to perform research on virtual reality itself and to employ it as a tool for scientific visualization. It took approximately one year and half to design and build the system but, once completed, its flexibility paid off, proving that the Kyb3 was open to an even wider range of applications than the ones it was devised for.

While mainly employed to visualize the results of microstructured materials analysis (Steel Fibre Reinforced Concrete [8,12,16]), a recent interest in 3D scanning and photogrammetry, led to the decision to employ the Kyb3 for a semi-immersive visualization of the scanned objects as well.

2   The Visualization System "Kyb3"

Being the first system of its kind in Estonia, the Kyb3 was conceived and built both as a tool for specific visualization tasks (Micro-structured materials analysis and visualization) and as a prototype to kick-start the research in the field of Virtual Reality in Estonia. The task of building a space and budget contained VR system that could also reproduce most of the real-size VE features, was not trivial and involved several months of accurate design. Every component of the system had to be chosen according to multiple constraint. While the budget-related ones might be obvious, the space related ones were instead the cause of more complex design choices. The full system had to fit into a space of no more than $2.5 \times 2.5 \times 2.5$ meters, while retaining a screen surface wide enough to grant a good semi-immersive visualization experience. Also, as mentioned, it had to be a scaled-down version of the features of real-size CAVE systems (table/floor screen, user tracking, etc).

2.1   Design Choices of the Kyb3 Related to Space

To deal with the space constraint, the fundamental choices have been: short throw projectors and a mirror system to further reduce the throw distance necessary for the projected image to achieve the chosen size. While with a traditional projection system, the projectors would have needed approximately 2.7 m distance to achieve a screen size of 110 cm × 80 cm, with the use of the short-throw projectors and mirrors, less that 75 cm where necessary. To properly position the hanging projectors, filters and mirrors, a special, configurable mounting was self-designed. This way it was possible to obtain a system fitting in a parallelepiped ($H \times W \times L$) of no more than 2.35 m × 2.04 m × 1.77 m, see Fig. 1.

The whole system is supported by a self-designed aluminum frame (the material was chosen to avoid excessive interference with the electromagnetic fields of the tracking system), tailored on the specific configuration needs of the Kyb3, and built with the practical support of Dimentio OÜ.

2.2   Design Choices of the Kyb3 Related to Budget

The budget constraint influenced all the design choices made: A single tower computer with 4 high-end NVIDIA 4000 graphics card was chosen instead of the now common setup with one computer per screen. A low cost electro-magnetic user tracking system, the WintrackerIII is employed instead of the more commonly used, but high price, optical systems. Consumer hardware (Nintendo Wiimote and Razer Hydra 6-DOF joysticks) is used to manage the user interaction.

Both, to keep the price low and to have a research-friendly system, only open-source freely-available software was installed on the machine. The whole input is managed through VRPN [17] and VRUI [10] Device Daemon, while the main software used for the applications are: ParaView for visualization of several types of scientific data-sets (vectors and tensors fields, CFD simulations, volumetric data), and VRUI, a VR platform supporting a wide set of software to visualize mesh data, LIDAR data, scalar/vectorial/tensorial volume data, VRML scenes and more. Further VMD and jReality are currently being configured to extend the fields of application to molecular dynamics and mathematical geometry.

A recent addition is BlenderCAVE. This list of software offers a wide choice of supported data-sets to researchers and users from various fields to visualize their data on the 3D screens of the Kyb3.

3   Application Within Cultural Heritage

One possible application of Virtual Reality and 3D scanning is, of course, in cultural heritage. It can be used to share information about and discuss artifacts with colleagues online, or to build a virtual museum for the public. In some cases it may not be possible for visitors to access the historic site, due to a remote location or the risk of damage, but nevertheless it would be beneficial to show it to the public to create interest in its preservation and exploration. Another possibility is that virtual exhibitions can be easily transferred from one place around the world to another and can take place in several locations at the same time and could be arranged in small towns or even villages, therefore being accessible by more people.

During the course of the academic year 2013 and 2014, having several MS Kinect camera available from previous user-tracking experiments, and being interested in further increasing the interaction between the Kyb3 and the real world, we turned our attention to 3D scanning options.

For the use of VR in a museum, several other points need consideration:

- The usability of applications by visitors to the museum
- The need to create different user interfaces depending on the target group
- The ability to integrate multimedia content, creating moments of edutainment effective
- The maintenance cost of the solution
- The cost of staff training

Most of these points are not addressed by our study, however some of the design choices we made have proven to be beneficial to maintanance costs.

The backprojection screens used by us are scratch resistant and washable, which is a large benefit when dealing with user groups and children. Also the Razer Hydra, used as a wand, is relatively cheap and as being gaming equipment also robust. It doesn't get damaged immediately when accidentally falling down and could be replaced without large costs if damaged. The optically tracked wands, used in large commerical VR environments, need readjusting of the tracker markers by the manufacturer after falling down, which causes downtime of the system and is expensive.

The main aim here is to show, how a general purpose VRE can be opened up for cultural heritage as a new application field, thus increasing the amount of possible users of the system and therefore increasing its value for the institution maintaining it.

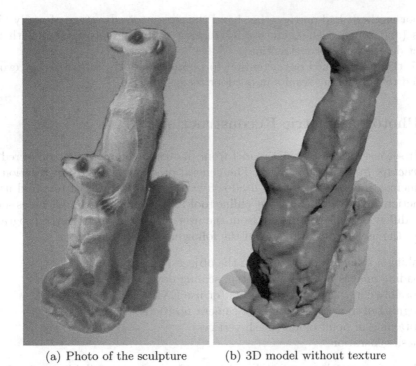

(a) Photo of the sculpture   (b) 3D model without texture

Fig. 2. Kinect scan of a meerkat sculpture

4   3D Scanning with a Depth Sensor

Due to the available equipment, the most obvious one seemed to be the reconstruction of an object through the automatic registration and merging of multiple point clouds derived from the depth sensor of the Kinect, using the Point Cloud Library (PCL) [15].

Three months of experiments that involved a BSc thesis, resulted in a partial success. Through the use of key-points registration and loop-closure detection to reduce errors, we obtained a self-developed software able to scan a small object (up to 30x30x30 cm), Fig. 2, or a human bust, with no textures and a limited level of depth resolution. The whole process, including scanning and reconstruction took approximately 20 minutes, resulting in a mesh file compatible with most of the 3D Visualization software.

The limitation of the method appeared though quite obvious when we tried using the same software to scan much larger objects and environments. On room-sized indoor areas, after tweaking of the parameters it was possible to obtain reasonable meshes, despite several external factors. Some examples are the type and intensity of lights and the color of the objects, conditioning negatively the quality of the Kinect depth image. Outdoors, these problems amplify, including the limitations due to having a cable-bound camera. More traditional LIDAR outdoor methods had on the other hand the serious disadvantage of really high prices (and some of the same reconstruction problems encountered with the Kinect depth-cloud reconstruction).

We therefore turned our attention to photogrammetry, whose recent evolution led to astonishing results in outdoor reconstruction.

5   Photogrammetric Reconstruction

The (re-)construction of a 3D model from photos is commonly also referred to as *Structure from Motion* (SfM). The general process for the reconstruction is, in principal, independent of the used software, but the degree of required user-interaction differs drastically. The online tool 123D Catch for example hides some of the different steps completely from the user, while the open-source programs require the user to perform each of the following steps separately:

- taking a sequence of pictures of the object
- loading images into software, resp. scaling down
- possibly enter camera parameters (or use EXIF data)
- aligning of images, determining camera positions
- obtaining of point cloud (mesh vertices)
- mesh generation

There are several commercial and free software tools available, some of the more popular ones seem to be:

- Agisoft PhotoScan: commercial
- Autodesk Smart3DCapture: commercial, can use GPS position
- Autodesk 123D Catch: free online tool using the core of Smart3DCapture, amount of pictures limited, restrictive license (content belongs to whom?)
- Python Photogrammetry ToolBox [3]: open-source front-end for OSM-Bundler, CMVS, PMVS [2]
- VisualSFM [18]: open-source, graphical user-interface
- OpenMVG [1]: open-source library
- MeshLab [5,6]: open-source mesh creation and processing software

As the rest of our 3D system is build on free and open-source software (FOSS), it is natural for us to concentrate on free software, meaning preferably open-source or at least usable free of charge.

In order to create a three-dimensional representation of an object of interest it is necessary to cover the subject with a good photo set, taking between 50 and 70 photographs of the subject from different angles and with overlap. During the process the lighting conditions should stay the same, it is preferable not to have anything blocking the view and the subject should not be moved as features from the whole photograph are used to stitch together the model. It is also preferable not to have any disturbances in the background.

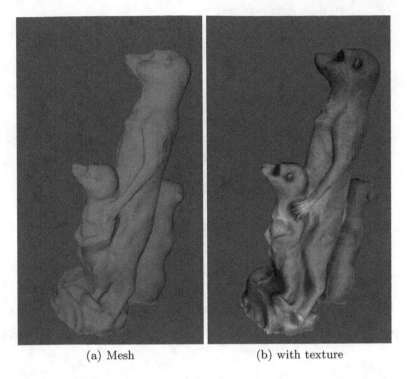

(a) Mesh   (b) with texture

Fig. 3. Photogrammetric model of a meerkat sculpture obtained with 123D Catch

5.1   123D Catch

Autodesk 123D Catch provides a simple and user-friendly way to record three-dimensional data without the need for specialized equipment or technical skills. It is accessible to anybody with a consumer camera. Autodesk 123D Catch finds common features on all the photographs and uses them to reconstruct a three-dimensional scene. To create a model of the statue of *Juulius*, the eternal student (Fig. 4) and the mascot of our university, we took about 50 photographs sequentially around the statue, each showing the whole statue, uploaded them to 123D Catch and received a three-dimensional scene representing the statue. Such a three-dimensional scene can easily be exported as a mesh object and opened in Blender where it can be modified, and represented interactively to a user using Blender game engine.

As mentioned before, the process is straightforward, the reconstruction in 123D Catch requires no adjustments by the user. In our case, it took about half an our to upload the pictures and obtain the model, the result is very detailed and presented in Fig. 5 for Juulius and in Fig. 3 for the meerkat skulpture for comparison with the Kinect scan in Fig. 2.

Fig. 4. Photo of Juulius, the eternal student, mascot of Tallinn University of Technology

5.2   Python Photogrammetry ToolBox

The Python Photogrammetry ToolBox (PPT) is a GUI for several tools to simplify the reconstruction process. Using PPT only some mouse-clicks are necessary to obtain structure from the images, however the process is not as automatized as with 123D Catch. The components invoked by the GUI are Bundler and PMVS, CMVS. After MeshLab needs to be invoked to create the mesh. PPT can take a mix of pictures from different cameras, but for all cameras the width of the CCD sensor needs to be known.

The following steps are performed:

- check camera database and enter parameters if necessary
- run Bundler, in this case we used the siftvlfeat for feature matching and the images have been scaled down to 1200 pixels
- then PVMS was used to create the point cloud
- in MeshLab the Poisson Surface reconstruction is used, here it may be necessary to remove points belonging to the surrounding

The result of the reconstruction is shown in Fig. 6. The result is slightly less precise as the one obtained by 123D Catch, but this might be due to a non-optimal choice of parameters or the scaling of the pictures.

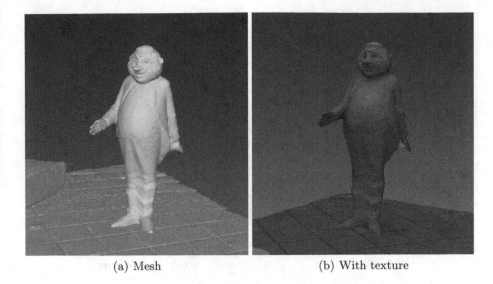

(a) Mesh   (b) With texture

Fig. 5. Mesh of Juulius obtained with 123D Catch

5.3   VisualSFM

Creating three-dimensional reconstructions using VisualSFMs graphical user interface is similar to using 123D Catch. First, the user needs to select the photographs to work with, then, with two button clicks, it is possible to receive a sparse reconstruction based on those. With one more button click it is possible to receive a dense reconstruction, computing which takes time -? for us it took about two hours to compute a dense reconstruction of the statue of Juulius. It is possible to run VisualSFM on the command line and change some of its parameters, giving the user more control over the steps of the reconstruction process. The resulting point cloud with the camera positions is shown in Fig. 7. Being able to see the camera positions gives the possibility to see possible reasons in case the model has holes or lacks details in some areas, due to sparse photo coverage.

6   BlenderCAVE

One possible category of software to create an interactive museum are game engines (e.g. the CryEngine has been used before [9]), and within this category, Blender [4] with the BlenderCAVE [13,14] is an interesting candidate. Blender was an in-house tool of the Dutch animation studio Neo Geo and Not a Number Technologies (NaN), in 2002 it was released under the GNU General Public License. While the learning curve is steep, the work-flow within Blender has been designed by modeling and animation professionals, and is very efficient.

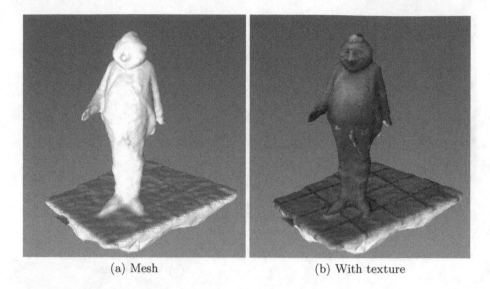

(a) Mesh   (b) With texture

Fig. 6. Mesh of Juulius obtained with Python Photogrammetry ToolBox and MeshLab

Implemented in 2012/2013 at the Computer Science Laboratory for Mechanics and Engineering Science (LIMSI), a CNRS Laboratory associated with Paris-Sud University, BlenderCAVE (BC) offers an adaptation to the open-source Blender Game Engine (BGE) module of Blender able to run in a scaleable way on any Virtual Reality architecture (N hosts, K screens), supporting stereoscopic viewing in all the most common techniques (passive, active, side-by-side, etc) and integrating a VRPN plugin to manage user tracking and interaction.

The flexibility of the BGE, together with the powerful features of Blender itself, provides the user an interactive 3D scene manager that is both simple to setup and flexible in the format of data that can be displayed. By integrating a physics engine (Bullet Engine), BGE can take, under the BC control, extremely interesting interactive scenes to a wide range of devices, from simple desktop environments to full-sized CAVE systems.

Thanks to a flexible implementation, BC allows most of the existing BGE scenes to work on a VE with barely a couple of lines of additional codes to their logic managers.

During the starting phase of Cultural Heritage visualization on Virtual Reality Environments, despite a wide selection of existing software, BC became our chosen one due to several reasons. First of all thanks to Blender's own features, that allow us to import almost every existing format of meshes and additionally perform some post-processing and refinement of the meshes obtained through the photogrammetric reconstruction. Having the BGE integrated in the same working environment means that the process to bring interaction to the static objects is extremely straightforward, allowing therefore to immediately be able to navigate the meshes in immersive ways (as for example walking around and inside them).

Fig. 7. Point cloud with camera positions obtained with VisualSFM

Additionally, the scaleability of BC, allows the preparation of the scenes to be easily be performed on desktop and laptop computers, and then taken to the already configured BC on the Kyb3 system, without requiring any additional configuration.

Fig. 8. Showing the obtained model with BlenderCAVE in our 3D system

An ideal setup for prototyping, working and displaying results of the work done in the quickest possible way. Fig. 8 shows the 3D model of Juulius obtained by photogrammetry integrated into one of the example scenes of BlenderCAVE.

7   Conclusions and Outlook

In this paper we have discussed the main design choices for a low-budget VR system, that has the main features of a CAVE-like environment, and that is used for both, VR development and applications in material science, civil engineering and cultural heritage. For the application in cultural heritage, we presented a tool-chain to create 3D models from real objects from small artifacts to statues and possibly to houses. The tool-chain included either free-of-charge or open-source software and covered the full range from 3D scanning over model creation to modeling and presentation with BlenderCAVE in our VR environment.

In the future the authors plan to develop interactive physical games using the physics engine of Blender. The physics engine could also be used to animate objects and therefore create more lively representations.

Another plan is to try to use of remote controlled multi-copters to take aerial photos, e.g. to create models of houses, castles or churches. The whole process described in Section 5 implies one thing: that pictures are taken from all the directions around the subject of interest, to cover every possible exposed surface. This can be relatively easy in case of small objects whose size is no larger than a human body, but what happens if the necessity of completely reconstructing a building arises? One possibility that we consider for the future are multi-copters, which are readily available now, many of them already endowed with HD cameras.

By combining the pictures taken from the ground and those taken from the copter of the otherwise unreachable parts, it is possible to gather all of the pictures necessary for a high resolution and accurate 3D model of a building. Due to the copter maneuverability, it is also possible to focus on extruding features of the building (as small towers or gargoyles) and include them realistically in the final reconstruction.

Acknowledgments. The paper was compiled with the assistance of the Tiger University Program of the Estonian Information Technology Foundation (VisPar system, EITSA/HITSA Tiigriülikool grants 10-03-00-24, 12-03-00-11, 13030009 and travel grant for H.H. to present at Salento AVR 2014).

This research was supported by the European Union through the European Regional Development Fund, in particular through funding for the "Centre for Nonlinear Studies" as an Estonian national centre of excellence. This research was also supported by the European Social Fund's Doctoral Studies and Internationalisation Programme DoRa 4 (through a long time stipend for E.P.). Further, the IT Akadeemia 2013/2014 grant for E.P.'s studies is gratefully acknowledged.

We thank our interns Liis Harjo (Tallinn University of Technology) and Giorgos Psistakis (ERASMUS intern, University of Crete) for their contribution on 3D scanning with a Kinect (G.P.) and photogrammetry (L.H.).

References

1. openmvg: open multiple view geometry. http://imagine.enpc.fr/~moulonp/openMVG/
2. Osm-bundler, pmvs, cmvs. http://code.google.com/p/osm-bundler/
3. Python photogrammetry toolbox. https://github.com/archeos/ppt-gui/
4. Blender Online Community: Blender - a 3d modelling and rendering package (2013). http://www.blender.org, version 2.xx
5. Cignoni, P.: MeshLab, a tool developed with the support of the 3D-CoForm project. http://meshlab.sourceforge.net/
6. Cignoni, P., Corsini, M., Ranzuglia, G.: Meshlab: an open-source 3d mesh processing system. ERCIM News 2008(73) (2008). http://dblp.uni-trier.de/db/journals/ercim/ercim2008.html#CignoniCR08
7. Cruz-Neira, C., Sandin, D.J., DeFanti, T.A., Kenyon, R.V., Hart, J.C.: The cave: audio visual experience automatic virtual environment. Commun. ACM **35**(6), 64–72 (1992)
8. Herrmann, H., Eik, M., Berg, V., Puttonen, J.: Phenomenological and numerical modelling of short fibre reinforced cementitious composites. MECCANICA 49(8), 1985–2000 (2014). doi:10.1007/s11012-014-0001-3
9. Juarez, A., Schonenberg, W., Bartneck, C.: Implementing a low-cost cave system using the cryengine2 (2010). http://cryve.id.tue.nl/paper/paper.html
10. Kreylos, O.: Environment-Independent VR Development. In: Bebis, G., et al. (eds.) ISVC 2008, Part I. LNCS, vol. 5358, pp. 901–912. Springer, Heidelberg (2008)
11. Pastorelli, E., Herrmann, H.: A small-scale, low-budget semi-immersive virtual environment for scientific visualization and research. Procedia Computer Science 25(iii-iv), 14–22 (2013)
12. Pastorelli, E., Herrmann, H.: Virtual reality visualization for short fibre orientation analysis. In: Baltic Electronics Conference 2014 (accepted, October 2014)
13. Poirier-Quinot, D., Touraine, D., Katz, B.F.: Blendercave: A flexible open source authoring tool dedicated to multimodal virtual reality. In: 5th Joint Virtual Reality Conference (JVRC), pp. 19–22 (December 2013)
14. Poirier-Quinot, D., Touraine, D., Katz, B.F.: Blendercave: A multimodal scene graph editor for virtual reality. In: 19th International Conference on Auditory Display (ICAD) (October 2013)
15. Rusu, R.B., Cousins, S.: 3D is here: Point Cloud Library (PCL). In: IEEE International Conference on Robotics and Automation (ICRA), Shanghai, China (May 9-13, 2011)
16. Suuronen, J.P., Kallonen, A., Eik, M., Puttonen, J., Serimaa, R., Herrmann, H.: Analysis of short fibres orientation in steel fibre reinforced concrete (SFRC) using x-ray tomography. Journal of Materials Science **48**(3), 1358–1367 (2013)
17. Taylor, II, R.M., Hudson, T.C., Seeger, A., Weber, H., Juliano, J., Helser, A.T.: VRPN: A device-independent, network-transparent VR peripheral system. In: Proceedings of the ACM Symposium on Virtual Reality Software and Technology, VRST 2001, pp. 55–61. ACM, New York (2001)
18. Wu, C.: Visualsfm: A visual structure from motion system. http://ccwu.me/vsfm/

Augmented Reality for Allowing Time Navigation in Cultural Tourism Experiences: A Case Study

Alessandro Fiore[1(✉)], Luca Mainetti[1], Luigi Manco[1], and Palmalisa Marra[2]

[1] Department of Innovation Engineering, University of Salento,
Via Monteroni, 73100 Lecce, Italy
{alessandro.fiore,luca.mainetti,luigi.manco}@unisalento.it
[2] Links Management and Technology s.p.a., Via Rocco Scotellaro, 73100 Lecce, Italy
palmalisa.marra@linksmt.it

Abstract. In the past few years, mobile phones have become an increasingly attractive platform for augmented reality. This paper describes the development of an interactive visualization system based on Augmented Reality Technologies and the integration into a tourist mobile application for Android. The basic idea is to allow the time navigation of cultural points of interest by means of Augmented Reality. The real scene is enhanced by ancient images to increase the cultural experience of the tourist, who can realistically come back in the past.

Keywords: Augmented Reality · Mobile · Enhanced Environments · Tourism · Image Recognition

1 Introduction

Augmented Reality (AR) aims to enhance our view of the world by overlapping virtual objects to the real world in order to convince the user that the former are part of the real environment. Thanks to the recent spread of mobile devices (smartphones, tablets, glasses), which offer powerful platforms for supporting AR, the mobile augmented reality is one of the fastest growing research area [1]. Furthermore, current smartphones and tablets are equipped with fast processors and embedded sensors, making them particularly suitable for both indoor and outdoor AR.

This paper presents an example AR for improving the user experience in the field of cultural tourism. The example we propose is one of the results of "Apulian Tourism Lab", a research project funded in 2013 by the Apulian Region within the "Apulian ICT Living Lab" funding initiative. The project aims at designing and implementing a technological platform for delivering services targeted to tourists in order to enhance the attractiveness of the cultural tourism, and the accessibility and logistics of the points of interest. The tourist services have been designed and developed in order to be provided in multi-device and multi-channel mode. They offer a complete set of solutions for accessing to in-depth information about cultural sites, for sharing travel experiences according to the social paradigms, and for buying tickets for entering in cultural sites and accommodations. In the field of information services for cultural sites, a "Cultural Compass" prototype has been developed and experimented, in order to help users in planning their visit, by guiding them along the lines

L.T. De Paolis and A. Mongelli (Eds.): AVR 2014, LNCS 8853, pp. 296–301, 2014.
DOI: 10.1007/978-3-319-13969-2_22

of time, space and semantics. The partners' consortium of the Apilian Living Lab project is composed by one ICT company, Links Management and Technology s.p.a. (which is the project lead), the GSA Laboratory of the University of Salento as the research partner, and by a set of local public authorities as final users representatives. As the project has adopted a living lab model, all partners participated in all project phases. Thanks to this approach, the final users have been involved not only into the experimentation phase but they also helped the project team in conceiving and prototyping the implemented solutions.

The Cultural Compass enables a complete navigation of cultural Points of Interest. It allows a exploration of the "cultural space" following three orthogonal axes: spatial exploration, semantics exploration, and time exploration. In particular, by means of the time navigation modality, the Cultural Compass becomes a kind of time machine through which the user can see the time evolution of Points of Interest. The user can see directly on the screen of its own device the historic images of a monument overlapping the real-time images of the same monument, captured by the camera.

Being the AR a key feature of the Cultural Compass, particular attention has been paid in designing a suitable software architecture. The Wikitude SDK is the technical tool we used to integrate AR features in the software prototype. It provides all the functionalities necessary to the temporal navigation modality.

The paper is organized as follows: section 2 provides the reader with a brief introduction to the software architecture and data model of the Cultural Compass prototype; section 3 demonstrates the application working on a real cultural POI; section 4 briefly reports on key related work in the area of AR; finally, in section 5 the conclusions summarize our key messages and sketch future research directions.

2   Architecture and Data Model

In Fig. 1 the Cultural Compass software architecture is depicted. The AR features, managed by AR MODULE, are built on top of the Wikitude API. Wikitude is a mobile AR software library that offers image recognition technologies. In contrast with location-based AR, the image recognition can be used also for providing AR capabilities in indoor environments without the need of using GPS or wi-fi connections for calculating the user's position. For this reason, we preferred Wikitude amongst AR frameworks. Every image that must be recognized (Target Image) is processed by an algorithm in order to extract data useful for recognition. Then all target images are stored in a Target Collection. At runtime, the Tracker analyzes the live camera image and detects the targets stored in its associated target collection.

The Cultural Compass mobile application is based on a well-defined data model that supports the three cultural exploration modes (spatial, semantic and temporal). A UML schema of the data model that allows the time navigation is shown in Fig. 2. The Resource class can be a Point of Interest, a route, a service, an event, or news. All resources are associated with one or more multimedia files, represented by the Multimedia class. As we can see, the Multimedia class provides a "Date" property that enables a time ordering of several multimedia files, for example images, related to a cultural asset. In particular, the ancient graphical representations related to different historical periods of a POI are included inside the data model instance through the insertion of the correct period in the Date property.

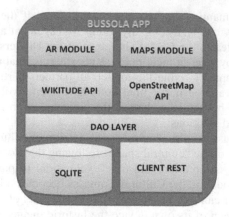

Fig. 1. Software Architecture of the Cultural Compass

By means of such a data model structure, the Cultural Compass can recognize a POI as temporally enabled, since the Multimedia objects associated with it contain the Data property and the application can superimpose the correct historical image on the one captured by the camera, depending on the historical period of interest by the user.

The application can use any recent image of a temporal POI as Target Image, in order to extract useful data for recognition. Such data, necessary for the proper functioning of Wikitude, are stored in the application level and they are not included in the data model. In this way, the information closely linked to the Wikitude framework hold a strong separation with those strictly necessary for the temporal navigation. So, the application architecture and the data model have been designed to be independent from the technology by which is implemented the AR.

3   Validation Scenario

A validation scenario has been defined to collect feedbacks form users and stockholders during the living labs activities. In this section, we describe a subset of this scenario, providing screenshots of the application prototype running in a temporal exploration session on the cultural Point of Interest "Santa Croce" Church, located in the old town center of Lecce (Italy).

When a tourist gets closer to an AR enabled Point of Interest (Santa Croce in this example), he/she can activate the temporal modality by rotating the device in landscape mode.

As we can see in Fig. 3, focusing the church's front, when recognized the application puts on top of it an image representing the same church but in an ancient time.

Tapping on the button near the church image, the user can activate an information bar that provide more details about the Point of Interest giving access among other to a photo gallery, as shown in Fig. 4.

It is easy to develop new features on top of Wikitude SDK, thanks to its flexibility. For example, we can use the date field in the Multimedia class to sort in chronological order images related to the same Point of Interest, but belonging to different time periods. Then, through Wikitude, we can nimbly put on the screen a footer bar implementing a time axis: tapping on different points on it, the user can have access to different images of the Point of Interest, superimposed on its main photo.

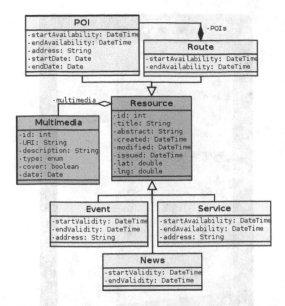

Fig. 2. Data Model of the Cultural Compass (time navigation)

Fig. 3. The AR image superimposed on the front of Santa Croce church

Fig. 4. The information bar

4   Related Work

In the following, we briefly report on AR projects in the cultural heritage and tourism field.

They include the early mobile augmented reality project Archeoguide [2], where ancient Greek architecture and Olympic sports events are displayed as visual overlays through a head mounted display direct at the site. Large and heavy backpacks with high technology gear, large GPS antennas and heavy uncomfortable head mounted displays were needed in order to reach the goal of positioning the user at the site and displaying context sensitive information on the spot.

The iTacitus Project was a European research project 2006-2009. One of system developed under the iTacitus program [3] was the augmented reality presentation system for remote cultural heritage sites. The system rendered augmented information on top of the camera feed of a commercial device. For positioning, the system relied solely on image-based tracking techniques.

Another interesting work is the MARCH (Mobile Augmented Reality for Cultural Heritage) Project [4]. Simply pointing the camera of a mobile device at prehistoric cave engravings, MARCH Project is useful for augmenting the captured image with the expert's drawings and highlighting in real time the animal engravings.

Authors in [5] propose a technique for model-driven generation of mixed reality virtual environments, applied to cultural heritage field. The study enables fast deployment of collaborative virtual environments for cultural explorations only providing new contents and a small set of parameters.

Finally, in [6] a mobile app uses AR technology to explain the history and architecture visually at a real building outdoors.

Whereas the reported relate work is more focused on the technology, we used a model-driven approach in order to enforce the software architecture and, consequently, we identified in the AR a way for allowing the temporal navigation.

5   Conclusions and Future Work

In this paper, we have presented a mobile application for cultural heritage and tourism that offers three navigation modes: spatial, semantic and temporal. In particular, the temporal navigation mode has been implemented exploiting AR techniques based on image recognition using the Wikitude framework. The main advantage of this technique is providing AR capabilities also in indoor environments.

In this way, the tourist can benefit of a direct link between the real object in the present and the virtual object in the past, thanks to a superimposition of ancient images of the cultural asset.

There are several aspects that may be considered for future work. At the present it's needed to use a web-based tool provided by Wikitude for extracting data useful for recognition from the target image. In the future, we want develop a custom tool for automate the process of data injection based on a own algorithm of data extraction.

Acknowledgements. This research has been partially supported by the P.O. FESR 2007-2013 – Asse 1 – Linea 1.4 – Azione 1.4.2 – Apulian Region funded WS7PSV5 "Apulian Tourism Lab" project, and Links Management and Technology S.p.A. The authors wish to thank all the people who worked on the project.

References

1. Butchart, B.: Augmented reality for smartphones. Technical report, JISC Observator (2011)
2. Vlahakis, V., N.I.J.K.M.T.M.G.: Virtual reality and information technology for archaeological site promotion. In: Proceedings of the 5th International Conference Business Information Systems, pp. 24–25 (2002)
3. Zollner, M., Keil, J., Wust, H., Pletinckx, D.: An augmented reality presentation system for remote cultural heritage sites. In: Proceeding of the 10th International Symposium Virtual Reality, Archaeology and Cultural Heritage (2009)
4. Choudary, O., Charvillat, V., Grigoras, R., Gurdjos, P.: MARCH: mobile augmented reality for cultural heritage. In: Proceedings of the 17th ACM International Conference on Multimedia, pp. 1023–1024 (2009)
5. Bucciero, A., Mainetti, L.: Model-Driven Generation of Collaborative Virtual Environments for Cultural Heritage. In: Petrosino, A., Maddalena, L., Pala, P. (eds.) ICIAP 2013. LNCS, vol. 8158, pp. 268–277. Springer, Heidelberg (2013)
6. Keil, J., Zollner, M., Becker, M., Wientapper, F., Engelke, T., Wuest, H.: The House of Olbrich — An Augmented Reality tour through architectural history. In: Proceedings of the 2011 IEEE International Symposium on Mixed and Augmented Reality - Arts, Media, and Humanities, pp. 15–18. IEEE (2011)

Easy Perception Lab: Evolution, Brain and Virtual and Augmented Reality in Museum Environment

Sara Invitto[1(✉)], Italo Spada[2], Dario Turco[3], and Genuario Belmonte[4]

[1] Department of Biological and Environmental Sciences and Technologies, University of Salento, Lecce, LE, Italy
sara.invitto@unisalento.it
[2] CETMA Consortium, New Media Area Manager, Mesagne, Italy
italo.spada@cetma.it
[3] Agilex S.R.L, Lecce, Italy
dario.turco@agilex.it
[4] Department of Biological and Environmental Sciences and Technologies, University of Salento, MAUS Museum of Environment – Unisalento, Lecce, Italy
genuario.belmonte@unisalento.it

Abstract. Within a route of Education Naturalistic Museum (MAUS), we configured various types of intervention and study related to new technologies and new scientific languages, depending on the objective of learning and involvement. The idea of this work was to increase and to enhance the usability of MAUS Museum through App of Augmented Reality and through Virtual Reality projections, related to natural stimuli (Plankton 3D and Tarbosaurus 3D), to a site storage of exhibits and geo-referencing of the same and all analysis and stimuli validation on the basis of new technologies and on the basis of the of the elements of interaction's characteristics. Easy Perception Lab is a project developed on Information Technology in which we validated/evaluated the activation produced by stimuli presented in 2D and 3D in MAUS museum, developed on evolutionary and neuroaesthetic hypotheses.

Keywords: Virtual Reality · Neuroaesthetic · Museum Learning · Evolution

1 Introduction

The use of new Information and Communication Technologies within Science Education is linked to date a series of interactive software that can play at a very high level of technology, making them extremely compelling in their interaction. These software applications are accessible by the user from the learner and have expanded the possibilities for experimentation of categories in which disable people can experience situations in ' protected way '. From this, MAUS Museum (Museum of Environment, University of Salento) have expressed the need to develop new educational tools for interactive users. The project aims to build a prototype of learning movie in virtual reality, to define new paradigms of intervention in education. The prototype Easy

© Springer International Publishing Switzerland 2014
L.T. De Paolis and A. Mongelli (Eds.): AVR 2014, LNCS 8853, pp. 302–310, 2014.
DOI: 10.1007/978-3-319-13969-2_23

Perception Lab allow a large set of users (school students of first and second degree and university students), to test a new approach to the use of a training related to virtual and augmented reality, based on the theories of neuroarchaeology and embodied perception [1-2] , specifically linked to perceptual immersion in an environment of a prehistoric animal. According to these theories, an immersive learning developments greater neural plasticity, memory, and emotional involvement. In Museum the users can move themselves in the environment of prehistoric animal or in plankton environment through the 3D perception, and this can be like a game or like a learning nice moment [3-6]. The work of perceptual sounds and the experimentation through psychophysiological EEG, were developed by the Laboratory of Human Anatomy and Neuroscience, the Virtual Reality (kinect, interaction) were developed by CETMA. Augmented Reality applications had been developed by Agilex srl. All the products were supervised by MAUS's Director Belmonte. Then, within a route of Education Naturalistic Museum (MAUS), we configured various types of intervention and study related to new technologies and new scientific languages, depending on the objective of learning and involvement. The idea of this work was to increase and enhance the usability of the MAUS through App of Augmented Reality and Virtual Reality projections, related to natural stimuli (Plankton Tarbosaurus 3D and 3D with moments of direct interaction), to a web-site storage of paleontological pictures, images and cards and geo-referencing of the same. All analysis and validation of the stimuli were based on the basis of new technologies and the characteristics of the elements of interaction according to neuroaesthetic [7-8] theory. Neuroaesthetic "is the study of the neural processes that underlie aesthetic behavior" More precisely, "there are forms of interaction with objects that can be called 'aesthetic,' " and "the job of neuroaesthetic is to identify these aesthetic functions and to investigate their neurobiological causes"[1]. Researchers who have been prominent in the field combine principles from perceptual psychology, evolutionary biology, neurological deficits, and functional brain anatomy in order to address the evolutionary meaning of aesthetic that may be the essence of perception and of learning in a structure like a Museum. In addition, and related to this topic, important recent developments in brain and cognitive sciences offer new avenues for productive cooperation between archaeology and neuroscience. Thus there is great prospect in the archaeology of mind for developing a systematic cross-disciplinary endeavor to map the common ground between archaeology and neuroscience, frame the new questions, and bridge the diverge analytical levels and scales of time. Neuroarchaeology [2] aims at constructing an analytical bridge between brain and culture by putting material culture, embodiment [9], time and long term change at center stage in the study of mind. In evidence of these theoretical paradigms, aim of this work is to assess, in a Museum of Natural History, how the stimuli that can be exposed, can elicit different cortical levels of activation related on the basis of phylogenetic characteristic of the stimulus, and, where the experience is 'contextualized' and where there is a immersive learning (Environmental learning and Virtual Reality learning) we can modulate cortical activation [10-12] in a direction of a greater arousal. In this study, we propose an experimental protocol in which we administered, through the software E-Prime 2.0 Presentation, a tachistoscopic presentation of objects, animals, plants, colored screen, fossils and pictures of planktonic elements during an EEG session. Some of these elements were showed in crossmodal way: 2D or 3D vision with sounds (the sounds could be consonant or dissonant with the image that we showed). The experimental study, based on psychophysiological techniques such as Event Related Potentials (ERP) and the Galvanic Skin Reflex, has provided an analysis of the cortical processing of information through the ERP analysis, after a immersive visit in MAUS and, later, as a result of a presentation in 2D and 3D stimuli / archeological finds of the MAUS. We also evaluated how different levels of cross-modal perception (visual and auditory) consonant and dissonant to the stimulus presented, have enabled different levels of attentional involvement [13-14].

2   Method

We prepared two steps of experiment: The First experiment with a ergonomic analysis of the stimulus, and the second with the immersive or 3D presentation in Virtual Reality.

Our Sample was composed by 24 university student, 12 men and 12 women (mean age 34 years s.d. 11). The sample of volunteers recruited had normal hearing, normal or corrected to normal vision and had a right manual dominance.

Subjects recruited had not previous experience of the MAUS Museum;

12 subject were insert in Baseline Condition Study (2D Vision) and 12 subjects in immersive Environment Condition (3 D, Real Experience). None of them had taken part in previous experiments. All participants gave written informed consent according to Helsinki declaration. Ethic committee (ASL Lecce) authorized the research.

2.1   Behavioral Tools

Anagraphic data of the subject (age, sex)

1-10 VAS (Visual Analogue Scale) for the discrimination of Familiarity with the Pictures

Reaction Time (recorded through E-Prime 2.0 Presentation).

2.2   Psychophysiological Tools

During the images presentation task we recorded an EEG 16 Channels of Brain AMP - Brain Vision Recorder, and Galvanic Skin Reflex (GSR).

We Considered in EEG tracks, the ERP (Event Related Potentials) for averaged waves for Reptiles, Maus Objects, Planktonic Elements and Colours, Dinosaurus 3D and Plankton 3

2.3   Conditions of Registration

The recordings were made through the use of a mounting international standard 16 electrodes / channels: EEG activity was recorded from the channels Fz, Cz, Pz, Fp1, Fp2, F3, F4, F7, F8, C3, C4, T7, T8, O1, O2 and GSR, using the Brain Amp device with the software Brain Vision Recorder (Products GmbH © 2010), during the course of a go-nogo task. The electrode for electro-oculogram (EOG) was applied over the left eye.

The band detected at 0.2 to 50 Hz, EEG sampled at 256 Hz for 1000 ms, with 100 ms basic pre-stimulus.

Finally, all data were analyzed and filtered through Brain Vision Analyzer software (Brain Products GmbH © 2010).

2.4   First Experiment

The images have been selected through a repertoire of neutral images (colored squares on a light background) and target images (fish, reptiles, mammals and MAUS objects and normal objects, plankton and Tabosaurus). All stimuli had a size of 240 x 210 pixels, and were displayed centrally on a light gray background and to the same level of brightness on the monitor of computer. The odd-ball task was administered using the software E-prime 2.0, application of software tools Psychology, Inc. The stimuli were 56 total including 10 target called "Mammals"; 10, referred to as "Fish"; 10, called "Reptiles"; 10, called "Objects"; 16 colored screen. The experimental task consisted of 4 trials; each trial, consisting of only one type of target alternating randomly in background-color, had a duration of 6000 seconds, with a stimulus duration of 2000 ms duration and interstimulus 1000 ms. Participants were instructed to stand upright with 75 cm ca between the front edge of the chair and the floor of the computer screen and press a mouse whenever they saw an image on the screen.

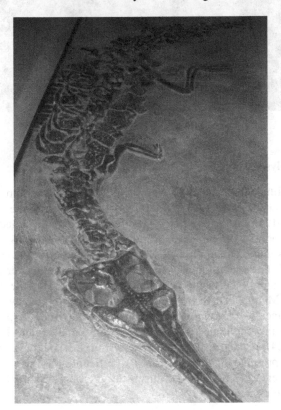

Fig. 1. MAUS Image/object – Teleosaurus Ancient big Reptile of Jurassic Period (MAUS-Unisalento)

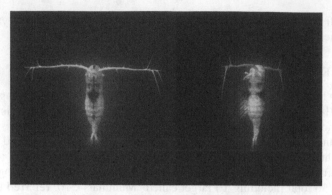

Fig. 2. Plankton, Acartia in 3D

Fig. 3. Tarbosaurus in 3D

2.5   Data Analysis

ANOVA on amplitude and latency, is significant in parietal amplitude F (6,156), p = 0.00 and Parietal latency F (3,190), p = 0.039; and amplitude in the occipital region F (7,069), p = 0.001. From the Post Hoc (Bonferroni Test) emerged on trials corresponding to categories of stimuli (Fish, Reptiles, Mammals, MAUS object and normal object), shows a significant amplitude in the parietal region for the category stimulus-versus Reptiles Fish, Parietal Latency for the category stimulus-versus Reptiles Fish, and a significant amplitude in the occipital region always for the category-Reptiles stimulus versus Mammals. ANOVA on Amplitude and latency, in lateralization shows a significance to the region in Left Parietal amplitude F (3,981), p = 0.035; Right in the parietal amplitude F (3,976), p = 0.035 and for the Right Occipital in amplitude F (4,924), p = 0,019. Post hoc (Bonferroni test), shows a trials corresponding to categories presented can be seen in a significant amplitude in the left parietal region for the category-Reptiles; in width in the region Parietal Right and Occipital Right for the Reptiles category.

2.6   Second Experiment

The objective of our study was to evaluate the perceptual characteristics of museum objects with evolutionary contents and natural sounds in a university museum, and how these characteristics can be fully elicited within the immersive environment an virtual reality. The assignment was a *Go no Go* task, carried out using a visual and auditory cross modal process. The visual stimuli consisted of two types of 2D images (colored screens and objects present in the museum fig.1) and two types of 3D ana-glyph images (Plankton fig.2 and Tarbosaurus fig.3) which were presented with the sounds of the Tarbosaurus or aquatic sounds in the background or no sounds at all.

The experimental group performed the task in the museum (13 volunteers, recruited in the university; avg. age 29.2; SD=4.2). The control group performed the task in the university (12 volunteers; avg. age 34; SD =6).

2.7   Data Analysis

N200: We found no significant different in N200 component in baseline condition.
In comparison between   Baseline condition vs Environmental context we found significant effect on Fp2 Amplitude (p=0,36) and F4 Amplitude (p=0,48) in direction of an increase in negative amplitude in Museum Conditions in all the trials.

P300: We found Significant Differences in F4Latency (p=0,025); O1 Amplitude (p=0,027); O2 Amplitude (p=0,006); F7Latency (p=0,022) and PZ in Latency (p=0,007) and Amplitude (p=0,011).

Analysis *MAUS Objects in Baseline and Museum conditions:*
In N200 ERP we find a significant effect on O1 Amplitude (p= 0,048) and P8 Amplitude (p=0,040) in direction of an increase in positive amplitude in Museum Condition and in 3 D condition (Plankton and Tarbosaurus)

In P300 ERP we found a significant effect in F4 Amplitude (p=0,048), in Cz Amplitude (p=0,000) and in Pz Latency (p=0,025).

The GLM considered the group, target condition and sound condition and showed a significant effect in ERP (Group α <.05; Target α <.05; Sound α <.05; Target *Sound α >.05). Post hoc analysis showed a significant effect in group condition in direction of ampler amplitude in frontal and occipital channels in an immersive environment. The 3D images activated ampler ERP in frontal and frontoparietal lobes with respect to the 2D images which activated ampler ERP in occipital lobes (fig.4, fig.5). 2D modality showed facilitation in latency in ERP for both sound conditions.

GSR Analysis: a General Linear Model Repeated Measures was performed in a design Image (4 levels) x sound (2 levels). Analysis didn't show any significant effect, but we can see a trend (fig. 6, fig.7) in image and in sound condition that are the same of ERP condition. We see a slower latency in 3D condition and in Tarbosaurus sound and an ampler GSR in Tarbosaurus sound condition.

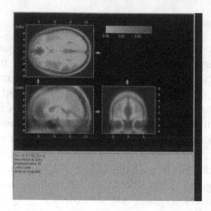

Fig. 4. Loreta Image during Tarbosaurus 3D Vision

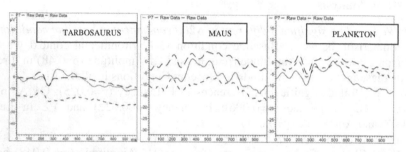

Fig. 5. Matching ERP in baseline condition (continuous line), water sound condition (long broken line), Tarbosaurus sound condition (short broken line) in images of Tarbosaurus 3D, MAUS 2D and Plankton 3D

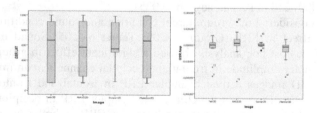

Fig. 6. GSR Latency and Amplitude in Image Condition

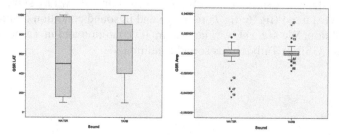

Fig. 7. GSR Latency and Amplitude in Sound Condition

Fig. 8. Immersive 3D Vision of Plankton (Globigerina) with active glasses

3   Conclusions and Discussion

Our data show that phylogenetically distant stimuli activate right hemisphere and activate a global analyses of the object , and that during a presentation and immersive 3D museum, there is a perceptual facilitation (due to cortical arousal) for the stimulus regardless of its difficulty of categorization. As already presented in our previous step of experiment and in other our works, in this protocol phylogenetically more distant stimuli activate different cortical processing, regardless of the familiarity of the stimulus presented too. The right hemisphere seems to be more sensitive to differences related to visual stimuli that are processed by eliciting a larger and slower activation; these stimuli correspond to those furthest from the evolutionary point of view. We show that phylogenetically distant stimuli engage the user in a higher cortical arousal stimuli closer than that and, in the process of engaging presentation in the museum, there is a facilitation of perceptual stimulus, regardless of its difficulty of categorization. From the above-mentioned paradigms of Neuroarchaeology and Neuroaesthetic, we can read these results as a confirmation of the need to perform the analysis on the characteristics of the stimuli that are to be exposed to the user: the stimulus, even if it is difficult to classify, according to its characteristics phylogenetic, is able to stimulate the emotional involvement and allow a more global analysis. In addition, an immersive learning environment (Museums and support related to Information Technology) greatly increases the power of discrimination and learning of the stimulus exposed. Indeed, the results of second experiment indicate that there is a greater arousal when the environment is immersive and even more so the stimulus is 3D and multi-dimensional in Virtual Reality.

In a context of nature and the environment, with a direct, multi-sensory learning we find a facilitation of cognitive activities implied not only allow it, but that can increase learning motivation and activation of sensory elements slightly stimulated in normal culture crystallized. According to our previous research, phylogenetically distant stimuli have differently activated the cortical processing, regardless of familiarity with the stimulus presented.

Within the paradigms of neuroarchaeology and neuroaesthetic, in response to these results, we can conclude that is necessary to carry out an analysis on the stimulus's characteristics that must be exposed to the user. The stimulus, although difficult to categorize, according to its phylogenetic characteristics, can stimulate the emotional involvement and enable a more global analysis and affective stimulus itself.

Furthermore, an immersive learning environment i.e., Museum and object in Virtual Reality (fig.8) greatly increases the ability of discrimination and learning of the stimulus exposed. Furthermore, we may conclude from our results, that when the Virtual Reality is accompanied by bodily interaction and sound perception, cortical activation is much larger, regardless of the fact that the visual stimulus is consonant with the sound accompaniment or dissonant with sound accompaniment, for example the Tarbosaurus image with a sound of water or the Plankton with a Tarbosaurus voices. Also the interaction in augmented reality, that we could not validate this work, but that we have produced for the project, in various levels, both with sounds that in movie, increases the interaction and hence the interest in learning object.

References

1. Zeki, S., Lamb, M.: The neurology of kinetic art. Brain 117(3), 607–636 (1994)
2. Malafouris, L.: Between brains, bodies and things: tecnoethic awareness and the extended self. Philosophical Transaction of the Royal Society of London, Series B 363, 1993–2002 (2008)
3. Panksepp, J.: At the interface of the affective, behavioral, and cognitive neurosciences: decoding the emotional feelings of the brain. Brain Cogn. 52, 4–14 (2003)
4. Van Le Q., Isbell L.A., Matsumoto J., Nguyen M., Hori, E., Maior, R.S., Tomaz, C., Tran, A.H., Ono, T., Nishijo, H.: Pulvinar neurons reveal neurobiological evidence of past selection for rapid detection of snakes. PNAS (October 28, 2013)
5. Toronchuk, J.A., Ellis, G.F.R.: Human becoming: phylogeny and ontogeny of affective social behaviour. Transdiscip. Sci. Relig. 4, 197–221 (2009)
6. Zink, C.F., Tong, Y., Chen, Q., Bassett, D.S., Stein, J.L., Meyer-Lindenberg, A.: Know your place: neural processing of social hierarchy in humans. Neuron 58, 273–283 (2008)
7. Ramachandran, V.S., Hirstein, W.: The science of art: a neurological theory of aesthetic experience. Journal of Consciousness Studies 6(6-7), 15–51(37) (1999)
8. Augustin, M. D., Wagemans, J.: Empirical aesthetics, the beautiful challenge: An introduction to the special issue on Art & Perception. Perception 3, 455–458 (2012)
9. Varela, F.J., Thompson, E.T., Rosch, E.: The Embodied Mind: Cognitive Science and Human Experience. The MIT Press, Cambridge (1992)
10. Massaro, D., Savazzi, F., Di Dio, C., Freedberg, D., Gallese, V., Gilli, G., Marchetti, A.: When Art Moves the Eyes: A Behavioral and Eye-Tracking Study. PLoS ONE 7(5), e37285 (2012)
11. Freedberg, D., Gallese, V.: Motion, emotion and empathy in esthetic experience. Trends in Cognitive Sciences 11, 197–203 (2007)
12. De Tommaso, M., Ricci, K., Laneve, L., Savino, N., Antonaci, V., Livrea, P.: Virtual Visual Effect of Hospital Waiting Room on Pain Modulation in Healthy Subjects and Patients with Chronic Migraine. Pain Research and Treatment, 1–8 (2013)
13. Invitto, S., Sammarco, S., Durante, N., Spada, I., Turco, D., Belmonte, G.: Museum ergonomy and evolution: 2D, 3D and multidimensional perception. In: 54th Annual Meeting, Society for Psychophysiological Research, September 10-14, Atlanta, Georgia (2014)
14. Invitto, S., Sammarco,S., Mignozzi, A., Durante, N.: Filogenesi e Percezione: Categorizzazione psicofisiologica di specie animali e oggetti. Psychofenia, Ricerca ed Analisi Psicologica, Pensa Multimedia, anno XV in press Codice (2014) ISSN 1722-8093

Visualization and 3D Modelling

On-Demand Generation of 3D Content Based on Semantic Meta-Scenes

Krzysztof Walczak[(✉)] and Jakub Flotyński

Poznań University of Economics,
Niepodległości 10, 61-875 Poznań, Poland
{walczak,flotynski}@kti.ue.poznan.pl

Abstract. In this paper, an approach to on-demand generation of inter-active 3D content based on queries to semantic meta-scenes is proposed. Meta-scenes are generalized content representations, which may be queried by different content consumers to create customized 3D scenes. The use of the semantic web techniques enables representation of content elements and queries at various levels of abstraction, using concepts related to 3D modeling in general and concepts specific to a particular application or application domain.

Keywords: On-demand content creation · Query-based content generation · 3D modeling · 3D meta-scenes · Semantic web · Virtual and augmented reality

1 Introduction

Widespread use of interactive 3D technologies on the web has been recently enabled by the significant progress in hardware performance, the rapid growth in the available network bandwidth as well as the availability of versatile input-output devices. 3D technologies can be successfully used in various domains, significantly enhancing possibilities of presentation and interaction with complex data and objects. Education, training, tourism, medicine, entertainment, social media and cultural heritage are examples of application domains, which can particularly benefit from the use of 3D technologies.

A common problem with the development and the use of 3D applications is the lack of relevant, up-to-date 3D content. Creating, searching and combining interactive 3D web content are much more complex and challenging tasks than in the case of typical web resources, as dependencies between components of such content may include, in addition to their basic meaning and presentation form, also spatial, temporal, structural, logical and behavioral aspects.

3D web content can be used in different contexts and for various purposes, and therefore it is critical that the content creation method can satisfy various requirements. Such requirements may be related to individual preferences and interests of content consumers (e.g., a specific level of detail or a specific subset of a scene), which are explicitly specified and may be satisfied on demand

© Springer International Publishing Switzerland 2014
L.T. De Paolis and A. Mongelli (Eds.): AVR 2014, LNCS 8853, pp. 313–332, 2014.
DOI: 10.1007/978-3-319-13969-2_24

through content customization. For instance, different engineers independently working on a common model of a complex machine may visualize only selected elements of the machine and switch on only selected animations of them. Such requirements may also reflect the context of interaction (e.g., user location or capabilities of the hardware and software used) and may be satisfied in contextual content adaptation, which may be considered as a kind of content customization performed implicitly with regards to the context of interaction or past activities of the consumer. For instance, a user walking through a city with a smartphone may obtain only a part of the historical model of the city for an augmented reality presentation, instead of obtaining the whole city model.

The available approaches to 3D content creation provide only limited capabilities of building customizable interactive 3D content, stressing the modification of selected content properties or the selection of particular content profiles depending on the context of interaction. The available solutions do not enable flexible content generation that can be performed on demand in response to queries issued by different content consumers, and which includes both explicit and implicit management of elements related to particular aspects of 3D content at different levels of semantic abstraction.

On-demand generation of interactive 3D web content may be facilitated by applying the semantic web technologies. The research on the semantic web aims at the evolutionary development of the current web towards a distributed database linking structured content and documents. Semantic description of web content makes it understandable for both humans and computers achieving a new quality in building web applications that can "understand" the meaning of particular components of content as well as their relations, leading to much better methods of content creation, management and presentation—representing diverse aspects of 3D content at different levels of abstraction and with regards to hidden knowledge, which may influence the created content.

The main contribution of this paper is a method of on-demand generation of interactive 3D content based on customizable generalized 3D content representations—*3D meta-scenes*. In the proposed method, final 3D content representations can be independently created by different content consumers querying common meta-scenes. Meta-scenes are customizable content representations, which are extensible sub- or super-sets of the generated final content representations. The use of the semantic web techniques enables the representation of queries and queried content, including their properties, dependencies and constraints, at different levels of abstraction—specific to 3D modeling as well as specific to an arbitrarily selected application or domain.

The remainder of this paper is structured as follows. Section 2 provides an overview of the current state of the art in the domain of semantic modeling of 3D content, 3D content adaptation and languages for querying content repositories. Section 3 provides an overview of the Semantic Content Model, which is the foundation of the proposed method. In Section 4, a new method of content generation based on the Semantic Content Model is proposed. Section 5 explains an illustrative example of on-demand 3D content generation. Section 6 outlines the implementation of the method. Finally, Section 7 concludes the paper and indicates the possible directions of future research.

2   Related Works

The background of the proposed content generation method covers aspects related to semantic modeling of 3D content, adaptation of 3D content and languages for querying semantically described resources.

2.1   Semantic Modeling of 3D Content

Several works have been devoted to semantic creation and description of 3D content. In [24], an ontology providing elements and properties that are equivalent to elements and properties specified in X3D has been proposed. Moreover, a set of semantic properties have been proposed to enable description of 3D scenes with domain knowledge. In [40–42], a method of creating 3D content on the basis of reusable elements with specific roles has been proposed. The method has been intended to enable 3D content design by non-IT-specialists. In [6,39], an approach to generating virtual environments upon mappings of domain ontologies has been proposed. In [15,18,20,21], an approach to building semantic descriptions embedded in 3D web content and a method of harvesting semantic metadata from 3D web content have been proposed.

Several works provide an overview of the use of semantic descriptions of 3D content in artificial intelligence systems. The idea of semantic description of 3D environments has been summarized in [27]. In [37], a review of the main aspects related to the use of 3D content in connection with the semantic web technologies has been provided. In [3], diverse issues arising from combining AI and virtual environments have been reviewed. In [8,29], abstract semantic representations of events and actions in AI simulators have been presented. In [26,28,43], a technique of integrating knowledge into VR applications, a framework for decoupling components in real-time intelligent interactive systems with ontologies and a concept of semantic entities in VR applications have been discussed.

The aforementioned approaches address semantic content description and creation using different ontologies and knowledge bases. However, in these approaches, 3D content is created by specifying instances of ontologies (knowledge bases) that determine the final form of the created content. The solutions do not permit creation of generalized content representations that could be customized on demand to enable generation of various forms of the final content representations adapted to specific requirements of particular content consumers.

2.2   Adaptation of 3D Content

The previous approaches to adaptation of 3D content have been designed mostly to permit content presentation on diverse hardware and software platforms. In [4,5], a rule-based framework using MPEG-7 has been proposed to enable adaptation of content for different access devices. Adaptation may include such operations as geometry and texture degradation as well as filtering of objects. In [23], a semantic model of virtual environments based on the MPEG-7 and MPEG-21 standards has been proposed to enable dynamic scaling and adaptation of the geometry and functions of virtual objects. In [10], an approach to 3D content adaptation for different devices and contexts of use has been proposed. In [30], a solution for streaming X3D content for remote visualizations with the adaptation of the level of detail based on several parameters (e.g., network bandwidth, device capabilities and user preferences) has been proposed. In [9], an approach to multi-platform 3D content presentation based on MPEG-4 has been presented. In [1], an approach to multi-platform visualization of 2D and 3D tourist information has been discussed. In [38], an approach to adaptation of 3D content complexity with respect to the available resources has been proposed. In [17], an approach to building multi-platform virtual museum exhibitions has been proposed.

The aforementioned approaches are mainly devoted to content adaptation depending on the target hardware and software platforms used. The solutions provide limited capabilities of modification of particular content elements, and they do not address semantic representation of content and flexible on-demand content generation.

2.3   Query Languages for Web Content

Several languages have been designed to enable generic domain-independent queries to semantic knowledge bases encoded in RDF, e.g., the RDF Data Query Language (RDQL) [35], the SPARQL (the successor to RDQL) [33], the SPARQL Update (SPARUL—the extension of SPARQL with capabilities of updating semantic graphs) [34] and the Second Generation RDF Query Language (SeRQL) [7]. These query languages have been intended for querying RDF data sources, and they do not provide specific support for the syntax, structure and semantics of RDFS and OWL, which are currently widely used for creating knowledge bases. To cover this gap, an approach to the use of the Semantic Web Rule Language, which is an OWL-based rule description language, for querying RDFS and OWL knowledge bases has been proposed [31].

Several languages have been designed to enable retrieval of multimedia content (in particular images, audio and video), e.g., the MPEG query format [36] and the Graphical Multimedia Query Language (GMQL) [44]. A number of works have been devoted to the analysis of building information models (BIM) using query languages, e.g., a query language with specific spatial and temporal operators has been proposed in [11]. The aforementioned languages have been intended for content exploration and they do not enable modeling and customization of 3D content.

3   The Semantic Content Model

The semantic content generation method, which is proposed in this paper, is strongly related to the content structure, which is determined by the Semantic Content Model (SCM—presented in [12–14,16,19,22]). The general scheme of a customizable 3D content representation (a meta-scene), which is compliant with SCM is depicted in Fig. 1.

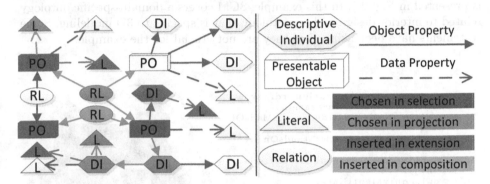

Fig. 1. The scheme of a meta-scene compliant with the Semantic Content Model (SCM) processed using the proposed method

The following elements of 3D content are distinguished in the SCM model: *presentable objects* (POs), *data properties* (DPs) with *literals*, *object properties* (OPs) with *descriptive individuals* (DIs) and *relations* (RLs). POs are the primary elements of the designed content that have independent representations (specific to the modality of content presentation), e.g., artifacts in a virtual museum exhibition, avatars in an RPG game, UI controls in a visual interface and sounds in an aural interface. Every PO is inextricably linked to some inherent properties that form it and give a sense of it in the selected presentation modality, e.g., the color map of a picture, the geometry of a 3D shape, the structure of a complex object, the sampling frequency of a sound, etc.

In addition to inherent properties, POs may be described by *data properties* (DPs) and *object properties* (OPs) that do not determine the basic meaning of the POs (are not obligatory), but specify additional features of the POs. While DPs enable specification of simple features, which may be expressed using single descriptive literals (e.g., scale, color and coordinates), OPs enable specification of complex features, which are expressed using multiple literals and DIs, which aggregate literals and other DIs (e.g., the material of a PO may be described by literals representing color, transparency and shininess).

Finally, multiple POs can be combined using *relations* (RLs). Every RL links at least two participants (POs), which are connected one to another by mutual dependencies related to some DPs or OPs that determine presentable effects of the RL, e.g., a relation that defines the relative position of some POs links these

POs and specifies their relative orientations and distances between them. RLs that link two POs are encoded using OPs (binary RLs), while RLs that link more than two POs are encoded using individuals that link the POs by OPs (n-ary RLs).

The aforementioned concepts of SCM enable representation of 3D content at different (arbitrarily chosen) levels of semantic abstraction (detail). An example of a semantic scene representation, which is a knowledge base encoded in SCM, is presented in Listing 1 (the RDF/Turtle format), while the view of the scene is presented in Fig. 2 [1]. In this example, SCM covers a domain-specific ontology related to interior design and an ontology that is specific to 3D modeling. Some statements have been skipped as they are not crucial for the example.

```
1:   ex:room,...,ex:decoration rdf:type
     scm:Room,...,scm:Decoration.
2:   ex:table,ex:decoration scm:isMadeOf
     "wood","metal".
3:   ex:tableFlowerpot scm:standsOn ex:
     table.
4:   scm:Flowerpot rdfs:subClassOf scm:
     Mesh;
5:      owl:equivalentClass
6:      [ rdf:type owl:Restriction;
7:          owl:onProperty scm:coordinates;
8:          owl:hasValue "..." ].
9:   ex:decoration scm:appearance ex:
     decorAppear.
10:  ex:decorAppear rdf:type scm:
     AppearanceDescriptor.
11:  ex:decorAppear scm:shininess "0.4".
12:  ex:decorAppear scm:color "gray".
```

Listing 1. An example of a semantic 3D scene representation encoded in SCM   **Fig. 2.** A view of the scene

The objects of the scene are specified in line 1. The domain-specific concepts: the scm:isMadeOf OP (2) and the scm:standsOn RL (3) determine the material and the position of the objects. The scm:Flowerpot PO class (4-8) and the scm:AppearanceDescriptor DI class (9-12) specify the shape (the scm:coordinates DP) and the appearance (the scm:color and scm:shininess DPs) of objects at the level that is specific to 3D modeling. Other examples of using SCM for 3D scene representation are described in [12,19,22].

4   The Content Generation Method

Although several approaches have been proposed for semantic modeling and adaptation of 3D content, they lack general and comprehensive solutions for

---

[1] In the scene, the 3D models of a table (http://resources.blogscopia.com/2011/05/ 19/bar-table-and-chairs/) and a flowerpot (http://resources.blogscopia.com/2010/ 04/22/flowerpot/) are used.

flexible on-demand generation of interactive 3D content that could be performed by different content consumers independently querying customizable 3D content representations.

In this paper, a new method of semantic on-demand generation of interactive 3D content is proposed. In the method, *content generation* means creation of a 3D content representation (a 3D object or a 3D scene), which satisfies individual requirements of a content consumer. A content consumer may be either a user or an application that retrieves 3D content for a specific purpose, e.g., related to content creation, management (indexing, searching and analysis) or presentation. Content generation may be performed simultaneously, on demand by different consumers executing independent semantic queries to common 3D meta-scenes.

The method is based on the semantic web techniques. The semantic concepts that may be used for building queries are imposed by the ontologies used within the SCM model in a particular queried meta-scene. The specification of queries and content representations can be performed at different (arbitrarily chosen) levels of semantic abstraction—either specific to 3D modeling (including, e.g., meshes, textures and animations) or specific to an arbitrarily chosen application or domain—abstract in the sense of final presentation (including, e.g., artifacts in a virtual museum, avatars in a game and buildings in a town model).

Semantic content representation at different levels of abstraction has been comprehensively discussed in the previous works [12,13,16,19,22]. The content generation method proposed in this paper is independent of the ontologies used for content representation (independent of the selected level of abstraction), and it may be used for content generation with meta-scenes based on different ontologies, which determine different levels of abstraction. The 3D content representations that are generated with the method, are transformed to final content representations that could be encoded in different content representation languages, such as COLLADA, VRML, X3D or ActionScript (using appropriate libraries), as explained in [14]. This paper focuses on on-demand content generation without going into details of semantic content representation and final content transformation, which have been discussed in the previous works.

A meta-scene is a customizable 3D content representation that is:

- *flexible*—it can represent content at different levels of abstraction: concrete—specific to 3D modeling and conceptual—specific to arbitrarily chosen application or domain (conceptual objects are mapped onto collections of concrete objects);
- *generalized*—it can represent a super-set of the presentable content (e.g., different variants of content configuration);
- *abstract*—it does not need to specify all elements that are required for final content presentation (e.g., appearance or positions of presentable objects);
- *extensible*—new elements may be added to a meta-scene to create the final 3D scene.

A *semantic query* is a knowledge base compliant with the semantic web standards—the Resource Description Framework (RDF), the Resource Description Framework Schema (RDFS) and the Web Ontology Language (OWL) and built according to semantic *Content Customization Patterns* (CCPs) proposed in this paper. Content generation can cover the following four activities:

– *selection* of content objects that are to be presented;
– *projection* of content objects by specifying their features and behavior to be presented;
– *extension* of objects by adding new features and behavior;
– *composition* of complex content objects.

Elements that are processed in the particular activities are indicated in Fig. 1. The first activity – content selection – provides basic objects to be assembled in the generated content, while the other activities configure and extend the selected content determining its final form, including content features and behavior. While content selection and content projection choose content elements to be presented, content extension and content composition modify the content by inserting additional content features and behavior.

The use of knowledge bases compliant with the semantic web standards as queries to 3D meta-scenes has an important advantage in comparison to the use of typical query languages (such as RDQL, SPARQL or SeRQL). Such solution enables 3D content representation at different levels of abstraction (concrete level and conceptual level) that is uniform in terms of syntax, structure and semantics and may be processed using a uniform approach (based on semantic reasoning). Hence, the overall complexity of content syntax, structure and content processing algorithms may be decreased. In the proposed method, reasoning is used for both query processing and for discovery of hidden knowledge, which may influence the content being modeled.

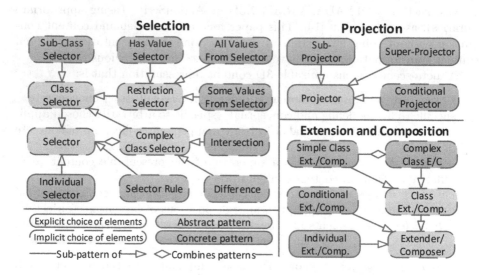

Fig. 3. *Content Customization Patterns* used for on-demand 3D content generation

In the proposed method, content generation is performed according to different Content Customization Patterns – CCPs (Fig. 3). In *Concrete CCPs*, a content consumer uses semantic concepts (classes and properties) to build a query. *Abstract CCPs* are not directly applied to query design (are too general), but form the pattern hierarchy. CCPs are firmly based on the semantic web standards (RDF, RDFS and OWL), which allow for declarative content creation.

Two groups of CCPs are distinguished in terms of query processing. The first group includes CCPs, in which content elements to be presented (POs, DPs, OPs and RLs) are explicitly (directly) indicated. The processing of such CCPs is relatively simple, as it requires only basic reasoning on content elements (classification into classes predefined in the method) based on relations between classes (the *sub-class* relations). The second group includes CCPs, in which content elements are implicitly indicated—by their properties and relations. The processing of such CCPs is more complicated, as in addition to the basic reasoning, it also requires classification that respects properties and relations of content elements. Activities within particular CCPs are described in detail in the following subsections.

4.1 Content Selection

Selection of 3D content indicates desirable POs, which occur in a semantic 3D meta-scene and are to be included in the generated scene. In general, the selection of POs for the generated scene may be performed explicitly or implicitly—depending on the complexity of the queried meta-scene, the acceptable complexity of the query and the consumer's knowledge of the meta-scene.

Explicit Selection of Presentable Objects. In an explicit selection, POs to be presented are directly indicated in a query. An explicit selection of POs is performed using the *individual selector* pattern in two steps. In the first step, a content consumer creates within the query a new *sub-class* of the *Selector* class, (which is predefined in the method). In the second step, every PO that needs to be included in the generated scene, is explicitly assigned to the created *sub-class*. The inclusion of a PO in the *Selector* class results in the selection of the PO for the generated scene and furthermore—in the final presentation of the PO. The *individual selector* pattern can be particularly useful when generating scenes that incorporate single representatives of PO classes that are known in advance (by identifiers), e.g., present the models of the Empire State Building and the Statue of Liberty from a 3D meta-scene that represents New York.

Implicit Selection of Presentable Objects. In an implicit selection, POs to be presented are indirectly indicated in a query. An implicit selection of POs is performed using the *class selector* pattern. This pattern can be useful when generating scenes that incorporate all POs that have common features, but are not known in advance or are not intended to be explicitly enumerated in the query (e.g., because of their number). In this pattern, a content consumer also creates a new *sub-class* of the *Selector* class. The new *sub-class* may be used in three different ways depending on the intended purpose of the content generation.

First, the *sub-class* may be specified as a super-class of a PO class, selecting all POs that belong to this PO class for presentation (the *sub-class selector* pattern). This pattern is useful when all POs of a common (previously created) class need to be presented (included in the generated scene), e.g., present all single-family houses included in a city model, present all artifacts located in a virtual museum, etc.

Second, the *sub-class* may be specified as an *OWL restriction* (the *restriction selector* pattern). This pattern is useful when the presentation should include all POs that have a common feature, but do not necessarily belong to a common previously created class. Three different *restriction selector* CCPs have been specified. The *has value selector* pattern enables the presentation of POs with a particular value of a particular property, e.g., present all sculptures made of wood. The *some values from selector* pattern enables presentation of POs that may have multiple values of a property, at least one of which is set to a desirable value, e.g., present all artifacts that include at least one transparent element. The *all values from selector* pattern enables presentation of all POs that are linked to some POs by the same property, e.g., present artifacts that have only wooden elements.

Third, the aforementioned CCPs are based on RDFS and OWL concepts, which do not enable some specific complex queries, in particular queries that condition the selection of POs upon properties of other POs. In the proposed method, semantically complex queries, which combine various individuals, classes and properties, are created using first-order logic rules (implications) that associate POs with the created *sub-class* of the *Selector* class (the *selector rule* pattern). For instance, present all museum artifacts that are made of the same material as the material of the David sculpture.

Classes created according to the above-mentioned CCPs may be combined using set operators (intersection and difference) according to the *complex class selector* pattern. This pattern is useful when POs should be selected according to logically complex requirements covering multiple features (but not semantically complex requirements as in the case of the *selector rule* pattern), e.g., present all single-family houses that are made of wood and have double-glazed windows (the *intersection* pattern), but their roofs are not made of asbestos (the *difference* pattern).

4.2   Content Projection

Projection of 3D content in the proposed method indicates desirable features or behavior of POs (chosen in content selection) that are to be presented in the generated scene. The features and behavior of POs are encoded by DPs with literals, OPs with DIs as well as RLs—linking different POs and properties that provide presentable effects of the RLs.

Choice of Properties and Relations. Content projection is performed in a few steps using the *projector* pattern, which permits the choice of properties and binary RLs. In the first step, a content consumer creates a new *property* (a DP or an OP) or a *binary RL* and specifies it as a sub-property/sub-relation of the predefined *Projector* concept. In the proposed method, all sub-properties/sub-relations of the *Projector* that are linked to some POs, are presented in the generated scene. Hence, all properties/relations that are sub-concepts of the created *property/binary RL* become presentable. The second step of the pattern depends on the complexity of the queried meta-scene and the acceptable complexity of the created query.

First, the created *property/binary RL* may be specified as a super-concept of a chosen DP, OP or a binary RL (the *sub-projector* pattern). In this manner, the chosen DP, OP or binary RL will be presented in the generated scene, as it becomes a sub-concept of the *Projector*. This pattern is convenient for presenting a particular property/binary RL as well as all properties/binary RLs with a common root concept for *all POs* included in the generated scene. For example, the pattern can be used to present all properties related to appearance (color, transparency, shininess, etc.) for all POs in the scene, present all RLs that determine relative locations of all POs, etc.

Second, the created *property/binary RL* may be specified as a sub-concept of a desirable DP, OP or binary RL and—in addition—as a sub-concept of the *Projector* (the *super-projector* pattern). Next, for a triple (a fact) in the meta-scene that needs to presented, a new triple is added to the query. The new triple includes the same subject and the same object as the base triple, but exchanges the base property/binary RL with the created *property/binary RL*. The created *property/binary RL* inherits all presentational effects from its base concept, so it may be used in the same way in content modeling. However, the explicit choice of the created *property/binary RL* instead of its base concept, enables the contextual presentation of the base concept—only for the desirable PO and prevents the presentation of the base concept for other POs. For instance, present all knights in a game, but only the king should be clad in armor.

In addition to the aforementioned CCPs for the explicit choice of properties and binary RLs, which is unconditional—determined in advance by the query, it is also possible to implicitly choose properties/binary RLs depending on specific conditions—by the use of the *conditional projector* pattern. In this pattern, a property/binary RL is classified as a sub-concept of the created *property/binary RL* by a rule, e.g., present colors of POs only if there is no PO with unspecified color in the meta-scene (for preserving the consistency of the generated scene).

Choice of n-ary RLs, which are encoded using individuals linking POs by OPs, is performed using CCPs designed for selection of POs (cf. Section 4.1).

4.3   Content Extension and Composition

In the proposed method, content modification encompasses *content extension* and *content composition*. Both operations introduce new content elements that are responsible for new features or behavior of the selected POs. Content extension introduces new DPs and OPs for describing selected POs, while content composition introduces new RLs for combining selected POs by specifying mutual dependencies, which are expressed by their properties (DPs and OPs). Since the representation of queries and the representation of meta-scenes is uniform— they are based on common semantic web standards—content modification may be performed in the same way as in the case of creating typical semantic 3D content representations with the SCM.

Neither an extension nor a composition may change the properties and RLs that are already set to some values. Otherwise, the specification of such property leads to an inconsistency in the generated scene. To enable the modification of a property/RL that already has a value in the meta-scene, a new generated scene, in which the property/RL is filtered out, needs to be created by a query to the meta-scene and then the generated scene should be used as a new meta-scene for a new query, which may extend the new meta-scene with a new value of the desirable original property/RL (content generation chain).

Like content selection, content modification including extension and composition may be accomplished explicitly or implicitly, using *extender/composer* CCPs.

Explicit Content Modification. In explicit content modification, new content elements are directly assigned to selected individual POs (the *individual extender/composer* pattern). For instance, present a particular building from a geometrical model of a housing estate and assign a color to it; select a model of the Earth and a model of the Moon and add a RL moving the Moon around the Earth.

Implicit Content Modification. In implicit content modification, new content elements are assigned to a class of POs (the *class extender/composer* pattern) using OWL restrictions (as in the case of the *restriction selector* pattern). If a DP is modified, the *simple class extender/composer* pattern is used to create a new *has value restriction* class that indicates a desirable value of the DP. Next, the class is specified as an equivalent to a previously created *class selector* class. In this way, all POs that are assigned to the *class selector* class in query processing are also linked to the desirable property indicated by the created *has value restriction* class. For instance, select all wooden objects and add shininess to their materials.

If an OP is modified, the *simple class extender/composer* pattern is used to create a new *some values from restriction* class that indicates the desirable target class of the OP. Next, the class is specified as an equivalent to a previously created *class selector* class (as in the case of modifying a DP). In the content generation, a semantic individual of the target class is created and connected to the POs by the OP. For instance, select all POs that have no material specified and assign wooden material to each of them.

Specification of multiple new elements to be introduced requires the use of the *complex class extender/composer* pattern, which is created using the intersection of the classes created according to the *simple extender/composer* pattern—in a similar manner as in the *complex class selector* pattern.

A conditional modification of a PO, which depends on properties of other POs, may be performed similarly to a conditional projection of a PO (using a rule—the *conditional extender/composer* pattern), e.g., set color of the ceiling to a value that is equal to the color of the walls in the room.

5 An Example On-Demand 3D Content Generation

An example of a semantic 3D meta-scene was created using the SCM model and customized using semantic queries constructed according to the CCPs. The queries are presented in Listing 2, while the resulting customized scenes are presented in Fig. 4. The creation of semantic 3D meta-scenes and final 3D content representations encoded in particular content representation languages have already been discussed in [12–14,19,22], hence, this example focuses on query-based content generation based on a given meta-scene.

The meta-scene includes six `smokers` (four made of clay and two made of metal) and six `stands` (for `smokers`). It is generalized, as it does not include some elements that are required for final content presentation (the `smokers` have no positions specified), so only an approximate presentation of the meta-scene is possible (Fig. 4A). 3D scenes have been generated on demand as the results of semantic queries to the meta-scene.

Query 1 (Listing 1, Part B) uses *selector rules* to declaratively specify constraints that assign one `smoker` to one `stand` (Lines 5-13). Every `smoker` that is not on any `stand`, is placed on a `stand`, on which there is no `smoker` yet. It is only important to deploy all `smokers` on some `stands`, but it is not important, on which `stand` a particular `smoker` is placed. In the rules, negation as failure and cut-off are used. Placing a `smoker` on a `stand` is performed by calculating the X, Y and Z coordinates of the `smoker` with respect to the coordinates of the `stand` (14-21). The resulting scene is presented in Fig. 4B.

Query 2 extends Query 1 with the selection of only the smokers that are made of clay (Part C). The selection is achieved using the *sub-class selector* and *restriction selector* CCP (23-29). The resulting scene is presented in Fig. 4C.

Query 3 extends Query 2 and it uses *selector rules* CCP to chose only the smokers, between which the distance is maximal (Part D, Lines 31-36; Fig. 4D). The rule verifying the maximal distance has been implemented using negation as failure and cut-off (like in Lines 9,12), and it is skipped in the listing. Furthermore, the *simple class extender* is used—for every `q:ClayObject`, components responsible for rotating the object after it is touched are created (according to the OWL restrictions) and assigned (37-40) to an instance of the `q:TouchSensor` (41-45), which is activated by a `q:RotatingInterpolator` (46-56), which is controlled by a `q:TimeSensor` (57-61).

In the example presented, the queries have been prepared using a semantic editor (Protégé). However, a specific tool supporting the creation of queries with CCPs could be developed.

```
 1:  Prefixes:
 2:      q−query, scm−Semantic Content Model,
 3:      ccp−Content Customization Patterns
 4:  # ————————— Part B —————————
 5:  q: standsOn(A, B) :−
 6:      q: smoker(A), q: stand(B),
 7:      q: notOnOthers(A), q: nothingOnIt(B).
 8:  q: notOnOthers(A) :−
 9:      q: standsOn(A, B), !, fail().
10:  q: notOnOthers(A).
11:  q: nothingOnIt(B) :−
12:      q: standsOn(A, B), !, fail().
13:  q: nothingOnIt(B).
14:  scm: x(A, AX) :− q: standsOn(A, B),
15:      scm: x(B, BX), AX = BX.
16:  scm: z(A, AZ) :− q: standsOn(A, B),
17:      scm: z(B, BZ), AZ = BZ.
18:  scm: y(A, AY) :− q: standsOn(A, B),
19:      scm: y(B, BY), scm: height(B, BHeight),
20:      scm: height(A, AHeight),
21:      AY = BY+(AHeight+BHeight)/2.
22:  # ————————— Part C —————————
23:  q: ClayObject
24:      rdf: type owl: Class ;
25:      rdfs: subClassOf ccp: ClassSelector .
26:      owl: equivalentClass
27:          [ rdf: type owl: Restriction ;
28:          owl: onProperty scm: madeOf ;
29:          owl: hasValue "clay" ] ;
30:  # ————————— Part D —————————
31:  q: remote(A, B) :−
32:      scm: x(A, AX), scm: x(B, BX),
33:      scm: z(A, ZX), scm: z(B, ZX),
34:      Distance^2 = (AX−BX)^2 + (AZ−BZ)^2,
35:      maximal(Distance^2).
36:  ccp: ClassSelector(A) :− q: remote(A, B).
37:  q: ClayObject rdfs: subClassOf
38:      [ rdf: type owl: Restriction ;
39:      owl: onProperty scm: sensor ;
40:      owl: someValuesFrom q: TouchSensor ] .
41:  q: TouchSensor rdf: type owl: Class ;
42:      rdfs: subClassOf scm: TouchSensor ,
43:      [ rdf: type owl: Restriction ;
44:      owl: onProperty scm: activates ;
45:      owl: someValuesFrom q: RotatingInterp].
46:  q: RotatingInterp rdf: type owl: Class ;
47:      rdfs: subClassOf scm: OrientationInterp ,
48:      [ rdf: type owl: Restriction ;
49:      owl: onProperty scm: key ;
50:      owl: hasValue "0 1.5 3" ] ,
51:      [ rdf: type owl: Restriction ;
52:      owl: onProperty scm: keyValue ;
53:      owl: hasValue"0 0 0 0 3.14 0 0 0 0"],
54:      [ rdf: type owl: Restriction ;
55:      owl: onProperty scm: controller ;
56:      owl: someValuesFrom q: TimeSensor ] .
57:  q: TimeSensor rdf: type owl: Class ;
58:      rdfs: subClassOf scm: TimeSensor ,
59:      [ rdf: type owl: Restriction ;
60:      owl: onProperty scm: interval ;
61:      owl: hasValue 3 ] .
```

Listing 2. Queries for an on-demand 3D content generation

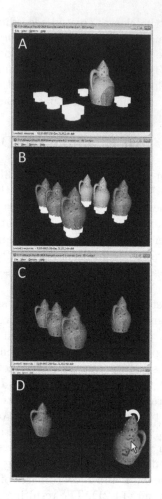

Fig. 4. A 3D meta-scene (A); a customized scene, in which every smoker is assigned to one stand (B); a customized scene including only the smokers made of clay (C) and a customized scene including rotating smokers, between which the distance is maximal (D)

Several other examples of 3D scenes generated with the method implementation are presented in Fig. 5. The meta-scenes have been conceptually modeled using an ontology with concepts reflecting selected elements of cities, and they have been customized by queries independently issued by different content consumers.

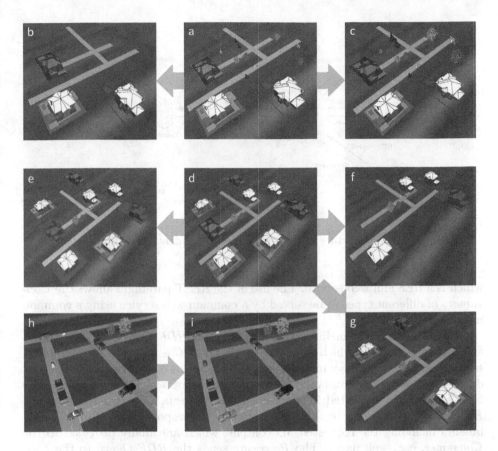

Fig. 5. **A meta-scene** (a), a customized scene without trees (b) and a customized scene, in which the trees that are far away from buildings are higher than the other trees (c).
A meta-scene (d), a customized scene, in which all buildings connected by a road are marked in red (e), and customized scenes, in which there are only the connected buildings (f) and only the buildings without a road (g).
A meta-scene (h) and a customized scene (i), in which all cars that are close to priority vehicles (fire trucks) being on the same road are marked red.

6   Implementation

A prototype system implementing the content generation method has been designed and partially developed as a Java-based web application. The architecture of the system is presented in Fig. 6.

A *Consumer* may be a user, who retrieves 3D content using either a *Web Browser* or another *Web Client* (in particular not limited to presenting HTML-based content), or a *Web Application* (e.g., indexing 3D content or preparing specific 3D scenes for users). A *Consumer* sends an *HTTP Request* to the *Provider*,

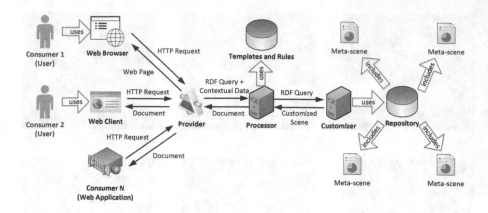

Fig. 6. The architecture of the on-demand 3D content generation system

which is a RESTful web service. The use of the REST paradigm allows the *Consumers* of different types to be served by a common web service using a common interface.

An *HTTP Request* includes two elements: an *RDF Query* for 3D content and *Contextual Data*, which is added by the *Web Client* or the *Web Application. Contextual Data* may include such parameters as consumer location, client device used as well as available 3D content browsers, which may influence the final form of the generated 3D content. Both elements are extracted from the *HTTP Request* and sent to the *Processor*, which is responsible for building documents including the requested 3D content, which are finally provided to the *Consumer*, e.g., web pages. The *Processor* sends the *RDF Query* to the *Customizer*. The *Customizer* retrieves a semantic 3D *Meta-scene* from the *Repository*. Meta-scenes have been implemented using the semantic web standards (RDF, RDFS and OWL), which permit the creation of semantic statements (facts) and the Prova declarative language [25], which permits the creation of horn clauses (rules) in the first-order logic. The *Processor* performs content generation based on reasoning on the *Meta-scene* and the *RDF Query*. Content generation has been implemented using the Pellet reasoner [32] and the Apache Jena SPARQL engine [2]—to process facts—and the Prova rule engine [25]—to process rules included in RDF queries and semantic 3D content representations. In consequence of the content generation, a *Customized Scene* is created, which satisfies requirements specified by the *Consumer*. The *Customized Scene* is delivered to the *Processor*, and it is transformed to the final representation encoded in one of the languages: VRML, X3D or ActionScript (with the Away3D library), which are representatives of both the declarative and imperative approaches to content representation. Next, the final document is built upon *Templates* as determined by *Rules* processing *Contextual Data*, which have been encapsulated in the *HTTP Request*. The generated *Document* is delivered to the *Consumer* via the *Provider*. Depending on the format of the 3D content generated, the content presentation may be performed using VRML and X3D browsers (e.g., Cortona3D or Bitmanagement BS Contact) or Adobe Flash Player.

7 Conclusions and Future Works

In this paper, a new method of semantic on-demand generation of interactive 3D content has been proposed. The method goes beyond the current state of the art in 3D modeling by enabling flexible 3D content creation and customization. The method is based on knowledge discovery and can be performed independently by different content consumers executing queries to semantic content repositories. The approach can improve content generation for VR/AR applications in various domains on the web.

The method has several important advantages in comparison to the available approaches to 3D content creation. First, the use of the semantic web techniques enables declarative content creation, which stresses the description of the results to be achieved, but not the manner in which the results are to be obtained. Second, it permits content creation and customization at different levels of abstraction regarding hidden knowledge, which may be inferred and used in the modeling process. Third, the method permits the reuse and assembly of common content elements, which may be described with shared ontologies and knowledge bases, and thus created and customized by different modeling users. Next, due to the conformance to the semantic web techniques, content generated with the method could potentially be further managed (indexed, searched and analyzed) in a simpler way in comparison to the content created with the other methods that do not rely on data semantics. Hence, the method could be convenient for the use with content repositories. Finally, the created semantically represented content is platform- and standard- independent and it can be presented using diverse 3D content presentation tools, programming languages and libraries thus liberating users from the installation of additional software and simplifying the use of 3D content.

A difficulty in the presented content generation method is related to the declarative rule-based description (logic-based programming) of projection of OPs (the *projector* pattern). Processing in this pattern requires recursive analysis of DIs and POs that are indicated by the OPs and RLs. This problem has been resolved by the use of SPARQL rules (created with the *construct* clause), which go beyond the first-order logic (supported, e.g., by Prova) and permit the representation of predicates (properties and relations) by variables in rules. Such SPARQL rules are used within the *Customizer*, so they are hidden from the modeling users and content consumers, which may use only first-order logic rules (compatible with Prova) in CCPs.

Possible directions of future research incorporate several facets. First, the proposed method can be evaluated in terms of the size and complexity of content representations (concrete, conceptual, customized and final representations as well as queries). Second, the method could be extended with semantic transformation of declarative rule-based descriptions of content behavior. Third, a visual tool supporting the creation of queries and on-demand content generation can be developed. Next, additional CCPs can be elaborated, e.g., to restrict the number of selected POs. Furthermore, query-based content generation can be extended to support the four-dimensional space (including time). Finally, the proposed method could be extended with parameters describing the context of interaction and information about the consumer's profile—to enable adaptation and personalization of 3D content.

Acknowledgments. This research work has been supported by the Polish National Science Center Grant No. DEC-2012/07/B/ST6/01523.

References

1. Almer, A., Schnabel, T., Stelzl, H., Stieg, J., Luley, P.: A Tourism Information System for Rural Areas Based on a Multi Platform Concept. In: Carswell, J.D., Tezuka, T. (eds.) W2GIS 2006. LNCS, vol. 4295, pp. 31–41. Springer, Heidelberg (2006)
2. Apache: Apache Jena. http://jena.apache.org/
3. Aylett, R., Luck, M.: Applying artificial intelligence to virtual reality: Intelligent virtual environments. Applied Artificial Intelligence **14**, 3–32 (2000)
4. Bilasco, I.M., Gensel, J., Villanova-Oliver, M., Martin, H.: 3dseam: a model for annotating 3d scenes using mpeg-7. In: ISM, pp. 310–319. IEEE Computer Society (2005)
5. Bilasco, I.M., Villanova-Oliver, M., Gensel, J., Martin, H.: Semantic-based rules for 3d scene adaptation. In: Proceedings of the Twelfth International Conference on 3D Web Technology, Web3D 2007, pp. 97–100. ACM, New York (2007)
6. Bille, W., Pellens, B., Kleinermann, F., Troyer, O.D.: Intelligent modelling of virtual worlds using domain ontologies. In: Proc. of the Workshop of Intelligent Computing (WIC), held in conjunction with the MICAI 2004 Conference. pp. 272–279. Mexico City, Mexico (2004)
7. Broekstra, J., Kampman, A.: Serql: An rdf query and transformation language (August 2004). http://gate.ac.uk/sale/dd/related-work/SeRQL.pdf
8. Cavazza, M., Palmer, I.: High-level interpretation in virtual environments. Applied AI **14**, 125–144 (2000)
9. Celakovski, S., Davcev, D.: Multiplatform real-time rendering of mpeg-4 3D scenes with microsoft xna. In: ICT Innovations 2009, October 25-29, pp. 337–344. Springer, Heidelberg (2010)
10. Dachselt, R., Hinz, M., Pietschmann, S.: Using the amacont architecture for flexible adaptation of 3d web applications. In: Proceedings of the Eleventh International Conference on 3D Web Technology, Web3D 2006, pp. 75–84. ACM, New York (2006)
11. Daum, S., Borrmann, A.: Definition and implementation of temporal operators for a 4d query language. In: Proc. of the ASCE International Workshop on Computing in Civil Engineering. ASCE (2013)
12. Flotyński, J., Walczak, K.: Semantic modelling of interactive 3d content. In: Proceedings of the 5th Joint Virtual Reality Conference. Paris, France (December 11-13, 2013)

13. Flotyński, J., Walczak, K.: Semantic multi-layered design of interactive 3d presentations. In: Proc. of the Federated Conf. on Computer Science and Information Systems, pp. 541–548. IEEE, Kraków (September 8-11, 2013)

14. Flotyński, J., Walczak, K.: Multi-platform semantic representation of 3d content. In: Proceedings of the 5th Doctoral Conference on Computing, Electrical and Industrial Systems, Lisbon, Portugal (April 7-9, 2014)

15. Flotyński, J.: Harvesting of semantic metadata from distributed 3d web content. In: Proceedings of the 6th International Conference on Human System Interaction (HSI), Sopot, Poland, June 6-8. IEEE (2013)

16. Flotyński, J.: Semantic Modelling of Interactive 3D Content with Domain-specific Ontologies. In: Procedia Computer Science, vol. 35, pp. 531–540. Elsevier (2014) ISSN: 1877-0509

17. Flotyński, J., Dalkowski, J., Walczak, K.: Building multi-platform 3d virtual museum exhibitions with flex-vr. In: The 18th International Conference on Virtual Systems and Multimedia, Milan, Italy, pp. 391–398 (September 2-5, 2012)

18. Flotyński, J., Walczak, K.: Attribute-based semantic descriptions of interactive 3d web content. In: Kiełtyka, L. (ed.) Information Technologies in Organizations - Management and Applications of Multimedia. pp. 111–138. Wydawnictwa Towarzystwa Naukowego Organizacji i Kierownictwa - Dom Organizatora (2013).

19. Flotyński, J., Walczak, K.: Conceptual Semantic Representation of 3D Content. In: Abramowicz, W. (ed.) BIS Workshops 2013. LNBIP, vol. 160, pp. 244–257. Springer, Heidelberg (2013)

20. Flotyński, J., Walczak, K.: Describing semantics of 3d web content with rdfa. In: The First International Conference on Building and Exploring Web Based Environments, Sevilla, Spain, January 27-February 1, pp. 63–68. ThinkMind (2013)

21. Flotyński, J., Walczak, K.: Microformat and microdata schemas for interactive 3d web content. In: Ganzha, M., Maciaszek, L., Paprzycki, M. (eds.) Proceedings of the 2013 Federated Conference on Computer Science and Information Systems Kraków, Poland, September 8-11, vol. 1, pp. 549–556. Polskie Towarzystwo Informatyczne (2013)

22. Flotyski, J., Walczak, K.: Conceptual knowledge-based modeling of interactive 3d content. The Visual Computer, 1–20 (2014). http://dx.doi.org/10.1007/s00371-014-1011-9

23. Gutierrez, M., Vexo, F., Thalmann, D.: Semantics-based representation of virtual environments. International Journal of Computer Applications in Technology **23**, 229–238 (2005)

24. Kalogerakis, E., Christodoulakis, S., Moumoutzis, N.: Coupling ontologies with graphics content for knowledge driven visualization. In: VR 2006 Proceedings of the IEEE Conference on Virtual Reality, Alexandria, Virginia, pp. 43–50 (March 25-29, 2006)

25. Kozlenkov, A., Paschke, A.: Prova Rule Language. https://prova.ws/

26. Latoschik, M.E., Biermann, P., Wachsmuth, I.: Knowledge in the Loop: Semantics Representation for Multimodal Simulative Environments. In: Butz, A., Fisher, B., Krüger, A., Olivier, P. (eds.) SG 2005. LNCS, vol. 3638, pp. 25–39. Springer, Heidelberg (2005)

27. Latoschik, M.E., Blach, R.: Semantic modelling for virtual worlds - a novel paradigm for realtime interactive systems? In: Proc. of the 2008 ACM Symp. on VR Software and Technology, Bordeaux, France, pp. 17–20 (October 27-29, 2008)

28. Latoschik, M.E., Frohlich, C.: Semantic reflection for intelligent virtual environments. In: IEEE Virtual Reality Conference 2007, Charlotte, USA, pp. 305–306 (March 10-14, 2007)

29. Lugrin, J., Cavazza, M.: Making sense of virtual environments: action representation, grounding and common sense. In: Proc. of the 12th Int. Conference on Intelligent User Interfaces, Honolulu, HI, USA, pp. 225–234 (January 28–31, 2007)
30. Maglo, A., Lee, H., Lavoué, G., Mouton, C., Hudelot, C., Dupont, F.: Remote scientific visualization of progressive 3d meshes with x3d. In: Proceedings of the 15th International Conference on Web 3D Technology, Web3D 2010, pp. 109–116. ACM, New York (2010)
31. O'Connor, M.J., Das, A.K.: Sqwrl: A query language for owl. In: Hoekstra, R., Patel-Schneider, P.F. (eds.) OWLED. CEUR Workshop Proceedings, vol. 529. CEUR-WS.org (2008). http://webont.org/owled/2009/papers/owled2009_submission_42.pdf
32. Parsia, C.: Pellet: OWL 2 Reasoner for Java. http://clarkparsia.com/pellet/
33. Prud'hommeaux, E., Seaborne, A.: Sparql query language for rdf (January 2008). http://www.w3.org/TR/2008/REC-rdf-sparql-query-20080115/
34. Schenk, S., Gearon, P., Passant, A.: Sparql 1.1 update. Tech. rep., W3C (2008)
35. Seaborne, A.: Rdql - a query language for rdf (member submission). Tech. rep., W3C (January 2004). http://www.w3.org/Submission/2004/SUBM-RDQL-20040109/
36. Smith, J.R., Döller, M., Tous, R., Gruhne, M., Yoon, K., Sano, M., Burnett, I.S.: The mpeg query format: Unifying access to multimedia retrieval systems. IEEE MultiMedia 15(4), 82–95 (2008). http://dx.doi.org/10.1109/MMUL.2008.96
37. Spagnuolo, M., Falcidieno, B.: 3d media and the semantic web. IEEE Intelligent Systems 24, 90–96 (2009)
38. Tack, K., Lafruit, G., Catthoor, F., Lauwereins, R.: Platform independent optimisation of multi-resolution 3d content to enable universal media access. The Visual Computer 22(8), 577–590 (2006)
39. Troyer, O.D., Kleinermann, F., Pellens, B., Bille, W.: Conceptual modeling for virtual reality. In: Tutorials, Posters, Panels and Industrial Contributions at the 26th Int. Conf. on Conceptual Modeling, Darlinghurst, pp. 3–18 (2007)
40. Walczak, K.: Flex-vr: Configurable 3d web applications. In: Proc. of the Int. Conf. on Human System Interaction, HSI 2008, Kraków, Poland, pp. 135–140 (May 25-27, 2008)
41. Walczak, K.: Structured Design of Interactive VR Applications. In: Proc. of the 13th Int. Symp. on 3D Web Technology (Web3D 2008), pp. 105–113. ACM; ACM Siggraph; Eurog Assoc; Web3D Consortium, ACM, Los Angeles, CA, (August 9-10, 2008)
42. Walczak, K., Cellary, W., White, M.: Virtual museum exhibitions. Computer 39(3), 93–95 (2006)
43. Wiebusch, D., Latoschik, M.E.: Enhanced decoupling of components in intelligent realtime interactive systems using ontologies. In: 2012 5th Workshop on Software Engineering and Architectures for Realtime Interactive Systems (SEARIS), pp. 43–51. Orange County, CA (2012)
44. Wu, Z., Xu, G., Zhang, Y., Cao, Z., Li, G., Hu, Z.: Gmql: A graphical multimedia query language. Knowl.-Based Syst. 26, 135–143 (2012)

Moka: Designing a Simple Scene Graph Library for Cluster-Based Virtual Reality Systems

Andrea Salvadori, Andrea Brogni$^{(\boxtimes)}$, Giordano Mancini, and Vincenzo Barone

Scuola Normale Superiore, Piazza dei Cavalieri 7, 56126 Pisa, Italy
{andrea.salvadori,andrea.brogni,giordano.mancini,
vincenzo.barone}@sns.it

Abstract. Clusters of PCs are widely employed in multi-screen immersive virtual reality systems. While this allows reducing the realization costs, it leds to an increase of complexity on the software side, since they require the development of distributed applications. Over the years, many frameworks supporting cluster rendering have been proposed, but none has established itself as the de-facto standard for immersive virtual reality application development. A new trend that is taking place consists in adding cluster-rendering support to one of the many freely available 3D engines. In this paper, we propose a convenient method to develop a lightweight distributed scene graph on top of a generic graphics engine. In particular, we describe the main mechanisms and design choices behind "Moka", a library for the development for cluster-based virtual reality applications. We also present "Caffeine", a virtual reality molecular visualizer based on the Moka library.

Keywords: Virtual reality · Cluster-based rendering · Molecular visualization

1 Introduction

Many immersive virtual reality systems (e.g. CAVE-like systems [1]) use multiple screens to surround the user with graphical representations of virtual environments, in order to increase the sense of immersion. The first systems of this kind employed expensive shared-memory graphics workstations with multiple video outputs. Thanks to the technological advances of personal computers' hardware, it has been possible to replace dedicated graphics workstations with a cluster of PCs equipped with high performance CPUs and GPUs, interconnected in a high bandwidth LAN. While this approach allowed the realization of multi-screen virtual reality systems at a fraction of the original cost, it led to an increase of complexity on the software side. In fact, these systems require the development of distributed applications consisting in at least one process for each node of the cluster, each one responsible to produce images for one of the screens of the Virtual Reality (VR) system, implying strict synchronization in order to keep coherency between screens.

In the following, we use the terms "cluster rendering" (CR) or "clustering" to refer to algorithms and applications related to the development of interactive graphical distributed applications, capable of producing a coherent and synchronized rendering on a cluster-based multi-display system.

© Springer International Publishing Switzerland 2014
L.T. De Paolis and A. Mongelli (Eds.): AVR 2014, LNCS 8853, pp. 333–350, 2014.
DOI: 10.1007/978-3-319-13969-2_25

Many of the techniques described are also employed in the realization of Net-worked Virtual Environments (NVEs) [2], although there are some important differences that must be taken into account. In particular, NVEs are designed to handle large numbers of network users, which concurrently modify the state of the virtual world. However, since each user has his/her own "vision of the world", transient inconsistencies are tolerated. In the case of applications for multi-screen virtual reality systems, instead, the virtual world is usually observed and manipulated by one or at most few users, but a much more strict synchronization is required to avoid inconsistences between the projected images, that would compromise the sense of immersion. Another related but distinct research field is the "parallel rendering" methods, in which parallel computing techniques and multi-GPUs systems and/or clusters of graphics workstations are exploited to speed up the rendering of complex datasets. The aim of these techniques is therefore orthogonal to the "cluster rendering", although the two methodologies can be combined (e.g. Chromium [3]).

Over the years, many VR frameworks supporting CR have been proposed, but none has been able to establish itself as a standard for immersive VR application development. Thanks to the availability of many mature and freely available 3D engines, a new trend is going on, adding CR support to one of them. We propose an efficient method to develop a lightweight distributed scene graph on top of a 3D graphics engine. In particular, we introduce "Moka", a library to simplify the development of applications for cluster-based immersive VR systems. Although Moka has been thought mainly for scientific visualization (with focus on molecular sciences), most of its mechanisms and design choices are general solutions that can be applied to any application field.

The paper is organized as follows: section 2 provides an overview of the most diffuse solutions to realize CR, while section 3 describes our motivations; in section 4, we present the "Moka" library; finally, in section 5 we present "Caffeine", a VR molecular visualizer based on the "Moka" library.

2   Cluster Rendering Approaches

The main drawback of cluster-based VR systems is that they require the development of distributed applications whose output image streams must be coherent across the screens. This requirement generally involves three different levels of synchronization [4, 5]. First, to obtain a correct stereoscopy, the generation of right and a left eye images must be synchronized across the multiple displays. This involves the synchronization of video signals (Gen-lock), a feature automatically provided by the current high-end GPUs. Second, each node of the cluster generates a new frame only when the others have finished producing the previous one (Frame-lock). This mechanism is not strictly necessary, but its lack may produce discrepancies across the generated images. On the other hand, it introduces a synchronization barrier that may have a negative impact on the frame rate. Finally, we have to synchronize the data used as input of the rendering process. Obviously, it is possible to implement this functionality at the application level, like in a generic distributed application. However, this approach significantly increases the development time, since the code dedicated to the replication of the application model between the nodes grows with the application's features and, furthermore, this code is very application-specific. The development could be simplified by using middleware that provides high-level functionalities such as object replication and remote method invocation (RakNet [6], ReplicaNet [7], Ice [8], Collage [9]).

A better solution consists in employing a framework specifically designed for this type of applications, which takes into account their common peculiarities. Over the years, several approaches have been proposed to realize generic toolkits for CR, trying to perform the data distribution in a way as transparent as possible for the programmer, so that the development of the applications would require only minor modifications with respect to a non-distributed one.

2.1 Input Event Distribution

In this approach, an identical copy of the application runs on each node of the cluster and the synchronization is obtained by broadcasting the data received from input devices (e.g. tracking systems) for all the instances. However, keeping the state of the application instances reasonably synchronized is difficult, because some computations (such as animations and physical simulations) are time dependent, in the sense that their results depend on the time they start/stop and on the time intervals between the executions of consecutives simulation steps. Since each application instance runs on a different machine, divergences may arise. Similar problems are caused by the use of random numbers and in general by the presence of any source of non-deterministic behaviors. To minimize these inconsistences additional synchronization mechanisms (such as the Frame-lock) are required. Finally note that, for similar reasons, the start of the application's instances should be synchronized and it is not possible to add further instances afterwards[1].

Despite its drawbacks, this approach is one of the most popular. It is employed, for example, as main mechanism to support clustering on VR Juggler [10–13].

2.2 Graphics Command Distribution

An interesting approach consists in intercepting the calls made by the application to the graphic API and streaming them over the network. Rendering slaves, running on each node of the cluster, receive these messages, decoding them and calling the corresponding graphic functions.

The main drawback is that, if the application performs many API calls per frame or if these calls manage many data, the network could be saturated, with consequent impact on the performance of all the services and applications sharing the same network. Moreover, like in input event distribution, it is not possible, in general, to "hot-plug" further rendering slaves once the application started. Finally, graphic libraries like OpenGL expose a vast and frequently expanded API, so implementing and keeping updated a corresponding proxy library requires a considerable development effort.

Examples of projects designed to exploit a similar approach are WireGL [14], Chromium [3] and XVR [15].

---

[1] More precisely, such a feature is possible but it should be explicitly implemented at the application level.

2.3   Scene Graph Distribution

Since scene graph structures are widely used in 3D graphics, another popular approach consists in replicating and keeping synchronized these structures on each node of the cluster. By doing so there is no need to run a complete copy of the application on each node, thus a master-slave architecture is usually employed: the "real" application acts as the master process, implementing the business logic, handling the input, and manipulating a proxy scene graph. The main purpose of this scene graph is not to render the 3D scene, but to keep track of the graph state and notify each change to the slaves. The slave processes, instead, have their own copy of the scene graph, keeping it updated according to the received messages, and drawing it on screen.

This technique has many points in common with the graphics command distribution approach: both employ master-slave architecture in which slaves are lightweight programs, whose only purpose is to render into the screen, and they are independent from the specific application that controls them. On the other side, the application (usually) does not perform rendering, so the workload is better distributed with respect to those approaches in which the whole application is replicated.

In contrast to previous approaches, the run-time insertion of further rendering slaves is quite simple to implement: when a new slave connects to the master, it is sufficient to perform a visit in which the whole graph is serialized and sent to the new slave.

The main drawback of this solution derives from the fact that, if the scene graph has not been designed from the beginning to be distributed, implementing such features afterwards could be very complicated and time consuming. That would usually consists in extending all the nodes' classes and override all the methods that change their internal state. However, real world's scene graphs are very complex libraries, so extending just a small subset of the available nodes would require a considerable effort. In some cases the problem can be circumvented by exploiting specific features of the used library, like in the case of Distributed Open Inventor [16]. Another possibility consists in wrapping the original scene graph within a set of classes that expose a smaller interface and implement data distribution. Although by doing so the interface of the original library is not maintained, it simplifies the addition of clustering support. For that reasons we choose to follow this path, as already done by other libraries like AVANGO [17]. Examples of libraries implementing a distributed scene graph are OpenSG [18, 19] , AVANGO [17], Distributed Open Inventor [16] and Syzygy [20].

3   Motivations

One of the first problems to face when developing a new VR application is to decide if relying on an existing framework, such as the open source projects VR Juggler [10, 13] and OpenSG [18], the free to use but proprietary XVR [15], commercial products like Unigine [21] and MiddleVR [22] for Unity [23] or other solutions. Other options are the development of an entire VR engine from scratch or the adoption of an intermediate solution by implementing a sort of "VR layer" on top of some pre-existing graphics engine. In particular, when choosing the right tools for the development of medium/large sized projects, many different aspects must be considered and evaluated, including: support of critical features in the applications; maturity of the project; documentation and maintenance; integration with other libraries.

Of course, it could be difficult to choose without making relevant compromises. On the other hand, today there are plenty of mature, freely available 3D engines (such as Unity [23], OpenSceneGraph [24], OGRE [25] etc.). Many of them are free to use also in commercial projects and are accompanied by a vast community providing support, documentation and numerous plugins that facilitate their integration with other libraries (such as GUI toolkits, physics engine etc.) and various kinds of devices (including the new low-cost VR-like devices such as the Oculus Rift [26]).

For these reasons, a new trend that is taking place is to add clustering support to these engines. Beside commercial products like MiddleVR [22], a few freely available plugins for popular engines can be found, but most of them are simplistic solutions based on the replication of the input data and/or of the view matrix. Libraries that implement a distributed scene graph on top of an existing engine are even less common and in most cases impose significant constraints, like requiring a static graph.

Use of an established traditional 3D engine would allow to meet all the requirements of our project (with the only important exception of CR), without onerous limitations, finding a way to implement clustering on top of it. However, we had to find a way to implement clustering on top of it in a limited amount of time. We introduced an abstraction layer on top of a pre-existing graphics engine, which exposes a simplified (but not simplistic) distributed scene graph. As expected the clustering functionalities are almost completely transparent to the developer, allowing the porting of an application using Moka to various kind of environments (from desktop to immersive VR systems) with only minor changes to the code. Furthermore, the structure and the content of the distributed scene graph can be dynamically manipulated and extended. It is important to note that we do not claim that our approach is the best possible, nor that the mechanisms we describe are particularly original. Instead, with this work we want to present a reasonable solution to a diffuse problem, in the hope that other people in similar situations may find it useful.

4   The Moka Library

The approach we adopted consists in developing a high-level scene graph on top of an existing graphics engine, providing a simpler and more concise interface and clustering support. The main characteristics and benefits of the approach we adopted are the following:

- By wrapping an existing scene graph instead of extending its classes, it is possible to expose a simpler interface, thus reducing the clustering related code.
- Thanks to the simplified interface, much of the complexity of the native engine can be hidden, thus accelerating the development process and making the library usable also by people with limited experience.
- Our approach does not rely on specific mechanisms provided by a specific engine (as [16]), thus making it applicable to other graphics engines. The substitution of one engine with another has a very limited impact on the applications' code.
- There are no constraints related to the scene graph structure, like it happens in many simplistic solutions: the structure and the content of scene graph can be dynamically modified, by creating and deleting nodes, removing a sub-graph from its

current position and attaching it to another node, loading a mesh from file, creating geometry and the related attributes procedurally, applying shaders etc.

- The mechanisms used to replicate the state of the scene graph can be exploited to create application-specific distributed objects, thus providing further flexibility.
- Frame-lock mechanisms may not be strictly needed.

The main drawback of our solution is that, due to the way it was conceived, it is better suited for applications that require only a subset of the functionality offered by the original engine. However, this fact does not impose constrains or prevent in any way to expose all the needed functionalities. In the worst case, in fact, the designer will define a scene graph as complex as the underlying one.

Moka has been implemented using OpenSceneGraph (OSG) [24] as native graphics engine, the Qt framework [27] as general-purpose library, Enet [28] for networking and GLM [29] as mathematics library. However, the concepts and mechanisms at the basis of Moka do not depend on specific technologies, so they can be easily adapted to other languages and toolkits.

4.1   The Basic Scene Graph

Each node of Moka wraps one of more OpenSceneGraph (OSG) nodes. As usual, the internal nodes of the graph represent a transformation to be applied to their children, while leaf nodes encapsulate the elements of the scene, such as meshes. At this stage, four different nodes have been defined to represent transformations: in addiction to a generic SGMatrixTransform class, specific nodes have been provided for translation, rotation and scaling. These last three classes also provide specific methods to animate the transformation over time (see section 4.5). As far as concerns the elements of the scene, two types of nodes have been defined: the *SGMeshFile* class allows to load a mesh from a file, while the *SGGeometry* class allows to define custom geometry (see section 4.6). Specific classes have been defined to represent materials, shaders and set of uniform variables. These kinds of objects can be dynamically attached to the *SGGeometry* nodes, obtaining custom graphical representations.

These classes can be used directly to develop desktop 3D applications, like any other scene graph. The most interesting part concerns, however, the mechanisms that allow the replication of these objects on each node of the cluster. With the exception of the initialization phase, these mechanisms are completely transparent to the programmer: thanks to polymorphism, the programmer can write his/her cluster-based application in the same way he/she would write desktop ones.

4.2   Distributing the Scene Graph

Suppose to have a set of objects living on the master process and a corresponding set of objects for each slave process. In order to keep all these instances synchronized, we need to inform the slaves about all the changes applied to the objects owned by the master. When a slave receives one of these messages it must be able to identify which one, between the objects he manages, corresponds to the object modified by the master and to update its state accordingly. In order to do so, each object must be associated to a unique global identifier such that:

- All the objects living within a single process must have different identifiers.
- Each object managed by the master and all its replicas must share the same identifier.

A convenient way to enforce these constraints is to generate a unique identifier every time the master creates a new instance. Then, when a message is sent to notify the slaves about the new object, the ID is included in the payload, so that they can assign it to the newly created object.

In Moka, the "*DistributedObject*" class has been defined to generate and store these identifiers. As the name suggests, this is the superclass of all the objects replicated between master and slaves (see Fig. 1). It provides two constructors:

- the first constructor does not accept any parameter; it is used only by the master process, and is responsible for the generation of unique global identifiers. Only positive IDs are generated in this way;
- the second constructor accepts an identifier as parameter, and it is able to create objects with a predetermined identifier. Slave processes use it when creating replicated objects but, as we will see in the following, it can also be employed on the master side to create application-level distributed objects.

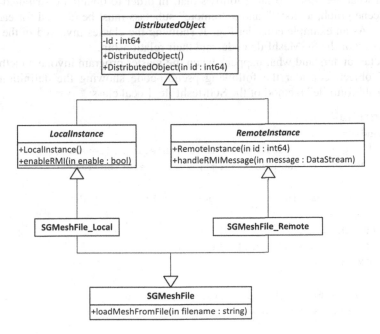

Fig. 1. Relation between the classes involved in the definition of a distributed object

In order to distinguish among the functionalities to be used by the master program and the ones designed for the rendering slaves, the DistributedObject class is specialized by the *"LocalInstance"* and *"RemoteInstance"* classes[2]. The purpose of these classes is to establish the basic mechanisms by which modifications applied to a "local" object are notified to the corresponding "remote" instances. Rather than collecting the changes in a list to be periodically distributed, as suggested in [18, 19], we preferred an approach more similar to the Remote Method Invocation (RMI). In particular, *LocalInstance* subclasses act as proxies, i.e. they encode each method call as a network message and broadcast it to the slaves. On the other side *RemoteInstance* subclasses act as "skeletons", decoding the received messages and calling the corresponding methods. Actually, there are some important differences between the classical RMI and the mechanism we employed:

- Unlike "stub" objects, *LocalInstances* maintain a complete internal state so to respond to "getter" methods directly, thus avoiding any unnecessary network communication and the consequent wait for a response.
- As a further consequence of the previous point, any return value can be provided directly by the *LocalInstance*, thus our pseudo-RMI mechanism does not support responses from remote objects.
- The communication is one-to-many and unidirectional, as in the publish/subscribe model.

From what described so far it follows that, in order to obtain a distributed version of the scene graph, a "local" and a "remote" subclass must be defined for each class of Moka. As an example consider Fig. 1, showing the classes involved in the distributed version of the SGMeshFile node, and their relationship.

To better understand what happens when the master program invoke a method on a "proxy" object, consider the following pseudo-code showing the definition of the "loadMeshFromFile" method of the SGMeshFile_Local class:

```
if(isRMIEnabled()) {
  // Sends the RMI message
  byte[] msg = encodeLoadMeshFromFile(this.id, filename);
  NetworkManager::sendMessage(msg); // See section 4.4

  // Prevents that further messages will be generated
  enableRMI(false);
  // Loads the mesh
  SGMeshFile::loadMeshFromFile(filename);
  enableRMI(true);
} else {
  // Loads the mesh without sending any message
  SGMeshFile::loadMeshFromFile(filename);
}
```

---

[2] Note that, here and in the following, we will use the term "local" class/object to refer to the classes/objects used in the main (master) application, and the term "remote" class/object to refer those used by the rendering slaves.

Since in general these operations may involve other (virtual) methods of *LocalInstance* subclasses, we must avoid that further network messages would be generated in the process. For this reason the *LocalInstance* class provides the "enableRMI" static method that allows to temporarily disable the pseudo-RMI mechanism.

4.3 The Distributed Objects Registry

The *DistributedObjectsRegistry* class, a singleton used only by the rendering slaves, implements several of the key functionalities required by the pseudo-RMI mechanism. Its main purpose is to dispatch the received messages to the corresponding remote object, but it is also responsible for their lifecycle.

In order to perform message dispatching, the *DistributedObjectsRegistry* manages a dictionary that associates all the distributed objects to their global identifier. Whenever a RMI message is received, it extracts the destination ID from the message and performs a look up on the dictionary to retrieve the corresponding remote object. The same mechanism is exploited to allow the manipulation of a remote scene graph. These operations are particularly tricky, involving the dynamic composition of remote objects in complex data structures. A simple solution can be derived by observing that the methods corresponding to these operations usually take one or more (distributed) objects as arguments. Therefore it is possible to insert the IDs of these parameters into the message corresponding to the operation. When the remote instance decodes this message, it queries the DistributedObjectsRegistry to obtain a pointer to the remote counterparts of the involved objects, and performs the requested operation using these pointers as parameters.

Some details must be provided on how our library is intended to be used from the developer's point of view. In particular, direct instantiation of Moka's classes is strongly discouraged. Instead the programmer is required to use a set of predefined factory functions that returns a pointer to a new heap-allocated object. These functions takes care of instantiating the right class according to the type of application under development: as an example, the "newSGMeshFile()" function returns an instance of the SGMeshFile class if we are developing a desktop application, a "SGMeshFile_Local" instance when developing the master program and a "SGMeshFile_Remote" object for slave programs. The application type must be specified by the developer by means of an initialization function. In the case of slave programs, this initialization function also takes care to register the factories into the DistributedObjectsRegistry, which manage another dictionary containing the associations between a string, which identifies the type of the nodes, and the corresponding factory function. In this way, whenever a LocalInstance is instantiated, its constructor sends a message containing the type identifier of the new object. The DistributedObjectsRegistry can therefore retrieve the corresponding factory and fulfill the creation request. The destruction of remote objects happens in a similar way: whenever a LocalInstance is being destroyed on the master process, and its destructor is invoked, a message carrying the object's ID is sent to the DistributedObjectsRegistry, asking for its destruction.

Finally note that, to maintain the same format between the pseudo-RMI messages and those directed to the DistributedObjectsRegistry, it was decided to assign to it the global identifier "0".

4.4   Network Communication

Most of the messages generated when modifying the scene graph must be delivered reliably, in order to guarantee the correct synchronization of the shared graph. There are cases, however, where unreliability should be preferred, as we will see in section 4.5. If both reliable and unreliable transport protocols are used to implement a single specific functionality (e.g. by means of "raw" TCP and UDP sockets), the implementation should deal with messages interleaved on two distinct communication channels and ensure that they are handled in the correct order. This way to proceed would lead to a significant increase of the complexity of the protocol.

For the reasons just exposed, we decided to make use of Enet [28], a simple and robust network library originally developed for the multiplayer first person shooter Cube [30]. Enet implements a dedicated protocol on top of UDP, providing features like reliable and ordered packet delivery, automatic fragmentation and reassembly of packets, connection monitoring, automatic connection retry etc.

For our purposes, the most important features offered by Enet are those related to reliability and sequencing, which can be enabled or disabled on a per-packet basis. In this way, the messages to be transmitted reliably can be mixed with the unreliable ones on the same logical channel, while preserving the delivery order.

To isolate the networking code from the rest of the system we wrote a small module dedicated to network communication. This module consists in a thread that exploits Enet to send and receive messages to/from the other processes, and in a singleton class (the "NetworkManager") acting as an interface between the communication thread and the rest of the application.

4.5   Animations

The visualization of dynamic systems is one of the fundamental tasks of the computer graphics. From a computer graphics point of view this corresponds to the generation of an animation, intended as a progressive time-dependent variation of the state of the graphical scene according to some mathematical model and/or to the user's input.

In this section, we describe an effective method to implement animations in a CR engine. This method is an adaptation of the techniques employed in NVEs [2] and does not employ Frame-lock synchronization, so small discrepancies may occur. However, the animations updates are frequent enough to make such discrepancies acceptable for the user in most of the cases, especially in research fields like molecular sciences. In our case, the aim is having not only visualization of data structures but also have continuous and effective interaction. This means that the collocation between visual graphical feedback and real position of the tracked hand will be a critical point for making this effective and simple. Our choice to do not implement the framelock, at this stage, comes from the priority to have fast visual responses when the user look at a specific point and try to interact with his/her finger.

Let us call "key frame" a given configuration of the animation, constituted by the initial state to be assigned to the node and all the information needed to compute (or approximate) its subsequent evolution. Also let us call "in-between" a portion of an animation between two key frames, which can be computed by applying a known function (e.g. a linear function) to the information provided with the last key frame. Then the master can use reliable messages to communicate only the key frames and, during the in-betweens, send small unreliable packets carrying the essential information to keep the computation adequately synchronized across the slaves.

In Moka, the methods that start an animation on a given node actually set a new key frame and, in the case of "proxy" objects, they generate a reliable pseudo-RMI message (see 4.2 and 4.3). To obtain an animation composed by multiple key frames, it is sufficient to call these methods whenever a new key frame must be set, without stopping the animation before each call. To ensure a correct synchronization in these cases, the "start" messages must include the current state of the node in their payload. For the same reason, the "stop" messages must be delivered reliably and must contain the state of the node at the end of the animation.

The animation steps are performed by the "update" method, which updates the state of the node as a function of the elapsed time from the last key-frame. We call this time span the "animation time". The "update" method is provided by any node of the scene graph (not only on those that support animations) and it propagates the call to each child. It is thus possible to invoke the update method on the root of the scene graph (letting the call to traverse the entire graph), without the need to keep track of the currently animated nodes. In order to keep the replicated scene graphs synchronized the animation time is periodically sent to each slave. In particular, each time the "update" method is executed on a currently animated local object, a message carrying the new animation time is generated and dispatched to the corresponding remote instances as usual, but with two important differences:

1. These messages are unreliable. However, their ordered delivery is ensured, even with respect to reliable messages.
2. When these messages are handled by a remote object, a special method is called instead of "update". This method has the only purpose of substituting the stored animation time with the received one.

From the previous discussion, it follows that the periodic update of the scene graph can be performed independently on the master and on each slave with different frequencies. In particular, on the slaves the update visit is performed once per frame, thus ensuring a smooth animation, while the master can adopt a lower frequency (e.g. 5-10 times per second), thus reducing the workload and the generated network traffic. From our experience, these update frequencies are sufficient to ensure a synchronization good enough to fool the human eye.

4.6 Procedurally Generated Geometry

Since our main research field concerns scientific visualization, with a strong focus on molecular structures, it was fundamental to have a way to define a new geometry at runtime (e.g. to visualize data resulting from numerical simulations or generated procedurally) and to apply to them custom graphical representations. For that reason, we defined the SGGeometry class, which allows defining a set of vertices and the related vertex attributes. The geometry is defined by specifying a vertex array, an optional array of indices and the type of geometrical primitives to be generated. Similarly, vertex attributes are assigned by providing an array containing a value for each vertex. Custom representations can be obtained by assigning a shader program to the geometry node. For that purpose, specific classes have been defined to load and encapsulate a shader program and a set of uniform variables. In a similar way, material properties are encapsulated in a dedicated object that can be attached to the geometry node.

An important problem has to be taken into account: since the various attributes and properties are set/added separately, the corresponding messages will be received and handled by the slaves at different times. It follows that the geometry may be rendered when it is still in an inconsistent state. For this reason, SGGeometry objects buffer all the requested changes, and apply them all at once when a specific method is called.

4.7   Local Sub-graphs

The design described so far requires that the master process is the only responsible for managing the application model and its graphical representation (in the form of a scene graph). The scene graph is then replicated and kept synchronized on each rendering slave. However, nothing prevents the slaves from extending the shared graph with specific local additions. This approach, also proposed in other systems like [16], may result useful in several ways, allowing to add ad-hoc functionalities to a specific subset of slaves. Although at first this may seem unnecessary, it can actually become an important feature in the realization of more articulated applications.

Consider, for example, an application running in a CAVE-like system [1] in which the user can interact by means of a tablet computer. Several today's tablets are in fact handheld PCs equipped with a desktop-class operating system, so they are able to run a custom client which acts both as a rendering slave (since it renders the shared scene graph) and as an input device. In that scenario the tablet does not just render a portion of the scene (like the other slaves does), but instead provides a different view of the virtual world, possibly enriched with additional information.

Another important application of this technique is related to head-tracked stereoscopy: to implement stereoscopy each slave must set the view and the projection matrix appropriately, in function of the physical characteristics of the driven display and of the current position of the user with respect to the screen [31]. It follows that it is not possible to use a shared "camera node", since each slave must be able to set the virtual camera parameters according to its individual configuration. For that reason, the "viewing branch" is not included into the shared graph, letting each slave to treat it autonomously as an extension of its local scene graph.

This choice also influences the way the data produced by the tracker are handled, since it would make little sense to gather that information on the master and then propagate them to the slaves. Instead, the data generated by the tracking device are "multicasted" to all the processes via UDP, thus minimizing both the network traffic and the latency [16]. Note that the tracker data can also be received and handled by the master process, since they represent an input for the application.

Our library permits to define custom sub-graphs owned by a slave. In particular, these sub-graphs can be constructed using the native graphics engine or by instantiating directly (i.e. without using factories) the non-distributed version of the Moka nodes. For those tasks commonly required in CAVE-like systems, like head-tracked stereoscopy and keystone correction, the library provides specific utility classes, which transparently manage a local "viewing sub-graph". Tracker data are received and handled directly by the slaves, but the master, if required by the application logic, can also process them.

4.8   Hot-Plug Synchronization

Being able to start a new rendering slave at any time and without particular constraints is a desirable feature, both where the user interacts by means of a dedicated client and when we want to improve the robustness of the system (thanks to the possibility to restart a slave after a crash/fault without restarting the entire application). Only few systems natively support such a feature. In particular, the feasibility of such a mechanism at the framework level also depends on the chosen data distribution model. Scene graph based approaches are naturally predisposed to support this feature, since it would just require a visit of the graph in which, for each encountered node, a sequence of messages is generated in order to reconstruct the node's state on the slave's side. In our implementation, each time a new slave is started, it sends a message to the master asking to be synchronized. On the master, this "hot-plug" synchronization consists in the following three sub-phases:

1. the graph is visited, asking to each node to prepare itself for the imminent synchronization (e.g. by stopping any running animation). Then the "NetworkManager" (i.e. the interface to the network communication module, see section 4.4) is asked to transmit all the future messages only to the newly connected slave;
2. the main visit of the graph is performed, in which each encountered node sends all the messages required to create a corresponding remote instance with the same internal state. Note that the generated messages are the same pseudo-RMI messages described so far, so as to exploit all the related pre-existing mechanisms;
3. a final visit is performed, notifying each node that the synchronization is completed, so that it can resume any possibly pending task. The NetworkManager is finally asked to broadcast all the future messages to any slave.

Except for the initial synchronization request, this entire procedure is completely transparent to the newly connected slave.

4.9   Application Level Distributed Objects

Our library can be extended in various ways. In addition to extend existing ones or add new classes, application-level distributed objects can be defined by using the same mechanisms and techniques we designed for scene graph replication. Given a regular class, the programmer can obtain a distributed version of it by implementing its "local" and "remote" subclasses and paying attention to assign to the local class a fixed, negative identifier. Then a factory function must be defined, returning a pointer to an instance the right class according to the type of application being developed (desktop, master or slave). For slave programs only, the factory function must also be registered to the DistributedObjectsRegistry, so that the remote instances can be automatically generated (see 4.3).

In general, the definition of application-level distributed classes is discouraged, for the reasons explained in section 2 and because the distribution of the scene graph has exactly the purpose to avoid this approach. There may be cases, however, in which this additional option can result useful.

4.10   Configuration Tools

Virtual reality applications usually require an initial configuration phase in which the employed devices are calibrated and the characteristics / settings of these devices and of the other software components are provided to the application. Since these settings are mostly independent from the specific application that use them, Moka provides a set of classes that can be used to load and save to files several common types of configurations, such as stereo settings, physical characteristics of the displays, network parameters, keystone calibration, simple scene parameters, optional transformations to be applied to the tracker data etc. We also developed some graphical programs to help the user in configuring the VR system. The resulting configuration is saved into a set of predefined files, which can be shared between multiple applications running on the same system.

5   Caffeine

We designed Moka as part of the "Caffeine" project, currently under development at the DreamsLab (Dedicated Research Environment for Advanced Modeling and Simulations) at Scuola Normale Superiore in Pisa. The group merges competences on theoretical and computational chemistry with interactive Virtual Reality technologies, working on the production and fruition of scientific and humanistic contents.

The aim of Caffeine project is to develop an integrated system for computational chemistry that will take maximum advantage from VR technologies in order to visualize and model complex molecular structures in a natural and effective way. Although designed for immersive VR systems, versions of Caffeine will be available for various environments, ranging from standard desktop systems to immersive VR environments. At the time of writing Caffeine is at an early alpha stage of development, but a first version of the molecular visualizer is stable enough to be used in our CAVE system (see Fig. 2a). In this scenario, the user can interact with the system by means of a simple application for Android devices we developed.

Fig. 2. a) Interacting with a hemoglobin, using Caffeine in our CAVE system. b) Rendering of an half of the Rat Liver Vault [32] molecule using Caffeine.

5.1 GPU-Accelerated Visualization of Molecular Structures

One of the fundamental features that Caffeine had to provide was the ability to visualize "all atoms" representations[3] of complex molecular structures at satisfactory frame rates. To this end we developed a set of shaders implementing a GPU-based ray-casting of implicit surfaces [33, 34], since this method has proven to provide very good results (both in terms of performance and image quality) when applied to the visualization of molecular structures [35–37]. This method consists in generating a simple proxy geometry (e.g. a cuboid or a point sprite) in place of each primitive surface to be drawn. The proxy geometry must enclose the corresponding surface in window space. Then, when the proxy geometry is being rasterized, a fragment shader evaluates the intersection between the surface and a ray starting at the camera position and passing through the center of the generated fragment. The resulting (closer) intersection point and the related normal vector are then used to shade the fragment and adjust its depth. If no intersection is found, the fragment is discarded.

Although a single shader could handle a full class of surfaces (as described in [33, 34, 36] for quadrics), and because we were interested in providing "all-atoms" representations of complex molecular structures, we implemented an optimized version of these shaders for spheres and cylinders. In particular, the proxy geometry is generated on-the-fly by a dedicated geometry shader (similarly to what proposed in [37]) and consists in just a quad for spheres and (at most) two quads for cylinders.

Finally note that since glyphs are common ways to represent scientific data, with Moka we provide specific classes to define sets of spheres and cylinders, in the hope to promote their reuse in other projects. These classes are not part of the scene graph, so they are unknown to the slaves. Instead, they simply encapsulate a SGGeometry node and the shaders implementing the ray-casting algorithm described before.

---

[3] In this class of representations the atoms are represented as spheres (balls) and the bonds connecting them are depicted as cylinders (sticks). Typical examples are "ball-and-stick", "space filling" and "liquorice" representations, which distinguish themselves according to the radius assigned to the atoms and to the visibility of the bonds.

5.2   A First Qualitative Performance Evaluation

To get a first qualitative evaluation of the performance of our system, we tried to load in Caffeine an half Rat Liver Vault [32] (PDB IDs: 2ZUO, 2ZV4 and 2ZV5), a complex molecule constituted by about 490 thousand atoms and 493 thousand bonds. The test was performed in our CAVE system, constituted by four slave nodes each equipped with 2 Intel Xeon E5645 processors, 24GB of RAM and a Nvidia Quadro 6000 GPU. Each slave drives a stereo projector with a resolution of 1400x1050 pixels.

The molecule was placed in a way to fill the front screen (to maximize the fragment processing workload), while remaining completely visible (to avoid that part of the geometry would be culled/clipped), as shown in figure Fig. 2b. The test was performed with head-tracked stereo enabled and the user was asked to move freely within the CAVE. Since, once finished loading, each slave runs independently from the others, we only measured the frame rate on the front slave.

During the test, we switched between "ball-and-stick" and "space filling" representations: the first produces a greater fill-rate (because of the increased atom's radius) but does not draw the cylinders, while the second doubles the number of elements to be drawn (because of the cylinders) but less fragments get involved. During the "space filling" test, we got frame rates comprised in the range 30-50 fps. This sensible variation results from the different fill-rates due to the changes of the user's perspective. The "ball-and-stick" test, instead, provided a more stable frame rate, comprised between 22 and 28 fps. In fact, in this representation, the variation of the fill-rate is more contained. However, the doubled number of elements to be drawn inevitably causes a drop in frame rate.

Although in future we plan to perform a much more accurate and targeted performance evaluation, this first simple test showed encouraging results. In fact, the frame rate remained at interactive levels also when almost two millions quadric surfaces[4] were ray-casted at the same time. We however noted a perceptible lag in the synchronization of the images across the screens when the user moved. This is due to the fact that we decided to not employ any frame-lock mechanism, so the images produced by different slaves may temporary diverge. However, a stringent frame-lock would have caused an inevitable drop in frame rate. Furthermore, these divergences are noticeable only when the system is under heavily stress, like in our test.

6   Conclusions and Future Work

In this work, we proposed a convenient method to develop a lightweight distributed scene graph on top of a 3D graphics engine. In particular, we described "Moka", a library to simplify the development of distributed VR applications supporting various types of environments: from standard desktop applications to cluster-based multi-screen immersive VR system like the CAVE.

The library is under development and it has been used in the implementation of a molecular visualizer, specifically designed for the research field of our group, solving our

---

[4] Ball-and-stick representation with "side-by-side" stereoscopy enabled.

needs to visualize structured scientific data in immersive technologies. In the near future, we are planning tests in terms of generic performances, with comparative studies.

In addiction, we are working on the extension of the Moka library both by exposing a much larger set of the features offered by the underlying graphics engine and by supporting some of the newer low-cost VR devices, like the Oculus Rift [26]. We would also like to provide a more comprehensive library for the visualization of scientific data, exploiting GPU-accelerated methods like the GPU-based ray-casting. Finally, we are improving the Caffeine project, with the aim to realize a truly innovative integrated system for computational chemistry, which takes maximum advantage from VR technologies.

References

1. Cruz-Neira, C., Sandin, D.J., DeFanti, T.A.: Surround-screen Projection-based Virtual Reality: The Design and Implementation of the CAVE. In: Proceedings of the 20th Annual Conference on Computer Graphics and Interactive Techniques, pp. 135–142. ACM, New York (1993)
2. Steed, A., Oliveira, M.F.: Networked Graphics: Building Networked Games and Virtual Environments. Morgan Kaufmann Publishers Inc., San Francisco, CA, USA (2009)
3. Humphreys, G., Houston, M., Ng, R., Frank, R., Ahern, S., Kirchner, P.D., Klosowski, J.T.: Chromium: A Stream-processing Framework for Interactive Rendering on Clusters. In: Proceedings of the 29th Annual Conference on Computer Graphics and Interactive Techniques, pp. 693–702. ACM, New York (2002)
4. Raffin, B., Soares, L., Ni, T., Ball, R., Schmidt, G.S., Livingston, M.A., Staadt, O.G., May, R.: PC Clusters for Virtual Reality. In: Virtual Reality Conference, pp. 215–222 (2006)
5. Guimarães, M.P., Bressan, P.A., Zuffo, M.K.: Frame lock synchronization for multiprojection immersive environments based on pc graphics clusters. In: Proocedings of the 5th SBC Symposium on Virtual Reality (2002)
6. RakNet 4. http://www.jenkinssoftware.com/
7. ReplicaNet. http://www.replicanet.com/
8. Internet Communications Engine (Ice). http://www.zeroc.com/
9. Collage. http://www.libcollage.net/
10. Bierbaum, A., Just, C., Hartling, P., Meinert, K., Baker, A., Cruz-Neira, C.: VR Juggler: a virtual platform for virtual reality application development. In: 2001 Proceedings of the IEEE Virtual Reality, pp. 89–96 (2001)
11. Allard, J., Gouranton, V., Lecointre, L., Melin, E., Raffin, B.: Net Juggler and SoftGenLock: Running VR Juggler with Active Stereo and Multiple Displays on a Commodity Component Cluster. In: Proceeding of IEEE Virtual Reality Conference 2002, pp. 273–274 (2002)
12. Bierbaum, Aron, Hartling, Patrick, Morillo, Pedro, Cruz-Neira, Carolina: Implementing Immersive Clustering with VR Juggler. In: Gervasi, Osvaldo, Gavrilova, Marina L., Kumar, Vipin, Laganá, Antonio, Lee, Heow Pueh, Mun, Youngsong, Taniar, David, Tan, Chih Jeng Kenneth (eds.) ICCSA 2005. LNCS, vol. 3482, pp. 1119–1128. Springer, Heidelberg (2005)
13. VR Juggler: The Programmer's Guide - Version 3.0. http://vrjuggler.org
14. Humphreys, G., Eldridge, M., Buck, I., Stoll, G., Everett, M., Hanrahan, P.: WireGL: A Scalable Graphics System for Clusters. In: Proceedings of the 28th Annual Conference on Computer Graphics and Interactive Techniques, pp. 129–140. ACM, New York (2001)

15. Carrozzino, M., Tecchia, F., Bacinelli, S., Cappelletti, C., Bergamasco, M.: Lowering the Development Time of Multimodal Interactive Application: The Real-life Experience of the XVR Project. In: Proceedings of the 2005 ACM SIGCHI International Conference on Advances in Computer Entertainment Technology, pp. 270–273. ACM, New York (2005)

16. Hesina, G., Schmalstieg, D., Furhmann, A., Purgathofer, W.: Distributed Open Inventor: A Practical Approach to Distributed 3D Graphics. In: Proceedings of the ACM Symposium on Virtual Reality Software and Technology. pp. 74–81. ACM, New York (1999)

17. Kuck, R., Wind, J., Riege, K., Bogen, M.: Improving the AVANGO VR/AR Framework - Lessons Learned. Virtuelle und Erweiterte Realität, 209–220 (2008)

18. Reiners, D.: OpenSG: A scene graph system for flexible and efficient realtime rendering for virtual and augmented reality applications (2002)

19. Roth, M., Voss, G., Reiners, D.: Multi-threading and clustering for scene graph systems. Computers & Graphics. **28**, 63–66 (2004)

20. Schaeffer, B., Goudeseune, C.: Syzygy: native PC cluster VR. In: 2003 Proceedings of the IEEE Virtual Reality, pp. 15–22 (2003)

21. UNIGINE Corp.: Unigine Engine. http://unigine.com

22. i'm in VR: MiddleVR for Unity. http://www.imin-vr.com

23. Unity Technologies: Unity. http://unity3d.com

24. OpenSceneGraph. Version 3.1. http://www.openscenegraph.org

25. OGRE (Object-Oriented Graphics Rendering Engine). http://www.ogre3d.org

26. Oculus VR Inc.: Oculus Rift - Virtual Reality Headset for 3D Gaming. http://www.oculusvr.com/

27. Qt Project. http://qt-project.org/

28. Salzman, L.: ENet Reliable UDP networking library

29. G-Truc Creation: OpenGL Mathematics (GLM). http://glm.g-truc.net/

30. Cube. http://cubeengine.com

31. Kooima, R.: Generalized Perspective Projection (2008). http://csc.lsu.edu/~kooima/articles/genperspective/

32. Tanaka, H., Kato, K., Yamashita, E., Sumizawa, T., Zhou, Y., Yao, M., Iwasaki, K., Yoshimura, M., Tsukihara, T.: The Structure of Rat Liver Vault at 3.5 Angstrom Resolution. Science **323**, 384–388 (2009)

33. Toledo, R., Levy, B.: Extending the graphic pipeline with new GPU-accelerated primitives. In: 24th International gOcad Meeting, Nancy, France (2004)

34. Sigg, C., Weyrich, T., Botsch, M., Gross, M.: GPU-based ray-casting of quadratic surfaces. In: Proceedings of the 3rd Eurographics/IEEE VGTC Conference on Point-Based Graphics, pp. 59–65. Eurographics Association (2006)

35. Tarini, M., Cignoni, P., Montani, C.: Ambient Occlusion and Edge Cueing for Enhancing Real Time Molecular Visualization. IEEE Transactions on Visualization and Computer Graphics **12**, 1237–1244 (2006)

36. Chavent, M., Vanel, A., Tek, A., Levy, B., Robert, S., Raffin, B., Baaden, M.: GPU-accelerated atom and dynamic bond visualization using hyperballs: A unified algorithm for balls, sticks, and hyperboloids. Journal of Computational Chemistry **32**, 2924–2935 (2011)

37. Bagur, P.D., Shivashankar, N., Natarajan, V.: Improved Quadric Surface Impostors for Large Bio-molecular Visualization. In: Proceedings of the Eighth Indian Conference on Computer Vision, Graphics and Image Processing, pp. 33:1–33:8. ACM, New York (2012)

Stereoscopic-3D Vision to Improve Situational Awareness in Military Operations

Alessandro Zocco[1](✉), Salvatore Livatino[2], and Lucio Tommaso De Paolis[3]

[1] Product Innovation and Advanced EW Solutions, Elettronica S.p.A., Rome, Italy
alessandro.zocco@elt.it
[2] School of Engineering and Technology, University of Hertfordshire, Hatfield, UK
s.livatino@herts.ac.uk
[3] Department of Engineering for Innovation, University of Salento, Lecce, Italy
lucio.depaolis@unisalento.it

Abstract. Situational awareness is especially important for an operator when carrying forward Network Centric Operations. The networking of knowledgeable entities allows them to share information and collaborate to develop a common operational picture. Increasing the number of commanded platforms may easily become overwhelming for an operator because of information overload and this results in making wrong decisions which may have disastrous consequences. This paper proposes the use of Stereoscopic-3D to increase the situational awareness and improve understanding of modern battle spaces in military operations. The advantage of using S3D visualization is evaluated by several users who operate LOKI, a Command and Control system for Electronic Warfare developed by Elettronica S.p.A. Different tasks and types of threats are considered. The obtained results are presented, which show clear advantages when the operator's interface benefits from S3D viewing.

Keywords: Stereoscopic 3D Vision · Human Computer Interaction · Network Centric Operations · Command and Control System

1 Introduction

Gaining a detailed understanding of battle space is nowadays essential for the success of any military operation.

Network Centric Warfare (NCW) [1,3,24] is the best term to describe changes in the operating environment of military organizations, and the emerging capabilities that affect the ability to understand and influence this competitive space in the *information age*. NCW can be accomplished thanks to a network of geographically distributed forces, granting a flow of increased contents, quality and timeliness of information, building up a shared *situational awareness*. The current situation and the relevant information such as, location of own forces, reconnoitered opponent troops and facilities, commands and orders from the superiors, platforms' status, etc. This information is generally displayed visually on scaled maps with regional properties of the mission area.

© Springer International Publishing Switzerland 2014
L.T. De Paolis and A. Mongelli (Eds.): AVR 2014, LNCS 8853, pp. 351–362, 2014.
DOI: 10.1007/978-3-319-13969-2_26

Being the visualized information the result of several inputs conveyed to the same displayed area, a state of *information overload* is likely to occur. In particular, the information flow rate may be greater than the operator's processing rate, leading to the creation of a wrong mental model of the mission scenario. This results in making wrong decisions that may lead to catastrophic situations [22].

An example scenario is described in Fig. 1. We have different platforms that have the capability of sensing some limited areas and each one has a personal limited awareness of its proximity. In Fig. 1(a) each platform sends collected data to a specific platform, known as Command and Control (C2). The C2 has the special task of fusing data, in a manual or automatic way. In Fig. 1(b) we see that the C2 sends the fused data to the different platforms, and in this way they will share the same enhanced situational awareness. This process is continuously repeated during the military operation. What the example shows, it is a typical example of Network Centric Operations (NCO), an operational situation related to NCW. NCO can be successfully accomplished thanks to enhanced situational awareness. The user's interface (UI), used to display current situation and relevant information, plays a key role when designing the architecture of a C2.

This paper proposes the use of Stereoscopic-3D (S3D) visualization in NCW user's interfaces to increase situational awareness and reduce information overload. The solution proposed is assessed on realistic NCW scenarios. The performed study is quite unique as nothing similar has been found in the literature works.

Next sections introduce to S3D visualization (Sect. 2) and related works (Sect. 3). The proposed solution is then presented (Sect. 4) followed by a description of our experiments (Sect. 5). Conclusions are eventually drawn (Sect. 6).

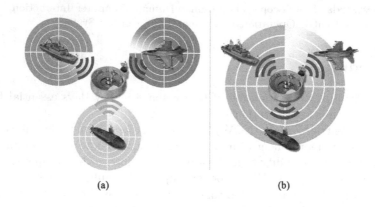

(a)   (b)

Fig. 1. Example of a Network Centric scenario

2   Stereoscopic 3D Visualization

S3D visualization artificially reproduces the mechanisms that govern human's binocular vision and it is therefore closer to the way we naturally see the world [7]. This aspect brings several benefits when compared to 2D monoscopic visualization, including greater comprehension and appreciation of presented visual inputs, perception of structure in visually complex scenes, spatial localization, motion judgment, concentration on different depth planes and perception of material surfaces. All these aspects help deliver a more vivid and realistic experience to a viewer, which explains why this technology is proposed in entertainment, e.g. in cinema and computer games [13,17]. S3D has also been proposed for serious applications as telerobotics and telemedicine [6,10,15,16]. S3D visualization presents also a number of drawbacks as it may cause eye strain, a double image perception, depth distortion, etc. [21], which may arise depending on the used technology.

Different technologies have been proposed to reproduce artificially stereoscopic visualization from 2D images. Stereoscopic visualization systems can be active, passive or autostereoscopic [4,16]. Passive stereo is a solution where light is differently filtered for the left and right eyes. This can be obtained in various ways. A well known approach is colour filtering, used in cinemas in the 1950s for the first time. Nowadays, the use of polarized filters (linear or circular) is very popular both in cinema and virtual reality applications. Passive stereo needs a specialized projector or two aligned low-cost projectors, an economical pair of polarized goggles and a silver screen. The active stereo requires active goggles synchronized over time with the a high-frequency projector (120 Hz) which alternately shows left and right eye images, therefore delivering to a user the stereoscopic viewing experience. The autostereoscopic approach allows for goggle-free stereo viewing but have restrictions on viewpoint observation and can typically be viewed by one observer at a time.

S3D can improve understanding of a modern battle space by enhancing depth perception and sense of presence, with clear advantage in terms of environment comprehension and fast-decision making.

3   Related Works

Several research groups have focused their activities on the design and development of new display paradigms and technologies for advanced information visualization.

Dragon [11] has been one of the first research projects in formalizing requirements for systems with the need to visualize a huge amount of information on tactical maps for real-time applications. A virtual environment for battlefield visualization has been realized with an architecture composed of interaction devices, display platforms and information sources.

Pettersson et al. [20] proposes a visualization environment based on the projection of four independent stereoscopic image pairs at full resolution upon a custom designed optical screen. This system suffers from apparent crosstalk between stereo images pairs.

Alexander et al. [2] presents some examples of augmented and virtual reality technologies, showing benefits and flaws, and the results of the experiments regard the evaluation of visibility and interactivity performances. This system however does not use S3D viewing.

Kapler and Wright [12] have developed a novel visualization technique for displaying and tracking events, objects and activities, within a combined temporal and geospatial display. The events are represented within an X, Y, T coordinate space, in which the X and Y plane shows flat geographic space and the T-axis represents time into the future and past. This technique is not adequate for an immersive 3D virtual environment experience because it uses an axis to describe the time evolution, which constrains the spatial representation on a flat surface. The altitude information, that is an important information in avionic scenarios, cannot be displayed. Nonetheless, it is remarkable the finding that by splitting geographical and logical information (e.g., health of a platform) the usability of the system can be enhanced.

4 Proposed Investigation

This paper proposes a new visualization system for NCW scenarios, (including displaying symbols and logical information on tactical maps), which exploits S3D visualization to increase the level of immersion of a viewer and reduce information overload. This is expected to improve operator's performance in terms of scene comprehension and decision-making.

4.1 High-Level Architecture of LOKI

The system proposed for experimentation is a S3D UI, which is part of *LOKI* a C2 system for Electronic Warfare (EW) consisting of a set of potentially heterogeneous platforms (e.g., air, surface, subsurface) with on-board sensors and actuators in the domain of electronics defense. Figure 2 shows the high-level architectural view of LOKI.

The LOKI Core component continuously executes an advanced multi-sensor data fusion process on the data retrieved from cooperating systems. Once these data are carefully fused, the system is capable to infer new important information such as a better localization of emitters and countermeasures strategy. This information is transferred to the LOKI HCI (Human-Computer Interface) using a communication middleware based on Data Distribution Service (DDS) paradigm [5].

The HCI Manager component provides a persistence mechanism to decouple the presentation layer from the core application logic. It is responsible for the communication with the core (i.e., receiving input data by the core and sending operator commands to the core) and for the translation of received data in a model understandable by the presentation layer.

The HCI Display component contains the elements that implement and display the UI and manage user interaction. It provides a high definition view of a realistic geographic environment. Platforms are positioned on the scene according to their geographic coordinates and are represented according to the Common Warfighting Symbology MIL-STD-2525C standard [18].

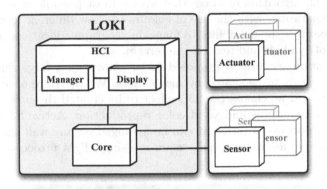

Fig. 2. LOKI architecture in the large

4.2   Design Choices for the UI

The UI has been designed with high modularity applying UI Design Patterns (UIDP) [8]. These patterns are structural and behavioral features that make applications more useful and usable. The main view of LOKI HCI is an application of the *Dashboard* pattern. EW scenario is displayed into a single tactical presentation updated regularly. *Data Brushing* pattern is used to offer a rich form of interactive data exploration. Multiple views of the same data are linked and synchronized so that certain manipulation (e.g., zooming, panning, selection) to one view are simultaneously shown in the others. According to *News Stream* pattern, data from different sources are dynamically updated and combined into one single stream. User can keep up with a news stream easily, since the latest items reliably appear on top with no effort.

In addition, structural patterns *Decorator* and *Composite* are used: the former allows to dynamically add properties (e.g., borders around a window) or behaviors (e.g., scrolling) to any component of the interface; the latter allows to compose interfaces as tree structures, to show part-whole structures, and lets to equally handle single objects and compositions [9].

Figure 3 shows a sample of the interface, built up in two different layers, as inspired by the research of Kapler and Wright [12]. A 3D terrain map, in the bottom part of the screen, is used to show both features of the selected terrain and geographic data of the elements of the scenario (e.g., real position, past track) and for elements that are not grounded, a transparent curtain is used to indicate their altitude. A parallel layer, that hosts the so-called logical view of the scenario, displayed above is used to represent other relevant non-geographic information (e.g., health status, lethality); it can be also used to visualize connections between the elements and to show elements that are outside the area of the operator is currently viewing in the geographic layer below. The geographical reference is maintained through connections between the two layers, using an algorithm of forces that avoids most possible crossing between lines. This separation, with the use of colours to show different levels of alerts, grants the operator the possibility to focus on geographic locations avoiding the overloading of symbols and text on the terrain.

The operation scenario is proposed to be shown on a large screen surface because view needs to be shared by many users. We therefore opted for a wall screen display and we choose the S3D effect to be created through active stereo because of its brightness and vivid color reproduction. Active S3D projection is also a good portable solution: it can be arranged on any wall and, compared with the polarized alternative, only requires a single light projector.

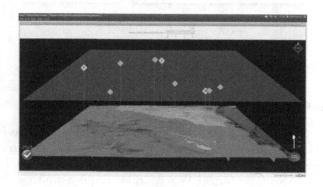

Fig. 3. Visualization of EW entities with their geographic location

5 Experimental Design and Test Procedure

5.1 Hardware and Software Choices

The system used for the experimentation illustrated in Fig. 4 includes:

- PC equipped with a Nvidia Quadro graphics card;
- Digital Light Processing (DLP) projector with a WUXGA (1920x1200px) resolution and a brightness of 7000 ANSI lumens;
- special eyewear comprising two infrared controlled Liquid Crystal Display (LCD) light shutters working in synchronization with the projector;
- large free wall surface (12m^2).

The simulator, where the scenario is developed and executed, is an integration with Commercial-Off-The-Shelf (COTS) products and proprietary software and is based on the principles of distributed and live simulation [23].

The software has been developed in Java language, using an OpenGL binding in order to talk to the OpenGL runtime installed on the underlying operating system. We worked on stereoscopic visualization parameters (accommodation and convergence) to obtain a well appearing negative screen-parallax, (shown 3D objects also appear in front of the wall). The Fig. 5 illustrates the achieved S3D effect.

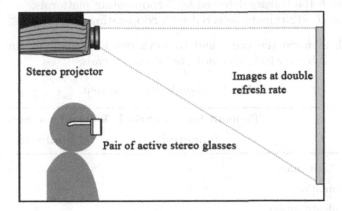

Fig. 4. Active 3D display system

Fig. 5. Binocular fusion of the stereo pairs

5.2 Usability Evaluation

The experimentation took place at the ELT facilities in Rome, where 12 members of the armed forces of different countries were asked to supervise a relatively big area of sea, the Strait of Sicily, where there is a large volume of traffic, generated by different types of vessels. The experimental trials were run using either 2D or S3D visualization mode.

Two realistic EW scenarios were simulated in order to evaluate effectiveness of S3D under different situations of information load:

- *Scenario I*: 100 threats detected by 3 cooperating platforms;
- *Scenario II*: 512 threats detected by 5 cooperating platforms.

On each scenario the users had to work out a solution to the five tasks described in Table 1 within the indicated time intervals.

Table 1. Scheduled tasks timeout

Task	Timeout for Scenario I [minutes]	Timeout for Scenario II [minutes]
Distance Estimation	1	3
DOA Estimation	1	3
Threats Identification	2	4
Threats Classification	2	4
Threats Correlation	3	5

The evaluation study was a within-subject evaluation designed according to the recommendations given in [14,19]. Test-users were experts in C2 systems with no experiences in using S3D, and an age between 32 and 46 (average 38.1). All participants executed all tasks of scenarios I and II using both 2D and S3D visualization. The assigned task and viewing situation (either mono or stereo) was scheduled according to a pre-determined order to counterbalance effects of fatigue and learning effects.

In order to measure operational behaviors, the following quantitative measurements were automatically acquired during the usability study:

- *Completion Time*: the time employed to complete all tasks within a scenario using a specific viewing mode (either mono or stereo);
- *Number of Failures*: the number of failed tasks in a scenario using a specific viewing mode (either mono or stereo).

In addition the following qualitative data, referring to the users' experience, were collected using questionnaires and interviews at the end of the test:

- *Depth Impression*: the extent of the perceived depth when observing the mission area;

- *Sense of Presence*: the sense of immersion and isolation from the surrounding worlds;
- *Situational Awareness*: the perception of the EW scenario elements and the comprehension of their meaning;
- *Viewing Comfort*: the level of tiredness and eye strain.

5.3 Results Analysis

The results of our experimentation are shown in Fig. 6 and Fig. 7 through bar diagrams for the descriptive statistics (mean value) and numerical figures shown right under each diagram for inferential statistics (Student's T distribution p-values). The (green) framed p-values indicate statistical significant result (p-value below 0.05).

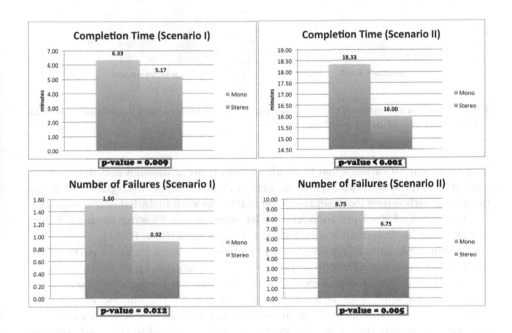

Fig. 6. Quantitative measurements: descriptive (mean values) and inferential statistics (Student's T distribution p-values)

The effect of stereo viewing on Completion Time and Number of Failures is significant on both scenarios (all p-values are below 0.05). This means that under stereoscopic visualization our users successfully completed more tasks in less time than under monoscopic viewing.

Under stereoscopic visualization (users') Depth Impression is significantly higher than under monoscopic viewing (p = 0.002). In particular, under complex EW scenarios monocular depth cues may not help and become ambiguous.

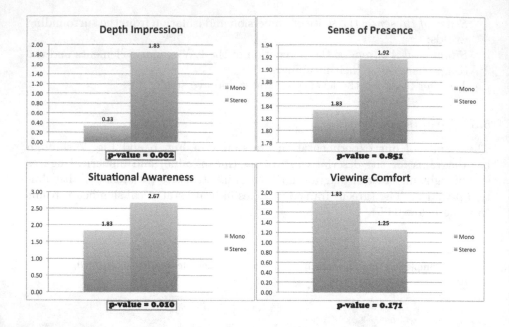

Fig. 7. Qualitative measurements: descriptive (mean values) and inferential statistics (Student's T distribution p-values)

This is a clear situation when binocular vision is an advantage and it allows for correctly estimating spatial relations, also in cases of minor discrepancies such as occurring with screen icons representing platforms with installed active emitters.

The Sense of Presence increases under stereoscopic viewing as mean value, however the improvement under S3D is not significant (p = 0.851).

A higher Situational Awareness is perceived by the majority of participants under S3D visualization. The improvement is significant (p = 0.010). Participants claimed that comprehension of the mission area was better and faster under S3D viewing. This is a fundamental aspect for the success of the military operation. The benefit of the improved comprehension is also shown by our quantitative results (figure 6). The best results are obtained in the most complex Scenario II, where users made less mistakes under S3D compared to 2D viewing (they are down of two errors as average, so obtaining a mean value of 6.75 versus the 8.75 under 2D viewing). The completion time is also reduced (16 minutes employed under S3D versus 18.33 minutes under 2D viewing).

There is no significant difference in Viewing Comfort between stereo and mono visualization (p = 0.171). This is a good results and we believe that it helped to keep the amount of screen parallax to a minimum value (experimentally estimated). Interestingly almost half of our users commented that they find more comfortable not wearing any device. Considering that NCO can last for several days, more tests should be performed in order to evaluate the long-term strain.

6 Conclusion

Inadequate situational awareness in NCW may lead an operator to make wrong choices with potential disastrous outcomes. Situational awareness is challenged by information overload. This makes the UI a key element in the design and development of the C2 systems for NCO.

This paper proposed an innovative UI that benefits from S3D visualization. We analyzed the role played by S3D visualization (compared to 2D visualization) in increasing situational awareness and reducing information overload, through an evaluation study where operator's performance is measured on a number of factors against quantitative variables (completion time and number of failures) and qualitative variables (depth impression, sense of presence, situational awareness, viewing comfort).

The results of the evaluation showed very clear trends with our users performing significantly better under S3D viewing in terms of completion time, number of failures, depth impression and situational awareness. Non significant difference were noticed in terms of sense of presence and viewing comfort.

S3D viewing is still sometime criticized because of the wearing and setup requirements (e.g. 3D glasses, projector system). Nonetheless it seems to be a burden our users are happy to bear because of the significant performance improvement brought by S3D visualization.

References

1. Alberts, D.S., Garstka J.J., Stein F.P.: Network Centric Warfare: Developing and Leveraging Information Superiority. CCRP Publication Series (1999)
2. Alexander, T., Renkewitz, H., Conradi, J.: Applicability of Virtual Environments as C4ISR Displays. In: Virtual Media for Military Applications (NATO HFM-136) workshop, New York (2006)
3. Braulinger, T.K.: Network Centric Warfare Implementation and Assessment. Master's Thesis, U.S. Army Command and General Staff College (2005)
4. Cyganek, B., Siebert, J.P.: An Introduction to 3D Computer Vision Techniques and Algorithms. John Wiley & Sons, UK (2009)
5. Data Distribution Service Portal. http://portals.omg.org/dds/
6. Dey, D., Gobbi, D.G., Slomka, P.J., Surry, K.J.M., Peters, T.M.: Automatic Fusion of Freehand Endoscopic Brain Images to Three-Dimensional Surfaces: Creating Stereoscopic Panoramas. IEEE Transaction on Medical Imaging 21(1), 23–30 (2002)
7. Drascic, D.: Skill Acquisition and Task Performance in Teleoperation using Monoscopic and Stereoscopic Video Remote Viewing. In: Human Factors and Ergonomics Society Annual Meeting, 35(19), pp. 1367–1371, San Francisco (1991)
8. Feng, S., Liu M., Wan J.: An agilely adaptive User Interface based on Design Pattern. In: IEEE 6th International Conference on Intelligent Systems Design and Applications, Jinan (2006)
9. Gamma, E., Helm, R., Johnson, R., Vlissides, J.: Design Patterns: Elements of Reusable Object-Oriented Software. Addison-Wesley, Massachussets (2005)
10. Intuitive Surgical. http://www.intuitivesurgical.com

11. Julier S., King, R., Colbert, B., Durbin, J., Rosenblum, L.: The Software Architecture of a Real-Time Battlefield Visualization Virtual Environment. In: IEEE Proceedings of Virtual Reality, Houston (1999)
12. Kapler, T., Wright, W.: Geotime Information Visualization. In: IEEE Symposium on Information Visualization, 4(2), pp. 136–146, Austin (2004)
13. Lipton, L.: The Last Great Innovation: The Stereoscopic Cinema. SMPTE Motion Imaging Journal **116**(11–12), 518–523 (2007)
14. Livatino, S., Koeffel C.: Handbook for Evaluation Studies in Virtual Reality. In: Proceedings of IEEE International Conference on Virtual Environments, Human Computer Interface and Measurement Systems (VECIMS), Ostuni (2007)
15. Livatino, S., Muscato, G., Sessa, S., Neri, V.: Depth-enhanced mobile robot teleguide based on laser images. Mechatronics **20**(7), 739–750 (2010)
16. Livatino, S., De Paolis, L., D'Agostino, M., Zocco, A., Agrimi, A., De Santis, A., Bruno, L.V., Lapresa, M.: Stereoscopic Visualization and 3D Technologies in Medical Endoscopic Teleoperation. IEEE Transactions on Industrial Electronics, Accepted for publication (To appear 2014)
17. Mahoney, N., Oikonomou, A., Wilson, D.: Stereoscopic 3D in Video Games: A Review of Current Design Practices and Challenges. In: 16th IEEE International Conference on Computer Games. Louisville (2011)
18. MIL-STD-2525C. http://www.mapsymbs.com/ms2525c.pdf
19. Nielson, J.: Usability Engineering. Morgan Kaufmann, San Francisco (1993)
20. Pettersson, L.W., Spak, U., Seipel S.: Collaborative 3D Visualizations of Geo-Spatial Information for Command and Control. In: International Conference of the Swedish Eurographics Chapter (SIGRAD), Gvle (2004)
21. Sexton, I., Surman, P.: Stereoscopic and Autostereoscopic Display Systems. IEEE Signal Processing Magazine **16**(3), 85–89 (1999)
22. Shanker, T., Richtel, M.: In New Military, Data Overload can be Deadly. The New York Times. New York (2011). http://www.nytimes.com/2011/01/17/technology/17brain.html
23. Sindico, A., Cannone, D., Tortora, S., Italiano, G.F., Naldi, M.: Distributed Simulation of Electronic Warfare Command and Control Scenarios. In: Symposium on Navy Operational Research and Logistics (SPOLM). Rio de Janeiro (2012)
24. U.S. Navy: Copernicus… Forward C4I for the 21st Century. Office of Chief of Naval Operations (OPNAV). USA (1995). http://www.navy.mil/navydata/policy/coperfwd.txt

Roll and Pitch Estimation Using Visual Horizon Recognition

Silvio Del Pizzo$^{(\boxtimes)}$, Salvatore Troisi, Antonio Angrisano,
and Salvatore Gaglione

Department of Science and Technology, Parthenope University of Naples, Naples, Italy
{silvio.delpizzo,salvatore.troisi,antonio.angrisano,
salvatore.gaglione}@uniparthenope.it
http://pang.uniparthenope.it/

Abstract. In guidance and automated control system, especially for unmanned vehicle, attitude determination is an important element. Generally this parameter is provided by sensors like INS (Inertial Navigation Systems), but it can be also estimated with a single camera that "looks" the horizon. This work presents the project of an embedded solution that uses visual information, captured by a consumer camera, to estimate the vehicle attitude. The system is designed to be mounted on board of a ship or a sail boat, in order to record the roll and pitch angles for safety purpose or to be used for real time application (e.g. during a regatta to overlap the values of the boat attitude with video output coming from a camera mounted on the masthead framing the race field).

Keywords: Photogrammetry · Computer vision · Orientation · Low-cost · INS · Attitude estimation

1 Introduction

The recent developments in computer vision and wide availability of low cost hardware, that is getting smaller and smaller, are a consolidate team able to occupy a main role in any scientific and technologic field, from medicine to engineer. The navigation is not an exception, indeed, even if the technology is not completely ready, it's getting to start the employ of artificial vision systems to support the traditional navigation systems e.g. in indoor navigation for mobile autonomous robot [1, 2], in terrestrial navigation [2] and aerial navigation [3, 4]. Such vision-based systems are very lightweight therefore it's easy to mount them on board of unmanned aerial vehicle, whose typical payload is extremely low.

Usually, every unmanned aerial vehicle (UAV) uses a built-in video camera for surveillance purpose or for anti-collision control through telemetry, but rarely it's employed for photogrammetric or remote-sensing surveys, because it's better to mount a specific camera for such purposes. Numerous authors employed a vision based navigation system on board UAV to extract attitude and velocity parameters by the monocular camera [1, 3, 5, 6].

© Springer International Publishing Switzerland 2014
L.T. De Paolis and A. Mongelli (Eds.): AVR 2014, LNCS 8853, pp. 363–380, 2014.
DOI: 10.1007/978-3-319-13969-2_27

In this work a new methodology to calculate the roll and pitch angles between a reference and a generic attitude is proposed, considering the single frame of a video as a gnomonic projection.

The paper describes the system setup used to evaluate the performance and reliability of the methodology, comparing the obtained results with the solutions of two external systems: photogrammetric and INS ones.

1.1   Related Works

Reliable estimation of "ego-motion" (trajectory and attitude of a moving body) is a fundamental task in several disciplines, especially in autonomous navigation for unmanned vehicles. Many authors employ Vision Navigation System (VNS) in their applications, even if this approach is still a challenging problem with many aspects to be explored. Specifically the use of horizon detection for attitude determination is an old idea: Todorovic et al. [4] implement a computer vision solution, based on horizon tracking, for flight stability and autonomy of MAVs (Micro Air Vehicles).

Other research groups, as well as single authors, have ongoing worked to this topic. Numerous approaches are able to detect the horizon with unsupervised systems. One of such approaches is based on the clustering of the image in two parts: the ground (or sea) and sky regions. The horizon line can be computed optimizing the clustering with statistical hypothesis [5-8]; another method uses a circular mask applied on the image that is invariant to the angles between horizon and x- axis of the image [9]. Another approach detects the horizon from a set of straight lines attained through the use of a pre-processed image followed by the Hough transform [3, 10, 11].

Currently, VNSs are employed to totally estimate the UAV ego-motion using known methods and algorithms based on Structure from Motion (SfM). The planar degeneracy of the scenario is often assumed, because it is rather typical, for UAV to fly at a high altitude, where the irregularities of the earth's surface become almost negligible [8]. The SfM resolution based on epipolar geometry is inherently ambiguous for the above-mentioned scenario [12], indeed the planar degeneracy leads to a solution with one degree of freedom. Such problem can be solved using a constrain on intrinsic camera parameters and by incorporating the co-planarity condition in the algorithm [13, 14].

However, the SfM classical algorithms don't fit to real time applications, such as UAV navigation requires, because they need a large base line between two consecutive acquisitions to obtain reliable results, hence they cannot be used to estimate the vehicle attitude with high frame rate [8].

Many good results have been recently reached using SLAM (*Simultaneous Localization And Mapping*) techniques for UAVs [15, 16]. Such works have highlighted how the ego-motion estimation of an aerial vehicle, and simultaneously the three-dimensional (3-D) layout of the scene employing multi-images triangulation methods, is achievable. Thanks to the recent GPU (*Graphics Processing Unit*), these methods reach the results in real-time (or near real time). The use of multi-image approach can solve the ambiguity of planar scenes, with the drawback of errors and computational complexity increase, and therefore the requirement of a powerful hardware.

All technics and approaches described above focus mostly on aerial and terrestrial navigation, where the unmanned vehicles prevail. This paper shows a new application for marine uses:

- for safety purpose, the data can be included in a classical black-box recorder;
- for near-shore single-beam hydrographic survey performed with low cost systems, the attitude obtained can be used to correct the unavoidable errors due to roll and pitch angles;
- for augmented reality purpose, the horizon detection and the obtained roll and pitch can be overlaid on the display system to provide extensive information.

2   Attitude Parameters Extraction by Single Camera

The most common sensors to measure the attitude are the Inertial Measurement Units (IMU, accelerometers and gyroscopic rate sensors), that have the advantages of high-rate and relatively small latency, but they are subject to significant drift (or significant cost). In outdoor scenario the inertial sensors are often aided by GNSS (Global Navigation Satellite System) sensors, that coupled with a Kalman Filter is able to provide a stable solution [17, 18].

The proposed vision system allows extracting a stable and precise solutions but with low frame-rate because it is characterized by high computational complexity; further, the system precision is strictly correlated with the precision of horizon recognition and with the knowledge of intrinsic camera parameters.

The proposed methodology can be divided in two distinctive phases:

1. Automatic Horizon detection;
2. Roll and Pitch computation.

During the first one the algorithm finds a straight line in the image that represents the marine horizon, by employing methods and procedures well-known in computer vision.

In the second phase the roll and pitch angles between a reference horizon and target horizon are evaluated .

2.1   Automatic Horizon Recognition

Many horizon line detection methods for any scenario are known [19, 20], they can be divided into three categories:

- Segmentation and Classification based algorithm;
- 2D Edge Detection and Hough transform based algorithm;
- *1D Edge Detection and Least Square* based algorithm.

The *segmentation and classification* based algorithm employs a clustering method to find two zones within the image: sky-ground or sky-sea separated by a line, which will be considered the detected horizon line. The optimal solution can be achieved with several clustering methods: *Otzu Segmentation* [21], *Recursive Intensity Clustering* [22], *k-means Clustering* [23, 24], *Regional Covariance Clustering* [6], etc. These methods can accurately detect the horizon line and they are able to be used in various scenarios; on the other hand, the high computational complexity makes them not suitable for real-time applications with a high frame rate. In marine or in planar scenario the horizon line is typically straight, the Hough transform allows to detect it in the image. The *2D Edge Detection and Hough transform* method is based on sequential process that can be summarized in two basic steps:

1) edge detection [25] on pre-processed image;
2) application of the Hough transform [26] to edges map.

The entire computational complexity of the method is strictly correlated to the density of Hough space.

Also in *1D Edge Detection and Least Square method* the edge detection is a fundamental phase, indeed this approach locates the position of the maximal local edge in the vertical direction for each column of the image. The optimal horizon line passes through the maximal local edge detected, and it can be identified using the least-square method [19]. This method has a low computational complexity but many outlier can be identified as maximal local edge, for this reason it is useful to perform a robust data snooping.

The approach presented in this work employs a customized version of 2D edge detection and Hough transform. The identification of the horizon starts with a pre-processing of the image. The image to be processed (initial image) will be a linear combination between R band of RGB space and Y band of CMY space, so an a priori RGB to CMY conversion is performed.

In order to reduce the possibility of false horizons, a smoothing convolution algorithm [27] is applied on the initial image followed by the equalization of the histogram. This pre-processing is very important because allows to delete the noise present on the image, even if an hard smoothing on the image risks to blur the horizon and consequently the result could be not precise. Figure 1 shows the difference between the same image and the equivalent edge map with pre-processing (on left side) and without it (on right side).

Canny edge detector [25] with automatic thresholding method is applied on smoothed image; the result is a black and white image called "edge map". Further it is necessary to compute the image gradient in order to establish an integrity parameter, as follows. All the horizon lines are usually characterized by a great image gradient magnitude and especially by a constant values of its direction along the entire line, as shown in the figure 2.

A robust method for detecting straight line segments in an edge map is through the Hough transform algorithm [28]. The method is based on accumulation matrix.

Fig. 1. Above are the original and filtered image, below their respective edge-map

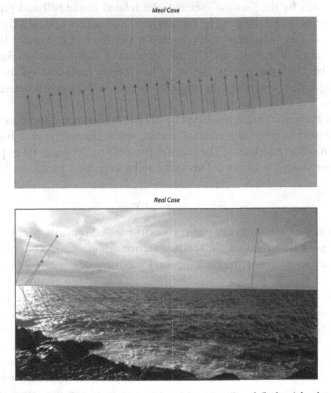

Fig. 2. Gradient directions along the ideal (above) and real (below) horizon line

Accumulation is performed using a discrete voting kernel defined by user. During this accumulation phase each pixel votes for several line parameter candidates, determined by the width of the voting kernel. Once the accumulation is completed, the list of line parameters for each edge pixel voted is reviewed, and the set of parameters with the twenty strongest overall votes in the list is selected as ideal candidates to horizon line.

In many instances, the strongest response (the longest line presents in the scene) from the Hough transform is taken as horizon detected [3, 5, 10]; this is true only for UAV navigation in planar scene, but in marine scenario several boats could be present or an irregular skyline due to coastline could be seen. Furthermore, the sea movements generate a dense random noise, which could create false horizons. For all these reasons the proposed algorithm chooses the line with the less values variation of image gradient angle, among the twenty possible candidate lines.

2.2 Algorithm for Roll and Pitch Evaluation

The image processing presented in the precedent sub-section is capable of detecting the horizon line in the image. This can be considered like a sensor front-end: the measure obtained by the "sensor" needs to be related to the roll and pitch angles of the camera and hence of the vehicle. Of course, if the camera optical axis is parallel to the longitudinal axis of vehicle, the vertical shift of the horizon in the image is connected with the pitch movements. On the other hand, its rotation is related with roll movements; but both parameters cannot to be directly measured on the image. The developed algorithm computes the attitude difference between a reference horizon and any other.

Generally, the real world is modelled by 3D Euclidean space where every point can be expressed with a three-dimensional vector, while the image is a bi-dimensional representation of the real world. The transfer from 3D to 2D space takes place when it is taken a photo with the camera. This step can be expressed by the projection matrix P:

$$x = PX \tag{1}$$

The projection matrix joins the camera's extrinsic and intrinsic parameters; the first describe the position of camera in space (exterior orientation), while the second are those necessary to modeling the basic internal geometry of the camera (interior orientation) [29].

It is useful to look at the interior orientation of a camera as its state of calibration; so the cameras may be distinguished in: calibrated camera, when the intrinsic parameters are known, or un-calibrated camera when they are completely unknown.

The calibrated camera has the great advantage to preserving the straight lines, furthermore the accurate knowledge of intrinsic parameters allows to calculate precise values of both attitude angles. In this work it's supposed an approach with calibrated camera: several calibration methods are developed to obtain the intrinsic parameters of an un-calibrated camera [30, 31].

An image is a bi-dimensional projective representation of real world and the angles are not preserved (principal point excluded) [12], for this reason it's not possible measure the angle directly on the image.

For a rigorous approach the image is regarded as gnomonic azimuthal map [32]. In cartography, the projection is a mapping of the Earth on planar surface; the gnomonic map is obtained by projecting a point onto a plane tangent to the globe looking from the center of the Earth. Let's assume the camera frame as projection plane, and a sphere centered in perspective center with radius equal to calibrated focal length as representing sphere (figure 3).

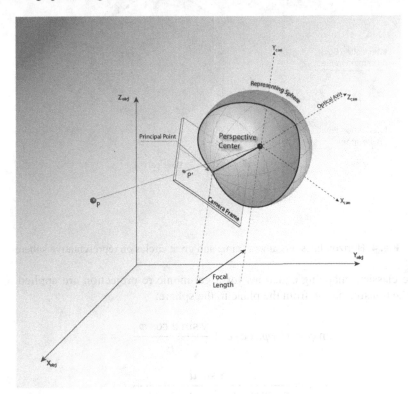

Fig. 3. Basic geometry in a tilted image. The representative sphere is centered in perspective center with radius equal to the calibrated focal length.

As shown in figure 3 the point of tangency is always the principal point, because this belongs to the frame plane and the sphere surface as well.

It's then defined a reference grid system on the sphere in accordance with the reference horizon, more precisely the reference horizon is projected as great circle on the representing sphere, this is considered as "equator". The great circle perpendicular to the "equator" that lies on the principal point is considered as "prime meridian" (figure 4). It's also defined a coordinate system centered in perspective center with z-axis perpendicular to the equatorial plane, x-axis which passes through the "prime meridian", the y-axis is set accordingly with a left-hand system.

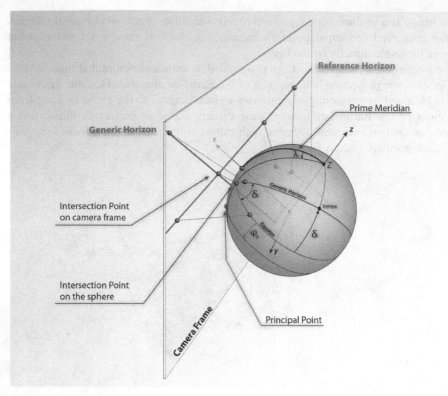

Fig. 4. Horizon lines on camera frame and great circles on representative sphere

The classical mapping equations for a gnomonic re-projection are applied to perform the transformation from the plane to the sphere:

$$\sin \varphi = \sin \varphi_0 \cos d + \frac{y \sin d \cos \varphi_0}{\rho}$$

$$\tan \lambda = \frac{x \sin d}{\rho \cos \varphi_0 \cos d - y \sin d \sin \varphi_0}$$

(2)

where

$$\rho = \sqrt{x^2 + y^2}$$
$$d = tan^{-1}(\rho)$$

A generic point **P** on the image plane with image coordinates x,y is re-projected on the sphere with spherical coordinates elevation and azimuth (φ, λ). In equations (2) φ_0 is the point of tangency elevation (principal point), ρ is the Euclidean distance onto image plane between the principal point and **P**, finally d is the angle between the optical axis and the vector perspective center – **P**.

Appling the equations (2) for two points lying on the generic horizon line a great circle on the sphere is defined together with its node azimuth λ_i and vertex elevation δ (figure 4) [33]. Starting from these last two parameters the roll ϕ and pitch angles θ can be attained by the following equations:

$$\phi = \delta_i \cos \lambda_i$$

$$\theta = \delta_i \sin \lambda_i \tag{3}$$

It is so evident that the roll and pitch angles cannot be directly measured on the image because the gnomonic projection is a conformal map only in the tangent point that, in our approach, has been chosen coincident with the principal point of the image.

3 Experimentation Approach

In order to evaluate the results obtained by means of the developed approach, several static trials have been carried out. This has permitted to validate the method and to estimate the achievable accuracies and precisions.

A qualitative analyses of results has been performed using the comparison with a low-cost INS while a more precise methodology (photogrammetry) is considered as reference for error analysis. The INS solution has been chosen as an alternative to the proposed horizon solution, investigating their characteristics and hypothesizing their integration.

3.1   Field Test Description

The equipment used for the proposed method performance evaluation was composed by two plates, on the top of which a set of photogrammetric circular targets was attached. The high plate is movable, whereas the plate located further down is fixed (figure 5). The static plate allows to give the photogrammetric acquisitions in the same reference frame. The movable plate is able to assume several attitudes; a locking device blocks it in a specific position, in order to fasten the sensors on it and to observe their behaviors.

On top of highest plate were placed: a camera Nikon D7100 for recording a video of the horizon, an X-Sens MTi-G used as low-cost sensor for INS measurements and a steel calibrated bar. A laptop was used for data acquisition and video recording.

In the first trial, the attitude angles between the upper plate and fixed one were detected by above-mentioned methodologies. Such quantities are considered as reference for the subsequent trials. Afterwards the movable plate was rotated and locked in several casual positions forming considerable angles of roll and pitch with respect to reference position.

Fig. 5. System setup for the different sensors and definition of coordinate system

3.2   Photogrammetry Approach

Generally, motion capture systems allow to obtain 3D trajectory of signalized points with high precision. Such systems imply the use of two or more synchronized digital recording devices managed by the photogrammetric algorithms [34].

Photogrammetry is a technique for obtaining information about the position, size and shape of an object by measuring images of it instead of by measuring it directly [35]. The results of a photogrammetry survey is a 3D position of generic point recognizable on at least two photos. In photogrammetry the position of a point in space is commonly defined by a three dimensional co-ordinate system. Origin scale and orientation may be arbitrary defined.

In this work photogrammetric techniques were employed to determine the precise coordinates of the circular target attached on the top of the two plates. A set of convergent images was acquired with calibrated camera for each trial. The lowest and fixed plate allows to define the same reference frame for all photogrammetric acquisitions, whereas the accurate scale is defined by the calibrated bar located on the higher plate.

Procrustes transformation method has been used to evaluate the attitude difference between the first and the subsequent trials. Of course, only the targets hold onto the highest plate have been interested by the transformation. The transform residuals are considered as figure of merit for the attitude accuracy.

Figure 6 shows the bundle rays of the camera station network in two different trials.

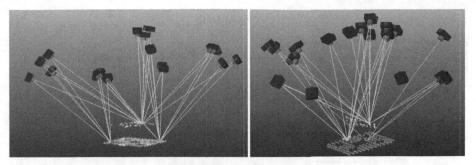

Fig. 6. Resulting bundles camera station network for two trials

3.3   INS with ZUPT Approach

The inertial navigation systems (INS) are self-contained and their performance is independent from the environment, conversely to GNSS. Moreover INS are more accurate in the short term, they can supply data continuously with very high rate and they provide all the navigation states, i.e. position, velocity and attitude. The main drawback of an INS is the performance degradation with time; in order to bound the errors to an acceptable level, regular updates are necessary and GNSS measurements are often used to this purpose. ZUPT (Zero Velocity Update) technique can be also used to bound INS errors; it consists of updating INS data by exploiting the information that the mobile object is static. ZUPT is often used in vehicular navigation, by stopping the car at regular intervals for some minutes, or in pedestrian application where the INS is placed on the foot and is at rest during the stance phase of the gait cycle [36].

In this work the adopted inertial sensors are based on MEMS (Micro-Electro-Mechanical Systems) technology, characterized by lightness, small size and low cost but with poor performance, hence the error would rapidly increase without applying a suitable technique to limit its growth. A static data collection has been performed and so it has been possible to apply the ZUPT technique for the whole data set, avoiding the typical performance degradation of INS solution. In figure 7 the scheme of the ZUPT technique is shown. The IMU (Inertial Measurement Unit) block include a triad of accelerometers and gyros, whose outputs (accelerations and angular rates) are processed by a navigation block which implements the inertial mechanization equations. The difference between the ZUPT and the INS velocities feeds the Kalman Filter in order to compute the corrections to navigation states and the calibration parameters, i.e. sensors bias and scale factor.

3.4   Horizon Approach

A Nikon D7100 reflex camera was used as video recording device; the video file is sent as input data to a software developed ad-hoc in Matlab environment able to extract automatically the horizon line and to evaluate the roll and pitch in every frame.

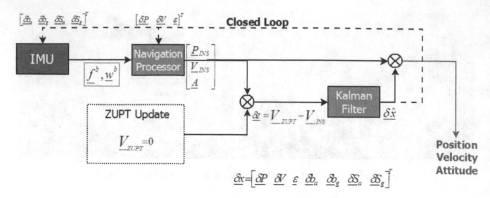

Fig. 7. ZUPT Scheme

As preliminary operation, reference horizon has to be accurately detected, and several frames are necessary to define it and its precision.

Statistical parameters for the reference horizon test are computed by the software, so as to obtain the attitude accuracy. In order to speed-up the testing and the further evaluation and recording operations a user-friendly interface was developed (figure 8).

A simple integrity value, based either on the gradient magnitude and its orientation along the horizon line, allows to assume if a line is to be considered as horizon or not.

Afterward the roll an pitch angles are estimated using the over-mentioned method. When a generic horizon is corrupted (the integrity value is zero) the attitude computation is skipped.

4   Results, Comparisons and Analyses

In order to validate the implemented method, several tests have been carried out in two different environments:

- clear scenario, data were acquired during a winter sunset with a good visibility and few annoying components, on the other hand, between the beginning and the end of trials the environment luminosity is critically changed (figure 9a);
- hostile scenario, data were acquired during a spring day with the presence of numerous and strong spoilers (figure 9b).

4.1   Clear Scenario

The video tape of test was acquired during a winter day, in order to have a clear scenario with only few trouble elements; furthermore the sunset moment was chosen to test the algorithm for high presence of light reflection on the sea waves.

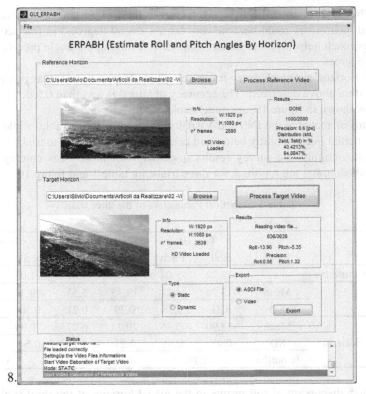

Fig. 8. User interface for evaluation and recording of attitude angles

(a)   *(b)*

Fig. 9. On the left the clear scenario, on the right the hostile scenario

A calibrated Nikon D800 camera with a 35 mm lens was used for the photogrammetric survey. All the acquisitions are composed by a dataset of at least 12 convergent images. The mean precision of the overall root mean square points for all acquisitions is 0.071 mm, that implies a potential accuracy on the angle computation less than 0.05 degrees. The results provided by this method were taken as reference, due to the high accuracy achieved.

The INS sensors are MEMS-based, therefore their performance degrade continuously and their errors could become very large (several degrees) in few seconds. The ZUPT approach helps to limit the aforesaid drift, bringing the angle precisions to less than 0.5 degrees.

In the Horizon approach every frame recorded (25 per second) was processed with the algorithm above described. The accuracy obtained is less than 0.5 degrees and the results, as shown in figure 10, are quite stable.

In terms of accuracy the INS and Visual solutions are comparable, while the precision the inertial one is slightly better and is more stable from trial to trial.

The photogrammetric survey results, together with those ones coming from the other methodologies are reported, for three trials, in table 1 and figure 10.

Table 1. Statistical Parameters of the three trials

		Trial 01		Trial 02		Trial 03	
	[deg]	Roll	Pitch	Roll	Pitch	Roll	Pitch
Photogrammetry		-13.79	-5.04	20.47	5.61	-21.05	-7.50
INS	Mean	-13.74	-4.81	19.35	5.53	-19.35	-6.93
	SD	0.31	0.38	0.29	0.21	0.30	0.35
Visual Horizon	Mean	-13.90	-5.35	20.24	6.07	-20.99	-7.25
	SD	0.48	0.81	1.21	1.21	0.54	2.12
	% outlier	1.19		4.49		3.23	

The high dispersion of roll results in the visual horizon of the third trial is due to the above mentioned condition of light reflections of the sun close to its sunset (figure 11). It is also evident that the difference in the mean results between photogrammetry and INS increase with the growing of the roll angle.

The relatively high values of standard deviation for visual horizon angle results are due to the presence of unavoidable outliers (in every trial less than 5% of data), that affect either roll and pitch angle.

4.2   Hostile Scenario

The algorithm was also tested in a critical scenario, that is often verified during the landing approach to the harbors for the increasing of the marine traffic (but quite rare event in open sea), with the aim to evaluate the percentage of horizon line detection failure.

The precision and accuracy of inlier cases are the same of the previous clear scenario, but their percentage is very poor, amounting to only 5%. To increase the number of inlier, in such scenarios, it is necessary a deep work on image preprocessing, joined to intensive use of algorithms for the automatic detection and tracking of marine vehicles and other obstacles [37]. On the other hand, the use of these algorithms rises the computational complexity, reducing the frame-rate of the acquisition for real time applications.

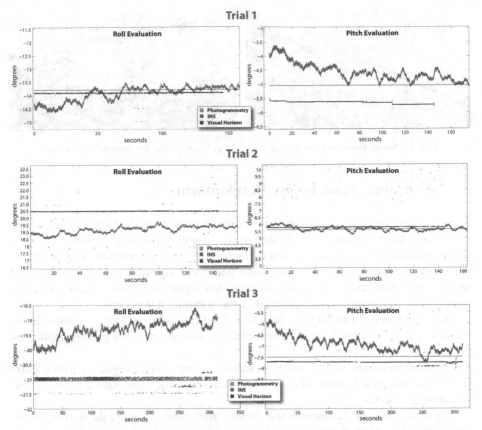

Fig. 10. Comparison of Roll and Pitch angles evaluated with Photogrammetry, INS and Visual Horizon in clear scenario

Fig. 11. A frame of third trial meaningful of the light conditions

The figure 12 is meaningful of the hostile conditions of the trial: in the scenes are present several maritime structures and vessels, which create several false horizon lines.

Fig. 12. Some frames of the hostile scenario video with the erroneous horizon line

5   Conclusions and Future Developments

The paper presents a new approach to compute the relative roll and pitch angles from the horizon position within an image. The investigation performed in clear scenario provides a competitive results compared to both INS and photogrammetric methods. Although the employment of re-projection gnomonic equation provide the expected results, in critical scenario the horizon detection algorithm is not reliable. An additional image processing needs to strengthen the solution in these cases.

Light reflections of the sun on the sea surface involve an increase of noise in the solution, the phenomenon could be reduced employing a polarizing filter applied on the camera lens.

The robustness obtained for open sea scenario suggests an integration with INS instruments through a Kalman filter, in order to control the unavoidable drifts of low-cost inertial systems.

The future steps of the research will include the improvement of the horizon detection in hostile scenarios and the development of a dynamic procedure for testing the obtained results. Furthermore the accurate knowledge of intrinsic camera parameters could improve the precision of the final results especially for the wide-angle cameras.

References

1. Dusha, D., Mejias, L.: Attitude observability of a loosely-coupled GPS/Visual Odometry Integrated Navigation Filter. In: Australasian Conference on Robotics and Automation (ACRA 2010) (2010)
2. Jones, E.S., Soatto, S.: Visual-inertial Navigation, Mapping and Localization: A Scalable Real-time Causal Approach. Int. J. Rob. Res. **30**, 407–430 (2011)
3. Dusha, D., Boles, W., Walker, R.: Attitude Estimation for a Fixed-Wing Aircraft Using Horizon Detection and Optical Flow. In: 9th Biennial Conference of the Australian Pattern Recognition Society on Digital Image Computing Techniques and Applications, pp. 485-492 (2007)
4. Todorovic, S., Nechyba, M.C.: Sky/ground modeling for autonomous mav flight. In: IEEE International Conference on Robotics and Automation (ICRA), pp. 1422–1427 (2003)

5. Neto, A.M., Victorino, A.C., Fantoni, I., Zampieri, D.E.: Robust horizon finding algorithm for real-time autonomous navigation based on monocular vision. In: 14th International IEEE Conference on Intelligent Transportation Systems (ITSC), pp. 532–537 (2011)
6. Ettinger, S.M., Nechyba, M.C., Ifju, P.G., Waszak, M.: Vision-guided flight stability and control for micro air vehicles. In: IEEE/RSJ International Conference on Intelligent Robots and Systems 2133, pp. 2134–2140 (2002)
7. Boroujeni, N.S., Etemad, S.A., Whitehead, A.: Robust Horizon Detection Using Segmentation for UAV Applications. In: Ninth Conference on Computer and Robot Vision (CRV), pp. 346–352 (2012)
8. Oreifej, O., Lobo, N., Shah, M.: Horizon constraint for unambiguous UAV navigation in planar scenes. In: IEEE International Conference on Robotics and Automation (ICRA), pp. 1159–1165 (2011)
9. Cornall, T., Egan, G., Cornall, T.D., Egan, G.K.: Measuring Horizon Angle from Video on a Small Unmanned Air Vehicle. In: 2nd International Conference on Autonomous Robots and Agents (2004)
10. Walia, R., Jarvis, R.A.: Horizon detection from pseudo spectra images of water scenes. In: IEEE Conference on Cybernetics and Intelligent Systems (CIS), pp. 138–144 (2010)
11. Zafarifar, B., Weda, H., et al.: Horizon detection based on sky-color and edge features. In: Electronic Imaging 2008, pp. 680–692 (2008)
12. Hartley, R.I., Zisserman, A.: Multiple View Geometry in Computer Vision. Cambridge University Press, ISBN: 0521540518 (2004)
13. Pollefeys, M., Verbiest, F., Gool, L.J.V.: Surviving Dominant Planes in Uncalibrated Structure and Motion Recovery. In: Heyden, A., Sparr, G., Nielsen, M., Johansen, P. (eds.) ECCV 2002. LNCS, vol. 2351, pp. 837–851. Springer, Heidelberg (2002)
14. Szeliski, R., Torr, P.H.S.: Geometrically Constrained Structure from Motion: Points on Planes. In: European Workshop On 3d Structure From Multiple Images Of Large-Scale Environments, pp. 171–186 (1998)
15. Kummerle, R., Steder, B., Dornhege, C., Kleiner, A., Grisetti, G., Burgard, W.: Large scale graph-based SLAM using aerial images as prior information. In: Proceedings of Robotics: Science and Systems (2009)
16. Steder, B., Grisetti, G., Stachniss, C., Burgard, W.: Visual SLAM for Flying Vehicles. Trans. Rob. **24**, 1088–1093 (2008)
17. Angrisano, A., Gaglione, S., Gioia, C.: Performance assessment of GPS/GLONASS single point positioning in an urban environment. Acta Geodaetica et Geophysica **48**, 149–161 (2013)
18. Angrisano, A., Petovello, M., Pugliano, G.: Benefits of combined GPS/GLONASS with low-cost MEMS IMUs for vehicular urban navigation. Sensors **12**, 5134–5158 (2012)
19. Libe, T., Gershikov, E., Kosolapov, S.: Comparison of Methods for Horizon Line Detection in Sea Images. In: The Fourth International Conference on Creative Content Technologies, pp. 75–85 (2012)
20. Lu, J.-W., Dong, Y.-Z., Yuan, X.-H., Lu, F.-L.: An Algorithm for Locating Sky-Sea Line. In: IEEE International Conference on Automation Science and Engineering, pp. 615–619 (2006)
21. Otsu, N.: A threshold selection method from gray-level histograms. IEEE Transactions on Systems, Man and Cybernetics **9**, 62–66 (1979)
22. Bajaj, M., Lay, J.A.: Image Indexing and Retrieval in Compressed Domain Using Color Clusters. In: IEEE Symposium on Computational Intelligence in Image and Signal Processing. CIISP 2007, pp. 271–274 (2007)

23. Lloyd, S.: Least squares quantization in PCM. EEE Transactions on Information Theory archive **28**, 129–137 (1982)
24. Mignotte, M.: Segmentation by Fusion of Histogram-Based K -Means Clusters in Different Color Spaces. IEEE Transactions on Image Processing **17**, 780–787 (2008)
25. Canny, J.: A Computational approach to edge detection. IEEE Transactions on Pattern Analysis and Machine Intelligence **8**(6), 679–698 (1986)
26. Hough, P.V.C.: Method and Means for Recognizing Complex Patterns (1960)
27. Gonzalez, R.C., Woods, R.E.: Digital Image Processing, 3rd edn., pp. 152–157. Prentice-Hall, Inc., Upper Saddle River (2006)
28. Duda, R.O., Hart, P.E.: Use of the Hough Transformation to Detect Lines and Curves in Pictures. Commun. ACM **15**, 11–15 (1972)
29. Mugnier, C.J., Forstner, W., Wrobel, B., Paderes, F., Munjy, R.: Manual of photogrammetry. American Society for Photogrammetry and Remote Sensing, pp. 215–223 (2004)
30. Brown, D.C.: Close-range camera calibration. Photogrammetric Engineering **37**, 855–866 (1971)
31. Remondino, F., Fraser, C.: Digital camera calibration methods: considerations and comparisons. In: International Archives of Photogrammetry, Remote Sensing and Spatial Information Sciences (2006)
32. Snyder, J.P.: Map Projections Used by the U.S. Geological Survey. U.S. Department of the Interior, Geological Survey (1983)
33. Royal Navy: Admiralty Manual of Navigation. Stationery Office (1987)
34. Nocerino, E., Ackermann, S., Del Pizzo, S., Menna, F., Troisi, S.: Low-cost human motion capture system for postural analysis onboard ships. In: Proc. Spie, vol. 8085, pp. 800–815 (2011)
35. Cooper, M.A.R., Robson, S.: In: Atkinson, K.B., (ed.) Close Range Photogrammetry and Machine Vision pp. 9–25. Whittles Publishing (2001)
36. Bancroft, J.B.: Multiple IMU Integration for Vehicular Navigation. In: Proceedings of ION GNSS 2009, vol. 1, pp. 1–13 (2009)
37. Fefilatyev, S., Goldgof, D.B., Langebrake, L.: Toward detection of marine vehicles on horizon from buoy camera. In: Proc. SPIE 6736 Unmanned/Unattended Sensors and Sensor Networks, pp. 673–676 (2007)

3D Model Visualization and Interaction Using a Cubic Fiducial Marker

Ihsan Rabbi[1,2](✉) and Sehat Ullah[1]

[1] Department of Computer Science and IT,
University of Malakand, Malakand, Pakistan
[2] Institute of Engineering and Computing Sciences,
University of Science and Technology, Bannu, Pakistan
{ihsanrabbi,sehatullah}@uom.edu.pk

Abstract. Fiducial markers are generally used for tracking the camera position and orientation in augmented reality applications. The tracking performance of existing markers degrades due to marker occlusion. Similarly it does not support 360^0 rotation in all axes and consequently it becomes difficult to achieve realistic/intuitive manipulation & visualization of virtual objects/contents. This paper presents the applications of a cubic marker in 3D models visualization and interaction and overcomes the above challenges. A cube having six fiducial markers, each on its face is used to be tracked from a single camera. The corners of the cubic marker are used to find its center. A 3D model is visualized on the center point of the real cubic maker. This cubic marker produces robust tracking results during occlusion. The visualization of 3D virtual models and interaction with these models are more realistic and ergonomic using the cubic marker.

Keywords: Augmented reality · Marker-based tracking · 3D Interaction · 3D visualization.

1   Introduction

Augmented Reality (AR) uses computer vision, image processing, and computer graphics techniques to augment the real world by digital information. AR needs real-time interaction between the users and the objects (real & virtual) [1]. A typical AR application consists of sensing, registration, tracking and interaction [2]. The task framework of a typical AR system is given in Fig. 1.

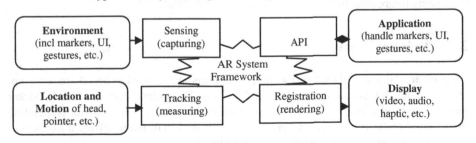

Fig. 1. Typical AR System Framework Tasks [2]

© Springer International Publishing Switzerland 2014
L.T. De Paolis and A. Mongelli (Eds.): AVR 2014, LNCS 8853, pp. 381–393, 2014.
DOI: 10.1007/978-3-319-13969-2_28

For the development of AR applications, the alignment of virtual contents with re-al-world object is the key challenge. The proper alignment of virtual information to the real world environment is called registration [3, 4]. Similarly, this alignment of virtual and real objects must be tracked as the user changes his/her viewpoints. Track-ing is the most important part of AR systems that is the process of estimating the camera pose (virtual or real) in the environment where augmentation takes place [5]. Therefore in AR applications, it is necessary to track the user movement in 6 Degree of Freedom (6DOF) relative to the environment.

In augmented reality applications, tracking can be performed using sensor-based, vision-based or hybrid techniques [6]. Sensors are placed in real environment for tracking in sensor-based tracking where as image information are used to track the camera pose in vision-based tracking [7, 8]. Vision-based tracking is the most widely used tracking technique in AR systems [6]. In marker-based approach, visual markers are placed in real environment for pose estimation. Markerless approach uses model-based or feature-based techniques to find the camera pose relative to real environment [9-12]. It is required to develop fast and accurate tracking system with less efforts, lower costs and minimum changes in the environment [13].

Marker-based approach uses 2D visual markers in real environment for tracking the environment. The main limitations of the existing 2D markers are occlusion and limited rotation. The existing marker fails to provide tracking even when they are slightly occluded. Similarly, these markers do not give 360^0 rotation in all axes, limit-ing their use in realistic manipulation/visualization of 3D virtual objects. This paper addresses the above challenges and discusses the applications of cubic marker in 3D models visualization and interaction. Six different patterns of markers are pasted on a cube that form cubic marker. Single camera is used to track the cubic marker. The corner points of the cube are used to calculate the actual center of the cubic marker. The center of 3D model is aligned with the calculated center of the cubic marker for visualization of model in 3D. This cubic marker produces robust tracking results dur-ing occlusion. The 3D model can be visualized from all the sides and provides effi-cient tracking than simple marker. Similarly the rotation of cubic marker has no effect on tracking.

The paper is planned as follow: First we discuss some related work in Section 2. Section 3 focuses on the overview of our proposed system. The process of visualiza-tion of 3D models using the proposed system is demonstrated in Section 4. We show our results and experimental analysis in Section 5. The paper is concluded in section 6 with some future directions.

2   Related Work

Fiducial markers are placed in the real environment for marker-based tracking ap-proach to develop augmented reality applications. The unique pattern of each marker makes it easy to identify its pose relative to the objects in the real-world. Depending on different patterns inside a marker, it allows the design of many different markers to enable continuous tracking inside a large building [14].

A real-time marker-based AR tracking [15] was developed to recognize and track unknown markers using corners information to estimate the camera position and orientation. Using corners information increase tracking robustness upto large distance and provide more reliable tracking system under severe orientations. A mobile phone tracking solution was presented that used color-coded markers [16]. Steinbis et al. [17] developed fiducial markers from a set of 3D cones that are more scalable in both indoor and outdoor tracking environments as these markers can be easily segmented into regions.   Maidi et al. [18] presented an approach by merging extended Kalman filter [19] with analytical method [20] to achieve direct resolution of pose parameters computation. It enhanced accuracy, stability and convergence of the pose parameters.

A real-time tracking method [21] was introduced that estimates 3D pose and track weakly textured planar objects. This method tracks each frame independently and use "tracking-by-detection" approach for tracking non-textured objects [21]. Tracking is failed by viewing the plane using a significantly oblique angle. Modeling the sampling and reconstruction process of an image is used to solve this tracking problem. Linear filter approach is used to correct the template that is calculated by using the tracked pose of the plane [22]. Lieberknecht et al. [23] developed a real-time tracking approach having the capability to track the camera pose in unknown environments that is based on a consumer RGB-D camera. In this system, it reconstructs a dense textured mesh. Seo et al. [24] presented an approach that handles the problem of occlusion and jitter in marker-based augmented reality applications. They used multiple keypoints and feature-tracking approaches to reduce the jitter effect and partial occlusion on marker tracking. This method requires more time to calculate the marker pose. Rabbi et al. [25] extended the functionality of ARToolKit to unprepared environments.

Researcher improved the marker-based technology to some extent but still there exists some challenges that need solution. These challenges include marker partial occlusion, marker rotation in all axes at 360^0 and virtual 3D model visualization and further analysis from all sides. This paper proposes a solution to the above challenges and discusses the applications of proposed method in 3D models visualization and interaction. The solution proposes the design of a cubic marker. This Cubic marker consists of six different patterns of markers on each side of the cube. Single camera tracks the cubic marker and the corner points of the cube are calculated. These corner points are used to find the center of the cubic marker. The center of 3D model is aligned with the calculated center of the cubic for visualization of model in 3D. This cubic marker produces robust tracking results during occlusion. The 3D model can be visualized from all the sides and produces efficient tracking than simple marker. Similarly the rotation of cubic marker has no effect on tracking performance.

3   Proposed System

Marker-based approach uses computer vision techniques to calculate the camera co-ordinates relative to the real-world marker. These coordinates are used to calculate the position of virtual camera and virtual images overlaid on real 2D marker [26]. Tracking failure occurs in existing markers due to marker occlusion and rotation beyond a certain limit. To solve these challenges, we propose a cubic marker and present its applications in 3D virtual models visualization and interaction.

For designing a cubic marker, a cube is structured using hard paper and six different patterns of markers are pasted on each side of the cube as shown in Fig. 2.

Fig. 2. Sample of Cubic Marker

This cubic marker is tracked using a single camera. The camera can see one, two or three attached markers based on cubic marker orientation. The four corners of the visible marker(s) are extracted as shown in Fig. 3.

Fig. 3. Marker Corner Points

These extracted four corner points P_1, P_2, P_3, $P_4 \in \mathbb{R}^3$ are used to find the missing corner points of the cubic marker (let say P_5, P_6, $P_7, P_8 \in \mathbb{R}^3$). Using the corner point's information, the center of cubic marker is calculated. Fig. 4 shows all the corner points of designed cubic marker.

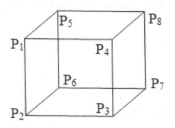

Fig. 4. Cubic Marker having all Eight Corner Points

All corner points are in three dimensional i.e. P_1 *is a Vector* $\begin{bmatrix} x \\ y \\ z \end{bmatrix}$.

The diagonal of the cub is calculated by using the corner points P_1 and P_7 (or other diagonal points). Mid-point (let say P_C) of the cube's diagonal is calculated which is the center of the cube. Mathematically we can represent P_C as:

$$P_{Cx} = (P_{1x} + P_{7x})/2$$
$$P_{Cy} = (P_{1y} + P_{7y})/2$$
$$P_{Cz} = (P_{1z} + P_{7z})/2$$

The center point is also in three dimensions and thus a vector of three values as:

$$P_C = \begin{bmatrix} P_{Cx} \\ P_{Cy} \\ P_{Cz} \end{bmatrix}$$

This PC is used to place the center of any 3D virtual model. The 3D virtual model is rotated and translated with the rotation and translation of cubic marker. The process of virtual 3D model visualization on cubic marker is illustrated in Fig. 5.

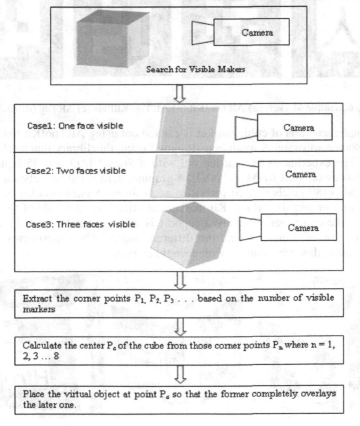

Fig. 5. Virtual 3D Model Visualization using Cubic Marker

The virtual model visualization on cubic marker starts with the placement of cubic marker in-front of camera. A toolkit may be used to track markers attached to cubic marker. The camera may identify one, two or three sides of the cubic based on the placement of cubic marker in-front of camera. The corner points of the visible markers are extracted which are used to calculate the remaining corner points of the cubic marker. These corner points are used to find the center of cubic marker. The 3D virtual model is visualized on the center of marker. As we rotate or translate the cubic marker in-front of camera, the virtual model is rotated and translated accordingly. The rotation of cubic marker at any axis does not affect the marker tracking performance.

4   Experimental Design

Artificial markers are placed in the real environment to develop augmented reality applications using marker-based approach. Toolkits have been developed using marker-based technique such as ARToolKit [27], ARToolKitPlus [28], ARTag [29], and ALVAR [30]. These toolkits use different patterns of markers (see Fig. 6) and provide a good framework for the development of an AR application.

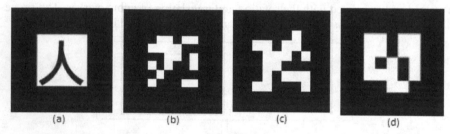

Fig. 6. Sample Markers (a) ARToolKit (b) ARToolKitPlus (c) ARTag (d) ALVAR

The implementation of cubic marker is carried out using ARToolKit library as it is an open source software. A module is designed using this library that tracks multiple markers. The experiments are carried out with a Sony VIAO core i5 laptop having 2.4GHz processor, 4GB RAM and NVIDA graphics card. Built-in webcam with resolution of 640×480 pixels is used for video acquisition. A cubic marker is structured using hard paper and six ARToolKit markers are fixed on each side of the cubic. To manipulate the cubic marker easily a support is attached as shown in Fig. 8. Fig. 7 shows the view of cubic marker from different angles. The experiments were conducted by using this cubic marker with a single camera.

Fig. 7. Experimental Design of 3D Cubic Marker

The primary aim of this cubic marker is to visualize 3D models at the center of this marker. For this purpose first we place a virtual cube as shown in Fig. 8. The virtual cube model is rotating with the rotation of real cubic marker. In this way the virtual model can be viewed from all the sides.

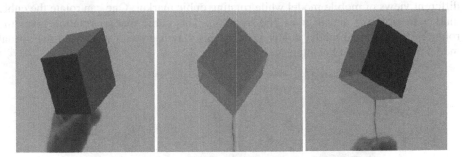

Fig. 8. Visualization of Virtual Cubic Model on Cubic Marker

Following this approach, one can visualize any virtual 3D model using the cubic marker. Fig. 9 shows the 3D model visualization and interaction of a user.

Fig. 9. User Performing 3D Model Visualization and Interaction

5   System Evaluation

In this section we present the evaluation of the cubic marker, comparing it with simple 2D marker in terms of occlusion, rotation and 3D model visualization and interaction.

5.1   3D Model Visualization

Our method is used to visualize 3D virtual models and further interacting with these models. For this purpose, we explain our technique using three different virtual models i.e. mobile model, human heart model and human brain model. Fig. 10 shows the different views of mobile model while rotating cubic marker. One can rotate the cubic marker in any axes and it gives 360^0 rotation. This cubic marker rotation gives the rotation of 3D virtual model at any axes. In this way users can visualized the virtual model from the side of his interest.

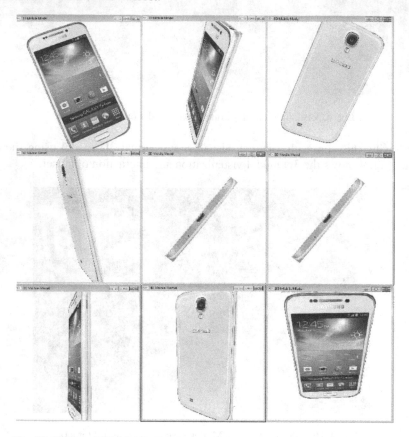

Fig. 10. Views of 3D Mobile Model from Different Angles using Cubic Marker

The cubic marker makes the interaction with virtual 3D models more simple and natural. The visualization and interaction with 3D heart and brain models are also shown in Fig. 11.

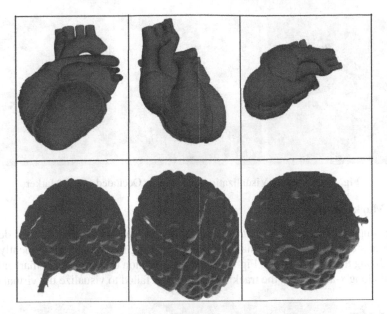

Fig. 11. Heart and Brain 3D Model Visualization from Different Angles using Cubic Marker

5.2 Marker Occlusion

Another problem using simple 2D fiducial markers is their tracking failure in case of partial occlusion. Here the marker is not recognized if a corner is occluded from the camera because the tracking process needs complete marker to be in view of the camera. This process is illustrated in Fig. 12.

Fig. 12. Marker Tracking using 2D Marker (a) without Occlusion (b) with Occlusion

In case of cubic marker the process of tracking is not affected if the later is partially occluded. Here the missing corner points are calculated from the visible corner points. Therefore the tracking process is not affected with partial occlusion. Referring to Fig. 13, we see that in spite of partial occlusion, the 3D model is properly visualized on cubic marker.

Fig. 13. 3D Model Visualization on Partially Occluded Cubic Marker

5.3   Marker Rotation

Another important problem associated with simple 2D markers is their limited degree of rotation in x and y axis. This limitation leads to tracking failure and consequently failure in visualizing the virtual model. Fig. 14 shows the rotation of a simple 2D marker beyond the limit along x-axis where the tracking process has failed to visualize the virtual cube.

(a)   (b)   (c)

Fig. 14. Marker Tracking during Rotation (a) and b) Within the Limit (c) Beyond the Limit Where Tracking Failed

The cubic marker is tracked from any side uniformly. Therefore rotating this marker along any axis produces accurate tracking. The camera moving around cubic marker has no affect on the tracking process performance. Fig. 15 illustrates cubic marker rotation and 3D model visualization.

Fig. 15. 3D Cubic Marker Tracking during Rotation

In order to evaluate the tracking performance of the cubic marker during rotation, we compare it with simple 2D marker. For his purpose the data of angular rotation along with corresponding tracking errors are recorded from the developed modules. Fig. 16 indicates that cubic marker is very less affected with marker rotation. On the other hand simple marker fails to be tracked when rotation angle exceeds a certain limit along x and y axis.

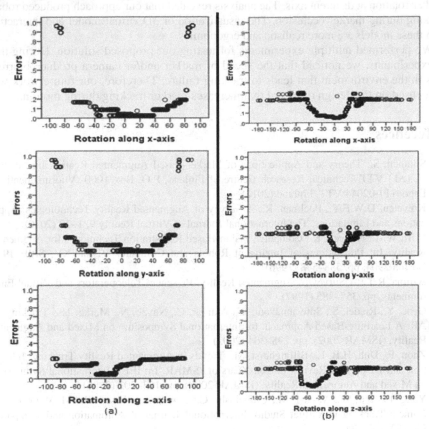

Fig. 16. Marker Rotation along axes (a) Simple Marker (b) Cubic Marker

The angles in the figure are measured in degrees. Fig. 16 indicates that the tracking process of simple marker fails during rotation of marker along x and y-axis. As the angle along x and y-axis exceeds from 80^0, the tracking error approaches to 1 i.e. no marker detection. The range of simple marker tracking angle along x and y-axis is -80^0 to +80^0 where less tracking errors are produced. On the other hand the range of rotation angle for cubic marker is 360^0 along all axis.

6   Conclusion and Future Work

This paper focused on the visualization of 3D virtual models using cubic marker for realistic interaction. The design of cubic marker with tracking methodology was presented.

Different 3D virtual models were visualized using our proposed approach. The approach makes the interaction and visualization of 3D virtual models (medical, industrial etc) more realistic and simple. It improves the marker tracking during occlusion and marker rotation in any axis. This approach can be used for visualization and interaction with 3D virtual models in medical organs and industrial machinery. The proposed approach was compared with existing approach during 3D model visualization, marker occlusion and marker rotation at different axis. The analysis revealed that our approach produced robust tracking during marker occlusion. The visualization of 3D virtual model and interaction with these models are more realistic and ergonomics.

We performed multiple experiments for testing our proposed solution. During these experiments, we noticed that the speed of marker and/or camera produce blurredness in the environment that leads to tracking failure. Therefore, our future work will be focused on the design of model that increases marker tracking during motion.

References

1. Siltanen, S.: Theory and Applications of Marker-Based Augmented Reality. In: Science, V. (ed.) VTT Technical Research Centre of Finland, P.O. Box 1000 (Vuorimiehentie 5, Espoo) FI-02044 VTT, Finland (2012)
2. Krevelen, D.W.F.V., Poelman, R.: A Survey of Augmented Reality Technologies, Applications and Limitations. The International Journal of Virtual Reality 9, 1–20 (2010)
3. Hoff, W.A., Nguyen, K.: Computer Vision-Based Registration Techniques for Augmented Reality. In: Proceedings of Intelligent Robots and Computer Vision XV, SPIE 1996. Boston 2904, pp. 538–548 (1996)
4. Azuma, R.T.: A Survey of Augmented Reality. Presence: Teleoperators and Virtual Environments, pp. 355–385 (1997)
5. Genc, Y., Riedel, S., Souvannavong, F., Akinlar, C., Navab, N.: Marker-less Tracking for AR: A Learning-Based Approach. In: International Symposium on Mixed and Augmented Reality, (ISMAR 2002), pp. 295–304 (2002)
6. Zhou, F., Duh, H.B.-L., Billinghurst, M.: Trends in Augmented Reality Tracking, Interaction and Display: A Review of Ten Years of ISMAR. In: IEEE International Symposium on Mixed and Augmented Reality, (ISMAR 2008), pp. 193–202 (2008)
7. Yang, P., Wu, W., Moniri, M., Chibelushi, C.C.: A Sensor-based SLAM Algorithm for Camera Tracking in Virtual Studio. International Journal of Automation and Computing 05, 152–162 (2008)
8. Bajura, M., Ulrich, N.: Dynamic Registration Correction in Video-Based Augmented Reality Systems. IEEE Computer Graphics and Applications 15, 52–60 (1995)
9. Comport, A.I., Marchand, E., Chaumette, F.: A Real-time Tracker for Markerless Augmented Reality. In: 2nd International Symposium on Mixed and Augmented Reality, (ISMAR 2003), pp. 36–45 (2003)
10. Chia, K.W., Cheok, A.D., Prince., S.J.D.: Online 6 DOF Augmented Reality Registration from Natural Features. In: 1st International Symposium on Mixed and Augmented Reality (ISMAR 2002), pp. 305–313 (2002)
11. Ferrari, V., Tuytelaars, T., Gool, L.V.: Markerless Augmented Reality with a Real-time Affine Region Tracker. In: 2nd International Symposium on Augmented Reality, (ISAR 2001), pp. 87–96 (2001)

12. Gross, M., Würmlin, S., Naef, M., Lamboray, E., Spagno, C., Kunz, A., Koller-Meier, E., Svoboda, T., Gool, L.V., Lang, S., Strehlke, K., Moere, A.V.d., Staadt, O.: Blue-C: A Spatially Immersive Display and 3D Video Portal for Telepresence. ACM Transaction Graphics, vol. 22, pp. 819–827 (2003)
13. Rabbi, I., Ullah, S.: A Survey on Augmented Reality Challenges and Tracking. ACTA Graphica 24, 29–46 (2013)
14. Naimark, L., Foxlin, E.: Circular Data Matrix Fiducial System and Robust Image Processing for a Wearable Vision-Inertial Self-Tracker. In: International Symposium on Mixed and Augmented Reality (ISMAR 2002), pp. 27–36 (2002)
15. Ababsa, F., Mallem, M.: Robust Camera Pose Estimation using 2D Fiducials Tracking for Real-Time Augmented Reality Systems. In: Proceedings of ACM SIGGRAPH International Conference on Virtual-Reality Continuum and its Applications in Industry (VRCAI 2004), pp. 431–435 (2004)
16. Möhring, M., Lessig, C., Bimber, O.: Video See-Through AR on Consumer Cell Phones. In: 3th IEEE/ACM international Symposium on Mixed and Augmented Reality (ISMAR 2004), pp. 252–253 (2004)
17. Steinbis, J., Hoff, W., Vincent, T.L.: 3D Fiducials for Scalable AR Visual Tracking. In: IEEE International Symposium on Mixed and Augmented Reality, (ISMAR 2008), pp. 183–184 (2008)
18. Maidi, M., Didier, J.-Y., Ababsa, F., Mallem, M.: A Performance Study for Camera Pose Estimation using Visual Marker Based Tracking. Machine Vision and Application 21, 365–376 (2010)
19. Bishop, G., Welch, G.: An Introduction to the Kalman Filter. In: SIGGRAPH 2001 (2001)
20. Dhome, M., Richetin, M., Lapreste, J.T., Rives, G.: Determination of the Attitude of 3D Objects from a Single Perspective View. IEEE Transaction. Pattern Analysis Machine Intelligence 11, 1265–1278 (1989)
21. Donoser, M., Kontschieder, P., Bischof, H.: Robust Planar Target Tracking and Pose Estimation from a Single Concavity. In: 10th IEEE International Symposium on Mixed and Augmented Reality (ISMAR 2011), pp. 9–15 (2011)
22. Ito, E., Okatani, T., Deguchi, K.: Accurate and Robust Planar Tracking Based on a Model of Image Sampling and Reconstruction Process. In: 10th IEEE International Symposium on Mixed and Augmented Reality (ISMAR 2011), pp. 1–8 (2011)
23. Lieberknecht, S., Huber, A., Ilic, S., Benhimane, S.: RGB-D Camera-Based Parallel Tracking and Meshing. In: 10th IEEE International Symposium on Mixed and Augmented Reality (ISMAR 2011), pp. 147–155 (2011)
24. Seo, J., Shim, J., Choi, J.H., Park, J., Han, T-d: Enhancing Marker-Based AR Technology. In: Shumaker, R. (ed.) Virtual and Mixed Reality, HCII 2011, Part I. LNCS, vol. 6773, pp. 97–104. Springer, Heidelberg (2011)
25. Rabbi, I., Ullah, S., Rahman, S.U., Alam, A.: Extending the Functionality of ARToolKit to Semi Controlled/Uncontrolled Environment. INFORMATION 17, 2823–2832 (2014)
26. Kato, H., Billinghurst, M., Poupyrev, I.: ARToolKit 2.33 Manual (2000)
27. ARToolKit. "ARTooKit", [visited January 14, 2013] Available from: http://www.hitl.washington.edu/artoolkit/
28. ARToolkitPlus. "ARToolKitPlus", [visited January 17, 2013]. http://studierstube.icg.tugraz.ac.at/handheld_ar/artoolkitplus.php
29. ARtag. "Augmeneted Reality system", [visited January 14, 2013] Available from: http://www.artag.net
30. ALVAR. "ALVAR – A Library for Virtual and Augmented Reality", [visited January 16, 2013] Available from: www.vtt.fi/multimedia/alvar.html

Posters

Intuitive Visualization of Reflectance Transformation Imaging for Interactive Analysis of Cultural Artifacts

David Vanoni$^{(\boxtimes)}$, Li Ge, and Falko Kuester

Center of Interdisciplinary Science for Art, Architecture, and Archaeology (CISA3), Qualcomm Institute, Calit2, University of California San Diego, La Jolla, CA, USA
{dvanoni,lge,fkuester}@ucsd.edu

Abstract. Reflectance Transformation Imaging (RTI) can be used to capture surface details including color and reflectance properties, enabling subsequent interactive rendering and re-lighting of digitized artifacts, enhancing and revealing otherwise obscured information. This paper presents a contextualized RTI visualization technique, transforming data analysis from desktop-based visualization into hands-on, interactive, intuitive, and collaborative data exploration that can augment RTI data directly on the physical artifact. Networked, mobile devices are introduced as visual interfaces to the data and as physical controllers for the intuitive manipulation of virtual light sources, including their position and characteristics.

Keywords: Augmented reality · Cultural heritage · Reflectance transformation imaging

1 Introduction

The visual appearance, geometry, and material of cultural artifacts all contribute important information needed for their analysis, interpretation, and understanding. While surface, sub-surface, and volumetric information is frequently needed to create a holistic view of the artifact, inspection in the visual range often provides the foundation for more advanced inquiries. When studying artifacts, the ability to discern subtle visual details plays a crucial role, and this level of inspection is usually best achieved while directly working with the physical artifact. However, physical access to an artifact is often limited, and thus it is beneficial to create a digital surrogate supporting effective and extensive visual inspection without requiring access to the artifact itself. Diagnostic imaging now allows for the creation of rich data records leveraging imaging techniques across the electro-magnetic spectrum to create the equivalent of a digital clinical chart for an artifact. One of these imaging techniques that has enjoyed great popularity with cultural heritage practitioners is Reflectance Transformation Imaging (RTI). RTI is a computational photography technique that captures details

© Springer International Publishing Switzerland 2014
L.T. De Paolis and A. Mongelli (Eds.): AVR 2014, LNCS 8853, pp. 397–404, 2014.
DOI: 10.1007/978-3-319-13969-2_29

of an artifact's surface, including color and reflectance properties. The distinctive advantage of the RTI method is that it enables interactive re-lighting of the digitized artifact from any direction, allowing the viewer to explore how light interacts with the artifact (Figure 1). Dynamic lighting can reveal material and texture details that conventional photography would fail to capture.

Interactive viewing of RTI data requires specialized algorithms to control and modify lighting parameters and is generally performed using desktop computers and displays accessed via keyboard and mouse interfaces. While these algorithms as well as software are readily available, interaction is limited to working exclusively with the digital record by modifying and moving virtual light sources via a 2D graphical user interface that controls how data is processed and visualized.

This paper presents a contextualized RTI visualization technique, transforming data analysis from desktop-based visualization into hands-on, interactive, intuitive, and collaborative data exploration that can augment RTI data directly on the physical artifact, using a video-see-through augmented reality (AR) approach. Networked, mobile devices are introduced as visual interfaces to the data and as physical controllers for the intuitive manipulation of virtual light sources, including their position and characteristics. All devices are context aware using the physical artifact itself or an arbitrary user-defined visual target for real-time tracking in 3D-space. The pervasive and robust nature of mobile devices ensures that RTI visualization can be made available to researchers, stakeholders, and the public at large in a broad range of different environments.

2   Background and Related Work

Reflectance Transformation Imaging (RTI) was originally introduced by Malzbender et al. as Polynomial Texture Mapping (PTM) [5], describing the fundamental data acquisition and processing techniques. Palma et al. subsequently proposed dynamic shading enhancement visualization techniques, aimed at improving the perception of features, details and shape characteristics [7]. RTI rapidly gained interest and support within the cultural heritage community, and in the field of archaeology in particular (eg. [4], [8]).

RTI acquisition involves photographing the desired artifact multiple times from a fixed camera position, while a light source is physically moved between photos. The image collection is then synthesized into a 2D RTI image, which

Fig. 1. RTI example showing changes to the visual appearance of a digitized artifact as a virtual light source is moved

encodes a view-dependent reflectance function for each pixel. Multiple interfaces for viewing and exploring RTI data have been developed over the years, such as the CHI RTIViewer [3] and the WebRTIViewer [6]. Figure 2 shows a screenshot of the widely used RTIViewer, providing access to rendering parameters such as color, specularity and highlight size as well as light source placement via a virtual trackball. Interactive zooming and re-lighting of the RTI data is supported through mouse-based interaction. In addition to its perceptual benefits, RTI is a relatively lost cost, time effective, versatile data acquisition technique, when compared against other popular imaging techniques such as 3D scanning.

The rise of networked, mobile devices such as smartphones and tablets, as well as the sensor package that they carry, is creating the opportunity to reimagine how RTI data is explored. A cyber-physical approach is now possible that allows for the physical artifact to be tightly connected with its digital surrogate, while concurrently enabling hands-on exploration and multi-user collaboration.

3   Technical Approach

Camera-equipped mobile devices can be used for spatially-aware input, using the artifact or a well-defined surrogate as a visual target that the mobile device can detect and subsequently track. Once a target is detected, the relative position and orientation of the mobile device can be determined and used for interaction (eg. [9], [12]). Here we use multiple collaborating devices that may serve as the display for the RTI visualization, a virtual light source, or both. Users may freely move collaborating mobile devices in 3D-space, and by doing so, define how virtual light sources are configured and where they are located relative to the display device that can be used to pan and zoom through the RTI image.

Fig. 2. Screenshot of RTIViewer showing the render window and its primary trackball interface for virtual light source placement

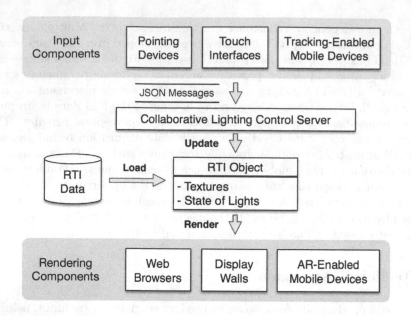

Fig. 3. Overview of the system architecture. Arrows represent data flow

Context-aware RTI visualization requires an integrative diagnostics methodology combining data acquisition and processing, with feature registration, tracking, data synthesis and rendering. This translates into a system architecture with several core components working together to enable flexibility in terms of interaction and rendering. Figure 3 shows an overview of the system architecture along with the flow of data through the various components. User input is passed from the desired input component to the *collaborative lighting control server* via JSON messages across the local network. These input messages, along with the desired RTI data, are then sent to any of the various rendering components for final visualization.

3.1   Data Preparation

Using community tools such as RTIBuilder [3], an RTI image can be prepared and exported to the Universal RTI format [2] and verified using RTIViewer. Data used in this paper was collected and curated by Antonino Cosentino and disseminated via Cultural Heritage Science Open Source[1].

For mobile device-based input we use natural feature tracking [10] to provide device localization. An image with "neutral" lighting conditions is first created by positioning the virtual light directly in front of the artifact and used to extract its feature description. This feature description is then supplied to the tracking system, allowing the mobile device to subsequently determine its position and orientation relative to the artifact.

---

[1] http://chsopensource.org/

3.2   Input Components

Our system provides various means of user input to control the position of the virtual light source. Input components allow the user to specify the horizontal and vertical position of the light source, which is represented as a 2D coordinate, (x, y), where each component is within the range $[-1, 1]$. The coordinate $(0, 0)$ corresponds to positioning the light directly in front of the artifact, the positive x direction corresponds to moving the light to the right, and the positive y direction corresponds to moving the light upward.

For input components such as standard pointing devices and touch interfaces, determining the light position is straightforward as there is a direct mapping between the input screen space and the light coordinates. This form of input behaves similar to that provided by RTIViewer and WebRTIViewer, and we have implemented a simple web page that enables input on both standard computers as well as touch-input devices such as smartphones and tablets. This web page sends the input coordinates to the lighting control server as JSON messages via a JavaScript web socket.

Tracking-Enabled Mobile Devices. To recreate the experience of physically moving a light source around an artifact, we developed an entirely new input mechanism using mobile devices by determining their pose—position and orientation—relative to the artifact being visualized (Figure 4). This input component analyzes the device's camera stream, searching for the image target which, in this case, is the pre-rendered image from RTIViewer mentioned above. When the image target is found, we retrieve the device's pose and calculate the light position via ray-plane intersection in which the ray originates from the device and points in the direction that the device's camera is facing. The

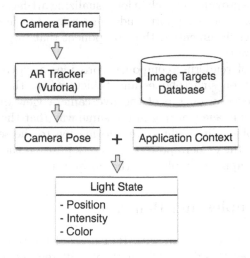

Fig. 4. Data flow for mobile device-based lighting control

resulting intersection point on the image target—corresponding to the desired light position—is mapped into the $[-1, 1]$ range and then sent to the lighting control server. In addition to light position, other light state parameters such as intensity and color can also be specified via the interface on the mobile device and passed along to the rendering.

3.3   Collaborative Lighting Control Server

The collaborative lighting control server is responsible for receiving the light state from the input components and making this state available to requesting rendering components. It is implemented as a node.js [1] application that receives light state updates from connected input components as JSON messages sent asynchronously via web sockets. The most recently received light state is stored by the server so that it is always available to any rendering component that requests it.Rendering components also connect to the server via web sockets and are responsible for polling the server for the latest light state.

3.4   Rendering Components

To facilitate RTI visualization across different devices, our system employs several different rendering components. These components load the desired RTI file into an OpenGL-based environment in which per-pixel data is loaded into OpenGL textures and then rendered with custom shaders that implement the RTI calculations. In addition to the data from the RTI file, these calculations also require the light state, which is retrieved from the lighting control server each time a new frame is rendered.

Our simplest rendering component is a WebGL-based implementation, similar to that developed by Palma, which allows visualization on compatible web browsers. While this provides a baseline for visualizing artifacts on most standard computing systems, we also support rendering on large-scale tiled display walls and virtual reality environments with a component that targets the CalVR [11] visualization framework.

Our final type of rendering component provides a video see-through augmented reality view on smartphones and tablets where the RTI visualization is rendered as an overlay on top of the live camera view of the device. This component performs image tracking in the same way that the input component does, but instead of sending light state information to the server, this rendering component uses the camera pose to correctly position the RTI visualization on-screen so that it appears in place of the image target.

4   Usage Examples and Benefits

We were able to test our system with RTI data of inscriptions carved into a wall, and we explored this data using multiple different system configurations. While the web-based input and rendering components provide the typical RTI

Fig. 5. Interactive RTI visualization on a tiled display wall. The user controls lighting with a smartphone.

Fig. 6. Interactive RTI visualization using multiple collaborating mobile devices serving as viewer and virtual light source

viewing experience as a baseline, the system becomes much more engaging when using a mobile device to control the virtual light. One such use case involves a tiled display system powered by CalVR which allows the user to physically walk around the visualization—moving back to get an overview or stepping forward to investigate details—while a smartphone tracks the visualization and provides lighting control (Figure 5). Another configuration uses a smartphone acting as the light source while rendering occurs on a tablet via an AR overlay (Figure 6). Both devices track the same image target—in this case the target is a physical printout of the artifact, but this same approach can be used with any representation of the artifact such as a digital image or the actual artifact itself.

When investigating artifact details such as these wall inscriptions, regular photos fail to provide the level of information needed to adequately perceive the true nature of the artifact. RTI provides an enhanced record that researchers can use to more effectively conduct analysis, and our system makes this experience both more accessible and more intuitive. Even a basic configuration using a web browser and a single smartphone—two components that are readily available to many researchers today—enables a much more intuitive experience because users feel as if they are physically manipulating an actual light bulb. Performing this physical action in proximity to the artifact promotes a mental recreation of the physical space which cannot be achieved with a standard mouse-based input method.

5   Conclusion and Future Research

This paper presents an augmented reality technique for the interactive and intuitive visualization and exploration of RTI data. This technique supports flexible, hands-on, investigation of artifact data, mediated by supporting numerous input and rendering methods. The use of collaborating mobile devices enables a new, intuitive avenue for visualization and lighting control, promoting examination and interpretation. In order to further explore the benefits of this approach, a formal user study is necessary. We are particularly interested in looking at the collaborative interactions that can take place when this approach is used for analysis by research teams.

Acknowledgments. This work was supported by the National Science Foundation under IGERT Award #DGE-0966375, "Training, Research and Education in Engineering for Cultural Heritage Diagnostics." Additional support was provided by the Qualcomm Institute at UC San Diego, the Friends of CISA3, and the World Cultural Heritage Society. Opinions, findings, and conclusions from this study are those of the authors and do not necessarily reflect the opinions of the research sponsors. The authors would also like to thank Antonino Cosentino of Cultural Heritage Science Open Source for the RTI data and Cultural Heritage Imaging for developing and promoting the RTI methodology.

References

1. node.js. http://nodejs.org/
2. Corsini, M.: Universal RTI Format - First draft (2008). http://classes.soe.ucsc.edu/cmps160/Fall10/labs/lab4/universal_rti_format_draft.doc
3. Cultural Heritage Imaging: Reflectance Transformation Imaging (RTI) (2013). http://culturalheritageimaging.org/Technologies/RTI/index.html
4. Earl, G., Martinez, K., Malzbender, T.: Archaeological applications of polynomial texture mapping: analysis, conservation and representation. Journal of Archaeological Science **37**(8), 2040–2050 (2010)
5. Malzbender, T., Gelb, D., Wolters, H.: Polynomial Texture Maps. In: Proceedings of the 28th Annual Conference on Computer Graphics and Interactive Techniques, pp. 519–528. ACM, NY (2001)
6. Palma, G.: Web RTI Viewer. http://vcg.isti.cnr.it/~palma/dokuwiki/doku.php?id=research
7. Palma, G., Corsini, M., Cignoni, P., Scopigno, R., Mudge, M.: Dynamic shading enhancement for reflectance transformation imaging. Journal on Computing and Cultural Heritage **3**(2), 1–20 (2010)
8. Palma, G., Siotto, E., Proesmans, M., Baldassari, M., Baracchini, C., Batino, S., Scopigno, R.: Telling the Story of Ancient Coins by Means of Interactive RTI Images Visualization. In: Archaeology in the Digital Era, pp. 177–185 (2014)
9. Pears, N., Jackson, D.G., Olivier, P.: Smart Phone Interaction with Registered Displays. IEEE Pervasive Computing **8**(2), 14–21 (2009)
10. Qualcomm: Vuforia (July 2014). https://www.vuforia.com/
11. Schulze, J.P., Prudhomme, A., Weber, P., DeFanti, T.A.: CalVR: An Advanced Open Source Virtual Reality Software Framework. In: IS&T/SPIE Electronic Imaging. International Society for Optics and Photonics (2013)
12. Vanoni, D., Seracini, M., Kuester, F.: ARtifact: Tablet-Based Augmented Reality for Interactive Analysis of Cultural Artifacts. In: 2012 IEEE International Symposium on Multimedia, pp. 44–49. IEEE Computer Society (December 2012)

Euclidean Vectors in Physics Education Using Augmented Reality

Angel Chi-Poot and Anabel Martin-Gonzalez$^{(\boxtimes)}$

Facultad de Matemáticas, Universidad Autónoma de Yucatán,
Anillo Periférico Norte, Tab. Cat. 13615, Mérida, Mexico
angel.linux91@gmail.com, amarting@uady.mx

Abstract. Augmented reality (AR) is one of the latest technologies that have demonstrated to be an efficient tool to improve pedagogical techniques. In this work, we present preliminary results of ongoing research in the development of an augmented reality system to facilitate learning of Euclidean vectors properties in physics. The system aids the user to understand physical concepts, such as magnitude and direction, along with operations like addition, subtraction and cross product of vectors, by visualizing augmented virtual components merged in a user-interaction environment.

Keywords: Augmented reality · Physics education · Educational technology

1 Introduction

Active evolution of technologies has had a positive impact on education, motivating the creation of new type of tools, applications, media, and environments in education to promote learning. Technological innovations such as virtual scenarios, wireless mobile devices, digital teaching platforms, virtual and augmented realities can enhance interest and motivation in students, as well as, the learning experience [1] [2] [3].

Augmented reality (AR) is a technology which augments the user's visual perception of the real world by superimposing virtual objects generated by a computer [4], [5]. Opposite to virtual reality (VR), where the user is completely enclosed in a computer-generated virtual environment, augmented reality permits the user to observe the real world, but with augmented virtual elements. Thus, AR complements reality, instead of totally replacing it.

Cai et al., remark that an AR learning environment coincide with concepts in education theories, supporting, for instance that learning is the result of associations formed between stimuli and responses. Moreover, an AR-based learning platform provides students with model constructing tools and scenarios, designed to be easily used by them [6].

Varied educative AR applications have been proposed to assist different academic subjects. In astronomy, an AR system was developed to learn about the

© Springer International Publishing Switzerland 2014
L.T. De Paolis and A. Mongelli (Eds.): AVR 2014, LNCS 8853, pp. 405–412, 2014.
DOI: 10.1007/978-3-319-13969-2_30

relationship between the earth and the sun by using 3D rendered earth and sun shapes [7]. In chemistry, a tangible user interface (TUI) called Augmented Chemistry (AC) was implemented, to show students 3D molecular models via AR [8]. Moreover, an augmented-reality-based 3D user interface was evaluated to enhance the 3D-understanding of molecular chemistry [9]. In biology, the anatomy and body structures can be studied by means of an AR system, like the Mirracle, which is an augmented reality magic mirror that shows virtual organs intuitively [10]. In mathematics and geometry education, the Construct3D system was designed to construct geometric virtual shapes by multiple users [11]. In physics, AR can be used to improve learning on kinematics properties [12] for example.

In mathematics, physics, and engineering, Euclidean vectors are geometric objects that characterize physical quantities having magnitude and direction (e.g. force, velocity, acceleration), contrary to scalar quantities that have no direction (e.g. time, temperature, displacement). A diversity of mathematical operations can be applied on vectors. Addition is the sum of two vectors, and represents, for example, the net force experienced by an object (i.e., the vector sum of all the individual forces acting upon that object). Substraction of vectors can be seen as an addition with a negative vector (opposite operation of addition). The cross product (also called vector product), $\mathbf{a} \times \mathbf{b}$, is a vector perpendicular to both $\mathbf{a}$ and $\mathbf{b}$ and is defined as

$$\mathbf{a} \times \mathbf{b} = \|\mathbf{a}\| \, \|\mathbf{b}\| \sin(\theta) \, \mathbf{n} \tag{1}$$

where θ is the measure of the angle between $\mathbf{a}$ and $\mathbf{b}$, and $\mathbf{n}$ is a unit vector perpendicular to both $\mathbf{a}$ and $\mathbf{b}$. The magnitude of the cross product is the area of the parallelogram with sides $\mathbf{a}$ and $\mathbf{b}$. The orientation of the cross product is orthogonal to the plane containing this parallelogram.

In this work, we present preliminary results of an augmented reality tool designed to enable the educator to use modern techniques for teaching physics concepts (e.g. vector properties and operations), and thus to help students to learn more completely through augmented reality environments.

2   Methods

2.1   System Setup

The AR system presented in this work, has mainly been developed for assisting education of physics concepts in classrooms. In particular, it focuses on the understanding of properties related to the euclidian vectors (magnitude and direction), and some operations of vectors (addition, subtraction and cross product).

Our system consists of a display device, a color and depth camera (see Figure 1). The display device is used to visualize the real world and corresponding augmentations. The color and depth camera belong to the Microsoft^{TM} Kinect sensor, developed for the Xbox 360 game console, which enables the use of gestures and body movement as a controller for the system. The main workstation for general processing has an Intel™ Core i7-3630QM processor at with 8GB RAM and Nvidia™ GeForce GT 640MB graphics card.

Fig. 1. Augmented-reality system setup. The user can visualize the augmented vectors on the screen while moving the hands to change their magnitudes and directions.

2.2   User Interface

The AR system permits the user to select among three different vector operations: addition, substraction or cross product. Every modality can be selected through virtual buttons displayed at a fixed location (upper part of the screen, approximately). Depending on the desired operation, the user has to placed the right hand at the corresponding button location for three seconds. The system modality will change according to the user selection.

The pose of the user has to be tracked based on the depth image using the NITE skeleton tracking software (www.openni.org). The real world 3D coordinates obtained by the Kinect sensor are transformed to the monitor 2D coordinate system through the OpenNI libraries. Finally, graphics are generated using the OpenGL libraries (www.opengl.org).

The 3D coordinates of the subject torso obtained by the Kinect is used as a common origin to form two angular vectors l and r. The 3D positions of the subject left and right hand are continuously tracked in order to get the ending points of the corresponding l and r vectors. The outcome vector on every operation is virtually generated and visualized within an AR environment.

3 Preliminary Results

Before each trial, the Kinect sensor needs to be calibrated for the user with a specific posture so that the sensor correctly tracks the user body. For this purpose, the user has to stand straight in front of the Kinect cameras with the hands above the head. Once the user is identified the AR system initiates the body tracking.

Addition of vectors is visualized in Figure 2. Positions of the left (blue) and right (red) hand of the user define ending points of the two vectors on which the addition will be computed. The resultant vector (addition result) is visualized in green. Position of the user torso is displayed as a yellow sphere, indicating the common origin of vectors. For this operation, the user can also move the hands back and forward to change magnitude and orientations of vectors, and observe different addition results.

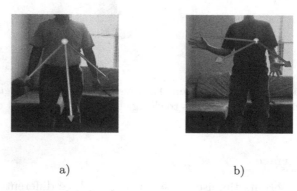

a)   b)

Fig. 2. Augmented view of addition of vectors by the AR system

Subtraction of vectors are shown in Figure 3. The system subtracts the blue vector from the red one. The final vector (subtraction result) is visualized in green.

Visualization of the cross product of vectors is shown in Figure 4. The cross-product vector (green) is the outcome of applying equation 1 to the blue and red vectors. We can observe the orthogonality property of the cross product in the augmented visualization.

We evaluated the augmented reality system for teaching vectorial operations with 10 undergraduates students and five teachers (Figures 5) through a survey with open-ended questions. Feedback from subjects were very positive and encouraging, also minor disadvantages of the system were indicated (e.g. losing hands tracking when the user is out of the sensor scope). During trials, the users did not need an extensive introduction to the system.

As we can observe in Figures 2, 3 and 4, the user can create vectors of various magnitudes and directions by using the hands in a dynamically way. The user

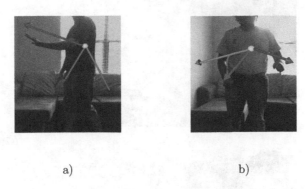

a)   b)

Fig. 3. Augmented view of the subtraction of vectors by the AR system

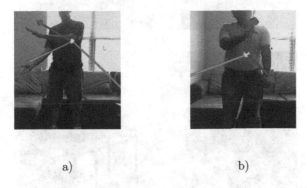

a)   b)

Fig. 4. Augmented view of the cross product of vectors by the AR system

can translate the hands to different 3D locations within the Kinect tracking area in order to generate virtual vectors with various magnitudes and directions.

The interaction of the subjects with the augmented system was very interesting to observe. Users were analyzing the generated virtual vectors they were controlling with their hands. They were trying several hand and body postures to watch and understand the effects on the operation outcome. By crossing the hands, they observed how the cross product vector changed 180° its direction. By changing vectors' magnitudes and/or directions, they observed differences in the result of addition of vectors. The majority of the students expressed that interacting with our system for the first time is a great tool to understand physical concepts like vector operations. Every user mentioned that the system interface is very easy to use, understand, and learn by interacting.

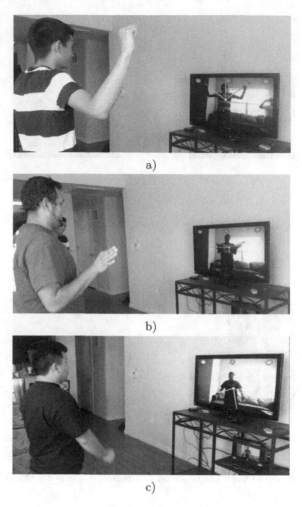

Fig. 5. Users interacting with the AR system

4   Discussion

In the traditional teaching methods, static materials do not show any information in a dynamic way such as motion or continuous movement [13] [14]. On the other hand, our system permits the user to interact with the elements to be understood. In the case of concepts like the cross product, which can only exist in a three-dimensional space, our AR system proposed seems to be efficient for an easier understanding of such kinds of concepts and their properties.

To develop a more complete AR system for teaching vectors, more properties and operations of vectors (e.g. vector projection, dot product) need to be considered, which is recommended for future work. Moreover, a survey with closed-ended questions may be applied to users in order to support current qualitative feedback with statistical results.

Even when existing learning methods work often adequately, there is always an increasing interest in developing more useful and practical methods to improve teaching experiences.

5 Conclusion

As technologies progress, educators are in constant search of more efficient pedagogical tools to enhance students learning process. This work presents preliminary results of the development of an augmented reality tool with a body-interactive interface to assist understanding and learning of properties and operations of vectors in physics. Users were able to virtually create vectors with different magnitudes and directions, and visualize their properties and operations. Most students had a positive attitude towards using an AR system for their learning in Euclidean vectors.

Acknowledgments. This work was supported by PROMEP 2013, grant number 103.5/13/6979.

References

1. Lee, K.: Augmented Reality in Education and Training. TechTrends **56**(2), 13–21 (2012)
2. Roussos, M., Johnson, A., Moher, T., Leigh, J., Vasilakis, C., Barnes, C.: Learning and Building Together in an Immersive Virtual World. Presence **8**(3), 247–263 (1999)
3. Nincarean, D., Alia, M.B., Halim, N.D.A., Rahman, M.H.A.: Mobile Augmented Reality: The Potential for Education. Procedia-Social and Behavioral Sciences **103**, 657–664 (2013)
4. Azuma, R.T.: A survey of augmented reality. Presence: Teleoperators and Virtual Environments **6**(4), 355–385 (1997)
5. Azuma, R.T., Baillot, Y., Behringer, R., Feiner, S., Julier, S., MacIntyre, B.: Recent advances in augmented reality. Computer Graphics and Applications **21**(6), 34–47 (2001)
6. Cai, S., Chiang, F.K., Wang, X.: Using the augmented reality 3D technique for a convex imaging experiment in a physics course. Int. J. Eng. Educ. **29**(4), 856–865 (2013)
7. Shelton, B.E., Hedley, N.R.: Using augmented reality for teaching Earth-Sun relationships to undergraduate geography students. In: The First IEEE International Augmented Reality Toolkit Workshop, Darmstadt, Germany (2002)
8. Fjeld, M., Fredriksson, J., Ejdestig, M., Duca, F., Btschi, K., Voegtli, B.M., Juchli, P.: Tangible user interface for chemistry education: comparative evaluation and redesign. In: SIGCHI Conference on Human Factors in Computing Systems, pp. 805–808. ACM, New York (2007)
9. Maier, P., Klinker, G.: Augmented chemical reactions: 3D interaction methods for chemistry. International Journal of Online Engineering **9**, 80–82 (2013)

10. Blum, T., Kleeberger, V., Bichlmeier, C., Navab, N.: Mirracle: An augmented reality magic mirror system for anatomy education. In: IEEE Virtual Reality Short Papers and Posters, pp. 115–116 (2012)
11. Kaufmann, H., Schmalstieg, D.: Mathematics and geometry education with collaborative augmented reality. In: SIGGRAPH 2002 Conference Abstracts and Applications, pp. 37–41. ACM (2002)
12. Duarte, M., Cardoso, A., Lamounier Jr., E.: Using augmented reality for teaching physics. In: WRA2005 II Workshop on Augmented Reality, pp. 1–4 (2005)
13. Craig A., McGrath, R.: Augmenting Science Texts with Inexpensive Interactive 3D Illustrations (2007)
14. Kühl, T., Scheiter, K., Gerjets, P., Gemballa, S.: Can differences in learning strategies explain the benefits of learning from static and dynamic visualizations? Computers & Education **56**(1), 176–187 (2011)

SLAM Map Application for Tracking Lights on Car Dashboards

Francesco Carotenuto[1]($\boxtimes$), Ugo Erra[2], and Vittorio Scarano[1]

[1] Dipartimento di Informatica, Università di Salerno, Fisciano, Italy
francesco.carotenuto@gmail.com, vitsca@unisa.it
[2] Dipartimento di Matematica, Informatica ed Economia,
Università della Basilicata, Potenza, Italy
ugo.erra@unibas.it

Abstract. Recent studies conducted by some insurance companies highlighted that the most part of drivers do not know the meaning of the dashboard lights. This leads drivers to be dangerous for others and themselves. Hence, the need to provide drivers with tools that support them to always be aware of the state of their cars. This paper proposes a system for mobile devices that uses augmented reality to be able to give information on a particular dashboard lights. The system is implemented by combining the use of Simultaneous Localization and Mapping (SLAM) maps with central moment computation widely used in computer vision. Preliminary research results show that the proposed system achieves its goal enables a a real-time visual feedback.

1 Introduction

Recent studies carried out of some insurance agencies [6] [8] have highlighted that the most part of drivers do not know the car components, and, in particular, the meaning of the dashboard lights. This lack of knowledge of drivers is dangerous because unknown car malfunctioning can lead to incidents and, as a consequence, to be injured, or, in the worst cases, to dead. For this reason, car manufacturers provide drivers with a printed maintenance guide. However, it is tedious and time consuming to leaf through a long printed car maintenance guide and, as a consequence, several drivers give up keeping cars in an unsafe state. To avoid this dangerous behavior, some applications mobile augmented reality[4] have been implemented to replace printed guides and to allow drivers to obtain information in a simpler way. Usually in these applications the user points with the camera of the mobile device a component such as a car wheel and some information about it are shown, such as instructions to change a wheel.

However, a feature which lacks to these applications is the tracking of the lights on the dashboard. In order to take full advantage of this feature, it should be always performed even when the car stops in an area not served by any wireless connection. Moreover, systems providing this functionality should have two important requirements: working in any type of lighting condition and recognizing the lights even if partially occluded by steering wheel as illustrated in Figure 1.

L.T. De Paolis and A. Mongelli (Eds.): AVR 2014, LNCS 8853, pp. 413–420, 2014.
DOI: 10.1007/978-3-319-13969-2_31

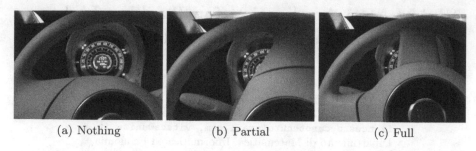

(a) Nothing   (b) Partial   (c) Full

Fig. 1. Examples of possible occlusions of the dashboard caused by the position of the steering wheel

The aim of this paper is to enrich the state of the art with a system based on augmented reality capable of giving information about dashboard lights in a simple and fast way and, at the same, satisfying the above mentioned requirements.

The idea is to associate with each light a relative position with respect to a marker (such as a portion of the speedometer). On the basis of these positions are derived from the frame of the segments that triggered the tracking. Within these segments, of fixed size, there should be a particular indicator. To detect the presence of this indicator, we proceed to search for a centroid located in a position close to the center of the segment.

In particular, the proposed system combines the use of Simultaneous Localization and Mapping (SLAM) maps, implemented through Metaio framework, with central moment computation obtained through OpenCV library.

The paper is structured as follows. Section 2 presents the background knowledge including description of SLAM framework implemented by Metaio and study of the moments and, in particular, of the central moment, performed by OpenCV. Section 3 presents the general architecture of the system and the steps that implement the lights tracking. Before concluding in Section 5, system tests are presented in Section 4.

2 Background Information

This section presents the two principal methodologies on which proposed system is based: SLAM and moment computation. SLAM [7] allows to realize a mapping of a 3D environment and can support a fast and stable tracking [3]. The produced maps are typically used by robots to be able to move in an environment or simply to give them an idea of their position within the environment. There are multiple ways to be able to trace the maps SLAM, some of these methods make use of certain devices such as GPS [1], laser and sonar[2]. These last two ones are usually installed on self-propelled devices.

However, it is also possible to construct a SLAM map by using a mobile device equipped with a camera [11]. In this way, it is possible to recover a particular

scene, identify a set of points that are placed on a 3D coordinate system. In this
work, we exploits Metaio SDK. It provides a set of APIs for the development
of augmented reality applications. In particular, it provides functionalities for
displaying multimedia content, but especially features that allow to make the
tracking using maps SLAM. For the creation of the maps, SLAM Metaio SDK
[5] uses an application called Toolbox available for both Android and iOS.

The second principal methodology is the moment computation. The moment
is a particular average intensity of pixels in an image. It is defined as:

$$M_{pq} = \int_{-\infty}^{+\infty} \int_{-\infty}^{+\infty} x^p y^q f(x,y) dx dy \tag{1}$$

In particular, this work considers the study of the central moments, as they form
a particular feature of an object represented in an image independently of its
location within the image itself. In the case of a binary image the coordinates of
the central moment is obtained with:

$$C = \left(\frac{M_{10}}{M_{00}}, \frac{M_{01}}{M_{00}} \right) \tag{2}$$

where M_{00}, M_{10}, M_{01} represent, respectively, the area of the object and the
center of mass of the object on x and y axis. In this work, we OpenCV [9] as
a library that provides functionalities to support applications that make use
of Computer Vision. In particular, OpenCV is used to calculate the moments
within the image that are the basis for the calculation of the central moment.

3   System Overview

This section presents the proposed system aimed at giving drivers information
about dashboard lights. In order archive its aim, the system uses the slam maps,
together with some pre-processed information. In particular, the system is composed of two modules: the first devoted to the acquisition of such information,
called *Training*, and the second one devoted to the tracking, named *Detection*.
The training module works to acquire the SLAM maps that make up the dashboard and some information that uniquely characterize the lights inside the
dashboard. Instead, the detection module uses the SLAM maps and information
produced by the training component in order to track dashboard lights.

The two components are used by different actors: training is used by car
maker whereas detection is used by the driver. Hereafter, more details about
system components are given.

3.1   Training

The training module of the system is illustrated in in Figure 2. From the diagram it is possible to note that before the training, there is a pre-training which

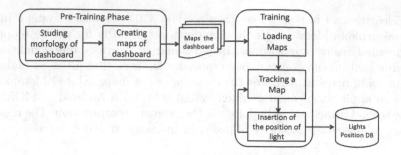

Fig. 2. Steps of training module

consists of two steps. The first step is devoted to the study of the morphology and arrangement of the lights on the dashboard. This step is useful to understand how many maps are needed to keep track of all lights. Using the information, we proceed to the creation of the SLAM maps using the application provided by Toolbox as shown in Figure 3.

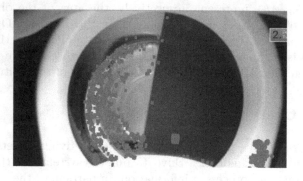

Fig. 3. SLAM map of a dashboard region

Subsequently, the generated maps are loaded into the training module as input. Using these maps, the user performs the tracking by pointing the camera of the device in the dashboard areas of interest. During the tracking an augmented object (AO) appears on the device screen. This augmented object can serve as a 3D placeholder to fix the position of the lights during the tracking as illustrated in Figure 4. Once the augmented object is placed on the light the user store its position in a database. Associated to the position of the light position further information can be inserted such as light name and more important a description of the meaning of the light. This process continues until all the 3D positions of all the dashboard lights are stored.

Fig. 4. Inserting of the positions of the light using training module

3.2   Detection

As illustrated in Figure 5, the detection module needs certain information such as those relating to the SLAM maps and the database with the positions of lights created in the previous phase.

In addition to this information, further data are required as the database of augmented objects(AO DB) that should be displayed in the case of tracking of one or more lights on. The AO associated with a single light is a tooltip which shows an icon and a brief description Figure 6.

The first step performed by detection module is to load all the positions of the lights

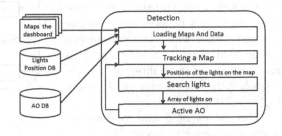

Fig. 5. Steps detection module

in the form of fictitious AOs. These objects are never displayed during the tracking of the portion of the dashboard where the user is pointing the camera for the light, but they only serve to obtain the position of the light in the scene. In detail, the detection module performs the tracking of a portion of the dashboard in order to obtain all the stored 3D position with the associated SLAM map. These positions, are mapped from 3D points in the world to 2D points using the camera device coordinates system.

Since the resolution and the aspect ratio of the display differs from those of the camera it is necessary to make the rescaling of the coordinate obtained in the previous step. After calculating all the coordinates of the lights in the area, we proceed with the capturing of the frame of the camera that triggered the tracking. Once obtained coordinates and the frame, it is possible to search the lights on in accordance with the steps described in Figure 7. The first step is to obtain

Fig. 6. AO visible on light on

segments of the image of a fixed size $n \times n$ whose the point at bottom-left is one of the obtained coordinates. Each one of these segments should contain a light.

For each of these segments, we calculate the center of mass of the objects present in the segment. Ideally, the center of mass of the light should be in the coordinated $C = (n/2, n/2)$. Since the front shot can translate some centimeters, then it is necessary to define a range within which the system can obtain that there is a light on. This range is defined in an interval $\lfloor n/2 \rfloor - \delta \leq C_x \leq \lfloor n/2 \rfloor + \delta$ and $\lfloor n/2 \rfloor - \delta \leq C_y \leq \lfloor n/2 \rfloor + \delta$.

The values of δ and n must be defined in order to avoid false positives and false negatives. A false positive occurs when the system detects the presence of a ligth on even if it is off, conversely as regards the false negative.

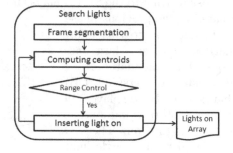

Fig. 7. Phases of search

High values of δ and n can lead to increase the number of false positives, whereas, small values increase the number of false negatives. In this work, the values of δ and n are defined empirically, taking as reference the resolution of the camera 320×240.

Whenever it finds a light on in the dashboard is inserted a new element in an array given in input to the last step of the Detection component. At the end, this last step views AO associated with the name of the light in the array.

4   Experiments and Results

This section presents preliminary experiments performed to test the proposed system. The carried out experiments take into account different occlusions and light conditions.

The lighting condition is considered to be primarily related to the maximum illumination of the instrument panel lighting, obtained using the mobile devices flash while shooting the scene. To better evaluate the robustness of the approach made and taking account of the absence of the flash from some mobile devices, such as tablet it was thought to perform tests also considering the condition of natural light. For natural light means the only light coming from the windows and windshield of the vehicle.

In particular, we consider four combinations of occlusions and lighting conditions:

- Scenario 1 (S1): absence of occlusion with full light.
- Scenario 2 (S2): absence of occlusion with natural light.
- Scenario 3 (S3): presence of occlusion with full light.
- Scenario 4 (S4): presence of occlusion with natural light

Moreover, since the system should be able to detect one or more indicators site in the same are, we consider two cases: situations with one light and dual lights adjacent. By summarizing, combining the defined modes with the aforementioned combinations of lighting and occlusion, we perform 8 tests. Each performed test is repeated five times and with different mobile devices.

The hardware configuration was based on a Samsung Galaxy Tab 2 GT-P7100, dual core 1GHz Tegra 2, 1GB of RAM, camera 3Mpixel with flash and a Motorola Moto G, quad core 1.2Ghz Snapdragon 200, 1GB of RAM, camera 5Mpixel with flash.

The evaluation of the proposed system is carried out by using the following scale:

- *yes*: tracking is performed within 30 seconds of the first shot dashboard.
- *partial*: tracking is performed within 45 seconds.
- *none*: tracking fails.

Table 1. Summary table of the tests performed

Configuration	S1	S2	S3	S4
Single Light	yes	yes	yes	yes
Multiple Light	yes	partial	yes	partial

The Table 1 shows the result of the performed experiments. As shown, the proposed system yields good performance obtaining the highest score in the 75% of the performed tests. We point out that these tests are preliminary and we are going to perform further experiments considering several users and a full day usage.

5   Conclusions and Future Works

This work is aimed at creating a system for mobile devices that helps the driver to better understand the instrumentation and controls as an easily and more appealing alternative to the car guide. As shown by the preliminary experiments, the proposed system yields good performance.

However, the proposed system tends to generate false positives due to the presence of unexpected occlusion objects within the camera view frustum. As for instance, an object with a color similar to light on can be detected as an objects with a contour and consequently possess a center of mass.

In the future, to reduce false positives we think to add a pre-processing step on the frame before breaking it up into segments. For example, this step could consist in the application of techniques for color segmentation [10] useful to remove all objects that do not match the color of the lights. In this way, we think to minimize the number of calculated centroids, and as consequence to increase the accuracy of the proposed system.

References

1. Carlson, J.D.: Mapping Large, Urban Environments with GPS-Aided SLAM. PhD thesis, Robotics Institute, Carnegie Mellon University, Pittsburgh, PA (August 2010)
2. Choi, J.W., Ahn, S., Chung, W.K.: Robust sonar feature detection for the slam of mobile robot. In: 2005 IEEE/RSJ International Conference on Intelligent Robots and Systems (IROS 2005), pp. 3415–3420 (August 2005)
3. Davison, A.J., Mayol, W.W., Murray, D.W.: Real-time localization and mapping with wearable active vision. In: Proceedings of the Second IEEE and ACM International Symposium on Mixed and Augmented Reality, pp. 18–27 (October 2003)
4. Fiat. Ciao fiat. http://www.fiat.it/ciao-fiat
5. Metaio GmB. Metaio sdk. http://www.metaio.com
6. Horton, P.: Dashboard warning lights confuse drivers (July 2013). http://www.lv.com/about-us/press/article/dashboard-warning-lights-confuse-drivers
7. Leonard, J., Durrant-Whyte, H., Cox, I.J.: Dynamic map building for autonomous mobile robot. In: Proceedings of the IEEE International Workshop on Intelligent Robots and Systems, IROS 1990, Towards a New Frontier of Applications, vol.1, pp. 89–96 (July 1990)
8. Megna, M.: Warning! drivers' knowledge of dashboard lights is running on empty (November 2013). http://www.insurance.com/auto-insurance/safety/what-does-dashboard-light-mean.html
9. OpenCV. Opencv. http://www.opencv.org
10. Skarbek, W., Koschan, A.: Colour image segmentation - a survey (1994)
11. Ventura, J., Arth, C., Reitmayr, G., Schmalstieg, D.: Global localization from monocular slam on a mobile phone. In: IEEE Virtual Reality (March 2014)

A Live Augmented Reality Tool for Facilitating Interpretation of 2D Construction Drawings

Stéphane Côté[1(✉)], Myriam Beauvais[1,2], Antoine Girard-Vallée[1,2], and Rob Snyder[1]

[1] Bentley Systems, Québec, QC, Canada
stephane.cote@bentley.com
[2] Département d'informatique, Université de Sherbrooke, Sherbrooke, QC, Canada

Abstract. Construction consists of a complex set of tasks in the 3D world based on instructions encoded in 2D drawings. Although the process is facilitated by the availability of 3D models displayed on digital tablets on construction sites, it is not always clear what is the exact 3D location of specific elements in 2D drawings. In this preliminary study, we propose a method based on a computer tablet and a head mounted augmentation system that enables the user to display a 3D element by clicking on its 2D representation on a construction drawing. Early results show that the method has potential, but highlights perception issues. We proposed and tested solutions to alleviate those issues.

Keywords: Augmented Reality · Construction · 3D model · 2D drawing

1 Introduction

Construction is a complex process involving a large number of tasks aimed at the development of physical infrastructure (the built environment). Infrastructure is inherently 3-dimensional. Designers propose a 3D building concept, and ultimately builders create the 3D object that corresponds to the designer's idea. Yet, the only design document that is legally approved for construction is the 2D drawing. Consequently, even though designers may have produced a 3D model of their design, drawings, because of their location-specific review and certification, are the only form of visual design communication that satisfies the legal framework required for construction. Since the process forces designers, architects and engineers to take one dimension out of their 3D design, drafting consists of a complex set of tasks aimed at accurately representing a 3D object with 2D representations.

For large infrastructure projects, the process may lead to the production of a very large number of drawings (e.g. thousands), each one referring to other drawings, through symbols that indicate their relative spatial relationship. The process is complex and must be done with great care, to ensure that when the builders read the drawings, they will be in a position to build the 3D building as it was designed. Faced with the increasing complexity of the task, nowadays builders often use digital tablets to display 3D models on site. Having such information on the construction site facilitates the construction process as it lowers the burden of having to build a complex mental image of the building based on 2D drawings. However, even when interactively displayed on a computer system on site, the model is still different from the physical

© Springer International Publishing Switzerland 2014
L.T. De Paolis and A. Mongelli (Eds.): AVR 2014, LNCS 8853, pp. 421–427, 2014.
DOI: 10.1007/978-3-319-13969-2_32

world: displayed elements may not have been built yet, or the corresponding built objects may have different visual properties, making the visual correspondence between the model and the building site difficult to establish for the construction worker. Consequently, even if displayed in the proper orientation and from the worker's position, the model and building task may still be difficult to interpret. We hypothesize that displaying the 3D model directly in the physical world, aligned in space and size with the building, would facilitate the builder's work. This way the model would appear with proper context, and the work required for building the infrastructure asset would likely become easier to understand.

Over the past decade, major advances have been made in the field of augmented reality (AR). By enabling the combined display of physical reality and digital models, AR facilitates data understanding by displaying it in its real context. The use of AR for construction has been investigated for several years [1]. Potential applications include: layout [2], building site monitoring and inspection [3], excavation work planning [4], etc. Aiming at facilitating construction work, some investigators have studied the potential of displaying 2D construction drawings in an augmented reality context, on the construction site. For instance, 2D drawings were used as an interface to visualize the corresponding 3D model using AR [5, 6]. Floor plans were draped onto the corresponding real floor surface in an industrial context [7]. Construction drawings were overlaid to spherical panoramic images at arbitrary locations in space [8].

The use of 3D CAD building models in an augmented reality context has been studied many times and shows high potential. For example, an AR system aimed at displaying BIMs in their physical world context is described in [9]. Another system, for the automated acquisition of point clouds from photos and their use for comparing with 4D BIMs in an augmented environment, was described in [10]. A short feasibility study [11] showed the potential of live mobile AR for construction work by overlaying 3D models with the physical world, facilitating the building task by displaying live instructions on what has to be assembled. In this latest study, the tracking system used was poor quality, and the absence of occlusion management affected perception.

Although the use of 3D models on-site is appealing, builders are used to work with 2D drawings: they understand drawings well, and they know how to interpret them. However, going from 2D drawings to 3D building is often a difficult mental step that does not seem to be made easier by having an electronic version of the 2D drawings or 3D model on site. Based on our discussions with users in the construction world, it appears some of the common questions they ask when looking at drawings is: "What did the architect / engineer mean when he drew that?" or "What does that line represent in 3D" or "How does this line refer to those lines in that other drawing?" 2D drawings or 3D models alone cannot easily answer those questions.

In this short study, we proposed a system that combines the use of 2D drawings and 3D models on-site in an augmented reality context, to facilitate the interpretation of 2D drawings. The system we propose consists of using a head mounted augmentation device and a tablet computer. The user uses both on-site: the 2D drawing is displayed on the tablet, and the augmentation device displays the 3D model within the context of the physical world. To facilitate the task of understanding the drawing, the system highlights the 3D elements that correspond to the 2D element selection on the 2D drawing.

2   Method

2.1   Hardware

Tracking. Considering that we wanted to concentrate on the problem of perception, we decided to solve the tracking problem by using a 8-camera 1.3 MPixel tracking system from OptiTrack. We attached a 3D marker to our visualization headset, and the Motive tracker software broadcast its position in real time on our local network.

Augmentation. Because indoor users are surrounded by walls, indoor augmentation may be facilitated by wide field of view headsets. To ensure a large field of view, we built our own augmentation headset based on an Oculus Rift equipped with 2 Genius 120-degree Ultra Wide Angle Full HD Conference Webcam for stereo capture of the environment (Fig. 1). The cameras were aligned manually, and the alignment was fine-tuned on the output video streams to produce a stereo video stream, which was fed back to the headset, as a basis for our video see through augmentation system.

Fig. 1. Headset composed of an Oculus Rift, 2 webcams, and a tracking marker

2.2   Software

The video stream, 6 DOF tracking data and 3D model were processed by an augmented reality prototype application developed in house in C++, based on the Ogre3D rendering engine. The virtual scene was captured using 2 virtual cameras, using the same inter-camera distance than the physical cameras installed on the Rift.

2.3   Model

The test environment was a small research lab, in which the tracking system was installed. A basic 3D CAD model of the room was created manually based on known room dimensions. That CAD model represented the existing infrastructure, to which we added a new wall to be built, with lower and higher cabinet, and used that new wall as an augmentation model (Fig. 2).

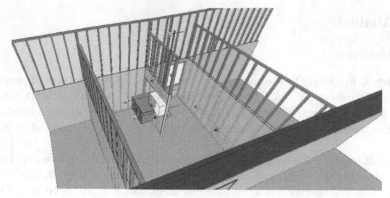

Fig. 2. Model of the room used for the experiment. An extra short wall with 2 cabinets, shown in the center of the back wall, was used as an augmentation model.

2.4   System Design

The system we proposed consists of 2 devices: a tablet computer, and an augmentation sub-system. The tablet computer is used to display 2D drawings, such as those that builders use on site. The augmentation sub-system is another device that is used for augmenting the physical world. In our experiment, we used the Oculus Rift augmentation setup described above, but in reality, it could as well be optical see-though glasses, or another tablet computer, or even the same tablet computer that is used for displaying the 2D drawing. Upon clicking on an element in the 2D drawing, the corresponding 3D element is displayed or highlighted in the augmented world, showing the user the exact 3D location of the 2D element he clicked on (Fig. 3). In our setup, the use of an Oculus Rift prevented the AR user from seeing the tablet, as the Rift covers the entire user's field of view. To circumvent that issue, in our experiment the selection of elements on the 2D drawings was done by another user. That limitation could easily be solved by using a higher resolution headset and cameras that would allow viewing the tablet display with sufficient resolution, or even by displaying the 2D drawing directly in the augmented view.

To make the highlight process automatic, a correspondence must be established between each element of the 2D drawings and corresponding element(s) in the 3D model. Although such correspondence could easily be obtained automatically (as 2D drawings are nowadays automatically generated from 3D BIMs), in this project the correspondence was established manually.

2.5   Tests

Early tests of the system revealed that it was working, but the low quality of the cameras induced latency, limited rendering speed due to their low acquisition rate, and created a small wobbling when moving the headset quickly due to their rolling shutter. In addition, tracking was fast but caused some model jitter. However, those issues were secondary as the resulting augmentation was sufficiently accurate for our tests.

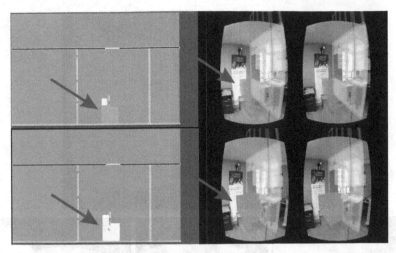

Fig. 3. Selecting a 2D element on the drawing (left) highlights the corresponding 3D element in the augmentation (right). Top images show unselected element, bottom images show selected. Element is indicated by arrow.

3   Results

Early tests of the method have shown that the proposed technique worked well. Clicking on a 2D element displayed on the tablet resulted in instantaneous highlight of the corresponding 3D element in the augmented scene. Two different 2D drawings were implemented, so that the same 3D element could be highlighted either by selecting its corresponding 2D element on a plan drawing or on a section drawing.

However, using the system we realized that displaying a 3D element alone is not always the best thing to do. For instance, the model we used for augmentation had a cabinet at a height of about 1,50 m. Displaying the cabinet alone in the augmented environment did not make much sense. The system displayed it at the right location, but the display of a floating cabinet was strange and kind of useless for construction. Indeed, builders need to know where exactly to build the cabinet, and a cabinet representation floating at an apparently approximate location appeared useless.

To improve perception, we proposed adding context to the element in 3 different ways: adding neighbor contextual elements (Fig. 4, top right), projection lines (Fig. 4, bottom left and center) and projection lines dimensions (Fig. 4, bottom right). Initial informal tests made with 3 subjects revealed that although adding neighbor elements was useful to facilitate perception of the position of the cabinet, the addition of projection lines was even more useful, as it helped subjects identify the actual 3D location of those floating objects with respect to objects in the physical world. The addition of dimensions seemed to make things even more clear. We hypothesize that this is caused by analogy with 2D drawings, in which users are used to see such dimensions. We further hypothesize that dimension lines would be even more useful to builders than simple augmentation of 3D elements, as they would see dimensions right before their eyes, and would no longer need to look at drawings to take measurements.

Fig. 4. Three techniques for enhancing perception of cabinet position. Figure shows: cabinet alone (top left), with contextual neighbor elements (top right), with projection lines on wall (bottom left), on floor (bottom center), and with added dimensions (bottom right).

4   Conclusion

In this paper, we proposed an AR system for the construction industry that might facilitate the construction process by displaying the 3D location of 2D drawings elements selected by a user on a tablet computer. Results show that the technique has potential, but revealed perception issues related with the perceived 3D location of displayed 3D elements. Further tests revealed that the display of vertical and horizontal lines along with dimension lines seemed to facilitate perception.

This preliminary study showed the potential of the technique, but would deserve another, more in depth investigation, to study specific elements that were highlighted in this study. For instance, it would be useful to study in detail the factors that improve 3D perception in a construction context, such as occlusion, shadow, texture, neighbor elements, etc. It would also be useful to verify whether the display of the 2D drawings themselves, in the 3D augmented view, would further facilitate their understanding. Finally, it would be useful to study how the 3D model could be adaptively displayed as the physical object is being built. We hypothesize that integrating the augmentation with 3D scans made on the site during construction might be part of the solution.

References

1. Rankohi, S., Waugh, L.: Review and analysis of augmented reality literature for construction industry. Visualization in Engineering **1**, 9 (2013)
2. Shin, D.H., Dunston, P.S.: Identification of application areas for Augmented Reality in industrial construction based on technology suitability. Journal of Automation in Construction, Elsevier **17**, 882–894 (2008)
3. Woodward, C., Hakkarainen, M.: Mobile Augmented Reality System for Construction Site Visualization. In: Proceedings of the International Symposium on Mixed and Augmented Reality (ISMAR) (2011)
4. Schall, G., Schmalstieg, D., Junghanns, S.: VIDENTE – 3D Visualization of Underground Infrastructure using Handheld Augmented Reality. GeoHydroinformatics: Integrating GIS and Water Engineering (2010)
5. Mackay, W. E., Pagani, D.S., Faber, L., Inwood, B., Launiainen, P., Brenta, L., Pouzol, V.: Ariel: Augmenting Paper Engineering Drawings. In: Proceedings of CHI 1995, pp. 421–422 (1995)
6. Fiorentino, M., Monno, G., Uva, A.E.: Published electronically, Tangible Interfaces for Augmented Engineering Data Management. In: Maad, S. (ed.) Augmented Reality, pp. 113–128. InTech (2010)
7. Appel, M., Navab, N.: Registration of technical drawings and calibrated images for industrial augmented reality. Journal of Machine Vision and Applications **13**(3), 111–118 (2002)
8. Côté, S., Trudel, P., Snyder, R., Gervais, R.: An Augmented Reality Tool for Facilitating on-site Interpretation of 2D Construction Drawings. In: Proceedings of the Construction Applications of Virtual Reality (CONVR) conference, London, England (2013)
9. Woodward, C., Hakkarainen, M., Korkalo, O., Kantonen, T., Aittala M., Rainio, K., Kähkönen, K.: Mixed reality for mobile construction site visualization and communication. In: Proceedings of the Construction Applications of Virtual Reality (CONVR) conference, Sendai, Japan (2010)
10. Golparvar-Fard, M., Peña-Mora, F., Savarese, S.: Integrated Sequential As-Built and As-Planned Representation with D4AR Tools in Support of Decision-Making Tasks in the AEC/FM Industry. J. Constr. Eng. Manage. **137**(12), 1099–1116 (2011)
11. Côté, S.: Exploring Augmented Reality for Construction. Blog post on BE Communities (2013)

Augmented Reality Simulator for Laparoscopic Cholecystectomy Training

Rosanna Maria Viglialoro[1]([✉]), Sara Condino[1], Marco Gesi[2],
Mauro Ferrari[1,2], and Vincenzo Ferrari[1]

[1] EndoCAS Center, Department of Translational Research on New Technologies
in Medicine and Surgery, University of Pisa, Pisa, Italy
rosanna.viglialoro@endocas.org
[2] Department of Translational Research on New Technologies in Medicine
and Surgery, University of Pisa, Pisa, Italy

Abstract. Augmented reality (AR) simulation, mixing the benefits of virtual and physical simulation, represents a step forward in surgical education. In preliminary studies, we demonstrated the possibility to correctly show AR information in case of deformations of the physical models thanks to the integration of electromagnetic (EM) tracking technologies into the simulation environment. In this paper, we describe an innovative AR simulator for laparoscopic cholecystectomy and in particular for the isolation of the cystic duct and artery, the most crucial phase of the intervention. The proposed simulator allows the AR visualization of these deformable tubular structures, which are covered by connective tissue and thus are difficult to identify. Moreover it provides an acoustic feedback as an alarm to the user in case of potential surgical errors.

Keywords: Augmented Reality · Surgical Simulator · Laparoscopic cholecystectomy

1 Introduction

Laparoscopic surgery is a counterintuitive technique due to loss of force feedback and 3D visualization, compromised dexterity, limited degrees of motion due to the fulcrum effect.

For these reasons a process of training at surgical simulators is important to achieve a level of competence in operations before surgeons are allowed to operate on real patients. Surgical simulators are effective training tools, because they allow the virtual or in vitro execution of surgical procedures and their repetition until satisfactory results are obtained. This leads to a shorter learning-curve and a reduction of medical errors improving the safety for patients. Existing simulators can be classified in: physical, virtual reality (VR) and augmented reality (AR) simulators [1,2]. Physical simulators can be of varying complexity: they range from simple box trainers including plastic tubes/rings to complex mannequins with realistic synthetic organ replicas. Generally, physical simulators are effective in learning basic tasks such as cutting, suturing, grasping or clipping. The principal advantage of these simulators is that they

© Springer International Publishing Switzerland 2014
L.T. De Paolis and A. Mongelli (Eds.): AVR 2014, LNCS 8853, pp. 428–433, 2014.
DOI: 10.1007/978-3-319-13969-2_33

provide a real force feedback during the practice allowing the actual interaction with the simulated anatomy. On the other hand, the major limits of these simulators are: the lack of a system for automatic evaluation of the user performance and the need to replace the simulator in case of destructive tasks.

VR simulators allow the trainees to interact with a virtual representation of an organ or a complete body region, reproducing tasks with different levels of difficulty or entire procedures [3,4].

VR simulators are generally expensive but are optimal for destructive tasks: the virtual scenario can be reset at the beginning of each trial without needing to buy new phantoms or to change spare parts. Moreover they can provide automatic and objective measurements of the trainee performance. A common limitation of these simulators is related to the haptic feedback which is difficult to be incorporated in a reliable and robust way.

Finally, AR simulators combine the benefits of physical systems offering real force feedback, virtual add-ons (to show hidden organs or to guide the user during the task execution), automatic and objective measurements of the performance [5].

In this work, we will describe an innovative approach for the laparoscopic cholecystectomy simulation, providing realistic physical replicas of involved anatomical structures coupled with innovative training aids based on AR and on acoustic feedback.

The most crucial phase of the laparoscopic cholecystectomy intervention indeed is the isolation of the cystic duct and artery, which are encircled by a sheath of dense connective tissue and can present several anatomical variations. One of the main causes of surgical errors are the misidentification of the common bile duct, or an aberrant bile duct; literature studies estimated that over 70% of bile duct injuries can be avoided by correct and safe identification of the cystic duct and artery [6]. The proposed AR based simulator offers advanced functionalities focalized on the training of this particular surgical skill.

2   Material and Methods

The proposed simulator integrates:

1. physical components comprising a mannequin with a patient-specific liver and gallbladder replicas, realistic reproductions of biliary ducts, arterial tree and connective tissue; realistic surgical instruments, laparoscopic camera and display;
2. AR functionality based on the use of electromagnetic (EM) sensors information;
3. an electrical apparatus to furnish sound alarms.

2.1   Physical Components

Details on the physical components of the simulator and their fabrication strategy are reported in [7, 8] and summarized below.

Patient-Specific Physical Models: Liver and Gallbladder
3D models of the liver and the gallbladder are obtained segmenting real CT images. Moulds to replicate the anatomical parts are designed and manufactured using a rapid prototyping process (Dimension Elite 3D Printer). The liver replica is obtained by pouring a platinum-cure silicone with colour pigments into the mould. The hollow gallbladder is obtained with a brush-on technique. Cotton fibers are added among silicone layers in order to obtain the optimal elasticity, thickness and robustness.

Synthetic Connective Tissue: Small Omentum
The small omentum (that covers the cystic duct and artery) is produced in the form of thin sheets of cured silicone reinforced with cotton fibers.

Tubular Structures: Biliary Ducts and Arterial Tree
The biliary ducts and arterial tree are fabricated using nitinol tubes covered by a layer of silicone to reproduce, without excessive alterations, the natural flexibility of vessels. The manufacturing process takes into account the need to sensorize these tubular structures for the implementation of AR functionality (see paragraph 2.2) and to simply detect the contact among them and the surgical instruments providing a sound alarm (see paragraph 2.3).

2.2   AR Functionality

The traditional intervention is guided by bidimensional laparoscopic images. The idea proposed in this work is to track in real time the laparoscope and the biliary ducts/arterial tree to augment the real laparoscopic images with virtual information showing in real time the position of these anatomical structures. For this aim an EM localizer (NDI Aurora V1 by Northern Digital) is integrated into the system and EM coils (EM sensors coils, 0.5 mm diameter - 8 mm length) are inserted inside the nitinol tubes used to fabricate both the biliary ducts and arterial tree. The number and position of EM coils can be varied to reproduce different anatomical configuration; an example of arterial tree sensorization is described in [9].

EM data are used to infer possible deformation of the sensorized tubular structures and consequently to update in real time the virtual scene. In particular dotted Bezier curve lines can be used to highlight the trajectory of the biliary ducts/arterial tree.

Finally, the implementation of a proper calibration routine allows the coherent integration of EM data, thus the virtual scene, and real laparoscopic images.

2.3   Acoustic Functionality

The constructive material of the biliary ducts and arterial tree is conductive. These structures and the surgical instrument (e.g. surgical hook) are electrically connected to an electronic acquisition board in such a way that the contact of the instrument with the cystic duct/artery causes a closing of the electric circuit and thus can be signalled with sound alarms (Fig.1) [8].

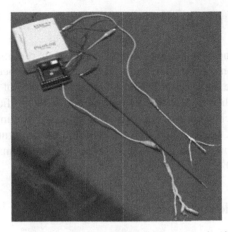

Fig. 1. Electrical connections for surgical instrument and conductive tubular structures

Figure 2 shows a global view of the simulation set up. The image grabbed by the laparoscope is augmented with information extracted from the EM data. The localizer follows in real time the position of sensorized tubular structures hidden by the connective tissue.

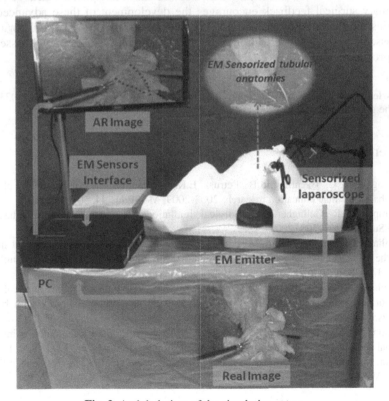

Fig. 2. A global view of the simulation set up

3   Preliminary Results

The components of the proposed simulator have been preliminary validated by a group of expert surgeons. A positive qualitative feedback has been received regarding the realism of the force feedback/mechanical response to the cut and the usefulness of the acoustic functionality to train the cystic duct/artery identification task. Good results have been also achieved as for the AR functionality: preliminary tests, in realistic surgical conditions, have shown that the maximum misalignment between virtual and real arterial sensorized structures does not exceed 0.99mm, with a mean and standard deviation of 0.35 and 0.22mm respectively[9].

4   Future Work and Conclusion

This work firstly presents the integration of AR and acoustic functionalities to enrich a realistic physical environment for the simulation of the most crucial phase of the laparoscopic cholecystectomy intervention: the isolation of the cystic duct and artery. EM tracking technologies are used to acquire information on deformable tubular structures and to render them in an augmented reality visualization. Simple electrical connections allow the implementation of a sound alarm to signal surgical errors. The preliminary surgical feedback encourages the development of these advanced functionalities. Further studies are needed for: the optimization of the simulator components assembly, the ingegnerization of the fabrication process, a complete assessment of the proposed system.

Acknowledgment. This work was financed by the SThARS project (code GR-2011-02347124) under the grant Giovani Ricercatori 2011-2012 by the Italian Minister of Health

References

1. McGaghie, W.C., Issenberg, S.B., Petrusa, E.R., Scalese, R.J.: A critical review of simulation-based medical education research: 2003-2009. Med Educ **44**, 50–63 (2010)
2. Champion, H.R., Gallagher, A.G.: Surgical simulation - a 'good idea whose time has come'. Br J Surg **90**, 767–768 (2003)
3. Moglia, A., Turini, G., Ferrari, V., Ferrari, M., Mosca, F.: Patient specific surgical simulator for the evaluation of the movability of bimanual robotic arms. Stud Health Technol Inform **163**, 379–385 (2011)
4. Turini, G., Moglia, A., Ferrari, V., Ferrari, M., Mosca, F.: Patient-specific surgical simulator for the pre-operative planning of single-incision laparoscopic surgery with bimanual robots. Comput Aided Surg **17**, 103–112 (2012)
5. Carbone, M., Condino, Ferrari, S.V., Ferrari, M., Mosca, F.: Surgical simulators integrating virtual and physical anatomies. In: CEUR Workshop Proceedings, pp. 13–18 (2011)
6. Imhof, M.: Malpractice in Surgery: Safety Culture of and Quality Management in the Hospital: Walter De Gruyter Incorporated (2012)

7. Condino, S., Carbone, M., Ferrari, V., Faggioni, L., Peri, A., Ferrari, M., et al.: How to build patient-specific synthetic abdominal anatomies. An innovative approach from physical toward hybrid surgical simulators. International Journal of Medical Robotics and Computer Assisted Surgery 7, 202–213 (2011)
8. Viglialoro, R., Ferrari, V., Carbone, M., Condino, S., Di Puccio, F., Ferrari, M., et al.: A physical patient specific simulator for cholecystectomy training (2012)
9. Ferrari, V., Viglialoro, R., Nicoli, P., Cutolo, F., Condino, S., Carbone, M., et al.: Augmented Reality visualization of deformable tubular structures for surgical simulators. Submitted to: IJCARS International Journal of Computer Assisted Radiology and Surgery

Tile Tracker: A Practical and Inexpensive Positioning System for Mobile AR Applications

Steven Maesen$^{(\boxtimes)}$, Yunjun Liu, Patrik Goorts, and Philippe Bekaert

Expertise Centre for Digital Media, Hasselt University - tUL - iMinds,
Wetenschapspark 2, 3590 Diepenbeek, Belgium
{steven.maesen,yunjun.liu,patrik.goorts,philippe.bekaert}@uhasselt.be

Abstract. In this paper, we propose a practical and low-cost positioning system that quickly determines the camera pose in an environment with pre-existing ground tiles, with the support of fiducial images. Such environment exists in many places, both indoors and outdoors, such as museums and parks. Our system is designed to be used on mobile devices (e.g. smartphone, tablets, etc.) with inexpensive cameras to fast calibrate cameras and to track the movement of a user. Contrary to other existing mobile tracking systems, our algorithm has minimal drift over time. To accomplish this, our approach, fully taking advantage of the existing rectangular tiles, labels them with markers that supports quick orientation determination and unique identification. Our algorithm recovers the camera pose based on the images taken of these marked tiles in real time, and thus provides basis for a wide range of applications such as navigational assistance and augmented or virtual reality.

Keywords: Optical tracking · Video tracking · Mobile AR · Marker · Fiducial · Low-cost

1 Introduction

Tracking is the process of locating moving objects or camera pose in consecutive video frames and is a field that has been long studied. It is a fundamental component of a variety of computer vision applications such as traffic monitoring control, security and surveillance, medical imaging, activity recognition and augmented reality. A typical strategy to solve the problem of object tracking in the 3D real world is to effectively extract features in each frame and reliably match corresponding features over time. Robust feature detection and matching algorithms, including SIFT [9], SURF [5] and FLANN [12], can be used for this purpose. However, since our goal is real-time tracking on mobile devices, these algorithms are computationally costly and impractical to implement on such devices with limited memory and processing power. Another widely-used approach is motion-based tracking algorithms that subtract the background from the moving object and determine the matching in subsequent frames using location prediction (e.g. Kalman filter). The object tracking methods proposed by

© Springer International Publishing Switzerland 2014
L.T. De Paolis and A. Mongelli (Eds.): AVR 2014, LNCS 8853, pp. 434–441, 2014.
DOI: 10.1007/978-3-319-13969-2_34

Han et al. [8] and Aggarwal et al. [4] follow this approach. These methods also require considerable amount of image processing. Instead of tracking complex objects in the scene, we transform the problem into a planar object tracking problem using markers. Existing markers include square shaped ARToolKit [1] and QR code, etc., circular ones proposed by Ababsa et al. [3] or line code using De Bruijn sequence proposed by Maesen et al. [10] In our approach, we propose to use existing ground tiles to create an optical tracking system with minimal drift. To get a global camera pose, we incorporate a simple dataset of unambiguous and easily-identiable 2D rectangular markers to be used on the existing ground grid. Due to the simplicity and fast speed, our approach has real-time performance on mobile devices. One significant advantage of our approach is its cost-effectiveness because we fully exploit the existing ground tiles to reduce marker tagging and alignment cost, besides their quality features that serve to be part of the markers.

2 Overview of Our Approach

We propose a low-cost and practical optical tracking system that can be used with low resolution cameras (e.g. smartphone or tablets cameras) in an environment with rectangular ground grid (e.g. ceramic tiles). The tiles in the grid are tagged with uniquely identifiable markers and are recognized in real-time to determine the camera pose. Our system works as follows (see Figure 2): First, a series of images or video sequences (we call them frames henceforth) are taken as the mobile device user walks through the space. Our system processes each frame, using computer vision techniques to detect the tiles together with markers on them (Section 4). Then we match the feature points on the processed frame with our data-set of marker patterns and find the corresponding marker (Section 3). Finally, from the matching result and the known world coordinates of the real tiles, we recover the camera parameters (Section 5).

3 Marking

Markers, also known as fiducial images, are a widely-used supporting element in vision-based tracking systems. The purpose of introducing markers into an environment for tracking is to support fast and deterministic identification and thus reliable localization. Once identification of the markers is accomplished, a homography can be established and the camera pose can be recovered from the image-world-correspondence.

3.1 Why Ground Tiles?

While markers enable fast recognition and tracking, they are not a free cake to take and a non-trivial cost comes with it. Besides a relatively insignificant raw material and printing cost, the primary cost involves a huge amount of human labour regarding tagging and aligning the markers in the physical environment in which object tracking is intended. This is tedious work and, depending on the scale of the environment, usually requires hours or days of work for more than one person, even with the assistance of optical measurement tools and alignment technology.

To reduce the amount of work, we propose a significantly faster marking approach that uses existing rectangular ground grid, e.g. ceramic floor tiles or square stone walkways, etc. We have observed that these grids exist in many places, such as supermarkets, museums, conference centres and parks (Figure 1). Many of these environments have the potential for AR or navigational applications. For example, a museum AR application can use visitors' tracked positions within the building to guide them through the artworks or exhibits, highlighting the pieces that might be of specific interests. A navigational application of a theme park can also pin-point the visitors and use this information to enhance their experience. As existing grids are already aligned, the labour of tagging in such environment is greatly reduced and becomes naturally effortless. The measuring of world coordinates of each tile is trivial as they can be calculated straightforwardly by adding an offset to an appointed origin in the grid. In our approach, we use rectangular tiles because they are simple, have clear computational advantages and yield great accuracy, potentially to sub-pixel level. However, the tiles are not required to be rectangular and any tiles that can emit four-point correspondences suffice.

Fig. 1. Examples of ground tiles in natural environment. Rectangular grid pavement outside Louvre Museum (left) [14], floor tiles inside exhibition space (middle) [14] and stone tiles around the Lincoln Memorial Reflecting Pool (right) [2]

3.2   Marker Design

Many marker designs exist and most commonly seen square markers are ARToolKit [1], ARTag [7], Tricodes [11], DataMatrix [15] and QR code [6]. Circular markers by Ababsa et al. [3] and line encoded markers by Maesen et al. [10] are also used for real-time tracking. The choice of the markers is directly related to the matching algorithm, therefore it is important to have good designs. There are certain criteria regarding how to choose good markers. As described by C.B.Owen et al. [13], the general guidelines are as follows:

- support unambiguous determination of position and orientation
- be easy to locate and identify using fast and simple algorithms

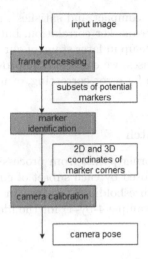

Fig. 2. System overview

– members of the marker dataset should be unique and unlikely be confused
with each other (i.e. minimal inter-marker correlation)

According to the guidelines mentioned above, we designed the marker dataset
to use the following pattern (to be experimented in our approach): The existing
ground grid serves as the border of the individual markers. (Please note markers
are not limited to fit inside one tile. They can also be bigger and consist more
than one tile.) A very distinctive advantage of rectangular marker is that it can
yield four corner points for tracking purpose. The straight tile edges allow corner
extraction to be less sensitive to noise in the vicinity or quantization errors. In our
experiment, we used a black-white binary 4-by-4 circular inner pattern, as shown
in Figure 3. The top-left dot is always white and the other three dots in the
outermost corners (namely, top-right, bottom-left and bottom-right) are always
black, and they are used to support the determination of unique orientation.
The other dots can be either black or white.

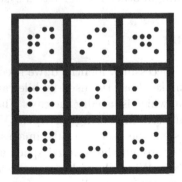

Fig. 3. Example of sample markers in our dataset

Our marker design is very compact and satisfies the first two criteria. However, it doesn't have zero inter-marker correlation, but for our initial testing, it suffices. When we have to scale up in later stage of our project, or in an environment with high amount of noises, we can easily improve our marker pattern by adding a few bits of checksum for error-correcting, or using orthogonal encoding whose cross correlation is low.

3.3 Determining the Match

After we got the subsets of corner points from processing the frame, we extract the corresponding region enclosed by each subset of corner points in the binary image we get from adaptive thresholding. This region can be warped to a common frame of reference (for example 4-by-4) for the identification of the marker in our dataset. (Figure 4)

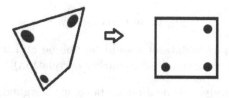

Fig. 4. The extracted image has to be warped and aligned before it can be compared with sample markers in the dataset

After the orientation of the warped image is determined by the three outermost black dots, we rotate the warped image so that it is aligned with the sample markers stored in the dataset . As dots are in fixed positions, we can read them out in a fixed order (based on orientation). The black dots signal the binary value 0, while white gives the value 1. Reading them out gives us an unique identifier ranging from 0 to 2^{n-4}, where n equals the total number of bits (16 in our experiment). This speeds up the identification in a hashed database compared to image matching in other marker based systems.

4   Frame Processing

Before the markers can be successfully identified, we need to detect the tile floor. The only assumption we make about the used mobile camera, is the fact that is has a fixed or manual zoom which is usually the case. Therefore we can calibrate the intrinsic camera parameters first using an OpenCV checkerboard pattern. After this pre-processing step, the user can take images at any arbitrary angle or position when he walks through the marked space as long as some ground tiles are present in the image. When the video sequences or images are taken of the tiles, they are first processed in the following a few steps to achieve a higher quality of recognition.

4.1 Binarization

First, a binary image is created through thresholding on the gray-scale image of the original frame. Simple thresholding straightforwardly separates the foreground from the background using a single global value as its threshold. This method does not give a satisfactory binarization in our experiment because it does not deal with varying illumination or noise (e.g. shadows from surrounding objects cast on the ground tiles). In our approach we use adaptive thresholding which gives an improved binarization that responds better to local features under non-uniform lighting.

4.2 Segmentation and Contour Detection

Because our goal is to determine the camera pose by correctly matching the four corners of corresponding tiles, we first have to identify the tile corners. Given all tiles have distinct straight-line borders, a fast way to find the tile corners, is to treat each tile as a separate segment and extract the vertices on its contour as its corners. With the binary image that we've got from the previous step, we look for all the segments using connected components labelling algorithm and extract contours from the result segments. The points are stored as subsets (one subset per contour). As an optimization, we only store the end points (i.e. x, y values) of horizontal, vertical and diagonal segments, instead of all contour points. This significantly reduces requirement on memory space which is highly limited on mobile devices. Fewer stored points also mean less data to process thus an increase of the processing speed and this makes real-time response possible even when most mobile devices do not yet have high computing power as compared to desktops.

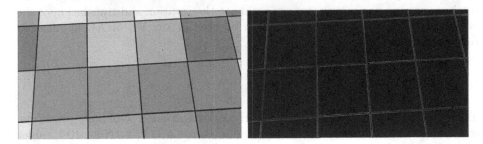

Fig. 5. Tiles are detected as segments using connected components labeling algorithm (left) and contours are extracted (right)

4.3 Corner Extraction

As we are only interested in points that are tile corners, now that we have subsets of contour points detected, we have to remove those that do not belong to the tiles. The idea is to use Ramer-Douglas-Peucker algorithm to simplify all the detected contours with fewer vertices. We choose an epsilon to preserve the approximate shapes of the contour and yet allow us to filter out the obvious non-rectangular-shaped outliers. To quickly remove non-tile points, we remove the contours that are geometrically not convex or consist of more than four vertices, because they cannot form a valid tile in the image. We notice that this step sifts out a big portion of outlier points that can otherwise be considered as valid tiles.

Fig. 6. Corners are extracted from contours (left) and marked on the input image (right)

5 Camera Calibration

Determination of the camera pose relative to an environment requires the correspondence of at least four identified 2D points in the camera image and their 3D world coordinates. If we incorporate the marker identification from Section 3, we can get the 3D world coordinates of each corner point. Because all points lay on a flat surface (the floor), a homography can be calculated which gives us a linear mapping between the camera plane (2D image points of the corners) and the floor plane. Using the standard pinhole model and the knowledge of the intrinsic camera parameters, we can estimate the rotation and translation of the camera and the mobile device. This can be used in any VR or AR application to generate the correct viewpoint.

6 Discussion

The work presented in this paper is still work-in-progress. Our first prototype works under controlled lab conditions on a Samsung Galaxy Note 10.1 tablet with a 1.4 GHz processor. Our first results look promising to further investigate the possible applications. Further testing in real world conditions is planned and extensive (latency) testing is needed on different mobile devices.

7 Conclusion

We presented a low-cost and practical optical tracking system that can be used in an existing environment with any rectangular ground grid. We proposed a simple and robust design of markers to be used with our system that supports quick orientation determination and unique identification. With the use of ground tiles, our system has very low cost and can be practically implemented with ease. Computationally, our algorithm is fast enough to be used on mobile devices with low resolution cameras. In the future we would like to incorporate inertial sensors for improved robustness. This also gives the opportunity of reducing the number of tiles that need markers to about one per square meter. We would also like to further optimize our algorithms to be more robust and faster.

References

1. http://www.hitl.washington.edu/artoolkit/
2. http://en.wikipedia.org/wiki/Lincoln_Memorial_Reflecting_Pool#mediaviewer/ File:Reflecting_pool.jpg (July 2005)
3. Ababsa, F., Mallem, M.: A robust circular fiducial detection technique and real-time 3d camera tracking. Journal of Multimedia **3**(4), 34–41 (2008)
4. Aggarwal, A., Biswas, S., Singh, S., Sural, S., Majumdar, A.: Object tracking using background subtraction and motion estimation in MPEG videos. In: Narayanan, P.J., Nayar, S.K., Shum, H.-Y. (eds.) ACCV 2006. LNCS, vol. 3852, pp. 121–130. Springer, Heidelberg (2006). http://dx.doi.org/10.1007/11612704_13
5. Bay, H., Ess, A., Tuytelaars, T., Van Gool, L.: Speeded-up robust features (surf). Computer Vision and Image Understanding **110**(3), 346–359 (2008). http://dx.doi.org/10.1016/j.cviu.2007.09.014
6. Denso: Qr code essentials (March 2013). http://www.nacs.org/LinkClick.aspx? fileticket=D1FpVAvvJuo%3D&tabid=1426&mid=4802
7. Fiala, M.: Artag revision 1, a fiducial marker system using digital techniques. Tech. rep., National Research Council (November 2004)
8. Han, M., Sethi, A., Hua, W., Gong, Y.: A detection-based multiple object tracking method. In: 2004 International Conference on Image Processing, ICIP 2004, vol. 5, pp. 3065–3068 (October 2004)
9. Lowe, D.G.: Distinctive image features from scale-invariant keypoints. International Journal of Computer Vision **60**(2), 91–110 (2004)
10. Maesen, S., Goorts, P., Bekaert, P.: Scalable optical tracking for navigating large virtual environments using spatially encoded markers. In: Proceedings of the 19th ACM Symposium on Virtual Reality Software and Technology, VRST 2013, pp. 101–110. ACM, NY (2013). http://doi.acm.org/10.1145/2503713.2503733
11. Mooser, J., You, S., Neumann, U.: Tricodes: A barcode-like fiducial design for augmented reality media. In: 2006 IEEE International Conference on Multimedia and Expo, pp. 1301–1304 (July 2006)
12. Muja, M., Lowe, D.G.: Fast approximate nearest neighbors with automatic algorithm configuration. In: VISAPP International Conference on Computer Vision Theory and Applications, pp. 331–340 (2009)
13. Owen, C., Xiao, F., Middlin, P.: What is the best fiducial? In: The First IEEE International Workshop on Augmented Reality Toolkit, pp. 8–16 (2002)
14. Ruault, P.: http://www.businessinsider.com/the-louvre-opens-islamic-art-wing-2012-9?op=1 (2012)
15. Stevenson, R.: Laser marking matrix codes on pcbs (December 2005). http:// www.thefreelibrary.com/Laser%20marking%20matrix%20codes%20on%20PCBS: %20the%20one-dimensional%20barcodes%20used...-a0140015287

Designing an Interactive and Augmented 3D Environment with Passive Tactile Feedback for Veterinary Training

Arnis Cirulis[1](✉) and Evija Liepina[2]

[1] Faculty of Engineering Vidzeme, University of Applied Sciences, Valmiera, Latvia
`arnis.cirulis@va.lv`
[2] Faculty of Veterinary Medicine, Latvia University of Agriculture, Jelgava, Latvia
`evija.liepina@llu.lv`

Abstract. The aim of the paper is to solve problems related to augmented three dimensional training environments for veterinary anatomy studies. Target group is veterinary medicine students. Project is inter-disciplinary bringing together information technologies and medicine. Practical approbation is based on a dog skeleton prototype and development of highly immersive visualization platform for veterinary studies with one to one scale and passive tactile feedback.

Keywords: Augmented reality · Tactile feedback · Veterinary training · Visualization · Intelligent scenarios

1 Introduction

Thanks to development of virtual and augmented reality technologies, due to improvements of performance parameters and increase of technologies availability, it is important to discover new innovative approaches of technologies usage in different branches. Medicine studies are long and complicated and our health must be supported by good specialists, the same is referable to veterinary medicine and health of animals. Three-dimensional training environments for veterinary anatomy studies improve quality and decrease training time and offer more accessible study materials. In this case target group is veterinary medicine students. Project is inter-disciplinary bringing together information technologies and medicine. Successful previous experience and research is done in field of virtual reality scenarios composition for industrial training and character recognition usage [1, 2]. Although in some technological aspects can be similarities with present project approbations, field of medicine has lot of specifics in model design, rapid prototyping, description and layered depiction. As for now there was no experience for Virtual and Augmented reality laboratory of Vidzeme University of Applied Sciences, thus why it is challenging our researchers to collaborate together with Latvia University of Agriculture, Faculty of Veterinary Medicine to provide them with modern interactive training environments. For the Vet-AR project the main goal is not to develop a platform with high intellectual feedback, but develop highly immersive visualization platform for veterinary studies with

L.T. De Paolis and A. Mongelli (Eds.): AVR 2014, LNCS 8853, pp. 442–449, 2014.
DOI: 10.1007/978-3-319-13969-2_35

one to one scale and passive tactile feedback [3]. The necessity for such solution is due to safety needs and health risks, because now students use exhibits which are kept in formalin which is chemical used to save exhibits structure. Secondly exhibits are in limited number and their usage provides mostly bone and skeleton information without blood system, muscles, organs, lymph etc. Additional important benefits of virtual and augmented reality use can be provided for example animation of body kinematics and physiological processes.

2   Problem Area and Global Practice in Anatomy Training

The benefits in use of VR technologies in medicine training is analyzed by several researchers and there are convincing evidences of process improvement [4, 5, 6, 7] whether it is anatomy training, whether surgery scenarios. According to their conclusions VR use is more and more common. However in this paper solution of augmented reality will be offered, it is important to consider as one type of VR solution which increases the immersion level even more.

Simulation when integrated into a well-structured curriculum has the potential to be a very powerful training and assessment tool when properly applied. Inappropriate application of simulation will lead the user to the belief that simulation does not work. Individuals in training should receive introductory instruction or education to set their training goal in context. At the same time, they could be acquiring basic skills training on a skills generalization focused VR trainer. Students would practice their skills on simulated tasks incorporating the principles of shaping and fading, with tasks becoming progressively more difficult. Trainees would not progress to the next task until they met objectively defined performance criterion consistently [4]. Technological advances have made available to health-care professionals a wide set of innovative training tools. Among these, virtual reality (VR) seems to have a great potential to enhance the learning process. First of all, virtual environments can provide modes of experiential learning; to the extent that VR provides high-level interaction with the learning content, it can foster active engagement by students and trainees. This contributes to raise motivation and interest, conditions that are recognized as crucial in the learning process [5].

Switching to augmented reality then the history of necessity to merge real and virtual environment is longstanding, however definitions are formulated just in last decades. If the first approaches of mixing real and virtual appeared in cinematography in 1950s, then definition appeared only in 1997 by Azuma [8]. History facts are summarized by Kent [9], and the first entry devoted to cinematographer Morton Heiling, who created Sensorama simulator in 1957, this simulator was patented and provided visuals, sound, vibrations and smell. The AR term appeared only in 1990 by Tom Caudell whose work was related to aircraft maintenance works. Azuma's definition [8] in 1997 prescribed AR as combination of real and virtual worlds in 3D with real-time interaction capabilities. Despite this definition, most of nowadays AR applications still offer real worlds augmentation with two dimensional data. Most of applications from Google Play and Apple's App Store for Android and iPhoneOS based smartphones and tablets provide two dimensional information. For example, text or image based descriptions or instructions, navigation arrows and instructions, or poorly interactive marker solutions with 3D object integration. Rapid growth of mobile devices usage and also technological leap of supported features makes professionals to think over new solutions in different economic sectors. Modern mobile and entertainment AR systems use one or more of the following tracking technologies: digital cameras and/or optical sensors (Nintendo Wii, Sony PlayStation Move, Microsoft Kinect), accelerometers, GPS, gyroscopes, solid state compasses, RFID and wireless sensors. These technologies offer varying levels of accuracy and precision. By Kent's literature analysis [9] most important is the position and orientation of the user's head. Tracking the user's hand(s) or handheld input device can provide 6DoF interaction technique. In Furht's turn [10] performance is relevant consideration. In spite of rapid advances in industry of mobile devices, their computing platform for real time imaging applications is still rather limited if done using cell phone's platform. As a result, many applications send data to a remote computer that does the computation and sends the result back to the mobile device, but this approach is not well adapted to AR due to limited bandwidth. Nevertheless, considering the rapid development in mobile devices computing power, it can be considered feasible to develop real-time AR applications locally processed. The usefulness of mobile devices use is also affirmed by Lee [11]. Mobile computing devices have been widely deployed to customers; the interest in mobile AR is increasing. As the need for mobility is growing, computing devices shrink in size and gain acceptance beyond an audience of tech-savvy specialists. With the help of enhanced computing power, small devices have sufficient computational capability to process complex visual computations. For example, a smart phone with a camera and wide screen can serve as an inexpensive AR device for the general public. Emerging wearable computers are also excellent platforms for enabling AR anywhere users may go.

3　Design and Composition of AR Training Environment

Today, image processing and computer vision technologies have been progressed to a stage that allows us to infer the 3D information of the world directly from the images. Because of the success of these technologies, more and more vision-based AR applications are emerged. Augmented reality refers to the combination of virtual objects and real-world environment, so that users can experience a realistic illusion when using the interactive virtual object to explore the real-world environment [12]. Several technologies and approaches of augmented reality implementations are available today. These technologies can be divided in two basic groups: marker-based systems and marker-less systems. Kan et al. [12] explains marker-based systems by use of specific marker for 3D tracking and positioning. This marker is employed to identify the corresponding virtual object that is to be placed in the real-world environment. When the marker is used as a tracking target, it has to be registered in the system in advance, as well as the virtual objects it associates with. However, since the registered information is independent for different AR systems, markers used in one system may not be applied in another system, unless an additional registration procedure is applied. For that reason in effective way RFID technologies could be used. Ginters et al. [13] introduced AR-RFID low cost visualization solution for logistics. To visualize the items in the storehouse which must be moved to assembly bay the AR-RFID solution is used ensuring additional possibilities of checking. That allows reducing the amount of potential errors and diminishing possible losses. RFID scanner reads the component code and 3D model of the item is visualized on the screen. AR-RFID by Ginters et al. [13] eliminates the problem of generating an equally stable and recognizable fiducial marker, because single marker is used only for tracking, not to recognize the 3D model. This makes it possible to use single marker with the highest stability. To identify the 3D model, an identification code, which is read from the RFID tag, is used. The 3D model is found using the identification code and displayed on the screen of the tablet PC. As well considerable marker-based version is described by Kan et al. [12] how traditional fiducial markers are replaced by QR codes, allowing to use AR in public domain systems. The QR code can be easily generated by any user and the AR system can track it no matter what the information it embedded. Thanks to FullHD video cameras and increase of computing performance, it is easier to pull down traditional marker restrictions, Seac02 company offers in its authoring platform LinceoVR to use self-taken photos as markers, providing limitless object-marker alignment options also solving the problem with fiducial marker hiding, which sometimes influences immersion level, if it is visible.

The second AR technologies group is based on marker-less solutions, meaning that marker-less pose trackers mostly rely on natural feature points which are visible in the users environment. Four requirements are summarized by Herling and Broll [14] to allow accurate pose determination from natural points. These requirements are as follows: fast computation time, robustness with respect to changing lighting conditions and image blurring, robustness against observation from different viewing angles, scale invariance or changing viewing distance. Numerous feature detectors have been proposed providing different properties concerning detection robustness or detection speed. Herling and Broll [14] divides exiting detectors in two classes: corner detectors spotting corner-like feature, blob detectors not spotting unique corner positions but image regions covering blob-like structures with a certain size.   From City3D-AR project experience these marker-less solutions cannot be used for new building layout in vacant environments and urban environments. They are more suitable for existing buildings and objects real-time overlay with additional data and for skeleton project Vet-AR as well.

4   Contents Preparation for AR Training

The challenging task for virtual environment composition is compilation of necessary 3D object set. Despite the many objects databases, it is still difficult to get appropriate objects in fast way. Usually there are limitation in object and authoring platforms compatibility and object format versions, objects availability and price. Modeling new photorealistic objects is very time consuming process. For objects of anatomy usually lack of precision and reality is a case. That is way CT (computer tomography) images with high resolution could be used to reconstruct precise 3D objects from human or animal bodies and organs. Lot of research is done to transform two dimensional CT images into 3D digital objects.

There are lots of complicated objects in anatomy for example coronary arteries. By the 3D volumetric data at hand, it is certainly useful to reconstruct a geometric model and create a 3D view of the coronary arteries. By using contrast enhancing agents, regions filled with blood exhibit higher intensities in CT images, which provide the possibility of extracting these regions from the rest of the given image. The segmentation of coronary arteries is challenging because coronary arteries are narrow tubular structures winding in-between and around heart chambers with branchings and complex curvatures, and due to the large size of image data, a fast and accurate segmentation approach is desired [15]. Training data for static shape models in the medical field will most likely consist of segmented volumetric images. Depending on the segmentation method used, the initial representation might be binary voxel data, fuzzy voxel data or surface meshes. Data originating from other sources of acquisition, e.g. surface scanning might be represented differently [16].

There are varieties of specific and useful methodologies to improve precision of objects and provide automatic 3D object generation. For Vet-AR project at the beginning phase free 3D test objects will be used available online for free.

5   Implementation of Augmented Skeleton and Exhibit Intelligence

There are several 3D environments available online which provide good quality resources for anatomy studies, e.g. Primal Pictures is very easy to use and understand, but still such solutions have lack of immersion and interaction. By use of traditional input and output devices it is impossible to achieve, but these 3D models of bones, organs, muscles, ligaments, arteries, veins, nerves, fascia and lymph is good platform for static augmented reality at the beginning, thus providing one to one scale and visual immersion for anatomy studies.

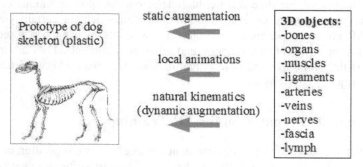

Fig. 1. Skeleton prototype augmentations

Virtual reality could bring such solution to the next level and similar solutions are introduced in field of industrial training for more than a decade. In simple way for one to one scale stereoscopic screen or monitor can be used. To bring anatomy studies to even more immersive and realistic level, augmented reality is the key. It is not enough only to look at the visualized object, it is important to touch the object, to move the object and to walk around it in real space. Lot of manipulation devices has been introduced to move your virtual avatar, but no device can replace real movements and no haptic devices can replace sense of real touch and force feedback. The introduced solution in paper (see fig. 1.) offers to use plastic skeleton of study object which are inexpensive and will work as passive tactile feedback and marker for placement of virtual objects (organs, muscles, ligaments, arteries, veins, nerves, fascia and lymph). It is like a prop solution in virtual reality, only there are not integrated sensors. Animated objects will increase immersion level, for example visualized blood circulation, heartbeat, muscle contractions etc. More complicated is implementation of natural kinematics of body movements or dynamic augmentation meaning that students moves skeleton bones and   virtual objects moves with the movements of bones. It is important also from physical side of skeleton prototype to allow only natural movements or system can analyse and make warning if trainee makes non-natural movements of skeleton.

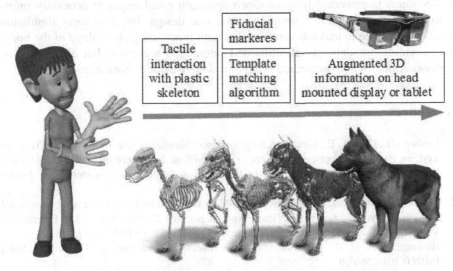

Fig. 2. Basic idea of Vet-AR project

For general visualization in augmented reality mode classical fiducial markers are used, but to achieve more detailed movements and precise virtual/real in Vet-AR alignment template matching algorithms can be used (see fig. 2.). High resolution head mounted display provides system with qualitative two dimensional video frames which should be processed. The tracking of a certain feature or target over time is based on the comparison of the content of each image with a sample template. Template matching algorithm can be found useful for several purposes. It can be used to detect the presence, or absence, of the object and to distinguish between different types of objects [17].

To improve precision both technologies can be used together and synchronized. Similar hybrid solutions are used in outdoor augmented reality by Karlekar et al. [18] only indoors we use fiducial marker instead of GPS localization.

For now the project is in beginning phase and still lot of work and future research must be done. This solution is the first step to build intelligent training environment by scenario virtualization and realistic feedback for study needs.

6   Conclusions

Virtual and augmented laboratory is equipped with latest head mounted displays from Vuzix, dog skeleton prototype and context for training scenarios will be provided by Latvia University of Agriculture, Faculty of Veterinary Medicine. Achieved results can be applied also to human anatomy training and health problem diagnostic's scenarios.

In future this solution will be merged with other research results related with human perception recognition and simulation modeling which are done in Sociotechnical Systems Engineering Institute. Such approach could augment necessary information for individuality in appropriate style and design, but data form simulation model can be taken to make an environment with functioning physiology of the body, thus providing not only visualization and interaction scenarios, but also medicine diagnosis scenarios with generated symptoms and visualized problematic areas.

References

1. Lauberte, I., Ginters, E., Cirulis, A.: Agent-Based Simulation Use In Multi-Step Training Systems Based On Applicant's Character Recognition. In: Proceedings of the 13th East-European Conference on Advances in Databases and Information Systems, pp. 16–22. Riga, Latvia (September 7-20, 2009) ISSN 0302-9743

2. Cirulis, A., Brigmanis, K.: Serious Game: Meat Grinder For Food Processing Vocational Schools. In Proceedings of the Virtual And Augmented Reality (VR/AR) In Education - VARE 2011, p.137. Valmiera, Latvia (March 18, 2011) ISBN 978-9984-633-18-3

3. Bowman, D.A. et al.: 3D user interfaces: theory and practice, p. 478. USA (2006) ISBN 0-201-75867-9

4. Gallagher, A., Ritter, M., Champion, H., Higgins, G., Fried, M., Moses, G., Smith, D., Satava, R.: Virtual Reality Simulation for the Operating Room Proficiency-Based Training as a Paradigm Shift in Surgical Skills Training. Lippincott Williams & Wilkins (2005)

5. Mantovani, F., Castelnuovo, G., Gaggioli, A., Riva, G.: Virtual Reality Training for Health-Care Professionals. Cyberpsychology & behavior, vol. 6(4). Mary Ann Liebert, Inc. (2003)

6. Larsen, C., Soerensen, J., Grantcharov, T., Dalsgaard, T., Schouenborg, L., Ottosen, C., Schroeder, T., Ottesen, B.: Effect of virtual reality training on laparoscopic surgery: randomised controlled trial. BMJ Research (2009)

7. Gallagher, A., Cates, C.: Approval of Virtual Reality Training for Carotid Stenting. What This Means for Procedural-Based Medicine. JAMA **292**(24) (December 22/29, 2004). American Medical Association

8. Azuma, R.: A survey of augmented reality. http://www.ronaldazuma.com/papers/ARpresence.pdf, Presence: Teleoperators and Virtual Environments, pp. 355–385 (August 1997)

9. Kent, J.: The Augmented reality Handbook - Everything you need to know about Augmented reality (2011)

10. Furht, B.: Handbook of Augmented Reality. Florida Atlantic University, p. 746. Springer, USA (2011). ISBN 978-1-4614-0063-9

11. Lee, T.: Multithreaded Hybrid Feature Tracking for Markerless Augmented Reality. Visualization and Computer Graphics, IEEE Transactions. Comput. Sci. Dept., Univ. of California, Los Angeles, pp. 355–368 (2009)
12. Kan, T.: QR code based augmented reality applications. Handbook of Virtual Reality, p. 339. Springer (2011)
13. Ginters, E., Martin-Gutierrez, J.: Low cost augmented reality and RFID application for logistics items visualisation. In: Annual Proceedings of Vidzeme of Applied Sciences ICTE in Regional Development (2011)
14. Herling, J., Beoll, W.: Markerless tracking for augmented reality. Handbook of Virtual Reality, p. 255. Springer (2011)
15. Yang, Y., Tannenbaum, A., Giddens, D.: Knowledge-Based 3D Segmentation and Reconstruction of Coronary Arteries Using CT Images. Georgia Institute of Technology, School of Electrical and Computer Engineering, Atlanta (2004)
16. Heimann, T., Meinzer, H.: Statistical shape models for 3D medical image segmentation. Medical Image Analysis 13. Elsevier (2009)
17. Ziaei, Z., Hahtoa, A., Mattilaa, J., Siukob, M., Semeraroc, L.: Real-time markerless Augmented Reality for Remote Handling system in bad viewing conditions. Fusion Engineering and Design 86, 2033–2038 (2011)
18. Karlekar, J., Zhou, S., Nakayama, Y., Lu, W., Loh, Z., Hii, D: Model-based localization and drift-free user tracking for outdoor augmented reality. In: 2010 IEEE International conference on Multimedia and Expo (ICME), pp. 1178–1183 (2010)

Investigation on Human Attentiveness to Video Clips Using Neurosky and LIRIS-ACCEDE Database

Edgaras Ščiglinskas[(⊠)] and Aušra Vidugirienė

Faculty of Informatics, Vytautas Magnus University, Kaunas, Lithuania
edgaras.sciglinskas@fc.vdu.lt, a.vidugiriene@if.vdu.lt

Abstract. The paper describes an investigation on human attentiveness to emotional video-clips stimuli using Neurosky Mindwave device to measure electric brain cortex signals. Software for video stimuli demonstration to the volunteers was created. LIRIS-ACCEDE database of video clips was used for construction of three experimental sets. Six volunteers participated in the initial tests where their reactions to emotional video clips were recorded in real time. The results showed that there were high correlations between the corresponding parts of the video sequences when neutral or positive video clips have been watched. The reactions to different kinds of emotional stimuli correlated in large diversity.

Keywords: Emotion elicitation · Dynamic stimuli · Emotional video clips · Attentiveness · Human-computer interaction

1 Introduction

Emotions are certainly significant in our lives. As virtual world is becoming a big part of our daily life, emotions have already entered to virtual environments as well. One of the cornerstones of the development of the next generation user interfaces (UI) is a more efficient human and computer interaction [1, 2, 3]. It is fundamentally important to develop the tools that enable to follow human condition, adapt to changes in the environment and are able to regulate emotional states (attentiveness, etc.) interactively in the areas as learning, operators' work, creative tasks, generating ideas, relaxing, etc [4, 5], [11]. Standard user interfaces does not track human emotional states as stress level, fatigue level, the level of attentiveness or other parameters. Undoubtedly, today's computer systems capabilities and advanced hardware has adequate means to reach these objectives. A new generation of user interface must ensure the effective human-computer cooperation, and these user interface principles could be applied to various areas [8, 9, 10]. Effective human and computer interaction, however, is not easy task, because of its complexity.

This study aims to investigate if different people react to the same video clips and same kind of video stimuli similarly in order to find out if there are any common tendencies that could be used to control human emotional state in later research. Human attention levels when watching sequences of video clips (neutral, positive, and negative) were tested.

© Springer International Publishing Switzerland 2014
L.T. De Paolis and A. Mongelli (Eds.): AVR 2014, LNCS 8853, pp. 450–456, 2014.
DOI: 10.1007/978-3-319-13969-2_36

2   Software for Emotion Elicitation

At first a thorough analysis on hardware selection for the experiments was performed. One of the most important criteria was comfort for a user as we aim to apply the results of the experiments in real life applications (with dynamical environment) and a device to measure user attentiveness has to be wirelessly connected to a computer, not expensive, easy to use and not requiring any additional effort to put it on (as compared to the devices where conductive gel between the sensors and the head is used). We have chosen Neurosky Headset [6], because it is in line with the mentioned requirements. NeuroSky technology allows low-cost EEG-linked research by using dry sensors. Neurosky safely measures brainwave signals and monitors the attention, meditation, different frequency signal intensities and RAW signals. This hardware has all the necessary tools for programming and software development and is compatible with different platforms what is essential to develop various user-friendly applications with emotional state monitoring.

Some tools for displaying a dynamic stimulus to a user are present [13], but they have a number of disadvantages that are essential to our study. Experiments require special measures that specific tools do not have or the appropriate tools are expensive. There are some cost-free tools [12], but special content format is required and the equipment to create these special formats is very expensive. A tool has to be compatible with Neurosky as well. These are the main reasons to create our own software for our experiments. Neurosky library ThinkGear.NET (that is compatible with .NET platform) was used for software development. The developed software displays video stimulus and records the measured bio-signals and pre-processed parameters in real time. Attention level, meditation level, RAW EEG signals, and different frequency intensities (Alpha, Beta, Gamma, Theta, Delta) are recorded.

A working window of the application includes a video window and a list of parameters to be measured (Fig. 1).

Fig. 1. A tool for presenting video clip sequences to a user and measuring its bio-signals

After connecting Neurosky device to the application, the video-clips stimulus from a list can be selected. When the experiment starts, the video-clips sequence stimulus is shown in full-screen mode to make sure that the volunteer is not distracted by parameter information on the screen. Bio-data of a user is recorded in real time. All the results and data are stored in text files.

At the moment the application is compatible only with NeuroSky series devices, but there are possibilities to extend compatibility and add support to other devices, because it is fully native application and programming language tools are versatile.

3   Experiment and Data

As the research is aimed to determine instant user's reactions to the stimulus, Liris-Accede database [7] of short annotated video-clips was suitable for the needs of a study. Video clips extracted from movies shared under Creative Commons licenses are used in the database. Video clips are sorted along the induced valence (from negative to positive) and arousal (from passive to active) axis. The annotation in this database was carried out by more than 3700 annotators from 89 different countries so the clips are annotated without cultural context differences what is very important in the study of human emotions.

At first three video sequences with different video-clips were created to determine the management capabilities of the human emotional state with dynamic video content.

All video clips were sorted in the groups in terms of their arousal and valence estimates, so each of these groups met an emotional state. Video clips were selected from these groups and video sequences were created from shorts video clips. Three groups (neutral, positive and negative) of annotated video clips were used. Videos from a group were selected randomly, as they have close estimates in each of the group. The videos did not repeat in the same sequence.

Experiment plan is presented in Tables 1-3. There are eight video clips in each of video sequence. Arousal and valence estimates, each video clip duration and video clip number in the database are also provided. Each video-clip in a sequence was separated by two seconds pause of neutral screen.

Table 1. Setting of video clips sequence no. 1. Video clips are selected from Liris-Accede database [7].

	1	2	3	4	5	6	7	8
Duration	11.14 s	10.58 s	9.47 s	10.55 s	10.56 s	9.58 s	10.58 s	10.57 s
Valence	5340	9468	5212	9708	4755	350	5048	4755
Arousal	5115	1287	4902	5264	5189	8688	4381	5189
State	Neutral	Positive	Neutral	Positive	Neutral	Negative	Neutral	Neutral
DB No.	91	4304	5364	667	28	889	4933	28

Table 2. Setting of video clips sequence no. 2. Video clips are selected from Liris-Accede database [7].

	1	2	3	4	5	6	7	8
Duration	9.20 s	10.59 s	9.42 s	8.44 s	11.58 s	8.22 s	11.52 s	10.57 s
Valence	9053	9647	4818	9107	4717	1262	4969	4392
Arousal	96	4025	4733	1674	4766	8260	5049	4818
State	Positive	Positive	Neutral	Positive	Neutral	Negative	Neutral	Neutral
DB No.	1340	396	4581	1774	4024	997	6010	4474

Table 3. Setting of video clips sequence no. 3. Video clips are selected from Liris-Accede database [7].

	1	2	3	4	5	6	7	8
Duration	11.21 s	10.58 s	9.23 s	10.46 s	9.04 s	11.12 s	11.03 s	11.02 s
Valence	140	7985	4818	8208	4678	236	4590	4784
Arousal	9624	7047	4733	56	4459	1061	4926	4967
State	Negative	Positive	Neutral	Positive	Neutral	Negative	Neutral	Neutral
DB No.	2922	1350	4581	4303	4148	4383	620	6434

Each state takes about ten seconds. This duration was chosen on purpose, because it is sufficient time to invoke human emotion and short enough to identify only these human emotions what are related to stimulus [7].

The sequence is formed so that it would be possible to analyse bio-signals of the same and different users when video clips from different groups are demonstrated and transitions between them are performed. The first video clip in a sequence was from a different group (neutral, positive or negative) in every of the three video sequences and the next seven video clips were from the same groups among the three video sequences. The majority of video-clips among the groups were different. Although there were video clips from the same group in a sequence, individual video-clips were not repeated in the same group.

The overall experiment scheme is shown in Fig. 2.

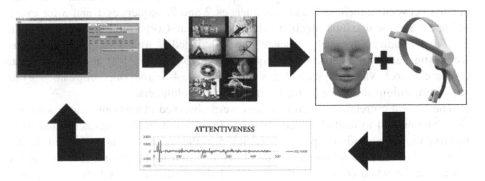

Fig. 2. Overall scheme of the experiment

At first a stimulus (video sequence) is chosen using a developed tool. The chosen sequence is demonstrated to a volunteer wearing Neurosky Headset. The measured signals are saved using a developed tool. Attentiveness levels were recorded one time per second, although one value of attentiveness level was calculated from five values of raw EEG signal in the device.

Six volunteers (students) participated in these initial experiments - 3 males and 3 females. All volunteers were from 19 to 26 years.

Signals of attentiveness levels of a Volunteer no. 3 when watching all three video sequences are shown in Fig. 3. Verticals lines indicates the segments that were analysed in more details: the first segment with the first video clip of a sequence from 0 to 10 second; the segment with the first and the second video clips from 0 to 22 second; the segment with the fourth and fifth video clips from 34 to 56 second; the segment with the seventh and the eight video clips from 68 to 90   second.

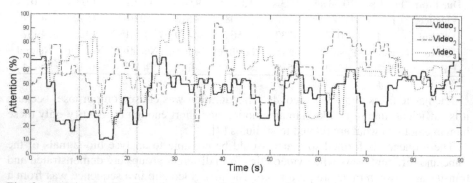

Fig. 3. Attention levels of a volunteer no. 3, for every video sequence. Solid line – video sequence no. 1, dashed line – video sequence no. 2, dotted line - video sequence no. 3

4   Results

After the data were collected during the experiments, correlation functions were calculated between sequences 1 and 2, sequences 2 and 3, sequences 1 and 3 for every volunteer and the maximal function values were taken. Correlation functions between each two volunteers for each sequence were calculated as well. Correlation functions were estimated for the entire video sequences (video clips no. 1-8) and parts of them (video clip no.1, video clips no. 1-2, video clips no. 4-5, and video clips no. 7-8) to see the transitions influence on the attentiveness of volunteers.

The highest correlation function values were observed in sections, where a transition from neutral to neutral (video clips no. 7 and no. 8 in the sequences) and from positive to neutral (video clips no. 4 and no. 5 in the sequences) is performed. In the first case highest correlation values are above 0.9, and in the second case the values are above 0.8 when comparing the signals of the same volunteer between different sequences and when comparing signals of the same sequence between different volunteers.

When comparing the signals that were recorded when watching the first video, the results are very different as the first video was from different emotionally annotated group in every video sequence. Some volunteers reacted similarly to different video clips and the maximal correlation function values were relatively high (around 0.6), the other reacted very differently with almost no correlation. Correlations between the people in each of video sequence were diverse as well and varied from very low values to relatively high values. When comparing the highest values of correlation functions for a block of the first and the second videos together in the sequence, the more stable situation is observed. The maximal correlation function values for this case are provided in Table 4 and Table 5.

Table 4. Maximal values of correlation functions between the pairs of the blocks (of the first and the second video clips in the sequences) for every volunteer are compared

	Participant no.					
	1	2	3	4	5	6
sequence 1-sequence 2	0.51	0.63	0.31	0.75	0.36	0.51
sequence 2-sequence 3	0.32	0.48	0.54	0.25	0.13	0.35
sequence 3-sequence 1	0.55	0.33	0.56	0.30	0.38	0.63

Table 5. Maximal values of correlation functions between each possible volunteer pair for the blocks (of the first and the second video clips in the sequences) are compared

Vol.	Sequence no. 1					Sequence no. 2					Sequence no. 3				
no.	2	3	4	5	6	2	3	4	5	6	2	3	4	5	6
1	0.36	0.32	0.47	0.40	0.40	0.50	0.68	0.63	0.52	0.52	0.22	0.40	0.25	0.38	0.49
2	-	0.55	0.55	0.33	0.12	-	0.45	0.58	0.55	0.36	-	0.54	0.50	0.26	0.56
3	-	-	0.59	0.31	0.14	-	-	0.66	0.27	0.48	-	-	0.39	0.56	0.54
4	-	-	-	0.23	0.10	-	-	-	0.52	0.40	-	-	-	0.23	0.46
5	-	-	-	-	0.58	-	-	-	-	0.47	-	-	-	-	0.33

5   Conclusions and Future Work

The results showed that the volunteers reacted similarly to some videos (sequence segment with video clips no. 4 and no.5 and segment with video clips no. 7 and no. 8. that were annotated as neutral and positive). Attention levels obtained when the first video clip was shown were diverse and the highest correlation function values when comparing different sequences for the same volunteer and the same sequence between each pair of the volunteers varied from very low to relatively high. When comparing a segment of the first two video clips, the correlations varied less. It can be assumed that the reactions to the first video clip in the sequences are differs more as every sequence started with the differently annotated video-clips. Recording attentiveness signal one value per second also can influence the results and different shape of the signal can be obtained if measuring frequency would be higher.

Further investigations will be continued with more accurate attentiveness signal analysis in the transitions intervals between the video clips. Influence of the previous emotional video clip to the attention level when watching the next emotional video-clip will be further analysed. We can also assume that the video clip sequences have to be prepared with more significant differences (between neutral, positive and negative annotations) for later experiments.

Acknowledgements. Postdoctoral fellowship of Aušra Vidugirienė is funded by European Union Structural Funds project "Postdoctoral Fellowship Implementation in Lithuania" within the framework of the Measure for Enhancing Mobility of Scholars and Other Researchers and the Promotion of Student Research (VP1-3.1-ŠMM-01) of the Program of Human Resources Development Action Plan.

References

1. Zimmermann, P., Guttormsen, S., Danuser, B., Gomez, P.: Affective Computing – A Rationale for Measuring Mood with Mouse and Keyboard. Int. J. Occup. Saf. Ergon. **9**(4), 539–51 (2003)
2. Brave, S., Nass, C., Hutchinson, K.: Computers that care: investigating the effects of orientation of emotion exhibited by an embodied computer agent. Int. J. Human-Computer Studies **62**, 161–178 (2005)
3. Hudlicka, E.: To feel or not to feel: The role of affect in human–computer interaction. International Journal of Human-Computer Studies **59**(1–2), 1–32 (2003)
4. Rached1 T.S., Perkusich A.: Emotion Recognition Based on Brain-Computer Interface Systems, Brain-Computer Interface Systems - Recent Progress and Future Prospects. In: Fazel-Rezai, R. (ed.). InTech (2013) ISBN: 978-953-51-1134-4, doi:10.5772/56227. Available from: http://www.intechopen.com/books/brain-computer-interface-systems-recent-progress-and-future-prospects/emotion-recognition-based-on-brain-computer-interface-systems
5. Liu, Y., Sourina, O., Nguyen, M.K.: Real-Time EEG-Based Emotion Recognition and Its Applications. In: Gavrilova, M.L., Tan, C., Sourin, A., Sourina, O. (eds.) Transactions on Computational Science XII. LNCS, vol. 6670, pp. 256–277. Springer, Heidelberg (2011)
6. Neurosky Headset description. http://neurosky.com/
7. LIRIS-ACCEDE database description. http://liris-accede.ec-lyon.fr/
8. Rezazadeh, I.M., Firoozabadi, M., Hu, H., Reza Hashemi Golpayegani, S.M.: Co-Adaptive and Affective Human-Machine Interface for Improving Training Performances of Virtual Myoelectric Forearm Prosthesis. IEEE Transactions on Affective Computing 3(3) (2012)
9. Kim, K.-S.: Effects of emotion control and task on Web searching behavior. Information Processing and Management **44**, 373–385 (2008)
10. Yadati, K., Katti, H., Kankanhalli, M.: CAVVA: Computational Affective Video-in-Video Advertising. IEEE Transactions on Multimedia 16(1), 15 – 23 (2014), doi:10.1109/TMM. 2013.2282128
11. Lewis, S., Dontcheva, M., Gerber, E.: Affective Computational Priming and Creativity. In: Proceedings of the SIGCHI Conference on Human Factors in Computing Systems, pp. 735–744 (2011)
12. Neurosky Headset description. http://store.neurosky.com/products/myndplay
13. OpenViBE software platform description. http://openvibe.inria.fr/discover/

Virtual Acoustic Reconstruction of the Church at the Lost Monastery of Santa Maria de la Murta

Ana Planells[2], Jaume Segura[1]([✉]), Arturo Barba[2], Salvador Cerdá[2],
Alicia Giménez[2], and Rosa M. Cibrián[3]

[1] Computer Science Department, ETSE, Universitat de València,
Avda Universitat s/n, 46100 Burjassot, Spain
jaume.segura@uv.es
[2] Applied Physics Department, Universitat Politècnica de València,
Camí de Vera s/n, 46022 Valencia, Spain
agimenez@fis.upv.es
[3] Physiology Department, Universitat de València, Av. Blasco Ibañez, 15,
46010 Valencia, Spain
rosa.m.cibrian@uv.es

Abstract. Archeological acoustics is a part of acoustics that studies ancient environments which were dedicated (completely or partly) to sound performing. The combination of this acoustic area in conjunction with room acoustics enables the study of the acoustic evolution of existing buildings (in terms of the historical documentation) or even, make the acoustic reconstruction of rooms which were destroyed or they are in a bad state or in ruins. In this work, an acoustical reconstruction of the church of the Hieronymites' monastery of the Murta from the XIV century, in Alzira, Spain has been developed. This building was abandoned in 1836 and now is in ruins. The work develops a geometrical model, together with a proposal of materials which were common in the churches of the same area, an acoustical study and finally an auralization of a choral performance has been done (as this monastery had its own musical chappele).

1 Introduction

Acoustical archeology aims to study previous acoustical stages in buildings or rooms or to recover old rooms, environments or buildings that has been lost. This part of the acoustic science also tries to analyze the historic acoustic evolution of emblematic buildings of our Cultural Heritage.

The main aim of this paper is to make a virtual acoustic rehabilitation of the ruined church of the Hyeronymite's monastery of Santa Maria de la Murta, according to several graphical and written documents.

© Springer International Publishing Switzerland 2014
L.T. De Paolis and A. Mongelli (Eds.): AVR 2014, LNCS 8853, pp. 457–464, 2014.
DOI: 10.1007/978-3-319-13969-2_37

1.1   Brief Historical Notes

The main purpose of this work is to retrieve the acoustics at the last stage of a Hieronymites' monastery. The ruins of this monastery are located in the Valley of the Murta (also called the old Valley of Miracles) at coordinates WGS84 (Latitude, Longitude): 39.128970, -0.361079. The monastery was founded in the 14th century by a group of monks coming from another monastery in the zone (Sant Jeroni de Cotalba). The building was ready in the second half of this century, thanks to several donations. [1][2]

One of the main patrons of this monastery was Lluís Vich Corbera, a "Mestre Racional" in the city of Valencia (this was the person in charge to control the treasurers in the Aragon Crown and the Kingdom of Valencia, this person also was in charge of all the counts of the kings and nobles). He donated many artworks and was buried in the church of this monastery.

The first church of the monastery (painting shown in Figure 1a) was located in the actual sacristy, which was in the place occupied by this vestry room after building the new church that was projected in 1516 by Guillén Ramón Vich (Archbishop in Xativa) and was finished in 1623. This long time was mainly due to some economical problems of the community of monks. The new church (painting shown in Figure 1 b) was next to the old church, so this place was used as a sacristy. [1]

1.2   Architecture of the Lost Monastery

The architecture of the new church shown a traditional building as a nave with chapels between counter-forts. A high choir at the feet and a high chancel was inherent to mendicant orders, as the Hieronymites. A cut in elevation showed the austerity of the classical architecture of the 15th century, only enriched with some tiles at the skirts of the church and some polychrome plaster rosettes [1].

This is an architecture that seeks the economy in the use of materials, which is a clear inheritance of the new mentality that comes after the Council of Trent and comes from the founder frantic activity patriarch Joan de Ribera. The orders and arches were made with stone, the walls made with masonry and the doorposts and vaults made with brick, although they were coated with some kind of plaster.

The use of brick allowed a reduction in costs and a faster construction. It was adapted to traditional forms (i.e. walls, vaulted ceilings, etc) and subsequently to other aimed at sphericity, which were made in Italian style, but also had reminiscences from the Valencia late-Gothic style. The bricked pendentive vaults were widely used in the Valencian architecture in the first half of the 16th century. The type of closure in the church of the Murta came at a turning point between the prevalence of these and barrel vaults with lunettes.[1][3]

After the confiscation of the properties of the Spanish Church in 1836 by Juan Álvarez Mendizábal, ministry of the regent queen María Cristina de Borbón, the monastery was abandoned and sold to private owners who left the building in a state of ruin.

Fig. 1. Paintings of the sacristy (old church) (a) and the new church (b) from 1846 and painted by M.Peris.

2   Methodology of the Virtual Acoustic Rehabilitation of the New Church of the Monastery

A geometrical model of the new church of the monastery has been developed using a CAD software. For this purpose, a measurement campaign was done in January, 2014. Figure 2 shows some photographs where the current state of conservation can be seen. This measurements were made with a handy laser rangefinder device.

The materials used were related to the referred in the bibliography of the monastery. At this moment, a specific study of the 'in-situ' materials has not been done yet, but it is scheduled by the end of September. The materials in Table 1 have been selected from the bibliography [4], taking into account the descriptions of the church in [1] [2] [3]. The model has been acoustically simulated by using the ODEON software [5]. In Figure 3, several views of the model of the church have been taken. The simulation has been done without taking into account the lining of the church (i.e. statues, paintings, altarpieces, organ, etc), because the model consider the last situation of the room in 1846 when the room was empty.

An omnidirectional source has been used in the simulation, located at the position (9.000, 28.000, 3.800). The receivers were located in the positions collected in Table 2. They are shown in Figure 4.

Fig. 2. Photographs of the current state of the church of the monastery. (a) Frontal part of the church with arch and the pigeon's tower. (b) Part of a side chapel (broken altar, some tiles on the floor and parts of plaster on the wall. (c) Measuring the height of the archs. (d) View of the back part of the church (similar view as in Figure 1)

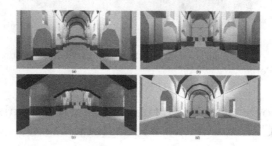

Fig. 3. Different views from the simulated model in ODEON: (a) view from the altar, (b) view from the middle of the church, (c) view from the back of the church, (d) view from the choir

Table 1. List of materials and absorption coefficients in the church based on frequency (in Hz)

Material	125	250	500	1000	2000	4000
Rough concrete	0.02	0.03	0.03	0.03	0.04	0.04
Ceramic tiles	0.01	0.01	0.01	0.01	0.02	0.02
Door wood	0.14	0.10	0.06	0.08	0.10	0.10
Crushed stone	0.41	0.53	0.64	0.84	0.91	0.63
Simple Glass	0.08	0.04	0.03	0.03	0.02	0.02
Wall plaster	0.02	0.02	0.03	0.04	0.05	0.05
Ceiling Plaster	0.02	0.03	0.04	0.05	0.07	0.08

Table 2. Positions of the 6 receivers in the church

Rec Nr	X	Y	Z
1	8.00	12.00	1.70
2	8.00	15.00	1.70
3	8.00	18.00	1.70
4	10.00	18.00	1.70
5	10.00	15.00	1.70
6	10.00	12.00	1.70

Also the graphical model has been developed with 3DMax Studio with textures, based on the documentation and the graphical information collected in-situ, in order to integrate auralization, by this moment as a video. This model is being transformed to IVE format in order to be easily integrated in an OSG navigator (or even in a CAVE). Figure 5 shows some captures of the texturized model.

3   Results and Discussion

After the acoustic simulation, the first result shows an average EDT reflected in Figure 6 and the statistics for RT30, C80 and D50, are shown in Tables 3, 5 and 4.

Table 3. Statistics of RT30 for the 6 receivers

Frequency	125	250	500	1000	2000	4000
Minimum	6.81	6.05	4.83	3.85	3.00	2.29
Average	6.83	6.06	4.84	3.87	3.02	2.32
Maximum	6.84	6.07	4.86	3.88	3.06	2.34

Table 4. Statistics of D50 for the 6 receivers

Frequency	125	250	500	1000	2000	4000
Minimum	0.05	0.05	0.06	0.08	0.11	0.14
Average	0.06	0.07	0.08	0.10	0.13	0.17
Maximum	0.07	0.08	0.10	0.12	0.15	0.19

These results make obvious that this church (with 8000 m^3 aprox.) was reverberant enough and the use of coating was necessary for different purposes (preaches, musical services, etc.). According to the empiric formula for the optimum reverberation time by Pérez-Miñana [6] for music at churches ($T_{opt} = 0.99 \cdot \sqrt[3]{V}$), this optimum reverberation time is 2.2 seconds, so the reverberation time of this church when the monastery was abandoned was higher than its optimum value.

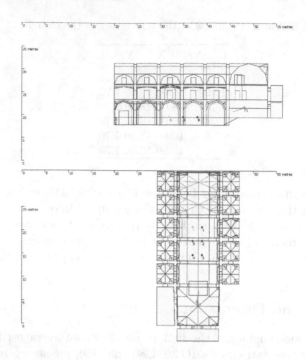

Fig. 4. Plan and section of the building with the receivers and source

Table 5. Statistics of C80 for the 6 receivers

Frequency	125	250	500	1000	2000	4000
Minimum	-9.8	-9.2	-8.2	-7.0	-5.7	-4.3
Average	-9.1	-8.6	-7.6	-6.5	-5.2	-3.8
Maximum	-8.7	-8.2	-7.2	-6.1	-4.9	-3.4

4   Auralization of a Musical Excerpt

One of the most important features of the acoustical simulation is the possibility
to obtain the impulse responses and thus to get auralizations of this lost building.
The church of the monastery of "Santa Maria de la Murta" has remained silent
for a very long time, and now, music can be listened in this environment. For this
work, a choral piece has been selected to be auralized in this environment. This
piece was composed by one of the Lluís Vich de Corbera's grandsons (also named
Lluís Vich) for a religious drama, called "Misteri d'Elx", based on the burial
of the Holly Virgin. This drama was declared Intangible Cultural Heritage by
the UNESCO in 2001. This piece is called "Ans d'entrar en sepultura" ("before
entering to the burial place") and it is for a men choir without instruments. This
piece was performed by the Capella del Misteri (current performers) in February
2014, and recorded with a binaural head (HeadAcoustics) in a dry environment.

Fig. 5. Texturized model for graphical representation into a video or an immersive device

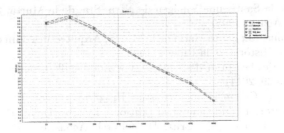

Fig. 6. EDT obtained in the simulation

The auralization was made in the position 1 of the Figure 4 and the audio can be heard in [7].

5 Conclusions and Future Work

In this work, a model of a lost building has been developed. This building has been acoustically simulated taking into account the dimensions of the ruins and the historical documentation. This first approach to the virtual acoustic rehabilitation of the monastery of "la Murta" has shown that the room had a high reverberation (RT30) and a poor definition for speech (D50), which is better at high frequencies.

Also the auralization of a choral work by Lluís Vich (grandson of one of the patrons of the monastery) has been done. This auralization has been performed within the empty church, without any ornament as this was the situation in 1846 when M.Peris make his paintings (shown in Figure 1).

This work is going to be extended by adapting this model to an OSG navigator and connecting a head-tracking with headphones system in order to detect the movement of the listener, adapting the sound according to the correspondent HRTF and interpolating between the different impulse responses in the room, pre-calculated from the acoustic model.

Acknowledgments. This project has been funded by the Spanish Ministry of Economy and Innovation with the grant ref. BIA2012-36896. The authors would like to thank also to Dr Aurelià Lairón, head of the historical archive in Alzira, and to professor Dr Carmel Ferragud for the review and the comments about this work.

References

1. Arciniega, L.: Santa María de la Murta (Alzira): Artífices, Comitentes y la "Damnatio Memoriae" de D. Diego de Vich. In: Simposium Los Jerónimos: El Escorial y otros Monasterios de la Orden. San Lorenzo de El Escorial, Instituto Escurialense de Investigaciones Históricas y Artísticas, vol. I, pp. 267–292 (1999)
2. Morera, J.B.: Historia de la fundación del Monasterio del valle de Miralles y hallazgo y maravillas de la Santíssima Ymágen de Ntra. Sra. de la Murta. Año 1773. Publ. Ajuntament d'Alzira (1995)
3. Tolosa, L., Framis, M.: Santa María de la Murta. Arquitectura d'un cenobi medieval. VI Assemblea d'Història de la Ribera (1993)
4. ODEON: Acoustic absorption data. http://www.odeon.dk/acoustic-absorption-data (visited in April 29, 2014)
5. Christensen, C.L.: Odeon Room Acoustics Program, version 10.1, User's Manual, Industrial, Auditorium and Combined Editions, Lyngby, Denmark (2009)
6. Fernández, M., Recuero, M., Cruz, D.: Church Acoustics. (RBA-05-015) Proc. Forum Acusticum, Seville (2002)
7. Auralization of "Ans d'entrar en sepultura" by Lluís Vich in the church of Santa Maria de la Murta. http://goo.gl/cEzplN

Author Index

Printed in the United States
By Bookmasters